Mastering
Dreamweaver MX Databases

The Scripting Tools

Dreamweaver MX is a powerful tool for building web applications visually, and it supports a wide variety of scripting languages and environments, including ColdFusion, Active Server Pages, ASP.NET, ADO.NET, JSP, and PHP—and the fundamental database language, SQL. If you've worked with any of these languages and need to add another one to your skill set, *Mastering Dreamweaver MX Databases* will give you enough of the essentials to get started. Or, if you have the opportunity to choose which language to use for a project, you can use these chapters to compare features and make an informed, appropriate choice. *See Chapters 11 through 16, and 18.*

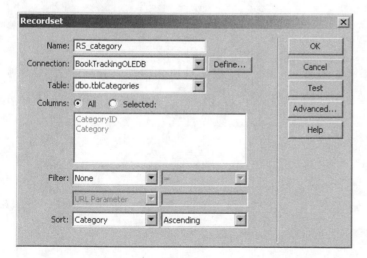

Working with Data (and Securing It)

Finally, *Mastering Dreamweaver MX Databases* shows how to secure your data and how to handle the essential data-manipulation tasks—retrieving, searching, and updating data. In this section, you'll also learn how to use templates and create master/detail page sets to both reduce your workload and give all the pages of your site a uniform look, and you'll be introduced to the add-in extension tools available through the Macromedia Exchange website. *See Chapters 17, and 18 through 24.*

Mastering™
Dreamweaver™ MX Databases

Susan Sales Harkins

Bryan Chamberlain

Darren McGee

San Francisco   London

Associate Publisher: Dan Brodnitz

Acquisitions Editor: Willem Knibbe

Developmental Editor: James A. Compton

Production Editor: Leslie E.H. Light

Technical Editor: Lucinda Dykes

Copyeditor: Pat Coleman

Compositor: Interactive Composition Corporation—Rozi Harris

Graphic Illustrator: Interactive Composition Corporation—Rozi Harris

CD Coordinator: Dan Mummert

CD Technician: Kevin Ly

Proofreaders: Amey Garber, Emily Hsuan, Laurie O'Connell, Laura Schattschneider, Yariv Ravinovitch, Nancy Riddiough, Monique van den Berg

Indexer: Nancy Guenther

Book Designer: Maureen Forys, Happenstance Type-O-Rama

Cover Designer: Design Site

Cover Illustrator/Photographer: Sergie Loobkoff

To Lexie—the reason I stay in this line of work.
—SH

I dedicate the part I played in this book to my wife, Sandy, and my children, Jacob and Rachel. You provide me with motivation, strength, hope, and happiness. Thank you.
—BC

My portion of this book is dedicated to Jay, my family (immediate and extended), and my friends who, over the years and most recently, showered me with faith, encouragement, patience, and support. Without all of you, I wouldn't have been able to write this—and, specifically, to you, Aunt Opal. I love you all. Also, to Mrs. Bain, Mrs. Unthank, Mrs. Cole, and Jim Moreton. You inspired me more than you'll ever know.
—DM

Acknowledgments

THANKS TO BRYAN AND DARREN for stepping in at the last minute, thanks to Sybex for staying with the book even when the project seemed impossible, and thanks to The Cobb Group editors for teaching me such an interesting marketable skill.
—Susan Harkins

I wish to thank Susan Harkins and Sybex for the opportunity to create this book. To The Cobb Group for providing such a great environment to learn and grow so much during my time there. I also wish to acknowledge that light is both a wave and a particle and that fast-food fries are much better while you are still in the car.
—Bryan Chamberlain

First and foremost, I'd like to thank Susan Harkins for her guidance and leadership on this project. Thanks to the folks at Sybex, too, for all your help and having patience with this hectic schedule. Special thanks to Troy Compton for his expert advice and additions to this book—KATE MIPS never fails! And thanks to those of you who find this book useful.
—Darren McGee

As a team, we'd also like to thank Macromedia, Inc., and particularly Heather Hollaender, for providing software that we used in writing the book, and for letting us distribute trial versions of MX software on the companion CD-ROM. Thanks also to Mariann Barsolo of Sybex, for coordinating the software, and to the Sybex CD team of Keith McNeil, Dan Mummert, and Kevin Ly. Special thanks to Leslie Light of Sybex for managing the book's production.

Contents at a Glance

Contents

Introduction

YEARS AGO, ONE OF US heard a sociology teacher say that technology advances exponentially. The professor used a snowball rolling down a hill to help us visualize the concept. The snowball starts off small, it grows quickly, and, after awhile, the snowball is, for most purposes, out of control and on an unknown course that we can't easily predict or refashion because it moves so fast and because it's so large. If it happens to roll over a few people on the way down, that's just the price we all pay. Eventually, a tree, a car, or even a change in gravity—something larger than its collective power—stops the snowball.

We gather around the now still but huge collection of snow and start grabbing pieces to compact into lots of smaller collections of the same snow. All that snow is eventually disseminated into lots of other snowballs as we continue to repeat the cycle. That's the way of technology, and most all of us have been a part of this amazing phenomenon via the Internet.

Our generation has witnessed one of the greatest growths in technology. Two decades ago, hardly anyone even knew the Internet existed. The snowball was just beginning to collect momentum. Now we are surrounded by snowballs at home, at work, and at play. Our grandmothers send e-mail, collect recipes off the Internet, and use media software to watch home movies of their grandchildren (sent via the Internet, of course). Some of you may even have a grandmother who's making her living using computers and the Internet! We even carry snowballs on our person in the guise of hand-held devices and phones that view e-mail and send instant pictures.

Sometimes growth applies a little pressure to keep up with and learn the latest technology. We seem to always want to push the envelope—to exploit the technology as far as we can and then to surpass it. Right now, developers of every ilk are finding their way onto the Internet because that's the current trend—developers are hearing a lot of "but we want it on the Internet."

It's becoming more and more difficult for the developer to stay on the cutting edge of technology. There are just too many things to know. We're wearing many caps and taking a lot of aspirin. The good news is, doors are opening, and opportunities are appearing where they never before existed. Since we can't know everything, technology is actually filling the void by creating products such as Dreamweaver MX—the technology has the expertise and does the work. Even if you have the expertise to do all the work yourself, why would you want to? There's no reason to spend hours writing script that Dreamweaver MX can produce in a matter of minutes.

Who Should Read This Book?

Anyone with a need to create and support a data-driven website will benefit from *Mastering Dreamweaver MX Databases*. You may be a novice or an expert. Dreamweaver MX makes the development experience much easier for the novice and more productive for the expert. Either way, you really can't lose. This book is a broad look at an even broader subject. It isn't aimed at the novice or the expert or even one specific technology—it focuses on using Dreamweaver MX to create a data-driven website.

Who Can Develop a Data-Driven Website?

Dreamweaver MX doesn't care on which side of the fence your expertise lies. The database developer can quickly produce dynamic web pages without knowing all the ins and outs of every scripting language and connection scheme. Dreamweaver MX takes care of the specifics. You just tell it where the database is and identify the data. On the other hand, the experienced web developer can easily connect a website to a database and start retrieving and updating data. The web developer doesn't have to speak in SQL or even understand every relational theory normalization rule.

If you're a web developer, you're way ahead of the database developer. On the other hand, if you're a database developer, you're way ahead of the web developer. In other words, your expertise will be enough to help you build this snowball.

The truth is, even a nondeveloper can produce dynamic web pages using Dreamweaver MX. Anyone can use Dreamweaver MX to create a data-driven website. As long as you're familiar with the database structure and the data, Dreamweaver MX will take care of all the connection and relational database magic.

What You Need

To try the techniques and examples in *Mastering Dreamweaver MX Databases*, you'll need Dreamweaver MX, a relational database system, a web server, and an Internet connection. Of course, you may have a much more sophisticated system already, but you don't really need it just to learn. You'll find that most of the technology choices are made for you rather than by you, and the operating system is a big factor. As you'll see if you check the system requirements listed on the Macromedia website (`www.macromedia.com/software/dreamweaver`), Dreamweaver MX runs on almost everything—it's the web server and database that limit your choices. Following are a few of the more common setup scenarios for Dreamweaver MX that you can use with this book:

Windows	IIS, SQL Server, using ASP, ASP.NET, ASP.ADO, or JSP
	IIS, Access, using ASP, ASP.NET, ASP.ADO, or JSP
	IIS, Oracle, using ASP, ASP.NET or JSP
	IIS, MySQL, using PHP
Linux	Apache, MySQL using PHP

How This Book Is Organized

This book is a conference call among you, management, the web, the database, the web server, and Dreamweaver MX. Each section focuses on one aspect of using Dreamweaver MX to create a database-supported website.

This book is unique in that the chapters don't necessarily build upon each other. You can certainly read the book chapter by chapter, but you won't have a finished website at the end of the last chapter. What you will have is the information you need to create one yourself—with Dreamweaver MX's help. In addition, you'll have a great reference tool as you're working.

Part I of this book demystifies the data-driven phenomenon. It isn't magic; it's all about knowledge, and Dreamweaver MX knows it all. We also introduce you to the Dreamweaver MX user interface and its many features. Then, we offer advice on applying consistent and professional coding practices. Finally, we review the workhorse of the whole model—the HTML form. If you're new to the web, we suggest that you not skip these chapters. You'll learn concepts that are vital to understanding the adventure on which you're about to embark.

Part II reviews four of the major relational databases on the market within the context of supporting a web-driven database: Microsoft SQL Server 2000, Microsoft Access 2002, Oracle9i, and MySQL. All four of these databases bring unique features to the web experience, and there are more (which we don't discuss). The good news is, Dreamweaver MX can support any relational database. If you have the luxury of choosing the system, you should probably read all four chapters so you can make a fully informed decision. In fact, we suggest you explore other systems as well. On the other hand, most of us are told which database to use. Perhaps it's one of the four we've reviewed, and if that's the case, we've provided a chapter's worth of information. Chapter 5 uses simple language and examples to tame an otherwise intimidating subject—relational database design. Database developers can probably skip this chapter.

In Part III, you'll learn about the scripting languages that claim the largest share of the market: ASP, ASP.NET, ADO.NET, JSP, and PHP. There are also chapters on ColdFusion, an application server, connection technologies, and web security. You won't become an expert on any scripting language, but you will secure a comfortable grasp on the ones we cover. This section should prove especially useful when you're working with existing systems that speak a language you don't know. Read the appropriate chapter, and once you have a general feel for the language, you should find it much easier to slip into the application and glean the information you need.

Anxious to actually start using Dreamweaver MX? That's what you'll do in Part IV. A full chapter is devoted to each data-manipulating task—retrieving, searching, and updating data. In addition, there's an introductory but fairly comprehensive chapter on SQL, the standard language of relational databases. If you've been meaning to learn SQL, but just haven't, now is a good time. In this section, you'll also learn:

◆ To use templates to reduce your work load

◆ About extensions that increase the functionality of your site

Every chapter contains good information, but not every reader will need each chapter. Each reader brings a unique level of expertise to the task at hand. That's one reason this book is so useful to such a wide audience—you don't have to read each chapter. Select the chapters that fill your information holes. For instance, web developers may benefit mostly from the chapters on database design and SQL, and the database developer will probably read the chapters on scripting languages first. There's something for everybody, and it's all written within the context of creating a data-driven website.

What's on the CD

The CD-ROM accompanying *Mastering Dreamweaver MX Databases* includes trial versions of four of Macromedia's most popular software tools:

◆ Dreamweaver MX for both Windows and Macintosh platforms

◆ Flash MX for both Windows and Macintosh platforms

◆ Fireworks MX for both Windows and Macintosh platforms

◆ ColdFusion Server for both Windows and Macintosh platforms

Finally, the CD includes sample database tables, scripts, and related files you can use as you try out examples throughout the book. These files are included for your convenience. Although we feel entering the scripts yourself will add to your learning experience, it isn't necessary. Feel free to use the scripts and files on the CD. Or, you might want to view the finished technique before you attempt to create it yourself. Finally, if you try, but your script simply won't work, use ours and move on. Chances are the problem is just a simple typo that you can't find, and that's not a good reason to hold up your learning experience.

NOTE   Throughout the book, the character _ appearing at the end of code lines in some listings marks a break introduced by the publisher to fit the printed page width; it is not part of the actual source code. The source code files on the CD do not have these introduced line breaks or _ characters.

Tell Us What You Think

We wrote this book to meet your needs, and only you can tell us how well we've succeeded. If there are topics you expected to find here that we haven't covered, or if you find any errors, let us know by going to the page for this book at www.sybex.com, and choosing the Submit a Review link. Of course, if this book has helped you in web development projects or if there are features we've included that you particularly like, we'd also love to hear about that. Good or bad, we'll use your feedback to build an even better book next time.

Part I

Data-Driven Web Pages

In these chapters you'll be introduced to:

- ◆ The data-driven world that web and database developers need to master
- ◆ Dreamweaver MX and its interface
- ◆ Coding practices for successful team development in Dreamweaver MX
- ◆ HTML forms, the basic tool for data input on the web

Chapter 1

An Introduction to the Data-Driven World

THE INTERNET IS CHANGING the way many of us work and play—the ball is rolling so to speak. Although some of us are shoved into the fray by job pressures, most of us are clamoring for more. More what? More information. We want to know everything there is to know, and we want to know it now. As consumers, we'd like it for free, but we're willing to pay for it if the information is vital. As vendors, we're scrambling to keep our customers happy and coming back.

With all this information comes responsibility and choices. Sometimes choices aren't easy, but to remain competitive and successful, you'll have to face them head on. Chances are, if you're reading this book, some decisions have already been made, and now it's up to you to turn your plans into reality. With Dreamweaver MX and this book, you're definitely up to the challenge.

In this chapter, you'll learn about:

- ◆ The benefits of offering dynamic data
- ◆ New technologies and terms
- ◆ Scripting for servers
- ◆ Matching a database to your needs

The Benefits of Offering Dynamic Data

Give web fanatics a static page and they'll demand dynamic data! Well, it's too late. The horse is out of the barn, and everybody thinks they need access to data any time they want it. Frankly, if you have clients to appease, you may have to meet their demands or go the way of the dinosaur. There are a few really good reasons to meet this challenge:

- ◆ You can automate many business-to-business communication tasks.
- ◆ You can simplify many work-related processes at once by creating one single interface for all accessing, updating, and so on.
- ◆ You can give your employees and your clients immediate and remote access to the information they need.

Business-to-Business Communication: Extranets

Suppose you run a small manufacturing plant that supplies customized gadgets for a really large manufacturing plant, and their specifications are now processed online. The whole thing is automated, and specifications are sent to you as soon as they're entered and approved. Are you going to insist that someone on the other side print out a spec sheet and fax it to you? If you want to keep this customer, you're going to climb on the technological assembly line by training someone to access the necessary data electronically. More than likely, someone in your organization will have to spend some time at the client's facilities, learning their system. Once the client gives your employee the necessary clearance to connect to their database, your employee can then sit at her own computer and download order information as required. What you do with the specifications once you've got them is entirely up to you, but at least you've met the client's needs.

The above scenario benefits from what's known as an extranet. That's a website for customers (or those needing limited access) rather than the general public that transmits across the Internet. Companies use them to gain access to all (or at least most) of their databases. Some use them for research.

Internal Communication: The Company Intranet

Now, let's suppose you have employees entering orders, maintaining accounts receivable and accounts payable, and updating inventory and fulfillment—and it's all going on at different locations all over the country. Do you really want to create an individual application for every department? It would be much more efficient and simpler if everyone were talking to the same database and using the same interface. And if you have personnel who are frequently on the road and need information such as current prices and inventory numbers, remote access to your internal site can be provided.

Such a system might include several different input screens that grant or deny access to any number of database applications. That way, employees can gain access to the data they need from any computer that can connect to the system.

This type of in-house website is known as an intranet. It serves employees, and although intranet pages may link to the Internet, there's no public access to the site. Intranets take advantage of Internet protocols and hypertext links to provide a standard means of sharing data internally.

Communicating with the Outside World: The Internet

As widespread as those two applications have become, by far the most common use of data-driven web technology is to exchange information with the outside world via the Internet. Do you have customers that would benefit from ordering from you directly online, bypassing sales personnel and telephone calls? If so, a data-driven site may be just the tool you need. These are just a few examples of the kinds of data-driven sites that Dreamweaver MX—and the languages and database systems it works with—can help you build. Dreamweaver MX does a great job of helping you build just the right site and the right web application for your purposes. However, we don't want to mislead anyone. For one thing, there is a learning curve. Not only do you need to understand Dreamweaver MX and the language and database system you're using, you also need to design exactly how the site will function. You should also consider some other issues before you open shop:

- Software, hardware, and support personnel will add to the costs.
- A database isn't a lockbox; it needs constant management and maintenance.
- Once you're online, your database is vulnerable to hackers. You'll need a good security plan and software and personnel to implement it.

Dreamweaver MX and this book can help you with the first point, but you'll need to deal with the others on your own. The goal of this book is not to provide "recipes" that take you through the steps of building each type of data-driven site; it is to show you how to use Dreamweaver MX and the related tools to build sites that make data accessible to your users.

New Technologies and Terms

Technological advances are driven by need, and that evolution is marked by small and large spikes. One of those large spikes was the introduction of HTML (Hypertext Markup Language) because it introduced hypertext, which meant that text information could be accessed in a nonlinear fashion via hyperlinks. HTML was so successful because it was incredibly easy to learn and use and because it worked. But once unleashed, these new capabilities just made users want more—they wanted interactivity and they wanted it to be as easy as HTML. The result is a technological smorgasbord— the only problem may be finding a place in line.

Learning the web technology hierarchy may be the biggest challenge for the nonprogrammer or even the programmer with no web development experience, because there really isn't one—at least not one that's easily laid out in clear terms. The diagram in Figure 1.1 offers a basic look at what happens with a web request; this process is the context in which web development takes place.

FIGURE 1.1

Processing data via the Internet

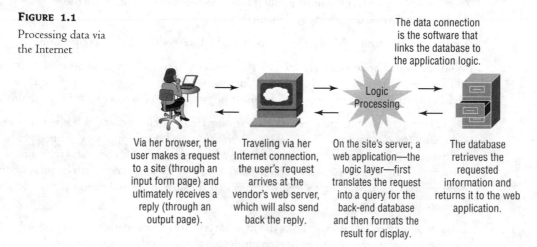

The data connection is the software that links the database to the application logic.

Logic Processing

Via her browser, the user makes a request to a site (through an input form page) and ultimately receives a reply (through an output page).

Traveling via her Internet connection, the user's request arrives at the vendor's web server, which will also send back the reply.

On the site's server, a web application—the logic layer—first translates the request into a query for the back-end database and then formats the result for display.

The database retrieves the requested information and returns it to the web application.

The user sits down at her computer keyboard and accesses your website, and information floods her monitor—seemingly with no effort. But there's a lot going on behind that monitor. First, her request is passed along to your web server via her Internet connection; the technology behind this connection is HTTP (Hypertext Transfer Protocol).

Your server interprets the request and sends it along to the appropriate application, which then processes the request. The results are then returned via the web server, which then routes it to her connection and on to her monitor. It's hard to believe all this happens in the few seconds she spent waiting for a request to be processed.

Through a process known as task switching (or multitasking), the web server manages to complete multiple tasks in a short period of time, making each user feel as though she is the only visitor at your site. A *web server* is the software technology that connects a browser to your database. Here's how it works:

1. As the server receives each request, it stores them in a queue (a list of items that's constantly updated).
2. The server chooses a predetermined number of tasks—known as threads—from the queue.
3. The server loads the first thread and works on it for a while, maybe for a few millionths of a second.
4. The server then loads the second thread and works on it for a while. The server continues in this fashion until the first thread is complete.
5. Once a thread is complete, it's removed from the queue.

The more threads you have, the slower each task is completed, but the loss in performance is hardly noticeable in most systems.

This process sees a request and the resulting processed data traveling across several layers of technology:

Browser Accepts requests from the user and displays data. Microsoft Internet Explorer and Netscape Navigator are the most popular browsers today. You'll often see the browser referred to as the client in web development documentation.

Internet connection Most of us connect to the Internet via HTTP connections.

Web server The software technology that allows you to connect to another system via your HTTP connection and then share data. Windows systems use Internet Information Services (IIS) and Personal Web Server (PWS). The most popular non-Windows server is probably Apache.

Logic layer An application server or a scripting language that processes both client- and server-side requests in regard to manipulating, formatting, and displaying data. This layer works in both directions—accepting requests from the client to the server for data and returning data from the server to the client's browser. The web server and application server can be one and the same. For example IIS 5, Microsoft's web server, is also considered an application server and is referred to as such by Microsoft.

Data connection This layer links the logic layer to the actual data. Connection solutions are specific to the operating system or, sometimes, to the actual database software.

Database This layer could comprise any number of database application files. It's simply the storage medium for your data.

Chances are you've visited a data-driven site. Most any time you request information and the browser displays the requested information, you're dealing with a *data-driven site*. What that means is that a database is actively providing information. Your web browser requests the information via a connection, the server passes that request on to the database, which then processes the request and returns it to your browser, via the server and the connection. Dreamweaver MX can help you build a fully dynamic website, even if you don't have the programming expertise to create such a site on your own.

Scripting for Servers

Dreamweaver MX is an HTML authoring tool and an application development tool that interprets multiple scripting languages to build data-driven websites. It runs on Windows and Mac systems and interacts with the majority of development operating systems. Dreamweaver MX supports most scripting languages, application servers, and database formats. In addition, Dreamweaver MX provides an easy-to-use graphical interface that integrates all these components.

Throughout this book, you'll see the term *script* in many forms. In a nutshell, a *script* is a set of statements pertaining to a particular scripting language. In this context, a scripting language is similar to any other language in that it's a combination of keywords, functions, and methods. However, scripting languages are considered *interpreted* languages. That means the server parses, compiles, and then executes the script all at once and as needed.

An interpreted language differs from other programming languages, otherwise known as compiled languages, in one respect. A compiled language can parse and compile code before the code is executed. As a result, the compiled language stores an already translated version of the code.

In this book, we'll use a variety of scripting languages in our examples. You can learn more about the following scripting languages in Chapters 12 through 16.

Active Server Pages (ASP)

Eventually, the quest for more flexible web languages led to several scripting languages. ASP is a server-side, language-independent scripting host from Microsoft. That means ASP interprets most scripting languages. In fact, ASP works with any scripting language that has a certified ActiveX Scripting Engine. The one requirement is that the language be compatible with the Microsoft Scripting Host. The following scripting languages are compatible with the Scripting Host:

VBScript   A subset of Visual Basic for Applications (VBA). We mention this one first because it's the default ASP scripting language.

JScript   Microsoft's counterpart to JavaScript. Neither is connected to Sun's Java language. Many developers consider JScript the common standard for browser scripting. JScript comes with ASP.

PerlScript   A subset of Perl, which has been around for a long time. It's used mostly with text. It doesn't come with ASP, but you can download it from www.activestate.com.

ASP.NET

Active Server Pages has been the Microsoft web staple for many years and has been supported in all prior versions of Dreamweaver MX (Drumbeat and Ultradev). ASP.NET is a complete rewrite of ASP for the .NET framework and provides many advantages over standard ASP. ASP.NET supports new providers when working with databases, particularly with Microsoft SQL Server 2000. Unlike standard ASP, which restricted the developer to working in VBScript or JScript, ASP.NET allows you to choose virtually any scripting language.

Don't confuse ASP (discussed in the previous section) and ASP.NET, because they aren't the same thing. However, ASP.NET is compatible with ASP to the extent that almost all ASP code is supported in ASP.NET (for now) for backward compatibility.

Hypertext Preprocessor (PHP)

PHP is another server-side scripting language that puts dynamic capabilities into the hands of the masses. PHP runs on Linux, many Unix variants (including HP-UX, Solaris, and OpenBSD), Microsoft Windows, Mac OS X, and RISC OS. Supported web servers include Apache, IIS, PWS, Netscape, and iPlanet. For the most part, you'll find PHP running on Apache servers and interacting with MySQL (a database), although PHP supports a number of databases, including dBase, IBM DB2, Oracle, and Sybase. Currently, PHP is an open-source language that can be freely distributed. You can download PHP at www.php.net.

In a nutshell, you insert PHP code inside your HTML code. When a client makes a request, your server executes the PHP code, just like any other scripting language. PHP's many capabilities include the following:

◆ PHP supports data-driven applications and supports cookies (or we wouldn't include it in this discussion).

◆ PHP authenticates and tracks users.

◆ PHP supports threaded discussions at your site.

◆ PHP is scalable across multiplatforms.

◆ PHP supports Extensible Markup Language (XML).

◆ PHP supports command-line scripting, which is ideal for scripts regularly executed by an operating system.

JavaServer Pages (JSP)

JavaServer Pages is an application server that uses XML-like tags and Java-based scripts to generate web pages. The technology is platform-independent and consists of Java server-side modules, known as servlets, that support and extend the web server. JSP is available for free from Sun Microsystems at http://java.sun.com/products/jsp/download.html.

JSP pages consist of three elements:

◆ Static components—HTML or XML

◆ JSP tags (unique to JSP)

◆ Java code, known as scriptlets to the Java developer

Anyone knowing HTML or XML should pick up JSP quickly. In fact, part of its appeal—and hence its growing market share—is its simple language. You don't have to be an experienced web developer to successfully use JSP.

If you're a Sun developer or if you're already familiar with Java, the jump to JSP will be painless. On the other hand, if you're coming from a Microsoft background, you'll find JSP very different from ASP. The main differences boil down to differences in shop technology—you're Sun or you're Microsoft. You can use JSP with Windows and IIS, but you can't use ASP with Sun.

The JSP engine is really a specialized servlet, supported by the servlet engine. JSP only deals with text, so you must use servlets to communicate with Java applets and applications. As a result of this arrangement, you may find servlets better suited to nondynamic tasks such as authentication, validation, and so on. Rely on JSP pages for your data-driven content.

Unlike most of the scripting languages we've reviewed, JSP code is stored separately from the static presentation within external JavaBeans components. The JSP page uses special tags to call these components as they're needed. When a change is made to the presentation template, the JSP engine automatically recompiles and reloads the JSP page.

JSP consists of three components: directives, scripts, and actions. Directives tell the JSP engine what to do with the JSP page. These directives are enclosed with the %@...% tag. Fragments of Java code, known as scriptlets, are enclosed in the <%...%> tag. Actions perform tasks such as instantiating objects and communicating with the server.

ColdFusion MX

Macromedia's ColdFusion MX is a web application server that lets developers create scripts for controlling data integration, logic, and user interface components for a website. In other words, Cold-Fusion MX processes the logic and scripting in your page and then lets your web server build the HTML to hand back to your user's browser.

NOTE   *An application server is a server that supports your web server. When your browser requests a ColdFusion MX page, your web server passes that request on to the ColdFusion MX application server, which then processes the request and hands it back to the web server for delivery to your browser.*

Using ColdFusion MX, you can quickly produce dynamic web pages without actually writing your own scripts—which can be tedious work even for the experienced web developer. This makes Cold-Fusion MX or any similar product the ideal solution for the nonprogrammer.

ColdFusion MX quickly produces HTML-like tags via its many wizards and auto-generating tags. For instance, you can combine ColdFusion MX tags to automatically generate a validation script (which you'd otherwise have to write yourself). The automatically generated script is ColdFusion Markup Language (CFML)—a tag-based server scripting language like HTML. You can download a demo copy of ColdFusion MX from www.macromedia.com.

Match a Database to Your Needs

Dreamweaver MX can connect to almost any database that runs on Unix or Windows. If an ODBC (Open Database Connectivity) or OLE DB driver exists, Dreamweaver MX will produce the code necessary to connect to and interact with the database. In this book, we'll review two of the largest full-system databases on the market: Microsoft SQL Server 2000 and Oracle9i. We'll also review the popular desktop database application, Microsoft Access, and the open-source relational database MySQL.

More than likely, as the application developer, you really had no choice over the database you'll be using. Your company chose it for a number of reasons: current costs and future needs were probably discussed. However, you probably ended up with the relational database that you already have. We're not endorsing a database, but we will use all the above in our examples throughout this book.

Working with Microsoft SQL Server 2000 and Access 2002

SQL Server 2000 is a powerful database and is fully web-enabled. You'll have no problem interfacing with it via Dreamweaver MX. It's also expensive and requires experienced personnel to administer and maintain the database. If you're a Windows fan and have the money, go with SQL Server 2000.

Access 2002 (also known as Access XP) is an alternative if you're running Windows, have limited resources, but anticipate a small amount of online traffic.

Relying on Open Source: MySQL

MySQL is fast, stable, runs on Unix and Windows, and it's free—do we need to say more? You can download MySQL at www.mysql.com. MySQL makes its money by selling technical support because the down side is that what you gain in fast, stable, and free open-source code, you lose in functionality. MySQL is a great alternative for the money-challenged but ready-to-learn-and-support crowd.

Oracle9i

Oracle is a SQL Server 2000 competitor and has been around for a long time. This industrial-strength database has friends in many places, and Dreamweaver MX has no problem talking to it.

Summary

We've tried to introduce you to the web-driven world, if that's possible in one short chapter. There are advantages and disadvantages, and as with any business decision, you have to weigh your unique needs and resources. But Dreamweaver MX can help you balance any disadvantages, such as the costs and the highly paid personnel that often accompany a web venture. In the end, there's simply nothing to replace experience. The remaining chapters will open the world of databases and show you how to use scripting languages to interact with databases. By the end of the book, you'll know the ins and outs of retrieving and interacting with dynamic data in several database formats.

In the next chapter, you'll launch Dreamweaver MX and have a look around.

Chapter 2

An Introduction to Dreamweaver MX

DREAMWEAVER HAS LONG BEEN the professional web developer's tool of choice for rapidly creating the user interface portion of a website. With Dreamweaver UltraDev, Dreamweaver provided tools and features that let the web developer interact with data tables as well as generate code targeted to specific web application servers. Now, with Dreamweaver MX, Macromedia has taken Dreamweaver to a new level, incorporating even better database tools, coding tools, and the ability to write and utilize code for several web application servers. Dreamweaver MX lets you create sites using HTML, XHTML, XML, ColdFusion, ASP.NET, ASP, JSP, and PHP. We'll cover the basics of Dreamweaver from a technical point of view in this chapter, taking you from a bit of Dreamweaver history to setting up your database connection and site management.

Topics in this chapter include:

◆ A bit of history

◆ Installing and running Dreamweaver MX for the first time

◆ Configuring Dreamweaver MX to suit your needs

◆ Setting up your PC/server environment

◆ Site management and transferring files

A Bit of History

"WYSIWYG, WYSIWYG! Wherefore art thou, WYSIWYG?" With apologies to the Bard, that's the chant that some of us designers and programmers were mumbling in the early days of web tools. Our standard web development tool, Notepad or some other text editor, just couldn't show us the fruits of our hard labor. We had to save the file, load it in our browser, and hope that we didn't miss a closing </tr> tag in the middle of our meticulously indented code. Unfortunately, many times we did miss that </tr> tag and had to spend at least a few minutes searching for the proper spot in which to insert it. Frustrating days those were, when all we really wanted to do was develop the slick data entry screen we were applying to our company's new online survey.

Then, magically it seems, along came tools such as NaviPress, HoTMetal, Webauthor, FrontPage (before Microsoft bought it) and Dreamweaver. These tools made it easier for the programmer to integrate the graphic designer's wishes with our effective and bug-free (right?!) code. We no longer had to waste time looking for the elusive, missed closing HTML tag or guessing at table widths and alignments. The age of WYSIWYG web development was here!

That was way back in 1997. Since then, many other WYSIWYG web tools have come and gone, and some have stayed. And they all have their little quirks and problems. True WYSIWYG still isn't possible in all cases, although you can pretty much count on WYSIAWYG, although none of the other tools have the robust feature set that Dreamweaver MX contains. But it took even the mighty Macromedia a while to get there.

WYSIWYG ("WHAT YOU SEE IS WHAT YOU GET") DEFINED

From NetLingo.com: "An acronym—this is a classic acronym for a technology that allows you to view or print a document exactly as it looks."

From FOLDOC (Free on-line Dictionary of Computing): "<jargon> (WYSIWYG) /wiz'ee-wig/ Describes a user interface for a document preparation system under which changes are represented by displaying a more-or-less accurate image of the way the document will finally appear, e.g. when printed. This is in contrast to one that uses more-or-less obscure commands that do not result in immediate visual feedback.

"True WYSIWYG in environments supporting multiple fonts or graphics is a rarely-attained ideal; there are variants of this term to express real-world manifestations including WYSIAWYG (What You See Is *Almost* What You Get) and WYSIMOLWYG (What You See Is More or Less What You Get)."

Dreamweaver started out as one of the first WYSIWYG tools that incorporated Dynamic Hypertext Markup Language (DHTML) and JavaScript generation into its bag of tricks. It progressed from its dynamic, yet humble roots to better and more powerful features, including the ability to use plug-ins that let you create objects that interface with web application servers such as (then) Allaire's ColdFusion. Macromedia continued to enhance Dreamweaver through additions and acquisitions. With the purchase of Elemental's Drumbeat, Macromedia added database connectivity and dynamic website development capability to Dreamweaver and called it Dreamweaver UltraDev. By then, Dreamweaver also was able to generate code directly into Active Server Pages (ASP) or ColdFusion Markup Language (CFM or CFML) pages. Dreamweaver MX builds on this legacy by generating code for a number of web application platforms, including ASP, ASP.NET, ColdFusion, JavaServer Pages (JSP) and PHP: Hypertext Preprocessor (PHP). It now incorporates numerous "behaviors" that let you customize the code Dreamweaver generates, includes the capability to enhance its core functionality with third-party extensions, and more. Dreamweaver has long been the professional web developer's choice. With this new release, Macromedia has positioned Dreamweaver to maintain that title for years to come.

Installing and Running Dreamweaver MX for the First Time

Before you can use Dreamweaver MX, you must install and configure it to match your local work environment. Like all software, Dreamweaver has a list of recommended minimum requirements that, if met, will run Dreamweaver in an acceptable fashion. Dreamweaver's power can only be maximized through an equitable system. Let's take a look at some of these requirements now.

Hardware and Software Requirements for the PC and the Mac

Macromedia has a list of minimum requirements that your PC or Mac should meet before you install and try to use Dreamweaver MX. Can you install Dreamweaver MX on a less powerful or capable system? Probably. But we wouldn't recommend it since Dreamweaver MX relies heavily on the network and graphics capabilities of your machine. The minimum requirements for Windows are as follows:

- Intel Pentium II processor or equivalent 300+MHz
- Windows 98, 2000, NT, Me, or XP
- Netscape Navigator or Internet Explorer 4 or later
- 96MB of available RAM (128MB recommended)
- 275MB available disk space
- 256-color monitor capable of 800 × 600 resolution (1024 × 768 millions of colors recommended)
- Microsoft Data Access Components 2.6 (or later). You'll find the latest version of MDAC at www.microsoft.com/data

The minimum requirements for the Macintosh are as follows:

- Power Mac G3 or better
- Mac OS 9.1 or higher, or Mac OS X 10.1 or higher
- Netscape Navigator or Internet Explorer 4 or later
- 96MB of RAM (128MB recommended)
- 275MB available disk space
- 256-color monitor capable of 800 × 600 resolution (1024 × 768, millions of colors recommended; thousands of colors required for OS X)

To actually use Dreamweaver without getting frustrated waiting on your machine, you probably want to use a faster machine than the minimum requirements. We recommend a Windows system comparable to at least the following specifications:

- Intel Pentium III processor (or better) 600+MHz
- Windows 2000, NT, or XP
- Netscape Navigator or Internet Explorer 5 or later
- 256MB of RAM
- Several GB available disk space for all your web development needs

For a Macintosh system we recommend the following:

♦ G4, single processor
♦ OS X or later
♦ Netscape Navigator or Internet Explorer 5 or later
♦ 512 MB of RAM
♦ Several GB available disk space for all your web development needs

Installing a Local Web Server

To use Dreamweaver MX properly, you'll need access to a web server. For quick testing purposes, you might want to install a local web server—a server on your local machine. Installing a web server on your local machine isn't that difficult, but you must be aware of which web server you need for your operating system. Also, if you're a Windows user, you'll have to know where to find the web server appropriate for your system. Table 2.1 will give you a bit of guidance as to which web server you need and where you can find it. PWS is Microsoft's Personal Web Server, IIS is Microsoft's Internet Information Services, and Apache is the open-source web server provided by the Apache HTTP Server Project.

TABLE 2.1: WEB SERVERS FOR SPECIFIC OPERATING SYSTEMS

OPERATING SYSTEM	WEB SERVER	WHERE TO FIND IT
Windows 95	PWS	NT Option Pack 4
Windows 98	PWS	Windows 98 CD
NT Workstation	PWS	NT Option Pack 4
Windows XP Home	Not Available	Not Available
Windows XP Professional	IIS	Choose Start ➢ Control Panel ➢ Add or Remove Programs
Windows NT Server	IIS	Choose Start ➢ Control Panel ➢ Add/Remove Programs
Windows 2000	IIS	Choose Start ➢ Control Panel ➢ Add or Remove Programs
Macintosh	Apache	Visit www.apache.org/dist/httpd/binaries/

Since each version and type of web server has its own installation instructions, we're not going to cover the specifics of each. However, we will point you to the informative instructions listed in the Dreamweaver MX help file. Start Dreamweaver, press F1, and search for "Installing a Web Server."

You'll find that actually installing the personal web server is quite painless. And hooking Dreamweaver into the web server isn't that difficult either. We'll show you that in the next section.

Installation Options

When you start the installation procedure for Dreamweaver MX, you're asked a few questions about how you want to configure the look and feel of your new software. Don't worry about the options you choose. If you don't like the setup once Dreamweaver MX is installed, you can change your initial options within the program.

You'll naturally be presented with the standard installation questions such as where do you want to install the program, but the first Dreamweaver MX–specific options you must decide are whether you want Dreamweaver MX to act as the default editor for certain file types. Figure 2.1 shows you the screen where you specify whether to use Dreamweaver MX as your default editor for ColdFusion files or keep your current ColdFusion Studio as the editor. Pay special attention to this screen, because you don't want to inadvertently break the link to the code editor you know and love.

FIGURE 2.1

Choose your default editor for various file types from the Default Editor screen.

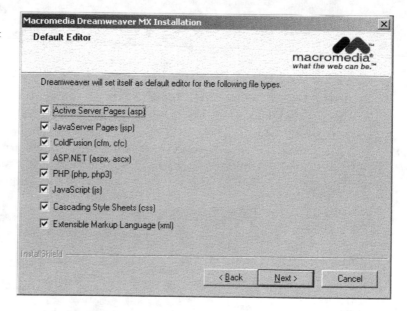

In the Start Copying Files screen, shown in Figure 2.2, you review and confirm the file types and extensions you selected. For example, if you selected PHP in the Default Editor screen, you'll see php and phpe under the Default Editor entry. If you find file extensions in this list for which you don't want to change the default editor behavior of your system, click the Back button and clear the check box for the appropriate file type.

FIGURE 2.2

Dreamweaver MX shows you the file types for which it will become the default editor after installation.

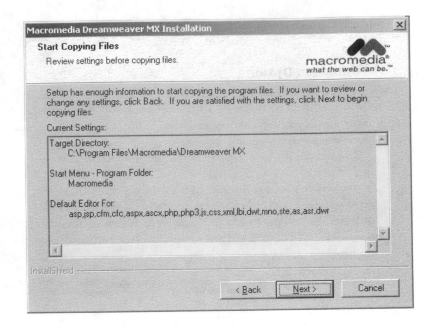

Running Dreamweaver MX for the First Time

As you can see in Figure 2.3, the first time you run Dreamweaver, it asks which type of workspace style you want to use, either the new Dreamweaver MX interface or the Dreamweaver 4 (and UltraDev) interface. The new Dreamweaver MX style follows the typical program style in which every toolbar, panel, and subwindow opens within the main program window. Macromedia is letting you get rid of the floating panel bars that tended to confuse many Dreamweaver users.

FIGURE 2.3

The first time you run Dreamweaver MX, you choose the style of interface you want to use.

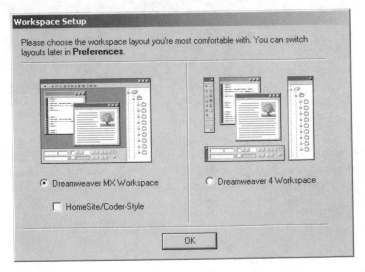

NOTE   To help curb software piracy and to encourage proper license use, Dreamweaver MX checks to see if another copy of Dreamweaver MX with the same serial number is running on your network. If Dreamweaver MX finds its serial number already running on a machine, it refuses to start and shuts itself down. Thus, if your single copy of Dreamweaver MX is installed on two machines (with the same MX serial number), you might be able to run it on only one machine at a time.

We believe that you'll find the new Dreamweaver MX style more comfortable to use, so you might want to ditch the floating-window concept. If you're a coder by nature—that is, a developer who prefers to work at the code level most of the time—you can also specify whether you'd like to start with the HomeSite/Coder-Style interface. If you choose this option, you'll start Dreamweaver MX in a coding window, as indicated on the left in Figure 2.4.

FIGURE 2.4

You can also choose a coding window as a default interface in Dreamweaver MX.

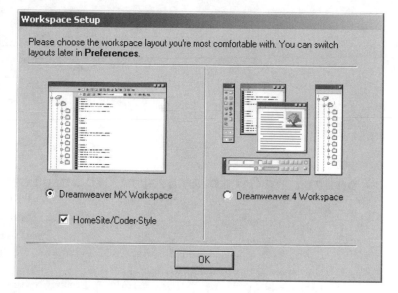

Remember, you can change your interface format at a later time if you don't like the one you chose. To do so, from the main menu, choose Edit ➢ Preferences ➢ General. As Figure 2.5 shows, you'll see a Change Workspace button in the middle of the window. Click it to display the Workspace Setup window, as shown in Figure 2.3 earlier.

WARNING   You'll have to restart Dreamweaver MX before your interface style changes take effect, so be sure you save your work before you restart!

FIGURE 2.5

You can use the Preferences window to configure Dreamweaver MX to your liking.

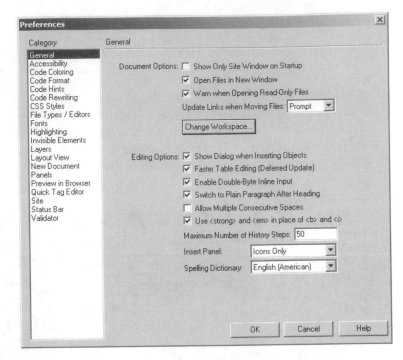

Configuring Dreamweaver MX to Suit Your Needs

Naturally, you'll want to personalize your nifty, new Dreamweaver MX installation to suit the way you work. Macromedia built dozens of configuration options into this new version of Dreamweaver so you can certainly make it conform to your work style as opposed to the other way around. To start you on your merry way, let's take a look at the Preferences menu, which is where you control almost all of the customization options available to you.

To customize Dreamweaver MX, choose Edit ➢ Preferences to open the Preferences window, shown earlier in Figure 2.5. We've already covered how to change your Dreamweaver MX workspace style, so let's explore some of the other options.

Adding Icons to the Panels and Adding the Launcher

If you're a designer, you're probably going to like this next feature. If you're a coder at heart, you're also going to find this next feature helpful, since it gives you quick access to the coding features you most often use. Instead of just using text to describe all these panels and options and menus (oh my!), wouldn't it be nice if you could see a helpful icon to visually indicate what all these options do? Well, surprise! You can. Select the Panels category, and then click the Show Icons In Panels And Launcher check box as shown in Figure 2.6. Once you do, you should notice a welcome, unobtrusive transformation of your Dreamweaver MX desktop—icons appear on the feature panels, and an additional, graphical toolbar called the Launcher is added at the bottom of your document window (see Figure 2.7). You can use this toolbar to launch some of the more frequently used features in Dreamweaver MX. Table 2.2 lists and describes the buttons on the Launcher toolbar.

FIGURE 2.6

You can transform Dreamweaver MX's simple text descriptions to eye-catching icons by choosing this option.

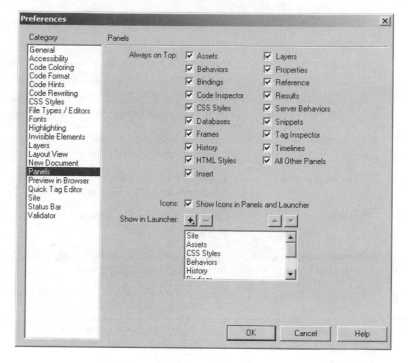

FIGURE 2.7

The Icon option also displays a toolbar, called the Launcher, at the bottom of your document window.

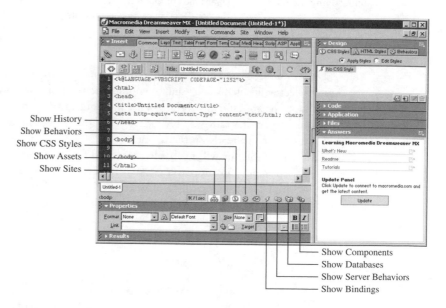

Show History
Show Behaviors
Show CSS Styles
Show Assets
Show Sites

Show Components
Show Databases
Show Server Behaviors
Show Bindings

TABLE 2.2: BUTTONS ON THE LAUNCHER TOOLBAR

BUTTON	WHAT IT DOES
Show Sites	Opens the Site tab under the Files panel, from which you control the sites in your work environment
Show Assets	Opens the Assets tab under the Files panel, from which you control the video, links, Flash, Shockwave, and so forth that are used in your sites
Show CSS Styles	Opens the CSS Styles tab under the Design panel, from which you control the CSS style sheets that are used in your site
Show Behaviors	Opens the Behaviors tab under the Design panel, from which you control the behaviors used in the pages you're creating
Show History	Opens the History panel, from which you can see the steps you've taken to modify the current document
Show Bindings	Opens the Bindings tab under the Application panel, from which you control the data bindings used in your pages
Show Server Behaviors	Opens the Server Behaviors tab under the Application panel, from which you modify the server-side behaviors used in your site
Show Databases	Opens the Databases tab under the Application panel, from which you control the databases used in your site
Show Components	Opens the Components tab under the Application panel, from which you control the non-Dreamweaver components you are using in your site

You can customize the options that appear on the Launcher by, you guessed it, going back to the Preferences window, selecting the Panels category, and clicking the plus sign button.

You can select which items you want on your Launcher, and you can also change the order in which the selected options appear using the arrows at the right of the panel. Figure 2.8 shows that we still have the Code Inspector, Frames, HTML Styles, and other options available to add to our Launcher. A grayed-out option is already on the Launcher.

The designers among us will probably prefer a different set of Launcher preferences than the programmers. But since Dreamweaver MX is targeted to both audiences, you'll probably find a mixture of options helpful, regardless of your profession. Here are our recommendations and ordering for each of the professions:

Designer	Programmer
Sites	Sites
Assets	Assets
CSS Styles	CSS Styles

Designer	Programmer
Behaviors	Behaviors
Server Behaviors	Server Behaviors
Bindings	Bindings
Databases	Databases
Timelines	Components
Code Inspector	Snippets
Reference	Code Inspector
History	Reference

FIGURE 2.8

Choose your Launcher options from the Panels category of the Preferences window.

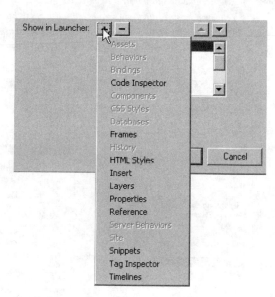

Preview in Browser

Probably the second thing you'll want to configure is the Preview In Browser setting. Dreamweaver MX lets you preview your work in an actual, live browser window. That is, it loads the page you're currently working on in a browser window so that you can view exactly how the page is going to appear to the public. Dreamweaver MX should automatically discover which browsers you have on your system during the installation process. But if you need to, you can manually add a browser or change which you use as your primary and secondary browsers through this setting.

Figure 2.9 shows the Preview In Browser category window. You'll notice that we set iexplore, which corresponds to Microsoft's Internet Explorer, as our primary browser. The F12 next to the name indicates that F12 is the hotkey by which we invoke the Dreamweaver MX preview mode for Internet Explorer. Now if Internet Explorer were our secondary browser or we also had Netscape Navigator, Opera, or some other browser installed, we'd see secondary browser with a CTLF12 next to it, implying that we invoke the secondary browser by pressing the Control key in conjunction with the F12 key. To add a secondary browser, click the Edit button to open the Add Browser dialog box (shown in Figure 2.9), and select the appropriate executable (.exe) file on your hard disk. You enter a name by which you want to refer to this browser (Netscape, IE, The Other Browser, or whatever), point to the executable file via the Browse button, and select whether you want to set this new browser as the primary or secondary browser. Once you click OK, you'll be ready to use the new setting. You may add as many browsers to this list as you wish, but you may have one Primary and one Secondary browser choice.

TIP   *Generally, you want to test your site on many different browsers and versions of browsers. Because of the rivalries among the various browser makers, they do not all adhere strictly to the HTML standards set forth by the World Wide Web Consortium (W3C). Even though most features you create will work on all browsers, invariably you'll find a feature that doesn't behave quite like you expect it to in one browser or another. By testing your code on as many brands of browsers as possible, you can find and trap for the odd behavior your users might encounter.*

FIGURE 2.9

Use the Add Browser dialog box to add a browser.

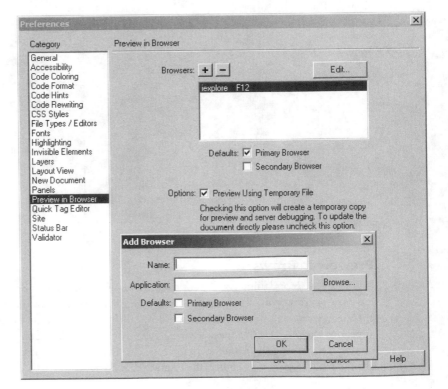

The Preview Using Temporary File check box tells Dreamweaver MX how to handle the preview step. If this option is checked, Dreamweaver writes your work to a temporary file and loads that file into the browser. You can change the default behavior by clearing the Preview Using Temporary File check box, which instructs Dreamweaver MX to automatically save your work and send the actual file itself to your browser. Keep in mind that if you select this option, you'll be working with the original version of your page; you won't have a copy to fall back on if you mess up your code or design. The temporary copy adds a small layer of protection for your original file. Plus, you can load the original file in one browser window for comparison and use the temporary version to review your most recent changes or additions.

Letting Dreamweaver MX Check Your Pages for Errors Before You Save Them

With all the updates to software, versions of programming languages, and versions of browsers, it's difficult to remember which HTML or other coding statement works in what combination. Does the Layer tag work with just version 4 browsers and later, or was that 4.5? Or maybe it was just Netscape 4.5? Or wait—was it the other way around? See what we mean? With Dreamweaver MX, you don't necessarily have to remember every nuance of every language and how it applies to every browser. You can have Dreamweaver MX check your work, or *validate* it, before you send it to the web server.

Using the Validator category in the Preferences window, you can tell Dreamweaver MX to validate your code against versions of HTML, XHTML (Extensible HyperText Markup Language), Internet Explorer, Netscape, ColdFusion, SMIL (Synchronized Multimedia Integration Language), WML (Website META Language), and JavaServer Pages. As you can see in Figure 2.10, telling Dreamweaver MX to validate against the different versions is as simple as clicking a check box. However, you might notice that you can't check all the versions of a particular language. Some newer code libraries— HTML, for example—incorporate the previous versions; so if you want to validate against HTML 4, it doesn't make sense to check HTML 1, 2, and 3. They're already in there.

Once you've set your preferences, you can start the validation process by choosing File ➢ Check Page from the main Dreamweaver MX screen. As you can see in Figure 2.11, you then have several options, only three of which we'll mention here. If you want to validate your HTML code, which you will probably do frequently, choose Validate Markup, or press the hotkey combination Shift+F6. If you want to validate an XML page, choose Validate As XML. Dreamweaver MX checks your code against the preferences you chose and displays a list of errors it finds, if any, in the Results pane at the bottom of your screen.

NOTE *If your page contains programming code such as ASP (Active Server Pages) and you're validating against HTML, you'll probably see errors about ASP tags in the list as well, since ASP isn't part of the HTML language.*

To make sure that your page works with a specific version of a browser, choose Check Target Browsers option to display a list of the current browser versions of Internet Explorer, Netscape Navigator, and Opera. Again, if Dreamweaver MX finds any incompatibilities with your page, it displays a list of errors in the Results pane.

FIGURE 2.10

Dreamweaver MX can check your work to ensure it adheres to a certain language syntax.

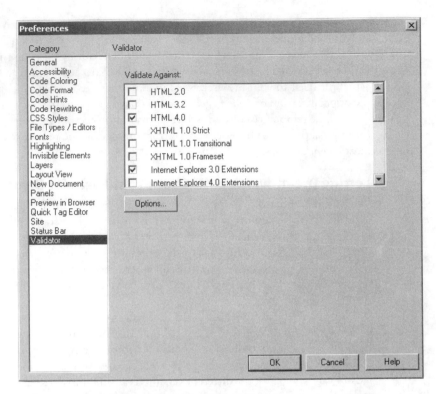

FIGURE 2.11

You can validate your work in several ways in Dreamweaver MX.

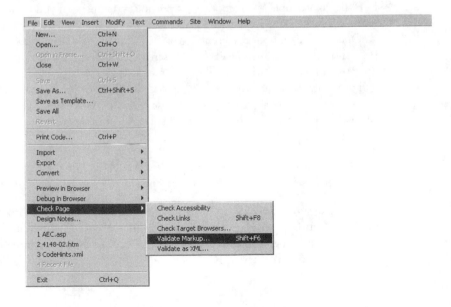

Letting Dreamweaver MX Rewrite (or "Fix") Your Code

Another category under Preferences is Code Rewriting. If you instruct it to, Dreamweaver MX tries to fix code so that it meets HTML standards when it opens a file. Depending on the user and the development task at hand, that can be either beneficial or counterproductive. The hardcore coder may find it annoying to have someone (or something) else rewrite their code, especially if the coder doesn't even know about it. More important, in ASP, ColdFusion, and other web server languages that tweak standard HTML to their own purposes, the "errors" Dreamweaver finds may not be incorrect and should not be "fixed." On the other hand, those new to HTML scripting may well appreciate having Dreamweaver MX do things such as remove extra closing tags. The settings under Code Rewriting give you considerable control over this behavior, so it's important to choose them carefully.

Figure 2.12 shows you the options available in the Code Rewriting category. The default behavior is to only rename forms when pasting into another page and to ensure that URLs and certain coding characters behave nicely. Naturally, you can change this default behavior. Click the Fix Invalidly Nested And Unclosed Tags check box, and several other options will activate as well. The Fix Invalidly Nested And Unclosed Tags option tells Dreamweaver MX to try to make sense of tags that aren't closed properly, such as nested tables that don't include closing </tr> tags and the like.

FIGURE 2.12

Dreamweaver MX lets you control how it will try to fix what it deems as erroneous HTML.

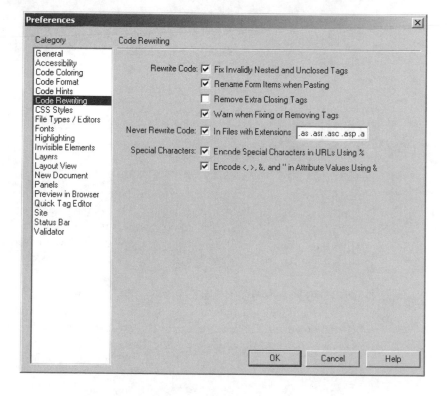

Early versions of programs such as FrontPage tried to fix these tags for you, which was fine, but they didn't warn you about it first! Plus, they rewrote and reconstructed meticulously created code that you may have spent hours on. Fortunately, Dreamweaver MX wants to play nice and gives us the option of warning us before it rewrites our code. It will even ignore files with certain extensions altogether so that there's no chance of it inadvertently creating bugs. If you have check the Warn When Fixing Or Removing tags option, Dreamweaver MX displays a window similar to Figure 2.13 when it encounters tag errors in a file that it's opening.

FIGURE 2.13

Dreamweaver MX will warn you when it changes your code.

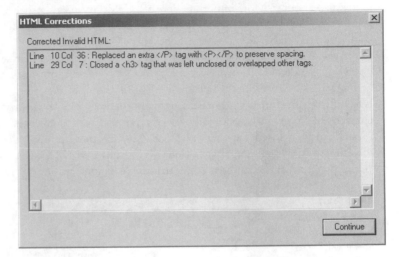

TIP   *Even though Dreamweaver MX tries to fix tag errors it finds, it's not foolproof. It may still leave unclosed tags if it can't quite interpret what you intended. Relying on Dreamweaver MX to fix your web pages is not an excuse for sloppy programming!*

Making Your Code Pretty and Readable

You designers out there probably won't care about the final preference setting we're going to cover.

But the coders will almost certainly want to tweak the Code Format category's options. This category lets you control how indention is configured—should indents be created using either tabs or spaces, for example—tab size, column wrapping, tag case, and more. Before you write your first line of code or create your first design, make sure these options conform to your coding style.

Exploring the Remaining Preferences Settings

We've explored many of the Preference settings in Dreamweaver MX, but by no means have we touched on them all. Those we've covered here will let you get Dreamweaver MX up and running in a manner that should aid your development process. Dozens more are available, so don't be afraid to explore the Preferences panel. And another thing—don't be afraid of the help (F1) key while you're exploring.

Setting Up Your PC/Server Environment for Dreamweaver MX

Naturally, you can't very well create and test robust, dynamic websites without a web server and database system in place. Although you don't need to duplicate the full setup of your production, or live, web server, you must be able to access minimal components in your development environment. Does your development system at home really need 1GB of RAM, a hot-swappable RAID hard drive system, and quad-2GHz processors? It would be nice, of course, but you don't need them to create your work. Let's explore a few options for setting up your development environment in a more realistic setting.

Know Your Web Server

Earlier in the chapter, we provided some guidelines for installing a web server. However, the process of choosing, installing, and configuring a web server is an enormous topic, mostly beyond the scope of this book.

As with other kinds of software, magazines are a good place to look for product comparisons that will help you choose a server. Once you've made the choice, you can learn about the administration of particular web servers from many books. For example, if you decide to use Apache, check out *Linux Apache Web Server Administration*, by Charles Aulds (Sybex, 2001). For purposes of this book, we're assuming that you have access to a functional, secure web server either at your workplace or at your home.

Several web servers are available for the various flavors of operating systems in the world today. Apache, MacHTTP, Internet Information Services, iPlanet, Lotus, Oracle—the list goes on and on. Part of the beauty of Dreamweaver is that it doesn't really care what your web server is, as long as it can serve up pages and connect to your database. You need to know how to specify your website's path on the server in order to set up Dreamweaver MX, and you need to know how to connect to the website's directory, but that's it. Once you give Dreamweaver MX those pieces of information, you can use the Dreamweaver MX Site Manager and its tools to maintain your site painlessly.

If you're developing websites at home and don't currently have a web server, you might want to obtain Microsoft's Personal Web Server or MacHTTP, depending on whether your computer is a Windows-based PC or a Mac. However, if you're running Windows 2000, Internet Information Services 5 is included, so you just need to set up your site.

Where Does the Database Go?

Once you know how to connect to your web server, where should you put your database? Again, in a workplace environment, you may have system and database administrators to set this up for you. If you're fulfilling the position of one or both of these roles, you'll need to decide where to put your database.

Ideally, in a production environment, your database lives on its own server, locked securely away in air-conditioned comfort behind firewalls, real walls (and doors), and other security devices. But your development environment may not be so secure and locked down. So where does the database go? It depends on the type of database you're using and the type of connection to the database. If you're using Microsoft's SQL Server, for example, you'll need to put the database on the server where SQL Server is installed. If you're using Microsoft Access or some other ODBC (Open Database Connectivity) or OLEDB-compliant database system, you can place your database wherever your web server can make an ODBC connection. Huh, you say?

Database servers such as SQL Server and Oracle require that you create and store the database on the machine on which you're running the server software. So if you're running SQL Server on a machine named Poseidon, your SQL Server database will live on Poseidon. On the other hand, database systems such as FoxPro, Access, dBASE, and others that are ODBC-compliant can live anywhere within the network. As long as you have a properly-permissioned ODBC connection from your web server to the database, you can get to your data. Speed and network traffic are issues in this type of setting though.

You don't necessarily want to clog your company's network with database traffic if you can avoid it. Your network administrator might get a bit angry with you. In a development environment (or even in some production environments), you might want to put the database on the web server itself if you're using a nonserver-based database. This arrangement will reduce the amount of network traffic between the web server and your database since the web server only has to look into one of its own directories for the data. You'll have to weigh the extra processing added to your web server against the network traffic you might generate by placing the RDBMS on a machine other than your web server.

You don't want to put the database in a folder of your website. You'll want to create a new folder, away from your web folders, and put your data in that folder. The new database folder should be completely separated from your web-publishing folders. Your website folder is exposed to the Internet, and you don't want the average user to be able to download your entire database through their browser!

NOTE   *Debate continues over whether you should use an RDBMS such as Microsoft Access in a web server environment. A quick search on the Internet yields heated discussions about costs, flaws, speed, features. . .you name it. Here's our take: If you're developing a site that (a) isn't going to be pounded by the public and (b) isn't ever going to contain much data, perhaps your needs will be met by Access 2000 (or later versions). If your targeted survey to 2000 people is only going to be live for a few months, or if your corporate news intranet has finally entered the development stage, explore Access. But if you already have a database server, by all means, use it! Microsoft Access cannot compete with the speed, security and features of a true database server.*

A Quick Look at the Database Menus

Dreamweaver MX makes it easy to create web pages that interact with a database. Using tools such as Server Behaviors and Bindings, you can add dynamic features to your web pages. We'll cover the use of these tools in later chapters. For now, let's take a look at the first steps you must take in order to use database connectivity on your site.

FIRST THINGS FIRST: SET UP YOUR SITE

There are a few steps you must follow before you can even get to the database. Dreamweaver MX requires that you create a site definition for your work. This site definition contains all the HTML or code files, graphics, media files, and so forth that your site will use.

Site Definition: Advanced Method

Figure 2.14 shows the Application panel and the tabs it contains. The first tab you'll typically seen in the Application panel is Databases. (Dreamweaver MX let's you customize the panels by moving tabs around. If you've customized your installation of Dreamweaver MX and reordered your tabs, your Databases tab may be elsewhere.) Before you can use a data table in your development, you must complete three steps:

1. Create a site.
2. Choose a document type.
3. Set up the site's testing server.

Creating a site basically means defining the characteristics of the local site. The document type essentially refers to the scripting language that works with the type of testing server for which you're developing—ColdFusion, JSP, PHP, ASP, ASP.NET, and so forth. The testing server is the web server on which you will develop a particular website.

Dreamweaver MX guides you through these steps. It orders them numerically and places a checkmark next to the steps as you complete them, as you can see in Figure 2.14.

FIGURE 2.14

The databases tab shows you the status of steps you must take to fully utilize Dreamweaver MX's database features.

However, if you're creating a site for the first time, this panel is grayed out and inaccessible. So, let's create a new page, which in turn, will let us create a new site. (You'll learn more about the Site Manager in the next section.) Choose File ➤ New from the main menu to open the New Document window, shown in Figure 2.15. From this window, you select the type of document you'd like to create. As you can see, you can choose from several categories of documents, as well as from Dynamic Page types within each category.

For our example, let's select the Dynamic Page category and ASP VBScript. Click Create to open an untitled ASP document. Your Databases tab should look similar to that in Figure 2.16. Notice that the steps in the Application panel's Databases tab have not been checked? We must go through the proper steps to get to our data.

In step 1, click the site link to open a Site Definition window, similar to that in Figure 2.17. (You might need to click the Advanced tab to display this screen.) Give your site a name—in our case, we'll call it Published Books. Don't confuse the name of your site with the HTML titles of your pages. The name you enter here is for your reference only; it will not appear in the browser.

FIGURE 2.15

Dreamweaver MX lets you create many types of documents, from ASP pages to Framesets to complete designs.

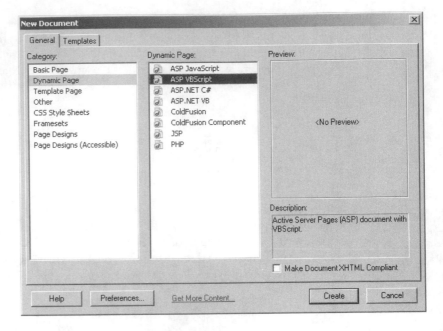

FIGURE 2.16

Since we're creating a new site, we need to define a few of the site's properties in order to use dynamic data.

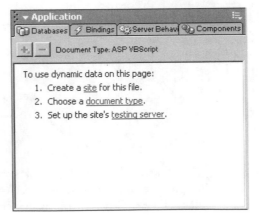

TIP *The Site Definition window lets you define many aspects of your site in any order. You can define all the required site information now and not worry about going back to the Databases tab to click the next step. Plus, from this window, you can set more of the site's options than the Databases tab offers.*

Next, you'll need to tell Dreamweaver MX where you want to locally store your files. That is, you need to specify where on your computer Dreamweaver MX saves the pages you create. Click the file folder icon to browse to the folder you want to use. If the folder doesn't yet exist, you can create it through the Choose Local Root Folder for Site file-browsing window. Leave the Refresh Local

File List Automatically option checked, since this will make certain that you have an updated file list from which to work.

FIGURE 2.17

You use the Site Definition window to set up a Dreamweaver MX site.

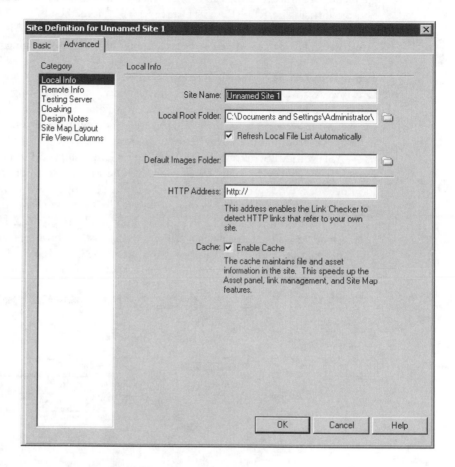

Dreamweaver MX automatically saves copies of images in your Default Images folder, which you can drag onto your active document from your desktop or other program. To set this folder, click the file folder icon and select the folder (or create it if it doesn't yet exist).

WARNING   *Nothing prevents you from setting your Local Root Folder to the actual web directory on your testing server. However, there are advantages associated with putting your Local Root Folder on your local machine. You will have two working copies of your site—one on your machine and one on the testing server. If you inadvertently scramble a file beyond repair or delete it, you can always copy the intact version from the testing server back to your local drive. On the other hand, if you set your Local Root Folder to your testing server, you won't have to go through the copy step to place your newly modified files onto the testing server; you'll be editing them directly. We recommend that you work locally and publish to your testing server.*

Remote Info   You use the Remote Info tab to specify how to connect to your remote, or live, web server. You'll probably need a user name and password, as well as pertinent connection information to set this up. Your system administrator should have this information, if you work in a corporate environment. Dreamweaver MX can connect via a local network, FTP, RDS, WebDAV, and even to a SourceSafe database. RDS (Remote Data Service), is the method by which you connect to ColdFusion's server. WebDAV (Web-based Distributed Authoring and Versioning) is a relatively new protocol used primarily on Unix-flavored servers. SourceSafe is Microsoft's versioning control software.

Define Your Testing Server Your testing server is important to your development process with Dreamweaver MX. This is the server on which you'll do your testing—surprise, huh? You need to define a testing server so that you can review how your pages will look and behave before you send them to your live website for the world to access. You define your testing server by clicking the Testing Server category in the Site Definition window. Choose the type of server model you're going to use—ASP with VBScript, ASP with JavaScript, ColdFusion, and so on. Once you choose a server model type, you'll need to tell Dreamweaver MX how to access your testing server—via FTP or your local network. Odds are that you'll be able to select Local/Network since you probably have your testing server in-house and can get to the web folder simply by browsing to it.

Your Site Definition window should now look similar to Figure 2.18. In order for Dreamweaver MX to load your site properly when you preview the site in a browser (remember the F12 key setup?), you'll need to enter the URL for the testing site in the URL Prefix text box. Once you click OK, Dreamweaver MX validates your entries and warns you if it finds something amiss.

FIGURE 2.18

Defining your testing server is crucial to Dreamweaver MX development.

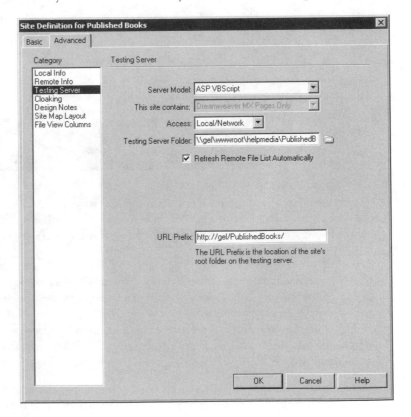

Site Definition: Basic Method

If you're not into tweaking everything manually and don't need the advanced features to define your sites, you can use the Basic method to get running quickly. Choose the Basic tab from the Site Definition window, as shown in Figure 2.19. Give your site a name—we're going to use PublishedBooks_ Basic. Click Next, and you'll get to choose the server technology you want to use.

FIGURE 2.19

You use the Basic tab to specify the minimum requirements for your site.

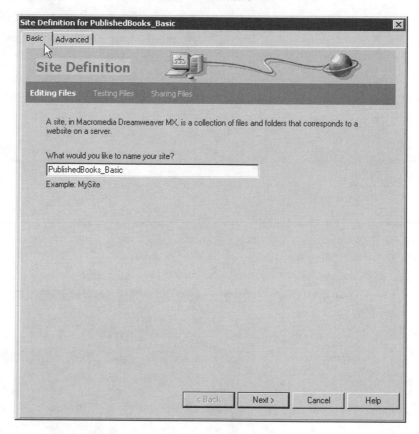

Click the Yes, I Want To Use A Server Technology option to display a drop-down list, which is shown in Figure 2.20. Again, we're going to choose ASP VBScript. Click Next, and specify how you want to work with local files. We're going to choose Edit Locally, Then Upload To Remote Testing Server. Specify the folder to contain your local files in the text box and click Next.

The next window, shown in Figure 2.21, lets you specify how you want to connect to your testing server—either through Local/Network, FTP, or RDS (if you're running ColdFusion). The options to connect to your server depend on the type of connection you're establishing. For example, if you choose FTP, you're presented with a list of options like those in Figure 2.21. Choose another, Local/Network, for example, and you're presented with corresponding file location options. We're going to use Local/Network for our example and specify the folder on our web server into which our files should be copied, as you can see in Figure 2.22.

FIGURE 2.20

The Basic tab guides you through a questionnaire to set up your site.

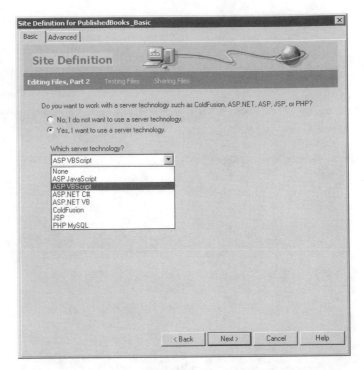

FIGURE 2.21

Your definition options depend on the type of testing server connection you elect.

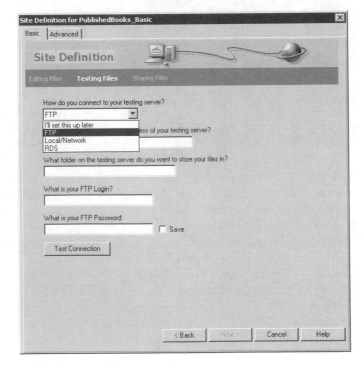

FIGURE 2.22

You specify a common network path when you choose Local/ Network as your connection type.

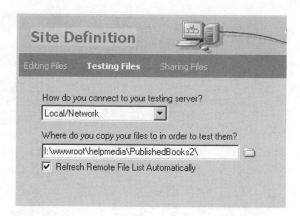

Next, you'll enter Part 2 of setting up your site, as the title bar will tell you. It's time to tell Dreamweaver MX the URL of your site's root folder. That is, Dreamweaver MX wants to know what address you will type into your browser to view your website on your testing server. It offers a default for those of you who are testing and developing on the same machine. But in a corporate environment you'll probably need to change this default. Once you specify your URL, you can have Dreamweaver MX immediately test the connection to ensure it can use the URL you've entered. Click the Test URL button. If successful, Dreamweaver MX displays a message like that in Figure 2.23. Otherwise, you'll see an error message requesting that you check the URL. Click Next to open the Sharing Files window, as shown in Figure 2.24.

FIGURE 2.23

After you specify the URL to use for your testing server, you can save debugging time by immediately testing whether Dreamweaver MX can connect to it properly.

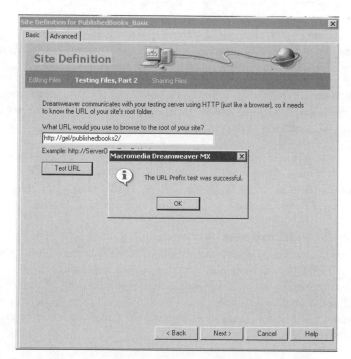

FIGURE 2.24

You need to decide
whether you want
to use Dreamweaver
MX's check-in/
check-out procedure.

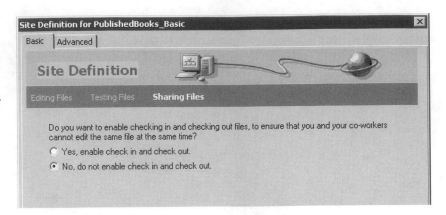

Now you'll need to decide whether you want Dreamweaver MX to apply a bit of traffic control to your development site. You can force designers and developers who are using Dreamweaver MX to check files in and out from your site when they need to modify them. Dreamweaver MX keeps track of who has what file open and helps prevent users from overwriting one another's work. Click Next once you've selected the check-in/check-out option that suits your needs.

WARNING   Even though Dreamweaver MX provides a check-in/check-out ability, it isn't fool-proof. Users who aren't using Dreamweaver MX can still gain access to the files and overwrite them through another program or folder-browsing utility such as Windows Explorer. Dreamweaver MX doesn't lock the actual file; it simply keeps internal track of who has a file open. Obviously, third-party programs can't read Dreamweaver MX internal messages, so they can't warn you that the file might be open. The only way to ensure that the Dreamweaver MX check-in/check-out feature is utilized properly is to establish a company policy that anyone who modifies website files must use Dreamweaver MX. This kind of policy isn't effective in most organizations if several development tools are used in website development.

The final screen you'll see in the Basic setup is the Summary screen, shown in Figure 2.25. This screen summarizes the options you selected for your site. Review these carefully to make sure Dreamweaver MX interacts with your website as you expect!

NOTE   Keep in mind that Dreamweaver is "smart" enough to know what it needs for the various types of sites you can create. If you're creating a ColdFusion site, you'll have the options to specify an RDS server, a ColdFusion data source, and other items related to ColdFusion. The same goes with the others—JSP, PHP, and so on You'll be asked to specify the items that Dreamweaver MX needs in order to connect to the site and data sources properly.

SECOND: CONNECT TO YOUR DATABASE

After you create your site, you can add a data connection to Dreamweaver MX. Click the + button on the Databases tab to display database connection options. If you're creating an ASP page, you'll see options similar to those in Figure 2.26. If you're creating a different type of page, JSP, for example, you'll see a completely different set of options. We'll delve deeper into these options in later chapters. For now, just be aware that Dreamweaver MX always changes the options to match the type of page you're creating.

FIGURE 2.25

The Summary screen shows you a summary of the options you've chosen for your site.

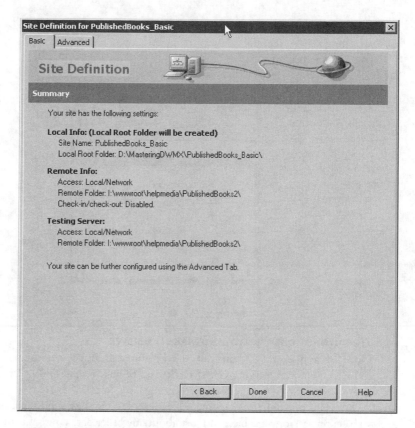

FIGURE 2.26

Options for creating a database connection from an ASP page

After you choose data connection type, you'll be presented with a list of options relating to that connection. For example, if you choose a DSN connection for an ASP page, you can specify options such as the connection name, the DSN name, the user name, the password, and so on. (See the corresponding chapters later in this book for connection information based on the type of page you're creating.) Once you establish your connection, you have access to the components in the database, as you can see in Figure 2.27.

FIGURE 2.27

After you establish a data connection, Dreamweaver MX gives you access to all the database components such as tables, views, and stored procedures.

THIRD: BIND TO YOUR DATA AND MAKE IT BEHAVE

Once Dreamweaver MX can connect to your database, you can use the Bindings tab to create queries to tie to your data. Bindings tie specific data to your forms, without your having to hand-code SQL queries. You can learn more about Bindings in Chapter 15.

Bindings not only tie dynamic data sources to databases, however. You can use form variables, web server session variables, and just about any other data content source that you can reach through a web page and the language you're using (ASP, JSP, and so on).

The Server Behaviors tab, which you can learn more about in Chapter 19, lets you add snippets of code to control your data. You can perform the standard add, edit, and delete functions through behaviors, as well as user authentication, data calculations, and even third-party behaviors.

Site Management and Transferring Files

Managing a website can be a major headache for even the most experienced web developers. As sites grow and change, they can become unwieldy, and you can inadvertently introduce broken links, orphaned pages, and general chaos in folder structure. Dreamweaver MX can help you keep your sites in order. In fact, some web developers think the site management features Dreamweaver MX provides are alone worth the cost of the software. The Site Manager modifies links within your pages to reflect new folder locations (for when you need to move files), checks links to verify they work, provides folder and file management, lets you move the site to your testing server and to your live server, and more. Let's take a quick look at some of the features that will make your website management easier.

What's on Those Menus?

Figure 2.28 shows the Site tab that's located on the Files panel. The buttons across the top of the panel give you access to the most frequently used options. Table 2.3 lists and describes these buttons.

FIGURE 2.28

The Site tab can be used to alleviate many of the head-aches associated with maintaining your website's structure and files.

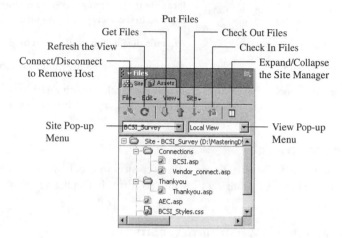

TABLE 2.3: BUTTONS ON THE SITE TAB

BUTTON	WHAT IT DOES
Connect/Disconnect To Remote Host	Connects you to the remote host (your live web server) if you've defined it in the Advanced tab of the Site Definition window. This button toggles to Disconnect From Remote Host if you're already connected. (The type of connection established to your remote host is defined in the Advanced tab of the Site Definition window.)
Refresh	Simply refreshes the local and remote file lists. Useful for refreshing the file lists if you deselected the Automatically Refresh File Lists option in the Site Definition window.
Get Files	Downloads the selected files from your live site or your testing server and copies them to your local site. This option overwrites any files, with approval, that exist in your local site, so make certain you want to copy these when you click the button. You specify the server from which to get the files using the View pop-up menu.
Put Files	Uploads a copy of your local site to your remote or testing server. You specify the server on which these files are placed using the View pop-up menu.
Check Out Files	If enabled in the Advanced tab of the Site Definition window, this button lets you check out a file by copying the file to your local site and marking the file as "checked out" on the server.

Continued on next page

TABLE 2.3: BUTTONS ON THE SITE TAB *(continued)*

BUTTON	WHAT IT DOES
Check In Files	Allows you to check in a file or files by copying the version from your local site to the testing server (or remote server, depending on which is selected in the View pop-up menu).
Expand/Collapse	Expands the Site tab to allow you to see more of the site.
Site Pop-Up Menu	Allows you to select a site from your defined site list.
View Pop-Up Menu	Allows you to select which view is active—Local View, Remote View, Testing Server, or Map View (shows you a map of your site).

Using the Site Tab

As we mentioned, the Site tab can help keep sites in order by aiding you in development tasks such as creating new folders, moving files, and so forth. Let's take a look at some of these useful features in more detail.

IMPORT AN EXISTING WEBSITE INTO THE SITE TAB

The Site tab is an invaluable tool in maintaining your site. You don't have to create a site from scratch to use it, either. Dreamweaver MX lets you import existing sites into the Site tab so you can take advantage of error checking, Site Map viewer, and other features. To import an existing website into the Site Tab, you must first add a site just as if you were creating a new site. To do so, from the main menu bar choose Site and then choose New Site from the pop-up menu to open the Site Definition window. Enter the appropriate settings for the new site (see the previous section for more information), and click OK. As you can see in Figure 2.29, we're calling our new site TestSite. Also notice that our Local View shows that there are indeed no files in our new site. Now, we want to switch to the server on which our site resides. Since we're going to import the files from our testing server, we'll choose Testing Server from the View pop-up menu.

FIGURE 2.29

The Local View of our new site shows there are no files yet in the site.

The Testing Server shows our site, just as we'd expect, so let's click the Get Files button. Dreamweaver MX asks for confirmation (Figure 2.30), so click OK to start the import process.

FIGURE 2.30

To import the existing site, switch to the proper view and click the Get Files button. You'll be asked for confirmation.

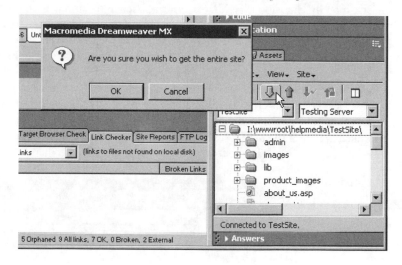

Once the import process is complete, switch back to Local View, and you should see a replica of your site, only this copy is in your local working folder. You can see the results of our import in Figure 2.31.

FIGURE 2.31

Our import of an existing site is a success!

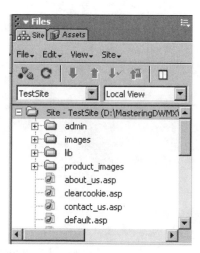

One last thing we need to do after an import is to tell the Site Manager what our default home page should be. We need to do this in order for features such as the Site Map to work properly. Setting the home page is easy—just right-click the file that should be the home page and choose Set As Home Page from the pop-up menu.

VIEW YOUR WEBSITE WITH THE SITE MAP

Once you've imported or created a site, you can view your site with the site map. You can launch the site map by choosing Map View from the View pop-up menu on the Site tab.

This feature shows you a map of your site, complete with links to other pages and whether those links are broken. Figure 2.32 shows the site map in action. Our default home page, `default.asp`, is at the top, followed by the subpages and links within those pages. This view also shows files that might be included as well. Notice the broken-link icons next to files such as `products.asp`, `index.asp`, and `about_us.asp`. Those are visual cues that these links might be broken. Dreamweaver MX adheres to strict syntax rules for specifying links and the like, so if you deviate at all from the "official" rules, Dreamweaver might not be able to interpret the link. In our case, our test site appears to have broken links because of the default behavior of ASP. We didn't specify an explicit `../` in the link to indicate relative paths in our links, so Dreamweaver is reminding us that we may have a bit of sloppy code.

FIGURE 2.32

The site map in action

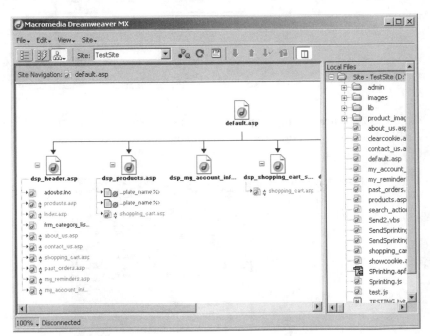

MANAGING LINKS

Dreamweaver is useful in managing links within pages, as well. It can track links from pages you create as well as those from imported sites and show you where broken links might reside. Obviously, this is a useful feature, especially when you're dealing with sites whose content changes frequently.

Finding Broken Links

Since we don't necessarily want to check the site map for broken links—can you imagine trying to do that for a site with hundreds of pages?—we can use one of Dreamweaver MX's features designed specifically for finding broken links; the Check Links feature. You can invoke the Check Links feature in a number of ways (like most features in Dreamweaver MX), but the quickest way is to click the Site menu in the Site tab, Check Links Sitewide. You can also use the hotkey combination of Ctrl+F8. Once you do, Dreamweaver MX checks your entire site's linking and inclusion structure. Anything it finds suspect, it displays in the Results panel, as you can see in Figure 2.33.

FIGURE 2.33
Dreamweaver MX checks our site for links it thinks might be broken.

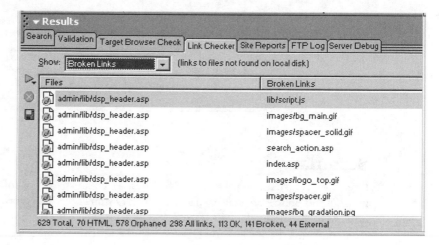

You can also view external links and orphaned files (files for which Dreamweaver can find no incoming link, or call). Click the Show drop-down menu in the Link Checker panel to get to these two extra categories.

To fix broken links, you can double-click the link to open the file and jump immediately to the offending link. Fix the link, save your file, and you're done!

TIP If you have a number of links to fix within a file, a judicious use of Find/Replace All will save you lots of time.

The Autoupdate Link Feature

One of the coolest features in Dreamweaver MX's link management repertoire is the Autoupdate Link feature. Suppose you need to move a document, or web page, from one folder to another. You can move the file, do a global search and replace through all your site files with the appropriate tag change, and then test the site to make sure you covered all your bases. Or, you can simply move the file into the new folder and let Dreamweaver MX do all the work. Drag the web page to its new location within the Site Tabpanel, and Dreamweaver displays a list of the files that refer to the file you're moving. You can choose to update or not by clicking the appropriate button, as shown in Figure 2.34. If you click Update, Dreamweaver MX takes care of the appropriate tag changes for you. Great, isn't it?

WARNING Unfortunately, Dreamweaver MX doesn't autoupdate links to graphics files and images. If you need to move these files, you'll have to revert to the old tried-and-true method of a global search and replace. Also, Dreamweaver MX cannot update links buried in custom-created scripts. There are simply too many possible variations in custom scripting, so Dreamweaver only checks and changes scripts that it creates as part of its feature set. If you have any custom scripts, you'll have to maintain those links by yourself as well.

FIGURE 2.34
Dreamweaver MX
can automatically
update links to
moved web pages
for you.

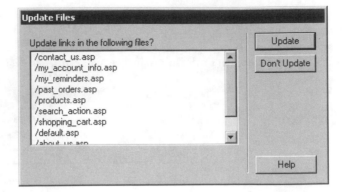

Summary

Dreamweaver MX is so packed with features, we could spend the entire book introducing them to you. But this book is about using databases with Dreamweaver MX, so we have to close the introduction now. By all means, explore the features you run across in your day-to-day use of Dreamweaver. Make sure you press the F1 key any time you find something you don't understand. Macromedia has created a great help file, and there's good support on the web at www.dreamweaver.com as well. Plus, you should also check out books such as the following: *Dreamweaver MX: Design and Technique*, by Ethan Watrall, and *Dreamweaver MX/Fireworks MX Savvy*, by Christian Crumlish, both published by Sybex in 2002.

In Chapter 3, we'll look at coding practices for database and web scripting. You'll learn about guidelines for every aspect of web development (and coding in general). We'll even show you a couple of ways Dreamweaver MX can aid you in maintaining your coding practices initiative.

Chapter 3

Coding Practices for Dreamweaver Development

THE BANE OR BOON, depending on your point of view, of every programmer is coding practices. The time it takes to make sure your program code adheres to your corporate code-development standard may seem ludicrous and all-consuming. The benefit of such work isn't readily apparent to most developers, especially those relatively new to the industry. However, seasoned and wise developers will tell you that there is no substitute for making sure your code, whether it be for compiled applications, web development, or stored procedures, is legible, understandable, and easy to follow—especially when that code needs to be modified six months after its creation to add a new feature to the system.

Unfortunately, most developers and, indeed, many companies don't have or enforce a coding practice standard that provides an easy way for other developers to "pick up and run with" a set of code. But you'll find, with a little upfront preparation and planning, you can make sure the code you create is informative, clear, and concise. By establishing a set of coding practices that you follow in every piece of code you create, you'll make sure that not only can other developers modify your code in the future, but that even you can make sense of what you wrote a year after you released the system.

We're going to cover some guidelines for coding practices in this chapter. We say guidelines because there are no hard-and-fast standards for coding practices—coding practices are as varied as the developers that create the code, and, therefore, what follows is necessarily subjective opinion. So take what we tell you here and apply it to your work environment, letting it guide you into a consistent coding standard that you follow religiously! And there's the key to success in following coding practices—consistency.

This chapter covers the following topics:

- ◆ Comment your code
- ◆ Web code structure
- ◆ Error checking and data validation
- ◆ Using the Tag Library Editor

Comment Your Code

Perhaps the most important step in programming that almost all developers overlook, either because of lack of time or for other reasons, is that of commenting their code. What exactly does commenting your code mean? It means that you take each chunk of code, each module, each variable, each tricky workaround, and so forth and describe its purpose, catches, caveats, and so on in detail. You provide this information in the code itself, using the comment tag (hence, "commenting") of the language you're using to basically tell the story of how your code works. You should comment everything. Everything. Can we say it again? Everything.

SOME "STANDARD" COMMENT TAG STRUCTURES

Almost all programming languages have a comment tag or statement of some sort. A statement or a symbol tells the code compiler or code interpreter to ignore the text that follows, since it won't be used as part of the actual code. Many programming languages, HTML included, have in-line comment and block comment tags. In-line comments can be included within a line of code. A block comment "blocks off" chunks of text within the code.

Here are some of the more familiar comment tags you will encounter. (We've included Pascal simply because it is the first language many beginning programmers learn.)

HTML

Inline Comment Marker: n/a

Opening Block: <!--

Closing Block: -->

COLDFUSION

Inline Comment Marker: n/a

Opening Block: <!---

Closing Block: --->

ASP

Inline Comment Marker: '

Opening Block: n/a

Closing Block: n/a

PASCAL

Inline Comment Marker: ;

Opening Block: /*

Closing Block: */

PHP

Inline Comment Marker: // OR #

Opening Block: /*

Closing Block:*/

Continued on next page

SOME "STANDARD" COMMENT TAG STRUCTURES *(continued)*

MySQL

> Inline Comment Marker: #
>
> Opening Block: /*
>
> Closing Block: */

MICROSOFT SQL SERVER

> Inline Comment Marker: --
>
> Opening Block: /*
>
> Closing Block: */

Document your code just as if you were telling a friend how to get to your new house. Mention everything that could even remotely be considered important because you are creating a roadmap that explains why you created the code in the way you did, what the variables do, and the purpose of the code. Remember, even though you have all this detailed information about your code in your head right now, you probably won't remember it a year from now. And, invariably, you'll need to modify code in a system at some point as your organization's needs change.

THE FIRST COMMENTING RULE OF THUMB: COMMENT AS YOU GO

Comment your code as you write it. Comment your design as you build it. Even though you may be on a roll and cranking out code faster than you ever have before, you still need to comment as you go. If you don't, chances are, you won't come back and do it later. In fact, even if you do come back to it, you'll probably take more time going back because you'll have to "relearn" what your code does in order to create accurate comments. Save time and effort and plan for the future by commenting as you go.

A few guidelines follow regarding commenting your code.

Create a Boilerplate Header Comment

Every page, function, and routine should include a comment structure that describes the page, function, or routine, gives its purpose, and so on. Developers like to include different information in the header comment such as variable purpose, time of last modification, and so forth. Create a comment boilerplate that fits your organization's needs while giving enough detail to explain your code. Then, make sure you include it at the top of at least every new file, if not every function and routine. A sample web page boilerplate header might look like the following:

```
<!--------------------------------------------------------
System:     Ad-banner display system
File:       /lib/include/GetUserInformation.asp
Client:     Sybex
```

```
Created by:      Darren McGee
Date Created:    8/9/2002
Last Modified:   9/6/2002

Purpose:    Gets all the information for a given user, including the ads
      viewed, the clicks made, and user type

History:    08/10/2002 - jdm - added password verification
            08/20/2002 - mhk - modified table display to 800x600 specs
            08/30/2002 - jdm - fixed pre-version-4 browser display bug

Calling pages:   DisplayUserInfo.asp; DisplayAllInfo.asp;
Called pages:    CalculatePageview.asp

Variables:  nClick - number of clicks on a particular link
            aUser - array containing user information

----------------------------------------------------------------------->
```

This sample contains a lot of information. Although providing this information does take time away from your coding , you can quickly and easily tell from the comment header what the file's purpose is, which files call it, which files it calls, and the history of changes to the file. Naturally, you'll want to customize such a header to suit your needs, but we recommend that you make it part of your standard program template. That way, whenever you create a new program file, the header will be automatically placed for you—all you have to do is change the appropriate information.

TIP   You can save files as templates within Dreamweaver MX by choosing File ➢ Save As Template. If you want to modify a template that Dreamweaver MX provides, open it as a new file, make your comment header changes, and then save the template with a new name.

Comment the Variables

You wouldn't get far in code development without the use of variables. We use variables to make our web pages and other code dynamic, since we can store information in variables, manipulate them, and delete them as we need. They're flexible and obviously handy to have around. But have you ever tried to debug someone else's code in which the variables weren't well documented? Trying to determine what purpose unknown variables serve can be a time-consuming puzzle, so comment every variable you use in the function or page you're creating. Regardless of whether you define the variables in the comment header, definitely add a comment describing the variable after its declaration. For example, the following snippet shows a few variables that without the defining comment would otherwise be obscure:

```
Dim intPlayerID      'Player ID Number
Dim strPlayer        'Player's full name
Dim lIsCaptain       'Logical for the captain?
Dim strTeamID        'Used to store Team ID Number
Dim strTeamName      'Used to store Team Name
Dim bHasCaptain      'Used to determine if team has a captain
Dim strStates        'Used as a full length string to populate state drop down
Dim intNewID         'Used to capture new player ID
```

Comment Chunks of Code That Perform a Particular Task

In addition to adding a header comment and commenting your variables, also comment chunks of code that perform a particular task. That is, comment chunks of code that work together within the same page. For example, as you can see in the following code snippet, the developer pointed out the code used for validation and gave a few notes about how it works.

```
Dim cnStreetball
Set cnStreetball = Server.CreateObject("ADODB.Connection")
cnStreetball.ConnectionString = Application("cnStreetball_ConnectionString")
cnStreetball.Open


'=====================================================================
' Validation
'=====================================================================
' IsAdmin overrides team check
' Use the passed Team ID and check it against the stored cookie.
'=====================================================================
If Not IsAdmin() Then
   If NOT Validate(strTeamID, Request.Cookies("streetballshowdown")
   ("teampwd"),2) Then
      Response.Redirect "TeamLogin.asp"
   End IF
End If

If Request.Form("action") = "1" Then
   '// Perform an Update
   '// If a PlayerID exists then update;else Insert

   If Len(Trim(intPlayerID)) = 0 Then
      '//Perform an Insert
      intNewID = InsertPlayer
      If intNewID > 0 Then
         Response.Redirect "Team.asp?TeamID=" & strTeamID &
         "&TeamName=" & Server.URLEncode(strTeamName)
      Else
         Response.Write "An insert error has occurred. Please
   contact a system administrator."
      End If
   Else
      '// Perform an Update
```

In this snippet, the developer chose to make the comments stand out a bit more from the code by using a double-slash (//) after the comment marker. Since comments can be hard to separate from code on a black-and-white printout, you may find this a good idea to adopt.

This code snippet also demonstrates a method of commenting that causes some controversy—the "clutter" comment used to separate the comment from other lines of code. Some developers and development companies suggest that you separate comments with chunks of white space. Frankly, we feel it doesn't have the same effect, as you can see by the modified snippet that follows. We suggest that you use whatever works best for you, your aesthetic tastes, and your work environment. But whichever style you choose, be consistent.

```
Set cnStreetball = Server.CreateObject("ADODB.Connection")
cnStreetball.ConnectionString = Application("cnStreetball_ConnectionString")
cnStreetball.Open


' Validation
'
' IsAdmin overrides team check
' Use the Passed Team ID and Check it with the Cookie.



If Not IsAdmin() Then
   If NOT Validate(strTeamID,
     Request.Cookies("streetballshowdown")("teampwd"),2) Then
       Response.Redirect "TeamLogin.asp"
```

General Comments about Commenting

There are numerous commenting methods and numerous commenting styles, and, of course, there is the lack of commenting. Developers don't like to do it, but they must if they want to maintain a clean, consistent, informative code design. Make commenting one of your standard practices, if you don't already.

Here are a few other guidelines regarding commenting.

◆ Comment anything that isn't readily understood or that might generate a question for developers modifying your code in the future.

◆ Comment control structures such as logic controls, loops, and other items that could take the logic flow in different directions.

◆ Make sure your comments are simple, clear, meaningful, and precise. We recommend you use complete sentences, since doing so helps force you to comment clearly and prevent ambiguity.

◆ You don't need to comment every line in the code. Comments should explain what your intention is for the code and what a particular code chunk does—not act as a translator for every statement you created.

◆ You might want to develop a few keywords to use in your comments that alert other developers to particularly important items. For example, you might want to use TRICKY for a piece of code that is complex to warn other developers to be careful when modifying it. Or you might use KLUDGY to indicate code that is a bit sloppy and needs to be improved. (You shouldn't be creating sloppy code at all, but sometimes time constraints don't let every developer generate the most elegant piece of code ever created. Sometimes, in today's business world, we have to get it done and then go back and make it elegant.)

◆ When you're editing your code, update your comments appropriately. You don't want to revisit the code seven months later to find that the code behaves nothing like its comments say it should.

◆ Generally, you do not want to put comments at the end of a line of code—except for variable declarations—because end-of-line comments are difficult to read and probably will end up wrapping in your code editor.

◆ Before you actually post the code on your production server, make sure your comments are clean and clear. Remove any superfluous or temporary comments that don't shed light on the code's purpose. Yes, this means erase the humorous comments you might have added about the design of the code or your boss's attitude.

Naming Conventions

How you name items will have great impact on the maintenance, readability, and usability of your code. Not only do individual languages and database systems have their own naming requirements for tables, variables, code pages, and so on, but you should also set your own requirements and publish them within the IT department as your company's Naming Convention List. Once you have a uniform naming scheme in place, you'll find it's easier for developers to work on one another's code when necessary and be able to interpret the meaning of the entire code base much faster. New recruits to the organization will learn your systems faster as well.

Again, we're going to give you a few guidelines to follow. Our choices for naming conventions won't fit everyone, so adapt what you learn to your needs. But, above all, be consistent in the application of your own schema.

Naming Variables

You can assign meaningful names to your variables in many ways. In fact, you'll find developers defending their naming scheme against another any time you bring up naming conventions because, naturally, their way makes more sense to them. Well, you should strive to follow certain guidelines, no matter how you name your variables.

Charles Simonyi, a Microsoft programmer for many years, created a schema for naming variables and other data items that has propagated throughout the technical world. It's affectionately known as "Hungarian" notation, apparently for two reasons: Simonyi is Hungarian, and the schema makes your variables look as though they're written in a non-English language. Although you probably won't want to adopt Simonyi's full schema, we recommend that you make a variation of that schema part of your standard coding practice policy.

TIP *Interested in reading more about Charles Simonyi's "Hungarian" notation? Check out the ten-page article on Microsoft's site at:* `http://msdn.microsoft.com/library/default.asp?url=/library/en-us/dnvsgen/html/HungaNotat.asp`.

Our version of Hungarian notation that works quite well for us in naming variables is as follows: Combine whole words to form your variable names so that the name indicates exactly what the variable contains; don't use cryptic variable names. Some good examples are *cFirstName, dDateSold, lHasCaptain,* and *nGrandTotal.*

◆ Proper-case significant words within your variables. For example, *FirstName* is combined from two whole, stand-alone words to form the variable name.

◆ Many developers like to indicate the type of their variables within the name. For example you might use a naming scheme such as the following:

`aUserList`	Indicates an array called *UserList*
`cFirstName`	Indicates a character variable called *FirstName*
`lHasCaptain`	Indicates a logical variable named *HasCaptain*
`nGrandTotal`	Indicates a numeric variable called *GrandTotal*

◆ There is a potential drawback to typing your variables within their names: if the datatype of the variable should change, you'll need to rename the variable in order to remain consistent. With global search and replace, though, this isn't such a big deal. We find the benefit of having the variable typed in its name well worth the potential cost of having to perform a global search and replace on the codebase. Decide on a scheme for your variable types, and apply it accordingly to your variable names. This type of identification helps in understanding code, especially if you're modifying code someone else wrote.

◆ Depending on the language in which you're developing, you might want to go so far as to add prefixes or suffixes to your variables to indicate their content types. For example, `str_User` for a structure variable or `sn_LoggedIn` for a session variable.

◆ You might want to include scope, as well: `g_VarName` for global, `l_varName` for local, and so forth.

◆ Don't go overboard with the naming prefixes, though. We know a developer who had so many prefixes that his prefix list was always longer than his variable names.

◆ When writing JavaScript code, you might want to follow the convention set forth by Dreamweaver itself: lowercase the first word of your variable names, but use proper casing (or an initial capital letter) for each word thereafter, such as `myGetDate`.

Whenever you're naming constants, you'll want to keep them in all uppercase letters. This makes the constant stand out clearly. You might also want to separate the words within constants by an underscore, to distinguish them even more clearly from a variable. For example, `DAYS_UNTIL_EXPIRATION` certainly makes more of an impact than `nDaysUntilExpiration`.

Name Boolean variables in such a way that they imply a logical true/false or yes/no answer. For example, `lIsRegistered` and `lHasPaid` lend themselves to a simple yes/no answer.

However you choose to name your variables, be consistent and be clear. Make certain that the developers in your organization understand the meanings of the schema you adopt. And make certain that everyone follows the same naming conventions.

Naming Data Tables

Just as in naming variables, following a few guidelines for naming data tables can save you time and confusion during your development process. Although you won't be "typing" your data tables with prefixes, you can certainly indicate the use of the data within the table name. For example, names such as "Employee," "RegisteredUser," and "ProductOnOrder" indicate the type of data in the table.

Naming linking tables can sometimes be a confusing process, since the link table contains keys from two or more tables. You could add the suffix `_omLink` to the end of the table for a one-to-many link table or `_mmLink` for many-to-many. (For more information about linking tables, see Chapter 5.)

Another convention you'll have to weigh within your organization is whether to name tables using plurals. We recommend that you do not use plurals in anything. In a multideveloper environment, plurals tend to cause more confusion than they're worth. Invariably, someone will forget to add the "s" for the Players table in a query, only to have to go back and debug the problem once the query fails. Plurals just aren't good in names. (On the other hand, if you must use plurals, make sure you do use them in every table name.)

Naming Data Columns

You can also make your development life easier if you adhere to a few guidelines for naming data columns and database field names. Again, you want to avoid plurals. Player or Players—it seems trivial just reading about it, but when you're in the midst of coding, you don't want to break your stride by having to look up the spelling of a table name.

Also, it's not a good idea to repeat the table name in the field name. For example, you shouldn't have a table named Player and a field named PlayerFirstName. The fact that the field resides in the Player table is sufficient to indicate that FirstName relates to Player.

Earlier, we mentioned naming your variables so that you know the datatype by reading the variable name. Don't adhere to this convention when naming table fields. It's not uncommon for table fields to change datatypes during the first phases of development of any system. Renaming table fields probably won't be as easy as renaming variables, since you'll have queries, forms and the like on which to perform a global search and replace.

You might want to separate your table field names with an underscore. That is, separate complete words in the name with an underscore, but save this practice for data columns. If you do so, you'll always know just by looking at the name which you're referring to—the field or the variable.

NOTE *If you name your data columns—or table fields—identically to variables used in your pages, Dreamweaver MX will try to automatically bind your variables when you use Server Behaviors. Even though this default behavior is nice, you might want to forgo this nicety for clearer, easily understood code.*

A Few Other Naming Guidelines

You can establish guidelines for anything that you must name in coding circles, so we'd like to give you a few more pointers on doing so. Although we certainly can't cover every possible item, using the following you should get an idea of how to name the entities we haven't mentioned.

◆ You can preface the name of a generic object with a lowercase o or obj, for example, oComment or objMemo.

◆ For connection objects, use conn plus the database name, such as connEmployee.

◆ You might want to preface query variables with qry, for example, qryGetAllUserInfo and recordsets with rst, for example, rstAllWithProduct.

◆ Since queries and stored procedures actually perform some type of action, you should probably include that action in the object's name, for example, qryInsertUserInfo or spGetSalesSummary.

◆ Don't use spaces in table or field names. Spaces can cause problems with some tools, such as external data access tools.

◆ Do not use reserved words (words that are actual commands) to name your tables. This can cause problems with the language or database you're using.

HTML Guidelines

When coding HTML or any program files, either by hand or using Dreamweaver MX, there are a few guidelines you can follow to make your HTML play nicely with browsers, servers, and users. The following guidelines are simply a starting point for your own list of HTML rules, so, as always, take what we show you and adapt it to your working environment. But above all, be consistent.

Filenames

There are many different types of web servers, and many of them are picky about filenames and, of all things, the case of filenames. If you follow these few simple rules, though, your filenames should not cause trouble.

- Don't use spaces in filenames. Spaces can cause all sorts of problems with servers, browsers, file listings, and so forth, since they can confuse a system into thinking the filename has ended.

- Use underscores to make your filenames clear and readable. Separate whole words with underscores, for example, `show_player_data.htm`.

- Don't use uppercase in filenames. Some Unix versions have problems with uppercase names, and some operating systems are case-sensitive. You can avoid both traps by simply using lowercase in all filenames. Besides, uppercase can make directory listings difficult to read.

File Components

Certain components of your HTML files can benefit if you apply a few consistent rules to them. Not only will the rules make your code clearer and easier to understand, but you'll find it functions better as well.

- Titles—any page that is displayed to a user should have a title. Titles are a good way to inform your users of where they are or what they should do in a site. Plus, some search engines use the title text in their data. (You don't need to give pages that aren't seen by a user, such as action pages, titles.)

- Meta tags—any page that you'd like a user to find in a search engine should have a meta tag list. Many search engines use the meta tags to categorize the pages they encounter, so a properly defined meta tag list could be very beneficial to your site traffic.

- Links—when linking to other pages within your site, you probably want to use relative paths as opposed to fully qualified domain names. If you're wanting to display an image stored in your image directory, you shouldn't use `<img src="http://your.site.com/images/imagename">`, since that kind of link causes more work for your server. Instead, use a relative path in the img tag such as `<img src="./images/imagename">`.

- Tables—in order to make tables display properly in all browsers, you should include non-breaking spaces in blank table cells. The ` ` character will put a blank space in the table. Some browsers won't properly display the borders of tables if the cell is empty. (You may see the non-breaking space character refered to as a "non-blanking" space. The World Wide Web Consortium [`www.w3c.org`], the ruling body of HTML standards, officially calls it the "non-breaking space.")

HTML Usability Rules

And of course, we have a few general rules we'd like to share.

Design for 800 × 600 screens. Most monitors today are designed to work better at a resolution of at least 800 × 600. (The optimal resolution for 17-inch monitors is 1024 × 768, but many users like the bigger type that an 800 × 600 setting on a 17-inch monitor provides.) Therefore, design your web pages with this resolution in mind.

Keep in mind while working on your high-speed corporate Internet connection that many users still rely on dial-up modems for their Internet connection, both at work and at home. Think about this before you fill a page full of heavy graphics. You don't want to chase off a potential customer by forcing them to wait a long time to load your site's pages.

Design for Netscape 4.5 and Internet Explorer 5 and later browsers. (Okay, let the controversy fly.) Many developers and companies proclaim that you should develop for version 4 browsers and later. Browsers are still free, and new versions are released all the time. Encourage your users to update their browsers by testing your code for browser versions earlier than Internet Explorer 5 (or Netscape 4.5), and guide users to the proper update pages if necessary. Of course, you don't want to alienate anyone, so test your code for version 4 compliancy and perhaps offer solutions to those using older browsers. (Yes, other browsers are available, as well, such as Opera, Mozilla, and so forth. These browsers take the two major browsers' features into consideration and operate in a similar manner.)

As features and options in HTML change and grow thanks to new technologies, new standards, and the like, web-usability standards may change. Although there are numerous books and articles on the best design rules, best usability rules, best user-interface rules, and best you-name-it rules, perhaps your best place to start looking for more information is the web itself. Check out Jakob Nielsen's site at `www.useit.com`. The irreverent among you will want to take a look at *Web Pages That Suck*, by Vincent Flanders and Michael Willis (Sybex, 1998) and *Son of Web Pages That Suck*, by Vincent Flanders and Dean Peters (Sybex, 2002). You can find Mr. Flanders' website at `www.webpagesthatsuck.com`. Another book you might want to obtain is *Don't Make Me Think*, by Steve Krug and Roger Black (Que, 2000).

Accessibility

Any site that hopes to reach all audiences and all peoples must make sure that its information is accessible to everyone—that includes people with disabilities that hinder or prevent their ability to gain access to your site's information. Unfortunately, those with disabilities are frequently overlooked when it comes to website design and construction. To remedy this situation, the World Wide Web Consortium's (W3C) Web Accessibility Initiative is striving to educate and urge the development community to apply its accessibility standards to websites.

With Internet access now reaching all aspects of American society and even proliferating in countries such as China whose control over Internet access was legendary, accessibility is becoming even more an issue. Millions of current and potential web users have disabilities and require sites that will work with hardware such as site readers, voice recognition systems, magnifiers, and so forth.

TIP   *You can read more about the W3C's Web Accessibility Initiative and find a complete list of guidelines at* `www.w3.org/WAI/`.

Web-accessible sites use the ALT tag on all images and animations; provide captioning and transcripts of audio and video; use hyperlink text that is sensible and descriptive when read aloud; provide style sheets that a user can override; and use many HTML 4.01 tags (such as ACRONYM for spelling out the title of an acronym for screen readers, for example, "World Wide Web" for WWW).

The W3C is offering a Quick Tips card for free, in quantities up to 500, to help spread the word about the Web Accessibility Initiative. You can also print a sample of the card from their website at www.w3.org/WAI/References/QuickTips. This Quick Tip card is available in several translations, including English, Danish, Dutch, Finnish, French, German, Italian, Norwegian, Portuguese, Spanish, and Swedish and also in Braille.

Dreamweaver MX can help you make your site compliant with web accessibility guidelines. When you turn on Accessibility Options in the Preferences window (choose Edit ➤ Preferences ➤ Accessibility), Dreamweaver MX lets you activate features about specific accessibility tags and settings related to various HTML objects. Figure 3.1 shows you the Accessibility options you can activate. As you can see, we've chosen almost all the options so that we can start making our sites W3C WAI compliant. (We haven't chosen Use Large Fonts because it doesn't apply to our web pages. This option causes Dreamweaver MX to display its fonts in a larger size during design time.)

FIGURE 3.1

Another strength of Dreamweaver MX is its ability to guide you in making your websites compliant with the W3C Web Accessibility Initiative.

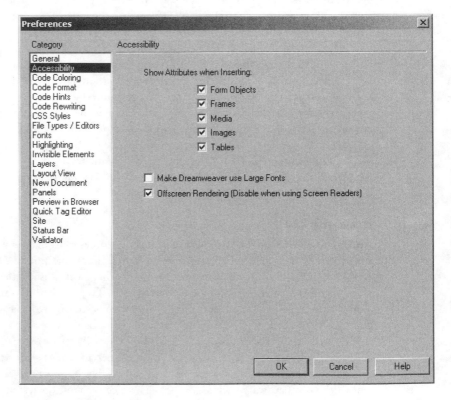

Once the Accessibility options are turned on, Dreamweaver MX will ask you for specific parameters related to making that option W3C WAI compliant whenever you add one of the activated options to a web page. For example, Figure 3.2 shows the options presented when you try to add a text field to a form after activating the Accessibility option for Form Objects.

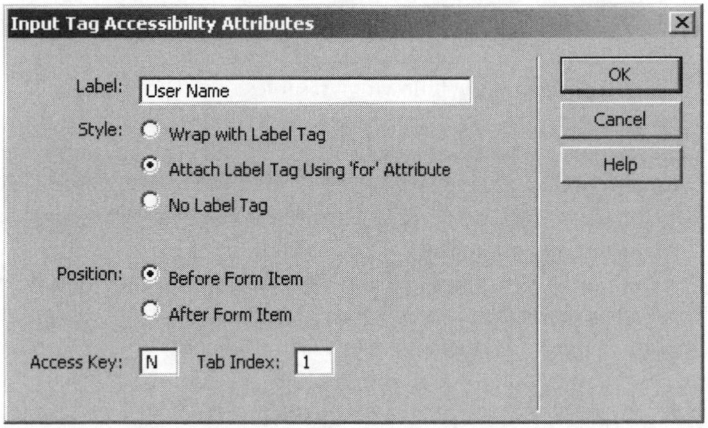

FIGURE 3.2

Dreamweaver MX asks for Accessibility components when you drop a text field onto a form.

Dreamweaver MX asks for features such as the type of label you want to use, an access key (hot-key), and so forth. One of the bonuses of the WAI recommendations is that web pages can now include features such as hotkeys. When you use the settings in Figure 3.2, Dreamweaver MX generates code similar to the following in a web page (we added the <u> tags around the access keys for formatting purposes):

```
<form name="form1" method="post" action="">
  <label for="textfield">User <u>N</u>ame</label>
    <input type="text" name="textfield" accesskey="N" tabindex="1" id="textfield">
    <br>
    <br>
    <label for="label2"><u>P</u>assword</label>
    <input type="text" name="textfield2" accesskey="P" tabindex="2" id="label2">
    </form>
```

The <label> tag allows the user to select the text box by either clicking the text box itself—which is the usual selection method—or clicking the label next to the text box, which is new functionality. This approach reduces the amount of precision needed to select a text box in order to enter data. The accesskey qualifier of the <input> tag is an HTML 4 tag that allows the user to press hotkeys to gain access to specific features. The results of this code is that the user can press Alt+N in a Windows environment to jump to the User Name field. Likewise, pressing Alt+P jumps to the Password field. This allows those unable to move a mouse to navigate a form with ease.

Web Code Structure

Now lets get down to the nitty-gritty of actually generating your code. All good developers have learned that applying a few simple rules to every code page they create saves them time and trouble in the future once the site or system is launched. Let's look at a few code development guidelines that can save you lots of time and headache once the code is complete.

Test for Passed Variable Existence

Always test for your variables' existence between page calls before you use the variable. What does that mean? Consider the following example:

Assume `payment.asp` accepts three variables from `shopping_cart.asp`: *nCartTotal*, *nCustomerId*, and *cSuggestedItem*. `Payment.asp` is the page that actually completes the transaction by letting the customer purchase their items. When all three variables are passed, everything works as it should. But if one of your developers forgets to send *cSuggestedItem* from `shopping_cart.asp`, the page can bomb, displaying an ungraceful exit to your user.

The developer or at least a beta tester should catch such a scenario. But, in large systems, where specific processing pages can be called by numerous other locations, it is possible for a few bugs to slip through. We've found that by testing to ensure that a variable we expected to be passed to a page actually *was* passed, we're not only able to protect our pages from disgraceful exits, but we can provide feedback to the programmer during the development process. Psuedocode for such a test trap might look like this:

```
IF DoesNotExist( cSuggestedItem ) THEN
   Display (" This page requires the following information: cSuggestedItem" )
   ( or other error processing routine)
   END PROCESSING
END IF
```

Testing for variable existence can save you time in debugging as well, since you'll already have some error checking in place. In a web development environment, there are numerous chances for your page to be called incorrectly. For example, suppose someone bookmarked our sample `payment.asp`, which then wouldn't be passed the variables? Testing for variable existence helps ensure that your pages remain clean and bomb-free.

Test for Variable Value

Not only should you test to make sure that passed variables actually exist before you use them, but you should also test to make sure they have a value. That is, never assume that the variable being passed contains a value. To make truly bullet-proof code, never assume anything in a web environment. You certainly don't want to just start adding values together, expecting a passed variable to have, say, a value of 5 or greater, only to find it has a value of Null. This not only wreaks havoc on your logic, but causes hard-to-find bugs. Again, there are too many chances for a web page to be called in ways you don't expect or plan for, so take the safe route and test for variable value. Yes, it takes a bit longer and seems tedious, but you'll be taking another step toward tight, clean, error-free code.

Declare Your Variables

Good programming practice, and indeed many programming languages, dictate that you must declare your variables before you use them. Not only does declaration of your variables force you to follow the programming language rules, but it can also act as a single place for variable information to a developer just encountering your code. Declare your variables near the top of your page, and in the declaration section, include all the variables you're going to use on that page.

Some languages, such as Active Server Pages (ASP), provide a statement such as Option Explicit that forces you to declare variables. Even though ASP lets you declare variables on the fly, declaring variables in a central spot in your code just makes good sense. Why?

◆ Variable declarations are easy to find.

◆ You can determine the variables used in the page by checking one central location.

◆ With settings such as Option Explicit (in ASP) turned on, the web application server will force you to declare your variables.

◆ Declaring your variables forces you to think more clearly about your code design. You're not as apt to throw a variable into the mix just because its convenient.

Logically Form Your Code Structure

One of the intangibles that is most difficult for a new developer to learn is to form good logic structure in programs. Learning how to properly test, branch, and execute based on those tests is a core component of programming development, and learning how to do it effectively and efficiently is the mark of a wise, seasoned developer. But logic control is just one piece of the logic structure puzzle. There's also the logical structure of how you put your code together. Do you have every bit of code related to a certain feature or function in a single page, or do you modularize it and break it out into separate files, as you should? The following guidelines will help with the learning curve.

◆ It's generally faster to test for the positive in control statements. Take the following pseudo-code for example: IF *TheTestExpression* = TRUE will save you a few milliseconds in almost all languages over a statement such as IF NOT(*TheTestExpression*).

◆ Programs will execute faster if you can avoid unnecessary IF-THEN statements and similar structures. Build your code logic so that you can reduce the number of tests since the server must evaluate every IF-THEN you create.

◆ Whenever possible, combine numerous IF-THEN statements into a CASE statement. Instead of using something like the following:

```
IF x = 3 THEN
do something with 3
END IF
IF x = 5 THEN
do something with 5
END IF
IF x = 7 THEN
do something with 7
END IF
IF x <> 3 AND x <> 5 AND x <> 7 THEN
    do something else with x
END IF
```

use a CASE statement such as:

```
SELECT CASE x
    CASE 3    do something with 3
```

```
      CASE 5    do something with 5
      CASE 7    do something with 7
      CASE Else  do something with x
END SELECT
```

CASE statements are faster in execution because once the computer hits the case that is true, it jumps to the end of the statement without evaluating the rest of the tests in the CASE statement. Most programming languages have a structure similar to the CASE statement, but it might be called something else, such as SWITCH, SELECT, or even SELECT CASE.

◆ Use temporary variables when you need them, but be judicious in their use. There's no need to use up system resources by using temporary variables just because you can. They not only consume memory, but they also make your code more difficult to follow. For example, suppose you have five counter loops in your code. As long as they're not nested loops, use the same counter variable for each. You don't need to use five counter variables when one will do.

◆ Use parentheses and brackets whenever you think a statement might be difficult to follow or ambiguous. A statement such as $x = y + t * v / pi$ might not only give you results that you didn't intend, but also force the reader to try to interpret what you mean. Parentheses make clear what you intended, as in: $x = [y + (t * v)] / pi$.

◆ Use functions or procedures to replace repetitive code bits. If you have a particular piece of code that you repeat several times—perhaps a series of calculations performed on several user-input fields—don't repeat the same bit of code over and over in your page. Put that bit of code into a function or a procedure call to make your code cleaner and more efficient. If you have to make a change to the calculations, you then only have one place to make the change.

◆ If you've created a section of code that another developer of your caliber would find difficult to understand, try rewriting it to make it clearer. Chances are, if you have to revisit this bit of code six months from the date you created it, you'll have a difficult time understanding it as well.

◆ Don't try to add patches and fixes to bad code. Rewrite the bad code, instead. Patches and fixes only make bad code worse. If you must apply a patch to bad code for time-constraint reasons, make a note of the inefficient code section and put it in the schedule to be rewritten. Bad code will come back to bite you.

◆ Whenever possible, test user input for validity before sending it to the server. There's more on this later in this chapter in the "Client-Side Validation" section.

◆ Before you try to make your code as efficient and fast as possible, make sure that you have it clear, correct, and bullet-proof. You can waste lots of time trying to generate the fastest way to calculate and display your data, only to find out that your results are wrong. Always complete the initial goal first, and then tweak and improve the code.

◆ Although flowcharts have basically gone by the wayside, there's still an advantage to creating a diagram of how your code should operate. A diagram provides a graphic representation of how your code is going to work. At the very least, create a site map so that you can see how your pages relate to one another, such as that shown in Figure 3.3.

FIGURE 3.3

A site map will help you keep your code's goal in perspective during development.

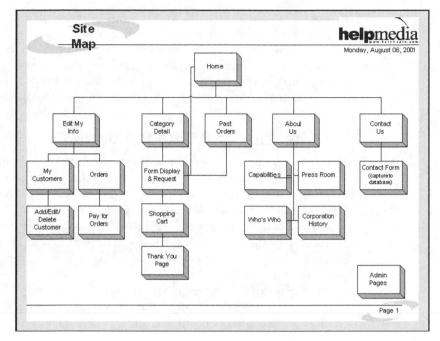

◆ Large systems with dozens of features may seem overwhelming from a development point of view. Save yourself time, headaches, and frustration by developing your code in small pieces. You can then put those pieces together to form the whole program. For example, if you're creating a system to manage library books, don't try to create the entire book maintenance routine in one chunk. Break it out into adding new books, searching for books, removing books, and so forth.

Keep Your Script Pages Independent

We've already touched on some of the points needed to keep your script, or code, pages independent of one another, but it bears repeating. Keeping your script pages independent ensures that an individual page can stand alone if someone should link to it directly—whether or not you intended for the particular page to be linked to directly.

A specific page can crash or return an error message to the user if the developer hasn't put code in the page to trap for such an occurrence. Many times overlooked by the developer, this type of error can be prolific in even the best of sites. Fortunately, you can apply simple methods to your code pages that will prevent this ungraceful exit from rearing its ugly head on your site. Use one or a combination of the following at the top of all pages that you do not want the user to find directly:

◆ The *HTTP_Referer* variable contains the page that the user was viewing before arriving at the current page. You can test to make sure that the previous page was the page you, the developer, were expecting. If it wasn't, send the user back to the previous page, or display a nicely formatted error message telling the user they shouldn't link directly to the page, or both.

◆ Testing to make sure that the current page has received all the form variables you were expecting it to receive ensures that your page won't crash. However, this method doesn't guarantee that the user came from the page you were expecting. Using HTTP Post routines, a sophisticated user can link directly to the page, passing in the form variables you expected, which may bypass any error checking of the data you applied to the data input page. This type of behavior may not concern you and, indeed, may be by design. Just be aware that this bypassing possibility does exist.

Error Checking and Data Validation

One way to keep your data tables clean and keep your system from bombing at the same time involves checking for errors in the data that are submitted to your site. If you verify that the data the user is entering falls within the parameters you expect, you shouldn't receive any nasty surprises that can crash your data or code. Suppose a user enters text in a numeric field—can your system handle that eventuality? Because, like it or not, the public will invariably enter the wrong type of information. And there's always the bored child at home who encounters your site and is just interested in seeing if they can crash it. Applying a bit of error checking isn't that difficult, and Dreamweaver MX can aid you in this respect.

You can verify that data entered in a web form meets expectations in two ways. You can use client-side validation or server-side validation. Advantages and limits are associated with both types, so you should use both in conjunction with each other to keep your data clean.

Client-Side Validation

Client-side validation refers to validation performed on the client side. That is, it's performed on the client's, also known as the user's, computer. Client-side validation is traditionally performed using JavaScript since the most popular browsers handle JavaScript equally well. This type of validation checks the information a user enters into a web form before it gets to the server. When the user clicks the Submit button, JavaScript ensures that the data conforms to your specifications before moving on to the action page. This kind of processing helps by doing the following:

◆ Reducing the amount of traffic to and from your web server since the data doesn't have to travel to the server before it gets checked (server-side validation). If an error is found in the data in server-side validation, the error must travel back to the user, who then corrects the problem and resubmits the data. This back-and-forth traveling can eat up precious bandwidth.

◆ Saving processing time on the server by ensuring that data is clean and clear before it gets to your database.

◆ Giving immediate feedback to your users since the processing is performed in their browser. The user doesn't have to wait for the data to travel to the server to be checked and a response to be sent. They know immediately whether they need to tweak the information they've entered.

TIP   Let's digress a moment here. JavaScript is not the same as Java. Java is a complete development language developed by Sun Microsystems. JavaScript originated with Netscape in 1995 as a means of helping developers and nondevelopers hook into Java. Microsoft then ported and released their version, called Jscript, in Internet Explorer. Don't make the common newbie mistake of referring to JavaScript as Java. Seasoned developers will laugh at you if you do.

Dreamweaver MX will help you with client-side data validation by letting you set behaviors to control what types of data each field in your form should receive. To set a Validate Form behavior, follow these steps:

1. Open the page that contains the form you want to validate.
2. From the Design panel, click the Behaviors tab, which you can see in Figure 3.4.

FIGURE 3.4
Dreamweaver MX behaviors save you time and effort by automatically creating useful scripts for you.

3. Click the + sign to add a new behavior, and choose Validate Form to open the Validate Form dialog box, a sample of which you can see in Figure 3.5.

FIGURE 3.5
You can validate a field as a number, as a numeric range, or as an e-mail address.

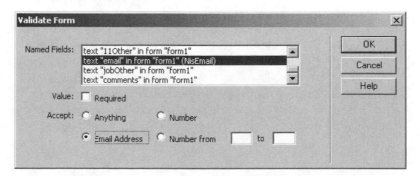

Our form contains several fields, including an e-mail address field. When you select text "email" in form "form1" (NisEmail) from the Named Fields list, Dreamweaver MX generates JavaScript (or VBScript, depending on the type of page you're creating) that verifies that the user has entered a valid e-mail address. A sample of this auto-generated code follows.

```
function MM_validateForm() { //v4.0
  var i,p,q,nm,test,num,min,max,errors='',args=MM_validateForm.arguments;
  for (i=0; i<(args.length-2); i+=3) { test=args[i+2]; val=MM_findObj(args[i]);
    if (val) { nm=val.name; if ((val=val.value)!="") {
      if (test.indexOf('isEmail')!=-1) { p=val.indexOf('@');
        if (p<1 || p==(val.length-1)) errors+='- '+nm+' must contain an e-mail
          address.\n';
      } else if (test!='R') { num = parseFloat(val);
        if (isNaN(val)) errors+='- '+nm+' must contain a number.\n';
        if (test.indexOf('inRange') != -1) { p=test.indexOf(':');
          min=test.substring(8,p); max=test.substring(p+1);
          if (num<min || max<num) errors+='- '+nm+' must contain a number
            between '+min+' and '+max+'.\n';
    } } } else if (test.charAt(0) == 'R') errors += '- '+nm+' is required.\n'; }
  } if (errors) alert('The following error(s) occurred:\n'+errors);
  document.MM_returnValue = (errors == '');
}
```

You can see that Dreamweaver MX makes the validation code concise. The code parses through the e-mail address making sure that it follows an e-mail address format—alphanumeric data, an @ symbol, more alphanumeric data, a period, and then more alphanumeric data. The code also contains a couple of other tests (for floating numbers and whether a field is required), since this function validates the entire form. But you might be wondering what Dreamweaver MX adds to the Submit button in order to accomplish this validation. Here it is, a function call automatically added to the Submit button's onClick event:

```
<input name="Submit" type="submit"
  onClick="MM_validateForm('email','','NisEmail');return
  document.MM_returnValue" value="Submit ">
```

Unfortunately, as you can see, Dreamweaver MX doesn't validate dates or other datatypes. However, recognizing that Dreamweaver MX wouldn't meet everyone's needs in every capacity, Macromedia made it extensible. You'll find numerous new and replacement behaviors on the Macromedia Exchange website at http://dynamic.macromedia.com/bin/MM/exchange/dreamweaver/main.jsp.

Some development languages, such as ColdFusion, also include their own auto-generated validation code routines. This means you could end up with lots of basically redundant JavaScript in your web pages, so you'll want to familiarize yourself with those options in your development language of choice and use the version that makes the most sense for you.

Keep in mind that since client-side validation uses JavaScript (most of the time), your validation routines will not work if the user has JavaScript turned off in their browser. Granted, most people don't turn off JavaScript, but as we mentioned before, you don't want to crash your system by letting bad data into it. That's where server-side validation comes in.

Server-Side Validation

Server-side validation consists of validating user input on the server. The user submits the form, the data travels to the server, and then the server checks the data based on the code you created—generally using IF-THEN statements or other control structures. Server-side validation is probably the most common type of validation, but again, it should be used in conjunction with client-side validation.

Even though you include client-side validation in your forms, server-side validation provides that extra, no-way-around-it step that ensures your data is clean and formatted as you expect. If the user has JavaScript turned off, the server-side validation you create will catch any errors.

Now you may be wondering why you need to use both server-side and client-side validation. Remember, client-side gives almost immediate feedback to the user without tying up your pipeline and your server. It provides a faster web-based experience for your users, which in today's rush-everywhere society is always a plus. And the user just can't escape the server-side checking, which won't tax your server too much if it is fed clean data, since you don't have to send error responses back to the user.

Server-side validation should consist of code in your action page that mirrors the validation action of each item you validate in your client-side portion—and even perhaps a bit more, depending on your system. If you validate a date and an e-mail address in your form, also validate the same date and e-mail address in your server-side validation to ensure that no data validation is skipped.

Using the Tag Library Editor

To aid you in your consistent code structure efforts, Dreamweaver MX provides a couple of tools. You can manipulate the rules Dreamweaver MX uses to format your code by setting Code Formatting Preferences, as discussed in Chapter 2. You can also use the Tag Library Editor, which lets you edit the way your tags will appear in your code. Let's take a quick look at this feature.

Using the Tag Library Editor you can control the line breaks, formatting, and case of every tag that Dreamweaver MX drops into your code. Follow these steps:

1. Choose Edit ➢ Tag Libraries, as shown in Figure 3.6, to open the Tag Library Editor, as shown in Figure 3.7.

2. We're going to change the formatting of the HTML body tag, so scroll down and select body in the Tags panel.

    You can control the spacing around the selected tag, in this case the <body> tag, by selecting a new setting in the Line Breaks drop-down list. You can change the actual formatting of the tag by choosing options in the Contents drop-down list. Changing the case of the tag is as easy as choosing Uppercase (or whatever) from the Case drop-down list. (You can make your casing choice a default for all tags by clicking the Set Default link.)

FIGURE 3.6

Launch the Tag Library Editor from the Edit tab.

FIGURE 3.7

The Tag Library Editor will also show you a preview of how your tag will appear in your code.

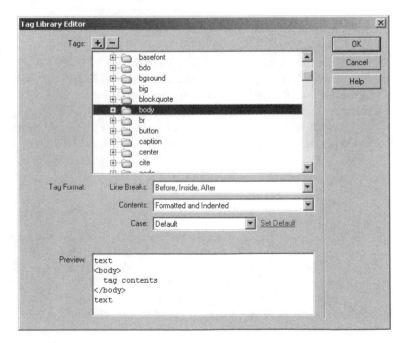

3. Choose Uppercase from the Case drop-down list, and Dreamweaver MX will show you how the tag will appear, as you can see in Figure 3.8.

FIGURE 3.8

We've changed the standard formatting of our HTML <body> tag.

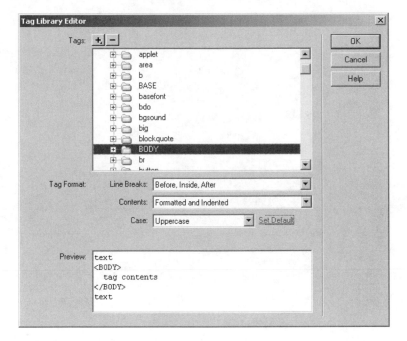

Summary

The best behavior you, as a developer, can adopt is consistently following a good, solid core of coding practices. Even though it may take you a little longer upfront during your development process to apply comments, declare variables, follow naming guidelines, and test for variables, doing so will invariably save you time in the long-run. Not only will your code be clean, tight, and easy to follow, but you'll be setting the stage for future developers to modify your code once you've moved on. Following the guidelines in this chapter will help ensure that the code you create resembles that of a seasoned developer—it will be slick, documented, and practically bug-free.

Chapter 4

An Introduction to HTML Forms

A DYNAMIC WEBSITE INTERACTS on two levels—with the database and with the user (or visitor). As with a regular database, the user doesn't really see what's going on behind the scenes; the user just initiates processing by making requests and sometimes by sharing data. The majority of this book will deal with interacting with the database; this chapter provides tools for the user to interact with the website.

A user interacts with the website for three reasons:

- ◆ To request data
- ◆ To modify existing data
- ◆ To enter new data

To accomplish any of these tasks, the user must communicate with the website.

For the most part, the web developer uses Hypertext Markup Language (HTML) forms to solicit information from the user. An HTML form is an element that turns a static page into an interactive page—by displaying elements that let the user interact with the page. Once the user enters data or clicks a button, the page interprets the request and processes the necessary scripts to comply with the user's request. In this chapter, you'll learn about HTML forms that let users interact with your page. Subjects include:

- ◆ An introduction to HTML
- ◆ What is an HTML form?
- ◆ HTTP headers
- ◆ Working with input elements
- ◆ Adding form objects and fields in Dreamweaver MX
- ◆ Post versus Get

An Introduction to HTML

It all begins with Hypertext Markup Language (HTML). Even though you may never have to write any HTML code, you should be familiar with it because the server typically translates all scripting languages into pure HTML and then returns all requests in pure HTML.

HTML, a subset of Standard Generalized Markup Language (SGML), conforms to International Standard ISO 8879 and has become the worldwide standard for web publishing. Almost all scripting languages interact with HTML, and many scripting languages include the ability to produce output in HTML. In addition, all browsers display almost any HTML file on any computer using any operating system—no wonder everybody uses it. (Experiences may vary, but exceptions to the preceding statement are rare.)

NOTE HTML *is a layout language that displays complex documents. A* complex *document contains both images and text.*

This language has only two components: the markup and the content. The *markup* consists of commands, known as tags, that are processed by the HTML engine. The *content* is the text or image displayed by the browser. The browser never displays HTML markup. Instead, the markup supplies specific instructions on how to display the content.

Thanks to HTML, users can format and display text and images, send requests to the server, create hyperlinks from one file to another (or one page to another), and accept input from other users.

What Is an HTML Form?

The HTML `form` element defines input elements that let the user interact with the page by entering data, choosing an item from a list, or clicking a button. For example, let's suppose a user must log on to a secured site. The solution is an HTML form, which in this case might be a couple of input elements—one for the user's name, and a second for the password. The page presents an input element in which the user enters their name and password. When done, the user probably clicks a button to submit their logon information to the server for processing and acceptance or rejection.

The `form` element works with the input elements, which tell the page what to display and then how to store any user responses. The `form` tag has the following syntax:

```
<form name="formname" action="URL" method="post|get" target="destinationframe">
```

The `name` parameter identifies the form, `action` is the URL where you want to send the data for processing, `method` specifies `post` or `get`, and `target` is the frame where you want the response to appear (if you're using frames). For example, the following `<form>` tag sends the data in the form named `frmLogIn` to a page named `LogIn.asp` using the `post` method:

```
<form name="frmLogIn" action="LogIn.asp" method="post">
```

Although all four parameters are optional, always name the form so that you can manipulate it (and the input elements) using client-side script. The `action` parameter specifies a new URL (page). If you omit this parameter, the form defaults to the current page. The `method` parameter accepts one of two predefined constants: `post` and `get`. We'll discuss these in detail later in the chapter, but in brief, the `post` method sends data in a single line. In contrast, `get` combines the form data and then appends it to the URL. For the most part, you'll use `post`, but the default method is `get`. When working with frames, the `target` parameter specifies the frame you want to display. If there is no frame, the browser opens a new (frame) window. The `target` parameter is optional and necessary only when the page uses frames or when you want a link to open a specific window. Don't worry if that last bit confuses you—you won't be working with frames or anything that complicated in this chapter. We just want you to be aware that the option exists.

Forms are an HTML element, but keep in mind that pure HTML is static. Scripting languages bring forms to life. Throughout the rest of the chapter, you'll see form and input elements mingled with Active Server Pages (ASP), a Microsoft server technology and scripting language. (In this chapter, we'll look at just the scripting language.) We chose ASP because of its universal popularity, but ASP is not the only option for forms processing. ASP can use many scripting languages. We chose to use VBScript with ASP because it's easy to learn, easy to use, and supported in Dreamweaver MX.

NOTE   *For an in-depth look at ASP, see Chapter 13.*

HTTP Headers

Visiting a web page is a lot like a conversation. Your browser initiates a discussion by asking to connect via an HTTP (Hypertext Transfer Protocol) request. When the server accepts, the client requests information, which the server then accepts, processes, and uses to process the request and then return the requested data in a web page—all via HTTP header requests. Fortunately, the client automatically transmits most of the data the server needs to see in the HTTP header in the form of server variables. These variables pass the IP address, the type of information requested, and any form content; query variables; and so on. The particular method used to pass all this header information depends on the scripting language you use.

Input Elements

If you're unfamiliar with web lingo, the context in which we're using some terms might be confusing. Think of an HTML form as an element that accepts data. The input element is defined by a second tag, `<input>`. First, the `<form>` tag spells out specifics about where the input is going and how; the `<input>` tag defines the type of input element the page will use to collect that data. There are several types of input elements.

Submit button   A Submit button sends the form contents to the server. For instance, the following statement displays a Submit button with the caption `"Submit"`:

```
<input type="submit" name="Submit data" value="Submit">
```

When you click the Submit button, the form element sends the form content (including user input) to the server for processing.

Reset button   A Reset button clears all input and resets the form to its original settings. For example, the following statement displays a Reset button element with the caption `"Reset"`:

```
<input type="reset" name="Reset" value="Reset">
```

When you click the button, the form clears the accompanying form.

General-purpose button   Clicking a general-purpose button executes a client-side script that defines and fulfills the button's purpose. You might display a button with the caption `"OK"` as in the following statement:

```
<input type="OKbutton" name="OK" value="OK", onClick="OKbutton()">
```

The `OKbutton()` parameter is a custom routine that performs a specific task when you click the button. Specifically, when you click the button, the form executes your `OKbutton()` routine. (`OKbutton()` isn't a real routine; it's just a fictitious name we're referring to for the sake of the example.)

Checkbox control   A checkbox control lets a user select more than one item in a list. For instance, the following statement displays a checkbox element with the text label `"Show Frame"`:

```
<input type="checkbox" name="chkFrameOn" value="FrameOn" checked>Show Frame</input>
```

When selected, this element returns the value `"FrameOn"`. The checked attribute selects the item when the page loads.

Radio button   Use a radio button to limit a user to only one item in a list or group. For instance, the following statement displays two radio button elements with the text labels `"Show Frame"` and `"Hide Frame"`:

```
<input type="radio" name="optFrame" value="Frame On" checked>Show Frame</input>
<input type="radio" name="optFrame" value="Frame Off">Hide Frame</input>
```

When selected, either element returns the value attribute. The checked attribute selects the item when the page is loaded. You should give all items in the same radio group the same name.

Image control   An alternative to the Submit button, the image control displays an image (or an icon) instead of the simple gray graphic button. For example, the following statement responds just as a submit button element, but displays a graphic file named `OKcheck.jif` instead of a button with a text caption:

```
<input type="image" src="OKcheck.gif">
```

Single-line text input   Use a single-line text input element when you have a single line of user input to capture. For instance, the following statement accepts an entry that's 15 or fewer characters:

```
<input type="text" name="txtLastName" value="" maxlength="15">
```

Password input   This element is the same as the single-line text input, but the password input displays asterisk characters (*) instead of the actual text the user enters. The following statement disguises the password entry as the user enters it:

```
<input type="password" name="pwdLogOn" value="">
```

Keep in mind that the password isn't disguised or encrypted when transferred to the server. A password form field isn't a secure way to transmit user identification information.

Multiline text input   This element accepts several paragraphs of text. For example, the following statement displays a text element that's 20 characters wide and 5 rows deep:

```
<textarea name="txtNote" cols="20" rows="5">Additional information</textarea>
```

Working with Input Elements

At this point, we want to actually display some of these input elements. To do so, you'll need to open Dreamweaver MX or a text editor to create the simple files and then display them in a browser. You'll also need to install a web server, if you haven't done so already. (See Chapter 2 for instructions on installing and setting up your web server.)

 We'll save our example files in a folder off the local system's web root directory—`C:\Inetpub\wwwroot\MasteringDreamweaver\Chapter4`.

We strongly encourage you to key in all the code to create the example files yourself. To check your work, compare your files with the example files on the CD accompanying this book.

The first step is to open Dreamweaver MX or a text editor and enter the script shown in Listing 4.1. In Dreamweaver MX, choose File ➤ New and then choose Dynamic Page from the Category list. Next, choose ASP VBScript from the Dynamic Page list and click Create. You can name the file anything you like, but be sure to save the file using the `.asp` extension if you're using a text editor. The example file is named `ch4list1.asp`.

At this point, we just want you to have the satisfaction of actually seeing a script work. In a real-world example, the form's `action` property would probably call a second script that performs a custom task or submits the form content to the server. Adding a second file to the mix might be a tad overwhelming for the novice. Our button simply calls the same file, although you do see a bit of action when clicking the button displays the button's value on the page.

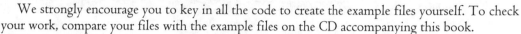

LISTING 4.1: *CH4LIST1.ASP*

```
<%@ Language=VBScript %>
<%
Response.Write Request.Form("SubmitTest")
%>
<html>
<head>
<title>Chapter 4, Listing 1 Example</title>
</head>
<body>
<form name="Click Me" method="post" action="ch4list1.asp">
...<input type="Submit" name="SubmitTest" value="It worked!">
</form>
</body>
</html>
```

TIP   The double quotation marks surrounding each attribute aren't always necessary. HTML requires these quotation marks only when the value contains a space character. We recommend you get in the habit of enclosing all attributes in quotation marks because it's so easy to forget them. In contrast, XHTML and XML require these quotation marks, which is another good reason to include them all the time. If you upgrade your HTML script to XHTML or XML, you'll save a lot of debugging time if your code already includes all the necessary quotation marks.

To run the `.asp` file, open your browser and enter the appropriate address. For our example, we're running Internet Information Services (IIS), Microsoft's web server, so the complete address is

```
http://localhost/MasteringDreamWeaver/Chapter4/ch4list1.asp
```

The result is the simple page shown in Figure 4.1. Click the button to display its value, "It worked!" and redisplay the button, as shown in Figure 4.2.

FIGURE 4.1

Our simple form displays a Submit button.

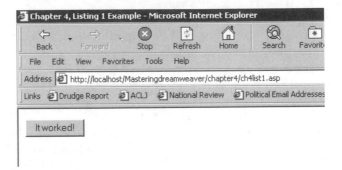

FIGURE 4.2

Clicking the button displays the button's value.

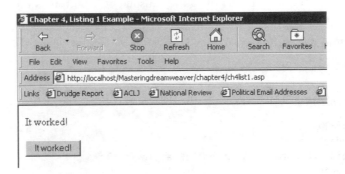

Now, let's run a more complex example—one that actually interacts with a sample database. Specifically, let's query the Northwind sample database that comes with Microsoft Access for orders pertaining to specific customers. (SQL Server has a version of this same database, named NorthwindCS.SQL, if you want to use SQL Server data.) A bit of preparation is involved before we can move on to the script.

First, copy the Northwind sample database to your web root folder. We'll be working from the folder `C:\Inetpub\MasteringDreamweaver`. You can work with almost any database; just be sure to copy it to the right web folder.

Then be sure the folder is shared by opening Windows Explorer and locating your sample web folder. Right-click the folder, choose Properties from the shortcut menu to open the Properties dialog box, and click the Web Sharing tab. Select the Share This folder option, and click OK. If Windows displays the Edit Alias dialog box, accept the default options and then click OK to close the Properties dialog box.

CREATING AN ODBC DATA SOURCE NAME (DSN)

Any time you want a web page to connect to data, you need a data link. Our current example uses an Open Database Connectivity (ODBC) Data Source Name (DSN). A DSN stores data such as the database name, its path, and user and password information. This information is required in order to connect to the database. Although OLE DB connections are superior technology, DSNs are quicker and easier to create. A DSN is more than adequate for our example. (For more information on OLE DB connections, see Chapter 10.)

There are two types of DSN: System and File. A System connection is available to all users on the system. You choose System when creating website connections. A File DSN requires a corresponding driver, and only those users with the appropriate driver installed can connect via a File connection. To create a System DSN on a Windows 2000 or Windows 98 system, follow these steps:

1. Choose Start button ➢ Settings ➢ Control Panel to open Control Panel.
2. Double-click Administrative Tools to open the Administrative Tools folder. (Windows 98 users can skip this step.)
3. Double-click Data Sources (ODBC) to open the ODBC Data Source Administrator dialog box.
4. Click the System DSN tab, and then click Add to open the Create New Data Source dialog box.
5. Locate the appropriate driver in the list, and then click Finish.
6. Back in the ODBC Data Source Administrator dialog box enter a name for the new DSN.
7. Enter a description for the connection.
8. Click Select to locate the file to which you're connecting.
9. Click OK. Windows adds the new System DSN to the System Data Sources list.
10. Close Control Panel.

If you're using Windows XP's default display theme:

1. Choose Start ➢ Control Panel.
2. Click Performance and Maintenance, and then click Administrative Tools to open the Administrative Tools folder.
3. Double-click Data Sources (ODBC) to open the ODBC Data Source Administrator dialog box.
4. Follow steps 4 through 10 earlier in this sidebar.

CREATING A LOCAL DSN

Now you're ready to create a connection to the sample database. To do so, create a System DSN. Our example connects to the Northwind sample database in the web root directory C:\Inetpub\wwwroot\ MasteringDreamweaver. To complete this last preparation, follow these steps:

1. Complete steps 1 through 4 (appropriate to your operating system) in the accompanying sidebar.
2. Select the Microsoft Access Driver, and then click Finish.
3. Name the DSN NorthWindDSN and enter the following description, "Connection to Northwind for Examples," as shown in Figure 4.3.

FIGURE 4.3
Name and describe
the DSN.

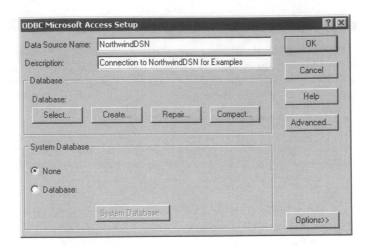

4. Click Select to open the Select Database dialog box and locate `C:\Inetpub\wwwroot\MasteringDreamweaver\Northwind.mdb` or the appropriate path for your system.

Make sure Windows adds the new DSN to the System Data Sources list in the ODBC Data Source Administrator dialog box, as shown in Figure 4.4.

FIGURE 4.4
Windows adds the
new ODBC DSN.

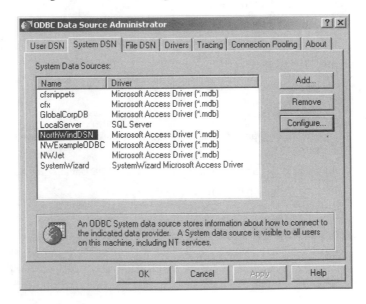

Now let's create a new form that queries the user for a specific customer name and then returns a list of orders for that customer. To do so, open your text editor, enter the script shown in Listings 4.2 and 4.3, and save the files as `.asp` files.

LISTING 4.2: *CH4LIST2.ASP*

```
<html>
<head>
<title>Chapter 4, Listing 2 Example</title>
</head>
<body>
<form name="frmChapter4Listing2" method="post" action="ch4list3.asp" >
<p> Enter the customer's name and then click the Submit button to see a list
   of orders.
<p>
<tr>
...<td width="45%">Customer </td>
...<input type="text" name="txtcompanyname">
</tr>
...<input type="submit" name="Submit" value="Submit">
</form>
```

LISTING 4.3: *CH4LIST3.ASP*

```
<%
Dim companyname
Set Conn = Server.CreateObject("ADODB.Connection")
Conn.Open "NorthWindDSN"
companyname = Request.Form("txtcompanyname")
SQL = "SELECT Customers.CompanyName, Orders.OrderID
   FROM Customers INNER JOIN Orders ON
   Customers.CustomerID = Orders.CustomerID
   WHERE CompanyName = '" & companyname & "'"
Set rst = Conn.Execute(SQL)
%>
<%Do While Not rst.EOF%>
...<%Response.Write rst("CompanyName")%> 
...<%Response.Write rst("OrderID")%>
...<BR>
...<%rst.MoveNext
Loop
%>
```

Now, open ch4list2.asp in your browser, which displays a simple text input element and a Submit button. Enter the customer name **Ernst Handel**, as shown in Figure 4.5, and then click the Submit button.

FIGURE 4.5

Enter a customer name.

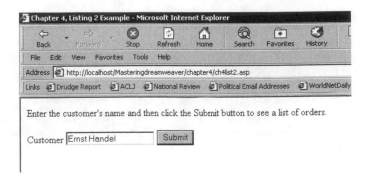

The results are shown in Figure 4.6—this customer has several orders. Notice that the filename in the address has changed from `ch4list2.asp` to `ch4list3.asp`. That's because the script instructed your browser to open the new page, `ch4list3.asp` in the `<form>` tag.

FIGURE 4.6

The page returns orders for the matching customer.

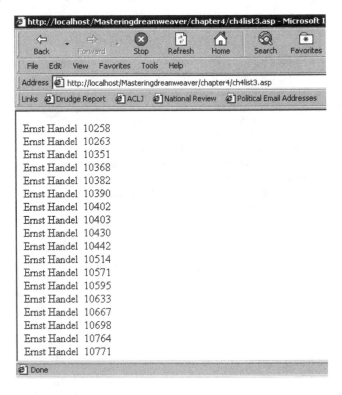

The form element and the input element in `ch4list2.asp` work together. The input element accepts data. When you enter a value in the input element named `txtcompanyname` and press Enter or click the Submit button, the `action` parameter in the form element passes that value to the script in `ch4list3.asp`.

The browser then opens ch4list3.asp and a connection to the NorthwindDSN data source (that we created earlier) and assigns the passed value to a variable named *companyname*. Next, the script opens a recordset named rst based on the SELECT statement, which includes the variable *companyname* in the statement's criteria. In the current example, this statement reduces to the following:

```
SELECT Customers.CompanyName, Orders.OrderID
    FROM Customers INNER JOIN Orders ON
    Customers.CustomerID = Orders.CustomerID WHERE CompanyName = 'Ernst Handel'
```

The Do While loop then displays the CompanyName and the OrderID values from each record in the resulting recordset in the browser. That's what you saw in Figure 4.6.

You don't have to use two .asp files to accomplish this task. Listing 4.4 combines both files. As you can see in Figure 4.7, your browser displays the results of the query in the same form instead of on a new blank page.

LISTING 4.4: *CH4LIST5.ASP*

```
<%Response.Clear%>
<body>
<form name="frmChapter4Listing4" method="post" action="ch4list4.asp" >
<p> Enter the customer's name and then click the Submit button
    to see a list of orders.
<p>
<tr>
...<td width="45%">Customer </td>
...<input type="text" name="txtcompanyname" value="">
</tr><input type="submit" name="Submit" value="Submit">
</form>
<%
Dim companyname
Set Conn = Server.CreateObject("ADODB.Connection")
Conn.Open "NorthWindDSN"
companyname = Request.Form("txtcompanyname")
SQL = "SELECT Customers.CompanyName, Orders.OrderID
    FROM Customers INNER JOIN Orders ON
    Customers.CustomerID = Orders.CustomerID
    WHERE CompanyName = '" & companyname & "'"
Set rst = Conn.Execute(SQL)
%>
<BR>
<%Do While Not rst.EOF%>
...<%Response.Write rst("CompanyName")%> 
...<%Response.Write rst("OrderID")%>
...<BR>
...<%rst.MoveNext
Loop
Set rst = Nothing
%>
```

FIGURE 4.7

The results of combining our two previous scripts

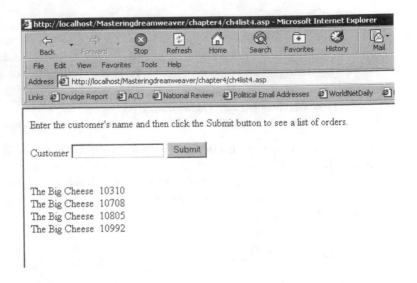

HANDLING HIDDEN VALUES

There's one last type of element that you should know about—the hidden element. This element stores values that you don't want displayed on the web page. For instance, you might store a value that will be re-evaluated on a subsequent form. To save the user the trouble of re-entering the data, you can store the data as a hidden value.

Those stored values aren't invisible, because the user can still view your source script and stored values by choosing View ≻ Source. Consequently, you'll want to use this attribute carefully. Don't use it to store confidential information such as passwords, user names, and so on. To store a hidden value, use the input type element in the form as follows:

```
<input type="hidden" value=returnedvalue>
```

The *returnedvalue* parameter is the value you're hiding from view.

NOTE   You'll learn more about implementing security on your website in Chapter 17.

Working with Select Elements

The previous section discussed input elements that required the user to actually enter data. Sometimes the user need only choose an item from a predefined list. If you're familiar with the Windows environment, you're already used to these types of controls—they're known as combo and list controls. HTML offers combo and list equivalents known as the drop-down and fixed list, respectively, although both are really the same element—the Select element. The user can select only one item from a drop-down list . Even though lists, by default, restrict the user to only one item, the user can select more than one item from a fixed list.

To create a drop-down list control, use the `<select>` tag with its many attributes in the following form:

```
<select name=elementname>
    <option selected value=value>optiontext</option>
    <option value=value>optiontext</option>
    ...
</select>
```

The *elementname* parameter is the name of the element, *value* is the option's value, and *optiontext* is the text displayed along with the item. The control returns the selected item's *value* unless there's no *value* attribute. In addition, the selected attribute value is selected by default when the form data is submitted. In that case, the control returns *optiontext*.

WARNING *Don't forget to enclose the* value *parameter in double quotation marks if* value *contains a space character. Otherwise, the control returns only the first word as the control's value.*

Creating a fixed list requires an extra attribute, the size attribute, in the following form:

```
<select name=elementname size=numberofitems>
```

The *numberofitems* parameter specifies the number of items initially displayed in the fixed list. If the list allows for more than one selected item, add the multiple attribute in the following form:

```
<select multiple name=elementname size=numberofitems>
```

Now, let's add a select element to our previous example. Specifically, we'll exchange the original input control for a list control that displays specific customer names. Doing so limits the potential for human error because the user must choose an item from the list instead of typing a value. The script then uses the selected item's return value as the query's criteria. When choices are restricted to an existing set of items, a list element is always preferable to user input.

The script in Listing 4.5 displays a fixed list of only two items. When you choose an item, the script displays the appropriate order records for that particular customer, as shown in Figure 4.8. When you delete the size attribute from the `<select>` element statement, the browser displays a drop-down control similar to the one shown in Figure 4.9.

LISTING 4.5: *CH4LIST5.ASP*

```
<%Response.Clear%>
<body>
<form name="frmChapter4Listing5" method="post" action="ch4list5.asp" >
<p> Enter the customer's name and then click the Submit button
    to see a list of orders.
<p>
  <tr>
    <td width="45%">Customer: </td><br>
...<select name="lstcompanyname" size="2">
......<option value="Ernst Handel">Ernst Handel</option>
```

```
......<option value="The Big Cheese">The Big Cheese</option>
...</select>
...<input type="submit" name="Submit" value="Submit">
</form>
</tr>
<%
Dim companyname
Set Conn = Server.CreateObject("ADODB.Connection")
Conn.Open "NorthWindDSN"
companyname = Request.Form("lstcompanyname")
SQL = "SELECT Customers.CompanyName, Orders.OrderID
   FROM Customers INNER JOIN Orders ON
   Customers.CustomerID = Orders.CustomerID
   WHERE CompanyName = '" & companyname & "'"
Set rst = Conn.Execute(SQL)
%>
<BR>
<%Do While Not rst.EOF%>
...<%Response.Write rst("CompanyName")%> 
...<%Response.Write rst("OrderID")%>
...<BR>
...<%rst.MoveNext
Loop
Set rst = Nothing
%>
```

FIGURE 4.8

The `<select>` element displays a fixed list.

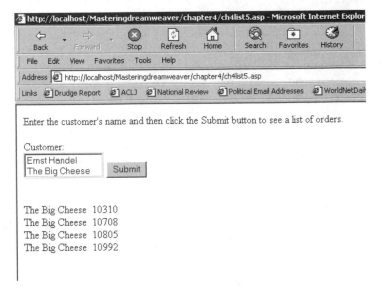

FIGURE 4.9

Use the `<select>` element to display a drop-down list.

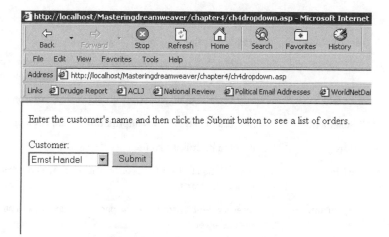

Adding Form Objects and Fields in Dreamweaver MX

Dreamweaver MX refers to form input types as form objects, and, fortunately, they're easy to insert. Simply choose Insert ➤ Form Objects, and then select one of the form objects from the submenu, or click the Forms tab of the Insert bar to display the Forms panel (see Figure 4.10). The form objects in Table 4.1 are listed in the same order as they appear in the Forms panel. The descriptions are the same for the items in the submenu.

FIGURE 4.10

Choose a form object from the Insert menu, or display the Forms panel to access form objects.

TABLE 4.1: FORM OBJECTS

OBJECT NAME	DESCRIPTION
Form	Inserts a form into the page. Dreamweaver MX inserts both the opening and closing form tags. (Be sure to position additional form objects between the form tags.)
Text Field	Inserts a text field, which will accept any type of alphanumeric entry.
Hidden Field	Inserts a field that stores information entered by a user, but isn't displayed.
Textarea	Inserts a multiline text field.
Check Box	Inserts a check box into the page. The user can choose more than one check box item in a group of options.
Radio Button	Inserts a radio button into the page. You can present several buttons, but the user can select only one.
Radio Group	Inserts a collection of radio buttons that share the same name.
List/Menu	Inserts a control that displays a number of items. In a list control, the user selects an item (or items) from a list of choices. A menu displays the option values in a pop-up menu and limits the user to only one item (unless the multiple attribute is included).
Jump Menu	Inserts a navigational list or pop-up menu. Each selection in the list is a link.
Image Field	Inserts an image field into a page.
File Field	Inserts a blank text field and a Browse button into the page.
Button	Inserts a text button into a page, which performs a predefined or scripted task.
Label	Inserts static text.
Fieldset	Groups other fields.

Both methods for inserting a form object or field open the Tag Editor so you can customize the form or field before Dreamweaver MX actually inserts it into the page. The properties are specific to the type of field you're adding. To select a form or field, simply click it.

Dreamweaver MX displays a red, dotted outline around a form object in Design view in the Documents window. All fields belonging to that form are enclosed in that outline. For instance, Figure 4.11 shows three fields in one form. As you add or delete fields, the outline expands or contracts, accordingly.

FIGURE 4.11

Forms are easily identified by the red dotted outline around them.

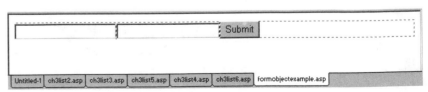

TIP *If the dotted line isn't visible when you insert form objects, check the Invisible Elements option by choosing View ➤ Visual Aids. If Invisible Elements isn't selected, select it.*

After selecting a form object, you can modify its properties via the Properties panel at the bottom of the screen. (Click the arrow to expand the panel.) Figure 4.12 shows the Properties panel for a new text field form object. Clicking the lightning icon displays a dialog box in which you can specify the data source for a dynamic form object.

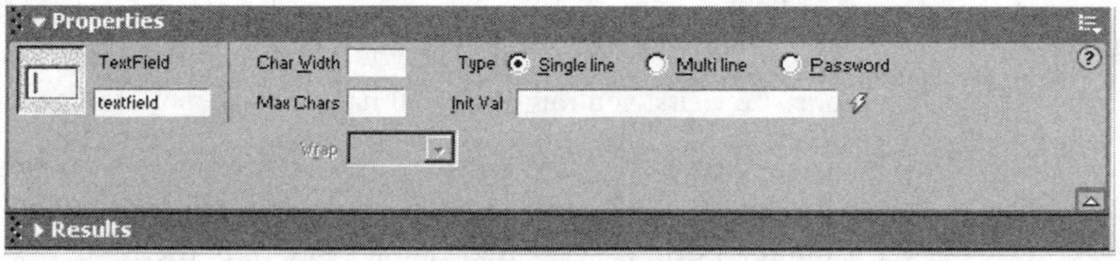

FIGURE 4.12

Open the Properties panel to modify a form object's properties.

Post versus Get

Earlier in this chapter, we mentioned that the Post method is preferable to the Get method and recommended that you always use Post unless you have a specific reason not to do so. The Post and Get options determine how a form's criteria is submitted to the server. The Post method sends data to the server in a single line, via the form's header. The Get method first appends the data to the URL before sending the data to the server. Consequently, you can't retrieve the data from the server using the Form collection (Request object). You can still get the data, but you must use the QueryString collection instead, which takes a bit more work. (You'll learn more about ASP's Form and QueryString collections in Chapter 13.)

Our examples rely extensively on the Form collection, so we can best illustrate this behavior by simply changing the Post method to Get in any of our scripts. (Be sure to save the change.) Then, open the page in your browser and try to execute the script. Unfortunately, the script returns an error message because the Form collection fails to return the values needed to complete the script. In addition, the URL also includes a lot of additional text . If you look closely, you'll see that the added text is simply the field names and values.

Figure 4.13 shows the URL after altering our first example script, `ch4list1.asp`. You might also recall that clicking the button simply displayed the text "It worked!" on the page, and that feature no longer works. Notice that the Get method concatenated script instructions to the address.

FIGURE 4.13

Using the Get method displays field names and values in the URL.

Since you can use either the QueryString or Form collection to send data to the server, you might think Post and Get are equivalent, but they're not. We recommend the Post method for the following reasons:

◆ Get limits the amount of data (to about 1000 characters).

◆ Get lets the user change the value, which probably isn't a good idea, especially if you've taken precautions (such as using specific fields and validating entries) in your script to limit entries.

◆ Get displays your variable names in the URL. If a user doesn't know how to use the variables, exposing these values probably won't matter. However, if someone intent on breaking into your site visits, you might as well have "Hack me" stamped across your page.

There's no clear advantage to using Get—if you view a site using Get (and you'll know by the URL), you can usually assume the developer simply doesn't know how to access variables from the server using the Form collection or doesn't care to bother.

NOTE *The Get option is still supported and is valid in XHTML. If you have only a small amount of data to transmit, Get transmits faster than Post. Also, if you want to invoke a server-side application without using a form (including passing parameters), you can do so using Get.*

Summary

The beginning of your web development ride begins and ends with HTML—that's because your server translates all requests from and to the web page into pure HTML. One of the most important and useful HTML tools you'll use is the HTML form. In this chapter, we showed you how to combine the HTML form element with input elements to gather information from the user. In the next chapter, we'll tackle database design.

Part II

The Databases

The chapters in this section will introduce you to:
- ◆ Database design concepts
- ◆ Oracle and SQL Server as competing platforms for web development
- ◆ MySQL as a free platform for web development
- ◆ Microsoft Access as a desktop platform for web development

Chapter 5

Designing the Database

THE SUCCESS OF YOUR dynamic website depends on the supporting database. Dreamweaver MX only makes the development process of creating an interactive site easier. If you can't retrieve the right data, all of Dreamweaver's fancy footwork is useless.

After all, a properly designed relational database is flexible, easy to use, and adapts well to change as the database grows. On the other hand, a poor design produces anomalies and frustration. An *anomaly* is simply an error that occurs when you try to work with your data—modifying, updating, adding, or even deleting information. As you can well imagine, working with a poorly designed relational database is difficult—getting the data from the tables to your website might prove almost impossible.

When discussing a website, the term *design* usually refers to the general look and feel of what you see. When discussing a relational database, the term *design* means the way the database is structured. This chapter is devoted to relational database theory and the design process. If you're not familiar with the driving force behind the relational database, welcome to Relational Database Theory 101. If you're well versed in relational database theory, you can probably skip this entire chapter. Here's what we'll cover:

◆ Redundant data—the purpose behind relational database theory

◆ Normalization—the solution behind the theory

◆ Primary and foreign keys

◆ The design process

◆ Taking on referential integrity

◆ Cascading options

Redundant Data—the Purpose Behind Relational Database Theory

Before relational database theory, flat-file storage was the critical issue. Memory was expensive and required lots of physical space. In addition, maintaining flat-file data took lots of human resources, which required salaries and office space.

The flat-file format stores every piece of data for every record, which can exponentially increase your storage needs and quickly lead to crushing demands on your resources. The main problem the relational model solves is redundant data. By using multiple tables that store each data item only once, the relational model significantly reduces storage needs.

RELATIONAL DATABASE HISTORY

Most of you have probably heard of Dr. E. F. Codd, the IBM researcher who reset the database time clock. His 1970 paper ("A Relational Model of Data for Large Shared Data Banks," which appeared in the June 1970 issue of *Communications of the ACM*) was the technological nudge the industry needed to grow. At the time, databases stored data in flat-file format (one table stores each field of data for every record) and were expensive and cumbersome to maintain—at that time, 64KB systems were the size of a piano crate.

Dr. Codd theorized a method that stored information in related tables, called *relations*, thus creating a storage medium that was efficient and easy to implement and use. Dr. Codd's paper became the basis for the *relational database model* on which all relational database systems (such as Microsoft Access, Microsoft SQL Server, Oracle, and so on) are based.

Eventually, this theory was realized in a marketable database known as DB2, an IBM relational database that still owns a large percentage of the database market. Another windfall was Structured English Query Language, or SEQUEL, the support language for multitable and multiuser data access. Today, we know this language as Structured Query Language (SQL), and it has become the industry standard for relational databases.

To understand the difference between a relational and a flat-file database, let's look at a simple example that we will work with throughout this chapter. Let's suppose we're creating a database that stores information on books. For each book, we want to include title, ISBN, category, and so on.

Suppose, in addition to information about each book, you also store address information for each book's author and publisher. The flat-file format forces you to enter each corresponding author and publisher address for each book. In other words, every time you enter a new book for an existing author or publisher, you must also enter the author and publisher address information.

In the relational model, you enter the author and publisher information just once in related tables that store only author and publisher data, respectively. When reviewing a book's author or publisher data, you simply rely on the relationship between the book and author or publisher tables to retrieve the corresponding author and publisher information for any book.

Normalization—the Solution Behind the Theory

Eliminating redundant data may be the need that gave rise to the relational model, but normalization is the process by which we put that purpose into action. *Normalization* is the process of dividing data into two or more related tables. We accomplish this task by carefully reviewing tables for groups of repeated data or inappropriate dependencies and then moving each group to a new table.

RELATIONAL DATABASE THEORY DEFINITIONS

A number of terms may be new to you, so let's review those before we tackle the actual subject of relational database theory:

Database   A collection of persistent data.

Relational database   A collection of persistent data that's stored in multiple, but related, tables.

Entity   A conceptual collection of one type of data.

Entity class   The complete collection of a single type of data.

Entity set   The known collection of a single type of data—the data of any given entity class that is stored in your database.

Table   A collection of related data that's stored in rows and columns, also known as a relation.

Field   The smallest unit of data in the database, commonly referred to as a field or a column. It defines a category of information within an entity.

Row   A combination of fields that together completes one entity.

Record   The data in one row—consisting of related data for one entity.

Scheme   The set of field names for a table.

Primary key   A value that uniquely identifies each record.

Foreign key   A field that refers to a related table's primary key field.

Relationship   An association between two tables based on a unique value known as the primary key.

Some of the terms listed here won't appear early in our discussion. However, they are terms you may see later, so you might as well learn them now. Specifically, let's look at the three rather cryptic "entity" terms as they refer to our database that stores information on books. Within that database, we have several tables, one of which is Books.

Following this scenario, an *entity* is all the information about any one book—its title, ISBN, category, and so on. The *entity set* is the information stored in our database on books, which might be 100 books or 100,000 books. In contrast, the entity *class* encompasses all possible books.

We're not going to try to teach you an entire semester's worth of relational algebra and its supportive terminology. However, introducing you to these terms does set the stage for what you're about to learn.

Almost always, you can reduce repeated entries to one record in a new table and then relate this record to each corresponding record in the original table via the primary and foreign key values. Generally, each table contains a primary key field that uniquely identifies each record in that table. Related tables use the primary key value as a foreign key to associate their data with the primary key value (or record). For example, suppose our Books database contains an authors table as well as a books table. Each book's unique identification number can be the primary key in the books table and a foreign key in the authors table. Both the primary and foreign key values are the same; however, their functions are different. The primary key value identifies a record, and the foreign key identifies an association between two records.

To normalize your data, you apply a set of rules (or constraints) known as *normal forms*. There are seven forms, but we'll review just the first four, since that level of normalization is usually adequate for most of the available Relational Database Management Systems (RDBMSs).

First Normal Form (1NF)   The compliant table contains no multivalued items or repeating groups. In addition each field must be *atomic*—that is, each field must contain the smallest data unit possible. Repeating and multivalued data should be moved to another table. The 1NF-compliant table must have a primary key. (The next section provides guidelines for choosing a primary key.)

Second Normal Form (2NF)   The table must be normalized to 1NF. Also, all fields in the table must refer to (or describe) the primary key value. In other words, each field must be fully dependent on the primary key value. (Don't worry if this concept of dependency seems dauntingly abstract; you'll see what it means in practice as we design a sample database later in this chapter.) When the primary key is based on more than one field, all non-key values must depend on the complex primary key, not just on one value (or field) within the key. Any non-key value that doesn't support the primary key should be moved to another table.

Third Normal Form (3NF)   The table should conform to 1NF and 2NF. All fields must be mutually independent. Any value that describes a non-key field must be moved to another table.

Boyce-Codd Normal Form (BCNF)   There must be no possibility whatsoever of non-key dependent fields. This subrule of 3NF catches values that might fall through 3NF cracks. Any field that shows a dependence on any non-key value must be moved to another table.

NOTE   *Developers disagree about the level of normalization needed to create the most efficient and easily maintained design. Many require that all tables be fully normalized to BCNF, while others are satisfied with 3NF, especially if BCNF begins to degrade performance. Some assert that current system speeds are fast enough to negate the performance issue in almost all instances and that consequently, performance isn't a valid excuse for not normalizing through BCNF.*

Demystifying Keys

Before we go any further, it's important that you understand the purpose of the primary and foreign key fields. Like so many issues in relational database theory, you'll find developers disagree on the subject of primary keys. We'd like to tell you that this section is the definitive resource on the purpose of keys and how to choose them, but that wouldn't be true. However, you'll find that most developers agree with the guidelines we're about to share with you. We just can't guarantee that you'll never end up arguing with a colleague or a boss over primary keys. This section will give you helpful ammunition should the need arise.

Primary Keys

A primary key field has one purpose: to uniquely identify each record in the table. Consequently, no normalized table can contain a duplicate record. Now, the data in every field other than the primary key field can be duplicated, but the primary key value must be unique—as long as that one field is unique, no record can be completely duplicated. We're splitting hairs, but it's necessary in order to grasp the nature of the primary key.

DUPLICATE RECORDS

The relational model doesn't allow duplicate records, even though many RDBMSs do. It's your job to enforce methods of preventing duplicates.

When speaking of duplicate records, we aren't referring to multiple entries of the same value in one field. We generally mean one of two things: either every field in the record is the same as at least one other record or every value in the primary key exactly matches that of another record. For instance, let's suppose your primary key is based on two fields: LastName and FirstName. You can have two or more LastName entries of Jones or two or more FirstName entries of Janice, but you can have only one Janice Jones.

We purposely kept this example simple to help explain what a duplicate record is. In reality, you wouldn't create a primary key based on just the first and last name fields because you can't guarantee the uniqueness of those fields.

Let's consider our example book database. Each record represents one book. The primary key value must uniquely identify each book. Sometimes, you can depend on naturally occurring data. For instance, a book's ISBN should be unique. Therefore, we can use the ISBN as the table's primary key field. The book's title might be duplicated in another record, and surely the book's author might appear in other records. But the ISBN (in theory, at least) should never be duplicated. Apply the following guidelines when considering key candidates:

- A primary key value can't be Null.

NOTE A Null value generally refers to an empty field, but it really means much more. In this context, a Null value doesn't necessarily mean there is no value, but rather that the value is unknown. The value might exist, but at the current time, we don't know what it is, or the value might not exist—the value is unknown. For the sake of this discussion, it's enough to understand that you must enter a value for a primary key field when you create the record—you can't leave a primary key field blank. In fact, many RDBMSs won't accept a record until you supply a primary key value.

- The primary key value must exist when the record is created and stored.
- The primary key must be stable. That means you can't change the primary key structure or its values.
- The primary key must be as compact as possible and contain the fewest possible attributes. (A primary key can consist of more than one field.)
- You can't change the primary key field. That includes adding fields to and deleting fields from the original key.

An RDBMS will allow you to break some of these rules, but don't. It's your job as the developer to enforce relational rules. The system's job is to be as flexible as possible.

NOTE A key candidate is any field or combination of fields that uniquely identifies a record. Not all key candidates make good primary keys.

Natural or Surrogate—the Ongoing Debate

What's the most foolproof way to create a primary key that conforms to the guidelines? *Natural* keys (the actual data) don't necessarily make good primary keys. Many developers instead rely strictly on *surrogate keys*, which contain system-generated, meaningless values. Many RDBMSs provide datatypes, such as AutoNumber in Access and Identify in SQL Server, that automatically generate sequential values for you. That's what we recommend, but it's a subject of heated debate. Developers have based primary keys on naturally occurring data since the inception of the relational model, and many of them maintain that natural keys are the best keys.

The biggest advantage advocates claim for natural keys is one of convenience—natural data is easily recognizable. Even though it isn't a primary key requirement, these developers want a primary key value to somehow identify the other values in the record. They want the user to be able to recognize record data by the record's primary key.

The rebuttal to this is that they've got the rule backward: the non-key fields must describe the primary key, not vice versa. The primary key uniquely identifies the record so that the RDBMS can relate that record to data in other tables; it isn't a convenience of happenstance for the user. And as you'll see later, in a well-designed database, users have no need to see the primary key value.

More important is how well the key values implement the basic requirements:

A primary key uniquely identifies the record.   A natural key is subject to input errors. With a surrogate key, a system-generated value is always unique and eliminates input errors.

A primary key value can't be null and must exist when the record is created and stored.   It's true that a record with a natural key can't be entered and stored until the data on which the primary key is based is known. Consequently, if the primary key value is unknown, you can't create the record. But a surrogate value is generated by the system when the record is created.

You can't change a primary key value.   Natural keys implement this poorly. Databases change as the business they support grows and changes. Information is added and deleted. No matter how stable you think a field is, it is subject to change if it contains natural data. But there's no reason to change a meaningless surrogate key value. In fact, many systems won't let you change an automatically generated value.

You can't change the primary key field.   Natural keys have the same disadvantage with database structure as with actual values; databases change as businesses change, and information is added and deleted. But neither a change in table structure or business rules affects the status of a surrogate key.

The primary key must be as compact as possible and contain the fewest possible attributes.   A natural key can have one field or consist of potentially all the fields in the table. By contrast, a surrogate key always contains one field.

It's hard to imagine that such a seemingly small issue can make or break a database, but it can. The most competent developer isn't a fortune-teller. You can only anticipate so much growth and change. In addition, no matter how well you safeguard your database, you can't fully protect your data from human errors.

We're not telling you that natural keys will doom your database. We're telling you that surrogate keys are more adaptable and remove the risk of human error.

Foreign Keys

Foreign keys are much easier to understand—there are no decisions to make. A foreign key is simply another table's primary key. A table can and often will contain both a primary and a foreign key. You need to remember only two rules:

◆ A foreign key value can be duplicated.

◆ A foreign key can be Null, but usually isn't without good reason.

NOTE *You might be wondering how a foreign key can remain Null if a foreign key value is simply another table's primary key value and a primary key value can't be Null. You simply leave the foreign key field blank when you enter the related record. Consequently, a query doesn't relate the record to its primary key value, but the record is still permissible. The reality is, few databases will need this much flexibility, and you should use extreme caution when applying this rule to a database. However, the fact remains that the relational database model does allow Null values in the foreign key field— but you might never put it to use.*

When finding related data, the system matches foreign and primary key values and then combines the data from any matching records to create a pseudo (or temporary) record. The original tables aren't modified; the data are simply displayed together.

Let's return to our book database example. Suppose you want to enter information for a new book that you've just acquired. Along with the book information (title, ISBN, and so on), you'll also identify the book's author. Let's further assume that the author is already listed in a table of authors, which lists each author's contact information. In addition, each author has a primary key value. Instead of entering the author's name in the book table, you enter the author's primary key value from the author's table. In this context, that value becomes a foreign key value in the book table.

You might be wondering just how the user finds a particular author's primary key value. Or, what do you do if the author doesn't exist yet? In a well-designed database, the book-entry form will include a list of available authors from which the user can choose. Then, when the system stores the record, the system also stores the appropriate primary key value, based on the user's choice. There's no reason for the user to ever view a primary key value or to even know that primary key values exist. The form also includes the means for entering new information for authors not yet listed and properly leads the user to enter that information before accepting and storing the new book record.

At this point, the books table has two keys, a primary key value and a foreign key field, that relate the book to the appropriate author in the authors table. To retrieve author information for the new book, query both tables. (Of course, the user probably doesn't know they are constructing a query at all, because your well-designed database has a clear, simple input form.) When the system encounters the author's primary key value in the books table, it tries to match that value in the author's primary key field. When it finds a match, the system combines the data from both records.

The Design Process

There's a lot more to learn about relational theory, but right now we're going to walk through the process of actually designing and normalizing some tables for our sample book database. The most important thing to learn from this phase is never to skip it. Few developers can correctly normalize their data in action—most of us need to work through the process on paper first. Doing so gives you a chance to work out flaws that could have serious repercussions in a working database. The development process is simple, although lengthy:

1. Gather information.
2. Define the database's purpose.
3. Create a list of all the data elements.
4. Divide the data elements into tables.
5. Normalize the tables.
6. Normalize new tables created during step 5.
7. Define datatypes, relationships and joins, foreign keys, and indexes.
8. Create the tables using the lists as reference.
9. Enter sample data.
10. Create prototype queries, forms, and reports.
11. Let the users evaluate the product.
12. Redesign based on user feedback.
13. Build actual forms and reports.
14. Repeat steps 11 through 13 as necessary.
15. Test beta.
16. Release product.
17. Maintain data and database.

Steps 1 through 7 are strictly design—you're creating your database on paper. Step 8 begins the development process. You'll implement and modify the original design throughout the development phase. Few developers are so intuitive that they know exactly what the database will look like when they begin step 8. (We'll only work through step 7 in this chapter. Steps 8 through 16 are often repeated and don't adhere to any strict order.)

Know Your Data

Perhaps one of the biggest mistakes a developer can make is to ignore the actual users. There's simply no way you can garner enough information to build a database by listening to the managers tell you what they want the database to do. Of course, you must give them your ear. But when they're done, speak to the users and pay close attention to their comments because they'll have the information you're really after—they'll tell you what the database needs to do. There's nothing worse than delivering a database spearheaded by managers that won't even use the product only to have the users tell you it doesn't get the job done.

We don't mean to put managers in a bad light, but managers seldom know how the work gets done; they just know how the finished product looks. On the other hand, the users have been getting the job done, despite inadequate processing support (why else would they have called you?), so they understand the mysterious process of gathering, manipulating, and reporting the data in a way the manager never will. There's no substitute for talking with the users and even watching them work if possible. Gather copies of the forms they use to gather data and the reports they generate.

Talk to the people actually doing the work, and talk to the people who know the future goals for the business and, most likely, the database. After your fact-finding mission is complete, compose a mission statement of sorts. It can be a paragraph or a page, but it needs to be as specific and realistic as possible in regards to the database's purpose. You don't need to list actual processing steps, but you must list the results of those steps.

After the users approve the mission statement, sit down with those forms and reports you gathered from users and managers, and start listing the actual data items that the database will store. If you're converting an existing database, start with those tables. Keep in mind that they may be improperly normalized or in flat-file format, but that's not important at this stage. Right now, you just need a comprehensive list of the data.

NOTE *Some developers find a series of mock-up forms created at this point help them through the normalization process that follows. Doing so certainly isn't necessary, but feel free to take a bit of creative license with the design process, and add the tools you find most helpful. Just make sure every data item on the paper forms and reports is represented in at least one of your mock-up forms. Others don't bother creating mock-up forms because they simply can't visualize forms at this stage without getting ahead of themselves and leaving holes.*

Now, let's put what we know to use by actually designing the sample book database we've referred to a few times in earlier examples. Specifically, let's suppose we're tracking books for a group or organization that accepts donated books and then lends them to others in the group (similar to a library). The following is a list of known items for our sample book tracking database: Title, ISBN, Category, Page Count, Author, Publisher, Type (hardback or paperback), Contributor, Borrower, Borrower's Address, Borrower's Phone, Lent Date, Due Date, and Return Date. Keep in mind that the number of data items can change during the design process. But this is where we'll start.

 All the tables we'll create in this chapter are available for you to review in the `Chapter05.mdb` file on the accompanying CD.

Applying Normal Forms

Once you have a list of data items, you're ready to start normalizing that data. At this point, you're just using pen and paper—don't attempt to create and normalize your tables without first working through the normalization process on paper. The first step is to identify the entities. An entity is a collection of one type of data (see the list of database definitions earlier in this chapter). For instance, our sample database stores data about books and information regarding the lending of those books. At this point, two entities are coming to light—books and lending information. (The number of entities might increase as we normalize our data.)

TIP *Forget the original paper forms and reports because most likely those forms aren't based on normalized data. They're helpful for identifying data items, but don't try to normalize your tables based on the how the data are arranged in those forms, or you'll bury yourself before you get started. Forget what you know about how the users have been getting the job done and stick to normalization rules. It can be difficult to take on the task without being influenced by what you've seen, but try.*

Once you identify the entities, start listing the data items under their appropriate categories. For instance, book title and page count describe the book, while borrower and lending data describe the lending process. After this step, our initial list has become two:

Books	Lending
Title	Borrower Name
ISBN	Borrower Address
Category	Borrower Phone
Page Count	Lent Date
Author	Due Date
Publisher	Return Date
Type	
Contributor	

At the end of this task, you might have several lists or just a few—each representing a table in your database. You'll probably end up with more by the time you're done, so don't worry if you have only a few tables in the beginning. In fact, some databases require only two or three tables.

MEETING 1NF REQUIREMENTS

At this point, you can begin breaking down the data items into the smallest possible units. For instance, author's name can be subdivided into author's first name and author's last name. The same is true of the contributor and the borrower. In addition, the borrower's address should comprise several fields: street address, city, state, and zip code. As you gain experience, you'll probably find that you do this automatically when creating the first list of items in step 3. The following lists have atomic fields—we've met the first condition of 1NF:

Books	Lending
Title	Borrower Last Name
ISBN	Borrower First Name
Category	Borrower Street Address
Page Count	Borrower City
Author First Name	Borrower State
Author Last Name	Borrower ZIP Code
Publisher	Borrower Phone
Type	Lent Date
Contributor Last Name	Due Date
Contributor First Name	Return Date

THE IMPORTANCE OF THE SMALLEST UNIT

If you've ever worked with an improperly normalized table, you already understand the importance of reducing each data item to the smallest possible unit. If not, names are a good way to illustrate the need for this step. You could enter a person's full name in one field. Furthermore, let's suppose that you enter the names in first name, last name format. How would you search those records or sort by last names? You could, but doing so would involve some serious programming tricks. In contrast, storing the last name and the first name in different fields satisfies normalization rules and makes searching, sorting, and manipulating the data easier.

Data items that need further division aren't always as obvious as names. In fact, the decision to subdivide may depend more on the database's purpose (business rules) and less on the actual data. Street addresses are a good example. Most of the time, you'll enter the street number and the street name in the same field, but that's not always the case. For instance, a real estate database might need to sort or search by street name or otherwise group addresses by numbered lots. To satisfy this need easily, you'd want to store each street address component in separate fields.

TIP   As you're working through the design on paper, jot down notes and unique situations that explain decisions that might not be obvious or might be quickly forgotten. Then, keep these sketches and lists with your documentation. Later, those penned-in details can prove invaluable to understanding and explaining early decisions.

Next, check each table for multivalued fields. Every entry should be just one instance of the item it represents. For instance, a book could have more than one category; a book could be both an adventure and a classic. So, we must move the category value to another table. Type is also a problem, since you could end up with both a hardback and a paperback version of the same book. Move the type value to another table. Now let's look at the lending list. There don't appear to be any multivalued fields, so we won't change that list during this step. The following books list meets the second condition of 1NF—there are no multivalued fields.

Books	**Categories**	**Types**
Title	Category	Type
ISBN		
Page Count		
Author First Name		
Author Last Name		
Publisher		
Contributor Last Name		
Contributor First Name		

The third 1NF condition is that you move repeating groups to another table. There will be a limited number of publishers, and eventually some or even all those publishers might be repeated, so let's move publishers in the books list to a new list. No repeating groups in the lending lists jump right out at us, so we'll not make any changes to that list. The following shows the books list and its resulting lists with no repeating group fields (we hope).

Books	Categories	Types	Publishers
Title	Category	Type	Publisher
ISBN			
Page Count			
Author First Name			
Author Last Name			
Contributor Last Name			
Contributor First Name			

NOTE   *Don't be surprised if your 1NF-compliant lists include new fields. Certainly each will include at least one new field if you use surrogate keys. In addition, subdividing your data may result in new fields.*

The final condition of 1NF is that each table must have a primary key. At this point, review each table for candidate keys—the field or fields that uniquely identify the record. If you're going to use surrogate keys, simply add a new field to each table, and properly identify it as the primary key. We'll add a system-generated datatype to each field instead of depending on natural data.

Those insisting on natural key primary keys will have a bit more work because:

♦ It's often difficult to find a set of fields that uniquely identify each record. In extreme cases, you may find the primary key requires every field in the table.

♦ Businesses change, and ultimately data and the purposes that data serves change. Adding a field to or deleting a field from a primary key can spell havoc for your database, no matter how deftly you attack the change. Anticipating the potential for long-term change this early in the design process is difficult, if not impossible.

All the lists below are normalized to 1NF.

Books	Categories	Types	Publishers	Lending
BookID (PK)	CategoryID (PK)	TypeID (PK)	PublisherID (PK)	LendingID (PK)
Title	Category	Type	Publisher	Borrower Last Name
ISBN				Borrower First Name
Page Count				Borrower Street Address
Author First Name				Borrower City

Books	Categories	Types	Publishers	Lending
Author Last Name				Borrower State
Contributor Last Name				Borrower ZIP Code
Contributor First Name				Borrower Phone
				Lent Date
				Due Date
				Return Date

NOTE *You might want to take a stab at assigning foreign key fields and establishing relationships. It might be a bit too early in the process to get them all exactly right. However, some developers do like to get this phase underway. Others wait until all the tables are fully normalized, to avoid confusion.*

MEETING 2NF REQUIREMENTS

Take your lists of 1NF tables and review each item carefully. Each field must provide information about (or describe) the primary key. Moving fields to other tables and even creating new tables are common occurrences during this stage.

Think back to your earlier categories from step 3, and make sure each value actually identifies, describes, or represents that entity. To do so, simply compare each field to your list of categories. If an item has characteristics that describe more than one category, you must move that field to another table. Which table you move the field to depends on the data. You might even have to create a new table.

Our original tables have a few problems. The books table list has two fields for the author and the contributor. Either one of the author fields could be said to describe the other more strongly than it describes the primary key value (the entity). The same is true with the contributor fields. So, move both to new tables. All the borrower information also fails this test, so move all the borrower data to a new table. Now the lists are normalized to 2NF.

Books	Categories	Types	Publishers	Authors	Contributors
BookID (PK)	CategoryID (PK)	TypeID (PK)	PublisherID (PK)	AuthorID (PK)	ContributorID (PK)
Title	Category	Type	Publisher	Author Last Name	Contributor Last Name
ISBN				Author First Name	Contributor First Name
Page Count					

Lending	Borrowers
LendingID (PK)	BorrowerID (PK)
Lent Date	Borrower Last Name
Due Date	Borrower First Name
Return Date	Borrower Street Address
	Borrower City
	Borrower State
	Borrower ZIP Code
	Borrower Phone

Some might see this as a 3NF issue, since we're dealing with non-key fields, but the two areas do seem to overlap sometimes. You can remove the first or last name for either the contributor or the author without adversely affecting the contents of the other name. In other words, deleting the author's first name field doesn't necessarily affect the contents of the author's last name field. That's why this particular problem seems to fall more into the 2NF arena. The two name fields aren't dependent on each other, but the names do describe each other more than they describe the entity (the book).

If you're using natural data and a primary key is based on more than one field, you have one more step. Each field must describe the primary key, as a whole. That means you can't have a field that describes only one field in the primary key. If you find such a field, move it to another table or create a new table.

MEETING 3NF REQUIREMENTS

At this stage, you want to rid your tables of inappropriate dependencies. By that, we mean you must remove any field that describes or depends on a non-key field. Basically, it's the same step you took in normalizing to 2NF, but in 2NF you secured dependency on the primary key. Now, you want to apply this logic to non-key dependencies.

TIP   An easy way to find non-key dependent fields is to imagine that you've deleted each field (one at a time) from the table and see if doing so affects any other field. This trick won't catch all non-key dependent fields, but it's an easy way to catch some of them.

The only list with a non-key dependency is the borrower list, and some people would ignore this one. As you probably know, zip codes depend on the address. You can leave the street address in the borrower's list, but the city and state will be repeating groups that need to go to another table. Yes, we probably could have caught them when looking for repeating data earlier, but this situation wasn't quite as obvious as the others we caught. The borrowers list quickly becomes two, and now our lists are all normalized to 3NF.

Borrowers	ZIP Codes
BorrowerID (PK)	ZIPCodeID (PK)
Borrower Last Name	City

Borrowers	ZIP Codes
Borrower First Name	State
Borrower Street Address	ZIP Code
Borrower ZIP Code	
Borrower Phone	

NOTE *The zip codes structure is more complicated than we've shown here because codes aren't always unique. Two different cities in different states could use the same zip code. In addition, a zip code often depends on the street address, and we didn't include that dependency in our example. We'll not attempt to resolve this issue in this exercise because we're simply illustrating the normalization process in the early stages of your design phase. To take the zip code system's true structure into account would unnecessarily complicate the task at hand. However, in real-world situations you will often find that the system you're trying to include in your normalizing scheme is inconsistent.*

MEETING BCNF REQUIREMENTS

BCNF is really a subrule of 3NF, but the two forms tend to merge in most discussions. In fact, if you really apply 3NF, there won't be anything left to change during this step. But, finding interdependencies among non-key fields can be difficult, and this is just one more chance to catch problems you missed.

This rule requires that there can be no chance of dependency, and it can be hard to define. Addresses are another good example because zip codes depend on city and state data. To fully normalize to BCNF, you must move these address dependencies to new tables, which we did in 3NF. However, you could take the whole matter a step further and move the city and state fields to yet another table, because there is still a possibility of dependency between the city and state fields.

Zip Codes	Cities
ZipCodeID (PK)	CityID (PK)
City	City
Zip Code	State

Such an arrangement can become complicated and actually slow down performance. You might have to choose between normalization and performance, and many developers often skip the BCNF step. However, as we mentioned earlier, with today's fast systems, performance isn't as persuasive an argument against BCNF as it used to be.

Do you recall how many lists we had in the beginning? Our two lists have been normalized into ten.

Don't consider your tables complete at this point. They're probably close, but we still have a few possible situations that could result in changes. First, the phone field in the borrowers list has the potential to be a problem if a borrower wants to leave more than one number. In such a simple database, one phone number is probably adequate, but this is one of those questions you might want to deal with now. Before entering any data, you could move the phone field to a new table and include a field to identify the type of phone each record represents: home, fax, cell, and so on, which means yet another table to list phone types.

At some time in the future, you might decide to add the contributor address information, especially if those contributors are interested in tax deductions for their donations. Doing so also might help resolve another problem that could arise—contributors with the same name. Although the primary key value solves this problem internally, there's no way for you to know that the existing contributor isn't the one you're currently dealing with unless you have more precise information. As with the phone situation, you might want to resolve this now before going any further.

If you decide to add address information, you don't need duplicate zip code and city tables; use the existing ones. The relationships can handle this arrangement.

Defining Datatypes, Relationships, Joins, Foreign Keys, and Indexes

Now you're ready to assign each field a datatype and to identify indexes and relationships between tables. You're still working with paper lists, so don't turn on your computer just yet.

Many developers still use field size to help limit data entry, but no longer worry about it in terms of resources because today's technology simply negates the problem. Most systems now have plenty of memory to go around, so limiting an entry's size to conserve on resources isn't the critical issue it once was. Old habits die hard though, and setting an appropriate field size is still an efficient development process.

In regards to datatypes, choose the type that most adequately accommodates the data. Doing so has two benefits: it's an easy form of validation, and you'll save on resources. For instance, a numeric field won't accept text, so assigning a numeric datatype is a field-level attempt at protecting the integrity of your data. In addition, if a two-character field is adequate, assign a two-character field size. Don't be stingy—allow enough room for the largest possible entry. Just don't waste your resources unnecessarily. Table 5.1 shows the tentative datatypes for all our fields:

TABLE 5.1: DATATYPES FOR FIELDS IN THE BOOK DATABASE

TABLE	FIELD	DATATYPE
Books	BookID	Numeric*
	Title	Text
	ISBN	Text
	Page Count	Text
Categories	CategoryID	Numeric*
	Category	Text
Types	TypeID (PK)	Numeric*
	Type	Text
Publishers	PublisherID (PK)	Numeric*
	Publisher	Text
Authors	AuthorID (PK)	Numeric*
	Author Last Name	Text
	Author First Name	Text

Continued on next page

TABLE 5.1: DATATYPES FOR FIELDS IN THE BOOK DATABASE *(continued)*

TABLE	FIELD	DATATYPE
Contributors	ContributorID (PK)	Numeric*
	Contributor Last Name	Text
	Contributor First Name	Text
Lending	LendingID (PK)	Numeric*
	Lent Date	Date/Time
	Due Date	Date/Time
	Return Date	Date/Time
Borrowers	BorrowerID (PK)	Numeric*
	Borrower Last Name	Text
	Borrower First Name	Text
	Borrower Street Address	Text
	Borrower ZIP Code	Text
	Borrower Phone	Text
ZIP Codes	ZIPCodeID (PK)	Numeric*
	City	Number
	ZIP Code	Text
Cities	CityID (PK)	Numeric*
	City	Text
	State	Text

Refers to the system's self-generating auto number datatype.

ABOUT RELATIONSHIPS

Establishing relationships between fully normalized tables is usually easy. At this point, you are so familiar with your data that the associations seem obvious. Keep in mind that these relationships are the tools you'll use to pull your data together into usable units. For instance, those books all have authors, but the author information is stored in the author table. That means you'll need to create a relationship between the two tables in order to view the author for each book or to view all the books written by a particular author. Indicate a relationship by drawing a line from table to table or by creating a legend that lists each relationship and identifies its type.

NOTE   This section won't attempt to teach you how to create relationships in any particular RDBMS. Those features are unique to each system. Refer to your system's documentation for specifics on creating and enforcing relationships.

Relationships are associations between tables. You'll use these relationships to pull together all that normalized data. In this section, we'll review three types of relationships:

One-to-one   A one-to-one relationship is probably the least common of the three. That's because this relationship relates one record to another, but limits the results of that relationship to just one record in either table. In other words, each record relates to none or only one record in the other table. You'll probably find that this relationship is most often forced by business rules and not the data itself. For instance, our example book database could force a lending rule that each lender can borrow only one book at a time, creating a one-to-one relationship between borrowers and available books. In this case, the relationship is forced by a business rule and doesn't flow naturally from the data—which will almost always be the case.

One-to-many   Almost all relationships falls into this category, in which one record in the primary key table relates to none, one, or even many records in the foreign key table. Following our book example, a book will have only one publisher, but each publisher can have many books. In this case, the publisher table contains the primary key value, and the book table stores the appropriate publisher primary key value as a foreign key. Figure 5.1 illustrates the relationship between these two entities.

FIGURE 5.1

The publisher primary key becomes the foreign key in the books table.

Foreign Key: Publisher

BookID	Name	Author	Publisher	Page Count	Price
1	Using Microsoft Access 97	2	1	825	$29.99
2	Using Microsoft Access 2000	2	1	734	$29.99
3	SQL: Access to SQL Server	2	2	698	$49.95

Primary Key: PublisherID

PublisherID	Name
1	QUE
2	Apress
3	Sybex

TIP   In discussions about relationships, you'll often see the tables in the relationship referred to as the one *table or the* many *table. These terms really refer to primary and foreign key placement. The* one *table contains the relationship's primary key, and the* many *table contains the relationship's foreign key. However, the* many *table contains a primary key of its own; it just won't be relevant to that particular relationship.*

Many-to-many   This relationship is a bit unique and a pain to work with because you're forced to create a third table to accommodate this relationship (in most RDBMSs). It's similar to the first type, the one-to-one relationship, except there's no limit—any record can match any number of records, and vice versa.

You end up with three tables: the two many tables as well as a linking table that contains the primary keys from both many tables as foreign keys. The linking table has a one-to-many relationship with both many tables, so there's no direct relationship between the two many tables in the end. Each record in the linking table relates to only one record in either many table. But both many tables may have many records in the linking table.

Our sample book database has a good example. Initially, you might want to treat the author primary key as a foreign key in the book table, to relate each book to a specific author. But some books have more than one author, and some authors write lots of books. The answer is to create a linking table that contains its own primary key and the primary key from both the books and authors tables. The books table will no longer contain a foreign key to the authors table. Figure 5.2 illustrates the use of the linking table between two many tables.

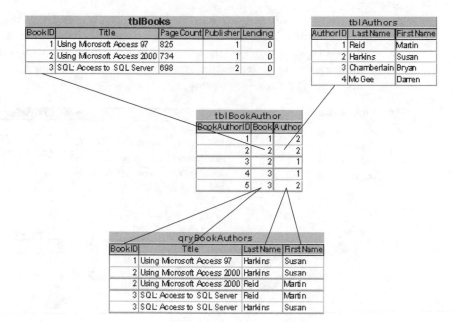

tblBooks				
BookID	Title	Page Count	Publisher	Lending
1	Using Microsoft Access 97	825	1	0
2	Using Microsoft Access 2000	734	1	0
3	SQL: Access to SQL Server	698	2	0

tblAuthors		
AuthorID	Last Name	First Name
1	Reid	Martin
2	Harkins	Susan
3	Chamberlain	Bryan
4	McGee	Darren

tblBookAuthor		
BookAuthorID	Book	Author
1	1	2
2	2	2
3	2	1
4	3	1
5	3	2

qryBookAuthors			
BookID	Title	Last Name	First Name
1	Using Microsoft Access 97	Harkins	Susan
2	Using Microsoft Access 2000	Harkins	Susan
2	Using Microsoft Access 2000	Reid	Martin
3	SQL: Access to SQL Server	Reid	Martin
3	SQL: Access to SQL Server	Harkins	Susan

JOINS

No discussion of relationships is complete without including information on joins. A *join* is a rule that further defines a relationship by determining which records are selected or acted upon. That means, like relationships, joins really don't come into play until you start querying records. The three most common types of joins are inner, left outer, and right outer.

Inner joins   Most relationships depend on an inner join to determine which records are acted upon. This simple join returns only those records from *both* tables in which there is a matching value in the related fields (primary and foreign key fields). Figure 5.3 is a graphic illustration of an inner join. Imagine that each circle represents a table on either side of a relationship. The intersection of the circles represents those records that contain a matching primary and foreign key value. The inner join returns only those records that intersect.

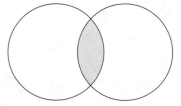

Using our book database, let's suppose you have several books listed but you haven't entered any publisher information yet. Running a query based on the books and publishers tables will return an empty recordset, as shown in Figure 5.4. That's because there are no matching values to relate the two entities. Later, once you've entered some publisher information, the query will return a list—but will return only those books for which the publisher foreign key matches a publisher primary key. In other words, if you have books for which you've not yet listed a publisher, the query won't return those books.

FIGURE 5.4

An inner join returns records only when there's a matching key value.

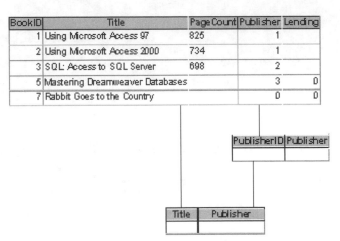

BookID	Title	Page Count	Publisher	Lending
1	Using Microsoft Access 97	825	1	
2	Using Microsoft Access 2000	734	1	
3	SQL: Access to SQL Server	698	2	
5	Mastering Dreamweaver Databases		3	0
7	Rabbit Goes to the Country		0	0

PublisherID	Publisher

Title	Publisher

Left outer join   The left outer join returns records from both sides of a relationship. However, the left outer returns all the records from one side of a relationship—even when there's no matching record in the related table. Any matching values in the related table are also returned. But the important point to grasp is that the "one" side of the one-to-many relationship returns all its records.

Once again, we can illustrate this join using circles. The circle on the left in Figure 5.5 represents the one table; the circle on the right represents the many table. Notice that the entire left circle is shaded, and that means the query returns all the records in that table. However, the query returns only those records from the many table (the circle on the right) in which the primary and foreign key values match. The resulting recordset will most likely contain seemingly incomplete records.

FIGURE 5.5

The shaded area represents the records returned by a left outer join.

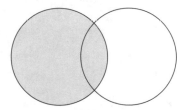

Now, let's suppose that the inner join we discussed isn't adequate for a particular need in the book database. We want to see a complete list of books and their publishers, even if the book doesn't have a listed publisher. In this case, we'd use a left outer join to return all the books in the books table (the one side of the relationship) and any matching values in the publishers table as shown in Figure 5.6 (the many side).

FIGURE 5.6

A left outer join returns all records from the one table.

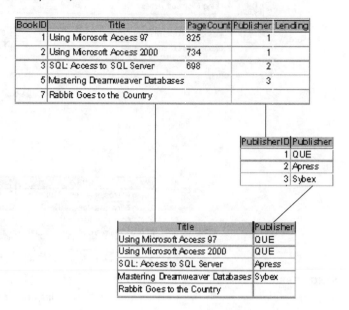

BookID	Title	Page Count	Publisher	Lending
1	Using Microsoft Access 97	825	1	
2	Using Microsoft Access 2000	734	1	
3	SQL: Access to SQL Server	698	2	
5	Mastering Dreamweaver Databases		3	
7	Rabbit Goes to the Country			

PublisherID	Publisher
1	QUE
2	Apress
3	Sybex

Title	Publisher
Using Microsoft Access 97	QUE
Using Microsoft Access 2000	QUE
SQL: Access to SQL Server	Apress
Mastering Dreamweaver Databases	Sybex
Rabbit Goes to the Country	

Right outer join The right outer join is similar to the left outer join. The difference is that the right outer join returns all the records from the right side of the relationship—or the many table. Records from the one side are included in the results only when the primary/foreign key values match.

Figure 5.7 uses the circles one last time to illustrate a join. The shaded circle on the right illustrates the many table, and a right outer join returns all the records in this table. The circle on the left represents the one table, and the shaded intersection represents those records in which the primary and foreign key values from both tables match.

FIGURE 5.7

The right outer join returns all the records from the many table and only those records that match a key value from the one table.

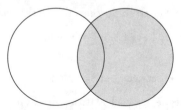

In our last example, we returned all the books regardless of whether they had a matching publisher. Let's suppose you want to return all the listed publishers and their books. The emphasis is on returning all the publishers, regardless of whether they have a book in the list. Figure 5.8 shows the results of this type of join.

FIGURE 5.8

Use a right outer join to return all the publishers and any of their listed books.

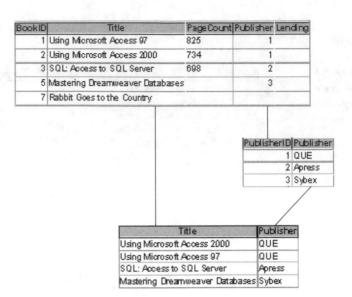

ASSIGNING FOREIGN KEYS

Choosing foreign keys is much easier once you define the relationships between your tables. (If you assigned foreign keys earlier, you might want to re-evaluate your choices now that the relationships are clear.) Simply put, one table's primary key becomes another table's foreign key. Of course, this means you add a new field to many of your tables. It's possible for a table to contain both a primary key and a foreign key, but there's no requirement that every table contain both. In addition, a table can have more than one foreign key (as you saw earlier in the table that links two many tables), but a table will never have more than one primary key. Apply the following guidelines for adding foreign keys to related tables:

One-to-one   Most of the time you can eliminate a one-to-one relationship by simply combining the data in one table.

One-to-many   Add the primary key from the one table to the related many table as a foreign key.

Many-to-many   Add the primary keys from both many tables to the third linking table as foreign keys.

Initially, most of the relationships between our sample tables are many-to-many:

Books	Datatype	Relationship Type	Foreign Key Field
BookID (PK)	Numeric*		
Title	Text		
ISBN	Text		
Page Count	Text		

Books	Datatype	Relationship Type	Foreign Key Field
Category (FK)	Numeric	many-to-many	Categories.CategoryID
Type (FK)	Numeric	many-to-many	Types.TypeID
Publisher (FK)	Numeric	one-to-many	Publishers.PublisherID
Author (FK)	Numeric	many-to-many	Authors.AuthorID
Contributor (FK)	Numeric	many-to-many	Contributors.ContributorID
Lending (FK)	Numeric	one-to-many	Lending.LendingID

*Refers to the system's self-generating auto number datatype.

At this point, you'll realize that the existing tables won't get the job done. We have several many-to-many relationships, and these relationships require a linking table. We can best illustrate this need by looking at the books and authors lists. Each book can have more than one author, and each author can have more than one book. Imagine trying to enter books with more than one author. The current lists simply can't handle this situation. Consequently, we need a linking table between the books and authors lists.

NOTE *Check your RDBMS documentation to see if it requires a linking table between many-to-many tables.*

A linking table will include a primary key of its own and the primary key from both the books and authors list as foreign keys. You won't need an author foreign key in your books list. When you need to review a list of books and authors, you query on three lists, not two: books, authors, and the linking lists between the two. Table 5.2 summarizes the tables in our database, including the linking tables added to handle the many-to-many relationships.

TABLE 5.2: A LAST LOOK AT OUR TABLES

TABLE	FIELD	DATATYPE	RELATIONSHIP TYPE	FOREIGN KEY FIELD
Books	BookID (PK)	Numeric*		
	Title	Text		
	ISBN	Text		
	Page Count	Text		
	Publisher (FK)	Numeric	one-to-many	Publishers.PublisherID
	Lending (FK)	Numeric	one-to-many	Lending.LendingID
Categories	CategoryID (PK)	Numeric*		
	Category	Text		

Continued on next page

TABLE 5.2: A LAST LOOK AT OUR TABLES *(continued)*

TABLE	FIELD	DATATYPE	RELATIONSHIP TYPE	FOREIGN KEY FIELD
Books-Categoriesmmlink	BookCategoryID (PK)	Numeric*		
	Book (FK)	Numeric	one-to-many	Books.BookID
	Category (FK)	Numeric	one-to-many	Categories.CategoryID
Types	TypeID (PK)	Numeric*		
	Type	Text		
BooksTypesmmlink	BookTypeID (PK)	Numeric*		
	Book (FK)	Numeric	one-to-many	Books.BookID
	Type (FK)	Numeric	one-to-many	Types.TypeID
Publishers	PublisherID (PK)	Numeric*		
	Publisher	Text		
Authors	AuthorID (PK)	Numeric*		
	Author Last Name	Text		
	Author First Name	Text		
Books-Authorsmmlink	BookAuthorID (PK)	Numeric*		
	Book (FK)	Numeric	one-to-many	Books.BookID
	Author (FK)	Numeric	one-to-many	Authors.AuthorID
Contributors	ContributorID (PK)	Numeric*		
	Contributor Last Name	Text		
	Contributor First Name	Text		
Books-Contributorsmmlink	BookContributorID (PK)	Numeric*		
	Book (FK)	Numeric	one-to-many	Books.BookID
	Contributor (FK)	Numeric	one-to-many	Contributors.ContributorID
Lending	LendingID (PK)	Numeric*		
	Lent Date	Date/Time		
	Due Date	Date/Time		
	Return Date	Date/Time		
	Borrower (PK)	Numeric		
Borrowers	BorrowerID (PK)	Numeric*		
	Borrower Last Name	Text		
	Borrower First Name	Text		
	Borrower Street Address	Text		
	Borrower ZIP Code (FK)	Numeric		
	Borrower Phone	Text	one-to-many	ZIPCodes.ZipCodeID

Continued on next page

TABLE 5.2: A LAST LOOK AT OUR TABLES *(continued)*

TABLE	FIELD	DATATYPE	RELATIONSHIP TYPE	FOREIGN KEY FIELD
ZIP Codes	ZIPCodeID (PK)	Numeric*		
	City (FK)	Number	one-to-many	Cities.CityID
	ZIP Code	Text		
Cities	CityID (PK)	Numeric*		
	City	Text		
	State	Text		

Figure 5.9 shows all the relationships in graphic format; we used Access's Relationships window. You probably never imagined that those original 2 tables would grow to 14. In the end, we have only one-to-many relationships in our database. Most systems can't handle a direct many-to-many relationship.

FIGURE 5.9

Join lines graphically define the relationships between our tables.

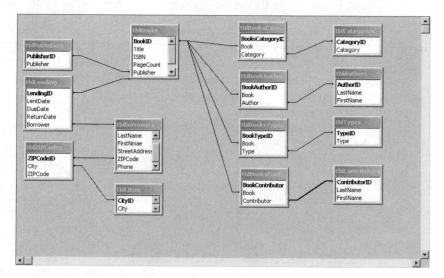

Once you think the tables are normalized and the relationships are all squared away, you're ready to tackle indexes. When you add your indexes is somewhat up to you—we think now is a good time, especially if you use surrogate keys. Keep in mind that a primary key automatically sets a unique index to avoid duplicate records. If you're using surrogate keys, your system will set that unique index to only one field—the field containing those meaningless values that constitute the primary key. That means you must remember to build any unique index, based on the data, yourself.

Indexes are unique to each database system, so it's difficult to define them specifically. The simplest explanation is that a nonclustered index is like a lookup table. The table stores key values that act as pointers to your data, making it easier for your system to search and sort data. When looking for data, the system refers to the lookup table for the pointer.

Some systems provide what's known as a clustered index, which stores data in a predefined order (such as alphabetical). All data are stored in this order. There's no pointer to the data as in the nonclustered data.

This chapter isn't the place for an intense discussion of indexes. We just want to make sure you attempt to include them in the design process. Refer to your RDBMS documentation for specific information on this subject.

At this point, you might consider adding three indexes, and those could change. First, add an index to the ISBN field in the books list because, theoretically, each book should have a unique ISBN. If there's any doubt, you could add the Title to create a complex index (an index based on more than one field).

This situation illustrates one of those real-world problems you'll have to deal with often. The truth is, publishers must maintain ISBNs, and that means duplicates do occur occasionally—by accident. If you include the title in the unique index, you negate the purpose of eliminating duplicate ISBNs—assuming the duplicate was in error. On the chance that the duplicate is in fact a mistake and does exist, you'd not be able to enter the second book in your database. In the end, regardless of which route you take, you'll have to take additional measures to guard against duplicate ISBNs that truly are in error.

NOTE *Unless you're maintaining a huge library, the chances of encountering a duplicate ISBN are so slight that the issue might not be important. If you're working on a voluntary project for a small group, you might not want to spend your time planning for a situation that might never arise. On the other hand, if you're creating a professional database, it might be best to cover all the possible problems, even small ones. If you're in doubt as to a particular solution's worth, discuss your concerns with whoever's paying the bill. Running up the client's bill on something they think is unimportant might not be in your best interest. Just make sure the client realizes there is a potential for trouble; you might even include your concerns in the accompanying documentation and then note the client's decision for historical support.*

Also add a complex index to the ZIP Codes and Cities lists. Specifically, add an unique index to the City and ZIP Code fields in ZIP Codes and the City and State fields in Cities.

The three indexes that we've suggested are for eliminating duplicates and won't necessarily improve performance. We've not added any indexes for the sole purpose of improving sort and search functions—none seem appropriate at this time.

Taking on Referential Integrity

Regardless of the medium you use to interact with the data, the database developer has one true goal—to protect the accuracy of the data. Getting the data to the web and vice versa takes a back seat while you're designing the database. In fact, you can completely forget that you're designing a database for the web and just treat your database as any other client/server project. Once the database is online, your job is to work with any constraints.

NOTE *The relational model enforces referential integrity. For a database design to truly meet relational database rules, it must also enforce referential integrity. Most systems provide referential integrity features, but it's up to you to enforce them. Check your RDBMS's documentation on how to enable referential integrity and which options it supports.*

Most RDMBSs provide a number of ways to protect data—from the simple elements such as appropriate datatypes to validation rules and even security. One method you might not be as familiar with is implementing referential integrity.

Integrity, in general, refers to a set of rules that maintain the relationships, and as a result, the data. There are three types of integrity rules:

Entity Each row must be uniquely identified. (This rule implies that a primary key value can't be Null.)

Referential A foreign key value must match a primary key value in a related table or be Null.

Business Enforce rules specific to the database, such as allowing each borrower to take only one book at a time.

All three of these rules protect your database from incorrect and missing data.

Referential integrity controls the data your users can modify, add, or delete by enforcing the relationships between tables. Specifically, this means the following:

◆ You can't allow users to enter a new foreign key value that doesn't match an existing primary key value in the related table. Such records are known as *orphans*, and they're not allowed in the relational model. Your RDMBS will probably allow you to enter orphans, so it's up to you to enforce referential integrity so that your users can't enter orphans.

◆ You can't allow users to delete an existing primary key value when it matches existing foreign key values in the related table. To do so would create orphans.

◆ You can't modify a primary key value if that value exists as a foreign key in a related table. You're not supposed to change a primary key value anyway. That's a great goal, but it might not be realistic, especially if your primary keys consist of natural data. If you do change a primary key value, you must also update all the matching foreign key values. Most RDBMSs can handle this task.

NOTE *Within the context of this section, the terms* primary key values *and* foreign key values *refer to the entire record, not just the value.*

You can't just apply referential integrity to any set of related tables. A few conditions must be met—and they all make sense when you consider the goal:

◆ The related fields must be a primary key or have a unique index.
◆ The related fields must be the same datatype.
◆ The related tables must be in the same database.

NOTE *The above rules are generally accepted practice, but that doesn't mean your RDBMS enforces them. Check your documentation if you're not sure.*

Most RDBMSs don't enforce referential integrity by default—you'll need to turn it on. Before doing so, your RDBMS will probably allow you to enter, modify, and delete any data at any time. Once you've turned it on, you can expect the following limitations:

◆ Your system will reject foreign key values if no matching primary key exists in the related table.
◆ Your system will reject your attempts to delete a primary key value when a foreign key value exists in a related table.

NOTE   *You can leave a foreign key field Null when entering a record, but referential integrity will be moot because your system won't be able to create the necessary join on the Null value.*

Let's apply some referential integrity rules to our book database. Specifically, there's a one-to-many relationship between the books and publishers tables. Each book has one publisher, but each publisher can have many books listed in our database. After enforcing referential integrity between these two tables you can expect your system to do the following:

◆ Reject any record in which the publisher value doesn't match an existing publisher primary key value in the publisher table. If the publisher doesn't exist, you must enter the publisher before entering the book record. (You can't add a foreign key value before the primary key value exists.)

◆ Reject any attempt to delete a publisher from the publishers table if a record in the books table still refers to that publisher. To delete the publisher, you must first delete (or change) the matching book record. (You can't delete a primary key value when a foreign key value still exists.)

Initially, referential rules can be stymied by a lack of records and your system's compliance to the relational model. For instance, if your system doesn't allow Null values as foreign keys with referential integrity enabled, you'll have to make sure there are no orphan records before you can turn on the feature. Consult your system's documentation for more information on enabling referential integrity.

Some Systems Support Cascading Options

All these restraints might seem to tie your hands a bit. No rule is absolute, and there may be times when you need to add, delete, and change without interference. Some RDBMSs offer cascading options to help with these situations.

WARNING   *We strongly recommend that you not permanently enable cascading options. Keep these options disabled until they are specifically needed. Changing and especially deleting data is a serious undertaking, and you definitely don't want to give this level of decision-making to users who are unfamiliar with all the repercussions of such serious actions. Deleting data can have far-reaching consequences and requires careful scrutiny and discretion.*

If you attempt to change a primary key value when foreign key values exist, you'll receive a referential integrity error message. Systems that support cascading options will allow such a change and even help you fully implement it by making the same change to all the matching foreign key values. For instance, if you change a particular publisher's primary key value in the publishers table with the cascading update option enabled, your system automatically updates any matching foreign key values in the books table.

NOTE   *Your RDBMS may or may not allow you to edit its system-generated, auto-numbering values used as surrogate key values. If you can't edit these values, cascading updates are a moot point. The option will still exist; you just won't be able to use it.*

The other cascading option allows you to delete primary key values when there are matching foreign key values in a related table. Enabling a cascading delete option allows your system to delete the matching foreign key values. The system will delete the primary key, but it will also delete any related records (foreign key values). This result may or may not be what you intended, so be careful when using this option.

Applying cascading options to our book database is a limited venture because we've used surrogate keys. If your RDBMS won't allow you to change a surrogate value that's generated by the system itself, you can't change your primary key value. That means any cascading update option is moot. But let's assume you used the ISBN as your primary key instead of a surrogate key. Furthermore, let's suppose you've found an incorrectly entered ISBN. With the cascading update feature enabled, you can change an ISBN number, and your RDBMS will update any foreign key values (in Books-Categoriesmmlink, BooksTypesmmlink, BooksAuthorsmmlink, and BooksContributorsmmlink) accordingly.

You can delete surrogate primary keys, so you might need a cascading delete option. Earlier, we discussed the possibility of using referential integrity to prevent you from deleting a publisher from the publishers table if a record in the books table refers to that publisher. (Remember, without referential integrity you can delete any record at any time.) Using a cascading delete option, you could delete a publisher if a related book record exists, but your RDBMS will also delete the book record. That may or may not be what you want, so be careful when using this option.

Summary

Nothing beats a good design—whether you're talking about sports cars or databases, the concept is the same. Start with a solid foundation, and you'll end up with a sleek, efficient, and well-tuned tool. The database developer can take a few creative liberties, but, for the most part, relational database theory is fixed. Although rules may seem limiting, they're there for a reason, so learn and apply them. In the end, you'll be glad you did. In our next chapter, we'll take a look at Oracle databases.

Chapter 6

Oracle and the Web

THE DATABASE YOU CHOOSE as a back end to your web application is among the most important and far-reaching development decisions you will make. As such, it's important to select a database application that not only meets your current needs but also scales to meet all your future needs. Oh, it would also be nice if this database application were ultra-secure, stable, and easily integrated into legacy systems. Stressed yet? Don't be. If you have the budget, the choice is easy—Oracle.

The Oracle system is the most popular database system available. It repeatedly beats all competition in features, performance, security, and stability. However, as the best of the best, it does come with a heavy economic and administrative price tag. To put it bluntly, Oracle is not for the faint of heart. If you're forking over the dough for an Oracle license (or two), you might as well budget for an Oracle database administrator (DBA). A database administrator manages every aspect of a database environment, overseeing database design, construction, and maintenance, establishing security roles and procedures, and administering the database system. Typically, an Oracle database administrator holds a degree in computer science and is Oracle certified. (Sometimes it takes an Oracle DBA just to figure out the Oracle licensing costs.)

Oracle is a large and complex system. Entire books are written about many of the features summarized in this chapter. Therefore, our goal in this chapter is to quickly familiarize you with Oracle product background and introduce you to the features and functionality you'll need to quickly begin using Dreamweaver MX and Oracle to build web applications.

- The Oracle product family
- Oracle datatypes
- Key Oracle functions
- Constructing SQL statements for Oracle
- Oracle connection options

If Oracle's complexity and power starts to turn you a bit Oracle-phobic, remember the great thing about Dreamweaver MX is that you don't have to intimately know every Oracle feature in order to use it as a database back end for your web application. Although you won't be taking full advantage of Oracle's powerful feature set, you can theoretically limit your Oracle interaction to establishing an Oracle database connection and dealing with Oracle's SQL idiosyncrasies.

The Oracle Product Family

Although the current version of the Oracle object-relational database is Oracle9i, there are many Oracle9i products from which to choose. Fortunately, as a web developer, you'll most likely interact with only these products:

- Oracle Server/Standard Edition
- Oracle Enterprise Edition
- Oracle Personal Edition
- Oracle Lite

Oracle Server/Standard Edition

Oracle positions the Oracle Server/Standard Edition as an entry-level database for a small number of users. Typically, when someone refers to Oracle8i or Oracle9i, they mean the Standard or Enterprise Edition. This product is available today for Windows NT, NetWare, and Unix platforms and for HP/UX, IBM AIX, Linux, and Sun Solaris.

Oracle Enterprise Edition

Oracle Enterprise Edition is targeted to large-scale deployments of database applications to serve a multitude of users. As such, Oracle Enterprise Edition offers scalability and reliability in both single- and multisystem configurations running on platforms ranging from Windows to most flavors of Unix. Enterprise Edition provides the most complete feature set of all the Oracle product family, including features focusing on database extensibility, performance, and management.

Oracle Personal Edition

Oracle Personal Edition is the single-user version of Oracle Enterprise Edition. Since the feature set matches that of the Enterprise Edition, Personal Edition is perfect for development or for learning Oracle. Using Personal Edition, you can write applications and later promote the application to the Standard or Enterprise editions.

Oracle Lite

Oracle9i Lite, targeted toward mobile computing, enables the delivery of web applications to a broad range of mobile devices. Oracle9i Lite is an add-on to the Oracle9i Application Server. Lite supports development for Windows, Palm Computing, EPOC, and different flavors of Windows CE such as Pocket PC and HPC-Pro.

Dreamweaver MX, Oracle, and SQL

As you know, Macromedia Dreamweaver MX is *the* tool for quickly creating data-connecting code to initiate straightforward selects, inserts, and updates of data with your database. However, no tool, regardless of how ingenious, is a substitute for knowledge and experience. Even Dreamweaver MX cannot craft the more complex SQL statements that are required to take advantage of the data relationships in your database tables. Nor can it know when to implement the staggering array of Oracle database functions. As such, you'll need to be at least somewhat familiar with the Oracle datatypes and key SQL functions, and you'll need to know how to construct SQL statements for Oracle and tune your SQL statements.

Oracle Datatypes

Each variable and value in Oracle has a datatype. Therefore, to successfully insert, manipulate, and update data in an Oracle database, you should be familiar with the datatypes. Don't worry, we won't cover every detail of Oracle datatypes; that would take the entire book. But we will introduce you to the datatypes you're most likely to use in your web development efforts. Before we dive in, it's helpful to know that Oracle stores data in one of three basic datatype families—character, numeric, and date.

Character Datatypes

Character data can be any string of data that will not be the object of an arithmetic operation. Basic character datatypes are CHAR, VARCHAR, NCHAR, NVARCHAR, LONG, and LONG RAW.

NOTE   Foreign languages often require special characters and character sets. NCHAR, NVARCHAR, and NCLOB can store national character set data, making these datatypes ideal for multilanguage applications. National character sets are lists of characters and character codes specific to a country or territory.

CHAR
CHAR is a fixed-length character string. The minimum size is 1 byte, and the maximum size is 2000 bytes. You are not required to specify a size with this character data. The default size is 1 byte.

VARCHAR
VARCHAR is a variable-length character string. The minimum size is 1 byte, and the maximum size is 4000 bytes. You must specify size when specifying a VARCHAR datatype.

NCHAR
NCHAR is a fixed-length character string. NCHAR can store national character set data.

NVARCHAR
NVARCHAR is a variable-length character string. The maximum size can be specified in characters or bytes. The number of bytes required to store each character determines the maximum size, with an upper limit of 4000 bytes. You must specify size when using an NVARCHAR datatype. NVARCHAR can store national character set data.

LONG
Character data of variable length with a maximum of 2 gigabytes, or $2^{31} - 1$ bytes.

LONG RAW
Raw binary data of variable length with a maximum of 2 gigabytes.

Large Datatypes

In addition to character data, Oracle provides several datatypes that support enormous amounts of information. These datatypes are typically used to store an unknown size or mixture of text, images, sound, video, and so on. Large datatypes are BLOB, CLOB, NCLOB, and BFILE.

BLOB

BLOB can hold a binary object with a maximum size of 4 gigabytes. Use this datatype to store images, sound, video, and so on.

CLOB

CLOB is a character object that can hold a maximum size of 4 gigabytes. Use CLOB to store large amounts of text.

NCLOB

NCLOB is a character object that can store a maximum size of 4 gigabytes. NCLOB can store national character set data. Use NLOB to store large amounts of text that can be encoded with different language character sets.

BFILE

BFILE contains a pointer to a large binary file located outside the database. BFILE's maximum size is 4 gigabytes.

Numeric Datatypes

Although it has half a dozen character datatypes, Oracle stores all numeric values under the NUMBER datatype. Numeric data can be any data that can take part in an arithmetic operation. Because all numeric data is grouped into one datatype and because numeric data can have a fractional component, it is highly suggested to set the precision and the scale.

Precision refers to the maximum number of digits in the value. *Scale* defines the number of digits pointing to the fractional component of the number, or the number of digits to the right of the decimal point. If you omit scale from the datatype, values are treated as integer numbers, and no decimal portion is stored. If you omit both scale and precision, the value is treated as a floating-point number. To demonstrate, you can use the following SQL statement to create a NUMERIC datatype with a precision of 12 and a scale of 6.

```
CREATE TABLE EXAMPLE (
NUMBER_U     NUMERIC(12,6)
)
```

The column this SQL statement creates can hold a maximum of 999,999.999999. Likewise, if you change the precision (the first number) of the numeric datatype to 7, the column can hold 9.999999. If you would like to set the datatype to maximum precision, use an asterisk as shown in the following SQL statement.

```
CREATE TABLE EXAMPLE (
NUMBER_U     NUMERIC(*,6)
)
```

Date Datatypes

The DATE datatype stores date and time information. It's important to note that Oracle stores date data in a proprietary format using the following information:

◆ Century

◆ Year

◆ Month

◆ Day

◆ Hour

◆ Minute

◆ Second

This format is slightly different from most other date formats, such as the ODBC (Open Database Connectivity) data format. Unfortunately, passing a date variable with a slight variant to Oracle is problematic. To store a value in a DATE datatype, the date value must be converted into the Oracle date format, using the Oracle To_Date function.

In most cases, Oracle can perform this conversion automatically. By default, Oracle converts a date in the DD-MON-YY format to its internal date format. Be forewarned, this default date format is specified in Oracle setup files and can be changed, so be sure to check with your Oracle DBA for the appropriate date format.

NOTE *The DD-MON-YY is a format mask for the date. DD refers to date, MON refers to the three-letter abbreviation for the month, and YY refers to the year. For example, the first day of the year would be written 01-JAN-03.*

Key Oracle SQL Functions

You use Oracle functions to accomplish many programming tasks from within your SQL statements. We've already mentioned the TO_DATE function, which is a Conversion function that converts one datatype to another. Conversion functions are just the tip of the iceberg. Oracle also has Grouping, Numeric, String, and Date functions (and many, many more). Being able to take advantage of Oracle's internal functions in your SQL statements has tremendous advantages. Let's take a look at the functions you might use in a typical web application.

Grouping Functions

You use Grouping functions to return values from groups of records defined in a SQL statement. Key Grouping functions include AVG, COUNT, MAX, MIN, and SUM.

AVG(EXPRESSION)

AVG returns the average of the values in a set of rows. You can specify DISTINCT or ALL in the AVG parameters. ALL (the default) uses all rows in the set of rows to calculate the average. DISTINCT uses only unique row values to calculate the average. For example, the following SQL statement discounts row value duplicates and returns an alias holding the value of 3 as the DISTINCT average of (2,2,3,3,4).

(An *alias* is a name that stands for a column or table. In our example, we create an alias named NUM_PAGES_AVG for the NUM_PAGES.)

```
SELECT
AVG(DISTINCT  NUM_PAGES) AS NUM_PAGES_AVG
FROM
BOOK
```

COUNT *(EXPRESSION)*

COUNT returns the number of rows in a recordset. If you include a column in the parameter, COUNT returns the number of rows in which the row value is not NULL. To demonstrate COUNT, the following SQL statement returns an alias holding the value of the total number of rows in the table.

```
SELECT
COUNT(*) AS COLUMN_1_COUNT
FROM
YOURTABLE
```

Likewise, the following SQL statement returns an alias holding the value of the total number of rows where COLUMN_1 is not NULL in the table.

```
SELECT
COUNT(COLUMN_1) AS COLUMN_1_COUNT
FROM
YOURTABLE
```

In some cases, Oracle's COUNT function can return decimal places with the generated count. To prevent such occurrences, wrap the COUNT function with the TO_CHAR function to drop the decimal places from the count value. For example, the following SQL code returns an alias holding the count value as a character datatype:

```
SELECT
TO_CHAR(COUNT(COLUMN_1)) AS COLUMN_1_COUNT
FROM
YOURTABLE  "
```

MAX*(EXPRESSION)*

MAX returns the largest value from a set of rows. For example, the following SQL statement returns an alias holding the largest value in COLUMN_1.

```
SELECT
MAX(COLUMN_1) AS COLUMN_1_MAX
FROM
YOURTABLE)
```

MIN*(EXPRESSION)*

MIN returns the smallest value from a set of rows. For example, the following SQL statement returns an alias holding the smallest value in COLUMN_1.

```
SELECT
MIN(COLUMN_1) AS COLUMN_1_MIN
FROM
YOURTABLE)
```

SUM(EXPRESSION)

SUM returns the total value for all values in a column. The following SQL statement returns an alias holding the total value of all values in COLUMN_1.

```
SELECT
SUM(COLUMN_1) AS COLUMN_1_SUM
FROM
YOURTABLE)
```

Numeric Functions

Although most scripting languages have their own set of numeric functions, passing the numeric function responsibility to an ultra-powerful database server such as Oracle can boost performance. Oracle key Numeric functions are ABS, GREATEST, LEAST, ROUND, and TRUNC.

ABS(NUMBER)

ABS removes the negative sign (if present) from a number and returns a positive value. For example, the following SQL statement returns an alias holding a positive value regardless of the actual COLUMN_1 value.

```
SELECT
ABS(COLUMN_1) AS COLUMN_1_ABS
FROM
YOURTABLE
```

GREATEST(VALUE1, VALUE2)

GREATEST returns the largest value in a list of values. To demonstrate, the following SQL statement returns an alias holding the greater value of COLUMN_1 and COLUMN_2.

```
SELECT
GREATEST(COLUMN_1, COLUMN_2) AS COLUMN_1_GREATEST
FROM
YOURTABLE
```

LEAST(VALUE1, VALUE2)

LEAST returns the smallest value in a list of values. For example, the following SQL statement returns an alias holding the least value of COLUMN_1 and COLUMN_2.

```
SELECT
LEAST(COLUMN_1, COLUMN_2) AS COLUMN_1_LEAST
FROM
YOURTABLE
```

NOTE   The GREATEST and LEAST functions are meant for the greatest or least values in the same row. If you want to return the greatest or least value in a set of rows, use MAX or MIN.

ROUND(NUMBER, DECIMAL PLACES)

ROUND returns a value rounded to a specified number of decimal places. The first parameter is the target number, and the second parameter specifies the number of decimals to round to. For example, the following SQL statement returns an alias holding the value 123.46—the 2-decimal rounded value of 123.456.

```
SELECT
ROUND(123.456,2) AS COLUMN_1_ROUND
FROM
YOURTABLE
```

TRUNC(NUMBER, DECIMAL PLACES)

TRUNC returns a value shortened to a specified number of decimal places. The first parameter is the target number, and the second parameter specifies the number of decimals to truncate. For example, the following SQL statement returns an alias holding the value 123.45—the 2-decimal truncated value of 123.456.

```
SELECT
TRUNC(123.456,2) AS COLUMN_1_TRUNC
FROM
YOURTABLE
```

String Functions

Many times you will want to manipulate a character string before displaying, inserting, or updating. You use String functions to apply string manipulations on entire columns of data. Oracles String functions are ||, INITCAP, LENGTH, LOWER, SUBSTR, and UPPER.

STRING || STRING

The || function appends several character values together. For example, the following SQL statement returns an alias holding the values in COLUMN_1, COLUMN_2, and COLUMN_3.

```
SELECT
(COLUMN_1 || ', ' || COLUMN_2 || ', ' || COLUMN_3) AS COLUMN_1_2_3
FROM
YOURTABLE
```

INITCAP(STRING)

INITCAP capitalizes the first letter of each word in a character string. This is a superb time-saver for capping the first letter in proper names. For example, the following SQL statement returns an alias holding "Macromedia Dreamweaver" if it finds the value "macromedia dreamweaver" in COLUMN_1.

```
SELECT
INITCAP(COLUMN_1) AS COLUMN_1_INITCAP
FROM
YOURTABLE
```

LENGTH(STRING)

LENGTH returns the number of characters in a character string. For example, the following SQL statement returns an alias holding the number of characters in COLUMN_1 of each row.

```
SELECT
LENGTH(COLUMN_1) AS COLUMN_1_LENGTH
FROM
YOURTABLE
```

LOWER(STRING)

LOWER converts all characters in a character string to lowercase. For example, the following SQL statement returns an alias holding "macromedia dreamweaver" from the value "Macromedia Dreamweaver" in COLUMN_1.

```
SELECT
LOWER(COLUMN_1) AS COLUMN_1_LOWER
FROM
YOURTABLE
```

SUBSTR(STRING, STARTING VALUE, NUMBER OF CHARACTERS)

SUBSTR extracts a section of a character string. The first parameter specifies the target character string. The second parameter sets the starting position of the substring you want to extract. The third parameter sets the number of characters to extract. For example, the following SQL statement returns an alias holding "Macro" from the value "Macromedia Dreamweaver" in COLUMN_1.

```
SELECT
SUBSTR(COLUMN_1,1,5) AS COLUMN_1_ SUBSTR
FROM
YOURTABLE
```

UPPER(STRING)

UPPER converts all characters in a character string to uppercase. For example, the following SQL statement returns an alias holding "MACROMEDIA DREAMWEAVER" from the value "Macromedia Dreamweaver" in COLUMN_1.

```
SELECT
UPPER(COLUMN_1) AS COLUMN_1_UPPER
FROM
YOURTABLE
```

Date Functions

Often in your web application, you will need to manipulate a date/time value within a SQL statement. The key Oracle Date functions are ADD_MONTHS, LAST_DAY, MONTHS_BETWEEN, NEXT_DAY, ROUND, SYSDATE, and TRUNC.

ADD_MONTHS *(DATE, NUMBER OF MONTHS)*

ADD_MONTHS adds (or subtracts if the value is negative) a number of months to a date value. For example, the following SQL statement returns an alias holding a value that is two months beyond the date in COLUMN_1.

```
SELECT
ADD_MONTH(COLUMN_1,2) AS COLUMN_1_ADD_MONTHS
FROM
YOURTABLE
```

LAST_DAY *(DATE)*

LAST_DAY returns the last day of the current month value. For example, the following SQL statement returns an alias holding the last day of the month in COLUMN_1.

```
SELECT
LAST_DAY(COLUMN_1) AS COLUMN_1_LAST_DAY
FROM
YOURTABLE
```

MONTHS_BETWEEN *(DATE1, DATE2)*

MONTHS_BETWEEN returns the difference between the two dates. To demonstrate, the following SQL statement returns an alias holding the months' difference between COLUMN_1 and COLUMN_2:

```
SELECT
MONTHS_BETWEEN(COLUMN_1, COLUMN_2) AS COLUMN_1_MONTHS_BETWEEN
FROM
YOURTABLE
```

NEXT_DAY *(DATE, DAY NAME)*

NEXT_DAY returns the first occurrence of the specified day after the date supplied. For example, the following SQL statement returns an alias holding the date the next Monday occurs after the supplied date.

```
SELECT
NEXT_DAY('10-MAY-2002','MONDAY') AS COLUMN_1_NEXT_DAY
FROM
YOURTABLE
```

ROUND *(DATE/TIME, FORMAT)*

ROUND returns the date/time rounded to a specified time unit. For example, the following SQL statement returns an alias holding the value "01-JAN-2002"—the rounded value of "10-NOV-2001".

```
SELECT
ROUND('10-NOV-2001','YEAR') AS COLUMN_1_ROUND
FROM
YOURTABLE
```

SYSDATE

SYSDATE returns the current date/time from the database server. For example, the following SQL statement returns an alias holding today's date/time value.

```
SELECT
SYSDATE AS COLUMN_1_ SYSDATE
FROM
YOURTABLE
```

TRUNC(DATE/TIME)

TRUNC removes the time component from the supplied date/time value. For example, the following SQL statement returns an alias holding the value "15-AUG-2002" from the date/time value in COLUMN_1.

```
SELECT
TRUNC(COLUMN_1) AS COLUMN_1_TRUNC
FROM
YOURTABLE
```

Conversion Functions

As we've mentioned, Oracle groups its datatypes into three families—character, numeric, and date. As such, you can convert one datatype to another using the Oracle functions TO_DATE, TO_CHAR, and TO_NUMBER.

TO_DATE (STRING, FORMAT)

TO_DATE performs character-to-date conversion. For example, the following SQL statement uses the Oracle To_Date function to convert the character variable to an Oracle compliant date.

```
INSERT INTO
        YOURTABLE
        (COLUMN_1,
        COLUMN_2)
    VALUES
        (COLUMN_1_VALUE,
        TO_DATE(VARIABLE,'DD-MM-YYYY')
```

TO_CHAR(DATE, FORMAT)

TO_CHAR converts numeric and date data to the CHAR datatype. For example, the following SQL statement uses the TO_CHAR function to convert the date variable to a formatted character string.

```
INSERT INTO
        YOURTABLE
        (COLUMN_1,
         COLUMN_2)
    VALUES
        (COLUMN_1_VALUE,
         TO_CHAR(VARIABLE, `MONTH DD, YYYY')
```

TO_CHAR(NUMBER, FORMAT)

Likewise, the following SQL statement uses the TO_CHAR function to convert the numeric variable to a formatted character string.

```
INSERT INTO
        YOURTABLE
        (COLUMN_1,
         COLUMN_2)
    VALUES
        (COLUMN_1_VALUE,
         TO_CHAR(VARIABLE, '$9,999,999'))
```

TO_NUMBER(STRING, FORMAT)

TO_NUMBER converts character data to the numeric datatype. For example, the following SQL statement uses TO_NUMBER to convert the character variable to a number.

```
INSERT INTO
        YOURTABLE
        (COLUMN_1,
         COLUMN_2)
    VALUES
        (COLUMN_1_VALUE,
         TO_NUMBER(VARIABLE)
```

Favorite Functions and Features

We've shown you the functions you will most likely use in your web development efforts. Now we want to introduce you to two functions, NVL and DECODE, that don't fit neatly into the previous function categories. All the same, we use these functions so often that we want to share them. In addition, we'll also show you a useful feature called ROWNUM.

NVL(EXPR1, EXPR2)

NVL (NULL value) is extremely useful for handling NULLs in your database. NVL allows you to specify how Oracle returns a NULL value. For example, the following SQL statement returns an alias holding 0 when a NULL is found in COLUMN_1.

```
SELECT
NVL(COLUMN_1,0) AS COLUMN_1_NVL
FROM
YOURTABLE
```

DECODE(EXPR1, EXPR2)

You use DECODE to create a programmatic value lookup. The first parameter in DECODE is the column you're selecting. Following parameters consist of value pairs. The first value in the pair sets the value to search. The second value in the pair sets the value the SQL statement should return if the search value is found. You can also specify a default return value in case no match is found. To do so, place the default value at the end of the pair values.

To demonstrate, `COLUMN_1` of our pseudotable holds gender information. Gender can have one of two values—M or F. You can use `DECODE` to attach the lookup values "Male" or "Female" to each M or F value in a returned recordset. As we mentioned, you can even set a default return value of "Unknown" if a row value does not match M or F. For example, the following SQL statement returns an alias holding "Male" or "Female" for each M or F value or holding "Unknown" for an unmatched value found in `COLUMN_1`.

```
SELECT
DECODE(GENDER,'M','MALE','F','FEMALE','UNKNOWN') AS FULLGENDER
FROM USERS
```

ROWNUM

`ROWNUM` is a pseudocolumn that Oracle attaches to each row in a recordset returned by a SQL query. (A *pseudocolumn* behaves like a table column, but is not actually stored in the table. You can select from pseudocolumns, but you cannot insert, update, or delete their values.) `ROWNUM` contains a number identifying the order the row was retrieved from the table. For example, the first row of a recordset has a `ROWNUM` of 1, the second row has `ROWNUM` of 2, and so on. You can use `ROWNUM` to limit the number of records your web page displays. To demonstrate, the following SQL statement returns a recordset of the first 20 rows of a table:

```
SELECT
COLUMN_1
FROM YOURTABLE
WHERE ROWNUM < 20;
```

WARNING   ROWNUM contains the order in which the row was retrieved from a table. This does not necessarily mean the rows in the recordset will be displayed according to ROWNUM. For example, if we append an ORDER BY COLUMN_1 to the sample ROWNUM SQL statement, Oracle selects the first 20 rows of a table. However, Oracle also sorts the recordset according to the COLUMN_1 series—not according to the pseudocolumn ROWNUM. Therefore, the rows in the recordset will not be displayed according to the ROWNUM.

Note that `ROWNUM` is only useful for less-than and equal-to comparisons. Greater-than comparison will always fail. The `ROWNUM` pseudocolumn only exists for actual rows returned in a recordset. For example, if you attempt to select a recordset with `ROWNUM` > 10, your query will fail. For the `ROWNUM` > 10 condition to be true, your query must return at least 11 rows—which it cannot do given the condition.

Constructing SQL Statements for Oracle

Although SQL was developed to provide consistent and easy access to relational databases, many databases have minor syntax variations in SQL syntax. In fact, Microsoft Access, Microsoft SQL Server, MySQL, and Oracle all use SQL, but there are enough differences in the individual syntax to make life difficult for the unaware.

Oracle SQL Guidelines

Before we discuss Oracle SQL syntax variations, though, let's look at a basic list of guidelines.

1. Names can be from 1 to a maximum of 30 characters.
2. Names must begin with a letter.
3. Names cannot be a reserved word.
4. Names cannot be a SQL command.
5. A name can begin with, end with, and contain illegal characters if it is enclosed in double quotes.
6. You can construct SQL statements using the standard A through Z character set, numbers 0 through 9, spaces, and + - * = ? @ ( ) _ . , < > | $ #.
7. Oracle strongly discourages you from using # and $.
8. Oracle does not distinguish between spaces and tabs, carriages returns, and multiple spaces. For example, Oracle considers the following SELECT statements identical:

```
SELECT BOOKS.BOOKID, BOOKS.TITLE FROM BOOKS


SELECT
BOOKS.BOOKID,
BOOKS.TITLE
FROM
BOOKS
```

9. SQL code is not case sensitive. However, Oracle variable names are case sensitive.

Comments

As discussed in Chapter 3, it is essential that you comment your code. Although you can comment around your SQL in the web-scripting language of your choice, you can also add comments within Oracle SQL statements. Comments do not affect Oracle's execution of the statement. A comment can appear between any keywords, parameters, or punctuation marks in a statement. You can create a comment in a SQL statement using two methods.

METHOD ONE

Method one lets you span a comment over several lines. Begin your comment with /* and end with */. Here's an example:

```
/* RETURN A RECORDSET
   CONTAINING THE BOOKID
   AND TITLE FROM THE BOOKS TABLE */
SELECT
BOOKS.BOOKID,
BOOKS.TITLE
FROM
BOOKS
```

METHOD TWO

Method two limits a comment to just one line. Begin the comment with --. Here's an example:

```
--  RETURN A RECORDSET
--  CONTAINING THE BOOKID
--  AND TITLE FROM THE BOOKS TABLE
SELECT
BOOKS.BOOKID,
BOOKS.TITLE
FROM
BOOKS
```

SQL Syntax Variations

For the most part, Oracle SQL statements match up well with the SQL syntax of other database systems. Straight Select, Insert, Update, and Delete SQL are all similar. However, Oracle does differ concerning joins. As we mentioned in Chapter 5, a *join* defines a relationship between data tables. The three most common types of joins are:

◆ Inner

◆ Left outer

◆ Right outer

INNER JOIN

Oracle does not support any of the "join" syntax. To create joins in Oracle, you must define the relationships between tables in the WHERE clause of the SQL statement.

For example, here is a simple join between the Book table and the Category table of the Books database sample:

```
SELECT
BOOKS.BOOKID, BOOKS.TITLE
FROM
BOOKS, CATEGORIES
WHERE
BOOKS.CATEGORY = CATEGORIES.CATEGORIESID
```

OUTER JOIN

Although Oracle does not support the "outer join" syntax, you can easily create a left or right outer join using a special operator, (+). Placing (+) next to a column specifies that the column can be padded with NULLs in the OUTER JOIN recordset. The following statement creates a left outer join in our sample database.

```
SELECT
BOOKS.BOOKID, BOOKS.TITLE
FROM
BOOKS, CATEGORIES
WHERE
BOOKS.CATEGORY = CATEGORIES.CATEGORIESID (+)
```

The resulting recordset looks like this:

BookID	CategoryID
1	1
2	1
3	3
4	4
5	<NULL>
6	<NULL>

Likewise, to create a right outer join, move the special operator as follows:

```
SELECT
BOOKS.BOOKID, BOOKS.TITLE
FROM
BOOKS, CATEGORIES
WHERE
BOOKS.CATEGORY(+) = CATEGORIES.CATEGORIESID
```

The resulting recordset looks like this:

BookID	CategoryID
1	1
2	1
<NULL>	2
3	3
4	4
<NULL>	5
1	1
2	1

NOTE *An Oracle idiosyncrasy is that you cannot use (+) on both sides of the equality to write a full outer join. Also, you cannot outer join the same table to more than one other table in a single SELECT statement.*

Tuning Your SQL Statements

Your primary goal as a web developer is to deliver information in a quick and efficient manner via the web. Unfortunately, poor database performance can dramatically slow your web application speed. Poor database performance can often be the result of poorly tuned SQL queries. Therefore, every SQL code tweak you can apply to shave off a few milliseconds of data access and retrieval time is vital. Fortunately, you can use a simple strategy to tune your SQL queries:

Say Exactly What You Want and Take Only What You Need

Specifically, avoid using * in SELECT statements. Using * forces Oracle to look up every column name in the database table and usually returns data you don't need in the recordset. Obviously, lookup and large data transactions take extra time and can slow performance. As an alternative, list every column name you plan to use in SELECT statements.

Likewise, list specific fields in INSERT statements instead of structuring the SQL statement to insert data based on column order. For example, the following statement:

```
INSERT
INTO YOURTABLE
VALUES
('To Kill a Mockingbird','ISBN-00001','01/01/2003')
```

ties your SQL statement to the column order of the table. To free you code and database from this dependence, list each column name in your SQL as shown in the following statement.

```
INSERT
INTO YOURTABLE
(BOOKTITLE,ISBN,CREATED_DT)
VALUES
('To Kill a Mockingbird','ISBN-00001','01/01/2003')
```

Oracle Connection Options

Establishing that first connection with Oracle will either be remarkably easy or mind-blazingly difficult. Due to many external factors such as the operating system of your Oracle server, the operating system of your web server, and your choice of a web-scripting language, Oracle connections can sometimes be problematic. But, at base, you have four connection options: ODBC (Open Database Connectivity), JDBC (Java DataBase Connectivity), OLE DB (Object Linking and Embedding Data Base), and native drivers. Each option uses a driver specific to the version and operating system of your Oracle server.

Connecting ASP to an Oracle Database

Microsoft ASP (Active Server Pages) let you connect to any Oracle database through an ODBC driver or an OLEDB driver. You can obtain ODBC drivers for Oracle 8i and 9i from Oracle (www.oracle.com) and from Microsoft (www.microsoft.com).

Connecting ASP.NET to an Oracle Database

Microsoft ASP.NET lets you connect to any Oracle database through an ODBC driver or an OLEDB driver. You can download ODBC drivers for Oracle8i and 9i from Oracle (www.oracle.com) and from Microsoft (www.microsoft.com).

Connecting ColdFusion to an Oracle Database

Macromedia ColdFusion let you connect to an Oracle database natively using JDBC or ODBC. Both the JDBC and ODBC drivers are installed with ColdFusion. However, you can download updated drivers from Macromedia (www.macromedia.com), Microsoft (www.microsoft.com), and Oracle (www.oracle.com).

Connecting PHP to an Oracle Database

Unfortunately, for PHP (Hypertext Preprocessor) development, Dreamweaver supports only the MySQL database system. Database systems such as Microsoft Access, SQL Server, and Oracle are not supported. Although Dreamweaver does not support direct connectivity to Oracle from PHP, PHP does support ODBC connections. Therefore, it is possible to create a PHP web application that connects to Oracle.

TIP   The Macromedia Exchange site (www.macromedia.com/exchange) offers third-party PHP extensions that provide server-side functionality comparable to Dreamweaver MX.

Connecting JSP to an Oracle Database

JSP (JavaServer Pages) lets you connect to an Oracle database using the JDBC driver for Oracle. You can download a list of drivers for Oracle databases at Sun's site (http://industry.java.sun.com/products/jdbc/drivers).

Taking JSP and Oracle one-step further, you can download a set of Dreamweaver MX extensions from Oracle.com to generate ServerBehavior extensions for Oracle 9iAS JSP tags. You can download the free Oracle Extensions for Macromedia Dreamweaver MX at the Oracle Technology Network (http://otn.oracle.com/products/ias/9ias_partners.html#Macromedia).

NOTE   Choosing the correct connection driver from the available Oracle drivers list is critical. In most cases, the version of Oracle being used dictates which driver should be used. In the past, simply finding the correct driver was a Herculean task. However, recently Oracle has made all versions of their drivers available on their website. To save you much time and trouble, be certain you are using the latest drivers designed for your version of Oracle.

FOR FURTHER INFORMATION

Because Oracle is the leading database choice in today's technology market, you have many avenues for finding more information on Oracle. The hardest part is determining the best resources on which to spend your time and/or money. The primary resource for all things Oracle is www.oracle.com. Here you can stay up-to-date with the latest version of Oracle, find a well-maintained knowledge base of Oracle issues and solutions, browse a large database of Oracle-related products and services, and peruse an online reference for Oracle training and education.

In addition to the Oracle website, check out these books: *OCP: Oracle8i™ DBA Architecture & Administration and Backup & Recovery Study Guide, OCA/OCP: Introduction to Oracle9i SQL Study Guide,* and *Mastering Oracle8i,* all from Sybex. To keep current with tips and techniques, we suggest The Oracle Professional at www.oracleprofessionalnewsletter.com and Exploring Oracle at www.elementkjournals.com. Finally, nothing substitutes for networking with people in the know, so check out your area Oracle User Group.

Summary

The Oracle product family is one of the most powerful and full-featured products available on today's market. Oracle is a highly advanced and complex tool that can provide your applications with tremendous speed and power. This chapter introduced you to the Oracle product family and reviewed the datatypes you will be using. In addition, we discussed common functions and features you will need in your web development efforts. However, this chapter is intended as an introduction and general roadmap to explore more of Oracle's considerable feature set. We encourage you to voraciously expand your knowledge and experience about this integral part of your web development environment.

Chapter 7

MySQL and the Web

MYSQL IS, ARGUABLY, THE most popular open-source database system available. The official MySQL website (www.mysql.com) notes that companies using MySQL as a production database include, among others, Yahoo!, MP3.com, and NASA. It's true that MySQL is not as full featured as some of the proprietary database systems we're looking at in this book; it doesn't have traditional stored procedures, triggers, or views, for example. But if your database-driven web application is on a tight budget, and you cannot sacrifice speed or performance, MySQL might just save the day for you. In this chapter, our objective is to get you up to speed on the basic functionality of MySQL and show you how to harness its capabilities for use in your web application.

This chapter covers the following topics:

◆ MySQL versions
◆ Dreamweaver MX, MySQL, and PHP
◆ MySQL datatypes
◆ MySQL functions
◆ MySQL syntax

MySQL Versions

MySQL is developed and primarily supported by MySQL AB, a Sweden-based company founded in 1995. Like most other projects in the open-source community, MySQL exists in a couple of different forms: the production (or stable) version and the development version. The production version (currently 3.23.x) is the one you will most likely be using if MySQL is your database platform. It is unlikely that MySQL AB will release any new features or improvements for the production version, but the company will continue to release bug fixes as needed. The development team is focused on the next release, which for now is the development version and includes the latest features.

MySQL is available for download from www.mysql.com in both source-code form and precompiled binary (ready-to-run) form. There are server versions for Windows, MacOS X, Linux, and various flavors of Unix (FreeBSD, Solaris, HP-UX, AIX, BSDi, and others). At the time of this writing, the available releases of MySQL are:

MySQL 3.23	Production
MySQL Max 3.23	Production
MySQL 4.x	Development

NOTE   Open-source software projects typically follow at least a couple of lines of development. One line is the stable branch of the code base. This is the version of the application that is recommended for use in production environments. It has typically undergone more extensive testing, is in wider use, and therefore is less prone to bugs and other problems. Another standard line is known as the development or current branch. This branch of the application normally contains "bleeding-edge" features and is rapidly changing as developers submit new code, sometimes daily. The MySQL team recommends that production users stick with the most recent version that they have labeled "stable," which at the time of this writing is 3.23. The next version, MySQL 4.0, is considered beta at this point.

MySQL 3.23

This production version of MySQL supports many features you have come to expect in a DBMS. MySQL utilizes a client/server architecture, which makes it more like Microsoft SQL Server or Oracle than a desktop system such as Microsoft Access. A wide range of datatypes are available within it. Additionally, MySQL supports full-text search and one-way data replication from a single master server to multiple slave servers.

MySQL Max 3.23

This version of MySQL is the same as the standard version, but includes built-in support for InnoDB and Berkeley DB table types. Either of these table types enables MySQL to handle full SQL transaction support, using the familiar SQL commands COMMIT and ROLLBACK.

MySQL 4.x

The current development line for MySQL is largely a rewrite of the source to provide a better foundation on which to build in SQL features missing from the current implementation. New features promised or talked about for forthcoming releases include direct support for Secure Sockets Layer (SSL), support for traditional UNION statements (which allows two SQL queries with the same column structure to appear to the client as a single result set), nested subqueries, stored procedures, and additional foreign key support (database-enforced data-integrity rules).

Dreamweaver MX, MySQL, and PHP

As difficult as the choice of which database system to use for your web application is, choosing the right development language to access that database from the web can be even more trying. Fortunately, if you selected MySQL for your database, Dreamweaver MX gives you the power of PHP (Hypertext Preprocessor) for development against that MySQL system out of the box. Although it is possible to use other web development languages with MySQL and it is also possible to use PHP with other database systems, the combination of the two within Dreamweaver MX is quite powerful.

Using Dreamweaver MX, you can take care of the connection from your web application to your MySQL database quickly. In the same way that you start Dreamweaver MX applications with other database systems, you will need to do the following:

1. Create the site.
2. Set the document type.
3. Configure the test server.
4. Establish the Dreamweaver MX database connection.

NOTE *Selecting PHP as the document type lets Dreamweaver MX know that you intend to use MySQL as your database platform because that is the only database directly supported within Dreamweaver MX for PHP web application development at this time.*

Here, we are concerned with step 4. The basic information required for establishing the connection to your MySQL server instance is as follows:

◆ Connection name
◆ MySQL server
◆ Username
◆ Password
◆ Database

Given this information, Dreamweaver MX constructs the following code to handle your web application's interaction with the MySQL server.

```php
<?php
# FileName="Connection_php_mysql.htm"
# Type="MYSQL"
# HTTP="true"
$hostname_WebProjDB = "localhost";
$database_WebProjDB = "WebDB";
$username_WebProjDB = "MyUser";
$password_WebProjDB = "MyPass";
$WebProjDB = mysql_pconnect($hostname_WebProjDB, $username_WebProjDB,
    $password_WebProjDB) or die(mysql_error());
?>
```

NOTE *See Chapter 10 for information about working with the MySQL Connection dialog box in Dreamweaver MX.*

MySQL Datatypes

Like other database systems we have looked at, MySQL stores data in one of several datatype families. In the case of MySQL, these families are numeric, character, and date/time. In addition to the standard datatypes, MySQL adds two character types—ENUM and SET—which we'll cover a little later.

Numeric Data

MySQL has some level of support for all the numeric datatypes specified in the SQL-92 standard. Furthermore, the MySQL team has given you a few more choices of datatypes to increase performance and reduce table size by using more precisely sized columns. For example, if you have a column whose value will always be in the range 0-255, you are correct in choosing the datatype `UNSIGNED TINYINT` as an alternative to the SQL-92 datatype `SMALLINT`. Making this one change cuts the storage requirement of that column in half, from 2 bytes to 1 byte. Although this is not a lot of savings for a small table, a large table, obviously, benefits a great deal.

For purposes of your web application, numeric data is any bit of data with which you need to perform arithmetic. The numeric datatypes supported by MySQL are `TINYINT`, `SMALLINT`, `MEDIUMINT`, `INT`, `BIGINT`, `FLOAT`, `DOUBLE`, `REAL`, `DECIMAL`, and `NUMERIC`. Also, you can use the MySQL-specific column definition attribute `UNSIGNED` to indicate a numeric column that stores only positive values. For example, a column to record visits to your website is a good candidate for an `UNSIGNED` column since you will always have 0 or more visits recorded.

WARNING *Although* `UNSIGNED` *can be valuable in designing the database to support your web application, exercise caution when using it. Particularly, keep in mind that this attribute is specific to MySQL and might not be available to you if you decide later to port your application to another database. Also, when performing mathematic operations in which one value comes from a column defined with the* `UNSIGNED` *attribute, the result of the operation is itself* `UNSIGNED`, *which produces incorrect results when performing operations that you expect to yield a negative result.*

TINYINT

`TINYINT` is an integer value ranging from −128 to 127; combined with the `UNSIGNED` attribute, this range (now excluding negative values) becomes 0 to 255. In the context of your web application, this column type is ideal for categorizing items into a relatively small number of groups. For example, a discussion website with a predetermined number of forums (and presumably fewer than 256) lends itself to having a forum identifier column defined as `TINYINT UNSIGNED`.

```
CREATE TABLE forums (
forum_id              TINYINT UNSIGNED,
   forum_description  VARCHAR (255)
)
```

You can also use `BIT` and `BOOL` interchangeably with the `TINYINT` datatype.

SMALLINT

`SMALLINT` is an integer value ranging from −32768 to 32767; combined with the `UNSIGNED` attribute, the range of values is 0 to 65535. Again taking a discussion website as an example, a table for current discussion topics might be defined as follows:

```
CREATE TABLE topics (
   forum_id           TINYINT UNSIGNED,
   topic_id           SMALLINT UNSIGNED,
   topic_description  VARCHAR (255)
)
```

MEDIUMINT

MEDIUMINT is an integer value ranging from −8388608 to 8388607; combined with the UNSIGNED attribute, the range of values is 0 to 16777215.

INT

INT or INTEGER is an integer value ranging from −2147483648 to 2147483647; combined with the UNSIGNED attribute, the range of values is 0 to 4294967295.

BIGINT

BIGINT is an integer value ranging from (get ready) −9223372036854775808 to 9223372036854775807; combined with the UNSIGNED attribute, the range of values is 0 to 18446744073709551615.

FLOAT

FLOAT is a single-precision, floating-point (real) number for which valid values can be 0 or are in the range of −3.402823466E+38 to −1.175494351E−38 and 1.175494351E−38 to 3.402823466E+38.

PRECISION—SINGLE AND DOUBLE

Computer science classes teach us that precision, in relation to the representation of numbers, corresponds to the number of decimal places that a number can have. If we store 3.1415 in a variable named *nPI*, we're telling the computer to store a value with 4 digits of precision (also called significant digits for you math whizzes out there) in the variable *nPI*. But the computer, of course, uses slots in its memory to hold variables and numbers (as well as everything else.) The larger the memory slot, the larger the number the computer can hold for any given variable. So, a single-precision variable has a given amount of memory it can use to hold a value. A double-precision has twice the amount of a single-precision.

Now, we're not intentionally being vague on the actual space allotted to single- and double-precision variables. The fact is, it varies with the computer. Typically, the definition of *single precision* is something like "the amount of memory corresponding to one computer word to store a number." So now we have a new term—a computer *word*. A computer word is the number of bits that you can store in one computer register. A computer register is... OK—enough of the computer science lesson. Suffice it to say that single-precision numbers are huge, and double-precision numbers are even larger.

DOUBLE

DOUBLE is a double-precision, floating-point number where valid values can be 0 or are in the range of −1.7976931348623157E+308 to −2.2250738585072014E−308 and 2.2250738585072014E−308 to 1.7976931348623157E+308. You can also use REAL interchangeably with the DOUBLE datatype.

DECIMAL

DECIMAL is also a double-precision, floating-point number. The effective range of a DECIMAL datatype is the same as that of a DOUBLE datatype; however, internally MySQL stores data of type

DECIMAL as a string, which allows the database designer more discreet control over the database storage requirement in terms of bytes used by a DECIMAL. You can also use NUMERIC interchangeably with the DECIMAL datatype.

NOTE   Unlike the integer datatypes described earlier, the floating-point datatypes do not have the range of values that they can support extended by including the MySQL-specific UNSIGNED attribute to the column definition. Instead, the effect that the UNSIGNED attribute has on a floating-point column is to simply disallow negative values.

Character Data

Character data is essentially any string of data that does not need to be numeric for the purpose of performing arithmetic operations with it. The character datatypes supported by MySQL are CHAR, VARCHAR, TINYTEXT, TEXT, MEDIUMTEXT, LONGTEXT, TINYBLOB, BLOB, MEDIUMBLOB, LONGBLOB, ENUM, and SET.

CHAR

CHAR is a datatype for containing a fixed-length string of data. The length of the column can be defined as 1 to 255. Technically, you can also define a CHAR column to have length of 0, but unless you understand the reasons for doing so and have a specific purpose, avoid defining a column that way.

VARCHAR

VARCHAR is a datatype for containing a variable-length string of data. The length of the column can be defined as 1 to 255.

NOTE   The primary difference between the CHAR and VARCHAR datatypes is in how MySQL stores data in the table and retrieves data from the table. A CHAR datatype pads values shorter than the defined length of the column with spaces when storing the value and trims spaces from the value when retrieving it. Therefore, a column defined with a length of 6 will take up 6 characters of storage space in the table regardless of the size of the value stored in it. A VARCHAR column also truncates values that are longer than the defined length of the column, but unlike CHAR, a VARCHAR allocates only as much space as is necessary to store the value—for values shorter than the defined length—plus 1 byte to record the actual length of the value.

TEXT, BLOB

TEXT, TINYTEXT, MEDIUMTEXT, and BIGTEXT are essentially all the same datatype and correspond with the related datatypes BLOB, TINYBLOB, MEDIUMBLOB, and BIGBLOB. These datatypes are all used to store large strings or binary objects, such as graphics. The difference between the TEXT types and the BLOB types is in how MySQL sorts the values. TEXT types are sorted without regard to case (case-insensitive), and BLOB types are sorted with regard to case (case-sensitive). Among the various versions of each of the TEXT and BLOB datatypes (TINY, MEDIUM, and BIG), the difference is the size of data that can be stored. Table 7.1 shows the lengths of these datatypes.

TABLE 7.1: MAXIMUM LENGTH OF DATATYPES

DATATYPE	MAXIMUM LENGTH (IN BYTES)
TINYTEXT, TINYBLOB	255
TEXT, BLOB	65535
MEDIUMTEXT, MEDIUMBLOB	16777215
BIGTEXT, BIGBLOB	4294967295

ENUM

The ENUM datatype lets you select a single string value from an enumeration of values defined at the time of table creation. If you attempt to set an ENUM field to a value not in the enumeration, MySQL inserts the value " " (empty string) instead. The ENUM datatype can support as many as 65535 individual values in the enumeration.

```
CREATE TABLE forums (
forum_id                TINYINT UNSIGNED,
    forum_description   VARCHAR (255),
    forum_status        ENUM("active", "inactive")
)
```

SET

The SET datatype is similar to the ENUM datatype in that it lets you specify a list of allowable values at the time of table creation. The difference between these two datatypes is that a SET column can be assigned multiple values from the list of valid choices. The member list of a SET column definition can contain, at most, 64 values.

```
CREATE TABLE topics (
    forum_id            TINYINT UNSIGNED,
    topic_id            SMALLINT UNSIGNED,
    topic_description    VARCHAR (255),
    topic_flags         SET("moderated", "public", "indexed")
)
```

Rows in this table might look like the following:

FORUM_ID	TOPIC_ID	TOPIC_DESCRIPTION	TOPIC_FLAGS
1	1	"General Discussion"	"public", "indexed"
1	2	"FAQ"	"public", "moderated", "indexed"
1	3	"Open Debate"	"public"

Notice that the value of the `topic_flags` column contains a combination of the possible values for the `SET` type column. The following is a typical SQL statement to return all the topics when `"indexed"` `topic_flag` is selected:

```
SELECT * FROM topics WHERE FIND_IN_SET('indexed', topic_flags) > 0;
```

Date/Time Data

The available date datatypes that MySQL provides are `DATETIME`, `DATE`, `TIME`, `TIMESTAMP`, and `YEAR`. Each datatype in the date/time family stores date- and time-related data with a different precision and has type-specific legal values.

DATETIME

The `DATETIME` datatype lets you store data that requires full date and time. A common use for this type is to record the exact date and time that a session within your web application began. For MySQL, the supported range of values for `DATETIME` is '1000-01-01 00:00:00' through '9999-12-31 23:59:59'.

DATE

The `DATE` datatype is useful if you do not need to record time-of-day. Good data fields for this column type include birthday, anniversary, and employment start date. The supported range of values for `DATE` is '1000-01-01' through '9999-12-31'.

TIME

The `TIME` datatype lets you store values that represent time. This datatype supports more than just a 24-hour range (HH:MM:SS); it actually provides the ability to store larger hour portions in the range of '–838:59:59' to '838:59:59'. This extended range of values makes a `TIME` column good for recording not only time-of-day data elements, but also elapsed time or other time counter values.

TIMESTAMP

The `TIMESTAMP` datatype lets you define a column that will record the time that `INSERT` or `UPDATE` operations are performed on a particular row of data in the table. You can define multiple columns as `TIMESTAMP`, but the first of these is the only one that the MySQL server will automatically modify.

NOTE A `TIMESTAMP` column lets you track the time that data was changed. MySQL automatically updates the first `TIMESTAMP` column defined in a table when data in the row is updated or when the row is initially created. You can override this feature by explicitly setting the `TIMESTAMP` column to another value at the time of `UPDATE` or `INSERT`. You can automatically set any `TIMESTAMP` column to the current date/time by passing `NULL` to MySQL in an `INSERT` or `UPDATE` statement.

YEAR

The `YEAR` datatype lets you store only the year portion of a date and does so in only 1 byte of storage space. The range is limited to storing values from 1901 to 2155.

WARNING Be careful when specifying dates in MySQL. In all cases that accept dates as values, MySQL performs only basic checks for validity. MySQL protects you from inserting date values with the month of 13, for example, but it does not verify that the February 29 is valid only in certain years and lets you specify a value of 09-31-2002 without complaint. MySQL simply checks that the month is between 01 and 12 and that the day is between 01 and 31.

MySQL Functions

MySQL functions give you the ability to perform data manipulation and aggregation at the server before the final result set of a query is returned to the client or manipulated by the server. There are many functions available for you to use, but we will hit only those that you will probably need in a typical web application with MySQL.

For a more complete reference to MySQL functions and syntax see the online documentation available at www.mysql.com.

Grouping Functions

Functions in this category allow you to return results based on aggregating a set of rows in the database. This would include finding the total number of rows in the result set (COUNT), determining the highest ordinal message number in a table of forum postings (MAX), and calculating the average number of messages posted by forum contributors (AVG).

AVG(EXPRESSION)

AVG calculates and returns the average value based on all the values of a particular field in a set of rows. This is useful for determining things like the average sale amount for an online store application.

```
mysql> SELECT AVG(total_sale) FROM purchases;
+-----------------+
| AVG(total_sale) |
+-----------------|
|           24.50 |
+-----------------+
```

MIN(EXPRESSION)

MIN finds the smallest value of a set of possible values. In a web application involving a discussion forum, this function might be used to find the earliest post in a particular forum.

```
mysql> SELECT MIN(post_date) FROM forum_messages;
+---------------------+
| MIN(post_date)      |
+---------------------+
| 2002-03-14 12:39:31 |
+---------------------+
```

MAX(EXPRESSION)

MAX finds the largest value of a set of possible values. As noted earlier, you might use MAX to find the largest message ID in a table containing all message posts to a particular forum.

```
mysql> SELECT MAX(message_id) FROM forum_messages;
+-----------------+
| MAX(message_id) |
+-----------------+
|           13768 |
+-----------------+
```

SUM(EXPRESSION)

SUM adds all of the values in a set of values and returns the result. This could be useful for determining the total sales in an online store application as in the following.

```
mysql> SELECT SUM(total_sale) FROM purchases;
+-----------------+
| SUM(total_sale) |
+-----------------+
|         9412.00 |
+-----------------+
```

COUNT(EXPRESSION)

COUNT returns a count of values in a set of rows. In order to quickly determine the total number of records in a table you could use COUNT(*). Another variation of COUNT is to count only unique occurrences of values in a set of rows. You would accomplish this by prefacing the expression with the keyword DISTINCT. For example, to determine the number of unique message posters in a table containing all messages and the user ID of the message poster, the following would give you the number of unique contributors of messages.

```
mysql> SELECT COUNT(DISTINCT poster_id) FROM forum_messages;
+---------------------------+
| COUNT(DISTINCT poster_id) |
+---------------------------+
|                         5 |
+---------------------------+
```

Numeric Functions

Functions in this category perform arithmetic operations within the MySQL server and return the result as part of the SQL statement. There are many more Numeric functions than are covered here. These are the more common functions you may need in your application.

ABS(EXPRESSION)

ABS returns the absolute value of a number. This has the effect of removing the sign from negative numbers and returning positive numbers unchanged.

```
mysql> SELECT ABS(-3), ABS(4);
+---------+--------+
| ABS(-3) | ABS(4) |
+---------+--------+
|       3 |      4 |
+---------+--------+
```

ROUND(EXPRESSION,PRECISION)

ROUND returns *expression* rounded to the nearest integer or to the specified precision (number of decimal places). The precision parameter is optional and will be assumed to be 0 if it is not specified.

```
mysql> SELECT ROUND(1.45), ROUND(1.55);
+-------------+-------------+
| ROUND(1.45) | ROUND(1.55) |
+-------------+-------------+
|           1 |           2 |
+-------------+-------------+

mysql> SELECT ROUND(123.456,1), ROUND(123.456,2);
+------------------+------------------+
| ROUND(123.456,1) | ROUND(123.456,2) |
+------------------+------------------+
|            123.5 |           123.46 |
+------------------+------------------+
```

TRUNCATE(EXPRESSION,PRECISION)

TRUNCATE returns *expression* truncated to the specified precision (number of decimal places). To truncate the entire decimal portion, specify 0 as the precision. This function differs from ROUND in that it simply cuts off any decimal portion larger than the specified precision.

```
mysql> SELECT TRUNCATE(1.45,0), TRUNCATE(1.55,0);
+------------------+------------------+
| TRUNCATE(1.45,0) | TRUNCATE(1.55,0) |
+------------------+------------------+
|                1 |                1 |
+------------------+------------------+
mysql> SELECT TRUNCATE(123.456,1), TRUNCATE(123.456,2);
+---------------------+---------------------+
| TRUNCATE(123.456,1) | TRUNCATE(123.456,2) |
+---------------------+---------------------+
|               123.4 |              123.45 |
+---------------------+---------------------+
```

String Functions

These functions allow you to manipulate string data at the MySQL server prior to your application receiving it (for SELECT statements) or prior to MySQL storing the value (for INSERT or UPDATE statements). Again, the available functions for string manipulation are numerous, so we'll just cover a few that you may find useful.

CONCAT(STRING1,STRING2,...)

CONCAT returns the string resulting from combining the argument strings. A typical use of this function is to combine parts of a person's name stored in separate fields in to a single full name value.

```
mysql> SELECT CONCAT('John', ' ', 'Doe');
+----------------------------+
| CONCAT('John', ' ', 'Doe') |
+----------------------------+
| John Doe                   |
+----------------------------+
```

INSTR(*STRING,FINDSTRING*)

INSTR returns the starting position of the string *findstring* within *string* or 0 if the string *findstring* is not found within *string*.

```
mysql> SELECT INSTR('abcdef', 'ef'), INSTR('abcdef', 'yz');
+-----------------------+-----------------------+
| INSTR('abcdef', 'ef') | INSTR('abcdef', 'yz') |
+-----------------------+-----------------------+
|                     5 |                     0 |
+-----------------------+-----------------------+
```

LCASE(*STRING*) / LOWER(*STRING*)

Both LCASE and LOWER change every character in the argument to lowercase.

```
mysql> SELECT LCASE('Macromedia Dreamweaver MX');
+------------------------------------+
| LCASE('Macromedia Dreamweaver MX') |
+------------------------------------+
| macromedia dreamweaver mx          |
+------------------------------------+
```

UCASE(*STRING*) / UPPER (*STRING*)

Both UCASE and UPPER change every character in the argument to uppercase.

```
mysql> SELECT UCASE('Macromedia Dreamweaver MX');
+------------------------------------+
| UCASE('Macromedia Dreamweaver MX') |
+------------------------------------+
| MACROMEDIA DREAMWEAVER MX          |
+------------------------------------+
```

LEFT(*STRING,COUNT*)

LEFT returns count characters from the beginning of *string*.

```
mysql> SELECT LEFT('Dreamweaver',5);
+-----------------------+
| LEFT('Dreamweaver',5) |
+-----------------------+
| Dream                 |
+-----------------------+
```

RIGHT(STRING,COUNT)

RIGHT returns *count* characters from the end of *string*.

```
mysql> SELECT RIGHT('Dreamweaver',2);
+------------------------+
| RIGHT('Dreamweaver',2) |
+------------------------+
| er                     |
+------------------------+
```

TRIM(STRING)

TRIM returns *string* with leading and trailing spaces removed. There are variations of TRIM that allow you to specify explicitly what character or string to remove. Additionally, you can control whether TRIM affects characters at the beginning or end of the string or both. You can also use LTRIM to remove leading spaces from a string and RTRIM to remove trailing spaces from a string.

```
mysql> SELECT TRIM('   Dreamweaver   ');
+--------------------------+
| TRIM('   Dreamweaver   ') |
+--------------------------+
| Dreamweaver              |
+--------------------------+
mysql> SELECT TRIM(LEADING '*' FROM '***Dreamweaver');
+----------------------------------------+
| TRIM(LEADING '*' FROM '***Dreamweaver') |
+----------------------------------------+
| Dreamweaver                            |
+----------------------------------------+
```

Date and Time Functions

One of the more common aspects of web applications will involve manipulating dates to determine things like new articles since the last visit by a user, recently modified links within a site, and for setting expiration dates on user submissions.

NOW()

NOW returns the current system date and time of the MySQL server. This is useful for recording events such as when a row in the database was last changed or the specific time a web user began a session with the web server.

```
mysql> SELECT NOW();
+---------------------+
| NOW()               |
+---------------------+
| 2002-08-31 10:23:40 |
+---------------------+
```

DAYOFWEEK(DATE)

DAYOFWEEK returns an index that can be used to determine the day of the week that a particular date represents. The return value is an integer from 1 through 7 where 1 = Sunday, 2 = Monday, 3 = Tuesday, 4 = Wednesday, 5 = Thursday, 6 = Friday and 7 = Saturday. For example to determine that the 4th of July 2002 fell on a Thursday, we would use the following

```
mysql> SELECT DAYOFWEEK('2002-07-04');
+------------------------+
| DAYOFWEEK('2002-07-04') |
+------------------------+
|                      5 |
+------------------------+
```

WARNING   There is another function in MySQL for determining the day of the week from a date called WEEKDAY. *Functionally, it is the same as* DAYOFWEEK, *the difference is that it uses a different indexing scheme to represent the days of the week. The index values returned by* DAYOFWEEK *correspond to the ODBC standard. The index values returned by* WEEKDAY *are integer values between 0 and 6 such that 0 = Monday, 1 = Tuesday, 2 = Wednesday, 3 = Thursday, 4 = Friday, 5 = Saturday and 6 = Sunday.*

DAYOFYEAR(DATE)

DAYOFYEAR returns the number of the day within the year represented by the date argument. The return value is in the range 1 through 366.

```
mysql> SELECT DAYOFYEAR('2002-08-30');
+------------------------+
| DAYOFYEAR('2002-08-30') |
+------------------------+
|                    242 |
+------------------------+
```

DAYNAME(DATE)

DAYNAME returns the name of the day represented by the date argument.

```
mysql> SELECT DAYNAME('2002-08-30');
+----------------------+
| DAYNAME('2002-08-30') |
+----------------------+
| Friday               |
+----------------------+
```

MONTHNAME(DATE)

MONTHNAME returns the name of the month represented by the date argument.

```
mysql> SELECT MONTHNAME('2002-08-30');
+-------------------------+
| MONTHNAME('2002-08-30') |
+-------------------------+
| August                  |
+-------------------------+
```

MySQL Syntax

Although MySQL supports most of the standard SQL syntax discussed in Chapter 18, there are those things that are slightly different, unusual, or enhanced. In this section, we will cover some of the basic rules you should keep in mind as you begin to develop your application using MySQL as the back-end database server.

Strings and Identifiers

MySQL allows you to delimit strings with either single quote (') or double quote (") characters. Either of the following is a valid string for MySQL: 'Dreamweaver MX' or "Dreamweaver MX".

TIP   MySQL also supports special characters in strings by means of an escape sequence using a backslash (\ ) as the escape character. Among the special escape sequences you may need to use are \' (to represent a single quote within a string) and \" (to represent a double quote within a string). It is good practice to scan character strings within your web application for characters with special meaning and escape them as appropriate before attempting to store the value in the database. For a complete listing of these escape sequences see www.mysql.com/doc/en/String_syntax.html.

You should exercise caution when naming identifiers within MySQL. Identifiers include table names, column names and database names. In general, MySQL is very flexible about the usage of special characters and even "reserved" words within or as identifiers. Database, table, and column names have a maximum length of 64 characters. MySQL allows database and table names to contain any character that your operating system will allow in a filename with the exception of '/' and '.' (Database names also must not contain a '\'). MySQL will allow identifiers to have the name of what would otherwise be considered a reserved word. The only thing you must remember is that if your identifier is a MySQL reserved word, you have to quote it with a (`) back tick character when you use it in your SQL statements. For example, "table" is a reserved word in MySQL (used when defining or changing a database table), however you are permitted to use a table that has the name "table" as in the following:

```
mysql> SELECT * FROM `table`;
+----------+------------+---------------------+
| table_id | table_name | table_description   |
+----------+------------+---------------------+
|        1 | table      | a listing of tables |
|        2 | users      | system users        |
+----------+------------+---------------------+
```

Be careful, though, if you forget that you have used a reserved word and do not quote it with a back tick, your application is bound for trouble:

```
mysql> SELECT * FROM table;
ERROR 1064: You have an error in your SQL syntax near 'table' at line 1
```

WARNING   *In practice, we would recommend that you avoid using identifiers that are reserved words in MySQL. While you are able to, your application may not be as easily ported to other database systems if that becomes necessary and your chances of encountering syntax problems, like those mentioned above, is greatly increased.*

Case Sensitivity

MySQL, in general, is not case sensitive when it comes to structuring your SQL statements. The following will return the same results:

```
mysql> select * from mytable;
mysql> SELECT * FROM mytable;
```

Because MySQL utilizes standard operating system files to contain the definition of databases and tables, it is dependent upon the underlying operating system to determine whether database names and table names are case sensitive. On Windows platforms, database and table names are not case sensitive, but on most Unix systems, database and table names are case sensitive. In other words, on Windows the tables "mytable" and "MyTABLE" reference the same table, but on Unix, creating a table as mytable and then referencing it as MyTABLE will result in an error because MySQL will be unable to find the table MyTABLE.

TIP   *To minimize errors and increase the likelihood that your application will run against a MySQL server on either Windows or Unix, you would be well advised to consistently name your tables and reference them using the same case throughout the application.*

Useful Statements

Obviously, the whole idea of creating a database-driven web application is to manipulate a set of data somewhere! To that end, you will find yourself using the basic SQL commands (SELECT, INSERT, UPDATE and DELETE) quite a bit. There are also some differences (or extensions) available to MySQL users. One notable extension to the SELECT statement is the ability of MySQL to limit the rows returned by a query. This is extremely valuable when working with a web application that requires a user to go through large amounts of data with a "screen at a time" approach (also called paging through the data).

SELECT ... LIMIT

To easily page through rows of data from your web application, you will find the LIMIT clause of the SELECT statement most useful. This allows you to specify a starting row and the number of rows to return in the result set. The syntax of the LIMIT clause is LIMIT [startingrow,] rowcount where the optional startingrow represents the starting row (if not specified MySQL starts with the first row of data) and rowcount represents the total number of rows to return. For example, if you have a table containing authors and titles for 300 books and you want to allow the user of your web application to page through these titles in groups of 20 you could use the following:

```
mysql> SELECT author, title FROM books LIMIT 0, 20
```

Providing the user with "Next" and "Previous" links from within your web application is as simple as keeping track of the starting record that was just used and issuing statements for the next 20 rows and the previous 20 rows. After using the above statement, to get the next 20 rows of data the following would be used:

```
mysql> SELECT author, title FROM books LIMIT 20, 20
```

Because the starting row defaults to the first row of data, if you want to retrieve the first 30 rows of data you could simply use:

```
mysql> SELECT author, title FROM books LIMIT 30
```

Finally, you can use the special value -1 as the `rowcount` parameter which tells MySQL to start at the specified row and return as many rows as are left.

```
mysql> SELECT author, title FROM books LIMIT 295, -1
```

WARNING *For purposes of the* LIMIT *clause, MySQL counts the rows starting at 0 for the first row instead of 1. A statement of:* SELECT author, title FROM books LIMIT 10, 20 *tells MySQL to start at the 11th row and return the next 20 rows.*

LOAD DATA INFILE

LOAD DATA INFILE allows you to quickly populate a table in MySQL (or bulk add rows to an already populated table). Before you can use this statement you must have "file" privileges on the MySQL server. The MySQL privilege and security system is complex and beyond the scope of this book, please refer to your MySQL system administrator or the online documentation for further details about MySQL privileges assigned to you.

The basic syntax of this statement is:

```
LOAD DATA INFILE 'MyFile.txt' INTO TABLE MyTable;
```

This will cause the server to read the file `MyFile.txt` and copy the rows of data in the table MyTable. By default, MySQL assumes that individual fields in the file are separated by a tab character, individual fields are quoted with single quotes ('), special characters are escaped with a (\ ) and lines are terminated with a new line character.

In Unix the new line is a single character: ASCII 10 or Line Feed. In Windows, a pair of characters represents the new line: ASCII 13 followed by ASCII 10 or Carriage Return and Line Feed. When importing text files created on Windows you'll need to override the line termination value with the optional clause LINES TERMINATED BY.

A more common file would be one of comma separated values where text fields are quoted with double quotes (") and lines are terminated with the Windows carriage return/line feed pair. The statement to load that file would look like this:

```
LOAD DATA INFILE 'MyFile.txt' INTO TABLE MyTable FIELDS TERMINATED BY ','
  OPTIONALLY ENCLOSED BY '"' LINES TERMINATED BY '\r\n';
```

For a complete discussion of the LOAD DATA INFILE along with numerous examples see the online documentation at www.mysql.com.

FOR MORE INFORMATION

There are a vast number of Internet resources available for further education on the subject of MySQL and a larger number of sites that rely on MySQL to support their own web applications. Check out MySQL's site at www.mysql.com. Or, browse through any of the tutorials on WebMonkey at www.webmonkey.com or simply do a search for MySQL at Google, Yahoo, or your favorite search engine. You'll find many resources available to you. One of the best sources of information about all aspects of MySQL is Ian Gilfillan's *Mastering MySQL* (Sybex, 2002).

Summary

While MySQL may not be as full featured and well known as some of the other database systems available, it is more than capable of handling most web application requirements. It is fast, flexible, and cost-effective. This chapter has provided a quick introduction to MySQL, surveying the different versions available, its close integration with the PHP language (covered in Chapter 16), and its datatypes, functions, and basic syntax. You'll learn more about SQL itself in Chapter 18. In the next chapter we'll look at another DBMS based on SQL, Microsoft SQL Server.

Chapter 8

SQL Server and the Web

WE COULD OPEN THIS chapter with personal opinions about SQL Server, but the gentle reader might suspect us of copying Microsoft's marketing hype. All things considered, SQL Server is probably the most comprehensive database product on the market—it's easy to implement and use, it's reliable and stable, and it's scalable. Furthermore, if you're already familiar with the relational database model, learning to use SQL Server shouldn't be too difficult. (Administrators might have a bigger, but still manageable, task at hand; but that statement would ring true for any database system.)

SQL Server has everything a database developer/administrator could want—analysis tools, replication, data mining, security, integration with .NET, indexed views, and so on. Most important (for the reader of this book) is that SQL Server 2000 is fully web-enabled. That means you should have no trouble getting a website to communicate with SQL Server 2000.

Topics in this chapter include:

- ◆ The SQL Server package
- ◆ Web support
- ◆ SQL Server components
- ◆ SQL Server datatypes
- ◆ Native functions
- ◆ Using Transact-SQL
- ◆ Migrating from Access to SQL Server
- ◆ Connection options

The SQL Server Package

SQL Server hit the market in 1988, but didn't seriously compete until Windows 3.1 was released in 1991. Windows and SQL Server were the perfect pair, and they've been together ever since. The most current version of SQL Server is SQL Server 2000. This version is available in several editions:

Enterprise Edition   The full version includes everything: meat, potatoes, dessert, and a cigar for later.

Standard Edition   This version is aimed at users in small- to medium-sized businesses. It lacks a few analysis tools and indexed views.

Developer Edition   This version includes all the features of the Enterprise Edition, but it isn't licensed for production. It's strictly a testing and development environment.

Desktop Engine   This is the upgrade to Microsoft Data Engine (MSDE 1). You can learn more about this version in Chapter 9.

Personal Edition   Similar to the Standard Edition for desktop and mobile use, but limited.

Windows CE Edition   This version is for handheld devices. It doesn't support stored procedures.

NOTE   *You can download a 120-day evaluation copy of SQL Server 2000 from* www.microsoft.com/sql/ evaluation/trial/2000/download.asp. *To learn more about specific SQL Server 2000 features, visit* www.microsoft.com/sql/evaluation/features/choosing.asp. *Microsoft also offers help for deciding which version is right for you at* www.microsoft.com/sql/techinfo/planning/SQLResKChooseEd.asp.

Microsoft recommends that you run SQL Server 2000 on Microsoft Windows 2000 Server (or later) on a Pentium or compatible system with a 166MHz processor and 128MB of RAM. For specific hardware and software requirements, visit Microsoft's SQL Server home page at www.microsoft.com/sqlserver.com.

Web Support

For the web developer, knowing that SQL Server 2000 is fully web-enabled is important. In general, that simply means that the relational database management system (RDBMS) makes it easy to access data via a web connection. SQL Server 2000 bases its web capabilities on existing standards such as SQL, ActiveX Data Objects (ADO), and Active Server Pages (ASP). It also offers other features such as:

◆ Extensible Markup Language (XML) with stored procedures to integrate data

◆ Analysis Services that integrate cube technology

◆ Uniform Resource Locator (URL) technology to get the data you need

NOTE   *Chapter 9 covers ADO and ASP in relation to Access. The information is essentially the same for SQL Server, so please see Chapter 9 for a brief introduction to these subjects. In addition, entire chapters are devoted to ADO.NET, ASP, and ASP.NET. For more in-depth information on these languages, see Chapters 13, 14, and 15.*

Extensible Markup Language (XML)

SQL Server 2000 takes Extensible Markup Language (XML) to a level far above simple support with XPath, URL queries, and XML Updategrams. *XML* is a platform-independent markup language that creates a *structured file*—a file that contains both text and nontext objects. For the most part, XML is used to transfer and share data between systems that aren't connected. XML is considered a web technology, and developers are using XML to publish interactive data on the web. XML documents run on the server or the client and are compatible with almost any browser using the following features:

◆ `OPENXML` provides a relational view on XML data. SQL Server enables queries to return data as XML using a SQL `SELECT` and the `FOR XML` clause. The `FOR XML` clause accesses a relational database. Then, a SQL `SELECT` and the `OPENXML` T-SQL keyword retrieve XML data. SQL Server 2000 also provides XML views, which access relational tables as XML documents.

◆ XML Updategrams update a SQL Server 2000 database, using XML. You specify the current state of the data and how you want the data to look, and the Updategram generates and executes the appropriate SQL statement required to produce the desired results. Bulk Load, a utility, loads large XML documents into a SQL Server 2000 database faster than Updategrams.

XML's main purpose is to publish interactive data to the web, but many developers are using it to share data, even when the web is not involved. XML is quickly becoming a standard, and SQL Server 2000 goes out of its way to accommodate the technology. For the most part, you'll rely on SQL and data-specific features to retrieve, insert, delete, and modify data via a web browser when you're dealing with a live connection. When working with data that rarely changes, you can save data to XML format and then display that data via an associated Extensible Stylesheet Language (XSL) file.

SQL Server can use XML to share data or import and export schema. Consequently, you can share a database's structure as well as its data. In fact, you can create an entire relational database by importing an Extensible Schema Data (XSD) file schema.

Here's our recommendation: more than likely, you won't encounter XML files when using Dreamweaver MX since XML is primarily a tool for transferring and sharing data, not accessing live data. Your website can use them, but you won't create them or interact with them in Dreamweaver MX.

NOTE   *For more information on using SQL Server 2000 and XML to integrate your data, visit* `www.microsoft.com/sql/techinfo/xml/default.asp`.

Web-Enabled Analysis

Customer information is a valuable resource to a company, and the web can provide tons of it, if you only know how to extract it. That's what SQL Server 2000's Analysis Services are about—accessing customer information from a website.

Cubes are dimensional views of data. Linked cubes make cubes (data) accessible to other servers, making the data (and its analysis) available to simultaneous users. Cubes present a multidimensional view of data. Linked cubes are simply cubes that are defined and stored on other servers. SQL Server 2000 also permits cube access over HTTP, enabling access to remote cubes over HTTP and through a firewall.

Here's our recommendation: this level of support won't be needed by the average site—this is for really large sites that support tons of data.

NOTE   *Download a white paper on SQL Server Analysis Services from* `www.microsoft.com/sql/evaluation/compare/analysisservicesWP.asp`.

Uniform Resource Locator (URL)

SQL Server 2000 provides several Uniform Resource Locator (URL) actions that access data. The following are just a few methods:

◆ Retrieve data by executing SQL queries using URL strings that reference a SQL Server 2000 virtual root. To do so, use the following URL form:

```
http://server/vroot?sql="validT-SQLstatement"
```

The appropriate instance of SQL Server returns the result as a standard rowset. If you specify the FOR XML clause, an XML document is returned instead.

◆ Retrieve database objects using the following URL form:

```
http://server/vroot/dbobject/xpath
```

The data isn't returned as XML, so you can retrieve database objects.

◆ Reference a template file using the following form:

```
http://server/vroot/vname?params
```

A template file is a valid XML document consisting of one or more SQL statements. When the URL specifies a template file, the SQL commands stored in the template file are executed. The results of the query replace the query itself, and then the entire XML document is returned.

◆ Execute an XPath query via an XML View using the following form:

```
http://server/vroot/vname/xpath?params
```

An XPath query retrieves specific data from relational tables via an XML View.

Here's our recommendation: the features in this section could possibly complement your work in Dreamweaver MX, but you won't manipulate them from within Dreamweaver MX.

SQL Server Components

SQL Server provides a number of services and utilities that help you manage your data and your database more efficiently:

Client Network Utility Manages the client Net-Libraries and defines server alias names. Also use it to set the default options used by a database library. Most users won't need this utility; it's a tool for administrators.

Server Network Utility Similar to the Client Network Utility, but you work with server behaviors.

Enterprise Manager Provides a window into your server environment in which you can view the network structure, each database, and even each object within each database.

Data Transformation Services Import/Export Wizard An import/export wizard that has a lot of bells and whistles.

Profiler   Runs efficiency reports on database components, which you can use to improve performance, reliability, and integrity.

Query Analyzer   A graphical tool that helps you create and execute queries and other SQL scripts.

Service Manager   Checks the state of SQL Server.

For the most part, all users need the Enterprise Manager and the Query Analyzer. That's where most of the work takes place. Beyond that, the tools you need depend on your level of involvement outside a particular database. Administrators will have a range of tools at their hands, and management will probably be interested in any number of analytical and management services available as add-ons.

SQL Server Datatypes

Like most RDBMSs, SQL Server 2000 supports different datatypes, in particular, the following:

Text   Alphanumeric data that doesn't respond to arithmetic operators.

Numeric   Numeric values stored with numeric characteristics and, most important, interpreted by arithmetic equations.

Image   Usually a large file that can contain a graphic, text or numeric values, but is viewed as one container, regardless of its content.

Table 8.1 lists and describes the SQL Server 2000 datatypes.

TABLE 8.1: SQL SERVER DATATYPE

SQL SERVER	DESCRIPTION
Binary	Binary data up to 8000 bytes
Char	Text up to 8000 bytes
VarBinary	Variable-length binary up to 8000 bytes
VarChar	Variable-length character up to 8000 bytes
Bit	Integers 1 and 0 only (yes/no; true/false)
Bit Null	Bit that allows Null
DateTime	Valid date stored as 8 bytes
SmallDateTime	Valid date stored as 4 bytes
DateTime Null	DateTime that allows Null
Decimal	Fixed precision and scale numeric data from $-10^{38} + 1$ through $10^{38} - 1$
Decimal Null	Decimal that allows Null

Continued on next page

TABLE 8.1: SQL Server Datatype *(continued)*

SQL SERVER	DESCRIPTION
Real	Floating precision numeric data from –3.40E+38 through 3.40E+38
Float	Floating precision numeric data from –1.79E+308 through 1.79E+308
Real | Float Null	Real or Float that allows Null
Image	Variable-length binary data with a maximum length of 2,147,483,647 bytes
TinyInt	Value from 0 through 255
SmallInt	Integer data from –32,768 through 32,767
Int	Integer data from –2,147,483,648 through 2,147,483,647
TinyInt | SmallInt | Int Null	TinyInt, SmallInt, Int that allows Null
SmallMoney	Monetary data value from –214,748.3648 through 214,748.3647
Money	Monetary data value from –922,337,203,685,477.5808 through 922,337,203,685,477.5807
Money | SmallMoney Null	Money, SmallMoney that allows Null
NChar	Unicode character
NText	Unicode text
Numeric	Functionally equivalent to decimal
Numeric Null	Numeric that allows Null
NVarChar	Unicode variable-length character
Text	Text
VarBinary	Variable-length binary
VarChar	Variable-length character

Native Functions

An RDBMS provides native (built-in) functionality in the form of functions that perform a predefined calculation or task. Generally, you provide a reference to values or information that the function processes within the confines of its defined job. You can use SQL Server functions in the following:

◆ A SELECT statement's field list to return a value

◆ A SQL WHERE clause search condition (SELECT, INSERT, DELETE, or UPDATE) to limit the returned rows

◆ Any expression

- ◆ A CHECK constraint or trigger to check for specified values when inserting data
- ◆ A DEFAULT constraint when inserting data

NOTE   A SQL Server function is either deterministic or nondeterministic. Deterministic functions always return the same result. DateAdd is a deterministic value because it returns the same result for the fixed set of input values. Nondeterministic functions return different results each time they are called, depending on the input values. For instance, GetDate returns the current date, which will always be a different value every time it's called (because the result also includes a time value). Only deterministic functions can be invoked in views and computed columns.

There are several types of SQL Server functions. In this next section, we review Date and Time, Mathematical, System, and String functions. This list isn't comprehensive by any means, but it does include the functions you'll probably use most often.

NOTE   Aggregate functions perform operations on groups of records. You can't limit the set based on criteria. The function processes the calculation on all the values in a single column. These functions are actually Transact-SQL functions and as such aren't truly native to SQL Server. You'll find more information on these functions in the "Using Transact-SQL in SQL Server" section later in this chapter.

DATE AND TIME FUNCTIONS

Date and Time functions use date arithmetic or serial values in their calculations. SQL Server supports dates from January 1, 1753, through December 31, 9999. Oddly enough, December 30, 1899, is considered the anchor date (instead of January 1, 1900, as you might expect). An anchor date has a serial value of 0. Several Date functions accept an argument that denotes a specific interval. Table 8.2 lists these constants.

TABLE 8.2: INTERVAL OPTIONS FOR SOME DATE FUNCTIONS

OPTION	DESCRIPTION
yyyy, yy, year	Returns a valid 4-digit year value
y	Returns a value between 1 and 365, representing the date's position within the year—between January 1 and December 31
mm, m, month	Returns the month as a value between 1 and 12
qq, q, quarter	Returns a value 1 through 4, denoting the quarter of the year
dd, d, day	Denotes day as a value between 1 and 31
dw	Denotes position of day within the week; a value between 1 and 7
ww, wk	Returns a value between 1 and 52, which represents the week of the year that the date falls within
hh, hour	Denotes hours as a value between 0 and 23
mi, n, minute	Denotes minutes as a value between 0 and 59
ss, s, second	Denotes seconds as a value between 0 and 59

GetDate()

GetDate() returns the current date and time value. The following statement returns the current date in a column named CurrentDate.

```
SELECT GetDate() As CurrentDate
FROM table
```

DatePart(datecode,date)

DatePart() returns a number of date components, and *datecode* is one of many options that define the time or date component. For instance, if the date field or variable contains August 10, 2002, the following returns the value 10.

```
SELECT DatePart(dd, date) As DayValue
FROM table
```

DateAdd(datecode, interval, date)

The DateAdd() function adds an interval to a specific date. For instance, if the date column contained the dates August 10, 2002, and September 10, 2002, the following statement returns September 10, 2002, and October 10, 2002—adding exactly one month to each date.

```
SELECT DateAdd(mm, 1, date)
FROM table
```

DateDiff(datecode, date, datestring)

The DateDiff() function returns the difference between *date* and *datestring*. That difference can be presented in any date component, as specified by **datecode**. For instance, if the date column contains the dates August 10, 2002, and September 10, 2002, and **datestring** is November 4, 2002, the following statement returns the values 86 and 55.

```
SELECT DateDiff(d, date, '11/4/2002')
FROM table
```

Day(date)

Day() returns a value between 1 and 31 that represents the day of the month of the specified date. The following statement returns 10 if the date in question is 8/10/2002.

```
SELECT Day(date) As DayValue
FROM table
```

Month(date)

Month() returns a value between 1 and 12, a value represents a month between January and December. The following statement returns 8 if the date in question is 8/10/2002.

```
SELECT Month(date) As DayValue
FROM table
```

Year(date)

Year() extracts the year value as a four-digit value from the specified date. The following statement returns 2002 if the date in question is 8/10/2002.

```
SELECT Year(date) As DayValue
FROM table
```

Mathematical Functions

Mathematical functions perform mathematical operations on numeric data and return the results. The user supplies the operands in the form of arguments, and the function processes those values within the context of its purpose.

Abs(value)

Abs() returns the absolute, or positive, value of a value or expression. The following statement returns the values 1, 2, and 3 if *value* contains the values −1, −2, and −3.

```
SELECT Abs(value) As AbsValue
FROM table
```

Ceiling(value)

Ceiling() returns the smallest integer greater than or equal to the given numeric expression. The following statement returns the value 2 if *value* is 1.21 or 1.63 and returns −1 if *value* is −1.21 or −1.63:

```
SELECT Ceiling(value) As GreaterThan
FROM table
```

Floor(value)

Floor() returns the largest integer less than or equal to the given numeric expression. The following statement returns 1 when *value* is 1.21 and 1.63 and returns −2 when *value* is −1.21 and −1.63.

```
SELECT Floor(value) As LessThan
FROM table
```

Rand(seed)

Rand() returns a random float value from 0 to 1. The following statement returns a series of random values, depending on the *seed* value.

```
SELECT Rand(seed) As RandomValue
FROM table
```

A query returns the same results if the *seed* value doesn't change.

Round(value,length,function)

Round() returns a value, rounded to the specified length, but it's flexible. You can use Round() to round or truncate a value. You can apply the following rules to round values:

◆ If *length* is negative and larger than or equal to the number of digits to the left of the decimal point, Round() returns 0. The following statements return 0.

```
SELECT Round(1.23, -1) AS RoundValue
FROM table
SELECT Round(1.23, -2 AS RoundValue
FROM table
SELECT Round(12.23, -3) AS RoundValue
FROM table
```

◆ Round() returns a rounded value when *length* is a negative number. The following statements return the values 10.00 and 100.00, respectively.

```
SELECT Round(12.23, -1) AS RoundValue
FROM table
SELECT Round(123.45, -2) AS RoundValue
FROM table
```

◆ Use the *function* argument (the default is 0) to truncate a value. When *function* is any value other than 0, the value is truncated. Generally, the *length* value needs to be 0 when truncating. The following statements return the values 12, 12.20, and 12.23, respectively.

```
SELECT Round(12.23, 0, 1) AS TruncatedValue
FROM table
SELECT Round(12.23, 1, 1) AS TruncatedValue
FROM table
SELECT Round(12.23, 2, 1) AS TruncatedValue
FROM table
```

◆ Expect normal rounding behaviors when *length* is a positive value and *function* is 0 (or omitted). The following statements return the values 120, 100, and 0, respectively.

```
SELECT Round(123, -1) AS RoundedValue
FROM table
SELECT Round(123, -2) AS RoundedValue
FROM table
SELECT Round(123, -3) AS RoundedValue
FROM table
```

SYSTEM FUNCTIONS

System functions operate or report on various system level options and objects by indirectly accessing information from system tables. Some functions are preceded with two at signs (@@). The following System functions return a corresponding identification value or name:

DB_ID() and DB_NAME()

The DB_ID and DB_NAME functions return a database identification value or name. The following statement returns the value 6 when Northwind is the current (active) database.

```
SELECT DB_ID() As DBID
```

The following statement returns Northwind when that database is current.

```
SELECT DB_NAME() As DBName
```

HOST_ID() and HOST_NAME()

These two functions return the host identification value or name, which will be unique to your system. Try the following to return the host identification value.

```
SELECT HOST_ID() As HostID
```

The following returns the host name, which should be the same as the current instance of SQL Server.

```
SELECT HOST_NAME() AS HostName
```

OBJECT_ID('name') and OBJECT_NAME(value)

These two functions return an object's identification value or name. To return a known object's identification value, use the following syntax:

```
SELECT OBJECT_ID('sysfilegroups') AS ObjectID
```

When you know the identification value and you want to know the object's name, use the following syntax:

```
SELECT OBJECT_NAME(24) AS ObjectName
```

USER_ID() and USER_NAME()

Use these functions to return the user identification value and name. The following statement returns the user identification value.

```
SELECT USER_ID() AS UserID
```

This statement returns the user name.

```
SELECT USER_NAME() AS UserName
```

@@Identify

Use `@@Identify` after inserting data to return the last-inserted identify value. For instance, the following statement inserts new values into `table` and then returns the latest identify value from that operation.

```
INSERT INTO Employees (lastname, firstname, ssnumber)
VALUES ('Smith', 'Janice', '555-55-5555')
SELECT @@IDENTITY As 'Identity'
```

META DATA FUNCTIONS

Meta Data functions are a type of System function; they return information about the database and database objects. There are several Meta Data functions, and all are nondeterministic. We'll review just a few of them in this section.

COL_LENGTH('table','column')

This function returns the length of a specific column. The following statement returns the value 4—the length of the OrderID column in the Northwind Orders table.

```
USE Northwind
SELECT COL_LENGTH('Orders','OrderID')
```

COL_NAME('tableid','columnid')

This function returns a column's name. The following statement returns the column name EmployeeID.

```
USE Northwind
SELECT COL_NAME(OBJECT_ID('Employees'),1)
```

ROWSET FUNCTIONS

Rowset functions return an object that can be used in a Transact-SQL statement in place of a table reference. They're all nondeterministic.

OpenDataSource(providername,initalizestring)

The OpenDataSource() function provides connection information without using a linked server name. The *providername* argument is the registered name of the PRODIG of the OLE DB provider. Use any of the keywords in Table 8.3 as the *initializestring* argument.

TABLE 8.3: *OpenDataSource* KEYWORDS

KEYWORD	OLE DB PROPERTY	VALID VALUES AND DESCRIPTION
Data Source	DBPROP_INIT_DATASOURCE	Name of the data source (connection). Providers interpret this in different ways. For a SQL Server OLE DB provider, this indicates the name of the server. For a Jet OLE DB provider, this indicates the full path of the MDB file or XLS file.
Location	DBPROP_INIT_LOCATION	Location of the database (connection).
Extended Properties	DBPROP_INIT_PROVIDERSTRING	The provider-specific connect-string.
Connect Timeout	DBPROP_INIT_TIMEOUT	Time-out value after which the connection attempt fails.
User ID	DBPROP_AUTH_USERID	User's identification value.
Password	DBPROP_AUTH_PASSWORD	Password to get past security.
Catalog	DBPROP_INIT_CATALOG	The name of the initial or default catalog when connecting to the data source.

Use this function in the following form:

```
SELECT *
FROM OPENDATASOURCE('SQLOLEDB','Data Source=servername;
    UserID=userid;Password=password'). database
```

STRING FUNCTIONS

String functions perform various operations on character and binary string values. Most can be used only with Char, NChar, VarChar, and NVarChar datatypes. When passing a literal string to the function, you must usually enclose the string in single-quotation delimiters in the form 'string'.

Substring(searchstring, begin, length)

Substring() retrieves a portion of a string. For example, the following statement returns the string 'bcde'—it begins to extract characters at the second letter in the specified string and extracts four characters.

```
SELECT Substring('abcdef', 2, 4)
```

Soundex() and Difference()

These two functions search for similar sounds in a character string. `Soundex()` converts a character string to a 4-digit code. The function ignores vowels and terminates when encountering a non-alphabetic character. Both strings in the following statement return the value S25.

```
SELECT Soundex('Susan'), Soundex('Suzanne')
```

The two strings, `'boy'` and `'toy'`, return the values B000 and T000. (Those are zeros, not upper-case O's.)

```
SELECT Soundex('boy'), Soundex('toy')
```

The `Difference()` function compares the results of running the `Soundex()` function on the specified strings and then returns a value from 0 through 4, 4 being the best match. The two sets of strings from the `Soundex()` example return the values 4 and 3, respectively—implying that Susan and Suzanne are more similar than boy and toy:

```
SELECT Difference('Susan', 'Suzanne')
SELECT Difference('boy', 'toy')
```

Stuff(string, begin, length, substring)

The `Stuff()` function replaces characters in one string with another, beginning at a specified position within the target string and replacing existing characters with a specified number of characters from the substring. The following statement replaces the third character with the letter *o* to return the word *block*.

```
SELECT Stuff('black', 3, 1, 'o')
```

NOTE   *This section is by no means comprehensive. You can find more information on SQL Server functions at* http://msdn.microsoft.com/library/default.asp?url=/library/en-us/acdata/ac_8_con_03_9rar.asp *or in Books Online, which comes with SQL Server 2000.*

Using Transact-SQL in SQL Server

SQL Server 2000 uses Transact-SQL (T-SQL), a vendor-specific version of the standard SQL. If you're familiar with Jet SQL, you'll find T-SQL similar. SQL Server uses T-SQL to process all its queries in the form of views, stored procedures, and even user-defined functions. In this section, you'll learn how to talk directly to SQL Server using T-SQL.

TIP   *For in-depth coverage of SQL, see Chapter 18.*

SQL Server Views

SQL Server uses a view to display the results of a SELECT statement. A *view* is simply a virtual table, which means the view doesn't actually contain data; a view shows a picture of the underlying tables, and the data stored there. Working with views is better than working directly with tables for the following reasons:

- ◆ Views prevent users from modifying the underlying tables.
- ◆ Views protect confidential data because you can limit the data the user sees.
- ◆ Views free up resources and reduce network traffic by retrieving only the data the user needs at the requested time.

To create a view, use the following syntax:

```
CREATE VIEW [databasename.][owner.]viewname[(column [n,...])]
[WITH attribute [n,...]]
AS
validselectstatement
[WITH CHECK OPTION]
```

Table 8.4 lists the attribute options for the WITH clause.

TABLE 8.4: *WITH* OPTIONS

OPTION	DESCRIPTION
ENCRYPTION	Encrypts the definition of the view. Be sure to keep the original scripts so you can modify the view if you choose. This option is useful only when you have a serious security requirement.
SCHEMABINDING	Prevents the user from making any changes to the underlying table.
VIEW_METADATA	Permits the use of client-side cursors with ODBC and OLEDB APIs.

To execute a view, simply call it in a SELECT statement in the following form:

```
SELECT fieldlist FROM dbo.viewname
```

Let's look at a simple example using the Northwind sample database that comes with SQL Server. Follow these steps:

1. Open the Query Analyzer.
2. Open a blank query window (if necessary) by choosing New from the New Query tool.
3. Double-click Blank Query Window, or connect to the appropriate server by choosing File ➢ Connect.
4. Specify Northwind by selecting it in the database drop-down list, which we've circled in Figure 8.1.
5. Create the following view, which displays each company and its orders:

```
SELECT VIEW dbo.vw_CustomerOrders
AS
SELECT dbo.Customers.CompanyName, dbo.Orders.OrderID
```

```
FROM dbo.Customers INNER JOIN dbo.Orders ON
    dbo.Customers.CustomerID = dbo.Orders.CustomerID
```

To view the results shown in Figure 8.1, open a new blank query window and refer to the view in the SELECT statement:

```
SELECT * FROM dbo.vw_CustomerOrders
```

FIGURE 8.1

Call a view in a SELECT statement to see its results.

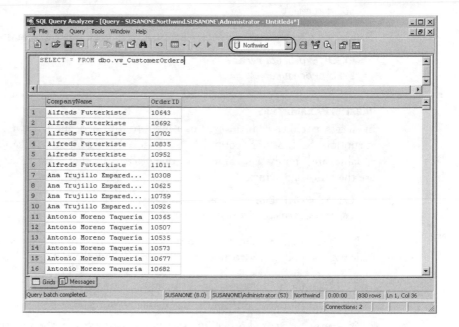

NOTE *SQL Server 2000 introduced indexed views because views, as simple as they sound, can actually slow things down because they're not optimized. All the computations take place when you execute the view. An indexed view has a unique clustered index. The query optimizer compiles an execution plan for the indexed view, so the evaluated view exists in physical storage. Consequently, the view runs much faster—almost immediately.*

SQL Server Stored Procedures

A *stored procedure* is simply a set of precompiled T-SQL statements that are stored with the SQL Server database. Access users will find them similar to Access queries, but there's no graphical interface to help you write them—you must know T-SQL. Stored procedures provide many benefits, and you'll rely on them often for the following reasons:

◆ They execute quickly because all checks and compiling have been performed.

◆ They reduce network traffic by replacing Active Data Objects (ADOs) to retrieve data.

◆ They improve security because users have access to the stored procedure, not the actual data on which the stored procedure is based.

CREATING AND EXECUTING A STORED PROCEDURE

Creating a stored procedure is simple, although the language used within a stored procedure can be extremely complex. To create a stored procedure use the CREATE PROCEDURE statement in the following form:

```
CREATE PROCEDURE procedurename
AS
SQLstatement
```

To execute a stored procedure use the EXECUTE or EXEC statement in one of the following forms:

```
EXECUTE procedurename
EXEC procedurename
```

PASSING PARAMETERS

In Access, parameter queries pass user input to the query and thereby limit the results of the query at runtime. SQL Server's equivalent is the stored procedure that accepts parameters, which act as variables and simply pass values from one place to another. To create a parameter stored procedure use the following syntax:

```
CREATE PROCEDURE procedurename
(@parametername datatype)
```

Now, let's create a simple stored procedure that returns all the item records for a specific order, which you supply in the form of a parameter. Follow these steps:

1. Open the SQL Server Query Analyzer.
2. Select Northwind from the Database drop-down list.
3. Enter the stored procedure shown in Listing 8.1 in the Query Analyzer, as shown in Figure 8.2.
4. Press F5 to save the stored procedure.
5. To display all the items in order number 10428, enter the following statement in the Query Analyzer:

   ```
   EXEC sp_customer_parameter '10428'
   ```

   as shown in Figure 8.3. To display detail records about any order, simply execute the procedure and specify the orders corresponding to OrderID value.

We strongly encourage you to key in all the code to create the example files yourself. To check your work, compare your files with the example files on the CD accompanying this book.

LISTING 8.1: STORED PROCEDURE WITH PARAMETER

```
CREATE PROCEDURE sp_customer_parameter
@OrderID int
AS
```

```
SELECT *
FROM [Order Details]
WHERE [Order Details].OrderID = @OrderID
```

FIGURE 8.2

Enter the stored procedure in the Query Analyzer.

FIGURE 8.3

Call the stored procedure.

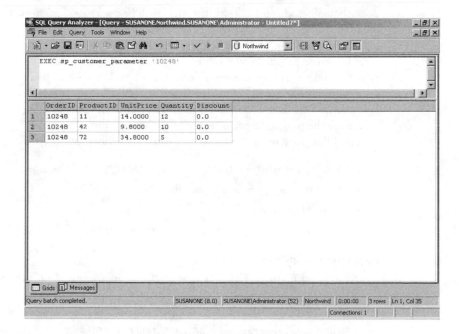

TIP *If the* EXEC *fails, make sure Northwind is selected in the Database drop-down list and try again.*

Adding a Default to the Parameter

When providing a parameter stored procedure, the user might forget to provide the parameter, which will produce an error message. One way around this is to provide a default value, when applicable. Include a default parameter by specifying the default when you specify the parameter in the following form:

```
@parametername datatype = defaultvalue
```

For instance, the parameter statement in sp_customer_parameter might resemble the following:

```
@OrderID int = '10428'
```

If you include the default value of 10428, you can execute the stored procedure without specifying a parameter value, and the call will return all the records for order 10428. Of course, you can still pass any valid value, other than the default, at any time. The default provides a shortcut when you use one value more than another, and it protects against errors if you forget to pass the parameter value.

SQL Server User-Defined Functions

User-defined functions (UDF) are new to SQL Server 2000, and it's about time! Other systems, such as Oracle and DB2, have provided them for a while. A *UDF* is a subroutine of encapsulated T-SQL code that you can call via T-SQL code, much like a native function. The major difference between a native function and a UDF is that you define the UDF's task and write the code necessary to get the job done. In addition, you can then modify the UDF at any later time.

A UDF can return a scalar value or a table variable (which is also new to SQL Server 2000). A *table variable* is similar to a temporary table in that it provides a set of temporary records, but it's available only within the scope of the calling function. The table variable is available to the user executing the function and while the function is in use. In addition, you can call a UDF from a SELECT statement. These are the major strengths of the SQL Server UDF.

The UDF may seem similar to the stored procedure, but the UDF provides different benefits:

◆ You can execute a UDF from a SQL SELECT or SQL action query.

◆ A UDF can return a table variable.

◆ You can join to a UDF.

◆ A UDF doesn't require much error-handling because T-SQL stops the function if an error occurs.

CREATING A UDF

To create a UDF, use the CREATE FUNCTION statement in the following form:

```
CREATE FUNCTON ownerprefix.functionname
(@parameter AS datatype = defaultvalue ...)
RETURNS scalardatatype | RETURNS TABLE | RETURNS
  @returnvariable TABLE tabledefinition
WITH option
AS
BEGIN | RETURN
        T-SQLstatement
END
```

Like a stored procedure, you can pass parameters in the form of the optional @parameter argument. Table 8.5 lists and defines the CREATE FUNCTION arguments.

NOTE *T-SQL requires the* ownerprefix *component to avoid ambiguous references. You might notice that many SQL Server developers include this prefix even when not required.*

TABLE 8.5: *CREATE FUNCTION* ARGUMENTS

ARGUMENT	STATE	DESCRIPTION
ownerprefix	Required	Identifies the function's owner—dbo by default.
functionname	Required	Identifies the UDF by name. It must be unique within the database and to the owner.
@parameter	Optional	Allows the user to specify a passed value.
datatype	Required with parameter statement	Declares the parameter's datatype.
defaultvalue	Optional	Specifies a default value for the parameter.
RETURNS	Required	scalardatatype: Defines the UDF as a scalar function.
	Required	TABLE: Defines the resulting table variable in the SELECT statement.
	Required	@returnvariable TABLE tabledefinition: Specifies a table variable, identified by the @returnvariable argument, and tabledefinition defines the table datatype.
WITH	Optional	SCHEMABINDING: Binds the UDF to a table after which you can't make changes to the table.
	Optional	ENCRYPTION: Encrypts the code and should be used with great care.

A SCALAR UDF

A *scalar* UDF returns a single value. To create a scalar UDF, use the following syntax:

```
CREATE FUNCTION ownerprefix.functionname
(@parameter AS datatype = defaultvalue...)
RETURNS scalardatatype
WITH option
AS
BEGIN
    T-SQLstatement
END
```

For example, the UDF in Listing 8.2 accepts a parameter and returns a single value that represents the number of pages in a document, with 2200 being the approximate number of characters per page.

The user supplies the total number of characters in the document when running the UDF. Figure 8.4 shows the results of passing the value 35,000 to the UDF. As you can see, it returns 15—the estimated number of pages for a document with 35,000 characters.

NOTE   When calling the UDF, you must enclose the arguments in parentheses as shown.

LISTING 8.2: PAGE COUNT UDF

```
CREATE FUNCTION dbo.fnt_pagecount
(@characters int)
RETURNS int
AS
BEGIN
   RETURN(@characters/2200)
END
```

FIGURE 8.4

You can pass a parameter to a UDF.

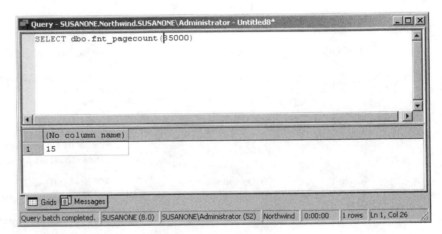

A TABLE-RETURNING UDF

A UDF can also return a *table variable*—a datatype that's new to SQL Server 2000. Table variables are similar to temporary tables, but more optimized, which makes them faster in most cases. You'll use a table-returning UDF to limit, modify, and insert new data. There are two types of table-returning UDFs:

Inline   Consists of a simple SELECT statement.

Multistatement   Can contain many statements.

An Inline UDF

Because an inline UDF consists of a single SELECT statement, that statement defines the resulting table. These UDFs use the following syntax, which defines the table's columns and datatypes in the SELECT statement:

```
CREATE FUNCTION ownerprefix.functionname
(@parameter AS datatype = defaultvalue ...)
RETURNS TABLE
WITH option
AS
RETURN selectstatement
```

Listing 8.3 is an example of an inline UDF. It returns orders for a particular customer. Use the following SELECT statement to return orders for the customer represented by the text value VINET as shown in Figure 8.5:

```
SELECT OrderID, ShippedDate
FROM dbo.fnt_shippedordersbycustomer('VINET')
```

LISTING 8.3: UDF THAT RETURNS ORDERS

```
CREATE FUNCTION dbo.fnt_shippedordersbycustomer
(@CustomerID nchar(5))
RETURNS TABLE
AS
RETURN (SELECT *
    FROM dbo.Orders WHERE dbo.Orders.CustomerID = @CustomerID)
```

FIGURE 8.5

This UDF returns orders for a specific customer.

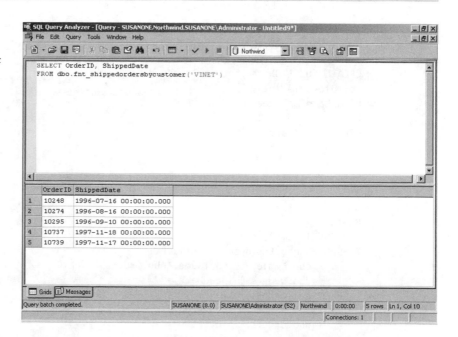

A Multistatement UDF

A UDF can require multiple SQL statements to return a table. When this is the case, you simply enclose each statement in a BEGIN/END block. The most significant difference between the inline and multistatement UDF is that the multistatement, also known as a multiline, defines the table's columns and datatypes in the TABLE statement. Use the following syntax to create a multistatement UDF:

```
CREATE FUNCTION ownerprefix.functionname
(@parameter AS datatype = defaultvalue ...)
RETURNS @returnvariable TABLE tabledefinition
WITH option
AS
BEGIN
    T-SQL code
    BEGIN
        T-SQL code
    END
END
```

The UDF shown in Listing 8.4 defines the table variable and then inserts the results of a SELECT statement into the table. To create the UDF, enter it in the Query Analyzer window and then press F5. To return all the shipped dates for Nancy Davolio, as shown in Figure 8.6 run the following statement:

```
SELECT *
FROM dbo.fnt_EmployeeOrders(1)
```

LISTING 8.4: MULTISTATEMENT UDF

```
CREATE FUNCTION dbo.fnt_employeeorders
(@EmployeeID int)
RETURNS @EmployeeOrders TABLE
(
FirstName nvarchar(10),
LastName nvarchar(20),
OrderID int,
Shipped DateTime
)
AS
BEGIN
    INSERT @EmployeeOrders
    SELECT dbo.Employees.FirstName,
        dbo.Employees.LastName, dbo.Orders.OrderID,
        dbo.Orders.ShippedDate
    FROM dbo.Orders
    INNER JOIN dbo.Employees ON
        dbo.Orders.EmployeeID =
        dbo.Employees.EmployeeID
```

```
    WHERE dbo.Employees.EmployeeID =
        @EmployeeID
RETURN
END
```

FIGURE 8.6

Return all the orders for a specific employee.

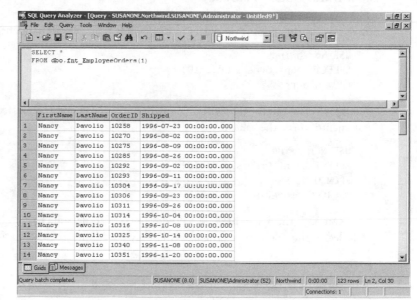

SQL Aggregate Functions

Unlike Access 2002, SQL Server doesn't provide domain functions. But you can use T-SQL aggregate functions to process sets of records and even limit those sets by using criteria in the form of a SQL WHERE clause. T-SQL aggregate functions aren't as limited as Jet SQL or Access 2002's domain functions because the WHERE clause supplies a means of filtering the data.

AVG(ALL | DISTINCT DOMAIN)

The AVG() function returns the average value of a set of values. For instance, the following statement returns the value 26.2185—the average unit price in the Order Details table in the Northwind sample database that comes with SQL Server.

```
USE Northwind
SELECT Avg([Order Details].UnitPrice) AS AvgPrice
FROM [Order Details]
```

The following statement limits the set of records considered in the calculation:

```
USE Northwind
SELECT Avg([Order Details].UnitPrice) AS AvgPrice
FROM [Order Details]
WHERE [Order Details].OrderID = '10248'
```

The average unit price for the order 10248 is 19.5333.

If you omit the ALL or DISTINCT predicate, T-SQL defaults to ALL. In this case, all the records are included in the calculation. The DISTINCT keyword limits the calculation to unique values.

COUNT(ALL | DISTINCT DOMAIN)

The Count() function returns the number of non-Null values in a set of values. The following statement returns the number of orders in the Orders table, which happens to be 830.

```
USE Northwind
SELECT Count(Orders.OrderID)
FROM Orders
```

The WHERE clause in the following statement limits the count to a particular customer. The following statement returns the value 5.

```
USE Northwind
SELECT Count(Orders.OrderID)
FROM Orders
WHERE CustomerID = 'VINET'
```

If you omit the ALL or DISTINCT predicate, T-SQL defaults to ALL. In this case, all the records are included in the calculation. The DISTINCT keyword limits the calculation to unique values.

COUNT(*)

This form of the Count() function counts the total number of rows. The result of a similar Count(domain) and Count(*) function can be the same. For instance, a quick count of the rows in the Employees table tells us there are nine employee records:

```
USE Northwind
SELECT Count(*)
FROM Employees
```

If you specify a count of the Region field, you find that only five employees have a geographical region listed:

```
USE Northwind
SELECT Count(Employees.Region)
FROM Employees
```

SUM(ALL | DISTINCT DOMAIN)

The Sum() function adds all the values in a set of values. For instance, the following statement returns the total unit price sum of all the orders, 56500.91, although business-wise, it doesn't make much sense to do so.

```
USE Northwind
SELECT Sum([Order Details].UnitPrice)
FROM [Order Details]
```

If you omit the ALL or DISTINCT predicate, T-SQL defaults to ALL. In this case, all the records are included in the calculation. The DISTINCT keyword limits the calculation to unique values.

MIN(DOMAIN)

The Min() function returns the smallest value in a set of records. The following statement returns the minimum unit price, 2.50.

```
USE Northwind
SELECT Min(Products.UnitPrice)
FROM Products
```

The following statement limits the search to only those products that are in a particular category—the resulting value is 4.50.

```
USE Northwind
SELECT Min(Products.UnitPrice)
FROM Products
WHERE CategoryID = '1'
```

MAX(DOMAIN)

The Max() function is similar to the Min() function, except it returns the largest value in a set of records. The following statement returns the maximum unit price value, which is 263.50.

```
USE Northwind
SELECT Max(Products.UnitPrice)
FROM Products
```

To find the highest-priced product in a particular category, use the following statement, which returns the value 43.90.

```
USE Northwind
SELECT Max(Products.UnitPrice)
FROM Products
WHERE CategoryID = '2'
```

STDEV(DOMAIN)

The StDev() function estimates the standard deviation for a set of records. The following statement returns the standard deviation for freight, which is 44.41, in the region represented by the value 'RJ'.

```
USE Northwind
SELECT StDev(Orders.Freight)
FROM Orders
WHERE ShipRegion = 'RJ'
```

StDevP(DOMAIN)

The StDevP() function evaluates the standard deviation for a population for a set of records. The following statement returns the standard deviation for population for freight, which is 43.75 in the region represented by the value 'RJ'.

```
USE Northwind
SELECT StDevP(Orders.Freight)
FROM Orders
WHERE ShipRegion = 'RJ'
```

Var(DOMAIN)

The Var() function estimates variance. The following statement estimates the variance for freight, which is 1971.85 on orders shipped to the region represented by the value 'RJ'.

```
USE Northwind
SELECT Var(Orders.Freight)
FROM Orders
WHERE ShipRegion = 'RJ'
```

VarP(DOMAIN)

The VarP() function evaluates the variance by population. The following statement evaluates the variance across the population for the freight, which is 1913.86 shipped to the region represented by the value 'RJ'.

```
USE Northwind
SELECT VarP(Orders.Freight)
FROM Orders
WHERE ShipRegion = 'RJ'
```

Migrating from Access to SQL Server

No doubt, both Access and SQL Server developers find themselves migrating an occasional Access database to SQL Server. Chapter 9 provides some hints for using the Upsizing Wizard in Access to do so. In this section, we'll offer some advice from the SQL Server side of the task. Basically, you're looking at a three-step process:

1. Create a working version of the application for SQL Server—the Upsizing Wizard in Access can help with this step.
2. Optimize the database for the client/server environment.
3. Optimize the database structure.

WHAT THE WIZARD CAN'T DO—MOVING THE FRONT END

SQL Server lacks a graphical interface environment, so you'll have to find some way to migrate the Access forms and reports or re-create them. Most likely, you'll convert the existing objects in another environment, such as Visual Basic or Active Server Pages (ASP) if you're creating a web application. The truth is, there's really nothing wrong with using Access as your front end.

The biggest challenge will probably be with an older Access database. If that file uses DAO, you must convert your DAO-based code to ActiveX Data Objects (ADO).

NOTE *You'll find a white paper on the subject of migrating from DAO to ADO at* `http://msdn.microsoft` `.com/library/default.asp?url=/library/en-us/dndao/html/daotoadoupdate.asp`.

Access forms and reports are usually based on a query or a `SELECT` statement by way of the form's Record Source property. (See Chapter 9 for more information on using SQL to specify an object's data source.) SQL Server will need a view or stored procedure to replace that query or SQL statement. An upsized form or report will return an error if any of the following is the case:

◆ A control refers to a parameter query. You must replace the reference with a stored procedure.

◆ A `WHERE` clause or a `SELECT` statement refers to a control. Try using the form's InputParameters property.

◆ Jet queries reference only the underlying data source's fields. SQL Server's T-SQL includes the data source, in the form `[tablename].[columnname]`. (The brackets are optional unless the name contains a space character.) Update all references to include the data source.

OPTIMIZING THE CLIENT/SERVER ENVIRONMENT

Once you have a working application with all the pieces in tact, you should optimize the SQL Server database application for the client/server environment. The following are a few guidelines that should improve performance across the network:

◆ Change Recordset object types to Snapshot if no updating is involved.

◆ Use pass-through queries when possible.

◆ Create local lookup tables for data that doesn't change, such as states, countries, and so on.

◆ Retrieve the smallest amounts of data possible.

OPTIMIZING THE STRUCTURE

SQL Server provides several graphical interface tools that can help you improve the database's structure. Once you've got the database application running smoothly in the client/server environment, consider testing the following and making the necessary improvements:

◆ Use SQL Profiler to record server activity in a trace file (`.trc`). Review it regularly to get an idea of what's going on behind the scenes that could possibly slow things down, such as errors, redundant objects, and so on.

◆ Review the Index Tuning Wizard for suggestions on more efficient index structure.

Executing T-SQL in Code

You can connect to a SQL Server database in several ways. When the connection involves a web page, you'll find the Command object superior to the Connection object. Chapter 9 contains a section on both the Connection and the Command ADO objects. The object is virtually the same for T-SQL and SQL Server. Refer to the "Executing Jet SQL in Code" section for a short introduction to these two objects. Chapter 10 provides a more thorough discussion.

TIP   *There's almost no way you can choose SQL Server and not eventually commit to learning ADO.NET. Right now, the .NET environment supports ADO, but who knows how long that will last? On the other hand, ADO.NET has a lot to offer, and it's worth at least looking into. For an introduction to ADO.NET, see Chapter 15.*

Connection Options

All the Dreamweaver MX supported languages will connect to a SQL Server 2000 database if you have the appropriate driver, with the exception of Hypertext Preprocessor (PHP). Your licensed copy of SQL Server 2000 is all you really need—the drivers should all be present. You can use ODBC or OLE DB with ASP, ASP.NET, or even ADO.NET to interact with a SQL Server database.

TIP   *For more specific information on connection options, see Chapter 10.*

Summary

You've just opened the box. SQL Server 2000 is one of the most advanced and efficient systems on the market, and we've just scratched the service. It can take months of intensive study and practice to reach a competent level of expertise with SQL Server 2000. But if you understand relational database theory and SQL, Dreamweaver MX can make quick work of the web development process. If you have the financial and personnel resources to support it, SQL Server definitely won't disappoint you in performance or functionality. On the other hand, if you've a small budget and few resources to call upon, you might want to consider Microsoft Access or MySQL. In the next chapter, we review Access 2002. You can learn more about MySQL in Chapter 7.

Chapter 9

Microsoft Access and the Web

MICROSOFT ACCESS IS THE most popular desktop database on the market. In fact, developers successfully push Access over the desktop edge—where no other desktop database dare go—to compete with the big boys—SQL Server, Oracle, and the rest. Despite the tricks Access can perform when exploited, keep in mind when choosing a database to support a website that Access wasn't designed to be a database server. On the other hand, if your application already exists in Access and it's currently getting the job done without user complaints about performance or stability, the chances are your Access application will make the switch to web application. In this chapter, we'll tell you what Access can handle, and what it can't, in the way of web support.

This chapter covers the following topics:

- ◆ The Access package
- ◆ Web support
- ◆ Jet datatypes
- ◆ Built-in functions
- ◆ Jet SQL
- ◆ Upsizing an Access database to SQL Server
- ◆ Connection options

The Access Package

Access has always been available as a stand-alone product. It's also available with Office. There are four versions of Office 2002, but only Office 2002 Professional and Office 2002 Developer include Access 2002. (Access isn't available for the Macintosh.)

Microsoft recommends that you run Office 2002 on Windows XP Professional, on a system with a Pentium III processor and at least 128MB of RAM. The Office 2002 (and Access 2002) minimum requirements are listed in Table 9.1. Except for the minimum hard disk space, the minimum requirements for Office 2002 and Access 2002 are identical.

TABLE 9.1: OFFICE 2002 (AND ACCESS 2002) REQUIREMENTS

REQUIREMENT	MINIMUM
Computer/Processor	Pentium 133MHz or higher processor
Operating System	Windows 98, Windows 98 Second Edition, Windows Millennium Edition (Windows Me), Windows NT 4 with Service Pack 6 (SP6) or later, Windows 2000, or Windows XP or later
Memory	All the following require an additional 8MB of RAM for each Office program running simultaneously:
	Windows 98: 24MB of RAM
	Windows 98 Second Edition: 24MB of RAM
	Windows Me: 32MB of RAM
	Microsoft Windows NT: 32MB of RAM
	Windows 2000 Professional: 64MB of RAM
	Windows XP Professional: 128MB of RAM
	Windows XP Home Edition: 128MB of RAM
Hard Disk	Office 2002 Standard: 210MB of available hard disk space
	Office 2002 Professional: 245MB of available hard disk space
	Professional Special Edition: 245MB of available hard disk space
	An additional 115MB is required on the hard disk where the operating system is installed.
	Stand-alone version of Access requires 170MB of hard disk space.
	Users without Windows XP, Windows 2000, Windows Me, or Office 2000 Service Release 1 (SR-1) require an extra 50MB of hard disk space for System Files Update.
Drive	CD-ROM drive
Display	Super VGA (800 × 600) or higher-resolution monitor with 256 colors
Peripherals	Microsoft Mouse, Microsoft IntelliMouse, or compatible pointing device

Web Support

We're changing the way we do business, and to Microsoft's credit, Access 2002 offers several data-integrating features. Most likely, Access will never be the web-support database of choice, but now, even the novice can get the job done using the following features:

◆ Using Access projects, you can access a SQL Server database.

◆ Data access pages are a quick solution for interacting with a database via a web browser.

♦ Access 2002's support for XML makes transferring data with non-Access systems easier than ever.

♦ Web components display dynamic data quickly.

In the next section, we'll explore built-in features that make Access web solutions easier than they've ever been.

Access Projects—SQL Server Desktop

Access projects use the OLE DB architecture to combine Access objects and the SQL Server engine. The result is SQL Server Desktop—SQL Server's power and efficiency in Access's easy-to-use interface. All database objects—forms, reports, data access pages, macros, and modules—are code-based or HTML-based. That makes these objects extremely easy to publish to the web.

NOTE   *OLE DB is a quick and efficient means to getting the data you want—regardless of its format—via network connections. For more information on OLE DB, see Chapter 10.*

An Access project (an ADP file) is a simple container for database objects. The tables are SQL Server tables and are stored on SQL Server. Although these objects all look familiar to their Access counterparts, they offer more options. To illustrate some of these differences, Table 9.2 compares Access 2002 table properties to those in a project, and Table 9.3 compares Jet and Transact-SQL (T-SQL) datatypes—ADP files use T-SQL, not Jet.

TABLE 9.2: COMPARISON OF ACCESS 2002 AND PROJECT TABLE PROPERTIES

ACCESS PROJECT	ACCESS 2002	DESCRIPTION
Column Name	Field Name	The field or column name.
Datatype and Field Size	Datatype	Specifies the column's datatype. Projects combine this property with Field Size for numeric datatypes.
Description	Description	Text that describes a column's purpose.
Length	Field Size	In Access, this property determines the size of a numeric or text datatype. Determines the size of a text or character field in a project.
Allow Nulls	Required	In Access, set the property to No to allow null values. When selected in a project, this property allows null values.
Default Value	Default Value	Enter a specific value for new records.
Scale	No equivalent property	Specifies the total number of digits for a value's decimal portion.
Precision	No equivalent property	Determines the total number of digits in a column.

Continued on next page

TABLE 9.2: COMPARISON OF ACCESS 2002 AND PROJECT TABLE PROPERTIES *(continued)*

ACCESS PROJECT	ACCESS 2002	DESCRIPTION
Identity	No equivalent property; use AutoNumber datatype	Returns a unique value for each record.
Identity Seed	No equivalent property at table level	Sets the first value for an Identity column.
Identity Increment	No equivalent property at table level	Determines the incremental value between each Identity value in a column.
Is RowGridRowGuid	No equivalent property, use AutoNumber datatype	Specifies that the row contain a GUID (globally unique identifier).
Formula	No equivalent property	Supplies an expression for a computed column.
Collation	No equivalent property	Sets the sorting order for a character column.
Format	Format	Sets column's display attributes.
Decimal Places	Decimal Places	Number of digits that follow the decimal point (from 0 to 6). The result affects display only.
Input Mask	Input Mask	Enters code that displays formatting during input.

TABLE 9.3: JET AND SQL SERVER (ACCESS PROJECT) DATATYPES

ACCESS PROJECT	JET	DESCRIPTION
text	Text	Stores any characters; limited to 2.14GB.
tinyint	Number, Byte	An integer value between 0 and 255.
smallint	Number, Integer	A short integer between -2^{15} and $2^{15}-1$.
int	Number, Long	A long integer between -2^{31} and $2^{31}-1$.
real	Number, Single	A single-precision floating-point value between $-3.40E+38$ and $3.40E+38$.
float	Number, Double	A double-precision floating-point value between $-1.79E+308$ and $1.79E+308$.
decimal	Number, Decimal	An exact numeric datatype that stores values between -10^{-28} and $10^{-28}-1$.
counter, autoincrement	AutoNumber	A long integer between $-2,147,483,648$ and $2,147,483,647$.
datetime	Date/Time	A valid time or date. Jet year values must be from 100 through 9999. Project year values are 1753 through 9999.

Continued on next page

TABLE 9.3: Jet and SQL Server (Access Project) Datatypes *(continued)*

Access Project	Jet	Description
bit	Yes/No	Integers 0 and 1 only (yes/no; true/false).
money	Currency	A scaled integer between -2^{63} and $2^{63}-1$.
image	OLE Object	Picture or object; limited to 2.14GB.
None	Hyperlink	An e-mail or website address.

Access projects are a great bonus in the following situations:

Limited financial resources   SQL Server Desktop is free with any version of Access.

Growing businesses   Projects are more stable and faster than the Jet database equivalent (MDB files).

Training needs   Becoming familiar with SQL Server Desktop projects may be the easiest way to learn SQL Server.

Licensing   You can avoid SQL Server licensing issues by installing a SQL Server runtime solution via a project.

Development environment   Projects provide a convenient testing and development platform for SQL Server.

The down side is that projects are limited to five concurrent users because Microsoft deliberately limits the number of processes. In addition, a project is limited to just 2GB of data (minus the system tables). This limitation is the same as an Access database. You get stability and new features—especially of interest to the web developer are the forms and reports, which are all HTML-based objects—but you're limited in the number of users and file size.

CONCURRENT USERS VERSUS CONCURRENT CONNECTIONS

Despite what you may have heard, you can use Access to support a data-driven website. In fact, Microsoft insists that Access can handle 255 concurrent connections. You can find more information on this assertion at http://msdn.microsoft.com/library/backgrnd/html/acmsdeop.htm.

On the flip side, many developers will warn you to steer clear of Access altogether. The real trick to using Access successfully in a multiuser environment is to understand the difference between concurrent user and concurrent connection.

A *concurrent connection* is a processed request—an action. A *concurrent user* is simply a user that's connected to the database. The concurrent user may consume none or several connections. An application that opens connections only as needed and then closes those connections as soon as the request is completed can consume just a few concurrent connections although those connections can support many concurrent users.

Here's our recommendation: if your website incurs a limited number of hits and the database is small, use an Access project instead of an Access MDB file. Your business may very well outgrow Access. When that happens, your Access project application will be much easier to upsize to SQL Server than an Access MDB application.

Data Access Pages (DAP)

Suppose you've got an Access application that runs well and efficiently. Then, you're asked to produce a prototype of a web application based on the existing application. Before you pull out the want ads and start job hunting, take a look at Data Access Pages (DAP). This relatively new technology saves an ordinary Access object as a DHTML (Dynamic HTML) file. The result is a browser-ready file that's ready to interact with your database. We can say a number of good things about DAP:

◆ You can save an existing object as a DAP, or you can build one from scratch. Either way, the Access Page Designer generates all the script for you.

◆ The client PC doesn't need Access to view a DAP.

◆ DAP can interact with a SQL Server database.

◆ You don't need Office 2002 Developer to distribute a runtime version of a DAP.

Unfortunately, the technology is demanding in other ways, which makes a DAP-based web solution a poor choice except for prototyping and for intranets:

◆ DAPs aren't cross-browser compatible. That means the viewer must be using Internet Explorer 5 or later.

◆ DAPs run only on Microsoft server technology—IIS 4.0 or later, to be exact.

◆ The script generated and used to display the page and interact with the linked database is difficult to modify—we don't recommend you even try unless you're knowledgeable in the area. Frankly, if you have that much knowledge, you're probably not going to rely on DAP technology.

◆ DAPs don't support subforms or subreports, although you can re-create the relationship using the Relationships Wizard.

◆ DAPs based on an existing form or report don't support the original object's event procedures. You must rewrite these procedures using the Microsoft Script Editor.

Here's our recommendation: a successful website must cater to as many technologies as possible, and DAPs don't cater to anything except Microsoft. That isn't necessarily bad. To the contrary, a tool that allows a novice to quickly build an interactive website is impressive. However, that's exactly what Dreamweaver MX does—without the restrictions imposed by a DAP. Don't even try to interact with DAP using Dreamweaver MX—create your pages from scratch using Dreamweaver MX and forget DAP.

Office Web Components (OWC)

Office Web Components (OWC) are ActiveX controls, and they're new to Access 2002. You'll use these controls—PivotTables and PivotCharts—to display data in an Access form. In addition, you can save a web component view as a DAP, which means you can also view these controls via a web browser. Unfortunately, web components are as restrictive as DAP technology. All the limitations we mentioned earlier for DAP also apply to web components—but it gets worse:

◆ The client PC must have a license for Microsoft Office 2002 to interact with a web component.

◆ The client with OWC installed but no Office 2002 license can view but not interact with the data.

◆ The client with neither OWC nor an Office 2002 license sees nothing.

Here's our recommendation: don't try to use OWC controls in Dreamweaver MX. There's no reason to—Dreamweaver MX controls are far superior to OWC.

Extensible Markup Language (XML)

Access 2002 supports Extensible Markup Language (XML), a platform-independent markup language.

You can use XML to publish interactive data on the web. More to the point, XML's main purpose is to ease the task of generating and reading data. Although XML is a web technology, it's quickly becoming the data-sharing technology standard—especially for systems that aren't connected and can't communicate with one another.

For the most part, you'll rely on SQL and data-specific features to retrieve, insert, delete, and modify data via a web browser when you're dealing with a live connection. However, you can increase performance by limiting those active connections when possible. When working with data that rarely changes, you can save data to XML format and then display that data via an associated Extensible Stylesheet Language (XSL) file. (An XSL file serves as a template for transforming data from one format to another.)

These XML data documents can be run from the server or the client and viewed on almost any browser that supports HTML 4. As needed, your web application can retrieve the XML document instead of hitting the server to process another data request. The resulting page is almost immediate.

Not only does XML share data—Access 2002 also imports and exports schema. Consequently, you can share an application's structure as well as the data it stores. You can create an entire relational database by importing an Extensible Schema Document. Developers can create entire relational databases or parts of databases simply by importing an XSD schema from the web.

Here's our recommendation: more than likely, you won't encounter XML files when using Dreamweaver MX since XML is a tool for transferring and sharing data, not accessing live data. We've included this short section because Access 2002 supports the technology.

Jet Datatypes

Datatypes are an integral part of every application, and a web application is no exception. It's vital that you understand the datatypes used in the Access database that's driving your website, and that you understand how your website will be impacted by those choices.

There are four types of Access datatypes (and this is typical of most RDBMSs):

Text   String data can be composed of almost any set of characters. The important thing to remember is that string data doesn't respond to any type of arithmetic operators.

Numeric   There are several numeric datatypes, and all store data with some type of number characteristic, meaning that the data can be interpreted by an arithmetic equation.

OLE Object   An OLE Object is a picture or an object. The picture or object can contain text or numeric values, but Access doesn't interpret them as such. Access sees only the larger container—that being the picture or object.

Hyperlink   This datatype is similar to text, but contains a web address or an e-mail address and has special linking properties. Some might put Hyperlink in the Text category.

Table 9.4 lists the many Jet datatypes and compares them to Access project datatypes. Use the Jet equivalent when creating and manipulating tables and fields using SQL. Keep in mind that comparable datatypes may not be exactly the same. Some may accommodate smaller or larger numbers of characters, require more or less memory, and so on. We're simply noting the datatypes that are the closest and that you'll most likely choose for the same types of data.

TABLE 9.4: ACCESS, SQL JET, AND PROJECT DATATYPES

ACCESS DATATYPE	DESCRIPTION	ACCESS PROJECT	JET EQUIVALENT
Text	Stores up to 255 characters.	VarChar, NvarChar	TEXT
Memo	Stores up to 65,536 characters.	Text	LONGTEXT
OLE Object	Stores pictures or objects up to 2.14GB. Use this datatype when storing documents or large amounts of formatted text.	Image	LONGBINARY
Yes/No	Integers 1 and 0 only (yes/no; true/false).	Bit	BIT*
Number: FieldSize = Byte	Any integer value between 0 and 255.	TinyInt	BYTE, TINYINT**
Number: FieldSize = Integer	A short integer between -2^{15} and $2^{15}-1$.	Short, SmallInt	SHORT
Number: FieldSize = Long	A long integer between -2^{31} and $2^{31}-1$.	Long, Int	LONG
Number: FieldSize = Single	A single-precision floating-point value from −3.40E+38 through 3.40E+38.	Single, Real	SINGLE
Number: FieldSize = Double	A double-precision floating-point value from −1.79E+308 through 1.79E+308.	Double, Float	DOUBLE
Decimal	An exact numeric type that stores values from -10^{-28} through $1^{-28}-1$.	Decimal, Numeric	DECIMAL**
Date/Time	A valid time or date. Jet supports dates from the year 100 through 9999.	DateTime, SmallDateTime	DATETIME

Continued on next page

TABLE 9.4: ACCESS, SQL JET, AND PROJECT DATATYPES *(continued)*

ACCESS DATATYPE	DESCRIPTION	ACCESS PROJECT	JET EQUIVALENT
Currency	A scaled integer between -2^{63} through $2^{63}-1$. A Currency field is accurate to 15 digits to the left of the decimal point and 4 digits to the right. Use Currency to prevent rounding errors.	Money, SmallMoney	CURRENCY, MONEY, SMALLMONEY**
AutoNumber: FieldSize = Long Integer	A long integer between $-2,147,483,648$ and $2,147,483,647$	Int (defined as Identity)	COUNTER, AUTOINCREMENT
Hyperlink	An e-mail or website address.	Char, NChar, VarChar, NVarChar (defined as Hyperlink)	LONGTEXT***
Number: FieldSize = ReplicationID	Globally unique identifier (GUID).	UniqueIdentifier	GUID

*Microsoft documentation recognizes the Jet SQL reserved word BOOLEAN, but tests from the SQL window and ADO code both failed.

**The following aren't available via the SQL window; they require ADO code: TinyInt, Decimal, SmallMoney.

***LONGTEXT creates a Memo, not a Hyperlink; currently, there isn't a Jet SQL Hyperlink equivalent.

NOTE *Access sorts on only the first 255 characters of a Memo field.*

CHOOSING THE CORRECT DATATYPE

One thing most RDBMSs have is plenty of datatypes from which to choose. If you're in doubt as to which datatype is the most efficient and accurate for your data, answering the following questions should help you decide:

◆ Will you use the data in any mathematical equations? If so, you definitely need a numeric datatype.

◆ How much storage space is required? If text data is large, it may require a memo field instead of a plain text field.

◆ Will you want to sort or index the field? You can sort and index both text and numeric values, but you can't sort or index an OLE Object field. Nor can you group on an OLE Object field.

◆ Should data sort as numeric or text values? For instance, the numeric values 1, 2, 3, 10, 100, and 200 will sort differently, depending on the datatype. When defined as a numeric datatype, the values sort as 1, 2, 3, 10, 100, and 200. When stored in a text field, these values sort alphanumerically as 10, 100, 2, 200, and 3.

Built-in Functions

Functions are predefined code that performs specific tasks or calculations. Often, you "plug in" values that interact with the function. For instance, the Sum() function has a predefined task—it adds the values you specify or reference. The arguments can be a literal value, a field or variable reference, or an expression that evaluates to one of the former.

Access supports two types of functions: built-in and user-defined. The built-in functions are predefined and come with Access. By predefined, we mean you can't alter or customize their purpose.

As a developer, you can create user-defined functions to accomplish unique tasks for specific applications. You'll use functions in criteria expressions (queries), calculated controls, VBA procedures, and SQL statements.

The main thing to remember about both types of functions is that both return a value instead of its name. You supply the function and any arguments it needs, but the function returns only the resulting value. For instance, if you execute a function via the Visual Basic Editor's (VBE) Immediate window, VBA returns only the results of the function, not the function itself, as shown in Figure 9.1. We used the Asc function to return the ASCII value of the lowercase letter *c*, which is 99.

NOTE   Throughout this section, we refer to both Access native (built-in) and Access project functions. In this context, Access project functions are the same as native SQL Server functions. Both Access native and native SQL Server functions can be available to you in an Access project. When working with a front-end object, such as a form or a report, use the native Access functions. When executing stored procedures, you must use the native SQL Server (and T-SQL) functions.

FIGURE 9.1

The Asc function returns only the resulting value.

A comprehensive discussion of all the built-in functions or how to create a user-defined function is beyond the scope of this chapter. However, it's worth mentioning that the built-in functions come in several categories:

- String manipulation
- Conversion
- Date
- Mathematical
- Financial

The following sections list many Access/VBA functions and their Access project equivalents, but the examples are of the native Access functions. For more specific examples of functions for an Access project file, see Chapter 8; SQL Server and Project built-in functions are the same.

String Functions

A String function performs some type of process on a string variable, field, or value. When passing a literal string to the function, you must enclose the string in double-quotation delimiters in the form `"string"`. The Access Project (T-SQL) equivalent delimiters are the single quotation mark—`'string'`.

ASC("CHARACTER")

Returns an Integer—the ANSI numeric value of a passed string argument. The Access Project/T-SQL equivalent is `ASCII('character')`. For example, the following function returns the ASCII value of 97 for the lowercase letter `"a"`:

```
=Asc("a")
```

CHR$(VALUE)

Returns a value's corresponding ANSI value. `CHAR(value)` is the Access Project equivalent/T-SQL equivalent. The following function returns the lowercase character `"a"`, which is the ANSI equivalent of the letter 97:

```
=Chr(97)
```

LCASE$("STRING")

Returns the lowercase equivalent of a passed string. `LOWER('string')` is the Access Project equivalent. The following statement returns `"abc"`:

```
LCase("ABC")
```

LEN("STRING")

Returns a long integer that represents the number of characters in a passed string. `DATALENGTH('string')` is the Access Project equivalent. The following statement returns the value 3 as a long integer:

```
Len("abc")
```

LEFT("STRING",NUMBER)

Returns a parsed string of a determined length as specified by the number argument and beginning at the passed string's leftmost character. The Access Project equivalent is `LEFT('string',number)`. The following function returns the string `"ab"`:

```
Left("abc",2)
```

LTRIM$("STRING")

Removes leading spaces from a passed string and returns just the string. The Access Project equivalent is `LTRIM('string')`. The following function returns the string `"abc"`.

```
LTrim$(" abc")
```

MID$("STRING",BEGIN,NUMBER)

Returns a specified number of characters from a passed string, as determined by the number argument, beginning at the position represented by the begin argument. The Access Project equivalent is SUBSTRING('string',begin,number). The following function returns the string "bcd":

```
Mid$("abcde",2,3)
```

RIGHT$("STRING",NUMBER)

Returns a specific number of characters from a passed string, specified by the number argument and beginning with the rightmost character. The Access Project equivalent is RIGHT('string',number). The following statement returns the string "de":

```
Right$("abcde",2)
```

RTRIM$("STRING")

Removes trailing spaces from a string and returns the passed string, excluding any trailing space characters. The Access Project equivalent is SPACE('string'). The following function removes the trailing spaces and returns just the string "abcde".

```
RTrim$("abcde     ")
```

SPACE$(VALUE)

Returns a specific number of space characters. The Access Project equivalent is SPACE(value). The following function returns the string "   " (which consists of three space characters):

```
Space$(3)
```

STR$(VALUE)

Converts the values of any numeric datatype to a string. The Access Project equivalent is STR(value). The following function returns the string value "123":

```
Str$(123)
```

STRCOMP("STRING1","STRING2")

Compares two strings and returns the result, either 0 or −1 as an integer. The Access Project equivalents are the SOUNDEX() and DIFFERENCE() functions. Although they're not interchangeable with StrComp, they're similar. The following function returns −1 because the two strings aren't identical:

```
StrComp("susan","suzanne")
```

UCASE$("STRING")

Returns the passed string in uppercase letters. The Access Project equivalents are UCASE('string') and UPPER('string'). The following function returns the string "ABCDE":

```
UCase$("abcde")
```

REPLACE("STRING","SUBSTRING","NEW")

Replaces occurrences of a substring in a target string with a new string. (There is no Access Project equivalent.) The following function returns the string `"black"`:

```
Replace("block","o","a")
```

SPLIT("STRING",DELIMITER)

Returns a one-dimensional array of substrings from the passed string, in which each substring consists of the characters that occur between each specified delimiter. If the delimiter is omitted, the space character is assumed. The example code returns each substring, the result of the `Split` function, in the Immediate window. For instance, if `"string"` equals the string `"Susan Harkins"`, and the delimiter is the space character, the code returns the two substrings, `"Susan"` and `"Harkins"`:

```
Dim a As Variant
Dim i As Integer
a = Split("string","delimiter")
For i = 0 To UBound(a)
    Debug.Print a(i)
Next i
```

STRREVERSE("STRING")

Reverses a passed string. The Access Project equivalent is `REVERSE('string')`. The following function returns the string `"edcba"`:

```
StrReverse("abcde")
```

VAL("STRING")

Returns the numeric value of *string*. There is no Access Project equivalent, but `CAST('string' AS datatype)` is close. The following function returns the value 123:

```
Val("123abc")
```

Conversion Functions

Conversion functions change a passed argument's datatype. They're tricky to work with because not all datatypes should be converted, so make sure you fully understand the implications of a conversion before applying it.

CBOOL(VALUE)

Converts any numeric or string value to a Boolean datatype. If the expression is 0, the result is False; any other value returns True. The Access Project function `CONVERT(bit,value)` isn't exactly the same, but it's close. For instance, the following procedure returns False if the passed value equals 0, but True when the passed value is any other value:

```
Function TestBoo(val As Variant)
    TestBoo = CBool(val)
    Debug.Print TestBoo
End Function
```

CBYTE(VALUE)

Converts a numeric value to the byte datatype. The passed value must be a value from 0 to 255; otherwise, the function returns an error. Use CONVERT(*tinyint,value*) in an Access Project. The following procedure returns the appropriate datatype of byte in the Immediate window only when the passed value is an appropriate value; otherwise, it returns an error message:

```
Function TestByte(val As Variant)
    TestByte = CByte(val)
    Debug.Print TypeName(TestByte)
End Function
```

CCUR(VALUE)

Converts a numeric or string value to the currency datatype. The following procedure returns the appropriate datatype of currency in the Immediate window if the passed value is also an appropriate currency value:

```
Function TestCurrency(val As Variant)
    TestCurrency = CCur(val)
    Debug.Print TypeName(TestCurrency)
End Function
```

The Access Project equivalent is CONVERT(*money,value*).

CDBL(VALUE)

Converts a numeric value to the double datatype. If the value equals 37,950, the following function returns the date 11/25/2003.

```
Function TestDate(val As Variant)
    TestDate = CDate(val)
    Debug.Print TypeName(TestDate)
End Function
```

The Access Project equivalent is CONVERT(*float,value*).

NZ(VARIANT,VALUEIFNULL)

Converts a Null value to 0, to a zero-length string, or to some other specified string value. There's no Access Project equivalent. An expression always returns Null if even one of the operands is Null. The following expression produces an error if either variant1 or variant2 is Null:

```
var = variant1 + variant2
```

To avoid the error, wrap both in an Nz() function as follows:

```
var = Nz(variant1) + Nz(variant2)
```

CINT(VALUE)

Converts a numeric value to the integer datatype. The following procedure returns the appropriate datatype of integer in the Immediate window if the passed value is also an appropriate integer value:

```
Function TestInt(val As Variant)
```

```
        TestInt = CInt(val)
        Debug.Print TypeName(TestInt)
    End Function
```

The Access Project equivalent is CONVERT(*smallint,value*).

CLNG(VALUE)

Converts a numeric value to the long integer datatype. The following procedure returns the appropriate datatype of long integer in the Immediate window if the passed value is also an appropriate long integer value:

```
    Function TestLng(val As Variant)
        TestLng = CLng(val)
        Debug.Print TypeName(TestLng)
    End Function
```

The Access Project equivalent is CONVERT(*int,value*).

CSNG(VALUE)

Converts a numeric value to the single datatype. The following procedure returns the appropriate datatype of single in the Immediate window if the passed value is also an appropriate single-precision value:

```
    Function TestSng(val As Variant)
        TestSng = CSng(val)
        Debug.Print TypeName(TestSng)
    End Function
```

The Access Project equivalent is CONVERT(*real,value*).

CSTR(VALUE)

Converts a variant value to the string datatype. The following procedure returns the appropriate datatype of string in the Immediate window if the passed value is also an appropriate string value:

```
    Function TestStr(val As Variant)
        TestStr = CStr(val)
        Debug.Print TypeName(TestStr)
    End Function
```

The Access Project equivalent is CONVERT(*varchar,value*).

CDATE(VALUE)

Converts a numeric value to a date value. The following procedure returns the appropriate datatype of date in the Immediate window if the passed value is also an appropriate date value:

```
    Function TestDouble(val As Variant)
        TestDouble = CDbl(val)
        Debug.Print TypeName(TestDouble)
    End Function
```

The Access Project equivalent is CONVERT(*datetime,x*).

Date Functions

Date functions use date arithmetic or serial values in their calculations. Fortunately, Access has a wide time period that it supports, from January 1, 100, to December 31, 9999. Each serial value represents a specific moment on any given day in the time period. For instance, the serial value for January 1, 100, is −657434, and the serial value for December 31, 9999, is 2958101. December 30, 1899, is known as an anchor date and has a serial value of 0. Any date that follows the anchor is a positive value; dates falling before the anchor are negative values.

Several Date functions accept an argument that denotes a specific interval. Table 9.5 lists and describes the constants that this argument accepts in Access and in an Access Project.

TABLE 9.5: INTERVAL OPTIONS FOR SOME DATE FUNCTIONS

ACCESS	ACCESS PROJECT	DESCRIPTION
yyyy	yyyy, yy, year	Returns a valid 4-digit year value
y	y	Returns a value between 1 and 365, representing the date's position within the calendar year—between January 1 and December 31
m	mm, m, month	Returns the month as a value between 1 and 12
q	qq, q, quarter	Returns a value 1 through 4, denoting the quarter of the year
d	dd, d, day	Denotes day as a value between 1 and 31
w	dw	Denotes position of day within the week; a value between 1 and 7
ww	ww, wk	Returns a value between 1 and 52, which represents the week of the year that the date falls within
h	hh, hour	Denotes hours as a value between 1 and 23
n	mi, n, minute	Denotes minutes as a value between 1 and 59
s	ss, s, second	Denotes seconds as a value between 1 and 59

DATE()

Returns the current system date and time as a string or variant value. The following function accepts no arguments and always returns the current date:

```
Date()
```

The Access Project equivalent is GETDATE().

DATEADD("DATEPART",INTERVAL,#DATE#)

Adds a specific number of intervals, which can be days, weeks, months, or years, to a specified date and returns the resulting date as a variant. The following function adds three days to August 19, 2002, and returns August 22, 2002:

```
DateAdd("d",3,#8/19/2002#)
```

The Access Project equivalent is DATEADD("*datepart*", *interval*, '*date*').

DATEDIFF("DATEPART",INTERVAL,#DATE#)

The returned integer value represents the difference between two dates in days, weeks, months, or years. The following function returns the difference between the two dates of August 22, 2002, and August 19, 2002—which is –3:

```
DateDiff("d",#8/22/2002#,#8/19/2002#)
```

The result is a negative value because the function expresses the greater date first, implying the subtraction necessary to compute the dates. If you reverse the order of the dates, the function returns 3. The Access Project equivalent is DATEDIFF("*datepart*", *interval*, '*date*').

DATEPART("DATEPART",#DATE#)

Returns an integer, the specified part of a date, such as a day, month, year, or day of the week. The following function returns the value 22, the day component of the specified date:

```
DatePart("d",#8/22/2002#)
```

The Access Project equivalent is DATEPART('*datepart*', '*date*').

DATESERIAL(YEAR,MONTH,DAY)

Returns a date string (variant datatype) based on the arguments. There's no Access Project equivalent. The following function returns the date string 8/22/2002:

```
DateSerial(2002,8,22)
```

DATEVALUE("DATESTRING")

Returns a date (variant datatype) based on a string. The following function returns the date string 8/22/2002:

```
DateValue(#8/22/2002#)
```

DAY(#DATE#)

Returns an integer value between 1 and 31 that represents a day of the month. The following function returns the day component 22 from the specified date:

```
Day(#8/22/2002#)
```

The Access Project equivalent is DATEPART('*dd*', '*date*').

HOUR(#DATE#)

Returns an integer value between 0 and 23 that represents an hour of the day. At 7:52 P.M., the following function returns the value 19:

```
Hour(Now)
```

The Access Project equivalent is DATEPART('*hh*', '*date*').

MINUTE(#DATE#)

Returns an integer value between 0 and 59 that represents a minute. At 7:53 P.M., the following function returns the value 53:

```
Minute(Now)
```

The Access Project equivalent is DATEPART('*mi*','*date*').

MONTH(#DATE#)

Returns an integer value between 1 and 12 that represents a month. The following function returns the value 8:

```
Month(#8/22/2002#)
```

You can substitute the actual date with the Now() function, and the function will return the value that represents the current month. The Access Project equivalent is DATEPART('*mm*','*date*').

NOW()

Returns, as a variant value, the date and time of a computer's system clock. The Access Project equivalent is GETDATE(). If the current date is August 22, 2002, the Now() function will return 8/22/2002.

SECOND(#DATE#)

Returns an integer value between 0 and 59 that represents a second. At 7:53:42 P.M., the following function returns the value 42:

```
Second(Now)
```

The Access Project equivalent is DATEPART('*ss*','*date*').

WEEKDAY(#DATE#)

Returns an integer value between 1 and 7 that represents a day of the week (1 = Sunday, 2 = Monday, and so on). The following function returns the value 5:

```
Weekday(#8/22/2002#)
```

August 22, 2002 is a Thursday, the fifth day of the week if Sunday is the first day of the week. The Access Project equivalent is DATEPART('*dw*','*date*').

YEAR(#DATE#)

Returns an integer value that represents a year. For instance, the following function returns the value 2002:

```
Year(#8/10/2002#)
```

The Access Project equivalent is DATEPART('*yy*','*date*').

TIMESERIAL(HOUR,MINUTE,SECONDS)

Returns the serial value of the time, expressed as a time string (string or variant datatype). There's no Access Project equivalent. The following time function returns the time string 5:52:43 P.M.:

```
TimeSerial(17,52,43)
```

The 17 argument represents 5 P.M. in a 24-hour clock.

TIMEVALUE("TIME")

Returns a serial value (variant datatype) that represents the time. For instance, the following function returns the time 2:24 P.M. as a time, not a string:

```
Timevalue("2:24PM")
```

The Access Project equivalent is `Timevalue('time')`.

Mathematical Functions

A Mathematical function generally performs some type of calculation that involves numeric values and mathematical operators. You supply the operands in the form of arguments, and the function processes those values within the context of its purpose.

INT(VALUE)

Returns the integer component of *value*. The following function returns just the integer portion, 345, of the value 345.67:

```
Int(345.67)
```

The Access Project equivalent is `FLOOR(value)`.

SGN(VALUE)

Returns an integer (−1, 0, or 1) that indicates *value*'s sign. The following functions return the values 1, −1, and 0, respectively:

```
Sgn(365)
Sgn(-4)
Sgn(0)
```

The Access Project equivalent is `SIGN(value)`.

RND(VALUE)

Returns a random value between 0 and 1 based on a seed value. The *seed* value determines the next random value. Think of it as a type of bookmark. For instance, the function `Rnd(value)` might return the value .01 or .9999999, or even any value between, depending on the current position of the seed value. The Access Project function, `Rand()`, also returns a random value, but behaves differently, so don't expect results to be the same.

UNDERSTANDING THE *RND()* FUNCTION

The Rnd( ) function accepts a single argument, and that argument substantially changes the results:

◆ If value is greater than 0, Rnd( ) returns the next random value in sequence, based on the seed value.

◆ If value equals 0, Rnd( ) returns the most recently generated value. That means the function repeats an already returned value.

◆ If value is less than 0, Rnd( ) returns the same value until you execute the Randomize( ) function. The Randomize( ) function resets the seed value.

Of equal importance is that a negative value resets the seed value to the previously generated random value in sequence, so be careful when using negative values with the Rnd( ) function. If you must and you don't want the impact of resetting the seed value, combine the Rnd( ) function with the Abs( ) function in the following form:

```
Rnd(Abs(value))
```

ABS(VALUE)

Returns the absolute value of *value*. ABS(*value*) is the Access Project equivalent. The following function returns the value 3:

```
Abs(-3)
```

Domain Functions

Domain functions are a subset of Mathematical functions. These functions are known as Aggregate or Domain functions. A *domain* is simply a set of records. For instance, you might want to sum or average all the values in a particular field. These functions are extremely flexible because you can specify criteria to limit the set. Don't confuse domain aggregates with SQL aggregates, which we'll review in the "Jet SQL" section later in this chapter. Domain functions don't have an Access Project equivalent—use Aggregate functions instead.

DSUM(FIELD,DOMAIN,CRITERIA)

Calculates the sum of a set of values. The following function sums the price values for all the items in the current order if txtOrderID (most likely a text box control in a form) contains the OrderID value:

```
DSum("UnitPrice","[Order Details]","OrderID = txtOrderID")
```

DCOUNT(FIELD,DOMAIN,CRITERIA)

Counts the values in a set. The following function returns the number of items (not the quantity of each) in the current order if txtOrderID (most likely a text box control in a form) contains the OrderID value:

```
DCount("OrderID","[Order Details]","OrderID = txtOrderID")
```

DStDev(FIELD,DOMAIN,CRITERIA)

Estimates the standard deviation across a set of values. The following function estimates the standard deviation for freight on orders shipped to the current shipping region in txtShipRegion:

```
DStDev("Freight","Orders","ShipRegion = txtShipRegion")
```

NOTE *You may have noticed that some of the domain references are enclosed in brackets and some aren't. Access requires the brackets only when the name in question contains a space character, as is the case with the Order Details table. Some developers enclose all references in brackets to avoid forgetting the brackets when they're required.*

DStDevP(FIELD,DOMAIN,CRITERIA)

Estimates the standard deviation across a population. To evaluate the population from the DStDev() example, use the following function:

```
DStDevP("Freight","Orders","ShipRegion = txtShipRegion")
```

DVar(FIELD,DOMAIN,CRITERIA)

Estimates variance across a set of values. The following function estimates the variance for freight on orders shipped to the current shipping region in txtShipRegion:

```
DVar("Freight","Orders","ShipRegion = txtShipRegion")
```

DVarP(FIELD,DOMAIN,CRITERIA)

Evaluates variance across a population. To evaluate the variance from the DVar() example across the population, use the following function:

```
DVarP("Freight","Orders","ShipRegion = txtShipRegion")
```

DMax(FIELD,DOMAIN,CRITERIA)

Determines the maximum value in a specified set of records. The following function returns the price for the highest-priced item in each order if txtOrderID (most likely a text box control on a form) contains the OrderID value:

```
DMax("UnitPrice","[Order Details]","OrderID = txtOrderID")
```

DMin(FIELD,DOMAIN,CRITERIA)

Determines the minimum value in a specified set of records. The following function returns the price for the lowest-priced item in each order if txtOrderID (most likely a text box control on a form) contains the OrderID value:

```
DMin("UnitPrice","[Order Details]","OrderID = txtOrderID")
```

DLookup(FIELD,DOMAIN,CRITERIA)

Finds a value in a particular field from a set of records. The following function returns the corresponding employee's name, based on the employee's identification number:

```
DLookup("LastName", "Employees", "EmployeeID = txtEmployeeID")
```

DAVG(FIELD,DOMAIN,CRITERIA)

Calculates the average in a set of values in a specified set of records. The following function returns the average price for all the items in the current order if txtOrderID (most likely a text box control in a form) contains the OrderID value:

```
DAvg("UnitPrice","[Order Details]","OrderID = txtOrderID")
```

Aggregate Functions

Aggregate Functions are similar to Domain functions in that they consider a set of records. However, you can't limit an aggregate set based on criteria. The Aggregate function names and arguments are the same in both an Access MDB file and an Access Project. It's important to remember that Aggregate functions aren't native functions; they're provided by SQL. As a result, you can't use Aggregate functions with Visual Basic for Applications (VBA). To learn more about Aggregate functions, see the "SQL Aggregate Functions" section later in this chapter.

Financial Functions

A Financial function is a highly specialized type of Mathematical function that returns financial statistics. Use the Access native functions in an Access Project; there are no comparable native SQL Server functions.

IPMT(RATE,PAYMENT,PAYMENTPERIODS,PRESENTVALUE)

Calculates the interest payment for a given period of an annuity based on periodic, constant payments and a constant interest rate. For example, the following function returns a monthly interest payment of $37.50 on a $10,000 loan over 48 months at 4.5 percent annual interest:

```
IPmt(.045/12, 1, 48, -10000)
```

PMT(RATE,PAYMENTPERIODS,PRESENTVALUE,FUTUREVALUE,TYPE)

Calculates the payment for an annuity based on periodic, constant payments and a constant interest rate. For example, the following function returns the monthly payment of $228 on a $10,000 loan over 48 months at 4.5 percent annual interest:

```
Pmt(.045/12, 48,-10000)
```

Note that *futurevalue* and *type* are optional arguments.

PPMT(RATE,PAYMENTPERIODSRANGE,PAYMENTPERIODS,PRESENTVALUE,FUTUREVALUE,TYPE)

Calculates the principal payment for a given period of an annuity based on periodic, constant payments and a constant interest rate. For example, the following function returns the monthly principal payment of $191.00 on a $10,000 loan over 48 months at 4.5 percent annual interest:

```
PPmt(.045/12,1,48,-10000)
```

NPER(RATE,PAYMENT,PRESENTVALUE,FUTUREVALUE,TYPE)

Calculates the number of periods for an annuity based on periodic, constant payments and a constant interest rate. For example, the following function returns the number of payments (48) at $228 that are necessary to pay off principal and interest on a $10,000 loan at 4.5 percent annual interest:

```
NPer(.045/12,228,-10000)
```

DDB(COST,SALVAGE,LIFE,PERIOD,FACTOR)

Calculates the depreciation of an asset for a specific period using the double-declining balance method or other method (which you specify). For example, the following function calculates the depreciation during the third year, which is $500, for a $10,000 asset that will depreciate by $8,000 over four years:

```
Ddb(10000,2000,4,3)
```

SYD(COST,SALVAGE,LIFE,PERIOD)

Calculates the sum-of-years digits depreciation of an asset for a specified period. For example, the following function calculates the sum-of-years' depreciation during the third year, which is $1,600, for a $10,000 asset that will depreciate by $8,000 over four years:

```
Syd(10000,2000,4,3)
```

FV(RATE,PAYMENTPERIODS,PAYMENT,PRESENTVALUE,TYPE)

Calculates the future value of an annuity based on periodic, constant payments and a constant interest rate. For example, the following function returns the future value of $11,966 for an investment of $228 made every month for 48 months earning 4.5 percent annual interest:

```
Fv(.045/12,48,-228)
```

PV(RATE,PAYMENTPERIODS,PAYMENT,FUTUREVALUE,TYPE)

Calculates the present value of an annuity based on periodic, constant payments to be paid in the future and a constant interest rate. For example, the following function returns the present value of $9,999 for an investment of $228 made every month for 48 months paying 4.5 percent annual interest:

```
Pv(.045/12,48,-228)
```

RATE(PAYMENTPERIODS,PAYMENT,PRESENTVALUE,FUTUREVALUE,TYPE,GUESS)

Calculates the interest rate per period for an annuity. For example, the following function returns a 3.74 percent rate per payment period for a loan of $10,000 with a monthly payment of $228 every month for 48 months:

```
Rate(48,-228,10000)
```

Jet SQL

Access uses Jet SQL. In fact, Access uses Jet SQL every time you run a query. You probably create a query in the Query Design window and then simply execute the query as needed without giving the relationship between that query and Jet SQL much thought. The Query Design window is a graphical interface, and Jet SQL doesn't talk in those terms. Instead, Jet SQL converts your graphically expressed question so that Jet (Access's database engine) can process your query. You're just unaware of the behind-the-scenes processes that occur between the time you execute your query and Jet returns the results.

The truth is, Access relies heavily on Jet SQL for almost all processing. That's why learning Jet SQL is an important part of using Access, whether you're working with a single-user desktop application or creating a data-driven website. In this section, you'll learn how Access uses Jet SQL.

The Query Design window isn't the only place you'll see Jet SQL pop up in your applications. Besides queries, you'll use Jet SQL statements as the data source for a number of objects (forms, reports, and controls) and code. In this section, we'll show you how to actually write and use Jet SQL statements in Access objects and code. If you're familiar with Jet SQL's relationship with Access, you can probably skip this section.

Jet SQL Queries

Open any query in Query Design view, and you'll see the graphical interface that lets you communicate with Jet without knowing its language of choice (Jet SQL). For instance, Figure 9.2 shows the Employee Sales by Country query from Northwind—the sample database that comes with Access—in Query Design view.

NOTE *Access Projects don't use queries; they use views and stored procedures in the same way SQL Server does. To learn more about views and stored procedures, see Chapter 8.*

FIGURE 9.2

Query Design view reveals a lot about a query.

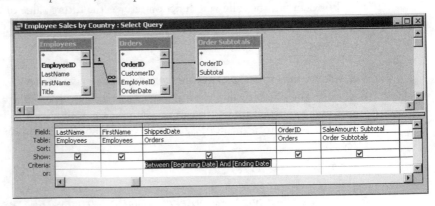

From the Query Design window we can learn a lot:

◆ The query is based on two tables, Employees and Orders, and on one query, Order Subtotals.

◆ The join line indicates a relationship between the EmployeeID fields in the two tables and the OrderID fields in the Orders table and the Order Subtotals query.

◆ The 1 and the infinity symbols displayed on the join line between the two tables tell us two things: that the relationship is a one-to-many relationship and that referential integrity is enforced. (Access displays these symbols only when referential integrity is enabled.)

You can set and view referential integrity properties by clicking the Relationships button on the Database toolbar to open the Relationships window. Then, double-click any join line to enable referential integrity or view the current settings in the Edit Relationships dialog box shown in Figure 9.3.

FIGURE 9.3

View referential integrity settings in the Edit Relationships dialog box.

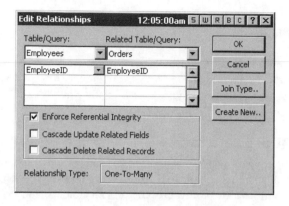

◆ The criteria expression, Between [Beginning Date] And [Ending Date], in the ShippedDate field tells us the query will return records between two dates. In addition, the brackets further indicate that the query is a parameter query. When this query is executed, Access prompts the user for a beginning date and an ending date and then incorporates the user's entries into the expression.

NOTE   *To learn more about referential integrity, see Chapter 5.*

Now, let's examine the Jet SQL equivalent to this query. To do so, click the View button on the Query Design toolbar and choose SQL View.

The Jet SQL statement is fairly complicated and identifies the following:

◆ The PARAMETER keyword identifies the query as a parameter query.

◆ The expression

```
Between [Beginning Date] And [Ending Date]
```

finds all the records between two dates.

◆ The first part of the SELECT clause identifies the fields the statement will include in the results.

◆ The FROM clause identifies the data source.

◆ The INNER JOIN clause

```
INNER JOIN (Orders INNER JOIN [Order Subtotals]
ON Orders.OrderID = [Order Subtotals].OrderID)
ON Employees.EmployeeID = Orders.EmployeeID
```

relates the Orders table and the Order Subtotals query on the OrderID field and the Employees and Order tables on the EmployeeID.

◆ The WHERE clause

```
WHERE (((Orders.ShippedDate) Between [Beginning Date] And [Ending Date]));
```

limits the results to only those records that fall between the two dates entered by the user in response to the parameter prompts when the query is executed.

TIP *The best way to learn Jet SQL is to use it. Begin by reviewing your queries in SQL View. Then, as you become more familiar with the language, start skipping Query Design View and try to write the SQL statements yourself in SQL View. Almost all the interactive commands you use to interact with Access data via the web will involve a SQL statement, so don't underestimate the importance of understanding Jet SQL.*

Using Jet SQL as a Data Source

Most Access objects have a specific data source. For instance, a form or a report is (usually) bound to a particular table or query. Controls also have a data source—a list or combo box might limit you to a list of items that the control captured from a table or query.

When using a table or fixed query as a data source, you simply identify the source by name. When using a Jet SQL statement, enter the appropriate Jet SQL statement as the data source.

A quick example is available in the Northwind Products form. Figure 9.4, shows this form open in Query Design view, and the Properties window is displaying properties for the SupplierID control. This combo box is bound to the SupplierID field in the Suppliers table, as noted in the Control Source property.

FIGURE 9.4

The SupplierID control uses a Jet SQL statement.

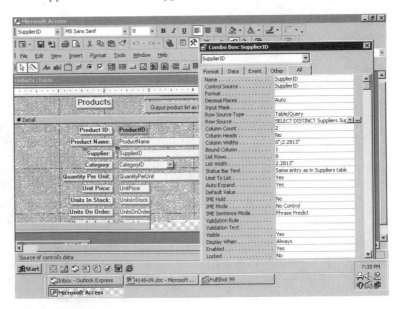

Right away you can see that the Row Source property is a Jet SQL statement. To see the entire statement, select the property and press Shift+F2 to view the property setting in the Zoom dialog box. The complete statement

```
SELECT DISTINCT Suppliers.SupplierID, Suppliers.CompanyName
FROM Suppliers ORDER BY Suppliers.CompanyName;
```

retrieves a unique list of values from the SupplierID and CompanyName fields and sorts those entries by the CompanyName field. You can use the form to view, update, and enter new product information. Instead of typing the supplier, the user selects a supplier from the control's drop-down list, as shown in Figure 9.5.

FIGURE 9.5

The Jet SQL statement populates the control with a unique list of suppliers.

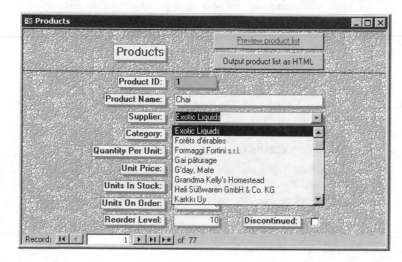

JET SQL VERSUS FIXED QUERIES

Many developers use Jet SQL statements to populate forms, reports, and controls. You can do so too, even if you don't know Jet SQL well enough to write the statements yourself. Simply create the appropriate query in the Query Design window. If the setting refers to a fixed query, open that query. Then, open the SQL window, highlight the statement, and press Ctrl+C to copy the SQL statement to the Clipboard. Next, select the appropriate form, report, or control property and press Ctrl+V to paste the statement into the Property field. The fixed query is no longer necessary. You can discard it without saving it, or delete it. Both the fixed query and the Jet SQL statement are optimized, so neither has an edge on performance. Using Jet SQL statements instead of fixed queries has only one real advantage—it removes clutter from the Database window.

NOTE *The Upsizing Wizard (the wizard that converts an Access database to SQL Server) creates a stored procedure for each Jet SQL statement it encounters as a data source. If any of your objects use the same statement, the wizard creates a stored procedure for each statement instead of creating only one statement. So, check your newly upsized application for duplicate stored procedures.*

Executing Jet SQL in Code

When you execute a query, open a form, or select a control, you execute a Jet SQL statement. Executing a query via code is similar—you use a VBA or ADO (ActiveX Data Objects) command to execute the query. From within an Access application, you can use the following methods to execute a SQL statement:

- The DoCmd object's RunSQL method
- The Database object's Execute method (DAO)
- The Connection object's Execute and Open methods (ADO)
- The Command object's Execute method

Most likely you'll never use the first two methods when connecting to a website, so we'll review just the last two. In addition, most of the scripting languages you'll use to interact with an Access database provide their own versions of the Connection and Command objects. The following is simply a review of the equivalent ADO objects you'll use in Access.

THE ADO CONNECTION OBJECT

The Connection object is the top-level object in the ADO hierarchy and represents the connection made to the data source through the OLE DB data provider. You can open a connection via the ADO Connection object in two ways:

- By using the Execute method
- By using the Open method

The Execute method uses the following form:

```
cnn.Execute validSQLstatement, recordcount, options
```

In this expression, *cnn* represents the Connection object, *validSQLstatement* is any valid SQL statement, *recordcount* stores the number of records modified by the action, and *options* indicates how the provider evaluates *validSQLstatement* (see Table 9.6).

TABLE 9.6: EXECUTE METHOD ARGUMENTS

CONSTANT	DESCRIPTION
adCmdUnspecified	Doesn't specify the command type argument.
adCmdText	Evaluates as a textual definition of a command or stored procedure call.
adCmdTable	Evaluates as a table name whose columns are all returned by an internally generated SQL query.
adCmdStoredProc	Evaluates as a stored procedure.
adCmdUnknown	Indicates that the type of command isn't known and is the default.
adCmdFile	Evaluates as a persistently stored recordset.
adCmdTableDirect	Evaluates as a table whose columns are all returned.

Continued on next page

TABLE 9.6: EXECUTE METHOD ARGUMENTS *(continued)*

CONSTANT	DESCRIPTION
adAsyncExecute	Executes *asynchronously*, which means that ADO returns control to the calling program without waiting for the operation to complete. Don't combine this option with the CommandTypeEnum value adCmdTableDirect.
adAsyncFetch	Retrieves remaining rows after the initial quantity is specified in the CacheSize property asynchronously.
adAsyncFetchNonBlocking	The main thread never blocks while retrieving. If the requested row hasn't been retrieved, the current row automatically moves to the end of the file.
adExecuteNoRecords	Command or stored procedure that doesn't return rows but only inserts data. Use this option only to pass as an optional parameter to the Command or Connection Execute method.
adExecuteStream	Results should be returned as a stream. Only passed as an optional parameter to the Command Execute method.
adExecuteRecord	Command or stored procedure that returns a single row, which should be returned as a Record object.
adOptionUnspecified	Command is unspecified.

NOTE *In the accompanying table, we use the term* asynchronous processing, *which means the controlling program continues to execute code before the processing completes. The alternative is synchronous processing, which means the program temporarily stops until the current process is complete. It then continues by processing the subsequent code.*

The following code sets a Connection object's Connection property to the current Access Project and then executes a SQL statement:

```
Dim cnn As ADODB.Connection
Set cnn = CurrentProject.Connection
strSQL = validSQLstatement
Debug.Print strSQL
cnn.Execute strSQL
Set cnn = Nothing
```

In this code, *validSQLstatement* is any valid SQL statement.

NOTE *The Execute method creates a read-only recordset with a forward-only cursor. If you need more functionality, use the Connection object's Open method.*

The previous example uses the Connection object's Execute method to run a SQL statement after setting the connection to the current project. Use the Connection object's Open and Close method to connect to an external data source using the following syntax:

```
cnn.Open connectionstring, userid, password, options
```

DEBUGGING WITH *DEBUG.PRINT*

The code shown in the Connection Execute method example contains a Debug.Print statement. We recommend you get in the habit of including a Debug.Print statement following any statement that defines a SQL statement to a variable (or almost any kind of variable definition statement for that matter). If the statement returns an error message, you can cut and paste the evaluated statement from the Immediate window to the SQL window for debugging. Specifically, run the evaluated statement as a regular query from the SQL window for more specific error messages. The evaluated statement proves invaluable when the statement includes variables, because the evaluate statement includes the actual value, properly concatenated.

In this example, *cnn* represents a Connection object, *connectionstring* identifies the connection, *userid* identifies the user, *password* is any assigned password if the application is password-protected, and *options* specifies synchronous or asynchronous processing. Table 9.7 lists and describes the arguments for *connectionstring*.

TABLE 9.7: THE *CONNECTIONSTRING* ARGUMENTS

ARGUMENT	DESCRIPTION
Provider	Specifies the connection's provider for the Access database, which is Microsoft.Jet.OLEDB.4.0
File Name	Specifies a provider-specific file
Remote Provider	Specifies a provider for a client-side connection
Remote Server	Specifies the path name of the server in a client-side connection
URL	Specifies an absolute URL, which generally identifies a file or directory

The following code uses the Open method to establish an external connection to the Northwind sample database:

```
Dim cnn AS ADODB.Connection
Set cnn = New ADODB.Connection
cnn.Open "Provider=Microsoft.Jet.OLEDB.4.0; " _
    & "Data Source=C:\Program Files\MicrosoftOffice\" _
    & "Office\Samples\Northwind.mdb;"
```

Although this chapter is about Access, Table 9.8 lists other provider strings.

TABLE 9.8: OLE DB CONNECTION STRING PROVIDERS

PROVIDER (PRODUCT)	PROVIDER STRING
Access	Microsoft.Jet.OLEDB.4.0
SQL Server	SQLOLEDB

Continued on next page

TABLE 9.8: OLE DB CONNECTION STRING PROVIDERS *(continued)*

PROVIDER (PRODUCT)	PROVIDER STRING
Oracle	MSDAORA
ODBC	MSDASQL
Index Server	MSIDXS
ActiveDirectory Service	ADSDSOObject

TIP   If you're using a Data Source Name (DSN), a connection string is as simple as identifying the DSN name in the form cnn.Open = "DSN=datasourcename"*, in which* datasourcename *is the name of the DSN you're using in the connection. Be aware that ADO assumes all defaults in this statement, so any passwords or user name variables must be passed before executing this statement. For more information on just what a DSN is and how to create one, see Chapters 4 and 10.*

THE ADO COMMAND OBJECT

If there's any chance your Access application will be upsized, use the Command object since it's more compatible with SQL Server. This object is used more frequently in ADP (Access Projects), but both Access and SQL Server Desktop support the Command object. The Command object represents a SQL statement, a stored procedure, or a command that's processed by the data source.

Use the following syntax to create and establish a connection via the Command object:

```
Dim cmd As ADODB.Command
Set cmd = New ADODB.Command
With cmd
    .ActiveConnection = validconnectionstring
    .CommandText = CommandTypeConstant
    .Execute
End With
```

In this example, *validconnectionstring* is CurrentProject.Connection or a combination of the arguments listed in Table 9.7. If populating a Recordset object, replace the Execute method with the following statement:

```
Set rst = .Execute
```

NOTE   For more specific information on the ADO Connection and Command objects, see Chapter 10.

SQL Aggregate Functions

In the earlier section, "Built-in Functions," we looked at a number of functions, including Domain functions that consider an entire set of records. You can use these built-in Domain functions with VBA, but you can't use them in SQL statements. Fortunately, SQL provides a number of equivalents, known as SQL aggregates.

The main difference, besides the environment in which you can use these functions, is that SQL aggregates can't be limited by criteria as Domain functions can. SQL aggregates accept only one argument—a reference to a field or an expression that refers to a field. Remember that the field always refers to the underlying data source, and not to a form, a report, or a control. Table 9.9 lists the SQL aggregate functions.

TABLE 9.9: SQL AGGREGATE FUNCTIONS

FUNCTION	PURPOSE	ACCESS/VBA EQUIVALENT	T-SQL (SQL SERVER DESKTOP)
Avg	Returns the average or mean value of a set of values	DAvg()	Avg
Count	Returns the number of non-Null values in a set of values	DCount()	Count
Count(*)	Counts the total number of rows	DCount(*)	Count
Sum	Sums the values in a set of values	DSum()	Sum
Min	Returns the smallest value in a set of values	DMin()	Min
Max	Returns the largest value in a set of values	DMax()	Max
First	Returns the value in the first row of the specified field	NA	NA
Last	Returns the value in the last row of the specified field	NA	NA
StDev	Returns the sample standard deviation for a set of records	DStDev()	StDev
StDevP	Returns population standard deviation for a set of records	DStDevP()	StDevP
Var	Returns sample variance for a set of records	DVar()	Var
VarP	Returns population deviation for a set of records	DVarP()	VarP

Upsizing an Access Database to SQL Server

Once an Access database outgrows the system, you might decide to upsize it to SQL Server. (For more information on SQL Server 2000, see Chapter 8.) The upsizing process isn't rocket science, but it can be labor intensive, especially if your database wasn't originally written with conversion in mind.

Regardless of your reasons and your experience, upsizing can be a difficult process if you go into it unprepared. Knowing what the wizard can and can't handle before you start can mean the difference between a successful conversion the first time and repeating the process a few times until you finally get it right. In this section, we'll discuss the hot spots and how to defuse them before running the Upsizing Wizard.

DEVELOP WITH AN EYE TO THE FUTURE

If there's any chance SQL Server is in your future, you can enforce a couple of simple rules when developing an Access database that will simplify any upsizing process:

◆   Don't include a space character in object names. Access and SQL Server both require any table or field name that contains a space character to be enclosed in brackets ([ ]). Access automatically adds the brackets, but SQL Server doesn't. The wizard will upsize the tables, but in SQL Server, you must remember to add the brackets yourself. Avoid potential errors (forgotten brackets) down the road by eliminating the cause—omit space characters in your Access object names.

◆   If you're in the habit of using SQL statements as the data source for controls, forms, and reports, start using fixed queries instead. The wizard will upsize these controls by converting the SQL statements to views or stored procedures. Unfortunately, the wizard can't distinguish one statement from another, which means all statements are converted, even duplicates. If you have multiple controls based on the same statement, you'll end up with a lot of duplicate views (or stored procedures)—one for each occurrence of the SQL statement. You'll have to delete all the duplicates and reset the appropriate source properties to the one remaining source. That can take some time and can be avoided by using fixed queries—at least when you have more than one object using the same query.

Upsizing Options

Moving an entire database to an entirely new format isn't a task to undertake lightly. Fortunately, the Access 2002 Upsizing Wizard has several versions under its belt, and with each new version it gets easier and more efficient. With the inclusion of Access Projects (ADP files), the Upsizing Wizard offers more than ever in the way of upsizing options:

◆   You can convert an Access MDB file to an ADP file, which utilizes SQL Server 2000. All the data and objects are actually stored on SQL Server, but the familiar Access interface is still available, and that can mean a lot to the developer unfamiliar with SQL Server. An ADP project is not only a great database product, it can be an effective training tool for the would-be SQL Server developer. (Even though you're using Access objects, Jet is no longer an issue.)

◆   You can link server tables to local Access tables and keep your Access MDB file intact, and you end up with a typical front-end/back-end arrangement. You're really just creating an ODBC link to the newly upsized tables on SQL Server. Unlike the other options, you won't have to modify the forms and reports. On the other hand, if performance is a serious issue, keep in mind that the queries are still processed locally, which may slow things down.

◆   You can upsize the data to SQL Server 2000 by creating an entirely new database on SQL server without altering the Access application you upsized.

NOTE   *To run the Access 2002 Upsizing Wizard, choose Tools ➤ Database Utilities. Select Upsizing Wizard, and choose one of the three options discussed in the accompanying section.*

Before You Start

You can't just jump into the upsizing process willy-nilly—preparation is the key to a successful conversion. Before you actually do anything, you must deal with a few matters.

Contact your SQL Server administrator to check your security roles. You must have permission to create a new database in SQL Server before you can upsize an Access file. In addition, the process requires Jet Read Design permission on all Access objects you plan to convert. If VBA modules are password-protected, you'll need that password.

NOTE   Access MDE *files can't be upsized. You must upsize the original* MDB *file.*

Create a backup of the Access database before you start the Upsizing Wizard. Store that copy in a safe place—ideally on another server.

TIP   Use the Access Documenter feature to run a report that lists all the properties for the tables, queries, fields, indexes, and relationships. Once you've upsized to SQL Server, you can refer to this list to ensure that everything made the conversion and to re-create those items that didn't. To run this feature, choose Tools ➤ Analyze, and then select Documenter.

Preparing the Access *MDB* File for Conversion

In a perfect world, a simple click would thoroughly convert everything in your Access MDB file to SQL Server, but that's not how it happens. The wizard can't yet handle several incompatibilities between the two systems. However, knowledge does give you an upper hand. If you know what to modify before upsizing, the process is often trouble free.

FIND AND DELETE UNSUPPORTED DATES

One of the biggest discrepancies between the two systems is the dates each system supports. Access 2002 supports dates from January 1, 100, to December 31, 9999; SQL Server supports dates from January 1, 1753, through December 31, 9999.

This seemingly simple difference creates one of those between-a-rock-and-a-hard-place issues if you have dates that fall before January 1, 1753. The wizard won't upsize any table that contains an invalid date—and, yes, we mean the entire table. The wizard doesn't just skip the record with the offending date; it skips the entire table.

NOTE   When encountering any type of error in a table, the wizard generally refuses to upsize the entire table. This decision actually makes sense. You're much more likely to realize a table's missing than a lone record.

Finding the Dates

To find problem dates, run a query on any table that contains a date field and use the following expression to find dates that falls outside SQL Server's date range:

```
datefield < #1-1-1753#
```

Once You Find the Dates

There's no easy way to deal with these records. The best solution is to simply delete any dates that SQL Server can't interpret. If you must keep the record, consider converting the date field to a text field and then writing a stored procedure or a user-defined function (within SQL Server 2000) that does the date arithmetic for you.

ADD A UNIQUE INDEX TO EACH ACCESS TABLE

The wizard requires that each Access table have a unique index. If there's no unique index, the wizard won't upsize the table. The solution is simple enough:

- Open the table and add an AutoNumber field to the table.
- Or, choose an existing field and add the index.

To add an index to an Access table, open the table in Design view and then select the appropriate field row. Next, select Yes (No Duplicates) in the Indexed property. Just remember to remove the AutoNumber field or the index from the table afterward.

WARNING *The Upsizing Wizard won't upsize a table that contains an index based on more than three fields.*

REVAMPING DUPLICATE SQL STATEMENTS

Many Access developers use SQL statements as the data source for controls, forms, and reports. You can even use the same statement for multiple objects. The wizard converts these statements into views or stored procedures, but it creates one for each instance—even if there are duplicate statements.

To avoid the laborious task of removing all those duplicate views (or stored procedures) and then resetting each object's source property, check your Access objects for duplicate SQL statements and convert them to fixed queries in Access, before you upsize.

MODIFY FIELD SIZE PROPERTIES

Access lets you create a primary and foreign key relationship on fields in which the field size settings are different; SQL Server doesn't. Check your primary and foreign key field size properties and make the necessary changes before upsizing. The wizard will refuse to upsize any tables in which the field size settings aren't the same.

DELETE SQL *DISTINCTROW*

SQL Server doesn't support the SQL `DISTINCTROW` keyword. As a result, the wizard will refuse to upsize any query that contains this keyword (and that includes SQL statements used as the data source for an object). Most of the time, you can simply substitute `DISTINCT` for the `DISTINCTROW` keyword . Be sure to carefully test the query after modifying because the two keywords aren't always interchangeable.

NOTE *Jet security won't upsize at all, and there's nothing you can do on either side of the conversion process to save any piece of it. Simply forget Jet security and learn SQL Server security.*

When It's All Over

Don't be discouraged if your first attempt to upsize an Access MDB file fails miserably. However, if you follow the advice in the previous section, you have a good chance of upsizing without too many errors. Do expect a few problem spots though; upsizing is seldom completely trouble free. In the worst case, you can note the major problems, return to the Access MDB file, make changes to avoid those problems, and then try again. In fact, you might have to repeat the process several times if you're working with a complex database.

If you're unfamiliar with SQL Server, the first thing you might notice is the absence of any queries. SQL Server doesn't use queries—it relies on views, stored procedures, and user-defined functions (UDFs).

You might find that a few queries didn't upsize at all. For instance, the wizard will try to upsize a subquery by upsizing the outer SELECT (the main SELECT) first. If the wizard encounters a problem, it will abandon both SELECT statements. In this case, you'll have to rewrite the query in SQL Server yourself.

As a general rule, Select, Append, Delete, Make-Table and Update queries update to a stored procedure. Any action query that contains a nested query or a parameter, crosstab, SQL Pass-Through, Data Definition Language, or Union query must be converted manually to a view or a stored procedure.

TIP   *If you find yourself faced with reconstructing a query that simply won't upsize to SQL Server, cut and paste the SQL statement from the Access SQL window to the SQL Server Query Analyzer and begin the process there. The analyzer will provide insight into Jet SQL's incompatibilities with T-SQL. Take advantage of the analyzer's error messages—don't try to rewrite the query on your own unless you're an expert at SQL.*

SQL Server 2000 supports Access 2002's extended properties, and the wizard should successfully convert most of them. However, you'll have to manually deal with any property not in the following list:

- Description
- Format
- Input Mask
- Caption
- Decimal Places
- Hyperlink (is upsized, but doesn't work)
- Row Source Type
- Row Source
- Bound Column
- Column Count
- Column Widths
- List Rows
- List Width
- Limit to List

In addition, SQL Server converts all Validation Rule settings to constraints. Be sure to open each table and check each constraint to make sure it converted properly. You might need to modify a few slightly.

Connection Options

All the Dreamweaver MX supported languages will connect to an Access database if you have the appropriate driver, with the exception of Hypertext Preprocessor (PHP). If you have a licensed copy of Access, you already have the drivers you need to interact with your database using ODBC or OLE DB. For the most part, you'll probably use ASP, ASP.NET, or even ADO.NET to interact with an Access database. However, if you choose JavaServer Pages (JSP), you can obtain an applet from Microsoft's site:

```
http://msdn.microsoft.com/downloads/samples/internet/default.asp?url=/Downloads/
    samples/Internet/author/datasrc/jdbcapplet/default.asp
```

NOTE   For more information on specific connection options, see Chapter 10.

Access as a Platform for Web Development

Under the right circumstances, Access can support a website, the biggest obstacle being traffic. Access simply can't handle heavy traffic. If you have an existing application in Access that you want to upgrade to the web, go ahead and try it out. A working application that gets the job done will probably continue to do so on the web.

If you're going to create the database, but you're stuck with Access, just keep the concurrent user issue in mind. Close all connections as soon as possible, and you'll find that Access handles more traffic than you expect.

On the other hand, if financial and support personnel resources are available, and you can choose the database system, don't choose Access. Don't even consider Access for a heavy-duty e-commerce site that's destined for heavy traffic.

Summary

This chapter is just a brief introduction to Access. You can't possibly learn everything you need to know in one chapter. Fortunately, you can connect to an Access database using ODBC and OLE DB drivers, so you should have no trouble interacting with an Access database over the web.

Part III

Paving the Way:
The Languages

In this section, you will learn how to:
- ◆ **Understand Database Connections and Scripting**
- ◆ **Work with ColdFusion and Dreamweaver**
- ◆ **Use JavaServer Pages (JSP) and Dreamweaver**
- ◆ **Use Active Server Pages (ASP) and Dreamweaver**
- ◆ **Work with ASP.NET and Dreamweaver**
- ◆ **Use ADO.NET and Dreamweaver**
- ◆ **Work with PHP and Dreamweaver**
- ◆ **Tackle Database Security over the Internet**

Chapter 10

Connections and Scripting

As much as the birth of web server scripting languages, web database connectivity has allowed static HTML to evolve into fully dynamic web applications. Dreamweaver MX is the ideal tool to develop a web application with web database connectivity. As you'll see in the following chapters, Dreamweaver MX can work with many web development languages set in a variety of environments. In addition, you've seen in the previous chapters that Dreamweaver MX can use web development languages to connect to almost any SQL-compliant database.

The glue that binds a web application to a database is the database connection. However, there are an astounding number of database connections to choose from. In fact, the number of possible database connections far outweighs the number of web scripting languages and databases combined. With that many choices, how do you choose the right database connection for your web application? Luckily, your choice of a web development language and an accompanying database will narrow the playing field.

That said, this chapter focuses on the various types of database connections available to you per your scripting language choice. As you'll see, some database connections are common across all Dreamweaver MX supported web development languages. We'll begin with an introduction to how Dreamweaver MX handles database connections in a web application and define the connection types. Then we'll move on to creating database connections for each supported web development language.

This chapter covers the following topics:

◆ Dreamweaver MX and database connections
◆ Managing an existing data connection
◆ Troubleshooting data connections

Dreamweaver MX and Database Connections

If you plan to use a database with your web application, you need to create at least one database connection. Without one, your web application won't know where to find the database or how to connect to it. With the exception of ColdFusion web applications, you can create database connections in Dreamweaver MX by providing the information the web application needs to establish contact with a database. When you create a database connection, Dreamweaver MX stores the connection information in a file in the Connections folder of your website. Interestingly, Dreamweaver MX does not actually use that database connection in your web application until you define a recordset on a page. At that point, Dreamweaver inserts an `include` directive in your page. As the web server executes your web page, the `include` directive inserts the connection code establishing a database connection.

As we mentioned, before Dreamweaver MX can use any database connection, you must provide the connection's basic requirements, such as the appropriate driver for your database, the database name and location, and the database username and password. Most of this information can be gleaned from the database documentation and installation or through your web server environment. However, before we move into creating database connections, you need to become familiar with the types of database connections. As you may know, Dreamweaver MX can work with a wide variety of database connections—ODBC (Open Database Connectivity), OLE DB (Object Linking and Embedding Database), JDBC (Java DataBase Connectivity), and native drivers. Let's briefly look at each type.

Open Database Connectivity (ODBC)

Microsoft developed ODBC to meet developer needs for an easy way to connect to a variety of databases. To that end, an ODBC connection is actually a connection to a driver whose sole purpose is to connect and translate common instructions (typically SQL) in a way that a specific type of database will understand. For example, an ODBC connection to a Microsoft SQL Server database uses a driver specifically written to translate commands for SQL Server. An ODBC connection to a MySQL database uses a completely different driver written specifically with the MySQL database in mind. In most cases, the driver required to create an ODBC connection to a database is probably included with the operating system you are using. Even if this is not the case, you can usually download the appropriate driver from the websites of the publishers of your chosen database or operating system or even third-party providers. The great thing about using an ODBC connection to link your web application and a database is the simplicity of its creation and the independence between the ODBC connection and your web application.

You can create an ODBC connection on the web server of your web application typically through a control panel provided by the operating system. The only bits of information you need are a name for the connection and the target database name, type, and location. The one word name for the ODBC connection is the data source name (DSN). You'll hear DSN referenced a lot by developers and in documentation. The important thing to remember is that a DSN is how you reference and use the ODBC database connection in your web application.

Just as an ODBC connection exists independently of your web application, your web application also functions independently of the ODBC connection. Your web application doesn't need to know the database name, version, or location. In fact, the database doesn't even have to be on the same computer as your web application. As we mentioned, all your web application requires to use the database connection is the DSN. Knowing this, you can see how useful it is to have such independence between the ODBC connection and your web application. For example, you can switch the source database your web application uses by simply altering the ODBC connection on the web server.

Likewise, you can quickly pack up and move your web application to almost any other web server with an identically named ODBC connection.

NOTE *ODBC connections are also used to apply a level of security to web applications. Typically a web application has a content presentation side accessed by the public and a content administration side accessed by content administrators. Obviously, the public requires different database access than your web content administrators. Therefore, many developers create two ODBC connections to link to their web application and database. One connection is for the public side of a web application and typically has read-only permission to the database. The second connection is for the content administration side of the web application and has full read, write, and delete permissions.*

Although you can create a DSN using Dreamweaver MX, at times you'll need to create a DSN on a web server through the Windows operating system. To create an ODBC connection on a Windows web server, first open the Control Panel, and then locate and click the ODBC Data Source Administrator icon to open the ODBC Data Source Administrator dialog box, as shown in Figure 10.1. (In Windows 2000 and later, you will find the ODBC Data Source Administrator under Administrative Tools.)

FIGURE 10.1

The ODBC Data Source Administrator dialog box

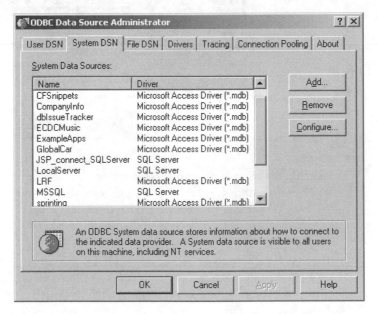

The three basic data connection types are File, Local, and System. A File DSN is an independent file that contains all the information required to connect to a database. Any application with permissions to the file can use the File DSN and move it as easily as moving a file. A Local data connection is stored in the Windows Registry and limits access to the connection to only the creator of the data connection. A System data connection is also stored in the Windows Registry and is available to every application on the server that has the proper access permissions. As such, System data connections are ideal for web applications.

To demonstrate how to create a DSN, let's create a System DSN for a Microsoft Access database version of our Books database. To do so, follow these steps:

1. In the ODBC Data Source Administrator dialog box, click the System DSN tab. At this point, you will see a list of System Data Sources currently defined on the web server.

2. To create a new System DSN, click the Add button to open the Create A New Data Source dialog box, as shown in Figure 10.2.

FIGURE 10.2

The Create New Data Source dialog box

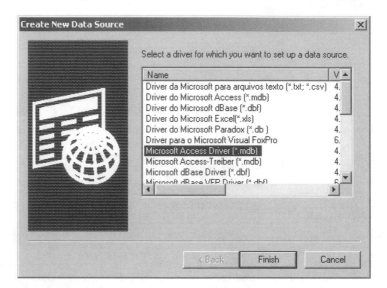

3. Select the appropriate driver for your database and click Finish. For our example, we are choosing Microsoft Access Driver. (If you cannot find the appropriate driver for your database, you will need to install it on the web server and begin again. Typically you can find the correct ODBC database drivers on the Microsoft website or on the website of the publisher of your database.)

4. The next few dialog boxes depend on the ODBC driver you choose, but generally they ask you for a one-word DSN, the name and location of the database, and a username and password (which is optional). In our example, enter *booktracking* for the DSN in the ODBC Setup dialog box.

5. Next, click the Select button to open the ODBC Microsoft Access Setup dialog box, as shown in Figure 10.3. Locate and select the MDWMX_Books.mdb database, and then click OK to save the booktracking System DSN.

As you can see in the System DSN tab of the ODBC Data Source Administrator dialog box (see Figure 10.4), a new booktracking System DSN is defined on your server. You can use this System DSN to access the Books Access database using Dreamweaver MX and any development language. What could be simpler?

FIGURE 10.3

The ODBC
Microsoft Access
Setup dialog box

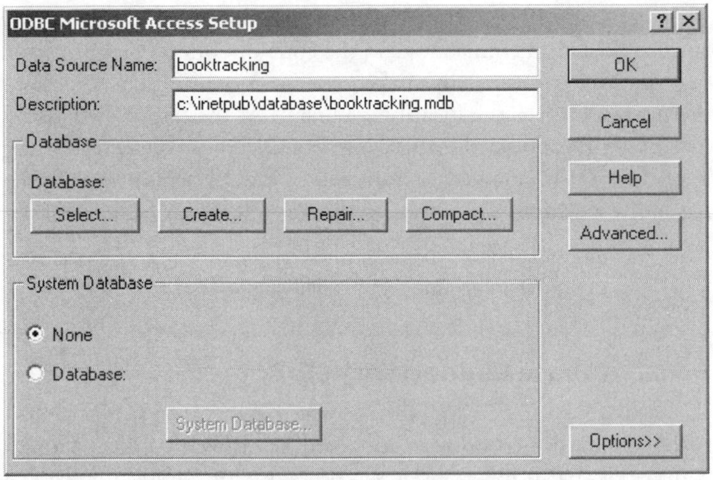

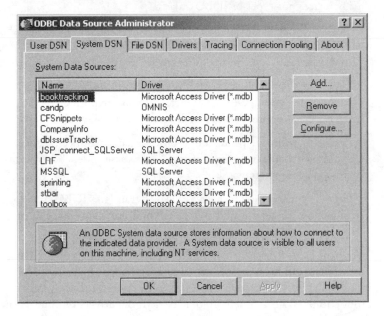

FIGURE 10.4

The ODBC Data
Source Administrator
dialog box

Object Linking and Embedding Database (OLE DB)

From a pure performance perspective, using OLE DB is the best way to connect to a database in Windows. In fact, an ODBC connection is actually a wrapper around an OLE DB connection to your database. Consequently, it makes sense that a direct OLE DB connection is faster than an ODBC connection. So why not use OLE DB connections all the time? Although OLE DB is certainly popular and efficient, ODBC remains the easiest to set up and maintain.

Instead of specifying the database and connection criteria in a System DSN as in ODBC, you specify OLE DB connections in the code of your web applications. For an OLE DB connection, you need to supply much of the same information that you supply for an ODBC connection—a provider or driver, the location and name of the target database, and any necessary security information. For example, the following is an OLE DB connection string in an ASP (Active Server Pages) application that connects to SQL Server. Simply replace *myWebServer*, *databasename*, *username*, and *password* with the appropriate information for your SQL Server.

```
Provider=SQLOLEDB; Data Source=myWebServer; Initial Catalog=datbasename;
    User ID=username; Password=password;
```

Java Database Connectivity (JDBC)

JDBC is to Java-coded applications what ODBC is to applications written in other languages. JDBC is the standard method for connecting a JSP web application to a database and issuing standard commands that JDBC translates as necessary for the specific database type. Similar to ODBC, JDBC relies on the concept of a DSN to identify a connection to a database.

There are four types of JDBC drivers.

Type 1   The first JDBC method of connection, Type 1 establishes a bridge between JDBC and ODBC so that JDBC can connect to a database. As such, ODBC drivers must also be installed on the server. Although the easiest to set up, this type is the slowest and most unreliable.

Type 2   Also establishes a bridge; however, this bridge connects JDBC directly with the target database, bypassing ODBC. In fact, it doesn't require ODBC to be installed on the server at all. Type 2 may require you to install access software specific to your database choice.

Type 3   Fully independent of ODBC or database-specific connection software, Type 3 is a pure Java driver that translates JDBC into a database-independent protocol that is then translated in native database commands.

Type 4   Also a pure Java driver, Type 4 translates JDBC commands directly into native database commands. Type 4 is best suited for connecting a web application and a database.

Dreamweaver MX comes with Type 4 JDBC drivers for IBM DB2, Oracle, MySQL, and Microsoft SQL Server. If you need to connect to some other database, you can use the Sun JDBC-ODBC Bridge. This type of bridge connection is fine for testing and development, but download and install a Type 4 JDBC driver specific to your database if you plan to move your web application into production. You can usually find Type 4 JDBC drivers on the website of the database publisher or through third-party companies. In addition, Sun maintains a list of available JDBC drivers at their website, `http://industry.java.sun.com/products/jdbc/drivers`.

Native Drivers

Native drivers connect your web application directly to a database, circumventing the traditional ODBC methods. Native drivers are typically faster and let you use database-specific features. However, to use a native driver, you typically need to install the database client software on your web server. To use a native driver in Dreamweaver MX, you need to consult the native driver documentation to construct a custom connection string.

Database Connections for ASP Developers

In this section we'll show you how to create a database connection for an ASP web application. You will need access to an ASP development environment that includes Internet Information Services (IIS) or Personal Web Server (PWS). Dreamweaver MX provides two default connection methods for an ASP application: Data Source Name (DSN) and Custom Connection String. The Data Source Name (DSN) option lets you connect via a Local or a System DSN. The Custom Connection String lets you craft your own connection using connection types such as ODBC, OLE DB, or a DSN-less connection. To demonstrate how to create a data connection in Dreamweaver MX, we'll create an Access version and a SQL Server version of the Books database and then create a System DSN connection, an OLE DB connection, and a DSN-less connection.

CREATING AN SYSTEM DSN CONNECTION

To create a System DSN connection in an ASP application in Dreamweaver MX, follow these steps:

1. Choose Windows ➤ Databases to open the Databases panel. Open any ASP page in your site, click the plus (+) sign, and choose Data Source Name (DSN) to open the Data Source Name (DSN) dialog box, as shown in Figure 10.5.

FIGURE 10.5

The Data Source Name (DSN) dialog box

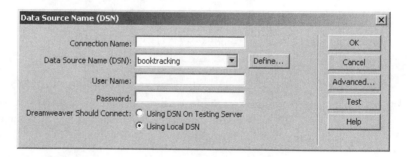

In this dialog box, you can connect using a System DSN or using a Local DSN. In almost every case, you'll want to connect using a System DSN on the testing server.

2. Click the Using DSN On Testing Server option to display a slightly altered Data Source Name (DSN) dialog box, as shown in Figure 10.6.

    The next step is to select a System DSN from the testing server. As you may recall, we created a System DSN to an Access version of our Books application in the "Open Database Connectivity (ODBC)" section. If you happened to skip that step, revisit the section and create that System DSN.

FIGURE 10.6

The Data Source Name (DSN) dialog box

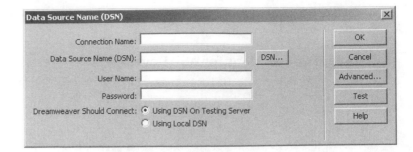

3. In the Dreamweaver MX Data Source Name (DSN) dialog box, click the DSN button. Dreamweaver MX queries the testing server and displays a current list of System DSNs in the Select ODBC DSN dialog box, shown in Figure 10.7. Select the booktracking DSN, and click OK to return to the Data Source Name (DSN) dialog box.

FIGURE 10.7

The Select ODBC DSN dialog box

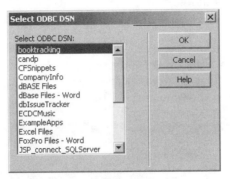

The last steps are to provide a name for the Dreamweaver MX data connection and test your connection. In our example, we'll use BookTrackingAccess as shown in Figure 10.8. Dreamweaver MX will use the data connection name as the filename of the ASP file that saves the data connection information.

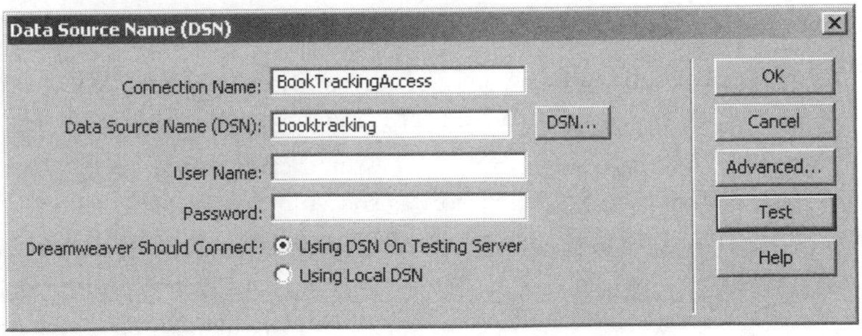

FIGURE 10.8

Define a Dreamweaver MX data connection name.

4. In the Connection Name box, enter a name for your connection, and then click the Test button to validate the connection string. If the test is successful, all is well. Click the OK button to save your connection as an ASP file in the Connections folder of your site.

CREATING AN OLE DB CONNECTION

To create an OLE DB connection to SQL Server in an ASP application using Dreamweaver MX, follow these steps:

1. Choose Windows ➤ Databases to open the Databases panel. Open any ASP page in your site, click the plus (+) sign, and choose Custom Connection String to open the Custom Connection String dialog box, as shown in Figure 10.9.

FIGURE 10.9

The Custom
Connection String
dialog box

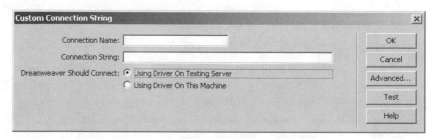

In this dialog box, you can enter a name for your Dreamweaver MX data connection and craft your own database connection string.

2. In the Connection Name field, provide a name for the Dreamweaver MX custom connection string. In our example, we'll use BookTrackingOLEDB, as shown in Figure 10.10. Dreamweaver MX will use the data connection name as the filename of the ASP file that saves the data connection information.

3. Now you need to enter the connection string to connect to the Books Access database. Enter the following as one line of code in the Connection String text field, adapting the placeholders (identified by [ ]) to connect to your SQL Server development environment.

```
Provider=SQLOLEDB; Data Source=[myWebServer]; Initial
     Catalog=[databasename]; User ID=[username]; Password=[password];
```

4. To create an OLE DB connection to an Access database, you can use the following line instead.

```
Provider=Microsoft.Jet.OLEDB.4.0: Data Source=[c:\databasepath]; User
     ID=[]; Password=[];
```

5. As with creating a System DSN connection, you can connect using a driver on the testing server or using a local driver. In almost every case, you'll want to connect using a driver on the testing server.

   Click the Using Driver On Testing Server option.

FIGURE 10.10

OLE DB Connection
in the Custom
Connection String
dialog box

Custom Connection String	
Connection Name:	BookTrackingOLEDB
Connection String:	4.0: Data Source=[c:\databasepath]; User ID=[]; Password=[];
Dreamweaver Should Connect:	⦿ Using Driver On Testing Server ○ Using Driver On This Machine

OK
Cancel
Advanced...
Test
Help

6. Before closing the dialog box, click the Test button to verify that the connection string works. If successful, click OK to save the data connection. If the test fails, you'll need to troubleshoot the problem. See "Troubleshooting Data Connections" at the end of this chapter.

CREATING A DSN-LESS CONNECTION

As an alternative to File, Local, and System DSNs, ASP lets you create a DSN-less connection. A DSN-less connection is simply an ODBC connection defined within your code rather than through the web server operating system. Developers often prefer this type of connection because they can create or alter the connection from within the web application code.

To replace our System DSN connection with a DSN-less connection, follow these steps:

1. Choose Windows ➤ Databases to open the Databases panel. Open any ASP page in your site, click the plus (+) sign, and choose Custom Connection String to open the Custom Connection String dialog box.

2. Enter a name for the Dreamweaver MX data connection. Then enter the following connection string to connect to the Access version of our Books database. The username and password parameters are optional.

```
Provider=MSDASQL; Driver={Microsoft Access Driver (*.mdb)}; UID=[ username];
    PWD=[=password];
```

3. Finally, click the Test button to validate the connection string. If the test is successful, all is well. Click the OK button to save your connection as an ASP file in the Connections folder of your site.

Database Connections for ASP.NET Developers

To create data connections for a Microsoft ASP.NET web application, you need access to an ASP.NET development environment that includes IIS or PWS and the .NET Framework. (For more information about creating your development environment in ASP.NET, check out Chapter 14.) There is one connection method for ASP.NET—OLE DB Connection. However, when you installed the .NET Framework, you installed another option—the Managed Data Provider for SQL Server. To demonstrate creating a data connection in Dreamweaver MX, we will create an OLE DB connection to the Access version of the Books database and use the Managed Data Provider for SQL Server to create a connection to the SQL Server version.

OLE DB CONNECTION

To create an OLE DB connection to our Books Access database in an ASP.NET application in Dreamweaver MX, take the following steps:

1. Choose Windows ➤ Databases to activate the Databases panel. Open any ASPX page in your site, click the plus (+) sign on the Databases panel, and choose OLE DB Connection to open the OLE DB Connection dialog box, as shown in Figure 10.11.

In this dialog box, you can build a connection string through a Dreamweaver MX DataLink Properties dialog box or load a Connection String template. Let's begin with building a connection string through the DataLink Properties dialog box.

FIGURE 10.11

The OLE DB
Connection
dialog box

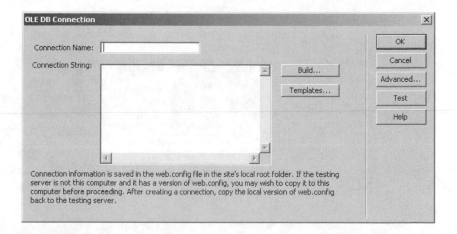

Using the DataLink Properties Dialog Box

1. Click Build to open the DataLink Properties dialog box, click the Provider tab, and choose Microsoft Jet OLE 4.0 Provider, as shown in Figure 10.12.

FIGURE 10.12

The Provider
tab of the Data-
Link Properties
dialog box

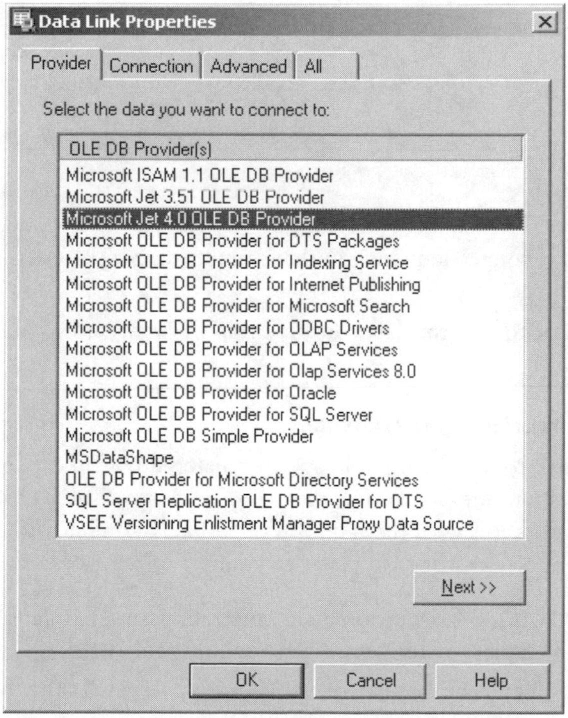

2. Click the Connection tab, which is shown in Figure 10.13. Enter the path to the Books Access database, and enter any username or password you have added to the database.

FIGURE 10.13

The Connection tab of the Data-Link Properties dialog box

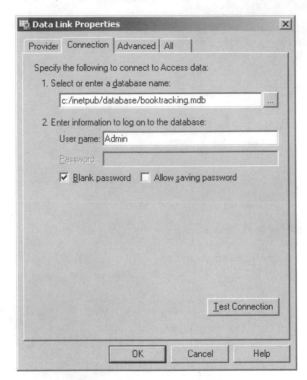

3. Click the Test Connection button to validate your data connection. If successful, click OK to insert the connection string in the Connection String text field of the OLE DB Connection dialog box.

4. Click OK to save the data connection in the web.config file in the root folder of your ASP.NET site.

Loading a Connection String Template

As an alternative to the DataLink Properties dialog box, you can load one of the many connection string templates into the Connection String text field of the OLE DB Connection dialog box. By now, even if you don't know what they are, you're probably familiar with the connection string templates. To use the connection string templates to connect to the Access Books database, follow these steps:

1. In the OLE DB Connection dialog box, click the Templates button to open the Connection String Template dialog box, as shown in Figure 10.14.

2. In the Select Template list, select Microsoft Access 2000 (Microsoft Jet 4.0 Provider), and then click OK to return to the OLE DB Connection dialog box.

FIGURE 10.14

The Connection
String Template
dialog box

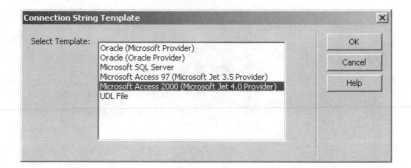

3. As you can see in Figure 10.15, Dreamweaver MX loads the familiar connection string template into the Connection String text field. All you have to do now is replace the placeholders with the appropriate information and click OK to save the data connection in the `web.config` file in the root folder of your ASP.NET site.

FIGURE 10.15

The Microsoft
Access 2000
connection
template loaded
in the Connection
String text field

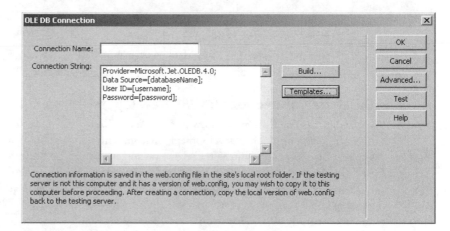

MANAGED DATA PROVIDER FOR SQL SERVER

If you're creating an ASP.NET web applicaton to connect to SQL Server, the Managed Data Provider for SQL Server is your best option. The Managed Data Provider for SQL Server is optimized for SQL Server and is blazingingly fast. The following steps demonstrate how to use Dreamweaver MX to create a data connection using the Managed Data Provider for SQL Server:

1. Choose Windows ➢ Databases to open the Databases panel. Open any ASPX page in your site, click the plus (+) sign and choose SQL Server Connection to open the SQL Server Connection dialog box, as shown in Figure 10.16.

2. You will see a familiar connection string template in the Connection String text field. Simply replace the placeholder information with your SQL Server and database information.

FIGURE 10.16

The SQL Server
Connection
dialog box

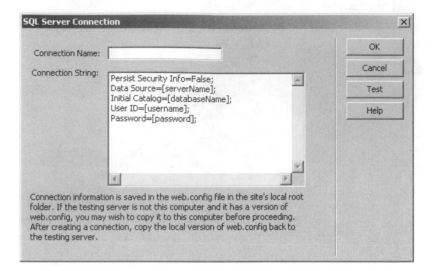

3. In the Connection Name text field, enter a Dreamweaver MX data connection name.

4. Click the Test button to validate the data connection. If the test is successful, click OK to save the data connection in the `web.config` file in the root folder of your ASP.NET website.

Database Connections for JSP Developers

In this section, we'll show you how to create a database connection for a JSP web application. Before beginning, you need a JSP development environment, which includes a web server, a JavaServer Pages application server (sometimes these are one and the same), and a JSP site defined in Dreamweaver MX. In our example, we are using IIS and Macromedia JRun 4, and we'll connect to the Access and SQL Server versions of the Books database. Further, we'll look at the three data connection methods provided by Dreamweaver MX in a JSP application—a JDBC-ODBC Bridge, Type 4 JDBC drivers, and a Custom JDBC Connection.

JDBC-ODBC BRIDGE

To connect a JSP web application to a database, you must use a JDBC driver. However, you can use a JDBC driver to connect to an ODBC-compliant database. As you may recall, a JDBC-ODBC bridge allows you to accomplish just this. For example, we can create a Dreamweaver MX data connection in our JSP web application that connects to the System DSN that points to our Access version of the Books database. To establish this connection, follow these steps:

1. Choose Windows ➢ Databases to open the Databases panel. Open any JSP page in your JSP web application site, click the plus (+) sign, and choose Sun JDBC_ODBC Driver (ODBC Database) to open the Sun JDBC_ODBC Driver (ODBC Database) dialog box, as shown in Figure 10.17.

2. You can specify whether Dreamweaver MX uses a driver on the local machine or a driver on the testing server. Choose Using Driver On Testing Server.

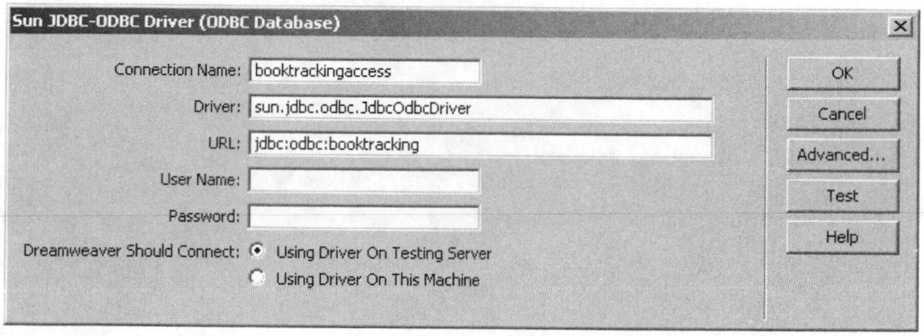

FIGURE 10.17

The Sun JDBC_
ODBC Driver
(ODBC Database)
dialog box

3. In the Connection Name field, enter a name for the Dreamweaver MX data connection. As we've mentioned, Dreamweaver MX will name the connection JSP page based on the Dreamweaver MX data connection name you provide. Then, in the URL text field, replace [odbc dsn] with the booktracking System DSN you created earlier, as shown in Figure 10.17.

4. Click the Test button to validate the data connection. If the test succeeds, click OK to save the data connection as a JSP file in the Connections folder of your JSP site.

TYPE 4 JDBC DRIVERS

As you may recall, Type 4 JDBC drivers allow a JSP web application to connect directly to a target database. Dreamweaver MX has five Type 4 database drivers you can use to connect directly to your database:

◆ IBM DB2 App Driver (DB2)
◆ IBM DB2 Net Driver (DB2)
◆ MySQL Driver (MySQL)
◆ Oracle Thin Driver (Oracle)
◆ INET Driver (SQL Server)

Each of these drivers requires similar information: the host server name, the port on which the database server communicates, the database name, and the username and password. To demonstrate, we'll use the INET Driver to connect to our SQL Server version of the Books database.

1. Choose Windows ➤ Databases to open the Databases panel. Open any JSP page in your JSP web application site, click the plus (+) sign, and choose INET Driver (SQL Server) to open the INET Driver (SQL Server) dialog box, as shown in Figure 10.18.

2. You can specify whether Dreamweaver MX uses a driver on the local machine or a driver on the testing server. Choose Using Driver On Testing Server.

3. Enter a name for the Dreamweaver MX data connection.

4. In the URL text field, replace [hostname] with the name of the IP address of your SQL Server, replace [port] with the port to which you've set SQL Server (the default port is 1433), and replace [database] with the database name.

FIGURE 10.18

The INET Driver
(SQL Server)
dialog box

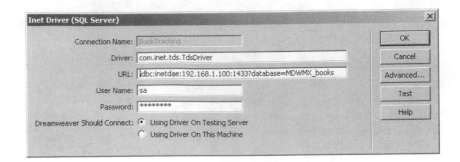

5. Click the Test button to validate the data connection. If the test succeeds, click OK to save the data connection as a JSP file in the Connections folder of your JSP site.

CUSTOM JDBC CONNECTION

Although Dreamweaver MX comes with five direct drivers that can connect to the most popular database servers, you may find yourself working with a more obscure database. In such a case, you can still use Dreamweaver MX to create a data connection through the Custom JDBC Connection method if you can find a JDBC driver for your database. As you can see in the Custom JDBC Connection dialog box shown in Figure 10.19, this method is wide open to whatever parameters your database demands. Unfortunately, Dreamweaver MX can offer you little assistance in determining these parameters. Your best bet is to install the JDBC driver on the web server and then consult the JDBC driver and your database documentation.

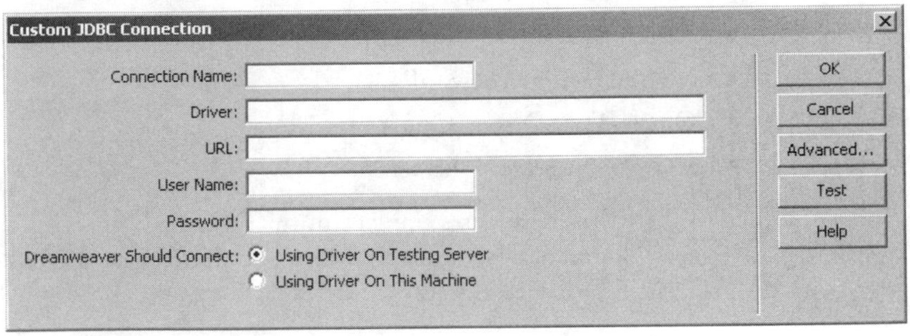

FIGURE 10.19

The Custom
JDBC Connection
dialog box

Database Connections for ColdFusion Developers

Unlike ASP, ASP.NET, JSP, and PHP, you cannot actually create a data source connection through Dreamweaver MX for Macromedia ColdFusion. Instead, you define the data source connection through the ColdFusion administrator. You can then view and select the data sources from within Dreamweaver MX. However, before Dreamweaver MX can connect to ColdFusion data sources, several requirements must be satisfied.

◆ You must have access to a web server such as IIS, PWS, or Apache Tomcat for Linux.

- ◆ You must install the ColdFusion application server on the web server.
- ◆ You must define a ColdFusion site in Dreamweaver MX.

When all these requirements are met, you can see all ColdFusion data sources in Dreamweaver MX. To demonstrate how ColdFusion data sources appear in Dreamweaver MX, we'll use the SQL Server version of our Books database.

1. Open the ColdFusion Administrator and navigate to the Data Sources section. In the Data Source Name text field, enter a ColdFusion data source name. This is the data source name that Dreamweaver MX displays in the Database window of your ColdFusion website.

2. Specify a driver to connect to the Books SQL Server database. You can use a ColdFusion-supplied SQL Server driver or select ODBC Socket to choose a System DSN from your web server. For our example, choose the Microsoft SQL Server driver from the Driver drop-down list box, as shown in Figure 10.20, and then click Add to open the Microsoft SQL Server Data Source dialog box

FIGURE 10.20

The Data Sources section in the ColdFusion Administrator

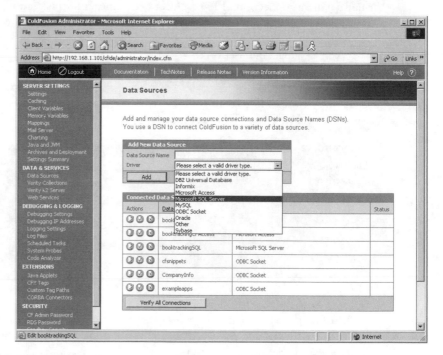

3. Enter the Books database name, the server it resides on, and the username and password to connect to the database. Click Submit to create the ColdFusion data connection.

4. Return to Dreamweaver MX and open your ColdFusion website. Open any CFM page in your site and choose Windows ➢ Databases to open the Databases panel. As you can see in Figure 10.21, Dreamweaver MX displays the ColdFusion data sources ready for use.

FIGURE 10.21

The Databases tab in Dreamweaver MX displaying data sources from the ColdFusion Administrator

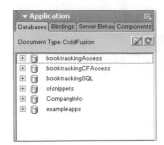

Database Connections for PHP Developers

Concerning PHP development, Dreamweaver MX supports only the MySQL database. However, PHP is a powerful open-source language that supports many types of database connection methods, including ODBC. Therefore, you can always take matters into your own hands and manually script your database connections. However, for the purposes of this section, we are going to demonstrate how to create a data connection to the MySQL database. To begin, you will need access to a PHP/MySQL development environment, including a web server and the PHP application server.

To create a data connection to a MySQL database, follow these steps:

1. Choose Windows ➤ Databases to open the Databases panel.
2. Open any PHP page in your site, click the plus (+) sign, and choose MySQL Connection to open the MySQL Connection dialog box, as shown in Figure 10.22.

FIGURE 10.22

The MySQL Connection dialog box

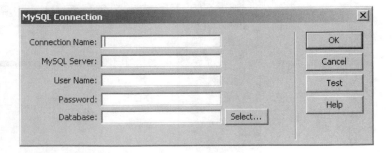

3. Enter the name of your Dreamweaver MX data connection, the name of your MySQL Server, the username and password to connect, and the database you want to connect.
4. Click the Test button to validate the data connection. If successful, click OK to save the data connection as a PHP file in the Connections folder of your PHP site.

Managing an Existing Data Connection

Once you've created a working Dreamweaver MX data connection, you may find you need to test the data connection again. To do so, open a page from your website, open the Database window, right-click on a connection, and choose Test. If the test fails, or for many other reasons, you might find you need to alter the settings of the data connection. To edit a data connection, open a page from your website, open the Database window, right-click a connection, and then choose Edit Connection from the drop-down menu to open the Data Connection dialog box. You can alter every setting but the name of the data connection.

If you want to change the name of a data connection, your best bet is to duplicate the data connection and correctly name the duplicate. To duplicate a data connection, open a page from your website, right-click the data connection in the Database window, and choose Duplicate to open the Data Connection dialog box. This dialog box displays the settings of the original data connection and lets you name the duplicate data connection.

To delete a data connection, you have several options. First, open a page from your website, and select a data connection in the Database window. To delete, you can click the minus (−) button, press the Delete key, or right-click the data connection and choose Delete.

Troubleshooting Data Connections

Data connection errors are one of the most troubling elements for dynamically driven websites. Problems will occur. Actually, inexplicable enigmatic problems will occur that can only be solved using the arcane art of exception error numerology. OK, a bit of an exaggeration, but tracking down a data connection problem is actually a hybrid of science and art. When a data connection error occurs, your web page will most likely bomb. In most cases, it will bomb and display an error message. That error message will undoubtedly have an error number and an explanation. In most cases, that explanation will mean next to nothing to you. However, the number is the clue. Start with that error number and comb through documentation and websites. In almost all cases, someone else has received that exact same error message and has already deciphered it. Have faith that their experience and solution have been documented—all you have to do is find it. Not to completely leave you out in the cold, the following section lists some of the more common data connection problems and provides a few solutions.

TIP   If your web page bombs but you do not see an error message, the most likely reason is that the page has bombed in the middle of writing an HTML tag. This means the error message is there—it's just hidden in the source code of the page. To view the error message, choose View ➤ Source in your browser, and scan to the bottom of the source code page. You should find the error message there.

Microsoft Error Messages

Since Microsoft developed the ODBC, the Windows operating systems, one of the most popular web servers available, and two major databases (Access, and SQL Server) and acquired FoxPro a few years ago, you can bet you will see more than your share of Microsoft data connection error messages. Fortunately, Microsoft and the rest of the world are phenomenal about documenting both problems and solutions. In addition to the common Microsoft error messages we detail in this section, you might also want to consult www.microsoft.com and www.macromedia.com, newsgroups dedicated to web programming or your chosen database, and the major search engines.

Access Permission Problems

If you are using Access as a back-end database for your website, the web server will need the appropriate read and write permissions to the database file. IIS runs as a web service typically under the user account IUSR_<*machine name*>, but most web administrators immediately change the user account the web service runs under to something else for security reasons. If you do that, you must also add the new, renamed web service user account to the access rights of the database file. If the web server does not have read and write permissions to the database, you can see any of the following error messages.

```
Microsoft OLE DB Provider for ODBC Drivers error '80004005' [Microsoft][ODBC
    Microsoft Access 2000 Driver] Couldn't use '(unknown)'; file already in
    use.

Microsoft OLE DB Provider for ODBC Drivers (0x80004005) [Microsoft][ODBC
    Microsoft Access Driver] The Microsoft Jet database engine cannot open
    the file '(unknown)'. It is already opened exclusively by another user,
    or you need permission to view its data.

Microsoft OLE DB Provider for ODBC Drivers error '80004005' [Microsoft][ODBC
    Microsoft Access 2000 Driver] Couldn't lock file.
```

To apply appropriate permissions, you need to get to the Properties ➤ File Security window for you Access file on your web server computer. Be certain that the user under which the web server is running has access to the file. In addition, make sure the web server user has read and write access, as shown in Figure 10.23.

FIGURE 10.23

The web server must have access to your database file

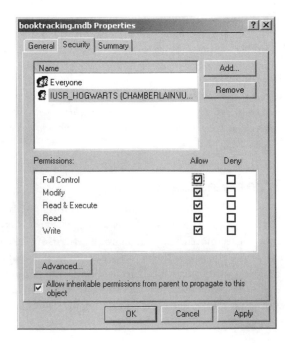

SQL Server Login Failed

One of the most common SQL Server connection errors occurs when you attempt to connect to SQL Server. You receive the following error message:

```
Login failed for user 'NULL'. Reason: Not associated with a trusted
    SQL Server connection
```

This error is typically caused by an authentication setting and is usually easily resolved. To do so, you'll need to alter your SQL Server security settings. Follow these steps:

1. Choose Start ➤ Programs ➤ Microsoft SQL Server ➤ Enterprise Manager to open SQL Server Enterprise Manager.

2. Right-click on your server, and choose Properties from the shortcut menu to open the SQL Server Proprieties (Configure) dialog box, as shown in Figure 10.24.

FIGURE 10.24

The Security tab in the SQL Server Properties (Configure) dialog box

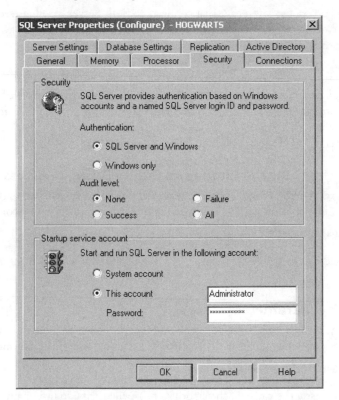

3. Click the Securities tab, and in the Authentication section, click the SQL Server and Windows option.

4. Click OK. SQL Server prompts you to stop and restart SQL Server. When SQL Server restarts, you can access the databases in the server.

Data Source Name Not Found

When you attempt to view a dynamic web page, you receive the following error message due to a number of possible scenarios. The DSN may be missing or corrupt, the DSN may not be a System DSN on the web server, or the Access database may be in use and locked.

```
80004005–Data source name not found and no default driver specified
```

To solve the problem, first be sure that the DSN exists on the web server as a System DSN. If the DSN exists as a Local DSN, delete the Local DSN and create a System DSN. If you suspect the Access database file is locked because someone else is accessing it, locate the Access file on the server and search for a locked file. The locked file will have the extension .1db. Delete the locked file, restart the server, and try to access the dynamic page again.

SQL Server Logon General Error

When you try to view a page that connects to SQL Server, you may see the following error message. This error message is typically generated when SQL Server does not authenticate the account or password that the web page is submitting to access a database.

```
80004005–Logon Failed()
```

Typically this error is born of permission problems. In the "SQL Server Login Failed" section, we've already suggested setting SQL Server security to Server and Windows Security. Another possible solution is to check for an underline (_) in the name of the SQL account name used to log into SQL Server. SQL Server does not allow an underscore in SQL account names.

Updating a Date Column to an Empty String in Access

You'll receive the following error message if one of your web pages attempts to update an Access Date/Time column with an empty string or a value that cannot be converted to a Date/Time value.

```
80040e07–Data type mismatch in criteria expression
```

To avoid this error message, simply avoid inserting or updating a Date/Time column if you have no value to insert.

Too Few Parameters

When your web page attempts to pass a SQL statement to a database and references a data column that does not exist in the table, you may receive the following error message.

```
80040e10–Too few parameters
```

In most cases, the cause of the error is a misspelled data column name. Carefully compare the data column names in your SQL statement with the data column names in your database table.

Summary

We've covered a lot of ground in this chapter. We've discussed the ODBC, OLE DB, JDBC, and native types of connections and demonstrated how to use Dreamweaver MX to create those database connections types in ASP, ASP.NET, ColdFusion, JSP, and PHP web applications. Keep in mind that all this database connection information is written from a Dreamweaver MX state of mind. You can connect to a database in many more ways than Dreamweaver MX can currently handle and than we've shown in this chapter.

Now that you know how to use Dreamweaver MX to create a connection between a web application and a database, the next step is to use that connection to retrieve data from the database and display it on a web page. To do so, we'll explore the Dreamweaver MX–supported web scripting languages and look at how to use them to create database-driven sites.

Chapter 11

ColdFusion and Dreamweaver MX

COLDFUSION, ONCE THE BRAINCHILD of the Allaire Corporation, now belongs to Macromedia, the creators of Dreamweaver MX. Since its inception many years ago, ColdFusion has provided the web developer an easy-to-use, powerful platform on which to build dynamic websites without being locked into the Microsoft suite of products. In fact, ColdFusion was born before ASP (Active Server Pages), PHP (Hypertext Preprocessor), and JSP (JavaServer Pages) and has added more and more power through its growing years. In fact, the latest version of ColdFusion, ColdFusion MX, was completely rewritten to run on a J2EE (Java 2 Enterprise Edition) platform, offering even more cross-platform coverage and compatibility.

Now that Macromedia guides the growth of this incredibly powerful web development platform, it's no wonder that Dreamweaver MX has a special affection for ColdFusion. Dreamweaver MX provides many features to aid your development of ColdFusion applications. We'll cover those features in this chapter, as well as introduce you to the ColdFusion application server and its language.

This chapter covers the following topics:

◆ ColdFusion—the web application server
◆ ColdFusion—the language
◆ ColdFusion—the development environment

ColdFusion—the Web Application Server (or Host)

ColdFusion has been around for nearly 10 years and has become more and more popular among web development teams every year. Fortune 500 companies as well as small development shops use ColdFusion not only because of its rapid application development features, but also because it is simply one of the more powerful web development language/application server combinations available.

You control how the host environment, the ColdFusion web application server (or just ColdFusion Server), behaves using the new ColdFusion Administrator, shown in Figure 11.1. You can launch the ColdFusion Administrator either through the web interface (typically `http://yourserver/cfide/administrator/index.cfm`) or through the Start ➤ Programs menu (in Windows). You have access to nearly 30 categories of settings to control everything from how ColdFusion treats pages that are taking too long to process, to e-mail, to logging error messages and events. Although we certainly can't cover every feature of the ColdFusion Administrator in one chapter, we can explore those items that will immediately make your web application development even more enjoyable with ColdFusion.

FIGURE 11.1

You use the ColdFusion Administrator to control how the ColdFusion Server behaves.

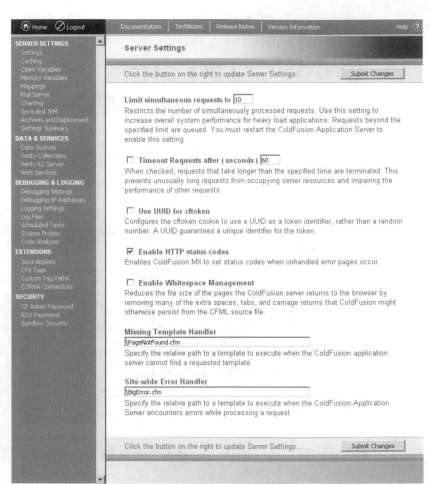

Server Settings—Settings

Under the Settings category, you'll find a few general behaviors that don't quite fit into any other category. This category, however, controls a few important aspects of ColdFusion that can greatly affect your site visitor's experience with your application.

Limit Simultaneous Requests

The Limit Simultaneous Requests setting controls how many requests your ColdFusion Server will process at any one moment. Let's suppose that you have just launched a web application that proves to be popular with the Internet community. As more and more people visit your site, it seems to get slower and slower, eventually bogging down to the point where even loading the home page takes forever. Well, until you move your application to a clustered server, you can try manipulating this setting so that your ColdFusion Server doesn't get hit with 100 simultaneous requests to load the home page at exactly the same moment.

This setting tells ColdFusion to handle only the number of requests you specify at any one moment. The rest of the folks have to wait in a queue until the server can get to them. This allows ColdFusion to respond rapidly to those that are in the immediate-process space so that it can then get to the other waiting users. You might need to experiment with this setting to find the optimal value; ColdFusion defaults to 10 requests. You'll have to stop and restart the ColdFusion Server in order for a change to this value to take effect.

Timeout Requests

This setting tells ColdFusion to watch over how long pages are taking to execute and stop them if they exceed the amount of time you specify. The default value, in seconds, is 60. Depending on your application, that may be more than enough time for any given procedure to run. Or, if your application performs intricate searching and logging of data, you might need to increase this setting.

The Timeout Requests setting helps keep your web server operating properly by canceling those pages that hang, for whatever reason. Perhaps a bug gets by you and causes your pages to never return a result to the user; the page simply loops and eats up your server's memory. With Timeout Requests enabled, you don't have to worry about that happening, since after 60 seconds, for instance, the page will simply stop and not crash the server.

Missing Template Handler

This setting lets you specify a page that the server shows to the user instead of a 404 error if a page can't be found. Nothing is as inelegant as going to a professional website and receiving a 404, or Page Not Found, error. The ColdFusion Administrator let's you ensure that your site visitors will never receive a nasty-looking 404.

We've all received these errors. Perhaps we misspell a page name in a URL and receive something like the default Internet Explorer 404 error page shown in Figure 11.2, which doesn't give the user any information specific to the site. A well-behaved site will trap for these kinds of mistakes and show the user a page that is a bit more friendly. Our example in Figure 11.3, which isn't by any stretch of the word professional, at least doesn't show the cryptic error number to the user, and it includes links to other pages in the site. You might also include a phone number to call for technical assistance.

Site-Wide Error Handler

The Site-Wide Error Handler setting does the same thing as the Missing Template Handler for errors other than missing page errors. Again, it's always better to show a "controlled crash" error page to your user than an inelegant, standard system error page.

FIGURE 11.2

A 404, or Page Not Found, error is not an elegant way to handle a missing page error.

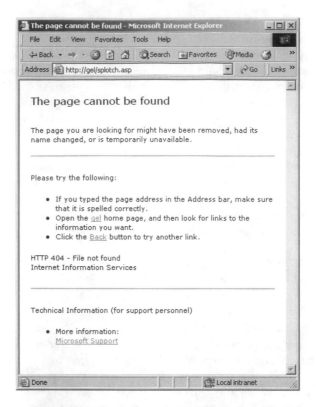

FIGURE 11.3

ColdFusion let's you specify a custom page that should be shown to the user when it can't find the page that was requested.

Server Settings—Client Variables

The Client Variables setting, shown in Figure 11.4, controls where ColdFusion Server stores client variables—variables that persist for clients across user sessions. The default setting, which we highly recommend you change, is to store this information in the system Registry. If you're running Windows, you know that this is a bad idea. You generally don't want variables stored in your system Registry. Not only will this cause Registry bloat, but it also slows down the system.

FIGURE 11.4

You should immediately set client variables to a data source instead of using the default of the system Registry.

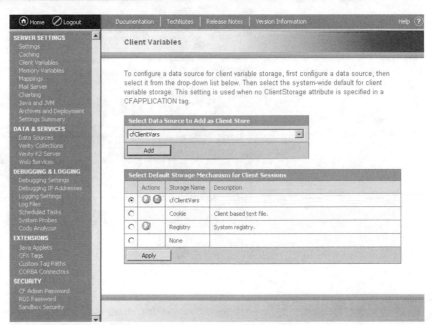

Fortunately, ColdFusion Administrator allows you to store client variable information in a database, as well. You do have the option of storing client variables in cookies, but you have more control over the variables if you store them locally in a table. So create a data source and set the default storage to the table specified in the data source (see Chapter 4 for more information).

Server Settings—Memory Variables

The Memory Variables setting lets you control how ColdFusion Server handles application and session variables. As you can see in Figure 11.5, you can specify the default timeout and the maximum timeout settings. The special control file, `Application.cfm`, can also control how long these variables exist on your server. However, the settings you specify here override the `Application.cfm` file. That's why you have a Maximum Timeout value. If your application states that an application variable should last for 7 days, but your server has a Maximum Timeout value of only 2 days, the variable will expire in 2 days.

This setting is especially useful in multi-application settings where many developers build applications. You can enforce server-setting policies through the ColdFusion Administrator since it always overrides `Application.cfm`.

FIGURE 11.5

You control how long ColdFusion Server stores memory variables through the Memory Variables setting.

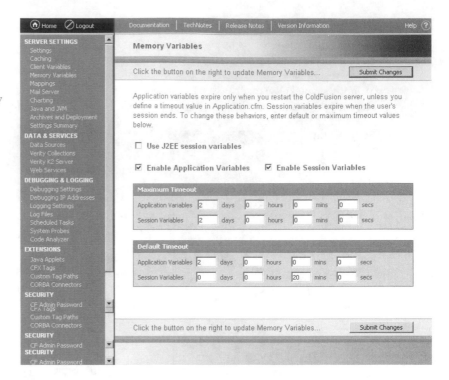

APPLICATION.CFM—THE AUTOMATIC INCLUDE FILE

Every Cold Fusion application can contain a special file named Application.cfm. This file is executed before every page in the application. ColdFusion looks first in the current page's directory for Application.cfm. If it doesn't find it, ColdFusion Server goes up one branch in the directory tree. It keeps searching until it finds an Application.cfm file.

Application.cfm is an optional file that is, in effect, automatically included at the top of every .cfm page that executes. Since ColdFusion looks in the current page's directory for the Application.cfm file, you can have more than one Application.cfm file per web application. Perhaps you need a set of variables to contain differing values depending on whether Sales or Marketing is using the system. You can set specific values for each department in an Application.cfm file for each folder (assuming, of course, that all Sales pages are in a Sales directory and all Marketing pages are in a Marketing directory).

Application.cfm is a regular .cfm file, and as such, can contain any ColdFusion code. Typically, Application .cfm is used to define default values for variables, data sources, application variables, and so forth. Login processing generally occurs in an Application.cfm file as well, since you can enforce a login check for every page.

Server Settings—Settings Summary

The Settings Summary category creates a report of all your ColdFusion Server settings. Figure 11.6 shows a small section of a sample report. This report is a great aid in making sure your Cold-Fusion Server is configured the way you want it. It certainly beats clicking every category and then scrolling through the page to check settings. If only early versions of ColdFusion Server had provided such a tool.

FIGURE 11.6

The Settings Summary gives you a report that details every value for every setting in your ColdFusion Server.

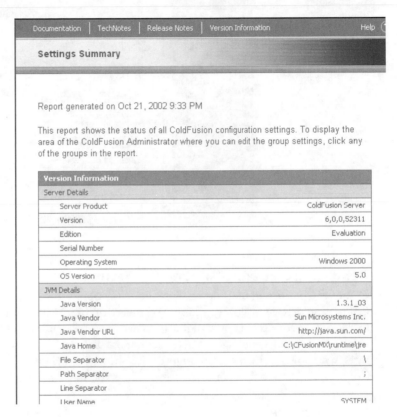

Data & Services—Data Sources

The Data Sources category controls the data connections your ColdFusion Server is going to use. As you can see in Figure 11.7, you can connect to a number of database sources. And for those databases that aren't listed, you can probably use ODBC (Open Database Connectivity) as a connection protocol.

Every data source that your ColdFusion application is going to use must be defined in the Administrator before you can use it, since the CFQuery tag (more on that later) uses the data source name found here. (You can find more about database connections in Chapter 10.)

FIGURE 11.7

The Data Sources
window lets you
manage the data
source connections
used in your
ColdFusion
applications.

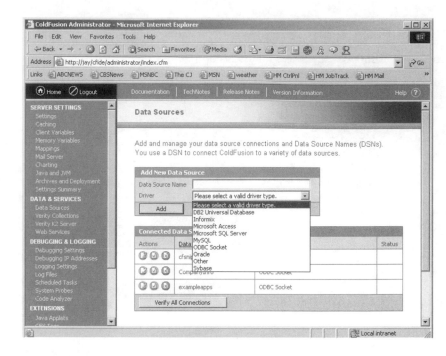

Debugging & Logging—Debugging Settings

One of the best-loved tools developers find in ColdFusion is its debugger. The capabilities in the
ColdFusion debugger allow you to see every piece of information you could hope for when it comes
to debugging your programs. ColdFusion's debugger will automatically append debugging information to the end of your pages. You control most debugging settings in the Debugging Settings
category, shown in Figure 11.8. Figure 11.8 shows the default debugging settings provided by
ColdFusion. Let's look at some of those settings you might want to change.

ENABLE DEBUGGING

To enable debugging, you must select the Enable Debugging check box and click Submit Changes.
When you do, each time you launch a `.cfm` page, you may see information like that in Figure 11.9,
where we're debugging our "hello world" application. We say "may" because you actually must tell
ColdFusion to show you the information. We'll cover how to do that shortly.

DEBUGGING OUTPUT FORMAT

You can display debugging information in two formats—*classic* and *dockable*. The classic format is
shown in Figure 11.9. By simply scrolling through the page, you have immediate access to information
such as the file that was running (Template), how long it took the page to execute (Execution Time),
various variables, cookies, and more.

FIGURE 11.8

The Debugging Settings category will become one of your favorite ColdFusion Administrator areas.

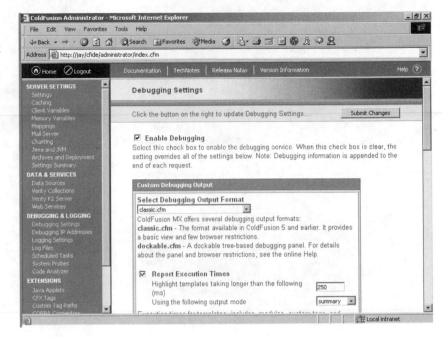

FIGURE 11.9

The debugging information you see may look similar to this.

Hello World

Debugging Information

ColdFusion Server Evaluation 6,0,0,48097

Template	/fusiontest/helloworld.cfm
Time Stamp	21-Oct-02 01:47 AM
Locale	English (US)
User Agent	Mozilla/4.0 (compatible; MSIE 6.0; Windows NT 5.0; T312461; Q312461; .NET CLR 1.0.3705)
Remote IP	192.168.1.120
Host Name	192.168.1.120

Execution Time

Total Time	Avg Time	Count	Template
0 ms	0 ms	1	C:\Inetpub\wwwroot\FusionTest\HelloWorld.cfm
140 ms			STARTUP, PARSING, COMPILING, LOADING, & SHUTDOWN
140 ms			TOTAL EXECUTION TIME

red = over 250 ms average execution time

Scope Variables

CGI Variables:

```
SCRIPT_NAME=/fusiontest/helloworld.cfm
HTTPS_KEYSIZE=
CERT_KEYSIZE=
AUTH_USER=
SERVER_NAME=xanadu
REQUEST_METHOD=GET
AUTH_PASSWORD=
```

Figure 11.10 shows you a sample of the dockable format. By clicking the appropriate debug link in the main page, you can hide or show the debug window or dock it within the main page, as you can see in Figure 11.11.

FIGURE 11.10

You can display the debugging information in its own window.

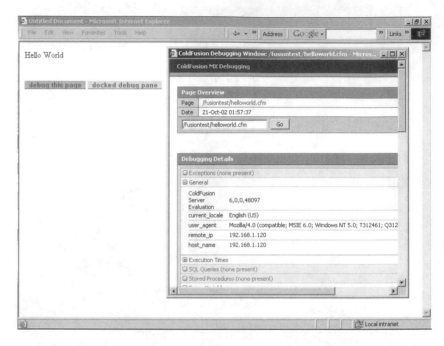

FIGURE 11.11

Or you can dock the debugging information within a pane of the current page.

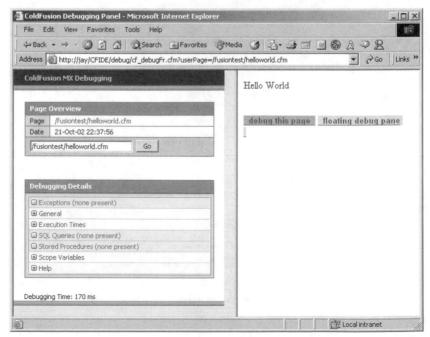

REPORT EXECUTION TIMES

This debugging setting can be invaluable when trying to make your pages load faster or for trying to find where a breakdown in speed lies. Report Execution Times tells you how long it takes your page to execute, from start to finish, including load time. Pages that exceed the millisecond count you specify are highlighted in red in the data summary.

VARIABLES

When it comes to debugging, you may find that there's no such thing as too much information. We recommend that you leave all the default settings in the Debugging Settings category, but also add the unchecked variables. That way, you can see every variable that could possibly affect your pages. Now, this is great if you're using the dockable debug window. If you're using the classic format, you may get tired of scrolling through all the information and want to uncheck the variable types you don't select that often.

Debugging & Logging—Debugging IP Addresses

We mentioned earlier that you actually need to tell ColdFusion to show you the debugging information when you've enabled the debugging option. You do that through the Debugging IP Addresses category. Figure 11.12 shows you the Debugging IP Address window, in which you enter the IP address of each computer for which you want to receive debugging information. If you have a team of developers, you can enter each of their specific IP addresses, and they'll see the debugging information for their pages. IPs that aren't listed here, perhaps the conference room computer, won't receive the debugging information.

FIGURE 11.12

To actually see the debugging information, you either enter a list of IP addresses or remove all the IP addresses.

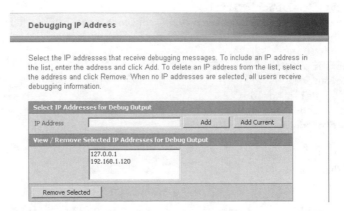

Now, if you remove all the IP addresses from the list, every user receives the debug information. Be careful when changing this setting on your production, or live, servers. You don't want the world to see all the debugging information for your website. Not only is it embarrassing, but it could pose a big security risk!

ColdFusion—the Language

By now, you know that ColdFusion files have a `.cfm` extension. These files contain ColdFusion Script, a tag-based markup language, generally called CFML. CFML (ColdFusion Markup Language) is similar to HTML (Hypertext Markup Language), which is also tag-based, but CFML also includes built-in functions similar to those built into ASP, PHP, and others.

As you do with these other languages, you create an application file, and the server interprets that file and delivers dynamically created HTML to the user.

Unlike some other web development languages, ColdFusion doesn't include constructs such as the Request object in ASP. Instead, it simplifies the day-to-day operations of development by consolidating many steps into single tags.

Using ColdFusion Script and CFML, you can create dynamic websites that can be as complex as you want to make them. Let's take a brief look at some of the more common tags and commands to get you started in your ColdFusion development.

The Pound (#) Symbol

The pound (#) symbol has special meaning to ColdFusion. It is used in pairs around variable names when those variables appear by themselves and not necessarily as part of a ColdFusion function or command. For example, the simple code in Listing 11.1 tells ColdFusion to store the string `"Darren"` in the variable *cMyName* and display it. You can see the results in Figure 11.13.

We strongly encourage you to key in all the code to create the example files yourself. To check your work, compare your files with the example files on the CD accompanying this book.

LISTING 11.1: *HELLOWORLD.CFM*

```html
<html>
<head>
<title>HelloWorld</title>
<meta http-equiv="Content-Type" content="text/html; charset=iso-8859-1">
</head>
<body>
<cfset cMyName = "Darren">
<cfoutput>
    Hello World
    and Hello #cMyName#
</cfoutput>

</body>
</html>
```

FIGURE 11.13

The simple output from our script displays the contents of the variable *cMyName*.

The *<cfset>* Tag

The `<cfset>` tag defines a variable in ColdFusion. It takes the following form:

```
<cfset variableName = value>
```

in which *value* can be either an expression or a literal value. If the variable you're defining already exists, ColdFusion just sets it to the new value. The `<cfset>` tag is similar to `DIM` in ASP, except you can immediately assign a value to your variable as you define it.

The *<cfoutput>* Tag

This tag is a data output tag that is used to display ColdFusion variables, queries, and other operations. You can use several options with the `<cfoutput>` tag, such as `query`, `group`, and `startRow`. Each of these options (and others) controls things such as where the data that you're going to display comes from, at what row in the data the output should start, and so forth. You can also just use it as we did in our Listing 11.1 to wrap a section of code. This tells ColdFusion that you're including some ColdFusion-specific tags or variables that it needs to interpret. Listing 11.2 and Figure 11.14, in the next section, show you the code and the results of using `<cfoutput>` with a query. The `<cfoutput>` tag works like `Response.write` in ASP, but also has the added functionality of being able to loop through a recordset itself.

The *<cfquery>* Tag

The `<cfquery>` tag allows you to create and execute a query on a table or other data source. As you can with other ColdFusion tags, you can apply many attributes to the `<cfquery>` tag, but in its simplest form, as you can see in Listing 11.2, it simply requires a name and a data source. The SQL code to be used in the query is enclosed within the opening and closing tags. The `<cfquery>` tag combines into one tag what takes in ASP at least four lines of code, plus the SQL statement.

NOTE   *To run this program, you need to create a DSN (Data Source Name) for the sample database, following the instructions in Chapter 10. Then use that DSN in the* `datasource=` *statement.*

LISTING 11.2: *SHOWAUTHORS.CFM*

```
<html>
<head>
<title>ShowAuthors</title>
<meta http-equiv="Content-Type" content="text/html; charset=iso-8859-1">
</head>

<body>

<cfquery name="MyQuery" datasource="Books">
    Select FirstName, LastName, AuthorId from tblAuthors
</cfquery>

<cfoutput query="MyQuery">
    <hr width="25%" align="left">
```

```
        Author_ID: #AuthorID# <br>
        First Name: #FirstName# <br>
        Last Name: #LastName#
</cfoutput>

</body>
</html>
```

FIGURE 11.14

The `<cfoutput>`
and the `<cfquery>`
tags work in
conjunction to
display a list of
records.

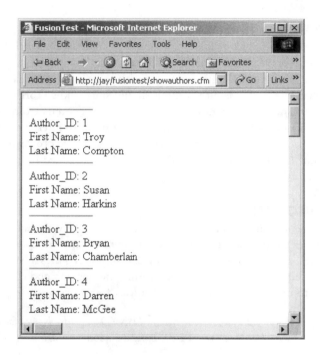

The *<cfabort>* Tag

This tag works like `Response.end` in ASP: it simply halts processing of the page. This tag comes in handy when you're debugging a page and want to stop processing at a specific point. Simply throw in a `<cfabort>` tag where you want the page to stop, and ColdFusion will not process anything else in the page.

ColdFusion—the Development Environment

As we mentioned, Dreamweaver MX works well with ColdFusion. Using the forms and panels in Dreamweaver MX, you can include a large part of the ColdFusion command set just by clicking your mouse. When you're working with a ColdFusion page, Dreamweaver MX places three ColdFusion-specific tabs across the Insert bar: CFML Basic, CFML Flow, and CFML Advanced. These three tabs provide quick access to the major components and tags within ColdFusion, along with pop-up windows to guide you in creating the tag. Let's take a look at a few of those.

The CFML Basic Tab

Figure 11.15 shows the CFML Basic tab and its components. These items are some of the most commonly used ColdFusion tags and components. Dreamweaver MX provides an easy way to apply these to your code—simply click the button to display a window containing text fields and settings appropriate for the tag.

FIGURE 11.15

The CFML Basic tab gives you quick access to some of the commonly used ColdFusion tags.

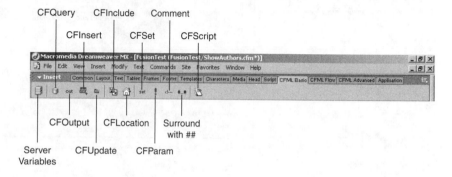

FIGURE 11.16

Entering server variables into your code is a snap.

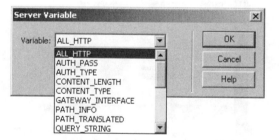

THE SERVER VARIABLES BUTTON

ColdFusion, naturally, can use server variables just like ASP. In Dreamweaver MX, you can quickly access many of these server variables by clicking the Server Variables button to open the Server Variable dialog box, which will be similar to that in Figure 11.16.

THE CFQUERY BUTTON

You don't have to remember the syntax of the many-optioned `<cfquery>` tag when you click the CFQuery button on the Insert bar. Figure 11.17 shows how Dreamweaver MX pops up a window to guide you through the options.

THE COMMENT BUTTON

Clicking the Comment button throws a comment into your code. That is, it adds the opening and closing brackets for a comment. And, if you highlight the text that you want to turn into a comment and click the Comment button, Dreamweaver MX simply wraps the text with the comment tags for you, as you can see in Figure 11.18. This is a great way to temporarily block out chunks of code when you're debugging an application.

FIGURE 11.17

Specify your choices for the `<cfquery>` tag by concentrating on the data and not the syntax of the tag.

FIGURE 11.18

You can instantly turn a chunk of code into a comment by selecting it and clicking the Comment button.

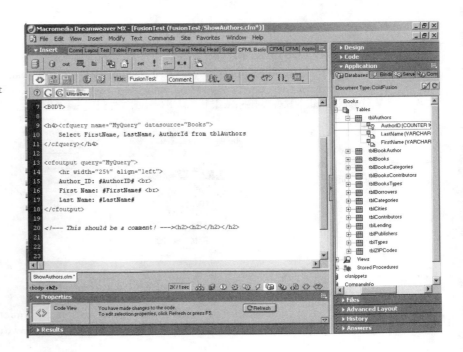

THE SURROUND WITH ## BUTTON

Just like the Comment button, the Surround With ## button wraps the selected text in pound signs. Many times, while cranking out code, you may forget to add the pound signs around your variables. You can simply highlight your variables and click the Surround With ## button to place the pound signs around them.

The CFML Flow Tab

The CFML Flow tab (see Figure 11.19) contains buttons for quick access to constructs that affect the logic flow of your application. Many of these, such as CFTry and CFCatch, require more explanation than this chapter allows. But let's explore a couple of the options so you can get the feel of what's on this toolbar.

FIGURE 11.19

The CFML Flow tab gives you access to flow-control constructs.

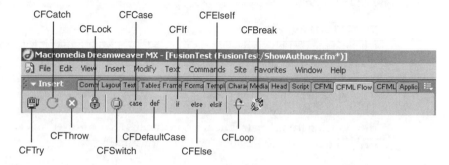

THE CFLOCK BUTTON

Clicking the CFLock button effectively prevents any other user from executing code that exists within the `<cflock></cflock>` tags. This helps you maintain integrity in your application when you're updating variables that can be shared across the application or even sessions. Figure 11.20 shows a sample CFLock window. You give the lock a name, set a timeout value so that the lock frees up if it can't lock the code within the time specified, and you set the type and scope of the lock. The code this generates looks like the following:

```
<cflock name="UpdateApplicationVariable"
     timeout="2"
     throwontimeout="no"
     type="exclusive"
  scope="application">
</cflock>
```

You place variable setting code between the opening and closing tags to make sure that only the current process can update a variable at a given moment.

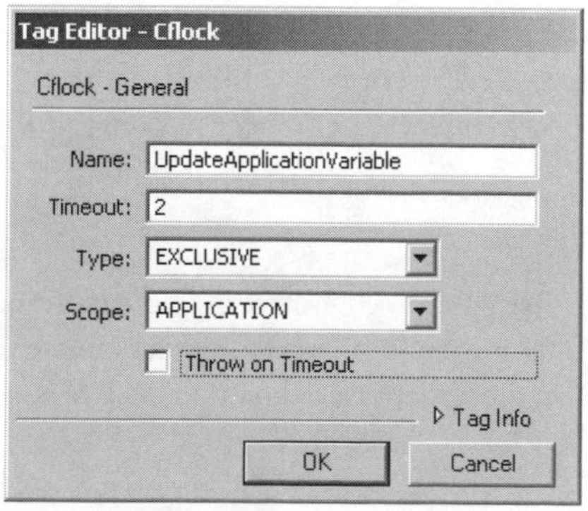

FIGURE 11.20

Lock your application and session variable updates to ensure that their integrity remains intact.

THE CFIF, CFELSE, AND CFELSEIF BUTTONS

Clicking any of these three buttons simply places the opening tag in your code. Clicking one of these buttons doesn't open a dialog box, but it does save typing. For example, if you click the CFIf button, Dreamweaver MX inserts `<cfif></cfif>` in your code and places the cursor at the space character within the opening `<cfif>` tag so you can immediately type the IF condition for which you're testing.

THE CFLOOP BUTTON

Clicking the CFLoop is the same as using a For-Next or Do-While loop in other languages; however, it's more powerful and more flexible. You can use CFLoop to create five types of loops, as you can see in Figure 11.21. The Index loop is like a For-Next loop. The Conditional loop is like a Do-While loop. The next three loop through a Query, a List, or a Collection, executing the loop once for every item in the type. This saves you from having to calculate the number of items in a construct and then looping from 1 to that number. Naturally, Dreamweaver MX adjusts the fields in the CFLoop dialog box to ask for the appropriate information.

FIGURE 11.21
CFLoop is a powerful command that creates looping structures using any of five different types as the key.

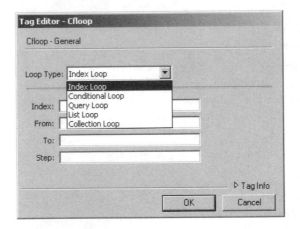

The CFML Advanced Tab

The CFML Advanced tab, shown in Figure 11.22, gives you access to more advanced features of ColdFusion's code base. Although clicking these buttons gives you access to the most common features of the item represented, you'll want to spend some time with the documentation, help files, or online forums to learn the power of these items. We're going to show a couple, however, to get you started.

THE CFCOOKIE BUTTON

To set cookies, you can click the CFCookie button. You can actually set six options for a cookie tag, and Dreamweaver MX makes it easy for you to use those options, as you can see in Figure 11.23. Just enter the values you want in the appropriate box and click OK, and you have instant cookie code.

FIGURE 11.22

The CFML Advanced tab gives you access to some of the real power behind ColdFusion.

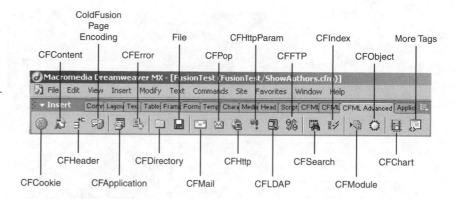

FIGURE 11.23

ColdFusion has its own method for setting a cookie, and Dreamweaver MX aids you in setting the cookie.

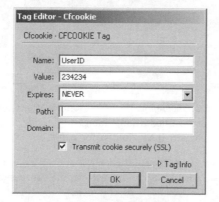

THE CFAPPLICATION BUTTON

The `<cfapplication>` tag is a special tag that typically goes in the `Application.cfm` file. It sets values for the application name, session timeout values, application timeout values, and so forth. (See Figure 11.24.) (Remember, your application can set these values, but the ColdFusion Administrator settings always override the application if they should disagree.) The settings we entered create code similar to the following:

```
<cfapplication name="MyApplication"
   clientmanagement="yes"
   sessionmanagement="no"
   setclientcookies="no"
   setdomaincookies="no"
   sessiontimeout="120"
   clientstorage="ClientVar">
```

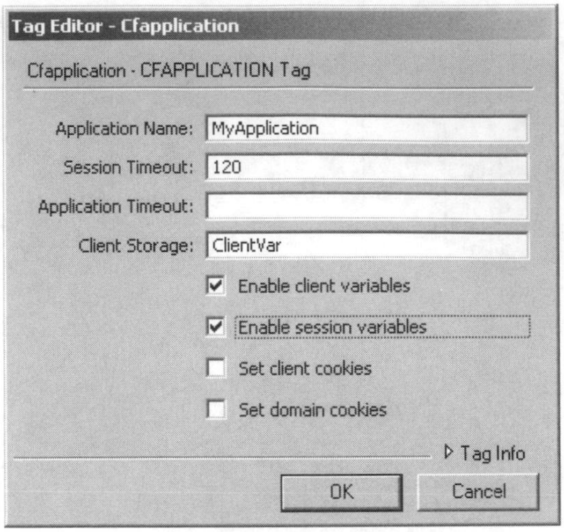

FIGURE 11.24

You can quickly set your `<cfapplication>` tag code by clicking the CFApplication button on the Insert bar.

FOR MORE INFORMATION

If you're serious about using ColdFusion, explore the vast resources Macromedia has devoted to ColdFusion on their website. You'll find tons of documentation, hints, sample code, and online forums where you can ask questions and share experiences with other ColdFusion users.

You might also want to check out *Mastering ColdFusion MX* or *ColdFusion MX Developer's Handbook*, both from Sybex, or any of Ben Forta's books. Some favorite online sources of ours are Ben Forta's site at www.forta.com and Webmonkey at www.webmonkey.com.

Summary

This chapter has given you a very quick and very brief overview of ColdFusion. We've covered some of the more important aspects of the ColdFusion Administrator settings that can affect your everyday coding experience. We've touched briefly on how ColdFusion differs from other web application development languages in that it has simplicity yet power built in. And we've touched on how Dreamweaver MX interfaces with ColdFusion.

Chapter 12

JavaServer Pages

JavaServer Pages (JSP) allows web developers to mix the power of HTML (Hypertext Markup Language) with the strength of Java to create web applications with unlimited potential. Although other web technologies, such as ColdFusion, can parse and execute text files containing programming commands mixed with HTML tags, JSP has the advantage of being intrinsically related to Java 2 Platform, Enterprise Edition (J2EE). This relationship allows JSP to leverage the full power of the Java language in a much simpler development environment. Another inherent difference between JSP and other web technologies is that JSP compiles script pages into Java servlets, small programs that a web browser can access without forcing the web server to interpret the script page each time it is called. This approach significantly reduces the resource demands on a web server.

To fully utilize JavaServer Pages and Dreamweaver MX, you need access to a JSP development environment. In addition, you need an understanding of the objects and syntax that make up JSP. The full breadth of Java and JSP are well out of the range of material we can cover in one chapter, so we'll focus our discussion on the most commonly used areas of the JSP language.

This chapter covers the following topics:

◆ JavaServer Pages—the host

◆ JavaServer Pages—the language

◆ JSP Elements

◆ Working in JSP

Overview

A JavaServer Pages (JSP) script file is a text file containing any combination of JSP and HTML code. However, as the JSP web server processes the text file, the server compiles the JSP script file into a servlet. *Servlets* are Java programs that can accept HTTP requests and send HTTP responses through a JSP web server. Typically, this process can be broken into several steps.

1. A web browser requests a page at a specific web address, such as www.sybex.com.
2. The web server hosting the www.sybex.com website accepts that request, locates the targeted page, and prepares to "serve" the page to the requesting web browser.

3. If the request is for a JSP page, the server passes the request to the server's servlet container. The servlet container controls the creation, use, and destruction of servlets. If this is the first request for the JSP servlet, the servlet container compiles the servlet from the JSP page and loads the servlet into memory. At this point, the servlet is ready to accept HTTP requests and send HTTP responses.

4. The server forwards the HTTP request to the servlet, which subsequently sends the resulting HTML to the requesting web browser.

NOTE *Java servlets are small programs written in Java to run within a Java Servlet Engine on a web server. Servlets can be a powerful web development tool. Java servlets are easily portable from one web environment to another and scalable from small to large implementations. In addition, servlets, which are compiled once and actually run inside the web server process, are typically less of a drain of a web server's resources than traditional web-scripting technologies that compile and render a script page upon each request.*

This overview is just the tip of the iceberg. Since the code in a JSP page is actually Java, you're not limited to a single operating system or web server technology. In fact, you can easily port a JSP web application to any operating system and web server technology that supports the Java standard, which includes Windows and most flavors of Unix.

J2EE

The primary focus of Java 2 Platform, Enterprise Edition (J2EE) is to simplify enterprise application development. J2EE accomplishes this goal in three ways. First, J2EE has sets of standardized, modular components that add additional functionality to the JSP language. Second, J2EE provides a complete set of web services to these standardized components. Third, J2EE automatically handles many details of application behavior—without requiring complex programming from the developers.

In addition, J2EE provides the same features that have made Java such a popular development tool—"Write Once, Run Anywhere," JDBC (Java Database Connectivity) for database access, CORBA (Common Object Request Broker Architecture) technology to interact with legacy enterprise systems, security to protect data, and full support for JavaBeans components, Java Servlets API (application programming interface), JavaServer Pages, and XML (Extensible Markup Language).

JavaServer Pages: Selecting a Host

To develop or host a JSP web application, you need access to a web server with a JSP engine. Setting up and administrating such a system is a complicated task, and you will need to make many decisions. Two of the most important decisions are which operating system to use and which web server and JSP engine to install. Macromedia JRun and iPlanet (now renamed to Sun ONE Application Server 7) are just two of the available technologies that add a JSP engine to existing web servers such as Microsoft IIS (Internet Information Services). In addition to the web server, you must also install the latest version of Sun Java Development Kit (JDK), which can be found at http://java.sun.com/j2se/1.4/.

The examples in this book use Macromedia JRun installed on a Windows server running Microsoft SQL Server. If you would like to duplicate the development environment we use in the JSP examples in this book, you can download evaulation versions of this software from Macromedia and Microsoft. Evaluation and development versions typically last for 30 to 90 days. Table 12.1 lists products that offer a built-in or add-on JSP engine as of this writing. For a more up-to-date listing, visit `http://java.sun.com/products/jsp/industry.html`.

TABLE 12.1: WEB SERVERS AND JSP ENGINES

SERVER AND ADD-ON ENGINE	PRODUCT TYPE	JAVA SERVLETS SUPPORT	JSP SUPPORT	LINK
Apache Tomcat	Server	2.3	1.2	`http://jakarta.apache.org/tomcat/index.html`
BEA WebLogic Server 7	Server	2.3	1.2	`www.beasys.com/products/weblogic/server/index.shtml`
Borland Enterprise Server, AppServer Edition	Server	2.3	1.2	`www.borland.com/besappserver/index.html`
Caucho Technology Resin	Add-on Engine	2.3	1.2	`www.caucho.com/products/resin/index.xtp`
Computer Associates Advantage Joe	Server	2.3	1.2	`http://www3.ca.com/Solutions/Overview.asp?ID=257&TYPE=S`
Fujitsu INTERSTAGE	Server	2.3	1.2	`www.fsw.fujitsu.com/interstage/products/index.htm`
Gefion Software Lite WebServer	Server	2.2	1.1	`www.gefionsoftware.com/LiteWebServer/index.jsp`
Hewlett Packard Total-e-Server	Server	2.2	1.1	`www.hp.bluestone.com/SaISAPI.dll/SaServletEngine.class/products/Total-e-Server/default.jsp`
IBM WebSphere Technology for Developers	Server	2.3	1.2	`http://www7b.boulder.ibm.com/wsdd/downloads/wstechnology_tech_preview.html`
IBM WebSphere Application Server 4	Server	2.2	1.1	`http://www-4.ibm.com/software/webservers/appserv/`

Continued on next page

TABLE 12.1: WEB SERVERS AND JSP ENGINES *(continued)*

SERVER AND ADD-ON ENGINE	PRODUCT TYPE	JAVA SERVLETS SUPPORT	JSP SUPPORT	LINK
IONA Orbix E2A Application Server Platform, J2EE Edition	Server	2.3	1.2	www.iona.com/products/appserv-j2ee.htm
Jetty	Server	2.3	1.2	http://jetty.mortbay.org/jetty/index.html
Lutris Technologies Enhydra	Server	2.2	1.1	www.lutris.com/
Macromedia JRun 4	Server and Add-on Engine	2.3	1.2	www.macromedia.com/software/jrun/
New Atlanta ServletExec	Add-on Engine	2.3	1.2	www.newatlanta.com/products/servletexec/index.jsp
Oracle 9i Application Server	Server	2.3	1.2	www.oracle.com/ip/deploy/ias/index.html
Orion Application Server	Server	2.3 PFD2	1.1	www.orionserver.com/
Pramati Server 3	Server	2.3	1.2	www.pramati.com/product/server30/index.htm
Secant Technologies ModelMethods Enterprise Server	Server	2.1	1.0	www.secant.com/products/ES/index.html
Servertec Internet Server	Server	2.2	1.1	www.servertec.com/products/iws/iws.html
Novell eXtendApplication Server 4 Beta	Server	2.3	1.2	www.silverstream.com/Website/app/en_US/AppServerBeta
Sun™ ONE Application Server 7, Platform Edition (formerly iPlanet™ Application Server)	Server	2.3	1.2	wwws.sun.com/software/products/appsrvr/home_appsrvr.html
Sybase EAServer	Server	2.3	1.2	www.sybase.com/easerver

Continued on next page

TABLE 12.1: WEB SERVERS AND JSP ENGINES *(continued)*

SERVER AND ADD-ON ENGINE	PRODUCT TYPE	JAVA SERVLETS SUPPORT	JSP SUPPORT	LINK
Tagtraum Industries jo!	Server	2.1, 2.2	1.1	www.tagtraum.com/
Trifork Application Server 3.1	Server	2.3	1.2	www.trifork.com/

JavaServer Pages: The Language

As we've mentioned, JSP consists of server-side scripting mixed with static HTML or XML (Extensible Markup Language). These script pages are subsequently translated into Java servlets at the web server. Advanced developers experienced with Java can access the full power of Java through JSP pages. For the beginning or intermediate developer, JSP provides a standard library of tags to easily accomplish most dynamic content operations.

To use a standard library of tags, the server needs to differentiate blocks of JSP from other contents of the page. JSP uses <% to identify the start of a JSP section and %> to identify the end of a JSP section. The JSP web server attempts to interpret JSP tags found between the opening and closing JSP tags. (All our JSP examples are wrapped by the beginning and end JSP script tag.)

NOTE   Although all current JSP engines accept only Java, the language creators did not limit JSP to Java. In the future, other scripting languages such as JavaScript or VBScript could be used as well.

JSP tags are case sensitive. For example, if you type <%@ Page %>, instead of <%@ page %>, the JSP server will not recognize your code tag, and the page will throw an exception. Furthermore, some attributes on the tags require case-sensitive values.

JSP Elements

You will see four types of JSP tags or elements enclosed in the opening (<%) and closing (%>) JSP tags—expressions, scriptlets, declarations, and directives.

Expressions

An expression's single purpose is to evaluate and return a string value. An expression begins with <%= and ends with %>. The = immediately after the opening JSP tag marks the following information as an expression to evaluate. Listing 12.1 shows a JSP page that returns the date of the server and displays it in the web browser. Figure 12.1 shows the result once the page is requested through a web browser.

We strongly encourage you to key in all the code to create the example files yourself. To check your work, compare your files with the example files on the CD accompanying this book.

LISTING 12.1: *HELLOWORLD.JSP*

```jsp
<%@ page contentType="text/html; charset=iso-8859-1" language="java"
    import="java.sql.*" errorPage="" %>
<html>
<head>
<title>Hello World</title>
<meta http-equiv="Content-Type" content="text/html; charset=iso-8859-1">
</head>

<body>
Hello World, today is <%= new java.util.Date() %>
</body>
</html>
```

FIGURE 12.1

Viewing the output from `helloWorld.jsp` in Internet Explorer

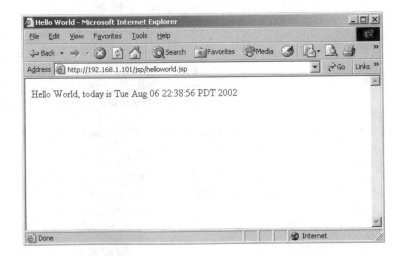

Scriptlets

Scriptlets are the simplest type of JSP element. A scriptlet is simply Java code enclosed in the opening and closing JSP tags. Scriptlets can contain any amount of valid Java code, including functions, declarations, and expressions. However, keep in mind that scriptlets cannot span multiple web pages—they are born and die with the beginning and end of a web page request. Listing 12.2 shows a simple example of a scriptlet containing a For/Next loop to output a series of numbers to a web browser window. Figure 12.2 shows the result in the browser window.

LISTING 12.2: SCRIPTLET EXAMPLE

```jsp
<%@ page contentType="text/html; charset=iso-8859-1" language="java"
    import="java.sql.*" errorPage="" %>
<html>
```

```
<head><title>Scriptlet Example</title>
<meta http-equiv="Content-Type" content="text/html; charset=iso-8859-1">
</head>

<body>
<% for (int listNumber = 0; listNumber < 5; listNumber++) { %>
    List # <%= listNumber %><br>
<% } %>
</body>
</html>
```

FIGURE 12.2

Viewing the output from **scriptlet .jsp** in Internet Explorer

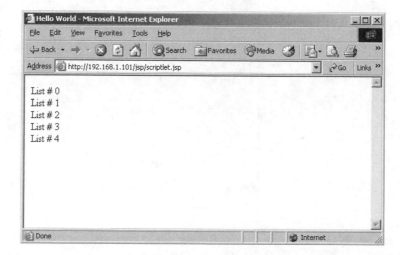

Declarations

Declarations initialize variables and methods. Declarations begin with the <%! and end with %>. The declaration element must be vaild Java code. Therefore, you must end a declaration with a semicolon. Variables and methods declared in a JSP page can be used by scriptlets and expressions within the same JSP page. Listing 12.3 adds a declaration element to our previous code example. You can see the results in Figure 12.3.

LISTING 12.3: DECLARATION EXAMPLE

```
<%@ page contentType="text/html; charset=iso-8859-1" language="java"
    import="java.sql.*" errorPage="" %>
<html>
<head>
<title>Declaration Example</title>
<meta http-equiv="Content-Type" content="text/html; charset=iso-8859-1">
</head>
<%! String listName = "My List"; %>
<body>
```

```
<% for (int listNumber = 0; listNumber < 5; listNumber++) { %>
    <%= listName %> # <%= listNumber %><br>
<% } %>
</body>
</html>
```

FIGURE 12.3

Viewing the output from `declaration.jsp` in Internet Explorer

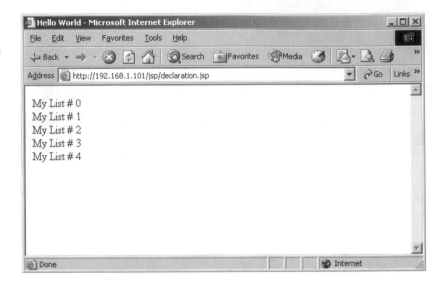

Directives

As we mentioned, when a JSP page is requested, the web server passes the JSP page to the servlet container. The servlet container manages all facets of the life of the servlet (JSP page). The servlet container makes many of its servlet management decisions through information passed to it through directives. Directives begin with `<%@` and end with `%>`. The three types of directives are `page`, `include`, and `TagLib`.

THE *PAGE* DIRECTIVE

The `page` directive defines attributes such as `language`, `extends`, `import`, `session`, `buffer`, `autoFlush`, `isThreadSafe`, `info`, `errorPage`, `contentType`, and `isErrorPage`. Typically, although not required, you place the `page` directive at the top of your JSP page. Listing 12.4 shows an example of the `page` directive. Table 12.2 defines each attribute.

LISTING 12.4: PAGE DIRECTIVE EXAMPLE

```
<%@ page contentType="text/html; charset=iso-8859-1" language="java"
    import="java.sql.*" errorPage="" %>
<html>
<head>
<title> Page Directive Example</title>
<meta http-equiv="Content-Type" content="text/html; charset=iso-8859-1">
```

```
</head>
<%! String listName = "My List"; %>
<body>
Page Directive Example
</body>
</html>
```

TABLE 12.2: THE PAGE DIRECTIVE ATTRIBUTES

ATTRIBUTE	MEANING
autoFlush	Used in conjunction with the buffer attribute, the autoFlush attribute flushes the buffer content automatically. The default value is True.
buffer	Controls the size of the buffer that holds page content written by the JSP page before sending the content to the web browser. The default is 8KB.
contentType	Defines the contentType of the generated content by the JSP page. The contentType attribute can be HTML, text, PDF, and so on. The default is text/html; charset-ISO=8859-1.
errorPage	Defines a custom error page to handle an error exception thrown from the current page.
extends	The name of the Java class you want to use as a subclass for the current JSP page.
import	Specifies Java packages or classes to import into your JSP page. By default, the java.lang.*, javax.servlet.*, javax.servlet.jsp.*, and javax.servlet.http.* are imported into your JSP page.
info	This value can be any string and can be accessed by the current JSP page through the getServletInfo() function.
isErrorPage	Specifies whether the current page is designed to handle errors. The default value is False. If set to True, the JSP can access the Exception object containing the exception thrown by the page that declared the current page as an error page.
isThreadSafe	Specifies whether the JSP page can handle multiple requests simultaneously. The default value is True. If the value is set to False, the servlet handles one HTTP request at a time.
language	The default value for this attribute is java. At this time, Java is the only accepted language.
session	Specifies whether the current JSP page is to participate in sessions. The default value is True.

THE *INCLUDE* DIRECTIVE

The include directive allows one JSP page to be included and processed with the current JSP file. The include directive allows a developer to structure a certain level of modularity into their website architecture. For example, when you use Dreamweaver MX to connect to a database (covered in Chapter 10), Dreamweaver MX creates and saves the connection information in a separate JSP page. That JSP page holds the information to connect to a database. When Dreamweaver MX needs that connection information, Dreamweaver MX inserts an `include` directive to that database connection JSP page into every JSP page that will connect to a database. An example of the `include` directive is shown in Listing 12.5.

@INCLUDE VERSUS INCLUDE ELEMENT

You can include a file in a JSP page using two methods—the `include` directive and the `jsp:include` element. Although both methods function similarly, the timing and result is different.

```
<%@ include file="Connections/db_connection.jsp" %>
```

The `include` directive takes in the target file when the server begins to translate the JSP code. Once the calling JSP script page is compiled into a scriptlet, modifying the `include` file will have no effect on the compiled scriptlet until you force a recompile. Methods of forced recompile vary from server to server, but one sure-fire method is to restart the web server. This `include` method is useful for dynamic content, such as JSP code.

```
<jsp:include page="dsp_header.html" flush="true" />
```

The `jsp:include` element includes the target file at page request time. Since the included page is taken in each time the calling page is requested, any change you apply to the `include` file is immediately seen in the calling file. This method is useful for static information such as headers, footers, graphics, and so on.

As you can see in Listing 12.5, the `include` element references a `db_connection.jsp` file. This file is generated by Dreamweaver MX and contains code to connect your servlets to a database. We'll cover database connections more in Chapter 10.

LISTING 12.5: *INCLUDEDIRECTIVE.JSP*

```
<%@ page contentType="text/html; charset=iso-8859-1" language="java"
    import="java.sql.*" errorPage="" %>
<%@ include file="Connections/db_connection.jsp" %>
<html>
<head>
<title>Include Directive Example</title>
<meta http-equiv="Content-Type" content="text/html; charset=iso-8859-1">
</head>
<body>
This example includes the database connection JSP file (db_connection.jsp) in
    the directory Connections.
</body>
</html>
```

THE *TagLib* DIRECTIVE

We've already mentioned that JSP provides a standard set of tags to help you develop web applications. JSP also let you create your own set of tags. To use custom tags in your JSP page, you must load your custom tag library into a JSP page. The `TagLib` directive specifies the tag library to load. The `TagLib` directive accomplishes three things:

1. Specifies that the current JSP page uses an extended tag library
2. References a special JAR file that defines the tags and the operations of the new tag library. A JAR file is a collection of files that compose a Java application.
3. Defines a special tag prefix to uniquely identify the new tags

There are two `TagLib` attributes and both are required—`URI` (Uniform Resource Identifier) and `PREFIX`. The `URI` attribute sets the path to the Tag Library Descriptor, which defines the tag library. The `PREFIX` attribute sets the prefix to uniquely identify the new library tags. Listing 12.6 shows an example of the `TagLib` directive and calls to tags defined in the custom tag library shipped with Macromedia JRun. Figure 12.4 shows the result.

LISTING 12.6: *TAGLIB.JSP*

```
<%@ taglib uri="jruntags" prefix="jrun" %>
<html>
<head>
<title>TagLib Example</title>
<meta http-equiv="Content-Type" content="text/html; charset=iso-8859-1">
</head>
<body>
This example includes the my_taglib tag library (my_taglib.jar) in the
    directory taglib.
<jrun:form name="category" action="category.jsp">
Enter a new category: <jrun:input name="Category" type="category"/>
<input type="submit" value="Submit"/>
</body>
</html>
```

To properly use custom tags in Dreamweaver MX, you must import your JSP custom tag library into Dreamweaver MX. To do so, follow these steps:

1. Open a JSP script page.
2. Choose Edit ➤ Tag Libraries to open the Tag Library Editor.
3. From the menu, choose JSP, and then select Import From File (*.tld, *.jar, *.zip), Import Jrun Server Tags From Folder, or Import From Server (web.xml).
4. Dreamweaver MX asks you to supply a `URI` and a `PREFIX` for the imported custom tags.

FIGURE 12.4
Viewing the output
from taglib.jsp
in Internet Explorer

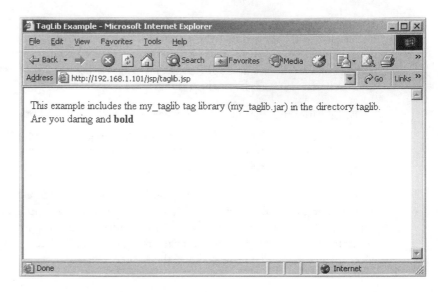

Working in JSP

Although Java is an expansive language, when working in JSP, you'll spend much of the time interacting with just a few elements. These elements allow your JSP pages to react to form submissions, redirect page requests, and transfer data back and forth between your database and the client browser. Therefore, it's important to be familiar with the following objects:

The HTTP Response   Sends information to the client

The HTTP Request   Retrieves information from the client

JDBC   Communicates with databases

JavaBeans   Communicates with Java classes

The HTTP Response

One of three things happens when the server responds to a request from a web browser: the server redirects the request, returns data, or returns an error. Regardless of the response, there are two components, a header and the data. The HTTP header contains a great deal of information, such as the type of content, the expiration date, cookies, and so on. In this section, we'll show you how to accomplish two common tasks: write a cookie through the client's web browser and redirect the client's request to another page.

WRITING A COOKIE

As you know, cookies are small text files of information that your servlet can write to the client browser. Cookies are extremely useful to establish such things as where and when the user accessed your site or whether the user is a new or returning visitor. With JSP, you have detailed access to cookies and the data stored in cookies. A cookie can have a name, a value, and several optional attributes such as a comment, path and domain qualifiers, a maximum age, and a version number. However, some web browsers have bugs in how they handle the optional attributes. Therefore, use optional attributes sparingly.

For a cookie to persist on the client's computer, you must write three attributes: name, value, and expiration. To see how to write such a cookie, take a look at Listing 12.7. This page, `cookiewrite.jsp`, writes the database ID of the site visitor to the visitor's computer and displays the cookie's value, name, and time of expiration, as shown in Figure 12.5. At a later time, you can then retrieve the visitor database ID to properly identify the visitor. As you can see, the following lines create a key and a value in the cookie. The key, userSID, is a name to set or retrieve the cookie value of 50. The next line sets the expiration date of the cookie.

LISTING 12.7: *COOKIEWRITE.JSP*

```
<%@ page contentType="text/html; charset=iso-8859-1" language="java"
    import="java.sql.*" errorPage="" %>
<%
    Cookie cookie = new Cookie ("userSID", "50");
    cookie.setMaxAge(365 * 24 * 60 * 60);
    response.addCookie(cookie);
%>
<html>
<head>
<title>Cookie Write Example</title>
<meta http-equiv="Content-Type" content="text/html; charset=iso-8859-1">
</head>
<body>
<%=cookie.getName()%><br>
<%=cookie.getValue()%><br>
<%=cookie.getMaxAge()%><br>
</body>
</html>
```

FIGURE 12.5

Viewing the output from `cookiewrite.jsp` in Internet Explorer

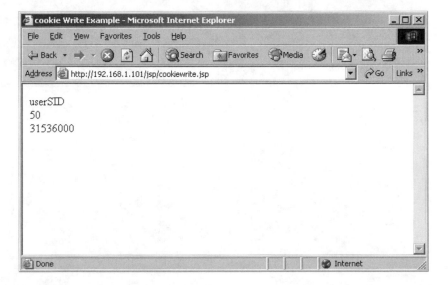

> **NOTE** *Cookies are messages passed to a web browser from a web server. If allowed, the web browser saves these messages as text files on a user's computer. The cookie is then forwarded back to the web server with each subsequent page request the user makes to the website. Web servers and web applications primarily use cookies to identify users. However, as the developer, you can store any piece of information that fits into the three parts of a cookie—a variable name, a value, and a date or time of expiration.*

REDIRECTING REQUESTS

Another task you can accomplish with the HTTP response header is a server-side redirect, which sends a visitor to a completely different URL. A perfect example of a redirect is to require a username and password to protect a page. If the correct username and password are not passed to the page, the page redirects the user to a login page. We'll talk more about security in a later chapter.

Since the redirect occurs in the HTTP header, further processing of the current JSP script file stops and the visitor is sent to a different URL. Listing 12.8 demonstrates a simple redirect to the `helloworld.jsp` page. You can see the results in Figure 12.6.

LISTING 12.8: *REDIRECT.JSP*

```
<%@ page contentType="text/html; charset=iso-8859-1" language="java"
    import="java.sql.*" errorPage="" %>
<% response.sendRedirect("helloworld.jsp"); %>
<html>
<head>
<title>Redirect Example</title>
<meta http-equiv="Content-Type" content="text/html; charset=iso-8859-1">
</head>
<body>
</body>
</html>
```

FIGURE 12.6

The result of redirecting to the `helloworld.jsp` page

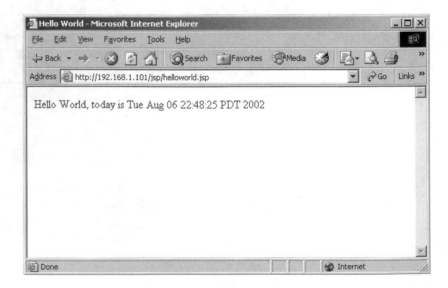

Hello World, today is Tue Aug 06 22:48:25 PDT 2002

The HTTP Request

When a web browser requests a page, it passes additional information through the HTTP header. Your JSP pages have access to all the information in that incoming request. Essentially, the HTTP header consists of a data structure of information sent by the browser to the server. All this information is accessible to you through JSP. In this section, we'll demonstrate how to access data submitted through a form and through the URL address, how to read the value of a cookie on the client's computer, and how to retrieve traditional server variables.

ACCESSING FORM AND URL DATA

Unlike other web technoligies, JSP makes no distinction between form data submitted by the Get and Post methods. Therefore, both submitted form data and variables passed through the URL address are available to you through the same two functions—`getParameter()` and `getParameterValues()`.

The getParameter() *Function*

The `getParameter()` function returns the first value attached to the named parameter. For example, the form in Listing 12.9 targets the JSP page in Listing 12.10. The targeted JSP page prints out the submitted form value of the passed form field `"Name"`. Figures 12.7 and 12.8 show the browser results.

LISTING 12.9: *HELLOWORLD_FORM.HTM*

```
<!DOCTYPE HTML PUBLIC "-//W3C//DTD HTML 4.01 Transitional//EN">
<html>
<head>
<title>Hello World Form</title>
<meta http-equiv="Content-Type" content="text/html; charset=iso-8859-1">
</head>
<body>
<form name="HelloWorld" method="post" action="helloWorld_action.jsp">
 <label>Your Name:
 <input name="Name" type="text" size="25" maxlength="25"></label>
 <input name="" type="submit" value="Submit">
</form>
</body>
</html>
```

LISTING 12.10: *HELLOWORLD_ACTION.JSP*

```
<%@ page contentType="text/html; charset=iso-8859-1" language="java"
    import="java.sql.*" errorPage="" %>
<html>
<head>
<title>Hello World Form Action</title>
```

```
<meta http-equiv="Content-Type" content="text/html; charset=iso-8859-1">
</head>
<body>
Hello World, my name is <%= request.getParameter("Name") %>
</body>
</html>
```

FIGURE 12.7

Viewing
helloWorld_
form.htm in
Internet Explorer

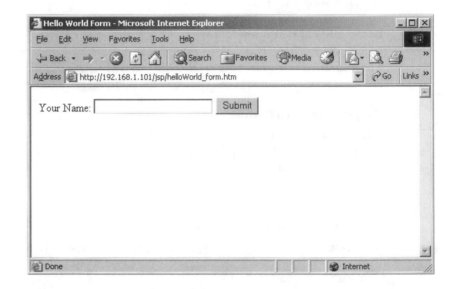

FIGURE 12.8

Viewing the output
from helloWorld_
action.jsp in
Internet Explorer

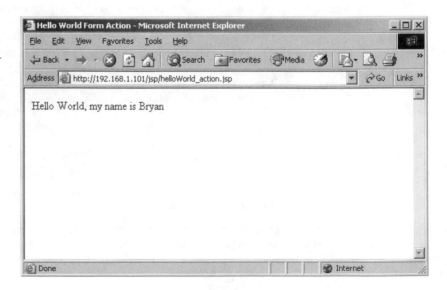

The getParameterValues() *Function*

In cases of multiple form fields such as check boxes or text fields, you use getParameterValues() to return every value attached to the named parameter. For example, the form in Listing 12.11 targets the JSP page in Listing 12.12. The targeted JSP page places the multiple values in an array and loops through the array, printing the submitted form values of the form field "Name". Figures 12.9 and 12.10 show the browser results.

LISTING 12.11: *HELLOWORLD_FORM2.HTM*

```
<!DOCTYPE HTML PUBLIC "-//W3C//DTD HTML 4.01 Transitional//EN">
<html>
<head>
<title>Hello World Form 2</title>
<meta http-equiv="Content-Type" content="text/html; charset=iso-8859-1">
</head>
<body>
<form name="HelloWorld" method="post" action="helloWorld_action2.jsp">
 <label>Your Name:<br>
 <input name="Name" type="checkbox" size="25" maxlength="25"
     value="Clark"></label>Clark<br>
 <input name="Name" type="checkbox" size="25" maxlength="25"
     value="Lois">Lois<br>
 <input name="Name" type="checkbox" size="25" maxlength="25"
     value="Jimmy">Jimmy<br>
 <input name="" type="submit" value="Submit">
</form>
</body>
</html>
```

FIGURE 12.9

Viewing
helloWorld_
form2.htm in
Internet Explorer

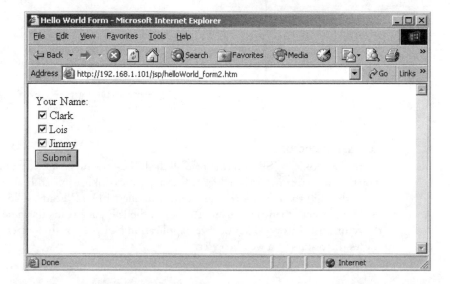

LISTING 12.12: *HELLOWORLD_ACTION2.JSP*

```
<%@ page contentType="text/html; charset=iso-8859-1" language="java"
    import="java.sql.*" errorPage="" %>
<html>
<head>
<title>Hello World Form Action 2</title>
<meta http-equiv="Content-Type" content="text/html; charset=iso-8859-1">
</head>
<body>
Hello World, my name is: <br>
<%
String names[] = request.getParameterValues("Name");
for (int i = 0; i < names.length; i++) { %>
<%= names[i] %><br>
<% } %>
</body>
</html>
```

FIGURE 12.10

Viewing the output from helloWorld_action2.jsp in Internet Explorer

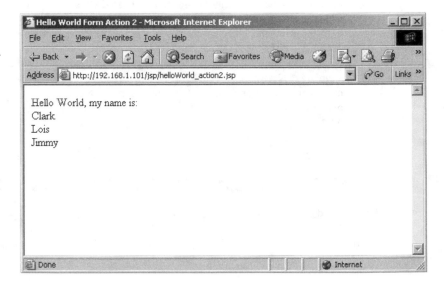

ACCESSING COOKIES

To read a cookie in JSP, you first read all the URL-attached cookies from the request HTTP header. You then loop through the cookies to find a specific cookie name and value. For example, Listing 12.13 loops through the cookies contained in the request HTTP header—looking for a cookie named userSID. When it finds the userSID cookie, the JSP page reads its value to find the database ID of the returning visitor (which our web application had previously written in a cookie). Figure 12.11 shows the results in a web browser.

LISTING 12.13: *COOKIEREAD.JSP*

```
<%@ page contentType="text/html; charset=iso-8859-1" language="java"
    import="java.sql.*" errorPage="" %>
<%
Cookie nameCookie = null;
String cookieName = "userSID";
String cookieValue = "";
Cookie[] cookies = request.getCookies();

for (int i=0; i < cookies.length; i++) {
   nameCookie = cookies[i];
   if (nameCookie.getName().equals(cookieName)) {
   cookieName = nameCookie.getName();
      cookieValue = nameCookie.getValue();
   }
}
%>
<html>
<head>
<title>Cookie Read</title>
<meta http-equiv="Content-Type" content="text/html; charset=iso-8859-1">
</head>
<body>
Your userSID is <%= cookieValue %>
</body>
</html>
```

FIGURE 12.11

Viewing the results of cookieread.jsp in a browser

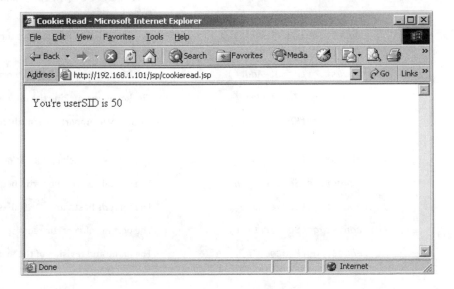

SERVER VARIABLES

If you are familiar with other web technologies, you are probably familiar with server variables—collections of information derived from the HTTP header information and sometimes from the web server. For example, you can discern the virtual path of the executing script page from the server variable *request.getServletPath()*. Although you won't be using server variables every day, they are a core resource you should be familiar with while you develop JSP web applications. Table 12.3 shows the most common server variables available to JSP, and Listing 12.14 shows the server variables used in a JSP page.

TABLE 12.3: SERVER VARIABLES

VARIABLE	DESCRIPTION
request.getAuthType()	If the web server supports user authentication, this is the authentication method.
request.getContentLength()	The length of the CONTENT_TYPE.
request.getContentType()	For requests with attached information, such as a HTTP POST and PUT, this is the data content type.
request.getPathInfo()	The path information of the request. For example, relative paths, such as pdfs/mypdf.asp, can access request pages. The extra information in the path information is sent as PATH_INFO.
request.getPathTranslated()	The translated version of PATH_INFO with virtual-to-physical mapping. In the PATH_INFO example, the PATH_TRANSLATED value may be C:\inetpub\wwwroot\test\pdfs\mypdf.pdf.
request.getQueryString()	Any information that follows the question mark (?) in the URL of the current page.
request.getRemoteAddr()	The IP address of the remote host making the request.
request.getRemoteHost()	The hostname making the request.
request.getRemoteUser()	If the server supports user authentication this is the authenticated username.
request.getMethod()	The form submission method of the request.
request.getServletPath()	The virtual path to the script being executed.
request.getServerName()	The server's hostname, DNS alias, or IP address.
request.getServerPort()	The port number of the request.
request.getProtocol()	The name and revision of the information protocol.

LISTING 12.14: *SERVERVARIABLES.JSP*

```
<%@ page contentType="text/html; charset=iso-8859-1" language="java"
    import="java.sql.*" errorPage="" %>
<html>
<head>
<title>Server Variables</title>
<meta http-equiv="Content-Type" content="text/html; charset=iso-8859-1">
</head>
<body>
request.getAuthType(): <%= request.getAuthType() %><br>
request.getContentLength(): <%= request.getContentLength() %><br>
request.getContentType(): <%= request.getContentType() %><br>
request.getHeader("Xxx-Yyy"): <%= request.getHeader("Xxx-Yyy") %><br>
request.getPathInfo(): <%= request.getPathInfo() %><br>
request.getPathTranslated(): <%= request.getPathTranslated() %><br>
request.getQueryString(): <%= request.getQueryString() %><br>
request.getRemoteAddr(): <%= request.getRemoteAddr() %><br>
request.getRemoteHost(): <%= request.getRemoteHost() %><br>
request.getRemoteUser(): <%= request.getRemoteUser() %><br>
request.getMethod(): <%= request.getMethod() %><br>
request.getServletPath(): <%= request.getServletPath() %><br>
request.getServerName(): <%= request.getServerName() %><br>
request.getServerPort(): <%= request.getServerPort() %><br>
request.getProtocol(): <%= request.getProtocol() %>
</body>
</html>
```

JDBC: Connecting to a Database

We've reviewed the more common aspects of the JSP language; however, any sophisticated website requires a database. To enable your JSP pages to communicate with a database, you use a JDBC connection. With a JDBC connection to a database, you can pull and push data from your JSP web application. Luckily, Dreamweaver MX gives you the choice of seven JDBC connection options right out of the box:

- Custom JDBC Connections
- IBM DB 2 App Driver (DB2)
- IBM DB 2 Net Driver (DB2)
- MySQL Driver (MySQL)
- Oracle Thin Driver (Oracle)
- Inet Driver (SQL Server)
- Sun JDBC-ODBC Driver (ODBC Database)

As you can see from the list, many of the connection options, such as the Oracle Thin Driver, allow your JSP web application to connect natively (directly) to the database. This typically increases response time and can speed up your application. However, to use the native database connection drivers, you need a bit of technical information about your database and the server it resides on, plus you need to be somewhat knowledgable about the connection driver (version, eccentriciities, that sort of thing). If you do not know or do not want to deal with this additional information, we suggest the good old JDBC-ODBC Driver. With JDBC-ODBC, the only information you need is the name of the ODBC connection to the database server. For example, to connect to our sample Books database, we know our database administrator has created a connection on the web server called `"bookTrackerPublic"`. So, to establish a connection to our database in Dreamweaver MX, we open the Sun JDBC-ODBC Driver (ODBC Database) dialog box, as shown in Figure 12.12. Next, we enter a name for our connection and replace [`odbc dsn`] with our ODBC connection name. All that's left to do is close the dialog box and begin pulling data. Simple as can be.

FIGURE 12.12

The Dreamweaver MX Sun JDBC-ODBC Driver (ODBC Database) dialog box

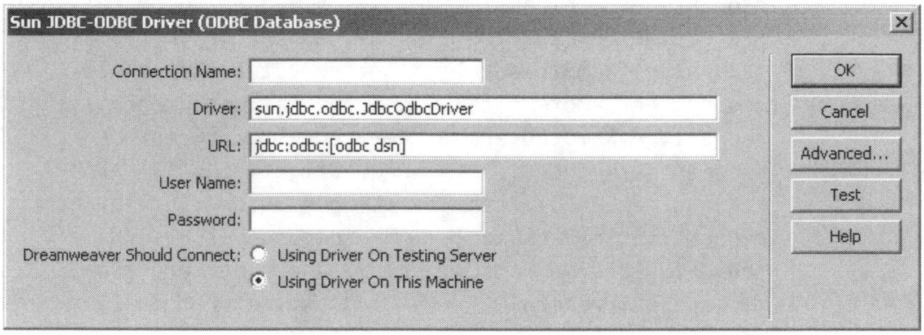

JavaBeans: Communicating with Java Classes

Up to now, you've seen how you can incorporate Java code directly into your web pages. Those JSP web pages are compiled into servlets and respond to web page requests to quickly build dynamic web pages. This model of compiling JSP script pages is powerful and fast. However, as you can imagine, the more complex the code, the longer it takes to compile a JSP script page into a servlet. JavaBeans to the rescue. JavaBeans allow you to permanently compile complex Java code and access the compiled JavaBean through a JSP script page.

A JavaBean is actually a complied Java class—a bit of software you can execute from your JSP script pages. Essentially, a JavaBean must follow only two rules:

1. You must be able to communicate with a JavaBean.
2. You must be able to create an instance of a JavaBean without passing it any dependent values.

How do you know when and what code you should move from a JSP script page to a JavaBean? It's helpful to think of your web application from a functional perspective. If you can recognize code that is used over and over again through your web application, it might make sense to extract the code into a Java class and compile it into a JavaBean. You then simply access the compiled JavaBean from all your JSP script pages.

Dreamweaver MX deals with JavaBeans in a way that is similar to the way it deals with other sources of data such as a database. JavaBeans even appear in the Bindings panel, allowing you to expand a JavaBean to view its properties. You can also drag and drop the properties onto your JSP script page. Of course, to access a JavaBean in this way, Dreamweaver MX must have complete access to the Bean class. Therefore, a copy of the Bean class must be in the `Configuration/classes` folder under the main Dreamweaver MX application folder. However, if you are developing with Dreamweaver MX on your web server, it is acceptable to have the Bean class in the normal system classpath.

Dreamweaver MX makes it simple to access a JavaBean through a JSP page. You can choose to define a JavaBean or a JavaBean collection in the Bindings panel, or you can click the Use JavaBean button on the JSP toolbar. To define a JavaBean or a JavaBean collection in the Bindings panel, follow these steps:

1. Activate the Bindings panel.

2. Choose Panel ➢ JavaBean or Panel ➢ JavaBean Collection.

3. In the resulting dialog box, configure the JavaBean or JavaBean collection.

In the example in Figure 12.13, we've chosen the TestCollection.MusicCollection Macromedia sample JavaBean. Typically, if Dreamweaver MX can find your Bean class, Dreamweaver will display it as a class choice.

FIGURE 12.13

The JavaBean Collection dialog box

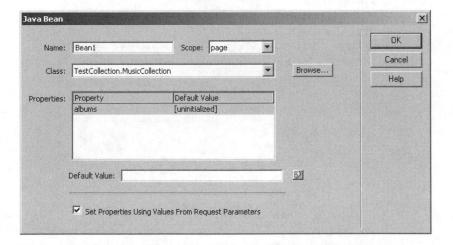

After you configure the JavaBean or JavaBean collection, you'll see the properties in the Bindings panel as shown in Figure 12.14.

To use a JavaBean in your JSP page, simply click the Use JavaBean button to open the UseBean dialog box, as shown in Figure 12.15, and enter the information requested. You can instantiate a JavaBean using nothing more than the ID and Scope attributes.

FIGURE 12.14

The Bindings panel

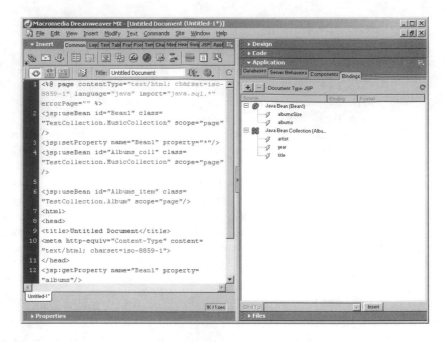

FIGURE 12.15

The Dreamweaver
MX UseBean
dialog box

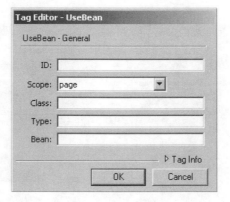

After you create an instance of the JavaBean in your JSP script page, you can interact with the JavaBean by setting JavaBean properties or getting JavaBean properties. To set or get a JavaBean property, use the GetProperty and SetProperty commands. Both of these commands are also available on the Dreamweaver MX JSP toolbar and in the Bindings panel. GetProperty gets the value of a bean property so you can display it in a result page. SetProperty sets a bean property value. Figures 12.16 and 12.17 show the SetProperty and GetProperty dialog boxes. Alternatively, if you registered your JavaBean or JavaBean collection in the Bindings panel of Dreamweaver MX, you can simply drag and drop your JavaBean properties into your JSP script page.

FIGURE 12.16

The Dreamweaver
MX SetProperty
dialog box

FIGURE 12.17

The Dreamweaver
MX GetProperty
dialog box

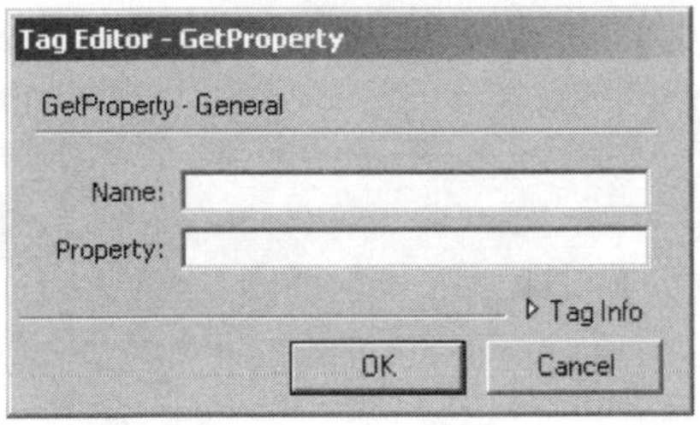

FOR FURTHER INFORMATION

You'll have no trouble finding information about Java and JSP, but we wanted to list a few of our favorite sites. The primary site, of course, is that of the creator of Java, Sun Microsystems. At `http://java.sun.com/products/jsp/`, you can find information about Java, JSP, and Sun's own JSP web server. Speaking of web servers, Macromedia's JRun (`www.macromedia.com/software/jrun/`) is one of the most stable and easy to administrate available. Plus Macromedia keeps extensive content online for JRun JSP devotees. In addition to the corporate sites, don't forget the information portal sites such as the JSP Resource Index (`www.jspin.com/`) and the newsgroups at Google (`http://groups.google.com/groups?hl=en&lr=&ie=UTF-8&oe=UTF-8&group=comp.lang.java`). Finally, check out these JSP and Java books by Sybex: *Enterprise Java 2, J2EE 1.4 Complete*, *Mastering JSP*, *Mastering Java 2, J2SE 1.4*, and *Java Developer's Guide to E-Commerce with XML and JSP*.

Summary

We covered a lot about JSP in this chapter. We defined what JSP is and how it works in terms of a web application, we explored the operating systems and web server choices you must make to develop your own JSP web system, and we delved into how you can use the JSP language to develop your own web applications. And we're not done yet. In later chapters, we'll explain, step by step, how to use Dreamweaver MX to build database-driven web pages. But even with all we have and are about to accomplish, there are literally mountains more Java to learn. It's an extremely powerful and fascinating language, and we encourage you to immerse yourself in all things Java.

Chapter 13

Active Server Pages

As YOU MAY KNOW, an Active Server Pages (ASP) script file is a text file containing any combination of scripts and HTML code processed and delivered as HTML to a web browser by the Microsoft IIS (Internet Information Services) web server. (IIS is included with every version of Windows, starting with Windows NT.) In theory, the process is nearly as simple as delivering static HTML. Once an IIS server accepts a browser's request and locates the page, it executes the commands listed in the ASP script file, renders the result as HTML, and sends it off to the browser.

ASP script commands can do anything from scanning a directory to connect and search a database to read and write files on the requestering computer. You can even access ActiveX objects for even more customized functions. Your options are only as limited as your creativity. That's the beauty of a tool such as Active Server Pages—if you can dream it, you can build it.

However, to fully utilize Active Server Pages and Dreamweaver MX, you need a basic understanding of the objects and script languages that make up ASP. We're not going to hit on every object, function, and method in the ASP script language, just the most commonly used elements.

This chapter covers the following topics:

◆ Active Server Pages—the host and the scripting languages
◆ ASP objects

Active Server Pages—the Host and the Scripting Languages

The host. Sounds ominous. The host simply refers to the script host that exists on the IIS web server. A script host defines the properties of a script language, its syntax, and all execution rules. For example, the Microsoft Windows Scripting Host is an example of the ASP script host. It reads and executes the following script languages:

VBScript A subset of Visual Basic for Applications (VBA). We mention this one first because it's the default ASP scripting language and it's the language we'll be using with our Dreamweaver MX examples.

JScript Microsoft's counterpart to JavaScript. JScript is packaged with ASP. Neither is connected to Sun's Java language, although you might consider them similar. Many developers consider JavaScript the common standard for browser (client-side) scripting.

WARNING   *Personal Pet Peeve: People often refer to JavaScript as Java. They are not the same thing—not even close. Don't do it. If you catch someone doing it, pinch them. Pass it on.*

PerlScript   A subset of Perl, which has been around for a long time. It's used mostly with text. It doesn't come with ASP, but you can download it from `www.activestate.com`. Since the ASP default is VBScript, you must include the option `<%@language=PerlScript%>` in your ASP document.

CLIENT-SIDE AND SERVER-SIDE SCRIPTING

Client-side scripting in web development refers to manipulating the browser and its HTML contents. As you know, the server sends web pages to the requesting web browser, the client. Once the web page leaves the server, the server can no longer affect the page in any way. Therefore, any page manipulation must occur on the client side through the web browser. Most web browsers have a built-in scripting component that lets you manipulate the contents of an HTML page. You can use client-side scripting to tell a browser to carry out many tasks with JScript, VBScript, and JavaScript. A perfect example of client-side scripting is a roll-over image. Many sites use JavaScript to tell the browser to swap one image for another as you roll your mouse over the image.

Server-side scripting in web development refers to programmatic tasks carried out by the web server before it delivers HTML content to a web browser. A good example of server-side scripting is connecting to a database, retreiving a list of states, and creating the HTML code to display the list.

As we've mentioned, you can use ASP to combine HTML and JScript or VBScript scripts to dynamically serve HTML. When a browser requests an ASP page from an IIS web server, the server processes the VBScript or JScript code and forwards the HTML result to the web browser.

The IIS web server determines which files are ASP script pages by the extension in the filename. If the filename has an `.asp` extension, the server searches the contents of the file for blocks of ASP script.

The server can differentiate blocks of ASP script from HTML because ASP script always begins with `<%` and ends with `%>`. If both opening and closing tags are found, the web server examines and attempts to execute the script between the opening and closing tags. (All our ASP examples are wrapped by the beginning and ending ASP script tag.)

WHAT YOU NEED TO RUN ASP SCRIPT FILES

If you are new to ASP development and you have not yet created your ASP development environment, you have two options. The first is obtain access to an IIS web server. The second option is to download the free Microsoft Personal Web Server from `www.microsoft.com`. Personal Web Server installs a mini–web server on your computer that can execute ASP script files. Although the first option is preferable, the second option will certainly work. For more information about IIS and Personal Web Server, visit `www.microsoft.com`.

An alternative to running a Microsoft web server is to run the Sun ONE Active Server Pages (previously Chili!Soft ASP.) Sun ONE Active Server Pages enables the Sun ONE and Apache web servers to run ASP web applications on Sun Solaris, Linux, Microsoft Windows, HP-UX, and IBM AIX operating systems. For more information about Sun ONE Active Server Pages, visit `www.chilisoft.com`.

ASP Objects

When you work in ASP, you interact with the seven basic objects of the language. It's helpful to think of objects as virtual items that you can create, set, query, and destroy. For example, the values of all form fields submitted to a target web page are kept within a collection of variables in the Request object. Therefore, to find the value of a specific form field named "name", you request its value from the Forms collection of the Request object.

```
request.form("name")
```

Although there are seven objects in ASP, much of the time you interact with only a few objects that let you transfer data back and forth between your database and the client browser. However, you need to be familiar with all the following objects:

Response   Sends information to the client

Request   Retrieves information from the client

Server   Communicates with the server

Application   Stores information about your application

Session   Stores information about a specific browser instance

ObjectContext   Initiates and controls transactions

ASPError   Obtains information about errors during ASP engine processing

The Response Object

When the browser requests data from the server, the server does one of three things:

- Redirects the request
- Returns the requested data
- Returns an error

In each case, the server takes action by way of the Response object. Regardless of the response, there are two components: a header and the data. The header contains a great deal of information, such as the type of content, the expiration date, cookies, and so on. Elements of the Response object that you might use in web-database development are `Response.Cookies`, `Response.Buffer`, `Response.Write`, `Response.Flush`, `Response.End`, and `Response.Redirect`.

RESPONSE.COOKIES

As you may know, cookies are messages passed to a web browser from a web server. If allowed, the web browser saves these messages as text files on a user's computer. All cookies specific to the current website are then forwarded as a collection of cookies to the web server with each subsequent page request the user makes to the website. Web servers and web applications primarily use cookies to identify users. However, as the developer, you can store any piece of information that fits into the three parts of a cookie—a variable name, a value, and a date or time of expiration. To write to the collection of cookies on a user's computer, you use the `Response.cookies` command. Using the Response object, you can write a variable name, a value, and an expiration date to the visitor's computer as a cookie. Cookies are extremely useful if you want to establish where and when the user accessed your site or if you want to know whether the user is a new or returning visitor. For example, the script in Listing 13.1 writes the database ID of a new visitor to the visitor's computer. You can then retreive the visitor database ID at any time to properly identify the visitor.

You'll find all the listings in this chapter on the accompanying CD.

LISTING 13.1: *COOKIEWRITE.ASP*

```
<% Response.cookies("userSid") = "007"
   Response.cookies("userSid").expires = "12/31/2030" %>
<html>
<head>
<title>Cookie Write</title>
<meta http-equiv="Content-Type" content="text/html; charset=iso-8859-1">
</head>
<body>
</body>
</html>
```

RESPONSE.BUFFER

As your ASP script file generates HTML data, that output is usually held in a temporary buffer until all the ASP script processes are complete. You can turn this buffer off or on using `Response.Buffer`. To set the buffer, insert `Response.Buffer = TRUE` in the first line of your ASP script file, as shown in Listing 13.2:

LISTING 13.2: *RESPONSEBUFFER.ASP*

```
<% Response.Buffer = TRUE  %>
<html>
<head>
<title>Hello World</title>
<meta http-equiv="Content-Type" content="text/html; charset=iso-8859-1">
</head>
<body>
Example of RESPONSE.BUFFER
</body>
</html>
```

RESPONSE.WRITE

You use `Response.Write` to write data to the browser screen. There are two methods for using `Response.Write`, `Response.Write` and a shortcut notation `<%= %>`. As you can see in Listing 13.3, both methods output `"Hello World!"` to a browser screen. You can see the results in Figure 13.1.

LISTING 13.3: *RESPONSEWRITE.ASP*

```
<html>
<head>
<title>Hello World</title>
<meta http-equiv="Content-Type" content="text/html; charset=iso-8859-1">
</head>
<body>
<% response.write("Hello World!")%>
<br>
<%= "Hello World!" %>
</body>
</html>
```

FIGURE 13.1

Viewing the output from response-Write.asp in Internet Explorer

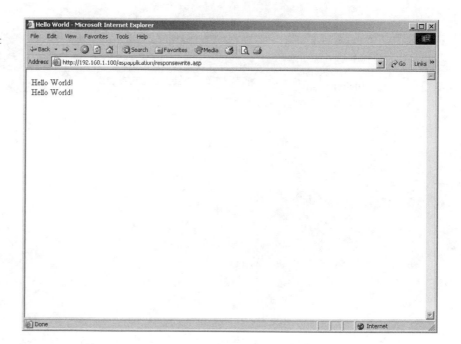

RESPONSE.FLUSH

Response.Flush sends all current output data held in the buffer of an ASP script page to the requesting browser. To use Response.Flush, Response.Buffer must be set to True. Being able to send all data to the browser is of great benefit when you are executing a long function or script. You can use Response.Flush to send bits of data to the screen as data is generated instead of waiting until the script ends. Listing 13.4 shows an example of the Response.Flush command. You can see the result in Figure 13.2.

LISTING 13.4: *RESPONSEFLUSH.ASP*

```
<% Response.Buffer = TRUE  %>
<html>
<head>
<title>Hello World</title>
<meta http-equiv="Content-Type" content="text/html; charset=iso-8859-1">
</head>
<body>
This is sent to the screen...
<% response.flush %>
...before this line.
</body>
</html>
```

FIGURE 13.2

Viewing the output from **response-Flush.asp** in Internet Explorer

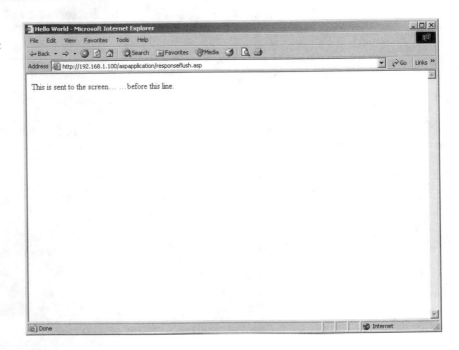

RESPONSE.END

Response.End stops all processing in the current ASP script file. Combining Response.Flush and Response.End is a common debugging technique among ASP programmers. It effectively allows you to insert break points in your ASP script file to more effectviely track down programming bugs. For example, in our script example of Response.Flush, we send one line to the browser before another line can execute. Suppose we suspected that the second line caused an ASP error on the page. By inserting Response.Flush and Response.End at different points on the page, we could effectively confirm our suspicion that the error is caused by the second line. To demonstrate, Listing 13.5

flushes the beginning portion of the script page to the browser and stops all processing before our suspected ASP error line appears. You can see the result in Figure 13.3.

LISTING 13.5: *RESPONSEEND.ASP*

```
<% Response.Buffer = TRUE  %>
<html>
<head>
<title>Hello World</title>
<meta http-equiv="Content-Type" content="text/html; charset=iso-8859-1">
</head>
<body>
This is sent to the screen and processing stops...
<% response.flush %>
<% response.end %>
...before this line which may have an error.
</body>
</html>
```

FIGURE 13.3

Viewing the output from response-End.asp in Internet Explorer

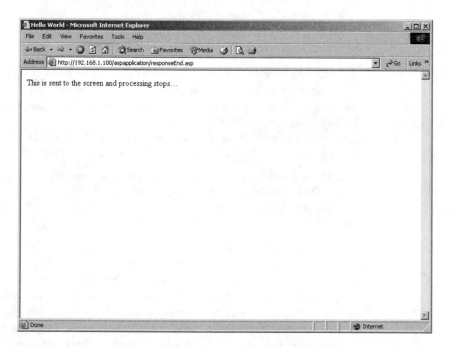

RESPONSE.REDIRECT(URL)

Response.Redirect stops further processing of the current ASP script file and sends the visitor to a different URL. A typical implementation of Response.Redirect is a script that protects a page with a login procedure. The basic concept is to include this script, which you might name pageSecurity.asp, at the top of any ASP page you want to protect from the general public. The pageSecurity.asp looks for a passed form field and compares the value to an authorized login. If the login values do not match, the pageSecurity.asp redirects the user to the login.asp page shown in Listing 13.6.

LISTING 13.6: *LOGIN.ASP*

```
<!DOCTYPE HTML PUBLIC "-//W3C//DTD HTML 4.01 Transitional//EN">
<html>
<head>
<title>Login Form</title>
<meta http-equiv="Content-Type" content="text/html; charset=iso-8859-1">
</head>
<body>
<form name="Login" method="post" action="pageSecurity.asp">
  <label>Your Name:</label>
  <input name="Name" type="text" size="25" maxlength="25">
  <input type="submit" value="Submit">
</form>
</body>
</html>
```

To create a script that can secure a page from unauthorized prying eyes, let's begin with our earlier example demonstrating how to request the value of the submitted Name form field. Next add a bit of IF THEN logic and the Response.Redirect command and you have the pageSecurity.asp shown in Listing 13.7.

Let's take the pageSecurity.asp page one step at a time. In the first line, we use the following:

```
<% if len(trim(request.form("Name"))) = 0 then
      response.redirect("login.asp")
   end if
%>
```

to see if the form field Name has been passed to the page and if the passed form field has a value. To do so, we use the LEN command to return the number of characters of the value in the Name form field. If the form field was passed, the LEN command returns a positive value. If the Name form field was not passed, the LEN command returns 0. Also notice we use the TRIM command to remove any spaces from the form field value. The TRIM command ensures that we test only real values and not a space. In the end, if the number of characters in the passed Name form field is 0, the Name form field doesn't exist. If the Name form field does not exist, we use Response.Redirect to send the visitor to a login page. If the number of characters in the passed Name form field is greater than 0, the Name form field was passed and it has a value. At this point, we can move on to comparing the Name form field to an authorized value.

To do so, we add a bit more IF THEN logic to our script. We add an ELSE to the script and check to see if the passed Name form field value matches our authorized Name "admin". If the Name form field value does not match our authorized login value, the script redirects the viewer to login.asp. However, if the Name form field was passed and the Name form field value is "admin", the page executes as normal. Pretty simple, but very effective. What's more, to quickly protect any page you like from unauthorized view, you can simply copy and paste the following code into the top of any ASP page.

```
<% if len(trim(request.form("Name"))) = 0 then
      response.redirect("login.htm")
   else
      if trim(request.form("Name")) <> "admin" then
         response.redirect("login.htm")
      end if
   end if
%>
```

LISTING 13.7: *PAGESECURITY.ASP*

```
<% if len(trim(request.form("Name"))) = 0 then
      response.redirect("login.asp")
   else
      if trim(request.form("Name")) <> "admin" then
         response.redirect("login.asp")
      end if
   end if
%>
<!DOCTYPE HTML PUBLIC "-//W3C//DTD HTML 4.01 Transitional//EN">
<html>
<head>
<title>Page Security Example</title>
<meta http-equiv="Content-Type" content="text/html; charset=iso-8859-1">
</head>
<body>
If you've logged in appropriately, you can see my page.
</body>
</html>
```

The Request Object

Similar to the Response object, which sends content to the browser, the Request object receives content from the browser. It does so in the shape of collections of variables that encapsulate the data for each request. Essentially, the Request object consists of collections of information sent by the browser to the server. You will often use the following Request collections in your ASP development—Request.Form, Request.Querystring, Request.Cookies, Request.ServerVariables, and Request.clientcertificates.

REQUEST.FORM

When a form using the submission method Post is targeted to the current ASP page, the collection of submitted form values are available to you through the Request.Form command. For example, HelloWorld_form.htm shown in Listing 13.8 targets an ASP page (HelloWorld_action.asp, shown in Listing 13.9) that prints out the submitted form values. Figure 13.4 shows the input form as viewed in Internet Explorer, and Figure 13.5 shows the page displayed after the user clicks Submit.

LISTING 13.8: *HELLOWORLD1_FORM.HTM*, THE INPUT FORM FOR AN ASP PAGE THAT USES *REQUEST.FORM*

```
<!DOCTYPE HTML PUBLIC "-//W3C//DTD HTML 4.01 Transitional//EN">
<html>
<head>
<title>Hello World Form</title>
<meta http-equiv="Content-Type" content="text/html; charset=iso-8859-1">
</head>
<body>
<form name="HelloWorld" method="post" action="HelloWorld1_action.asp">
  <label>Your Name:
  <input name="Name" type="text" size="25" maxlength="25"></label>
  <input type="submit" value="Submit">
</form>
</body>
</html>
```

FIGURE 13.4

Viewing Hello-
World1_form.htm
in Internet Explorer

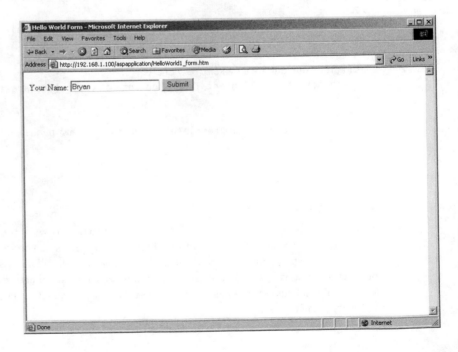

LISTING 13.9: *HELLOWORLD1_ACTION.ASP*, WHICH TAKES INPUT FROM *HELLOWORLD1_FORM.HTM*
VIA *REQUEST.FORM*

```
<!DOCTYPE HTML PUBLIC "-//W3C//DTD HTML 4.01 Transitional//EN">
<html>
<head>
<title>Hello World Action</title>
<meta http-equiv="Content-Type" content="text/html; charset=iso-8859-1">
</head>
<body>
Hello World, my name is <% Response.Write(Trim(Request.Form("Name"))) %>
</body>
</html>
```

FIGURE 13.5

The results of
HelloWorld1_
action.asp
displayed in
Internet Explorer

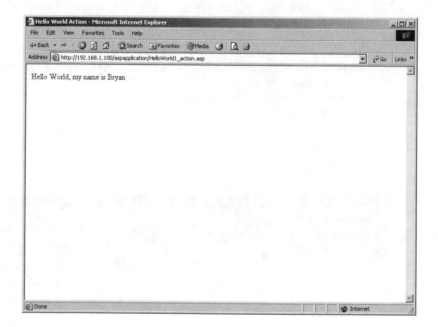

SUBMITTING FORMS

You can specify two methods to submit a form—Get and Post. Using the Get method, all form values are passed to the form Action target through the URL address. Therefore, the value red for the form text field "color" is passed to the action target form_action.asp as

    form_action.asp?color=red

Using the Post method, all form values are passed to the form Action target in the HTTP headers that are a part of every web page request.

REQUEST.QUERYSTRING

Request.Querystring is a collection of value pairs passed in the URL to an ASP page. For example, when a form using the submission method Get is targeted to the current ASP page, the collection of submitted form values are available to you through the Request.Querystring command. For example, the form in Listing 13.10 targets an ASP page (Listing 13.11) that prints out the submitted form values. Figure 13.6 shows the input form in Internet Explorer, and Figure 13.7 shows the resulting display.

LISTING 13.10: *HELLOWORLD2_FORM.HTM*, THE INPUT FORM FOR AN **ASP** PAGE THAT USES *REQUEST.QUERYSTRING*

```html
<!DOCTYPE HTML PUBLIC "-//W3C//DTD HTML 4.01 Transitional//EN">
<html>
<head>
<title>Hello World Form</title>
<meta http-equiv="Content-Type" content="text/html; charset=iso-8859-1">
</head>
<body>
<form name="HelloWorld" method="get" action="HelloWorld2_action.asp">
  <label>Your Name:
  <input name="Name" type="text" size="25" maxlength="25"></label>
  <input type="submit" value="Submit">
</form>
</body>
</html>
```

FIGURE 13.6

Viewing Hello-World2_form.htm in Internet Explorer

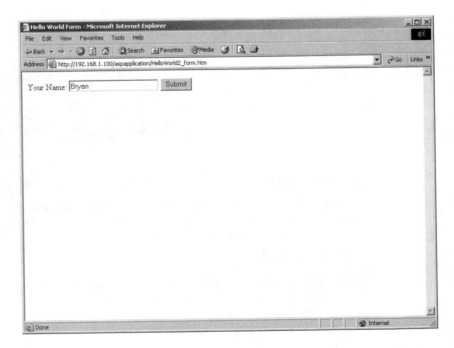

```
<!DOCTYPE HTML PUBLIC "-//W3C//DTD HTML 4.01 Transitional//EN">
<html>
<head>
<title>Hello World Action</title>
<meta http-equiv="Content-Type" content="text/html; charset=iso-8859-1">
</head>
<body>
Hello World, my name is <% Response.Write(Trim(Request.Querystring("Name"))) %>
</body>
</html>
```

FIGURE 13.7

The results of
`HelloWorld2_`
`Action.asp`
displayed in
Internet Explorer

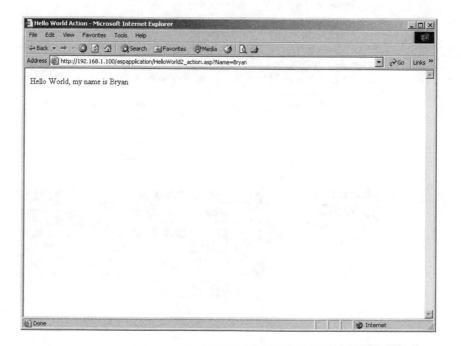

Likewise, you can pass variable names and values to an ASP page by hand-coding the variable name and value in the address targeting the ASP page. For example, the following link accomplishes the same thing as our Get method form.

```
<a href="helloworld2_action.asp?name=Popeye">Hello World</a>
```

REQUEST.COOKIES

`Request.Cookies` allows you to read a value from the collection of cookies your site has written to the user's computer. As mentioned earlier, cookies are extremely useful if you want to find out where and when the user accessed your site or if the user is a new or returning visitor. For example, the following line reads the database ID of the returning visitor (which our web application had previously written).

```
CurrentUserSID = Request.cookies("userSid")
CurrentUserSID_expires = Request.cookies("userSid").expires
```

REQUEST.SERVERVARIABLES

Any HTTP header information is available to you through the `Request.ServerVariables` command and its associated variables. The `Request.Cookies`, `Request.Querystring`, and `Request.Form` collections actually get most of their information from server variables. For example, when a form is submitted to an ASP page, the form method (Get or Post) is listed in the HTTP header of the form and can be determined by executing the following line:

```
Request.ServerVariables("Request_Method")
```

In addition to `Request_Method`, many other server variables are available to you. Fortunately, Dreamweaver MX makes it simple to choose one. Server variables is the first object Dreamweaver MX displays in the ASP tab in the Insert bar. To insert one of the server variables listed in Table 13.1, simply click the server variable icon shown here, and choose from the Server Variables dialog box shown in Figure 13.8.

FIGURE 13.8

The ASP tab in Dreamweaver MX

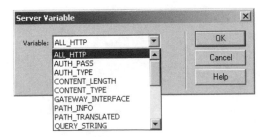

TABLE 13.1: SERVER VARIABLES FOR THE *REQUEST.SERVERVARIABLES* COMMAND

VARIABLE	DESCRIPTION
`Request.ServerVariables("ALL_HTTP")`	All HTTP headers sent by the client.
`Request.ServerVariables("AUTH_PASS")`	The password corresponding to REMOTE_USER as supplied by the client.
`Request.ServerVariables("AUTH_TYPE")`	If the web server supports user authentication, this is the authentication method.

Continued on next page

TABLE 13.1: Server Variables for the *Request.ServerVariables* Command *(continued)*

VARIABLE	DESCRIPTION
Request.ServerVariables("CONTENT_LENGTH")	The length of the CONTENT_TYPE.
Request.ServerVariables("CONTENT_TYPE")	For requests with attached information, such as a HTTP POST and PUT, this is the data content type.
Request.ServerVariables("GATEWAY_INTERFACE")	The revision of the CGI specification to which this server complies.
Request.ServerVariables("PATH_INFO")	The path information of the request. For example, relative paths, such as pdfs/mypdf.asp, can access request pages. The extra information in the path information is sent as PATH_INFO.
Request.ServerVariables("PATH_TRANSLATED")	The translated version of PATH_INFO with virtual-to-physical mapping. In the PATH_INFO example, the PATH_TRANSLATED value may be "C:\inetpub\wwwroot\test\pdfs\mypdf.pdf".
Request.ServerVariables("QUERY_STRING")	Any information that follows the ? in the URL address of the current page.
Request.ServerVariables("REMOTE_ADDR")	The IP address of the remote host making the request.
Request.ServerVariables("REMOTE_HOST")	The host name making the request.
Request.ServerVariables("REMOTE_IDENT")	If the HTTP server supports RFC 931 identification, this variable is set to the remote user name.
Request.ServerVariables("REMOTE_USER")	If the server supports user authentication, this is the authenticated user name.
Request.ServerVariables("REQUEST_BODY")	The body of the request. Used with Post messages to access the posted information.
Request.ServerVariables("REQUEST_METHOD")	The form submission method of the request.
Request.ServerVariables("SCRIPT_NAME")	The virtual path to the script being executed.
Request.ServerVariables("SERVER_NAME")	The server's host name, DNS alias, or IP address.
Request.ServerVariables("SERVER_PORT")	The port number of the request.
Request.ServerVariables("SERVER_PROTOCOL")	The name and revision of the information protocol.
Request.ServerVariables("SERVER_SOFTWARE")	The name and version of the information server software.

REQUEST.CLIENTCERTIFICATE

Request.clientcertificate is a collection of certification fields passed with a page request from the browser. If the browser is currently using the Secure Socket Layers (SSL) protocol, the protocol sends certificates to the server that identify the browser to the web server, allowing for secure data transactions. If the browser is not using the SSL protocol, the `Request.clientcertificate` collection is empty. Before you can use the `Request.clientcertificate` collection, you must configure your web server to request client certificates.

The `Request.clientcertificate` collection has one argument—Key. Key is a string that specifies the name of the field to retrieve. A certificate contains the seven fields listed and described in Table 13.2.

TABLE 13.2: *CLIENTCERTIFICATE* COLLECTION KEYS

FIELD	DESCRIPTION
Certificate	A string containing the binary stream of the entire certificate content.
Flags	Two flags provide additional client certificate information. The ceCertPresent flag indicates a client certificate is present. The ceUnrecognizedIssuer flag indicates the last certification in this chain is from an unknown user.
Issuer	A string containing the subfield values that provide information about the issuer of the certificate.
SerialNumber	A string that contains the certification serial number.
Subject	A string containing the subfield values that provide information about the subject of the certificate.
ValidFrom	The date when the certificate becomes valid.
ValidUntil	The expiration date of the certificate.

For example, to display the expiration date of the client certificate, you use the following:

```
<%= Request.ClientCertificate("ValidUntil") %>
```

Issuer and *Subject* have an additional argument to pass local information—*Subfield*. Table 13.3 list and describes the subfield arguments.

TABLE 13.3: *CLIENTCERTIFICATE* SUBFIELD VALUES

ARGUMENT	DESCRIPTION
C	The name of the country of origin
CN	The common name of the user
GN	A given name
I	A set of initials
L	A locality
O	The company or organization name

Continued on next page

TABLE 13.3: *CLIENTCERTIFICATE* SUBFIELD VALUES *(continued)*

ARGUMENT	DESCRIPTION
.OU	The name of the organizational unit
S	A state or province
T	The title of the person or organization

A NEEDLE IN A HAYSTACK

ASP is a forgiving language. If you aren't exactly sure what collection a variable is in, you can search the ASP collections for that variable. For example, you can reference the submitted form field "birthDate" as

```
request.("birthDate")
```

or as

```
request.form("birthDate")
```

However, we mention this alternative as a caution, not as an option. When you force ASP to search through all collections looking for a variable, it can slow execution time and create code that is difficult to debug. Furthermore, ASP returns the value of the first variable match it finds. Therefore, the returned value might or might not be the value of the variable you want.

The Server Object

The Response and Request objects send data to and from the server. In a web application, you often need information about the server itself, and that's where the Server object comes in. It provides access to server information in the form of properties and methods. You need to know the following properties and methods: ScriptTimeout, Execute, HTMLEncode, URLEncode, MapPath, GetLastError, and CreateObject. Using these properties and methods, you can create objects, execute code, translate paths, and perform other server-side tasks.

SCRIPTTIMEOUT

Infinite loops are bad. An infinite loop, or a process that continues to call itself forever, eventually consumes so many resources that your web server will crash. To avoid infinite loops, ASP is set to time out, or end a script, if the script executes longer than 90 seconds. However, at times a complicated script can require longer than 90 seconds to execute. The ScriptTimeout property lets you set the runtime in seconds for an ASP script. For example, use the following code to force a script to time out if its processing exceeds 200 seconds.

```
<% Server.ScriptTimeout = 200 %>
```

Likewise, you can retrieve the current ScriptTimeout value as follows:

```
<% ScriptTimeout = Server.ScriptTimeout %>
```

EXECUTE(PATH)

Execute lets you call another ASP script page from within an ASP script page. Once the called ASP script page executes completely, the calling ASP script page continues. From a programming perspective, Execute is similar to calling a function or a subroutine. For example, you can create an ASP script page named GetCurrentTime.asp whose sole purpose is to generate and display the current date, as shown in Listing 13.12.

LISTING 13.12: *GETCURRENTTIME.ASP*

```
<html>
<head>
<title>Get Current Time</title>
<meta http-equiv="Content-Type" content="text/html; charset=iso-8859-1">
</head>
<body>
<%= FormatDateTime(Date, 1)  %>
</body>
</html>
```

You could use Execute to run the GetCurrentTime.asp script page from any other ASP script page, such as your site's home page as shown in Listing 13.13.

LISTING 13.13: *DEFAULT.ASP*

```
<html>
<head>
<title>Default Home Page</title>
<meta http-equiv="Content-Type" content="text/html; charset=iso-8859-1">
</head>
<body>
   This is my home page. Below you can see the date.
   <HR>
<% Server.Execute("GetCurrentTime.asp") %>
</body>
</html>
```

HTMLENCODE

To print certain characters in an HTML page, you must use a special character code. For example, when a browser encounters the < character, it does not display the character. To display the < character in a browser, you use the charcter code <. Luckily, you don't have to memorize every character code. HTMLEncode lets you convert any character to the alternative HTML character code. To demonstrate, the following line displays the < character in a browser.

```
<% Server.HTMLEncode("<") %>
```

URLENCODE

Similar to HTMLEncode, URLEncode converts a string of characters to the URL-encoded format. Spaces are replaced with +, and special characters are converted to hexadecimal. For example, the following line converts "Have a nice day" to "Have+a+nice+day".

```
<% Server.URLEncode("Have a nice day") %>
```

MAPPATH(PATH)

MapPath returns the physical path on the server of a relative or virtual path. For example, to return the physical path on the server to the current directory of the executing ASP script file, you write the following:

```
<% PhysicalPath = Server.MapPath("\") %>
```

Likewise, to return the physical path to the currently executing ASP script file, you write the following:

```
<% PhysicalPath = Server.MapPath("\mypage.asp") %>
```

GETLASTERROR

GetLastError returns an instance of the ASPError object that lets you access detailed information about an error that has occurred. GetLastError stores the error information in nine properties: ASPCode, ASPDescription, Category, Column, Description, File, Line, Number, and Source. You must access these properties before any data is send to the client browser. Listing 13.14 is an example of accessing the ASPError properties.

LISTING 13.14: *ASPERROR.ASP*

```
<%
Dim objErrorInformation
Set objErrorInformation = Server.GetLastError

Response.Write("ASPCode = " & objErrorInformation.ASPCode)
Response.Write("ASPDescription = " & objErrorInformation.ASPDescription)
Response.Write("Category = " & objErrorInformation.Category)
Response.Write("Column = " & objErrorInformation.Column)
Response.Write("Description = " & objErrorInformation.Description)
Response.Write("File = " & objErrorInformation.File)
Response.Write("Line = " & objErrorInformation.Line)
Response.Write("Number = " & objErrorInformation.Number)
Response.Write("Source = " & objErrorInformation.Source)
%>
```

CREATEOBJECT(OBJECTID)

CreateObject lets you create an instance of a server object to use in an ASP script. The most common server object you create will be to connect to a database and retreive data. To do so, you work with an ADODB.Recordset server object.

The ADODB.Recordset server object represents an entire set of records pulled from a database table. Listing 13.15 demonstrates how to create, fill, and close a recordset with information from a database. Notice that we use an include statement to pull in the ASP file that defines our database connection we created in Chapter 10.

LISTING 13.15: *RECORDSET.ASP*

```
<%@LANGUAGE="VBSCRIPT"%>
<!--#include file="Connections/book_connection.asp" -->
<%
Dim Recordset1
Dim Recordset1_numRows

Set Recordset1 = Server.CreateObject("ADODB.Recordset")
Recordset1.ActiveConnection = MM_ book_connection _STRING
Recordset1.Source = "SELECT * FROM Titles"
Recordset1.CursorType = 0
Recordset1.CursorLocation = 2
Recordset1.LockType = 1
Recordset1.Open()

Recordset1_numRows = 0

Recordset1.Close()
Set Recordset1 = Nothing
%>
```

The Application Object

Through a process known as task switching (or multitasking), the server manages to complete multiple tasks in a short period of time, making each user feel as though they are the only visitor at your site. Here's how it works:

1. As the server receives each request, it stores the request in a queue (a list of items that's constantly updated).
2. The server chooses a predetermined number of tasks—known as threads—from the queue.
3. The server loads the first thread and works on it for a while, maybe for a few millionths of a second.
4. The server then loads the second thread and works on it for a while. The server continues in this fashion until the first thread is complete.
5. Once a thread is complete, it's removed from the queue.

The more threads you have, the longer it takes to complete each task, but the loss in performance is hardly noticeable in most systems. IIS gives you the choice of balancing the two needs: performance or multiple tasks. The ASP engine starts with three threads. You can increase or decrease this number depending on your needs—choose to process one thread quickly or to process several threads simultaneously. When sharing resources to process multiple threads, you'll use the Application object. Specifically, Application methods let you limit processing to only one thread.

The Application object is the sum of all ASP files within your web application. As such, you can share information across the application. You use the Application object to share, store, and retreive information pertinent to your entire web application. For example, a useful application variable is the e-mail address for all your forms. You set the e-mail address once as an application variable, and that variable is available to all threads running in your application. If you need to change the e-mail address throughout your application, you simply change it once. For example, the following code sets the e-mail address throughout the application.

```
<% application("emailAddress") = "webmaster@helpmedia.com" %>
```

WARNING   *Don't use the Application object to store your recordset data. Looking up data makes the Application object unavailable to other threads until the value is retrieved, which can seriously slow down all your threads.*

The Session Object

The term *session* is subject to the context in which it's being used. In simplest terms, a session refers to the time a client spends connected to your web application. Similar to the Application object, the Session object has start and end events. Specifically, a session begins when a browser makes a request and ends when the connection is terminated. The Session object stores values associated with a particular client, providing an easy method for storing and tracking individual client (user) IDs.

For example, when a client not currently connected to your website makes a request, the web server creates a Session object and assigns a session ID for that new client. This session is maintained even when the user requests different pages within the same application. Only when the session is terminated does the server destroy the Session object. For this reason, storing the ID of a visitor in a session variable is a great alternative to continually referring to the ID in a cookie. For example, the following code reads the `userSid` of the cookie we set in an earlier example and places it in a session variable that is available across all pages in your web application.

```
<% session("userSid") = Request.cookies("userSid") %>
```

You can control when a session terminates in two ways:

- Use the Timeout property to define a limit to inactivity.
- Use code to specify conditions for terminating the session.

If you don't need tight control, you have two other choices:

- Shut down IIS, which ends all sessions.
- Modify the `global.asa` file (see the next section), which stops all the applications and ends all sessions, but doesn't act until the next request by any browser.

The browser can also opt to end the session by refusing the SessionID cookie. Neither the application or IIS has any control over this choice, nor will the server know in advance which browser might refuse a cookie.

NOTE *A web server maintains a Session object only for browsers that support cookies.*

The *global.asa* file

The `global.asa` is a file that can reside in the root directory of your web application. If it exists, ASP locates `global.asa` as the first request is made to your web application. As an application and a session begin and end, the `global.asa` file executes commands based on the following events and in the following order:

1. Application_OnStart is executed when the first user requests a page from your ASP application. This event is reset if the web server is restarted or if you edit the `global.asa` file.

2. Session_OnStart triggers every time a new user requests a page from your ASP application. It occurs directly after the Application_OnStart event.

3. Session_OnEnd is triggered when a user or the site ends a session. This typically happens when a user has not requested a page for 20 minutes.

4. Application_OnEnd ends the application when the last user connected to the ASP application ends their session, when the server stops, or when the `global.asa` is altered.

You can use the `global.asa` file to initialize and define application and session variables or run processes. For example, you can place the application and session code examples in the web application `global.asa` file as shown in Listing 13.16. Notice that we added code to destroy the variables in the session and application end events.

LISTING 13.16: *GLOBAL.ASA*

```
Sub application_OnStart
   application("emailAddress") = "webmaster@helpmedia.com"
End Sub

Sub session_OnStart
   session("userSid") = Request.cookies("userSid")
End Sub

Sub session_OnEnd
   session("userSid") =  null
End Sub

Sub application_OnEnd
   application("emailAddress") = null
End Sub
```

The ObjectContext Object

You use the ObjectContext object to manage transactions with the Microsoft Transaction Server (MTS) that have been initiated by an ASP script file. The ObjectContext object lets you commit or abort a transaction and set a process to follow either event. When the `@transaction` directive is specified in the first line of an ASP script file, the file runs in a transaction until the transaction succeeds or fails. We mention ObjectContext for completeness. Initiating and managing transactions with ASP and MTS is outside the scope of this introductory chapter. For more information, consult `www.microsoft.com`.

The ASPError Object

The ASPError object exposes detailed information about the last error that occurred. This error information is stored in nine properties. To access this information, you must use the Server object, `GetLastError`. (See the "*GetLastError*" section earlier in this chapter.)

FOR FURTHER INFORMATION

You can utilize hundreds of resources to find out more about ASP. Three of the most-visited ASP-oriented websites are `www.microsoft.com`, `www.w3schools.com/asp/`, and `www.4guysfromrolla.com`. For some great training and reference books such as *Mastering Active Server Pages 3*, visit `www.sybex.com`. To keep current with tips and techniques, we suggest Active Server Developer's Journal at `www.element-kjournals.com`. Finally, nothing substitutes networking with people in the know, so check out your area ASP user group.

Summary

In this chapter, we introduced you to the ASP host, the language, and the seven ASP objects—Response, Request, Server, Application, Session, ObjectContext, and ASPError. We also demonstrated how to write scripts that access ASP's common functions, methods, and properties. As mentioned, we only touched on the most-used elements of ASP in web development. As always, we encourage you to continually expand your ASP knowledge.

Chapter 14

Dreamweaver and ASP.NET

ASP.NET IS THE NEXT step in web development evolution with the Microsoft .NET framework. However, ASP.NET is not simply an update of syntax and function to its precursor—Microsoft ASP (Active Server Pages). ASP.NET introduces a completely new framework to web development on Microsoft operating systems. As you know from previous chapters HTML (Hypertext Markup Language), ASP, and most other web development schemes function based on a client/server model. In the web client/server model, historically all interaction consists of a transaction beginning with a request and ending with fulfillment. For example, the client, a web browser, contacts the server, a website, and requests information. The server then sends the information back to the client. Thus, the transaction is complete. The server has no more interaction with the client until the client sends another request for a transaction.

ASP.NET does not end the transaction when it fulfills the web browser request. Instead, ASP.NET relies on an event-driven model to actually monitor and respond to events that happen on the client, your web browser. How does a web server know what's happening in a web browser on your computer? ASP.NET uses client-side scripting to listen to events as they happen in your web browser.

To fully utilize ASP.NET and Dreamweaver MX, you need an understanding of the .NET framework, the syntax of VB.NET or C#, and the objects and underlying structure of ASP.NET technology. Obviously, this is well more than we can cover in one chapter, so we'll focus on an introduction to ASP.NET, the .NET framework and commonly used areas of VB.NET, and the C# language.

This chapter covers the following topics:

- The .NET framework
- ASP.NET—the host
- ASP.NET—VB.NET or C#
- ASP.NET web forms
- Using ASP.NET server controls
- Active and passive events
- Specifying validation
- ASP.NET objects
- ASP.NET XML web services

Overview

An ASP.NET script file is a text file (.aspx) that contains any combination of ASP.NET code and HTML code. The first time a web server processes an ASP.NET web page, the web server compiles the ASP.NET script file. Once compiled, the ASP.NET page is quick to respond to any subsequent web request. If the original ASP.NET script file is altered, the page is compiled again on the next page request. All ASP.NET script files are managed by the Common Language Runtime (CLR) environment.

CLR manages and compiles code on several levels. For example, the first time the web server processes an ASP.NET script file, the ASP.NET script file is compiled into a language called Microsoft Intermediate Language (MSIL). MSIL is an intermediate language that is essentially a compacted version of your ASP.NET script file. From that point, CLR compiles the MSIL code into machine code and processes it for web requests. Typically this process is almost instantaneous, but it occurs in the following steps.

1. A web browser requests a page at a specific web address, such as www.sybex.com.
2. The web server hosting the www.sybex.com website accepts that request. If the ASP.NET script file has been altered from the compiled version or has not been compiled, it is compiled into MSIL. It is then compiled again into machine code. The compiled version is executed, and HTTP responses are sent to the requesting browser.
3. The server forwards the HTTP request to the compiled version of the ASP.NET script file, which subsequently sends the resulting HTML to the requesting web browser.

This overview is just the tip of the iceberg. Unlike other web technologies, there is not one specific ASP.NET programming language. ASP.NET actually supports multiple programming languages. Although more language choices may develop, right now you can choose to develop in the VB.NET, C# (C Sharp), or JScript.NET language. (Dreamweaver MX supports only the VB.NET and C# programming languages, so that will be our focus throughout this chapter.) Also, since ASP.NET is built on the .NET technology, you have access to every powerful feature and function in the .NET framework.

The .NET Framework

The .NET in ASP.NET is not just a clever marketing scheme. The .NET refers to the Microsoft .NET framework, a structure and collection of objects common to all Microsoft .NET technologies. By centralizing all Microsoft technologies on the .NET framework, all development efforts have access to key compatibility, security, and system features.

For example, we've already touched on how the CLR environment manages and compiles ASP.NET code into MSIL and then compiles it into whatever native machine code the target computer requires. That model is not specific to ASP.NET but to all .NET technologies. Thus, the Java prime directive "Write once, publish everywhere" can truly be achieved with .NET.

Central to the .NET framework is that everything is treated like an object. Each object is organized into groups called namespaces.

For example, all database-related objects are grouped in the SYSTEM.DATA namespace. To use objects in the SYSTEM.DATA namespace, your ASP.NET page simply loads the namespace before using the objects. You'll find numerous namespaces throughout the .NET framework, and you can even create your own. For a full list of all .NET namespaces, see the .NET framework documentation included with the ASP.NET Software Development Kit.

The important point concerning .NET namespaces is that ASP.NET has access to all of them. Moreover, an ASP.NET page is an actual object based on the SYSTEM.WEB.UI.PAGE namespace. Therefore, an ASP.NET page has its own properties and methods that you can reference and manipulate. You can begin to see how extensive and powerful the .NET framework makes ASP.NET.

ASP.NET—the Host

To develop or host a ASP.NET web application, you need access to a Windows server running Windows NT, 2000, or XP. (Windows NT will need a special option pack to run the .NET framework. The option pack is available in the download section of www.microsoft.com.) In addition, we suggest downloading the .NET Software Development Kit to install the .NET framework. The full Softwae Development Kit is a large download (more than 100MB), but it provides a multitude of documentation and code examples you can have at your fingertips. The .NET Software Development Kit is a free download from www.microsoft.com/net.

As well, you should choose between VB.NET or C# as the programming language in which you'll create your ASP.NET application. To help you make an informed choice, we'll use both VB.NET and C# in the examples in this chapter.

ASP.NET—VB.NET or C#

You can build web applications that utilize the full power of ASP.NET using either VB.NET or C#. However, they are different syntactically. For example, the following lines contain a comment, declare a variable, and assign it a value in VB.NET:

```
' myName is a String to hold a name
Dim myName As String
myName = "Bryan"
```

This line declares the same variable in C#:

```
// myName is a String to hold a name
String myName;
myName = "Bryan";
```

Most developers choose VB.NET because of their familiarity with Visual Basic, VBScript used in traditional ASP, and Microsoft VBScript for Applications. VB.NET is a quick-to-learn, powerful language that can make the transition from traditional ASP to ASP.NET painless. C# is a new programming language based on the powerful C and C++ programming languages. If you are familiar with C, C++, or Java, C# will be a comfortable fit.

ASP.NET Web Forms

Regardless of your programming language choice, the structure of ASP.NET pages is the same. Almost every ASP.NET script page can be broken into the following components—Page Directives, Code Declaration Blocks, Code Render Blocks, and Web Forms. To demonstrate each component, let's dissect the sample ASP.NET VB.NET script file shown in Listing 14.1 and the ASP.NET C# script file shown in Listing 14.2. The result of both scripts is the same; you can see the C# output in Figure 14.1.

We strongly encourage you to key in all the code to create the example files yourself. To check your work, compare your files with the example files on the CD accompanying this book.

LISTING 14.1: *HELLOWORLD-VB.ASPX* IN **VB.NET**

```
<%@ Page Language="VB" ContentType="text/html" ResponseEncoding="iso-8859-1" %>

<script runat="server">
    Sub tbName_Change(Sender As Object, E As EventArgs)
        lblWelcome.Text = "Hello " + tbName.Text
    End Sub
</script>
<!DOCTYPE HTML PUBLIC "-//W3C//DTD HTML 4.01 Transitional//EN">
<html>
<head>
<title>Hello World Form</title>
<meta http-equiv="Content-Type" content="text/html; charset=iso-8859-1">
</head>
<body>
<form runat="server">
  <label>Your Name:</label>
  <asp:textbox ID="tbName"  OnTextChanged="tbName_Change" runat="server"
    TextMode="SingleLine" />
  <asp:button ID="btSubmit" runat="server" Text="Enter" />
  <asp:label ID="lblWelcome" runat="server" ></asp:label>
</form>
</body>
</html>
```

LISTING 14.2: *HELLOWORLD-CSHARP.ASPX* IN **C SHARP**

```
<%@ Page Language="C#" ContentType="text/html" ResponseEncoding="iso-8859-1" %>

<script runat="server">
    void tbName_Change(Object Sender, EventArgs E) {
        lblWelcome.Text = "Hello " + tbName.Text;
    }
</script>
<!DOCTYPE HTML PUBLIC "-//W3C//DTD HTML 4.01 Transitional//EN">
```

```
<html>
<head>
<title>Hello World Form</title>
<meta http-equiv="Content-Type" content="text/html; charset=iso-8859-1">
</head>
<body>
<form runat="server">
  <label>Your Name:</label>
  <asp:textbox ID="tbName"  OnTextChanged="tbName_Change" runat="server"
     TextMode="SingleLine" />
  <asp:button ID="btSubmit" runat="server" Text="Enter" />
  <asp:label ID="lblWelcome" runat="server" ></asp:label>
</form>
</body>
</html>
```

FIGURE 14.1

Viewing the output from helloWorld-CSharp.aspx in Internet Explorer

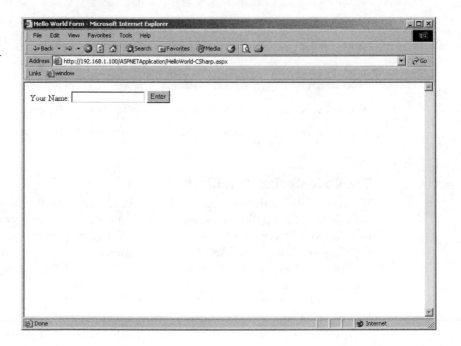

The Page Directive

Beginning at the top of both script files you'll notice

```
<%@ Page Language="VB" ContentType="text/html" ResponseEncoding="iso-8859-1" %>
```

and

```
<%@ Page Language="C#" ContentType="text/html" ResponseEncoding="iso-8859-1" %>
```

This is a Page Directive. You use Page Directives to tell ASP.NET how to handle the page. In this case, we've simply declared the type of programming language we'll be using throughout our page. In addition to declaring the default programming language of the page, you can also use Directives for many other tasks. Table 14.1 lists and explains the directives supported by ASP.NET.

TABLE 14.1: ASP.NET DIRECTIVES

DIRECTIVE	PURPOSE
@ Page	Defines page-specific attributes used by ASP.NET. The Page Directive can only be used in `.aspx` files.
@ Control	Defines control-specific attributes used by ASP.NET. The Control Directive can only be included in user control `.ascx` files.
@ Import	Imports a namespace into an ASP.NET page or user control.
@ Implements	Indicates that an ASP.NET page uses a specific .NET framework interface.
@ Register	Defines and applies an alias to namespace and class names. Hereafter, the alias can be used to include user and server controls in a page or user control.
@ Assembly	Links an assembly to the ASP.NET page or user control.
@ OutputCache	Controls the output caching of an ASP.NET page or a user control.
@ Reference	Links a page or a user control to the ASP.NET page or user control.

The Code Declaration Block

If you're familiar with JavaScript, you'll recognize that the next line begins a Code Declaration Block. A Code Declaration Block is nothing more than a section of the page that contains programming code. A Code Declaration Block always begins with the `<script>` tag and ends with the `</script>` tag. However, in the case of ASP.NET, the programming code is compiled by the server. In ASP.NET, any code or object you want the ASP.NET server to handle should include the `RUNAT="SERVER"` parameter, as our beginning code block does. As you can see in the VB.NET and C# sample code, the Code Declaration Block is defining a subprocedure that changes the text of our lblWelcome label to the value of the `tbName` text field once the Submit button is clicked.

The VB.NET version of the declaration block looks like this:

```
<script runat="server">
    Sub tbName_Change(Sender As Object, E As EventArgs)
        lblWelcome.Text = "Hello " + tbName.Text
    End Sub
</script>
```

The C# version looks like this:

```
<script runat="server">
    void tbName_Change(Object Sender, EventArgs E) {
        lblWelcome.Text = "Hello " + tbName.Text;
    }
</script>
```

The Code Render Block

If you're an ASP developer, you'll recognize the next line we call to your attention in both scripts:

```
<%= "Sample ASP.NET Script Page" %>
```

This line is referred to as a Code Render Block. There are two types, inline code and inline expressions. *Inline code* defines self-contained code blocks for more complex functions. *Inline expressions* are typically used as a shortcut for the RESPONSE.WRITE command, which outputs data to the HTML page. These types of Code Render Blocks were commonly mixed freely with HTML code in traditional ASP script files. However, ASP.NET script pages are more structured. ASP.NET script pages are typically organized with ASP.NET code at the top of the page and the user interface or presentation at the bottom of the page. Therefore, Code Render Blocks are of minimal use in ASP.NET. Still, they are handy to directly output a line, quickly declare a variable, or set a value.

The Web Form

The next block of lines demonstrates one of the most important concepts in ASP.NET—Web Forms. Web Forms are script pages that direct the server to dynamically generate HTML-compliant output to the target browser, such as a web browser or a mobile device. Web Forms provide much of the built-in web functionality of ASP.NET.

In addition, Web Forms allow developers to finally separate the visible portion of the page, the user interface or presentation, from the programming code and logic. The visual part of a Web Form is called the Page. The Page holds the HTML and ASP.NET server controls. The logic portion of the Web Form is held within Code Declaration Blocks that are compiled by the server.

Back in our sample ASP.NET script, notice that the <form> tag has the RUNAT="SERVER" parameter. This ensures that ASP.NET realizes this form is indeed a Web Form. When the server processes this Web Form, it translates it into HTML. For example, the Web Form looks like this in our example ASP.NET script file:

```
<form runat="server">
  <label>Your Name:</label>
  <asp:textbox ID="tbName"  OnTextChanged="tbName_Change" runat="server"
    TextMode="SingleLine" />
  <asp:button ID="btSubmit" runat="server" Text="Enter" />
  <asp:label ID="lblWelcome" runat="server" ></asp:label>
</form>
```

which is radically different from the following server-generated HTML that is sent to a web browser:

```
<form name="_ctl0" method="post" action="HelloWorld-CSharp.aspx" id="_ctl0">
<input type="hidden" name="__VIEWSTATE" value="dDwxMzc4MDMwNTk103Q8O2w8aTwwPjs+O2_
w_8dDw_7bDxpPDE+O2k8NT47PjtsPHQ8cDxwPGw8VGV4dDs+O2w8Y_
XNkZnNkZjs+Pjs+Ozs+O3Q8cDxwPGw8VGV4dDs+O2w8SGV_
sbG8gYXNkZnNkZjs+Pjs+Ozs+Oz4+Oz4+Oz4P44crQ5YQM_
qdaLaCekXk+vypiEg==" />
  <label>Your Name:</label>
  <input name="tbName" type="text" value="" id="tbName" />
  <input type="submit" name="btSubmit" value="Enter" id="btSubmit" />
  <span id="lblWelcome"></span>
</form>
```

NOTE *The above code has been formatted to fit the book page. The length of your lines of code may vary from what is shown here.*

Within a Web Form you can place server controls, which are form controls the server can programmatically monitor and then react to the events that affect them. For example, when you view the ASP.NET form in your web browser, the text field, label tag, and Submit button are actually server controls that can react to events and even communicate with the server at any given time. With ASP.NET, you no longer have to wait for the user to submit a form to react to events.

For example, in a simple login form scripted in traditional ASP, the user enters their login name and password. They then click Submit to send the form to the server. The server validates the login name and password and responds with a success or failure message to the user. If you script the same login form using server controls and ASP.NET, you can set the Login textbox and the Password box to validate and return a success and failure message as soon as the user enters information. In short, past techniques limited server processing and responses to a form submission. ASP.NET allows your server to process and respond to any action occurring to any control or object on a web page.

However, notice that our sample `<form>` tag has no Action page specified. Without an Action page defined, the form submits the form data to itself. This is referred to as *Postback Form* and is common practice in ASP.NET. Also notice that the ASP.NET web server has added a hidden text box to the HTML form block. This hidden text field allows one of the best, albeit simplest, features of a Postback Form with HTML server controls—server controls within the form retain their value when the form is submitted. So, if you enter your name in the text box and submit the form to itself, ASP.NET automatically populates the text box with the submitted text box value. In traditional ASP, a developer had to include several lines of code to accomplish this.

In our example, you can see that the text box, button, and label all include the `RUNAT="SERVER"` parameter specifying them as server controls. Also notice that the text box has an additional element that sets a call to the `tbName_Change` subprocedure declared in our Code Declaration Block. So, whenever the text box value is changed and the form is submitted, the subprocedure sets the value of the text box as the value of the label, as shown in Figure 14.2.

FIGURE 14.2

An event-driven
Web Form

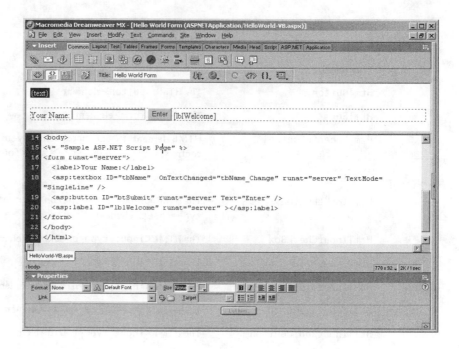

Using ASP.NET Server Controls

As we've mentioned, you can use ASP.NET server controls to easily create and programmatically reference and control objects in ASP.NET script pages. To make programming this large library of controls easier, each control has a base object model that contains the same properties, methods, and events. In our previous example, you saw a few HTML server control counterparts to some standard HTML form controls we all know and love. However, HTML server controls are only the beginning. There are 45 default ASP.NET web server controls that you can use for everything from controlling the value of a text box to managing the display of an ad banner system to binding a form field to a column in a database.

At this point, you may be wondering about the differences between HTML server controls and web server controls. Very simply, HTML server controls are standard HTML tags with the RUNAT=SERVER parameter that marks them as a server controls. HTML server controls lack the expansive attributes and control provided by web server controls. In addition, the ASP.NET web server won't generate HTML targeted to browser versions as web server controls will. Table 14.2 shows a list of common HTML server controls. (As you recall, most HTML elements can be transformed into HTML server controls by adding the RUNAT=SERVER parameter.) Table 14.3 lists and describes web server controls. Don't stop there. Hundreds of web server controls are freely available on the web. In fact, you can even create your own web server controls.

TABLE 14.2: HTML SERVER CONTROLS

CONTROL	WHAT IT CONTROLS
HTMLAnchor	The HTML <a> tag
HtmlButton	The HTML <button> element
HtmlForm	The HTML <form> element
HtmlGenericControl	HTML elements that are not specifically supported by existing server controls, such as <span>, <div>, and <font>
HtmlImage	The HTML <img> element
HtmlInputButton	The HTML <input type=button>, <input type=submit>, and <input type=reset> elements
HtmlInputCheckBox	The HTML <input type=checkbox> element
HtmlInputFile	The HTML <input type=file> element
HtmlInputHidden	The HTML <input type=hidden> element
HtmlInputImage	The HTML <input type=image> element
HtmlInputRadioButton	The HTML <input type=radio> element
HtmlInputText	The HTML <input type=text> and <input type=password> elements
HtmlSelect	The HTML <select> element
HtmlTable	The HTML <table> element
HtmlTableCell	The HTML <td> and <th> elements
HtmlTableRow	The HTML <tr> element
HtmlTextArea	The HTML <textarea> element

TABLE 14.3: WEB SERVER CONTROLS

CONTROL	PURPOSE
AdRotator	Displays an advertising banner
Button	Displays a push button
Calendar	Displays a one-month calendar with which the user can select dates and move to the previous and next months
CheckBox	Displays a check box control
CheckBoxList	Creates a group of check boxes that can be dynamically created by binding to a data source

Continued on next page

TABLE 14.3: WEB SERVER CONTROLS *(continued)*

CONTROL	PURPOSE
CompareValidator	Compares one form control value to another or to a specified value
CustomValidator	Validates based on user-defined parameters
DataGrid	Displays items from a data source in a table and allows the user to select, edit, and sort items
DataList	Displays items from a data source using templates that can be customized
DropDownList	Displays a drop-down list from which the user can select an item
HyperLink	Displays a link that directs the user to another page
Image	Displays an image defined by the ImageURL property
ImageButton	Displays an image and allows the server to handle click events
Label	Displays and manipulates static content on the page with the benefit of applying styles to the content
Literal	Displays and manipulates static content on the page without applying styles to the content
LinkButton	Displays hyperlink-style buttons
ListBox	Displays a single- or multiple-selection list box
Panel	Displays a panel as a container for other controls
PlaceHolder	Reserves a location in the page for programmatically added controls
RadioButton	Displays a radio button
RadioButtonList	Displays a radio button group that can be dynamically created by binding to a data source
RangeValidator	Validates that the value of a form control falls within a given range
RegularExpressionValidator	Validates that the value of a form control matches a specific pattern such as a date or a credit card number
Repeater	Displays the items from a data source in a layout dictated by repeating a single template for each item in the list
Table	Displays and manipulates a table
TableCell	Creates and manipulates a cell for the Table control
TableRow	Creates and manipulates a row for the Table control
Textbox	Displays a single or multiline text box

Continued on next page

TABLE 14.3: WEB SERVER CONTROLS *(continued)*

CONTROL	PURPOSE
RequiredFieldValidator	Validates that the user does insert a value into a form control before submitting the form
ValidationSummary	Displays a summary of all failed validation controls
XML	Used to output data to an XML document or text stream

In most cases, using a server control in Dreamweaver MX is simple. For example, to add a Form control to your page, follow these steps:

1. Create a new ASP.NET page in your defined ASP.NET site.
2. From the ASP.NET toolbar, click the Textbox button to open the TagEditor - Textbox dialog box, which is shown in Figure 14.3.

FIGURE 14.3

Dreamweaver MX inserts the Textbox server control

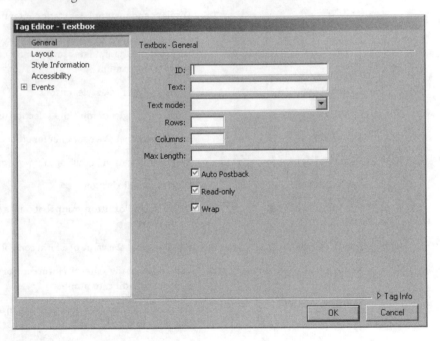

3. Enter the ID and TextMode, and click OK. Dreamweaver MX places the Textbox server control in your page.

Active and Passive Events

As we've mentioned, ASP.NET server controls expose and raise server events. However, because the server can handle only active events, it's important to understand the difference between active and passive events. Active events include clicking a button or a link, filling out a text box, pressing a key on the keyboard—anything you purposefully click, select, drag, or otherwise interact with. Passive events include moving the mouse to rollover an image or other page object or scrolling down a page.

As events occur, you can choose to have the server process them as they happen or to process them as a collection during a form submission. Keep in mind that "as they happen" sounds attractive, but it is connection and processor heavy. Consider a user entering their personal information in a web form. Each bit of information entered into each text box sends a Post to the server. To demonstrate, let's change our helloWorld web form example to contact the server as soon as the value in the text box changes. To do so, all we need to add is `autopostback=true` to the `tbName` text box as shown in Listing 14.3. Preview the page in a web browser. As you can see in the result shown in Figure 14.4, the event triggers the validation and the response as soon as you activate and leave the `tbName` text box.

LISTING 14.3: *HELLOWORLDAUTOPOST-VB.ASPX* IN **VB.NET**

```
<%@ Page Language="VB" ContentType="text/html" ResponseEncoding="iso-8859-1" %>

<script runat="server">
    Sub tbName_Change(Sender As Object, E As EventArgs)
        lblWelcome.Text = "Hello " + tbName.Text
    End Sub
</script>
<!DOCTYPE HTML PUBLIC "-//W3C//DTD HTML 4.01 Transitional//EN">
<html>
<head>
<title>Hello World Form</title>
<meta http-equiv="Content-Type" content="text/html; charset=iso-8859-1">
</head>
<body>
<%= "Sample ASP.NET Script Page" %>
<form runat="server">
  <label>Your Name:</label>
  <asp:textbox ID="tbName"  OnTextChanged="tbName_Change" autopostback=true
     runat="server" TextMode="SingleLine" />
  <asp:button ID="btSubmit" runat="server" Text="Enter" />
  <asp:label ID="lblWelcome" runat="server" ></asp:label>
</form>
</body>
</html>
```

Obviously, adding an active Post to each web server control could quickly bring your web form to a crawl and consume a great deal of server resources. That said, in almost every case, you want to handle all events as a collection.

FIGURE 14.4

Viewing the output from `helloWorldauto-post-VB.aspx` in Internet Explorer

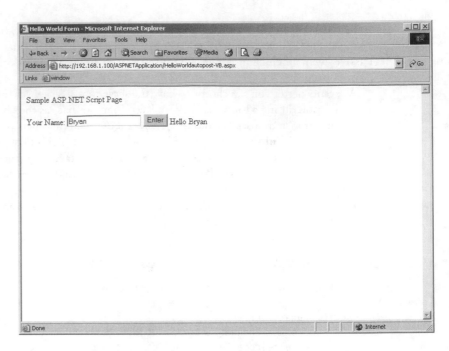

Whether actively or collectively, a server control sends information to the server in two pieces—an object that identifies the server control generating the event and an object that describes any pertinent event information. Typical trigger events are OnClick, OnDataBinding, OnDisposed, OnInit, OnLoad, OnPreRender, and OnUnload. Just as we did in our `helloWorld.aspx` example, you can take advantage of each of these events by wiring your server control to listen and then react to an event.

Specifying Validation

As we've pointed out, ASP.NET includes a set of validation server controls that provide an easy-to-use way to check HTML forms and controls for errors. Plus, you can create more complex validation schemes by adding multiple validation server controls to your form. However, let's limit our sample validation to just the `RequiredFieldValidator` server control.

You add the `RequiredFieldValidator` server control to a Web Form just as you add any other server control. Follow these steps:

1. In Dreamweaver MX, open your `helloWorld.aspx` file from your defined site.
2. Place the cursor next to the Enter button,
3. Click the More Tags button on the ASP.NET toolbar to open the Tag Chooser.
4. Highlight the ASP.NET Tags group, select the Validation server controls control, and choose ASP:RequiredFieldValidator as shown in Figure 14.5. Then click the Insert button.

As you can see in the dialog box shown in Figure 14.6, you need to set a number of Validation control parameters.

FIGURE 14.5

Dreamweaver MX
Tag Chooser for
ASP.NET

FIGURE 14.6

The Dreamweaver
MX TagEditor for
ASP.NET

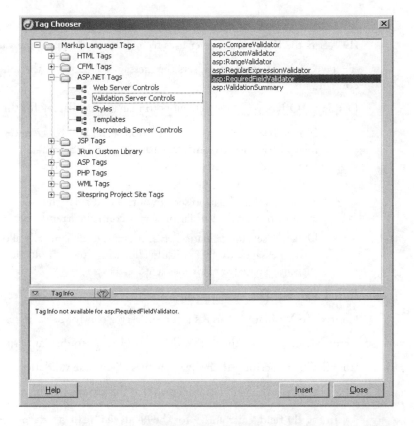

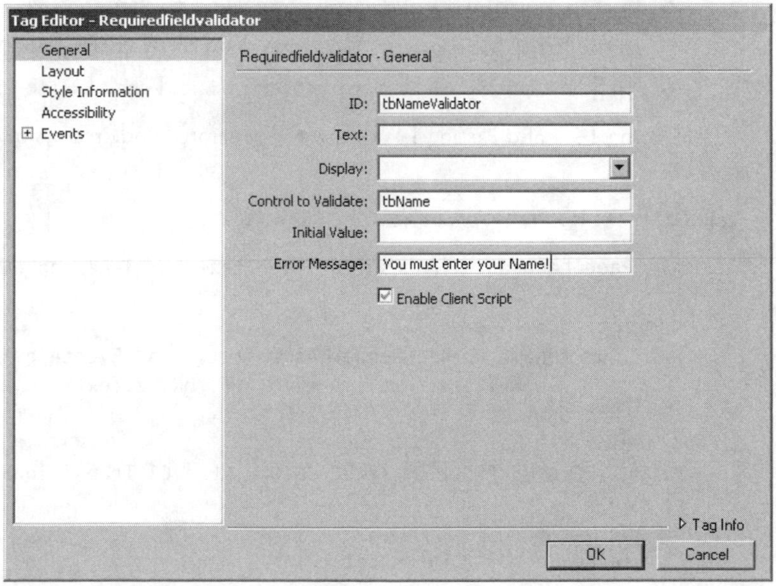

Let's take a look at the parameters.

ID   Sets the ID the web server uses to monitor and control the validation server control.

Text   Optional. If specified, sets the message to display if the validation of the targeted server control fails.

Display   Offers you three behaviors to manage the display for this validation control:

- None, the default, sets the validation server control to never display an error message but instead pass the error message to a ValidationSummary control. A ValidationSummary control gathers all error messages from all validation server controls and displays a summary of error messages.

- Static sets the validation server control to display the validation error message in whatever layout position the validation server control currently occupies.

- Dynamic sets the validation error message to dynamically allocate space on the page for the error messages. By dynamically allocating space, multiple validation controls can share the same space for error messages.

Initial Value   The value initially associated with the watched server control

Control to Validate   Targets a current server control to validate.

Error Message   Sets the text of the error message to display if the validation fails.

Enable Client Script   If checked, enables client-side validation.

All right, let's set the validation control for the `tbName` text box. Follow these steps:

1. In the ID field, enter an ID for the `RequiredFieldValidator` server control.

2. In the Control To Validate text box, enter **tbName**.

3. In the Error Message text box, enter **You must enter your Name!**

4. Click the Enable Client Script check box, and click OK to insert the control into your form.

Listing 14.4 and Listing 14.5 show the generated code results in our VB.NET and C# examples.

LISTING 14.4: *HELLOWORLDVALIDATE-VB.ASPX*

```
<%@ Page Language="VB" ContentType="text/html" ResponseEncoding="iso-8859-1" %>

<script runat="server">
    Sub tbName_Change(Sender As Object, E As EventArgs)
        lblWelcome.Text = "Hello " + tbName.Text
    End Sub
</script>
<!DOCTYPE HTML PUBLIC "-//W3C//DTD HTML 4.01 Transitional//EN">
<html>
<head>
<title>Hello World Form</title>
```

```
<meta http-equiv="Content-Type" content="text/html; charset=iso-8859-1">
</head>
<body>
<%= "Sample ASP.NET Script Page" %>
<form runat="server">
  <label>Your Name:</label>
  <asp:textbox ID="tbName"  OnTextChanged="tbName_Change" runat="server"
    TextMode="SingleLine" />
  <asp:button ID="btSubmit" runat="server" Text="Enter" />
  <asp:label ID="lblWelcome" runat="server" ></asp:label>
  <asp:requiredfieldvalidator ControlToValidate="tbName" ErrorMessage="You must
    enter your Name!" ID="tbNameValidator" runat="server" />
</form>
</body>
</html>
```

LISTING 14.5: *HELLOWORLDVALIDATE-CSHARP.ASPX*

```
<%@ Page Language="C#" ContentType="text/html" ResponseEncoding="iso-8859-1" %>

<script runat="server">
    void tbName_Change(Object Sender, EventArgs E) {
        lblWelcome.Text = "Hello " + tbName.Text;
    }
</script>
<!DOCTYPE HTML PUBLIC "-//W3C//DTD HTML 4.01 Transitional//EN">
<html>
<head>
<title>Hello World Form</title>
<meta http-equiv="Content-Type" content="text/html; charset=iso-8859-1">
</head>
<body>
<form runat="server">
  <label>Your Name:</label>
  <asp:textbox ID="tbName"  OnTextChanged="tbName_Change" runat="server"
    TextMode="SingleLine" />
  <asp:button ID="btSubmit" runat="server" Text="Enter" />
  <asp:label ID="lblWelcome" runat="server" ></asp:label>
  <asp:requiredfieldvalidator ControlToValidate="tbName" ErrorMessage="You must
    enter your Name!" ID="tbNameValidator" runat="server" />
</form>
</body>
</html>
```

Let's preview our sample validation script file in a web browser. As you can see in Figure 14.7, the web form appears the same as our original sample page. However, click the Enter button without a value in the text box. As Figure 14.8 show, ASP.NET kindly validates the text box and displays our error message.

FIGURE 14.7

Viewing the hello-WorldValidate-VB.aspx form in Internet Explorer

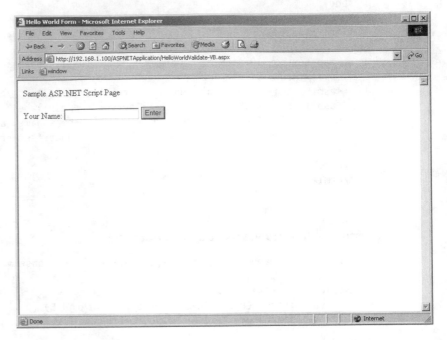

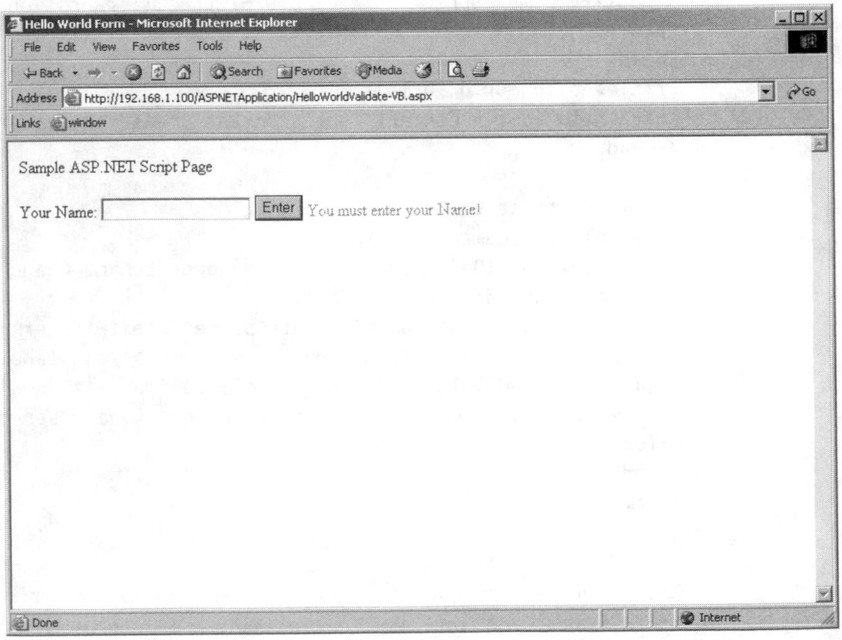

FIGURE 14.8

Clicking the Enter button without a value in the text box displays the helloWorld-Validate-VB .aspx error message.

ASP.NET Objects

Working in .NET framework and ASP.NET means you will interact with many objects. We're not covering every object available because that would take a couple of books. However, we are going to hit on the most common that you'll be using in ASP.NET. By now you should be familiar with the Response and Request objects, which are used in all the programming environments that are available to Dreamweaver MX and which are covered in Part III of this book. Because most of the ASP.NET objects are similar to the ASP objects covered in the Chapter 13, we are not going to review each in detail. In this section, we'll review the Response, Request, and Page objects. Finally we'll cover the `global.aspx` file for session and application management.

The Response Object

The server uses the Response object to create a header and data to communicate with the client web browser. Using the Response object, you can manipulate both the header and data.

THE *RESPONSE.WRITE* COMMAND

You may be somewhat familiar with the `Response.write` command from traditional ASP. However, as we've mentioned, ASP.NET expects a whole new web page structure. Remember, logic is typically placed at the top of the page, leaving the rest for the user interface. As you can see in our example in Listing 14.6 and the result in Figure 14.9, we've placed the `Response.write` command in the Page_Load event.

LISTING 14.6: *RESPONSEWRITE.ASPX*

```
<%@ Page Language="VB" ContentType="text/html" ResponseEncoding="iso-8859-1" %>

<script runat="server">
    sub Page_Load(obj as object, e as eventargs)
        Response.write("Response.Write Example")
    end sub
</script>
<html>
<head>
<title>ResponseWrite Example</title>
<meta http-equiv="Content-Type" content="text/html; charset=iso-8859-1">
</head>
<body>

</body>
</html>
```

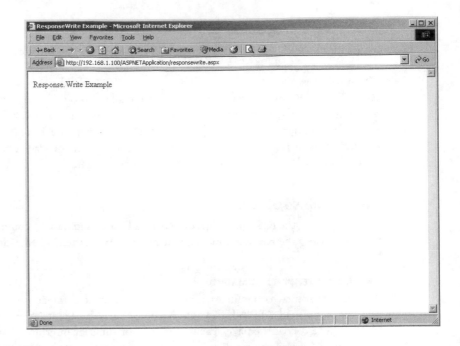

FIGURE 14.9
Viewing the output from `ResponseWrite .aspx` in Internet Explorer

THE *RESPONSE.BUFFER* COMMAND

As the web server compiles your ASP.NET script file and generates the header and date of the Response object, that data is usually held in a temporary buffer until all the script processes are complete. However, you can turn this buffer off or on using `Response.buffer`. To disable the buffer, insert `Response.buffer = FALSE` into the Page_Load event of your ASP.NET script file as shown in Listing 14.7.

LISTING 14.7: *RESPONSEBUFFER.ASPX*

```
<%@ Page Language="VB" ContentType="text/html" ResponseEncoding="iso-8859-1" %>

<script runat="server">
    sub Page_Load(obj as object, e as eventargs)
        Response.buffer = False
    end sub
</script>
<html>
<head>
<title>ResponseBuffer Example</title>
<meta http-equiv="Content-Type" content="text/html; charset=iso-8859-1">
</head>
```

```
<body>
Response.buffer example
</body>
</html>
```

THE *RESPONSE.REDIRECT* COMMAND

You use the Response.redirect command to send a user to a different URL without their knowledge. As we demonstrated in Chapter 12, a typical implementation of Response.redirect is to protect a page with a login procedure. As you may recall, the concept is to look for a passed form field and compare the value to an authorized login. If the login values do not match, the script redirects the user to another web page. You'll notice that the ASP.NET implementation of the PageSecurity script shown in Listing 14.8 is similar to the ASP version. However, the ASP.NET code is encapsulated in the Page_Load event. In short, the Page_Load event checks for a submitted form field called Name. If Name has not been submitted, Page_Load redirects the user to HelloWorld-VB.aspx. If Name does exist, Page_Load compares the submitted value of Name to the appropriate password "admin". If the value of Name does not equal the appropriate password, Page_Load redirects the user to HelloWorld-VB .aspx. If the value of Name does match the password, the rest of the current PageSecurity.aspx page loads and the user can see the content.

LISTING 14.8: *PAGESECURITY.ASPX*

```
<%@ Page Language="VB" ContentType="text/html" ResponseEncoding="iso-8859-1" %>

<script runat="server">
    sub Page_Load(obj as object, e as eventargs)
        if len(trim(request.form("Name"))) = 0 then
        response.redirect("HelloWorld-VB.aspx")
            else
                if trim(request.form("Name")) <> "admin" then
                response.redirect("HelloWorld-VB.aspx")
            end if
        end if
    end sub
</script>
<html>
<head>
<title>PageSecutity Example</title>
<meta http-equiv="Content-Type" content="text/html; charset=iso-8859-1">
</head>
<body>
</body>
</html>
```

The Request Object

The Request object receives content from the browser. It does so in the form of collections of variables that encapsulate the data for each request. There are several Request collections—`Request.Form`, `Request.Querystring`, and `Request.ServerVariables`.

THE *REQUEST.FORM* COLLECTION

When a form using the Post submission method is submitted to the current ASPX page, the collection of submitted form values is available through the `Request.Form` command. For example, to reference the submitted form value of a text box named FirstName, use the following command:

```
Request.Form("FirstName")
```

THE *REQUEST.QUERYSTRING* COLLECTION

`Request.Querystring` is a collection of value pairs passed in the URL address to an ASPX page. For example, when a page passes a variable and value through a URL address such as

```
http://www.sybex.com? FirstName =Bryan
```

the collection of passed form values is available to you through the `Request.Querystring` command. In addition to passing variables through the URL, you can also use the Get form submission method to pass value pairs of variables and values to a ASPX page. To reference the *FirstName* variable passed through the URL string in this example, you use this syntax:

```
Request.Querystring("FirstName")
```

`Request.Form` and `Request.Querystring` are useful collections carried over from traditional ASP. However, in contrast to traditional ASP, you will find you can accomplish most of the functionality of these collections with web server controls.

The Page Object

You can reference every ASPX page through the Page object. In addition, the Page object has several features and events you will find yourself using often. In fact, we've already used one of the events in several of our examples—Page_Load. Using the Page_Load event, we can direct ASP.NET to execute code as the page loads but before it renders HTML. This event is the perfect time to execute functionality such as authenticating users or redirecting users to established data connections.

Another feature of the Page object you will use often is the IsPostBack property. Remember we discussed a Postback Form, which is a form that submits data to itself. The IsPostBack property allows you to tell if the current page is being loaded for the first time or if the page is being loaded in response to a form submission. Listing 14.9 shows the IsPostBack property in action. As you can see in Figure 14.10 and Figure 14.11, when the page is loaded, the script uses the IsPostBack property to determine whether the page is loaded for the first time or in response to a postback generated by clicking the form's Enter button.

LISTING 14.9: *ISPOSTBACK.ASPX*

```
<%@ Page Language="VB" ContentType="text/html" ResponseEncoding="iso-8859-1" %>

<script runat="server">
    sub Page_Load(obj as object, e as eventargs)
        If Not IsPostBack
        lblMessage.Text = "This page is loaded for the first time."
        else
            lblMessage.Text = "This page is loaded is response to a post back."
          end if
    end sub

</script>
<html>
<head>
<title>IsPostBack Example</title>
<meta http-equiv="Content-Type" content="text/html; charset=iso-8859-1">
</head>
<body>
<form runat="server">
  <asp:label ID="lblMessage" runat="server" ></asp:label>
  <asp:button ID="btSubmit" runat="server" Text="Enter" />
</form>
</body>
</html>
```

FIGURE 14.10

Viewing IsPost-Back.aspx in Internet Explorer

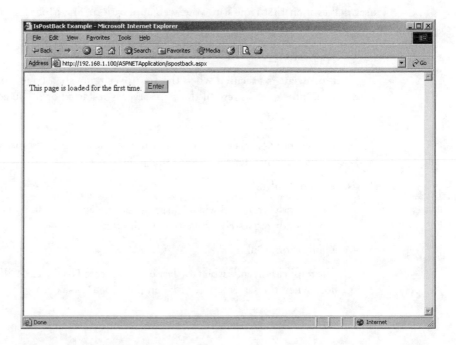

FIGURE 14.11

Viewing IsPost-
Back.aspx in
Internet Explorer

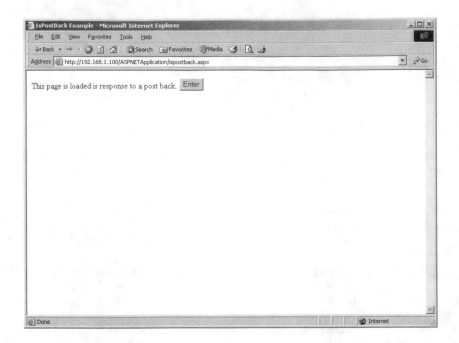

The *global.asax* file

The global.asax file is a tool for controlling both your application and the client session, and you can place this file in the root directory of your web application. ASP.NET looks for this file as a user makes their first request to your web application. The global.asax file controls the following events in the following order.

1. Application_OnStart

   This event is executed when the first user requests a page from your ASP.NET application. This event is reset if the web server is restarted or if you edit the global.asax file.

2. Session_OnStart

   This event triggers every time a new user requests a page from your ASP.NET application. It occurs directly after the Application_OnStart event.

3. Session_OnEnd

   This event is triggered when a user or the site ends a session. This typically happens when a user has not requested a page for 20 minutes.

4. Application_OnEnd

   The application ends when the last user connected to the ASP.NET application ends their session, when the server stops, or when the global.asax is altered.

Most developers use the global.asax file to initialize application and session variables or to run processes. For example, application and session code can be placed in the web application global.asax file as shown in VB.NET in Listing 14.10 and C# in Listing 14.11. It is your responsibility to add code that destroys session and application variables on the session and application end events.

LISTING 14.10: *GLOBAL.ASAX* **IN VB.NET**

```
Sub Application_Start(Sender As Object, E As EventArgs)
      application("emailAddress") = "webmaster@helpmedia.com"
End Sub

Sub Session_Start(Sender As Object, E As EventArgs)
  session("userSid") = Request.cookies("userSid")
  Session.Timeout = 1
End Sub

Sub Session_End(Sender As Object, E As EventArgs)
      session("userSid") =  null
End Sub

Sub Application_End(Sender As Object, E As EventArgs)
      application("emailAddress") = null
End Sub
```

LISTING 14.11: *GLOBAL.ASAX* **IN C#**

```
void Application_Start(object sender, EventArgs e) {
application("emailAddress") = "webmaster@helpmedia.com";
}

void Session_Start(object sender, EventArgs e) {
  session("userSid") = Request.cookies("userSid");
  Session.Timeout = 1;
}

void Session_End (object sender, EventArgs e) {
  session("userSid") =  null;
}

void Application_End (object sender, EventArgs e) {
 application("emailAddress") = null;

}
```

ASP.NET XML Web Services

ASP.NET greatly simplifies the development of logic and the user interface while still increasing the power of web pages for web users. Microsoft did not stop there. With ASP.NET XML Web Services, Microsoft expands the event-driven object architecture of .NET to provide multiple paths for applications and processes to communicate. For example, say you have a network consisting of several geographically distributed web servers hosting various corporate and subordinate company intranets and databases. Each site displays the corporate news. Imagine the complexity and the timing of continually rolling out new corporate messages. With .NET framework and ASP.NET, you can create a News XML Web Service on the corporate site, and the other sites can access and pull information as needed from this web service. No more worries about data replication or timing issues.

Although useful to illustrate the point, a news subscription is a simplistic example of the power of XML Web Services. Imagine a web application that is literally built on functions and processes spread across the world but exposed through XML Web Services. What's more, XML Web Services aren't limited to web browsers. Any application that can connect to the web can connect to XML Web Services. XML Web Services offer you a choice of connection protocols. Any application or process can access an XML Web Service through HTTP-GET, HTTP-POST, or Simple Object Access Protocol (SOAP).

HTTP-GET HTTP-GET is a standard protocol that you've probably seen used in HTML forms. HTTP-GET simply requests a web service through a URL and sends and receives data through HTML. Any parameters that should be passed are sent in the URL.

HTTP-POST HTTP-POST is the counterpart to HTTP-GET. The difference is that HTTP-POST sends parameters through the HTTP request message and not through the URL.

SOAP SOAP is an up-and-coming protocol that allows servers to send and receive data. SOAP depends on XML to pass and receive information. Obviously, XML can send and receive a great deal more information than the value-pair limitation of HTTP-GET and HTTP-POST. SOAP is the default protocol that web services use to transmit information.

XML Web Services promise a truly expansive method to deliver applications over the Internet. However, delving into XML Web Service programming, deployment, and accessing is outside the scope of this book. To give you an idea of web service programming, Listing 14.12 shows a simple script that creates an XML Web Service. Once you've saved this script you can access the web service through your site. ASP.NET automatically generates a web page to view the class, methods, and properties of the HelloWorld web service, as shown in Figure 14.12.

LISTING 14.12: *HelloWorld_WS.asmx*

```
<%@ WebService Language="VB" Class="HelloWorld" %>

Imports System
Imports System.Web.Services

Public Class HelloWorld :Inherits WebService
    <WebMethod()> Public Function HelloWorld() As String
```

```
        Return("Hello World")
    End Function
End Class
```

FIGURE 14.12

The `HelloWorld_WS.asmx` class description page

FOR FURTHER INFORMATION

You can utilize hundreds of resources to find out more about ASP.NET. Some of our most-visited ASP.NET-oriented websites are www.asp.net, and www.4guysfromrolla.com. For some great training and reference books such as *Mastering ASP.NET*, visit www.sybex.com.

Summary

In this chapter, we introduced you to the .NET framework and the ASP.NET Host, the languages, Web Forms, web server controls, and XML Web Services. We also demonstrated how to write scripts that access ASP.NET's events and server controls. Still, as much as we touched on this chapter, ASP.NET and the .NET framework are too richly layered with features to do them justice in one chapter.

Chapter 15

ADO.NET

SIDE BY SIDE WITH the Microsoft .NET framework is the next iteration of Microsoft data objects technology—ADO.NET. Although similar to ADO (ActiveX Data Objects), ADO.NET is built specifically to handle data interaction on the web and to integrate XML (Extensible Markup Language).

In this chapter, you'll learn about the ADO.NET framework and how to use ASP.NET and Dreamweaver MX to interact with data sources. In addition, you'll learn more about ASP.NET server controls and how to bind them to a DataSet.

This chapter covers the following topics:

◆ What is ADO.NET?

◆ ADO.NET Object Model

◆ SqlConnection and OLE DB managed providers

◆ DataSets

◆ Binding data in web forms

What Is ADO.NET?

The short answer is, it's an API designed to work within Microsoft's .NET framework. In order to handle data interactions on the web and support XML, ADO.NET allows ASP.NET developers to use an OLE DB (Object Linking and Embedding Database) connection to access any type of data—a database, a text file, XML data, and so on. As such, ADO.NET introduces a number of new data access objects to support its new disconnected data model. *Disconnected* refers to the new way ADO.NET creates and relinquishes a DataSet. As you know, one of the traditional behaviors of ADO was to create a recordset with a live connection to a database. Any change you apply to a row or a column in the recordset you could immediately apply to the database. However, the recordset was a static collection of data independent of any relationships it may have had in the database.

ADO.NET instead uses XML to transfer an independent representation of data to an application through a DataSet. A *DataSet* is a memory-only copy of the data. Therefore, modifying the data in a database is a two-step process—first apply the modifications to the DataSet and then apply the DataSet to the database.

NOTE   *This chapter focuses on the first step of the data-modification process. Unfortunately, committing a DataSet to a database under the custom events of the ASP.NET server controls is a long and complex issue because it is done completely outside the realm of Dreamweaver's help. Dreamweaver MX allows users to easily create an update form but not to customize script server controls with in-depth ADO.NET code. For more information on ADO, consult Sybex's* ADO and ADO.NET Programming, *by Mike Gunderloy. For more information on updating a database, consult Chapter 20.*

ADO.NET Namespaces

As you know, the .NET framework is structured around namespaces, which organize components into groups based on functionality and purpose. You can quickly add functionality to your .NET applications simply by loading a namespace. A .NET namespace is simply a library, or a collection, of objects. It's therefore not surprising that to establish easy access to data connections and data objects, Microsoft has organized ADO.NET into namespaces. You'll find ADO.NET separated into three .NET namespaces—System.Data, System.Data.OLEDB, and System.Data.SQLClient. The System.Data namespace allows you to create and manage ADO.NET data objects, and the System.Data.OLEDB and System.Data.SQLClient allow you to connect to OLE DB data sources and to Microsoft SQL Server.

ADO.NET Object Model

The ADO.NET Object Model is made up of two primary parts—the Managed Provider and the DataSet. The Managed Provider is the connection between the DataSet and the original source of data, such as the database or data store. The Managed Provider handles the connection, access, manipulation, and retrieval of data that is represented in the DataSet.

SQLCONNECTION AND OLE DB MANAGED PROVIDERS

ADO.NET offers two Managed Providers: the SQL Managed Provider and the OLE DB Managed Provider. The SQL Managed Provider is strictly for interaction with Microsoft SQL Server. The OLE DB Managed Provider interacts with any OLE DB-compliant data source.

Since both providers offer identical basic functionality, why would Microsoft create two different providers? The SQL Managed Provider is optimized for Microsoft SQL Server. The SQL Managed Provider allows for a direct connection to Microsoft SQL Server that doesn't require OLE DB, ADO, and ODBC (Open Database Connectivity). In fact, the SQL Managed Provider connection is managed by the same Common Language Runtime (CLR) environment that manages ASP.NET scripts. Therefore the connection and interaction between SQL Server and a DataSet is optimal.

Both Managed Providers perform three tasks:

◆ They provide protocols to connect to data stores and create and interact with DataSets.

◆ They create a Data stream for fast access to data stores. (A Data stream is similar to a DataSet but faster with less functionality.)

◆ They create connected objects that execute database-specific commands.

DATASET

As we've mentioned, the DataSet is an independent representation of data pulled from a data source. The DataSet completely replaces the Recordset object used in traditional ASP and ADO. Although useful in its time, the Recordset could not deal with multiple sets of data or maintain data relationships. The DataSet can not only manage multiple sets of data, but maintain complex data relationships between those sets of data. In addition, the DataSet provides a consistent programming interface for developers to access any type of data. As shown in Figure 15.1, the DataSet itself is made up of a hierarchy of objects.

FIGURE 15.1

The hierarchy of objects in a DataSet

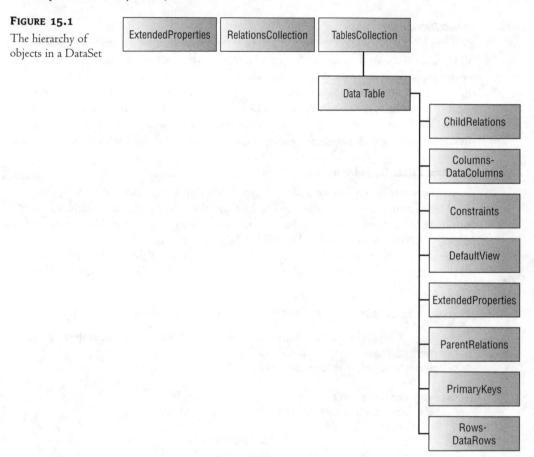

Yes, we know. Object hierarchies don't make a lot of sense until they are put into perspective. Imagine a neighborhood yard sale at your house. You and your neighbors bring items and drop them on a clothes table and a toys table. Obviously, someone must keep track of each item and its relationship—who originally owned the item and the purchase price once it's sold. The DataSet can accomplish all this.

The clothes table and the toy table are represented in a DataSet by a Clothes DataTable object and a Toys DataTable object in the TablesCollection object. In addition, there is an Owner Data-Table object. To define the relationships between the three data tables, the DataSet uses custom DataRelation objects held in the RelationsCollection object. The RelationsCollection object allows you to select from each table through simple queries. You no longer are required to craft complex joins to simply interact with data. The DataRelations object manages all the constraints and relations between the data tables.

Although simplistic and perhaps forced, our neighborhood yard sale example effectively illustrates the potential of the ADO.NET DataSet. The DataSet is indifferent to where the information items come from, how they were and are used, or where the data is going. The DataSet only cares how data is defined and related within its framework—which you specify, of course.

USING DATASETS

You can use a DataSet in your ASP.NET pages in three ways—to hand-code an empty DataSet and fill it with your own data, to hand-code a DataSet with data from a data source, or to use the Dreamweaver MX custom tag `MM:DataSet` to create a DataSet from a defined connection. You will see that the custom tag `MM:DataSet` is by far the easiest way to create a DataSet. However, you need to know at least the basics of hand-coding a DataSet in ASP.NET. First, we'll demonstrate how to hand-code a DataSet in memory, and then we'll show you how to hand-code a DataSet from a connected data source. Finally, we'll demonstrate how to use the Dreamweaver MX `MM:DataSet` custom tag.

Creating a DataSet in Memory

To demonstrate how to create a DataSet, let's take a look at an ASP.NET script page that creates a new DataSet in memory and fills it with data sans any connection to a database. To make matters simple, let's create the Owner's table we mentioned in our earlier neighborhood yard sale example. Listing 15.1 shows the sample ASP.NET VB.NET script file.

We strongly encourage you to key in all the code to create the example files yourself. To check your work, compare your files with the example files on the CD accompanying this book.

LISTING 15.1: *DATASET_CREATE.ASPX*

```
<%@ Page Language="VB" ContentType="text/html" ResponseEncoding="iso-8859-1" %>
<%@ import Namespace="system.Data" %>
<%@ import Namespace="system.Data.OLEDB" %>

<script runat="server">
    Sub Page_Load(Sender As Object, E As EventArgs)
        'Create a DataSet
        dim ds as new DataSet("MyDataSet")
        'Create an instance of a DataTable
        dim dTable as New DataTable("Owner")

        'Create the columns FirstName, LastName, OwnerID
    dTable.columns.Add("FirstName",System.Type.GetType("System.String"))
    dTable.columns.Add("LastName",System.Type.GetType("System.String"))
        dTable.columns.Add("OwnerID",System.Type.GetType("System.Int32"))
        dTable.columns("OwnerID").AutoIncrement = True

        'Add the DataTable to the DataSet
        ds.Tables.Add(dTable)

        'Define the OwnerID column as the PrimaryKey
        dim keys() as DataColumn = {ds.Tables("Owner").Columns("OwnerID")}
        ds.Tables("Owner").PrimaryKey = keys
```

```
      'Create an instance of a DataRow and add values
      dim dr as DataRow = dTable.NewRow()
      dr(0) = "Bryan"
      dr(1) = "Chamberlain"

      'Add the DataRow to the DataTable
      dTable.Rows.Add(dr)
   End Sub
</script>
```

As you can see, the first step is to identify VBScript as the language we'll be using in this ASP.NET script page. Next, we import the appropriate namespaces to create our DataSet and eventually establish a connection to a database. To do so, we use the following lines:

```
<%@ import Namespace="system.Data" %>
<%@ import Namespace="system.Data.OLEDB" %>
```

At this point, we need a page event that loads and executes our DataSet code. For that, we use the `Page_Load` event. As you recall from the ASP.NET chapter, the `Page_Load` event is triggered every time a page is loaded. The following code creates the event response.

```
<script runat="server">
   Sub Page_Load(Sender As Object, E As EventArgs)
...
   End Sub
</script>
```

Now create a DataSet object to eventually hold a DataTable object called Owner inside the `Page_Load` procedure. Next, create three columns in the Owner DataTable—`OwnerID`, `FirstName`, and `LastName`. Adding columns requires two parameters, the column name and data type. Notice that we use the `AutoIncrement` command to set the `OwnerID` column to increment automatically

```
      'Create a DataSet
      dim ds as new DataSet("MyDataSet")
      'Create an instance of a DataTable
      dim dTable as New DataTable("Owner")

      'Create the columns FirstName, LastName, OwnerID
   dTable.columns.Add("FirstName",System.Type.GetType("System.String"))
   dTable.columns.Add("LastName",System.Type.GetType("System.String"))
      dTable.columns.Add("OwnerID",System.Type.GetType("System.Int32"))
      dTable.columns("OwnerID").AutoIncrement = True
```

The next few lines add the Owner DataTable to the DataSet and set the `OwnerID` column as the PrimaryKey.

```
      'Add the DataTable to the DataSet
      ds.Tables.Add(dTable)
```

```
'Define the OwnerID column as the PrimaryKey
dim keys() as DataColumn = {ds.Tables("Owner").Columns("OwnerID")}
ds.Tables("Owner").PrimaryKey = keys
```

The final step is to create a DataRow object, fill it with data, and add it to the DataTable. The following lines accomplish this:

```
'create an instance of a DataRow and add values
dim dr as DataRow = dTable.NewRow()
dr(0) = "Bryan"
dr(1) = "Chamberlain"

'Add the DataRow to the DataTable
dTable.Rows.Add(dr)
```

Creating a DataSet from a Data Source

Now we've created a DataSet in memory that your ASP.NET script page can access, manipulate, and even send to a database. You've got to admit, creating a DataSet and adding DataTable objects is rather easy. Let's move on to pushing data from a database into a DataSet. To demonstrate, we'll create a script page that pulls the CategoryID and Category columns of data from the tblCategories table in our sample Books database. You can see the code in Listing 15.2.

LISTING 15.2: *DATASET_DATACONNECTION.ASPX*

```
<%@ Page Language="VB" ContentType="text/html" ResponseEncoding="iso-8859-1" %>
<%@ import Namespace="system.Data" %>
<%@ import Namespace="system.Data.OLEDB" %>

<script runat="server">
   Sub Page_Load(Sender As Object, E As EventArgs)

      'Create a DataConnection
      dim myconnection as new OleDbConnection("Provider=SQLOLEDB.1;Persist_
      Security Info=False;User ID=SA;Password=XXXXXXX;Initial_
      Catalog=MDWMX_BOOKS;Data Source=192.168.1.100")

      'open connection
      dim myCommand as new OLEDBDataAdapter("Select * from tblCategories",
         myconnection)

      'Fill DataSet
      dim ds as DataSet = new DataSet()
      myCommand.Fill(ds,"tblCategories")

   End Sub
</script>
```

As before, the script file begins by defining the default language and importing the Data and Data.OLEDB namespaces that allow us to create DataSets and connect to our database. Also as before, we position our DataSet code inside the Page_Load event. Next, we introduce two new objects to connect and pull data from our database—the OleDBConnection object and the OleDBDataAdapter object. Obviously, the OleDBConnection object creates the connection to our database. The OleDBData-Adapter object allows us to pass an SQL command to the database and retrieve data. As you can see in the code, the following lines create our data connection to an SQL Server version of our Books database.

```
'Create a DataConnection
dim myconnection as new OleDbConnection("Provider=SQLOLEDB.1;_
Persist Security Info=False;User ID=SA;Password=XXXXXXX;_
Initial Catalog=MDWMX_BOOKS;Data Source=192.168.1.100")
```

Then we use the OleDBDataAdapter object in the following lines to pass an SQL statement and return data.

```
'open connection
dim myCommand as new OleDbDataAdapter("Select * from tblCategories", myconnection)
```

At this point, we have only to fill a DataSet with the returned data of the OleDBDataAdapter. Doing so is even easier than our previous example of creating a DataSet. We can use the Fill command to literally dump the returned data of our SQL statement into a DataSet. The following lines direct the OleDBDataAdapter to create a DataTable in the Tables collection identical to the returned data from our SQL statement. The OleDBDataAdapter even names the DataSet for us.

```
'Fill Dataset
dim ds as DataSet = new DataSet()
myCommand.Fill(ds,"tblCategories")
```

The Dreamweaver MX MM:DataSet Custom Tag

Dreamweaver MX uses a custom tag to allow you to simplify the normal demands of coding an ASP.NET DataSet. MM:DataSet allows you to easily script and use DataSets in your ASP.NET pages. MM:DataSet also allows you to omit most of the required ASP.NET DataSet properties by setting these properties for you. The only required properties are ConnectionString, CommandText, and the standard RunAt ASP.NET setting. ConnectionString defines the connection to your database. CommandText defines the SQL statement or stored procedure to pull data from your database through the database connection. RunAt is the ASP.NET setting instructing the server to run the control at the server. Besides these three required properties, there are a multitude of other properties you should know in order to take full advantage of the MM:DataSet custom tag. Table 15.1 describes the MM:DataSet properties.

To use the DataSet Dreamweaver MX custom tag, you must properly register the tag in your ASP.NET script page. Fortunately, as you choose a Dreamweaver MX custom tag from the Dreamweaver MX interface, Dreamweaver MX automatically inserts the following code into your ASP.NET page for you.

```
<%@ Register TagPrefix="MM" Namespace="DreamweaverCtrls"_
    Assembly="DreamweaverCtrls,version=1.0.0.0,_
    publicKeyToken=836f606ede05d46a,culture=neutral" %>
```

TABLE 15.1: *MM:DATASET* PROPERTIES

PROPERTY	DEFAULT	DESCRIPTION
ConnectionString		[Required] Defines the connection string to connect to your database.
CommandText		[Required] Defines the SQL or stored procedure name to forward to the database. If IsStoredProcedure is False, Dreamweaver MX expects SQL. If IsStoredProcedure is True, Dreamweaver MX expects the name of the stored procedure. In place of variable names, you can use the question mark (?) as a placeholder for a parameter. For example, Select from tblCategories where categoryID = ?.
RunAt		[Required] Standard ASP.NET setting instructing the server to run the control at the server.
CreateDataSet	True	Specifies whether the server will preserve the DataSet created from the SQL in the CommandText property. For example, you definitely want to preserve the DataSet created from a SELECT statement. However, SQL commands such as INSERT, UPDATE, and DELETE do not produce results. Therefore, you want to set CreateDataSet to False.
Expression	True	Specifies under what condition the CommandText property is executed. For example, you want INSERT or UPDATE CommandText to execute only if all required fields are validated.
IsStoredProcedure	False	Specifies whether CommandText is sending SQL or specifying a stored procedure to execute.
TableName	"theTable"	Defines a name to use when you refer to records in a DataTable listed in the DataSet. For example DS.theDS["Categories"].DefaultView references the default view of the DataTable categories.
Debug	False	True activates debugging on pages that throw error exceptions. If True, the FailureURL property is ignored.
FailureURL	""	Defines a URL in which the server redirects a user if an error exception is thrown.
SuccessURL	""	Defines a URL in which the server redirects a user if no error exceptions are thrown.

Continued on next page

TABLE 15.1: *MM:DataSet* Properties (*continued*)

PROPERTY	DEFAULT	DESCRIPTION
CurrentPage	0	Defines the index of the displayed page based on the total number of records divided by the number of records defined in PageSize. For example, if PageSize is 10 and the total number of records is 40, the index of the current page could be 0, 1, 2, or 3. Each indexed page displays 10 records each from the total number of records beginning with the specific StartRecord. The StartRecord is always calculated from the index of CurrentPage × PageSize. So, if the CurrentPage index is 2 and the PageSize is 10, the calculated StartRecord is 20.
PageSize	0	If CreateDataSet is True, defines the number of records to retreive from the DataSet and display on your page.
MaxRecords	0	Defines the total number of records to retrieve.
StartRecord	0	Defines the record number you want to start collecting from the DataSet and display on your page.
GetRecordCount	True	If PageSize is greater than 0, defines the total number of records. GetRecordCount is performance heavy and should be avoided if possible.
RecordCountCommandTest	""	If PageSize is greater than 0 and GetRecordCount is True, sets an SQL statement to obtain a record count to improve performance. For example, SELECT COUNT (CategoryID) as MYRECORDCOUNT returns the number of records in the table.
DefaultView		[Read Only] Calls the default view of the DataSet through theDS.Tables[0].DefaultView.
EndRecord		[Read Only] The number of the final record of the collected records calculated by (CurrentPage + 1) × PageSize and RecordCount.
LastPage		[Read Only] If PageSize is greater than 0 and GetRecord-Count is True, the index of the final page in the index is calculated from PageSize and RecordCount.
RecordCount		[Read Only] If CreateDataSet is True and GetRecord-Count is True, the total number of records in the dataset is calculated and returned from the CommandText.
TheDS		If CreateDateSet is True, the .NET DataSet to hold records is retrieved as a result of CommandText.

As you can see, the code references a special file named `DreamweaverCtrls.dll`. This file contains all the functionality of Dreamweaver MX custom tags. Obviously, your web application must have access to `DreamweaverCtrls.dll`. Therefore, you must be sure `DreamweaverCtrls.dll` is in the `bin` folder of your website or virtual directory. You can do this in two ways:

◆ Copy `DreamweaverCtrls.dll` from the `Configuration/ServerBehaviors/Shared/ASP.Net/Scripts` directory of your Dreamweaver MX application directory to the `bin` folder of your website.

◆ Use the Dreamweaver MX Site Manager to deploy the `DreamweaverCtrls.dll` to your site. To do so, choose Deploy Supporting Files from the Site menu in the main Dreamweaver MX document window menu bar, choose Site ➢ Deploy Supporting Files to open the Deploy Supporting Files To Testing Server dialog box, as shown in Figure 15.2. Set the access method and the directory path to the `bin` directory of your website, and click Deploy.

FIGURE 15.2

The Deploy Supporting Files To Testing Server dialog box in Dreamweaver MX

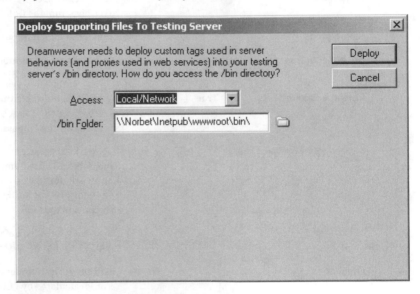

The next step is to create a connection for a DataSet to pull data from a database. In Chapter 10, we demonstrated how to create a database connection. Using Chapter 10 as a reference, open a new ASP.NET script page and create a data connection to the Books database. Once you create and test your database connection, you can use the Dreamweaver MX `MM:DataSet` custom tag to create a DataSet and add it to your ASP.NET script page.

To do so, follow these steps:

1. Open the DataSet dialog box in one of the following ways:
   ◆ Activate the Application panel group and click the DataSet icon.
   ◆ Choose Insert ➢ Application Objects ➢ DataSet.
   ◆ Activate the Bindings panel and choose DataSet(Query) from the panel menu.

You can view the DataSet dialog box (shown in Figure 15.3) in two modes—Simple or Advanced. In either mode, you can define the DataSet name, the data connection, the target table or columns, and the Failure page to redirect your users to in case of DataSet error. In Simple mode, you can select a table and columns and leave Dreamweaver MX to build the SQL statement to access your database. In Advanced mode, you can dynamically build the SQL query.

2. In the mode you're most comfortable with, enter **DS** in the Name text box, and choose your created data connection.

3. Dreamweaver MX queries the data source and returns a list of tables and columns in the Table drop-down list box. For our purposes, set the mode to Simple, select dbo.tblCategories from the Table drop-down list box, and click the All option in the Columns section.

FIGURE 15.3

Creating a DataSet

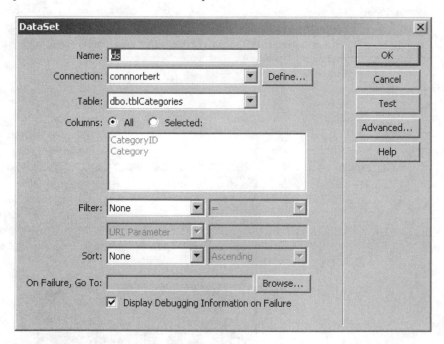

4. Click OK to create the DataSet and add the DataSet code to your ASP.NET script page.

Listing 15.3 shows the Dreamweaver MX-generated code that is inserted into your script page. In addition, Dreamweaver MX inserts the DS in the Bindings panel, as shown in Figure 15.4.

LISTING 15.3: *MMDATASET_CUSTOMTAG.ASPX*

```
<%@ Page Language="VB" ContentType="text/html" ResponseEncoding="iso-8859-1" %>
<%@ Register TagPrefix="MM" Namespace="DreamweaverCtrls"_
Assembly="DreamweaverCtrls,version=1.0.0.0,_
publicKeyToken=836f606ede05d46a,culture=neutral" %>
```

```
<MM:DataSet
id="DS"
runat="Server"
IsStoredProcedure="false"
ConnectionString='<%# System.Configuration.ConfigurationSettings._
AppSettings("MM_CONNECTION_STRING_connnorbert") %>'
DatabaseType='<%# System.Configuration.ConfigurationSettings._
AppSettings("MM_CONNECTION_DATABASETYPE_connnorbert") %>'
CommandText='<%# "SELECT * FROM dbo.tblCategories" %>'
Debug="true"
> </MM:DataSet>
<MM:PageBind runat="server" PostBackBind="true" />
<html>
<head>
<title>MMDataSet</title>
<meta http-equiv="Content-Type" content="text/html; charset=iso-8859-1">
</head>
<body>

</body>
</html>
```

FIGURE 15.4

The DataSet shown
in the Bindings panel

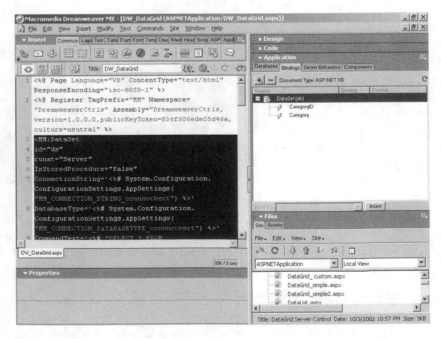

Binding Data in Web Forms

You've seen how to code your own DataSet and how to use the Dreamweaver MX MM:DataSet custom tag to create a DataSet. All well and good, but the awesome part of ADO.NET and ASP.NET is that you have instant access to all data stored in the memory-resident DataSet. Moreover, you can bind almost any web control in a web form to a DataSet. Binding a web control to a DataSet means, among other things, you can automatically populate web controls. Imagine—you will never have to loop through a recordset again to incrementally populate a list box!

You can bind data to an ASP.NET page in two ways. The first method uses the `DataSource` property of server controls such as the Listbox, DropDownList, RadioButtonList, CheckboxList, Repeater, DataList, and DataGrid. The second uses a data-binding expression, which is commonly referred to as Dynamic Text. Dynamic Text can be used with or without a server control. Regardless of the method you employ, the actual binding of data to a control or a page requires the `DataBind()` command.

You can choose to bind data to the script page itself using ASP.NET:

```
Page.DataBind()
```

or you can choose to bind data to specific controls by naming the control in the `DataBind()` command

```
Listbox1.DataBind()
```

However, if you are not specifically binding data to a control, Dreamweaver MX offers you a custom tag alternative to the ASP.NET `Page.DataBind()` command—`MM:PageBind`. `MM:PageBind` allows you to insert the Dreamweaver MX custom tag instead of inserting ASP.NET code. To insert the `MM:PageBind` custom tag, take these steps:

1. Activate the ASP.NET panel and choose the More Tags icon to open the Tag Chooser dialog box.
2. Choose ASP.NET Tags and Macromedia Server Controls.
3. Select `MM:PageBind` and click the Insert button to insert the custom tag in your script file. You can see an example of the `MM:PageBind` custom tag in Listing 15.3.

Now let's look at how to use a data-binding expression.

Data-Binding Expressions

You can use a data-binding expression, or Dynamic Text, anywhere in your script page. To do so you need only to insert an expression and the `DataBind` command into your ASP.NET page. As we mentioned, the `DataBind` command signals ASP.NET to bind data to controls in the script page. Let's demonstrate by using Dynamic Text to output the first value in the `Category` column of the DS DataSet. To do so, begin with the script page shown in Listing 15.3. As you recall, we've already created a DataSet of the tblCategories table. To bind Dynamic Text to the DataSet, follow these steps:

1. Place your cursor between the Body tags of the script page.
2. Choose Windows ➢ Server Behaviors to activate the Server Behaviors panel.
3. Choose Panel ➢ Dynamic Text to open the Dynamic Text dialog box.
4. Select the Category column from the Field list box, and click OK. Dreamweaver MX inserts the following line into your script page. You can see the script page in Listing 15.4 and the browser results in Figure 15.5.

   ```
   <%# DS.FieldValue("Category", Container) %>
   ```

LISTING 15.4: *DATABINDING_DYNAMICTEXT.ASPX*

```
<%@ Page Language="VB" ContentType="text/html" ResponseEncoding="iso-8859-1" %>
<%@ Register TagPrefix="MM" Namespace="DreamweaverCtrls" _
Assembly="DreamweaverCtrls,version=1.0.0.0,_
publicKeyToken=836f606ede05d46a,culture=neutral" %>
<MM:DataSet
id="DS"
runat="Server"
IsStoredProcedure="false"
ConnectionString='<%# System.Configuration.ConfigurationSettings._
AppSettings("MM_CONNECTION_STRING_connnorbert") %>'
DatabaseType='<%# System.Configuration.ConfigurationSettings._
AppSettings("MM_CONNECTION_DATABASETYPE_connnorbert") %>'
CommandText='<%# "SELECT * FROM dbo.tblCategories" %>'
Debug="true"
> </MM:DataSet>
<MM:PageBind runat="server" PostBackBind="true" />
<html>
<head>
<title>Data-bind Expression</title>
<meta http-equiv="Content-Type" content="text/html; charset=iso-8859-1">
</head>
<body>
<%# DS.FieldValue("Category", Container) %>
</body>
</html>
```

FIGURE 15.5

Dynamic Text result

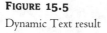

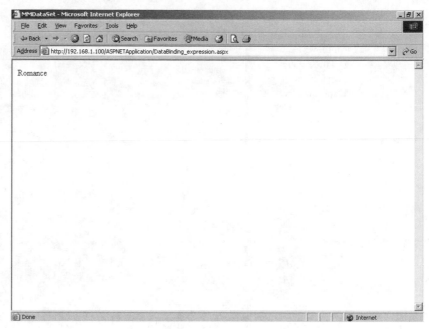

Data-Binding through a Control's Data Source

Now let's take data-binding a step further. Using the same script page, let's bind the DataSet to a DropDownList control through the control's `DataSource` property. Doing so populates the display text of the control with all the values in the `Category` column. As well, we want to push the like values of the `CategoryID` column into the values of the DropDownList control. But, before we can add our DropDownList control, we must add a form control around the Dynamic Text in the script page using the following code:

```
<form runat=server>
</form>
```

Now, remove the Dynamic Text we previously placed in the script page and insert a DropDown-List control. To do so, follow these steps:

1. Choose Insert ➤ ASP.NET Objects ➤ DropDownList to open the Tag Editor dialog box.

2. Select the General category from the category list, and set the ID to DropDownList1.

3. Select the Data category and insert the default DS DataSet view (`<%# ds.defaultview %>`) into the Data Source text field, insert Category into the Data Text Field, and insert CategoryID into the Data Value Field as shown in Figure 15.6.

FIGURE 15.6

The Tag Editor for a DropDownList. (top) The General category; (bottom) the Data category.

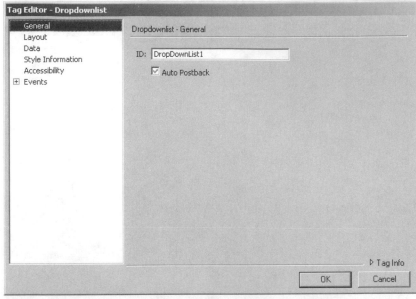

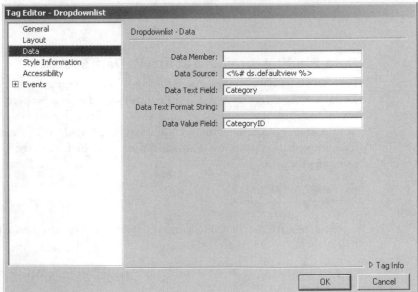

4. Click OK to insert the following DropDownList code into your script file. Figure 15.7 shows the browser result.

```
<asp:dropdownlist DataSource="<%# ds.defaultview %>" _
DataTextField="Category" DataValueField="Categoryid" _
ID="DropDownList1" runat="server"></asp:dropdownlist>
```

FIGURE 15.7

Data bound
DropDownList
browser result

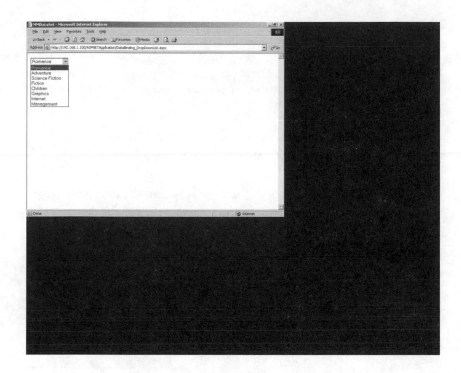

Data-Binding Web Server Controls

As we've shown, you can bind DataSets to many server controls through the `DataSource` property. However, three powerful data server controls in particular can alleviate a lot of development work: the Repeater, the DataList, and the DataGrid. They are a bit more complex than your standard server control. For that reason, you really need a bit of under-the-hood knowledge. Let's use Dreamweaver MX to create each data-bound server control and then examine them from a code perspective.

THE REPEATER SERVER CONTROL

The Repeater server control loops through all records of the DataSet to display the information according to predefined templates. *Templates* are collections of server controls and HTML (Hypertext Markup Language) that allow you to specify the layout of the generated web page. You can use four types of templates with the Repeater server control:

- ItemTemplate
- AlternatingItemTemplate
- HeaderTemplate and FooterTemplate
- SeparatorTemplate

The ItemTemplate, which is the default, generates HTML for each row in the DataSet. The AlternatingItemTemplate generates a row for every other row of the DataSet. The AlternatingItemTemplate is generally used to offset the style of the ItemTemplate, for example, to generate alternating row colors. The HeaderTemplate and FooterTemplate generate HTML before and after the Repeater control generates content for the DataSet. The SeparatorTemplate generates content between each data row. This may sound complicated, but once you see it in action, you'll love this server control.

To add a Repeater server control to our script file, follow these steps:

1. Remove the DropDownList box we created earlier.
2. Insert another instance of Dynamic Text bound to the `CategoryID` column and an instance bound to the `Category` column of our DataSet.
3. Add a <BR> tag.
4. Select CategoryID, Category Dynamic Text, and <BR> tag.
5. Activate the Server Behaviors panel and choose Repeat Region from the panel menu to open the Repeat Region dialog box, as shown in Figure 15.8.

FIGURE 15.8

The Repeat Region dialog box

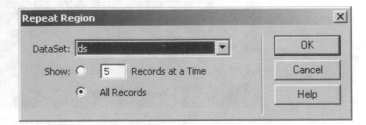

6. Select the DS DataSet in the DataSet drop-down list box, and in the Show section, click the All Records option.
7. When you click OK, Dreamweaver MX replaces the Dynamic Text code line with the following.

```
<ASP:Repeater runat="server" DataSource='<%# DS.DefaultView %>'>

    <ItemTemplate>
       <%# DS.FieldValue("CategoryID", Container) %>
<%# DS.FieldValue("Category", Container) %><br>
    </ItemTemplate>
  </ASP:Repeater>
```

This Repeater, while rather bare-bones, will output all the values in the `CategoryID` and `Category` columns of tblCategories. You can easily add templates to this code to make the display a bit more robust. Listing 15.5 shows the code for a more pleasing Repeater control for the Categories table of our Books database. Figure 15.9 shows the result in a browser. Let's briefly examine the code.

LISTING 15.5: *DW_REPEATER_EXTENDED.ASPX*

```
<%@ Page Language="VB" ContentType="text/html" ResponseEncoding="iso-8859-1" %>
<%@ Register TagPrefix="MM" Namespace="DreamweaverCtrls" _
Assembly="DreamweaverCtrls,version=1.0.0.0,_
```

```
publicKeyToken=836f606ede05d46a,culture=neutral" %>
<MM:DataSet
id="DS"
runat="Server"
IsStoredProcedure="false"
ConnectionString='<%# System.Configuration.ConfigurationSettings._
AppSettings("MM_CONNECTION_STRING_connnorbert") %>'
DatabaseType='<%# System.Configuration.ConfigurationSettings._
AppSettings("MM_CONNECTION_DATABASETYPE_connnorbert") %>'
CommandText='<%# "SELECT * FROM dbo.tblCategories" %>'
Debug="true"
> </MM:DataSet>
<MM:PageBind runat="server" PostBackBind="true" />
<html>
<head>
<title>Repeater</title>
<meta http-equiv="Content-Type" content="text/html; charset=iso-8859-1">
</head>
<body>
<form runat='server'>
  <ASP:Repeater runat="server" DataSource='<%# DS.DefaultView %>'>
    <HeaderTemplate>
  <table width=400 cellspacing=0 cellpadding=2 border=0>
    <tr>
      <td><strong>CategoryID</strong></td>
      <td><strong>Category</strong></td>
    </tr>
    <tr>
      <td colspan=2><hr width="100%" size="1" noshade color="#003399"></td>
    </tr>
</HeaderTemplate>

<ItemTemplate>
    <tr>
      <td><%# Container.DataItem("CategoryID") %></td>
      <td><%# Container.DataItem("Category") %></td>
    </tr>
</ItemTemplate>

<AlternatingItemTemplate>
    <tr>
      <td bgcolor=#CCCCCC><%# Container.DataItem("CategoryID") %></td>
      <td bgcolor=#CCCCCC><%# Container.DataItem("Category") %></td>
    </tr>
</AlternatingItemTemplate>

<FooterTemplate>
```

```
    </table>
  </FooterTemplate>

    </ASP:Repeater>
  </form>
  </body>
  </html>
```

FIGURE 15.9

The Repeater server
control

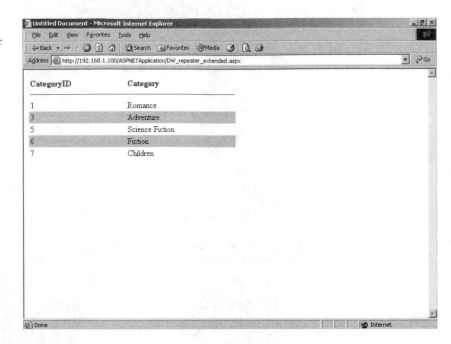

As you can see in the code listing, we begin by establishing a data connection to the Books database. Then we register the Dreamweaver MX custom tags with the script page and use MM:DataSet to create our DS DataSet. Next we wrapped the Repeater server control around the Dynamic Text. As you can see, the Repeater server control consists of an opening and closing Repeater tag and the appropriate opening and closing Template tags. In our example, we created an HTML table with alternating background colors of the rows. To accomplish this, first we use the required ItemTemplate to create one standard formatted table row for each row in the DataSet.

```
<ASP:Repeater id="Repeater" runat="server" >

<ItemTemplate>
  <tr>
    <td><%# Container.DataItem("CategoryID") %></td>
    <td><%# Container.DataItem("Category") %></td>
  </tr>
```

```
    </ItemTemplate>

    </ASP:Repeater>
```

The next step is to create the alternating rows with a contrasting background color. To do so, we add the AlternatingItemTemplate to the Repeater tag content—making sure to set the table cell background color to gray (# CCCCCC).

```
<ASP:Repeater id="Repeater" runat="server" >

<ItemTemplate>
   <tr>
      <td><%# Container.DataItem("CategoryID") %></td>
      <td><%# Container.DataItem("Category") %></td>
   </tr>
</ItemTemplate>

<AlternatingItemTemplate>
   <tr>
      <td bgcolor=#CCCCCC><%# Container.DataItem("CategoryID") %></td>
      <td bgcolor=#CCCCCC><%# Container.DataItem("Category") %></td>
   </tr>
</AlternatingItemTemplate>

</ASP:Repeater>
```

As you can probably guess, our code is missing the column headers identifying our data and the opening and closing Table tags. To add these to our Repeater control, use the HeaderTemplate and FooterTemplate.

```
<ASP:Repeater id="Repeater" runat="server" >
<HeaderTemplate>
  <table width=400 cellspacing=0 cellpadding=2 border=0>
    <tr>
       <td><strong>CategoryID</strong></td>
       <td><strong>Category</strong></td>
    </tr>
    <tr>
       <td colspan=2><hr width="100%" size="1" noshade color="#003399"></td>
    </tr>
</HeaderTemplate>

<ItemTemplate>
   <tr>
      <td><%# Container.DataItem("CategoryID") %></td>
      <td><%# Container.DataItem("Category") %></td>
   </tr>
</ItemTemplate>
```

```
<AlternatingItemTemplate>
   <tr>
      <td bgcolor=#CCCCCC><%# Container.DataItem("CategoryID") %></td>
      <td bgcolor=#CCCCCC><%# Container.DataItem("Category") %></td>
   </tr>
</AlternatingItemTemplate>

<FooterTemplate>
</table>
</FooterTemplate>
</ASP:Repeater>
```

Notice we did not include the SeparatorTemplate in our Repeater control. Because we utilized the AlternatingItemTemplate and displayed the Repeater data in an HTML table, the SeparatorTemplate was not necessary. However, if you would like to add it to the script file, the code would look something like the following:

```
<SeparatorTemplate>
   <tr>
      <td colspan=2><hr width="100%" size="1" noshade color="#003399"></td>
   </tr>
</SeparatorTemplate>
```

As you can see, ASP.NET makes use of a lot of templates in its server controls. Once you're comfortable with using templates with ASP.NET, you'll find that you write and reuse a lot of them. The perfect place to store your templates is in the Dreamweaver MX Library. Each template becomes a library item you can insert into your code at a moment's notice.

THE DATALIST SERVER CONTROL

You'll find the DataList server control similar to the Repeater server control, except for one important aspect. The DataList control allows users to interact and modify data presented in the control. Similar to the Repeater control, the DataList control loops through all records of the DataSet to display the information according to predefined templates. In addition to the four templates you are already aware of, the DataList server control supports the SelectedItemTemplate and EditItemTemplate. The SelectedItemTemplate generates a row of content only when the user selects an item from the DataList control. Typically, developers will change the presentation style of the row to identify the row currently selected. The EditItemTemplate generates a row of content when an item is put into edit mode. These templates work well to inform the user they have selected something or to empower the user to alter data.

To see how the DataList server control works, remove the Repeater control from our script file and then create the DataList server control. To do so, follow these steps:

1. Choose Insert ➤ ASP.NET Objects ➤ DataList to open the DataList dialog box, as shown in Figure 15.10. You can also open this dialog box by activating the Application panel group and clicking the DataList icon.

FIGURE 15.10

The DataList
dialog box

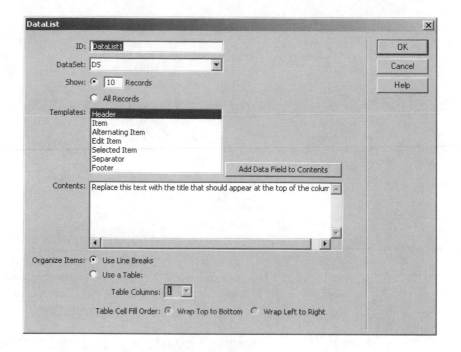

As you can see, the initial DataList dialog box includes far more property options than the Repeat Regions dialog box.

2. To create our sample DataList, name the control DataList1, choose DS as the DataSet, and click the All Records option in the Show section.

WARNING   *This Dreamweaver MX feature is misleading. You can choose to show a limited set of records, but doing so does not add the sorting functionality. It only sets attributes in the DataList control to trigger sorting functionality—which you must add on your own.*

Let's skip the Templates section for a moment.

3. In the Organize Items section, select the Use Line Breaks option. (We'll be making a table of our own using DataList templates.)

4. If you want DataList to create a table upon rendering, select the Use A Table option.

5. Specify the number of columns. If you set the number of columns to greater than 1, be certain to set the Table Cell Fill Order accordingly. The Table Cell Fill Order option Wrap Top To Bottom displays items in the DataSet from top to bottom in each column you specify. Similarly, the Wrap Left To Right option displays items in the DataSet left to right.

Now, you need to specify the properties in the Templates section. As you recall, DataList can use a Header, Item, AlternatingItem, EditItem, SelectedItem, Separator, and FooterTemplate. The ItemTemplate is the only required template.

6. In the Templates list, select Item.

7. To insert a variable into the ItemTemplate Content text area that corresponds to the `CategoryID` or `Category` column in the DS DataSet, click the Add Data Field To Contents button to open the Add Data Field dialog box, as shown in Figure 15.11.

FIGURE 15.11

Add DataField variables to the DataList Template Contents Area

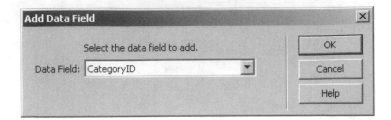

8. Choose CategoryID from the Data Field drop-down list, and then click OK.

9. Choose Category from the Data Field drop-down list, and then click OK. As you can see in Figure 15.12, Dreamweaver MX inserts the appropriate variables into the Contents section of the DataList dialog box. All that's left for you to do is define more DataList templates and add the necessary formatting and functionality.

FIGURE 15.12

Inserting template code in the DataList dialog box

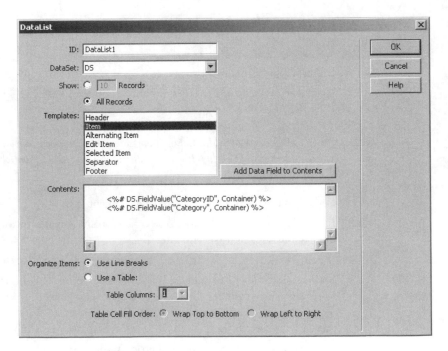

10. Click OK to insert the DataList control into our script page.

Listing 15.6 shows the Dreamweaver MX-generated code, and Figure 15.13 shows the DataList in Design mode.

LISTING 15.6: *DW_DATALIST.ASPX*

```
<%@ Page Language="VB" ContentType="text/html" ResponseEncoding="iso-8859-1" %>
<%@ Register TagPrefix="MM" Namespace="DreamweaverCtrls" _
Assembly="DreamweaverCtrls,version=1.0.0.0,_
publicKeyToken=836f606ede05d46a,culture=neutral" %>
<MM:DataSet
id="DS"
runat="Server"
IsStoredProcedure="false"
ConnectionString='<%# System.Configuration.ConfigurationSettings._
AppSettings("MM_CONNECTION_STRING_connnorbert") %>'
DatabaseType='<%# System.Configuration.ConfigurationSettings_
AppSettings("MM_CONNECTION_DATABASETYPE_connnorbert") %>'
CommandText='<%# "SELECT * FROM dbo.tblCategories" %>'
Debug="true"
> </MM:DataSet>
<MM:PageBind runat="server" PostBackBind="true" />



<html>
<head>
<title>Untitled Document</title>
<meta http-equiv="Content-Type" content="text/html; charset=iso-8859-1">
</head>
<body>

<form runat="server">

  <asp:DataList id="DataList1"
runat="server"
RepeatColumns="1"
RepeatDirection="Vertical"
RepeatLayout="Flow"
DataSource="<%# DS.DefaultView %>" >
    <ItemTemplate>
        <%# DS.FieldValue("CategoryID", Container) %>
        <%# DS.FieldValue("Category", Container) %>
    </ItemTemplate>
  </asp:DataList>
</form>
</body>
</html>
```

FIGURE 15.13

The DataList in
Design mode

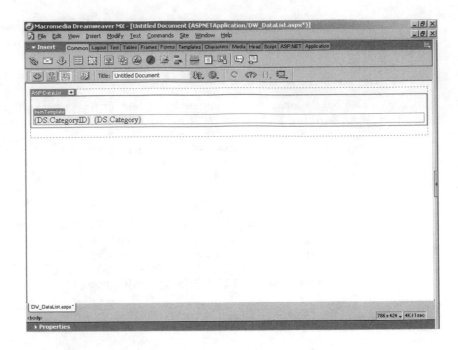

BUILDING ON THE DREAMWEAVER CODE

To further the formatting and functionality beyond the Dreamweaver MX basics, you can place
HTML and ASP.NET code in the appropriate Template section. Listings 15.7 through 15.11 show
sample template code.

The HeaderTemplate is used for the column headings of a table displaying data.

LISTING 15.7: THE HEADERTEMPLATE

```
<table width=400 cellspacing=0 cellpadding=2 border=0>
   <tr>
     <td><strong>CategoryID</strong></td>
     <td><strong>Category</strong></td>
   </tr>
   <tr>
     <td colspan=2><hr width="100%" size="1" noshade color="#003399"></td>
   </tr>
```

The ItemTemplate is used to display a default view of the items in a DataSet.

LISTING 15.8: THE ITEMTEMPLATE

```
<tr>
    <td><asp:linkbutton ID="linkbutton1" runat="server" commandname=Edit>_
<%# DS.FieldValue("CategoryID", Container) %></td>
    <td><%# DS.FieldValue("Category", Container) %></td>
</tr>
```

The AlternatingItemTemplate provides a different display for every other row of items in a DataSet. The alternate displays increase the readability of long tables of data.

LISTING 15.9: THE ALTERNATINGITEMTEMPLATE

```
<tr>
    <td bgcolor=#CCCCCC><asp:linkbutton ID="linkbutton1" _
runat="server" commandname=Edit><%# DS.FieldValue("CategoryID", Container) %></td>
    <td bgcolor=#CCCCCC><%# DS.FieldValue("Category", Container) %></td>
</tr>
```

The EditItemTemplate provides a unique view to edit the items in the current row of the DataSet.

LISTING 15.10: THE EDITITEMTEMPLATE

```
<tr>
    <td bgcolor=#CCCCCC>
        <asp:LinkButton commandname="Cancel" id="lbtCancel" _
runat="server" text="Cancel" runat="server" />
        <asp:LinkButton commandname="Update" id="lbtUpdate" _
runat="server" text="Update" runat="server" />
        <asp:LinkButton commandname="Delete" id="lbtDelete" _
runat="server" text="Delete" runat="server" />
    </td>
    <td bgcolor=#CCCCCC><asp:TextBox id="tbxCategory" runat="server" _
Text='<%# Container.DataItem("Category") %>' />
        <asp:TextBox id="tbxCategoryID" ReadOnly="true" _
runat="server" Text='<%# Container.DataItem("CategoryID") %>' />
    </td>
</tr>
```

The FooterTemplate provides a specialized display for the bottom of the DataList.

LISTING 15.11: THE FOOTERTEMPLATE

```
</table>
```

Keep in mind that to add true functionality to your DataList, you will also have to match the template code with events and procedures to accommodate templates that elicit actions such as the EditItemTemplate. Listing 15.12 shows a complete DataList script page ready for you to fill the event procedures with database functionality, and Figure 15.14 shows the results in a browser. Unfortunately, detailing the intricacies of custom scripting-server controls to dynamically update DataSets requires in-depth coverage of ASP.NET and is outside the range of this chapter. Don't let that stop you though. Check out http://msdn.microsoft.com/library/default.asp?url=/nhp/default.asp?contentid=28000440 to find out more about events and custom scripting.

LISTING 15.12: *DATALIST.ASPX*

```
<%@ Page Language="VB" ContentType="text/html" ResponseEncoding="iso-8859-1" %>
<%@ import Namespace="system.Data" %>
<%@ import Namespace="system.Data.OLE DB" %>

<script runat="server">
        'Create a DataConnection
        Dim myConnection As OLE DBConnection
        Dim myDataAdapter As OLE DBDataAdapter
        dim ds as DataSet
        Dim dt As DataTable
        Dim dr As DataRow

    Sub Page_Load(Sender As Object, E As EventArgs)

        myconnection = new OLE DBConnection("Provider=SQLOLE DB.1;_
Persist Security Info=False;User ID=SA;Password=superman;Initial _
Catalog=MDWMX_BOOKS;Data Source=192.168.1.100")

        myDataAdapter = new OLE DBDataAdapter("Select *_
 from tblCategories", myconnection)

            ds = new DataSet()
            myDataAdapter.Fill(ds,"tblCategories")
            'select data view and bind
            DataList1.DataSource = ds
            DataList1.DataMember = "tblCategories"
            DataList1.DataBind()

    End Sub

    Sub DataList1_ItemCommand(Sender As Object, E As DataListCommandEventArgs)
        DataList1.SelectedIndex = e.Item.ItemIndex
        DataList1.DataBind()
      End Sub
```

```
        Sub DataList1_EditCommand(Sender As Object, E As DataListCommandEventArgs)
            DataList1.EditItemIndex = e.Item.ItemIndex
            DataList1.DataBind()
        End Sub

        Sub DataList1_CancelCommand(Sender As Object, E As DataListCommandEventArgs)
            DataList1.EditItemIndex = -1
        DataList1.DataBind()
        End Sub

        Sub DataList1_UpdateCommand(Sender As Object, E As DataListCommandEventArgs)
            Dim tbxCategory As TextBox = e.Item.FindControl("tbxCategory")
            Dim tbxCategoryID As TextBox = e.Item.FindControl("tbxCategoryID")
                Dim Category As String = tbxCategory.Text
            Dim CategoryID As integer = tbxCategoryID.Text

        End Sub

        Sub DataList1_DeleteCommand(Sender As Object, E As DataListCommandEventArgs)
            Dim tbxCategory As TextBox = e.Item.FindControl("tbxCategory")
            Dim tbxCategoryID As TextBox = e.Item.FindControl("tbxCategoryID")

                Dim Category As String = tbxCategory.Text
            Dim CategoryID As integer = tbxCategoryID.Text

        End Sub
</script>


<html>
<head>
<title>DataList Server Control</title>
<meta http-equiv="Content-Type" content="text/html; charset=iso-8859-1">
</head>
<body>

<form runat=server>

<ASP:DataList id="DataList1" repeatlayout="Table" runat="server"
onItemCommand="Datalist1_ItemCommand"
onEditCommand="Datalist1_EditCommand"
onUpdateCommand="Datalist1_UpdateCommand"
onCancelCommand="Datalist1_CancelCommand"
onDeleteCommand="Datalist1_DeleteCommand"
DataKeyField="CategoryID" >

<HeaderTemplate>
  <table width=400 cellspacing=0 cellpadding=2 border=0>
    <tr>
```

```
                  <td><strong>CategoryID</strong></td>
                  <td><strong>Category</strong></td>
          </tr>
          <tr>
                  <td colspan=2><hr width="100%" size="1" noshade color="#003399"></td>
          </tr>
</HeaderTemplate>


<ItemTemplate>
     <tr>
             <td><asp:linkbutton ID="linkbutton1" runat="server" _
commandname=Edit><%# Container.DataItem("CategoryID")

%></asp:linkbutton></td>
             <td><%# Container.DataItem("Category") %></td>
     </tr>
</ItemTemplate>

<SelectedItemTemplate>
     <tr>
             <td bgcolor=#CCCCCC><%# Container.DataItem("CategoryID") %></td>
             <td bgcolor=#CCCCCC><%# Container.DataItem("Category") %></td>
     </tr>
</SelectedItemTemplate>

<AlternatingItemTemplate>
     <tr>
             <td bgcolor=#CCCCCC><asp:linkbutton ID="linkbutton1" _
runat="server" commandname=Edit><%#
Container.DataItem("CategoryID") %></asp:linkbutton></td>
             <td bgcolor=#CCCCCC><%# Container.DataItem("Category") %></td>
     </tr>
</AlternatingItemTemplate>



<EditItemTemplate>
     <tr>
             <td bgcolor=#CCCCCC>
                     <asp:LinkButton commandname="Cancel" id="lbtCancel" _
runat="server" text="Cancel" runat="server" />
                     <asp:LinkButton commandname="Update" id="lbtUpdate" _
runat="server" text="Update" runat="server" />
                     <asp:LinkButton commandname="Delete" id="lbtDelete" _
runat="server" text="Delete" runat="server" />
             </td>
             <td bgcolor=#CCCCCC><asp:TextBox id="tbxCategory" runat="server" _
Text='<%# DataBinder.Eval(Container.DataItem,
"Category") %>' />
```

```
            <asp:TextBox id="tbxCategoryID" ReadOnly="true" runat="server" _
Text='<%# DataBinder.Eval(Container.DataItem,
"CategoryID") %>' />
</td>
    </tr>
</EditItemTemplate>

<FooterTemplate>
</table>
</FooterTemplate>
</ASP:DataList>
</form>
</body>
</html>
```

FIGURE 15.14

DataList.aspx

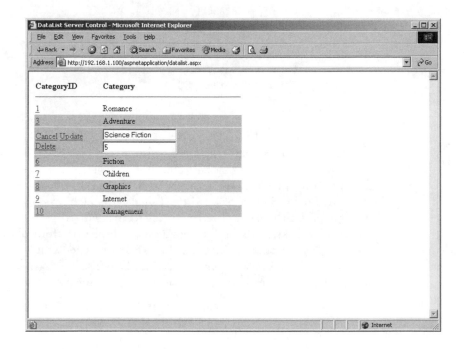

At the top of the script, DataList.aspx begins importing the required Data and OLE DB namespaces. It then establishes a data connection to the Books database, pulls data, and creates and fills a DataSet. Once the DataSet is filled, it is set as the data source to the DataList server control.

```
<%@ Page Language="VB" ContentType="text/html" ResponseEncoding="iso-8859-1" %>
<%@ import Namespace="system.Data" %>
<%@ import Namespace="system.Data.OLE DB" %>

<script runat="server">
        'Create a DataConnection
```

```
        Dim myConnection As OLE DBConnection
        Dim myDataAdapter As OLE DBDataAdapter
        dim ds as DataSet
        Dim dt As DataTable
        Dim dr As DataRow


    Sub Page_Load(Sender As Object, E As EventArgs)

        myconnection = new OLE DBConnection("Provider=SQLOLE DB.1;_
Persist Security Info=False;User
ID=SA;Password=superman;Initial Catalog=MDWMX_BOOKS;Data Source=192.168.1.100")

        myDataAdapter = new OLE DBDataAdapter("Select *_
 from tblCategories", myconnection)

        ds = new DataSet()
        myDataAdapter.Fill(ds,"tblCategories")
        'select data view and bind
        DataList1.DataSource = ds
        DataList1.DataMember = "tblCategories"
        DataList1.DataBind()

    End Sub
```

The next few procedures in DataList.aspx are event-driven. When the user selects an item to edit in the DataList server control or subsequently clicks a Cancel, Update, or Delete link, these special commands trigger an event that calls a function. These special commands can simply activate one of the DataList templates or execute custom code. For example, DataList1_ItemCommand activates the web content defined in the SelectedItemTemplate, and DataList1_EditCommand activates the web content in the EditItemTemplate. As you can see in Figure 15.14, DataList1_ItemCommand highlights the row a user clicks, and DataList1_EditCommand displays the form objects in the EditItemTemplate. DataList1_UpdateCommand, DataList1_CancelCommand, and DataList1_DeleteCommand are triggered when the user clicks similarly named links in the DataList. These commands typically run any custom database push-pull functionality you want to occur as the user manages the data in the DataSet.

```
Sub DataList1_ItemCommand(Sender As Object, E As DataListCommandEventArgs)
    DataList1.SelectedIndex = e.Item.ItemIndex
    DataList1.DataBind()
End Sub

Sub DataList1_EditCommand(Sender As Object, E As DataListCommandEventArgs)
    DataList1.EditItemIndex = e.Item.ItemIndex
    DataList1.DataBind()
End Sub

Sub DataList1_CancelCommand(Sender As Object, E As DataListCommandEventArgs)
    DataList1.EditItemIndex = -1
    DataList1.DataBind()
End Sub
```

```
Sub DataList1_UpdateCommand(Sender As Object, E As DataListCommandEventArgs)
    Dim tbxCategory As TextBox = e.Item.FindControl("tbxCategory")
    Dim tbxCategoryID As TextBox = e.Item.FindControl("tbxCategoryID")
    Dim Category As String = tbxCategory.Text
    Dim CategoryID As integer = tbxCategoryID.Text
End Sub

Sub DataList1_DeleteCommand(Sender As Object, E As DataListCommandEventArgs)
    Dim tbxCategory As TextBox = e.Item.FindControl("tbxCategory")
    Dim tbxCategoryID As TextBox = e.Item.FindControl("tbxCategoryID")
    Dim Category As String = tbxCategory.Text
    Dim CategoryID As integer = tbxCategoryID.Text
End Sub
```

The final, all-important section of the code is the DataList itself. As we've mentioned, the DataList is composed of the opening and closing DataList tags surrounding the Header, Item, SelectedItem, EditItem, and FooterTemplate tags. To add the event behaviors that react to the data and user interaction, we've placed trigger events in the opening DataList tag. Once you add trigger events to your DataList, you'll need to modify and commit the DataSet to your database. For more information about updating a DataSet through a DataList, go to http://samples.gotdotnet.com/quickstart/aspplus/default.aspx?url=%2fquickstart%2faspplus%2fdoc%2fwebdatabinding.aspx.

```
<ASP:DataList id="DataList1" repeatlayout="Table" runat="server"
onItemCommand="Datalist1_ItemCommand"
onEditCommand="Datalist1_EditCommand"
onUpdateCommand="Datalist1_UpdateCommand"
onCancelCommand="Datalist1_CancelCommand"
onDeleteCommand="Datalist1_DeleteCommand"
DataKeyField="CategoryID" >
```

THE DATAGRID SERVER CONTROL

The last, but most powerful, data-server control we're going to discuss is DataGrid. A DataGrid server control generates multicolumn tables from data sources such as a DataSet. You can format the columns in a variety of ways—data, button, hyperlink, templated, and so on. Using Dreamweaver MX to insert a DataGrid server control in a script page allows you to define an ASP.NET DataGrid server control from a dialog box interface.

The DataGrid server control is similar to both Repeater and DataList server controls. However, DataGrid provides much more functionality. DataGrid can generate a table column for each field in your DataSet or data source. DataGrid automatically chooses the best style to display data based on the data content. However, you can override the default column style and choose to display the column data in a variety of ways.

Bound　The default column type. You can specify which columns to display, in what order, and you can specify how the columns display through styles.

Button　Displays data as HTML buttons. This allows you to attach custom events and functionality to each piece of data.

Edit   Displays data in form objects. This allows the end user to modify the data right from the display page.

Hyperlink   Displays data in hyperlinks you define.

Template   Just as with previous data-bound server controls, you can create custom templates to display data any way you wish.

The so very cool part of DataGrid is that you can use it as is to simply show the data in a data source. Alternatively, DataGrid has an enormous number of properties that you can use to modify to the nth degree.

Let's examine a DataGrid example. We'll create a simple DataGrid. To do so, follow these steps:

1. Remove the DataList server control from the script page to make room for the DataGrid control.

2. Choose Insert ➢ ASP.NET Objects ➢ DataGrid to open the DataGrid dialog box, as shown in Figure 15.15. You can also open this dialog box by activating the Server Behaviors panel and choosing DataGrid from the panel menu.

FIGURE 15.15

The DataGrid
dialog box

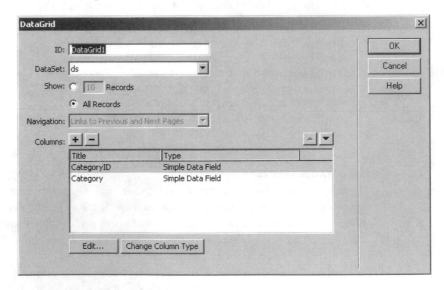

3. In the ID box, enter **DataGrid1**.

4. In the DataSet drop-down list box, select ds.

5. In the Show section, click the All Records option.

6. When you click OK, Dreamweaver MX inserts the DataGrid into your script page.

This simple implementation of DataGrid shown in Listing 15.13 and in Figure 15.16 automatically generates the columns and rows of our data source for us. As you can imagine, this example would take all of five minutes to use DataGrid to display the data in your data source.

As you can see, a number of properties are defined in this DataGrid example. We'll discuss more about using the full potential of the DataGrid server control to delete and modify data in Chapter 21. Some are presentation styles; others, similar to DataList, are Edit, Update, and Cancel events and functions. DataGrid still has an enormous number of properties you can manipulate. You should investigate all DataGrid properties, as this is a tremendously powerful control that can save you hours of development time.

LISTING 15.13: *DATAGRID_SIMPLE.ASPX*

```
<%@ Page Language="VB" ContentType="text/html" ResponseEncoding="iso-8859-1" %>
<%@ Register TagPrefix="MM" Namespace="DreamweaverCtrls" _
Assembly="DreamweaverCtrls,version=1.0.0.0,_
publicKeyToken=836f606ede05d46a,culture=neutral" %>
<MM:DataSet
id="DS"
runat="Server"
IsStoredProcedure="false"
ConnectionString='<%# System.Configuration.ConfigurationSettings._
AppSettings("MM_CONNECTION_STRING_connnorbert") %>'
DatabaseType='<%# System.Configuration.ConfigurationSettings._
AppSettings("MM_CONNECTION_DATABASETYPE_connnorbert") %>'
CommandText='<%# "SELECT * FROM dbo.tblCategories" %>'
Debug="true"
> </MM:DataSet>
<MM:PageBind runat="server" PostBackBind="true" />
<html>
<head>
<title>MMDataSet</title>
<meta http-equiv="Content-Type" content="text/html; charset=iso-8859-1">
</head>
<body>

<form runat="server">

  <asp:DataGrid id="DataGrid1"
  runat="server"
  AllowSorting="False"
  AutoGenerateColumns="false"
  CellPadding="3"
  CellSpacing="0"
  ShowFooter="false"
  ShowHeader="true"
  DataSource="<%# DS.DefaultView %>"
  AllowPaging="false"
>
    <HeaderStyle HorizontalAlign="center" BackColor="#E8EBFD"ForeColor="#3D3DB6"_
Font-Name="Verdana, Arial, Helvetica, sans-serif" _
```

```
              Font-Bold="true" Font-Size="smaller" />
                <ItemStyle BackColor="#F2F2F2" _
          Font-Name="Verdana, Arial, Helvetica, sans-serif" _
          Font-Size="smaller" />
                <AlternatingItemStyle BackColor="#E5E5E5" _
          Font-Name="Verdana, Arial, Helvetica, sans-serif" _
          Font-Size="smaller" />
                <FooterStyle HorizontalAlign="center" BackColor="#E8EBFD" _
          ForeColor="#3D3DB6" Font-Name="Verdana, Arial, Helvetica, sans-serif" _
          Font-Bold="true" Font-Size="smaller" />
                <PagerStyle BackColor="white" _
          Font-Name="Verdana, Arial, Helvetica, sans-serif" Font-Size="smaller" />
              <Columns>
                <asp:BoundColumn DataField="CategoryID"
                  HeaderText="CategoryID"
                  ReadOnly="true"
                  Visible="True"/>
                <asp:BoundColumn DataField="Category"
                  HeaderText="Category"
                  ReadOnly="true"
                  Visible="True"/> </Columns>
            </asp:DataGrid>
          </form>
          </body>
          </html>
```

FIGURE 15.16

DataGrid_
simple.aspx

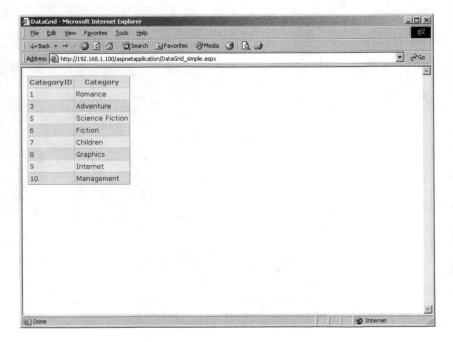

For Further Information

Individually, resources for ASP.NET, ADO.NET, and Dreamweaver MX are plentiful. However, precious few resources incorporate all three technologies. Some of our frequent haunts are www.gotdotnet.com/, http://msdn.microsoft.com/library/default.asp?url=/nhp/default.asp?contentid=28000440, and www.4guysfromrolla.com. A relatively new but fast favorite is www.udzone.com—a site to share and glean knowledge with the rest of the Dreamweaver MX community.

Summary

In this chapter, we introduced you to ADO.NET and discussed how it supports and interacts with ASP.NET. We also demonstrated how to create DataSets and bind them to server controls. Keep in mind that ADO.NET is a still a somewhat new initiative. Microsoft is constantly evolving and bettering .NET as a whole. Since the technology is evolving, you will run into problems that seem to defy both Macromedia and Microsoft documentation. As such, it is imperative that you not only keep up, but also actively seek out the latest technical documents and patches for .NET, Windows, and Dreamweaver MX.

Chapter 16

PHP and Dreamweaver MX

PHP STANDS FOR HYPERTEXT PREPROCESSOR, but the abbreviation comes from the original full name of Personal Home Page Tools. PHP has been around longer than most other application web servers, and it happens to be one of the technologies Microsoft doesn't like. It is nevertheless becoming incredibly popular for a couple of reasons. First, it's free. There are no license fees, no charges for downloading—simply no charges. Second, PHP is part of the open-source software movement.

This chapter covers the following topics:

◆ Introducing PHP
◆ Why PHP?
◆ Configuring PHP
◆ PHP—the language
◆ Dreamweaver and PHP

Introducing PHP

PHP started out as a set of CGI (Common Gateway Interface) scripts created by Rasmus Lerdorf and released to the general public on June 8, 1995. At the time of this writing, you can see the original announcement at: http://groups.google.com/groups?selm=3r7pgp$aa1@ionews.io.org. Lerdorf started the ball rolling on a product that has become amazingly popular in the last year. Figure 16.1 shows a NetCraft survey from PHP.net that illustrates the dramatic usage growth PHP has experienced in recent years.

PHP, like ASP (Active Server Pages), ColdFusion, and others, is a scripting language that resides on your server and lets you create dynamic web pages. PHP works like the others in that you embed PHP code within your HTML (Hypertext Markup Language) pages and the server interprets the PHP, generates the HTML code, and hands it to the user's browser. But PHP differs from the others in that it really isn't tag-based. It's more like a traditional programming language in which you can define variables and functions on the fly. You can even make recursive functions (functions that can call themselves) in PHP.

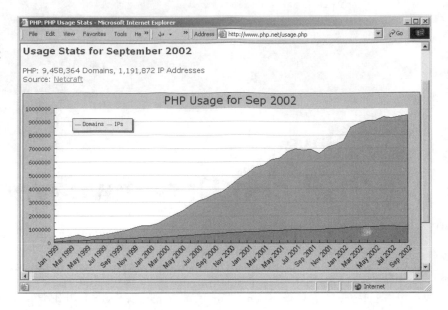

NOTE   *In this chapter, we're exploring the latest release of PHP, PHP 4.*

Why PHP?

Why would anyone want to use PHP? If it's not supported by a large company such as Oracle or Microsoft, why should we use it? Well, let's look at a few of the many reasons PHP runs on millions of websites.

PHP IS FREE

PHP, from its first release, has been free. This means you don't have to spend hundreds to thousands of dollars to license a web package from Microsoft, Sun, Oracle, Netscape, or even Macromedia. For those on a budget, *free* can be a big reason for using PHP.

PHP RUNS ON A FREE WEB SERVER

PHP is available to run on just about every possible web server. It's even available to run on the new Mac OS X. But the server that PHP is basically wedded to is the free Apache Web Server from the Apache Software Foundation, found at `www.apache.org`. The Apache Web Server runs on most Unix and Windows flavors, so it is available for almost all major platforms, including the new Mac OS X.

PHP is wedded to Apache in that it is built so that you can actually make PHP part of the Apache Web Server: you can actually compile PHP into the Apache Web Server. This makes it blindingly fast and stable. Normally, PHP sits "on top" of the web server, waiting to grab PHP commands from the web pages before the web server gets them. Being inextricably linked into the web server removes a layer of complexity that gives great performance boosts.

Apache is also a free web server, whose growth and stability are becoming legendary. It's already the leading web server, as Table 16.1 shows from a SecuritySpace.com survey.

TABLE 16.1: SecuritySpace.com Survey of Web Server Usage

Server	Number of sites using each web server in August	Aug. %	Number of sites using each web server in September	Sept. %	% Change
Apache	5,845,842	66.49	6,037,315	66.75	+0.26
Microsoft	1,923,409	21.88	1,974,123	21.83	−0.05
Netscape	110,609	1.26	107,183	1.18	−0.08
Zeus	74,702	0.85	71,919	0.80	−0.05
WebSTAR	50,003	0.57	57,913	0.64	+0.07
WebSite	29,502	0.34	32,583	0.36	+0.02
Other	757,554	8.62	763,991	8.45	+0.17

PHP Works with a Free SQL Database Server

MySQL, which we covered in Chapter 7, is a free database server. It's also fast and stable. You'll find "triad" packages all over the Internet that include PHP, Apache, and MySQL installation programs for various platforms. Visit your favorite web search engine and search for "php triad" to see what we mean. Or you can download the installation package from `http://sourceforge.net/projects/phptriad`.

PHP Is Open-Source Software

PHP is officially part of the open-source software movement, which encourages programmer, hacker, and code-tinkerer volunteers to freely copy and modify the code to make it better. Those that modify the code or create new features or modules for code submit their enhancements to the governing body of the software for inclusion into the next official release. Generally, open-source software is either free or inexpensive.

Open-source is great because you have basically the world of software developers working on a single product—potentially thousands and thousands of developers trying to improve a piece of software. There is a drawback though: generally, open-source software doesn't come with technical support. You can't pick up the phone, pay someone, and get your questions answered. However, with the Internet today, you can almost always find an answer or a lead to solve technical questions on just about every piece of popular software.

Open-source software also has a tradition of longevity and stability. Although corporate entities maintain tight reins on their software and tend to move slowly in patching bugs, the open-source movement tends to work much faster. Bugs are fixed sooner, and thus the product is more stable. Although corporate entities must make a profit in order to stay in business, open-source projects don't need to appease shareholders, so they're not necessarily going away any time soon.

PHP Is Basically a Traditional Programming Language

Unlike other web-development languages, PHP doesn't really have tags that you use to create its functionality. You'll see later in this chapter that even Dreamweaver MX doesn't provide a large number of button-inserted commands. We suspect this is because there really aren't tags for which you could assign buttons. The structure of PHP is C-like, so C programmers shouldn't have a problem learning PHP. But even though PHP has a traditional programming language structure, it's still relatively easy to learn.

Configuring PHP

PHP, like much of open-source software, has many configuration options. As you might expect, since you can compile PHP into the Apache Web Server itself or even compile a build for Windows, options control how your customized, compiled version will behave. You can decide whether to include XML (Extensible Markup Language) support, reside as an Apache module, build in database directories, include Java support, and so forth. All the options and their behavior are beyond the scope of this chapter, but you can find them at the PHP website (www.php.net).

PHP also uses an initialization file called php.ini, a portion of which is in Listing 16.1. This file contains lots of PHP startup options that let you quickly customize how some features of PHP should behave without your having to recompile the entire system. The php.ini file is well documented within for those of you interested in learning more about tweaking your PHP installation. But let's take a look at a few of the options that you might want to immediately adjust in your copy of PHP.

THE *PHP.INI-RECOMMENDED* FILE

PHP ships with the php.ini file set with default values tuned for a development and learning environment. PHP also ships with the php.ini-recommended file, which is set with default values tuned for a production environment. The PHP folks highly recommend that you use the php.ini-recommended file as the starting base for your production environments, since it tweaks performance and security issues.

LISTING 16.1: A SMALL PART OF THE *PHP.INI* FILE INCLUDED WITH A WINDOWS INSTALLATION OF PHP

```
;;;;;;;;;;;;;;;;;;;;
; Language Options ;
;;;;;;;;;;;;;;;;;;;;

; Enable the PHP scripting language engine under Apache.
engine = On

; Allow the <-d? tag.  Otherwise, only <-d?php and <script> tags are recognized.
short_open_tag = On

; Allow ASP-style <% %> tags.
asp_tags = Off

; The number of significant digits displayed in floating point numbers.
precision   = 12

; Enforce year 2000 compliance (will cause problems with non-compliant browsers)
y2k_compliance = Off

; Output buffering allows you to send header lines (including cookies) even
; after you send body content, at the price of slowing PHP's output layer a
```

```
; bit. You can enable output buffering during runtime by calling the output
; buffering functions. You can also enable output buffering for all files by
; setting this directive to On. If you want to limit the size of the buffer
; to a certain size, you can use a maximum number of bytes instead of 'On', as
; a value for this directive (e.g., output_buffering=4096).
output_buffering = Off

; You can redirect all the output of your scripts to a function. For
; example, if you set output_handler to "ob_gzhandler", output will be
; transparently compressed for browsers that support gzip or deflate encoding.
; Setting an output handler automatically turns on output buffering.
output_handler =
```

THE *SHORT_OPEN_TAG* OPTION

This .ini option controls whether PHP uses a short version of the open PHP tag. Dreamweaver MX uses the long open tag (<?php>), which is what you should use as well. By default, short_open_tag is on. We recommend you turn it off. When on, short_open_tag allows you to start PHP statements with just <? as an opening tag. This was used heavily in earlier versions of PHP, and rumor has it that this tag is going to be phased out, since it conflicts with some XML statements. Save yourself some future compatibility problems, and use the proper, long version.

THE *ASP_TAGS* OPTION

When set to on, this option allows you to use ASP-style tags (<% %>) as PHP-code delimiters. If you're running PHP in a Windows Internet Information Services (IIS) environment, you may get unpredictable results since, by default, ASP is active on newer installations of IIS. Therefore, make sure this option is set to off.

THE *OUTPUT_BUFFERING* OPTION

The output_buffering option controls whether you can send HTTP (Hypertext Transfer Protocol) header information to the browser after you've sent body content. This means, for more practical purposes, it controls whether you can set a cookie in a page and then redirect from that page. You set the number of bytes to allow in an output buffer, so set this to a nice-sized chunk. PHP recommends 4096.

THE *ALLOW_CALL_TIME_PASS_REFERENCE* OPTION

This option is basically another legacy option that controlled whether you could pass function arguments by reference. (The programmers out there know what this means. For you nonprogrammers, it basically means that any changes made to the variable through the function call persist when the function ends.) The preferred PHP method for specifying pass-by-reference behavior is now in the function call itself. We recommend you set this option to off.

THE *DISPLAY_ERRORS* OPTION

In a learning or development environment, you typically want to see all the error information you can when your page crashes. However, you generally do not want to show that kind of information to someone visiting a production website. Error information might divulge security information such as database names, file paths on your web server, and so forth. Make sure this setting is off in your live PHP environment. (You can still trap errors using error_log.)

THE *LOG_ERRORS* OPTION

You typically use this in conjunction with display_errors. The default value in php.ini is off, but in a production environment, you'll want it turned on. This controls whether PHP logs errors to a file on your web server. This file is controlled by the error_log setting.

THE *ERROR_LOG* OPTION

This setting controls where errors in your site are logged. PHP will create the file with the filename you enter for this setting. Use this file to trap errors when you have display_errors set to off.

THE *ERROR_REPORTING* OPTION

The error_reporting option can use any of 12 constants that control whether PHP reports errors such as fatal errors, warnings, notices, and so forth. You can combine some of the constants to choose exactly the type of errors you want to know about using the following symbols: & (and), | (or), and ~ (not). For example,

```
error_reporting = E_ALL & !E_NOTICE
```

tells PHP to show you all errors except notices. If you want to see only errors and no warnings whatsoever, use something like the following:

```
error_reporting = E_ERROR |E_CORE_ERROR|E_COMPILE_ERROR
```

See Figures 16.3 and 16.4 later in the chapter for a comparison of this behavior. For your production environment, we recommend you log all errors and warnings so that you can trap problems that occur on your live website.

PHP—the Language

As we mentioned, PHP looks more like a traditional programming language such as C, Pascal, or Visual Basic. It doesn't use the familiar tag structure you may be accustomed to, but it's not that difficult to grasp. PHP is quite powerful and has more in its bag of tricks than we can cover in this chapter. But, like the other language chapters in this book, we'll explore a few of the features that will get you started.

Language Overview

Before we get into a few of the more common PHP commands you use in your web development, you need to be aware of the way PHP handles some of its constructs.

CASE SENSITIVITY

PHP is a forgiving language. It does its best to never generate an error when running on your web server. And, for the most part, PHP isn't case sensitive in its language constructs. However, there is one point that can drive you batty if you're unaware of it. PHP is picky about the case of variables. That is, PHP is case sensitive with variable names. The variable *City* is not the same as the variable *city*.

UserID is not that same as *userid*. Keep that in mind when you start developing in PHP and save yourself some time. (Function names and command names can be mixed case, if you'd like—just don't mix-case your variables.)

VARIABLES START WITH A DOLLAR SIGN ($)

All variables in PHP are to be prefaced with a dollar sign ($). Using the example in the previous section, our PHP code should have *$City* or *$UserID* as the variable names whenever we use them. Without the $, PHP won't know that you're trying to use a variable. Also, the first character after the $ cannot be a number. The variable name *$76Trombones* would generate an error. If you need to include the dollar sign at the beginning of a text string, escape it using the backslash (\). For example, to print a dollar sign, include something similar to the following:

```
<?php print "\$sign" ?>
```

ALL STATEMENTS END WITH A SEMICOLON (;)

All statements in PHP must end with a semicolon (;). However, blocks and loops do not. The semicolon tells PHP that the current line has ended and that it should process the command.

CURLY BRACES DENOTE BLOCKS OF CODE ({ })

To include and execute blocks of code within IF statements or loops, you follow the C and JavaScript conventions of wrapping the block with curly braces ({ }). For example, an IF statement can take the following form:

```
IF TRUE
   {
print ("Hello world. <br>");
print ("Hello again, from the second line.");
   }
```

COMMON ESCAPE SEQUENCES

We demonstrated a sample escape sequence above with the dollar sign. Escape sequences are those character combinations that *escape* from the typical processor behavior and allow you to deviate from the standard processing of the code. You'll need to use escape sequences in double-quoted strings (more on that in the next section). Here's a list of common escape sequences you might need in order to display certain characters within PHP:

\$	Causes PHP to print a dollar sign
\"	Causes PHP to print a double quote
\\	Causes PHP to print a backslash

SINGLE-QUOTED VERSUS DOUBLE-QUOTED STRINGS

Single-quoted strings are treated differently than double-quoted strings in PHP. Single-quoted strings treat almost everything between them as literal characters, even if you include variable names. For example, the code

```
<?php print 'The name you entered was $cFirstName' ?>
```

displays the text shown in Figure 16.2. As you can see, PHP didn't interpret the variable as you might have expected. For PHP to interpret the variable correctly, use double quotes around the text string, as in the following:

```
<?php print "The name you entered was $cFirstName" ?>
```

FIGURE 16.2

Single quotes tell
PHP to take
everything literally.

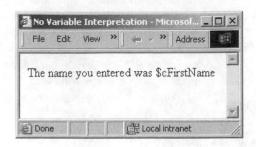

PHP IS FORGIVING

As we mentioned, even though PHP is more like a true programming language instead of a tag-based language, it is forgiving when you make an error in your code. PHP typically tries to continue to run when it encounters an error so that your page doesn't bomb out. For example, Listing 16.2 shows that we're trying to print the variable *cFirstName*, but we haven't defined it. You might expect an error, but depending on how you have the `php.ini` value set for `error_reporting` (`E_ALL` will show you notices), you might see something like Figure 16.3. PHP warned us that it couldn't find the variable, but continued processing the code. Figure 16.4 shows the same code, ran with `error_report` set to `E_ALL & ~E_NOTICES`.

LISTING 16.2: *PHP_NOTICE*

```html
<html>
<head>
<title> Variable Display</title>
<meta http-equiv="Content-Type" content="text/html; charset=iso-8859-1">
</head>

<body>

<?php print "The name you entered was $cFirstName" ?>
<br><br>
<?php print "You should see a notice from PHP above." ?>

</body>
</html>
```

FIGURE 16.3
PHP continues code processing when it encounters an undefined variable, but displays a notice.

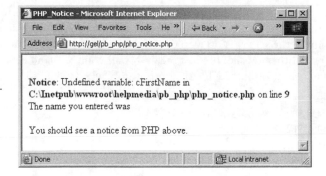

FIGURE 16.4
This is the same code with the `php.ini error_reporting` option set not to show notices.

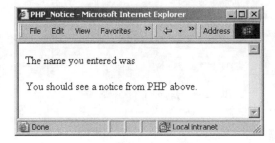

PHP's Comparison Operators

PHP's comparison operators are used to compare variables within expressions. Each language generally has a couple of operators that are different from other languages. PHP is no exception, so here's the list:

==	Equal To (not to be confused with the assignment operator '=')
!=	Not Equal To
>	Greater Than
<	Less Than
>=	Greater Than or Equal To
<=	Less Than or Equal To
===	Identical (only returns true if the variables are the same datatype and the same value)

Language Specifics

Now that you have an overview of the PHP language and understand some of its quirks, let's explore the commands and features that you will use in web development. Naturally, we're not going to cover all, but this discussion should give you a good idea where to start in PHP web development.

Writing to the Page—*PRINT* AND *ECHO*

Output—you've certainly got to have it in web development. Otherwise, there's not much sense in having a website, right? PHP has two primary commands for printing to a web page—`print` and `echo`.

These two commands perform the same function, but operate a bit differently: echo can take multiple arguments, and print can return a value to the calling routine if it's successful in actually displaying information to the screen. You won't need these differences in most instances, so it's best to settle on one or the other—echo, for instance—for all your printing needs. Here's an example of each of these tags in action that yields the output in Figure 16.5.

```php
<?php
 $cCityName = "Louisville";
 print "PRINT: The city name is $cCityName" ?>
<br><br>
<?php echo "ECHO: The city name is $cCityName" ?>
```

FIGURE 16.5

Both echo and print do basically the same thing.

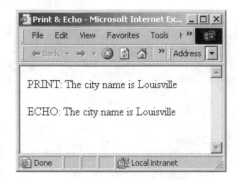

PASSING VARIABLES BETWEEN PAGES WITH GET

PHP, like other web-development languages, has its own method for retrieving values passed between pages. In ASP, in order to grab a value from an HTTP Get operation, you use request .querystring("varname"). In PHP, you use the command $http_get_vars to extract variables from the query string. The following code creates the form shown in Figure 16.6.

```html
<html>
<head>
<title>Passing Variables</title>
<meta http-equiv="Content-Type" content="text/html; charset=iso-8859-1">
</head>

<body>
<form action="Name_get_Action.php" method="get" name="GetName">

What is your name? <input name="Name" type="text" maxlength="50">
<br>
<input name="Submit" type="submit" value="Submit">

</form>

</body>
</html>
```

FIGURE 16.6

This simple form
uses the Get method.

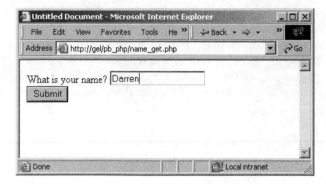

Notice that the form is submitted with a method of Get. The following code extracts the variable
from the query string that the Get method creates. You can see the value passed in the query string by
checking the URL in Figure 16.7. The following code retrieves the variable:

```html
<html>
<head>
<title>Untitled Document</title>
<meta http-equiv="Content-Type" content="text/html; charset=iso-8859-1">
</head>

<body>

<h2>Using Get</h2>
<br>
You entered: <?php print $HTTP_GET_VARS['Name']; ?>

</body>
</html>
```

Unlike most functions and commands in other web-development languages, `$http_get_vars`
uses brackets instead of parentheses, as you can see here. That may take you a few syntax errors to
get used to typing.

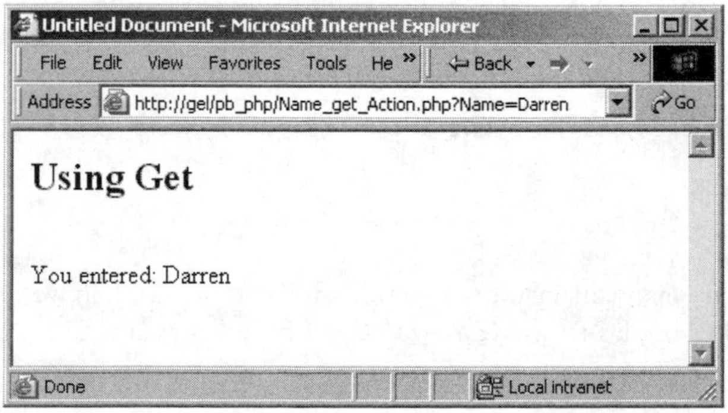

FIGURE 16.7

The HTTP Get
method passes form
variables in the URL
query string.

PASSING VARIABLES BETWEEN PAGES WITH POST

The preferred way to pass form variables to other pages is through the use of HTTP Post. This method passes the variables in the HTTP header so that the user doesn't see a query string. Plus, it's cleaner, doesn't have a size restriction, and is a bit more secure than Get. To retrieve variables passed using Post, you use the $http_post_vars command. For example, the following code is almost identical to the form code earlier, but notice that we're using Post as the method:

```html
<html>
<head>
<title>Untitled Document</title>
<meta http-equiv="Content-Type" content="text/html; charset=iso-8859-1">
</head>

<body>
<form action="Name_Action.php" method="post" name="GetName">

What is your name? <input name="Name" type="text" maxlength="50">
<br>
<input name="Submit" type="submit" value="Submit">

</form>

</body>
</html>
```

We retrieve the variable sent via the Post method using the following code that creates the same output, shown in Figure 16.8, as the Get. However, notice that there is no query string in the URL.

```html
<html>
<head>
<title>Using Post</title>
<meta http-equiv="Content-Type" content="text/html; charset=iso-8859-1">
</head>

<body>
<h2>Using Post</h2>
<br>

You entered: <?php print $HTTP_POST_VARS['Name']; ?>

</body>
</html>
```

There are many, many more functions and commands than we can cover here, so to learn PHP in depth, grab a book such as *Mastering PHP 4.1* from Sybex at your local book store or visit www.php.net for more information.

FIGURE 16.8

Post doesn't send the query string, so we use $http_post_vars to retrieve the variable.

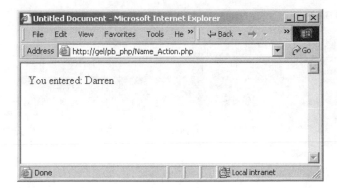

Dreamweaver and PHP

Dreamweaver MX can aid you in your PHP development, just as it helps with the other web-development languages. Although there isn't as much one-click support in Dreamweaver MX's PHP toolbars as, say, ColdFusion, Dreamweaver MX can still save you time in code entry and database calls.

Dreamweaver MX currently provides support for only the MySQL database when you're creating PHP pages. PHP can connect to other flavors of databases (see Chapter 10), but at this time, Dreamweaver MX doesn't support those other flavors. However, it does make MySQL database calls fast and easy. Let's take a look at Dreamweaver's handling of PHP.

THE PHP TAB

When you choose to create PHP pages, Dreamweaver MX adds a PHP tab to the Insert panel, as shown in Figure 16.9. The PHP options are as follows:

Button	What It Inserts at the Cursor Location
Form Variables	`<?php $HTTP_POST_VARS[]; ?>`
URL Variables	`<?php $HTTP_GET_VARS[]; ?>`
Session Variables	`<?php $HTTP_SESSION_VARS[]; ?>`
Cookie Variables	`<?php $HTTP_COOKIE_VARS[]; ?>`
Include	`<?php include(); ?>`
Require	`<?php require(); ?>`
`<?`	`<?php ?>`
Echo	`<?php echo ?>`
`/* */`	`/* */`
If	`<?php if ?>`
Else	`<?php else ?>`

FIGURE 16.9

Dreamweaver MX's
PHP tab

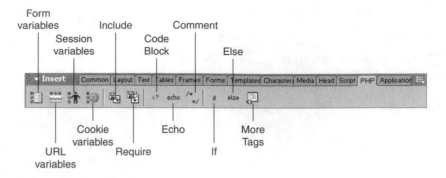

Two PHP functions on the Dreamweaver MX Insert bar are worth mentioning here: Include()
and Require(). You use these two functions to include the contents of another .php code file
within your code. Suppose you have a suite of database functions you've written to simplify
repetitive database tasks such as opening and closing a connection. Instead of typing these functions
into every page (or cutting and pasting the code), you can basically suck the function code into
every file by using one of these two functions. For example, the code snippet below includes the
file database_functions.php, which we'll assume contains a function called Open_Connection():

```php
<?php

include 'datase_functions.php';

Open_Connection();

?>
```

Now that the file is included, we can simply refer to Open_Connection() just as if we had typed
it in the code page ourselves. This is a great method by which you can save time and reuse code.

Include() and Require() are identical in every way except that if the file that you're including
doesn't exist, Include() will simply give you a warning, whereas Require() will return a fatal error
and stop processing the page. Basically, Include() won't bomb your code, but Require() will.

As you can see, Dreamweaver MX icon support saves you typing, but that's about all at this
point. But Dreamweaver MX's PHP support comes in handy when you start dealing with databases.
Dreamweaver MX can handle all the cryptic MySQL calls for you.

NOTE *PHP 4.1.0 deprecates the $http_type_vars arrays that Dreamweaver MX uses on its toolbar. Those variable
arrays are replaced with newer, automatically global arrays such as $_get, $_post, $_cookie, $_server, $_env,
$_request, and $_session. So you might want to start using these instead of Dreamweaver MX's default version
just to make sure your code is compatible with future versions of PHP. You use these new variable arrays just as you
use the older versions: instead of $http_post_vars['name'], you use $_post['name'].*

DREAMWEAVER MX'S PHP/MYSQL DATABASE SUPPORT

Making connections to the various flavors of databases can be quite frustrating, especially when
you're learning a new language. Every database and every language has its own specific manner in

which to communicate, and PHP and MySQL are no different from the rest. Although you can certainly take the time to learn the connection strings that are required to talk to a database (see Chapter 10 for more information), you don't necessarily need to since Dreamweaver MX can handle it all for you. To illustrate this point, let's create a screen that shows the list of authors from our Books database. Follow these steps:

1. Create a new PHP page and add it to your PHP site. We're calling our PHP site PB_PHP.

TIP   For information on how to create a new site, see Chapter 2.

2. To create a new Dynamic PHP page, choose File ➤ New, and select the appropriate options, as shown in Figure 16.10.

FIGURE 16.10

Create a new PHP Dynamic Page.

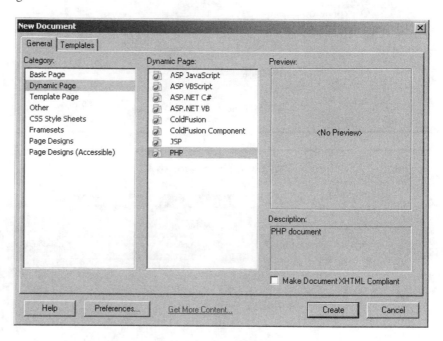

3. To create a link to the database, click the plus sign (+) on the Databases tab of the Application panel. You'll see that Dreamweaver MX offers only the MySQL connection since that is the only database support currently offered by Dreamweaver MX when using PHP.

4. Assuming you've created a MySQL database named PubBooks or are using the sample included on the CD, enter something similar to what you see in Figure 16.11. Give the connection a name, tell Dreamweaver MX what MySQL server to use, give the username and password, and then tell Dreamweaver MX which database to use.

5. Click the Test button to test your connection. (If your copy of MySQL and PHP are on the same computer, you can enter **localhost** as the server name.) If Dreamweaver MX can communicate with the database, it will give you a connection successful message like that in Figure 16.12.

FIGURE 16.11
We're building a
connection to our
MySQL table.

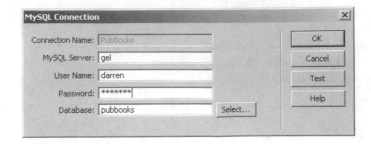

FIGURE 16.12
Our connection was
successful.

Now, we're ready to add the list of authors recordset to the Bindings tab of our Application panel.

1. Click the plus sign (+) on the Bindings tab, and choose Recordset to open the Recordset dialog box, which is shown in Figure 16.13.

FIGURE 16.13
We're going to select
the data, sorted by
last name, from the
tblauthors table.

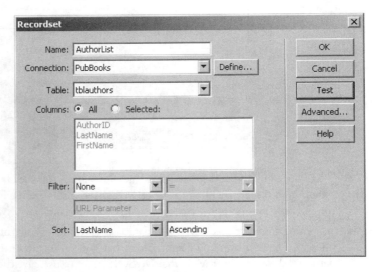

2. In the Name box, enter **AuthorList**, from the Connection drop-down list, select PubBooks, and from the Table drop-down list box, select tblauthors.

3. We want to sort by last name, so from the Sort drop-down list box, select LastName.

4. Click Test, and you should see a Test SQL Statement window similar to that in Figure 16.14, showing all the data from the table.

5. Click OK, and Dreamweaver MX will add some code to your pages that extracts the query.

FIGURE 16.14

We can test to make sure our query works before we leave the query configuration.

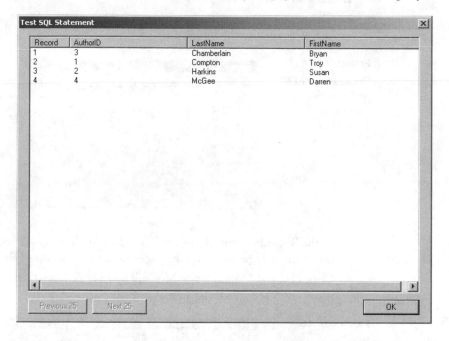

In our example, Dreamweaver MX added the following to the top of the page:

```php
<?php require_once('file:///J|/Inetpub/wwwroot/helpmedia/PB_php/
↳Connections/PubBooks.php'); ?>
<?php
mysql_select_db($database_PubBooks, $PubBooks);
$query_AuthorList = "SELECT * FROM tblauthors ORDER BY LastName ASC";
$AuthorList = mysql_query($query_AuthorList, $PubBooks) or die(mysql_error());
$row_AuthorList = mysql_fetch_assoc($AuthorList);
$totalRows_AuthorList = mysql_num_rows($AuthorList);
?>
```

and added the following to the bottom:

```php
<?php
mysql_free_result($AuthorList);
?>
```

This code tells PHP to load the connections setup file PubBooks.php. It then sets up the MySQL connection, builds the SQL string we want to execute, and gets the data. The last line frees up the connection so that PHP can return the used memory and other resources to the server. Isn't it nice that Dreamweaver MX handles this for us?

Now, we're ready to actually display the data. Currently our page is blank, so let's add a Dreamweaver MX Dynamic Table to the page. Follow these steps:

1. Click in your PHP page.
2. Choose Insert ➢ Application Objects ➢ Dynamic Table to open the Dynamic Table dialog box, which is shown in Figure 16.15.

FIGURE 16.15

Dreamweaver MX guides us through creating our dynamic table.

3. In the Recordset drop-down list box, select AuthorList—it should already be selected since this is the only recordset on the page—and keep the rest of the defaults at this point.
4. Click OK, and Dreamweaver MX will add a table with a repeating region in your page. You should now see something similar to Figure 16.16.

FIGURE 16.16

We now have a repeating region within our table.

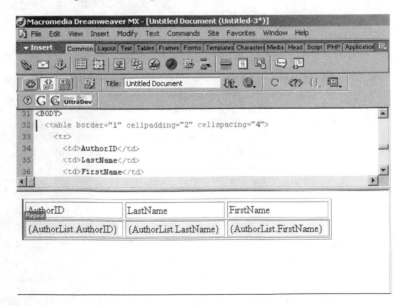

5. Add a header to your page, save it, and load it in your browser. You should see something similar to Figure 16.17, which shows our data list, sorted by last name, in an HTML table. And all we had to do was enter just a little bit of information. Dreamweaver MX makes it that easy.

FIGURE 16.17

We created our
dynamic PHP/
MySQL data page
with just a few
clicks and a little
information.

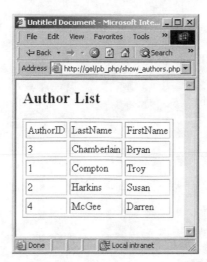

Summary

There's much, much more to PHP than we covered here. This brief introduction gives you just an inkling of what PHP can do and hopefully will give you enough information to spark your interest to learn more about PHP. Once you get into it, you'll find that PHP truly is a powerful web-development language. And as we covered here, since it's part of the open-source movement, it promises to only get better and more powerful and should be around for quite a long time. Remember, you can learn more about PHP at the PHP website (www.php.net) or at www.zend.net.

Chapter 17

Database and System Security for the Internet

SECURITY: "FREEDOM FROM RISK or danger; safety." It's a wonderful idea, isn't it? Unfortunately, 100 percent security doesn't exist, especially on the Internet. There is no such thing as a *secure* computer network, only *difficult-to-break-into* networks. And the Internet is a network of networks. As long as computers are linked together, there will be people who try to look at someone else's files. The latest and greatest security protocols are effective only until someone cracks them.

So, with that delightful thought in mind, what can you do to make sure your system is difficult to break into? Plenty. But you'll have to take the time to learn a tremendous amount about how networks operate, how TCP/IP (Transmission Control Protocol/Internet Protocol, the language of the Internet) works, how your operating system security works, how . . . you get the picture? Hundreds of companies out there focus on nothing but computer security—there's that much to learn and more.

But you don't need to be daunted by these seemingly horrific and negative statements. The average user can do quite a lot to make their computer challenging to those who would like to gain unapproved access. And if you have a bit of network understanding, you can take even more measures to keep a network in working order. This chapter will give you an overview of system security and a few tips on the steps you can take to keep your web server and database server safe from prying eyes in the age of the Internet. This chapter covers the following topics:

◆ Types of threats
◆ Protecting your intellectual property
◆ Protecting your web server
◆ Protect your database
◆ Using Dreamweaver MX to apply security to your pages

Types of Threats

Numerous threats can wreak havoc on your computer system. When people think of securing their computer systems, many think that they just need to protect themselves from computer viruses or hackers. They tend to forget that there's also an intrusion route through their own office, either intentional or accidental. Types of internal and external threats include:

Intentional threats   Computer viruses, theft, hacking (or cracking), vandalism, arson

Natural threats   Floods, fire, lightning, tornadoes, and earthquakes

Accidents   Lost passwords, lost product keys and serial numbers, spilled liquids, deletion of files

These are just a small sample of the types of threats around. To protect your computer system, you must take precautions to prevent or deal with all of them.

Protect Your Intellectual Property

The many facets of protecting your data include locking down the network as well as just making sure that poor programming won't corrupt it. But here we're talking about the data as a whole—the data, code, and supporting files as an investment piece of intellectual property. Following a few simple guidelines will help make sure that your current set of data is safe.

Back Up Your Data

Back up your data regularly. This includes not only your data files, but also the programs you use to create the data. You don't necessarily have to back up the program from the server itself, although you'll automatically save configuration files if you do. But you should make backup copies of the CDs or disks that contain the software you need to run your business. There may be legal limitations and liabilities for doing this, so be sure to read your software license. But most software vendors these days allow you to make a personal backup for use so that you can store the original away for safekeeping. System administrators should always use the backup copy when installing software on various machines and save the original in case the backup gets corrupted.

You can back up your data in many ways, including using software that splits your backups across CDs to multi-tape machines that grab the data from across the network. Figure 17.1 shows a sample of the Backup utility that ships with Windows 2000. It allows you to back up files, even across a network, but is limited in that it doesn't work across multiple media or back up SQL Server. If you have a large amount of data to back up, you might want to invest in a more automated type of backup system. Multitape backup systems rotate the tapes automatically based on a schedule you set to make sure they save all your data.

Some companies provide backup services via the Internet. Using a secure, generally Point-to-Point Protocol (PPP), you send your files and data on a scheduled basis to an offsite facility that takes care of creating a backup tape. Should you need access to the backup, you call the company, and someone brings you a tape, or you can download your files across the Internet, just as you sent them.

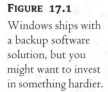

FIGURE 17.1

Windows ships with a backup software solution, but you might want to invest in something hardier.

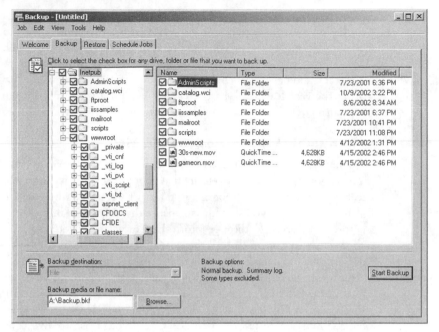

Test the Backup

Pat yourself on the back if you already back up your files regularly. But see if you get two pats—do you periodically test the backup to ensure its integrity? We've heard many horror stories of system administrators not being able to restore a backup set because the backup device had a flaw that prevented the making of accurate copies. Just because the text on the screen says "Backup Complete," doesn't necessarily mean you'll be able to restore from the backup. Backup tapes can lose their optimal tension over time, or they just wear out. Sometimes, backup software is simply buggy and may have a problem with the restore procedure.

To prevent adding your name to the victim list of failed restorations, immediately test the restoration capabilities of any new backup software or device you obtain. And you should periodically spot-check restoration from tapes, CDs, or whatever media you use for backups. Likewise, test the restoration capabilities of any online service you may employ. You don't really want to take another company's word that their software works without testing it, do you? You know, that old "trust, but verify" adage?

Keep Offsite Copies of the Backup

Kudos to you for implementing a backup plan in order to keep your data secure. You've guaranteed that you have backup copies of your critical files and software if disaster strikes and you need to restore the data. But suppose something happens to the office building—fire, flood, tornado—are your backup copies safe? Unless you're already storing your backup copies off site, you probably can't truthfully answer yes to that question.

Keeping copies of your backup media off site helps protect you in the event of catastrophic disaster. If the office burns to the ground, you've at least got a copy of your data you could port to another computer or server and be up and running with as little data loss as possible. Set up a schedule to store backup media off site, either with someone in-house whom you trust implicitly or with a company who will pick up your backup media regularly. Generally, companies that warehouse backup media as their business have fireproofed storage facilities, are bonded against disasters, and have great credibility. If you find one in the yellow pages, ask for a list of references, or, at the very least, call the Better Business Bureau to find out more about the company before you turn over your important data to them.

Thoroughly Wipe or Destroy Old Media

Obviously, you don't want other companies gaining access to your data, especially if they're competitors. You're going to take steps to ensure that your information is secure while it's on your servers. You need to carry this diligent behavior one step further to include when the information isn't on your servers. What we mean is, you should also ensure that any failed or replaced media are wiped clean of data before you dispose of them or return them or whatever you do with them. Just because a hard drive crashes doesn't mean that all the data on every sector of the disk is gone. It just means that the drive won't work in your computer any longer. If you plan on throwing the disk away, you'll either want to completely destroy the disk (take it apart, smash it, burn it) and scatter its parts across trash bins or wipe it with a bulk-magnetic eraser, also known as degaussing it. Just as an accountant will shred confidential documents, destroy your confidential files when the media on which they're housed must be destroyed. You don't want your trash to give away your company secrets, right?

TIP   Degaussers come in many shapes and sizes. They also have varying magnetic field strengths. You'll find degaussers that can handle video tapes, metal tapes, backup tape cartridges, and even complete hard disks. As you might expect, the prices for these machines range from anywhere less than $100 to several thousand dollars. Some companies offer degaussing services, however, at relatively inexpensive prices.

Protect Your Web Server

Protecting your web server is of the utmost importance in the age of the Internet. Hackers, crackers, computer viruses, and other malicious little beasts are out there trying to gain entry into whatever system they can. A vulnerable web server is just too easy an opportunity for these types of attackers to pass up. Fortunately, you can take steps to help keep your system secure.

Protect Your Web Server from Internal Mishaps

You may be surprised to learn that you need to protect your web server from internal forces. After all, anything internal is supposed to be safe, right? Again, we get into that reduce-the-possibility-of-accidents mode. Internally, you have developers who have access to the web server. If your security model isn't tight, you may have people who aren't developers who have access to the web server and its directories. Although the former isn't as bad as the latter, both open the possibility for disaster.

When it comes to server permissions and rights, give only those who need them the least amount of privilege they need to do their job. This means that you restrict rights to those groups and individuals who need them. Accounting doesn't need access to the web server's live directory. And developers don't usually need access to the accounting package folders. Following that logic, all your developers probably don't need access to the live web server, but they do need access to the development server.

After a long, hard shift of programming while trying to meet a tight deadline, a mapped drive to the live folder looks an awfully lot like any other folder, as you can see in Figure 17.2. The figure looks like any other folder view; which is exactly the point. We could have accidentally overwritten or deleted a folder on the live server if we weren't alert.

FIGURE 17.2

A mapped drive to the live server can be dangerous unless you're very alert

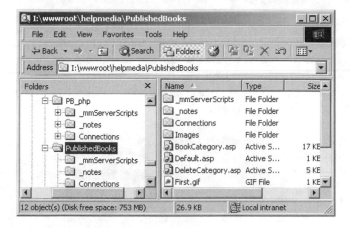

TIP   A good rule of thumb that you should adopt before installing new software or launching a new version of your website is back up the old version and data first! You don't want to accidentally lose updates to your tables or a tweak that someone made on the live site (against policy, mind you, but a tweak that works) that didn't make it to development code. Plus, in case something goes wrong and the new version doesn't work as you expect, you can replace it quickly with a backup. Making a backup of a website generally involves copying only the website folder and its database. So make sure you include this step in your new-version-release policy.

If you need to delegate responsibilities and need one or more developers to move files live on a regular basis, give those one or two developers security rights and permissions to do so. Remove the possibility of accidental deletion or overwriting of the files by disallowing access to everyone else. Remember, you generally want to give everyone the least amount of privileges with which they can accomplish their job. The "least privilege rule" may make you seem like an inflexible controller, but when it comes to securing your live web presence, a little explanation about why the rule is in place generally assuages any concerns your colleagues may have.

Protect Your Web Server from External Attacks

Needless to say, a greater number of possible attacks lurk outside your office than inside. New methods by which hackers, crackers, and computer viruses gain access are revealed almost weekly. With more than 60,000 identified computer viruses out there in Net land, you will learn that a good antivirus scanner is your friend if you don't already know it. You'll also come to find that a properly configured firewall will be your first defense against unauthorized intrusion. But one of your first tasks is to make sure you have the latest patches and security fixes for the operating system you use.

Operating systems are complex pieces of software. With hundreds of millions of lines of code, there are going to be weaknesses somewhere. (After all, humans wrote the software, and humans make errors.) Even though software companies run extensive beta tests on their software, invariably there will be flaws and security holes somewhere that a cracker will find and exploit. Once flaws are discovered, software companies are generally quick to fix them and release patches to their systems that plug these holes.

NOTE   Patches are files that you can usually download or receive on a CD that fix flaws in a piece of software without your having to reinstall the complete piece of software again. Patches generally don't interfere with how you've configured your software, which usually makes application of the patch seamless and trouble free.

Companies, and open-source movements as well, have tried to make patches easily accessible. For example, Microsoft even has an automated patching system called Windows Update to which they built a link in Internet Explorer, shown in Figure 17.3, that you can access from the Tools menu. When you launch Windows Update, your browser takes to you windowsupdate.com, the Windows Update site, shown in Figure 17.4.

FIGURE 17.3

Microsoft has made it quick and easy to get patches through Internet Explorer.

FIGURE 17.4

Windows Update will scan your system and report the patches that are available for your system.

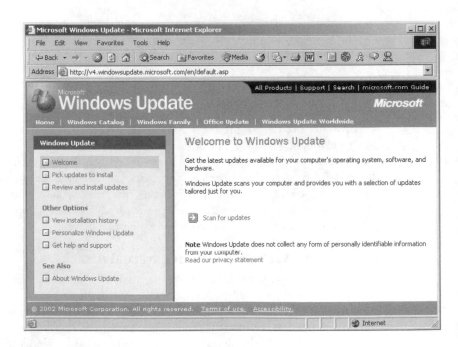

Sun has patches available for the Sun Linux products available at their Sun Linux Support page, shown in Figure 17.5 and found at `http://sunsolve.sun.com/patches/linux`.

Apple has patches for OS X on their support page—see Figure 17.6—found at `www.apple.com/support`. Regardless of the operating system you use, always obtain and apply the latest patches regularly.

FIGURE 17.5

You can find Sun's offering of patches for Linux at their patches site.

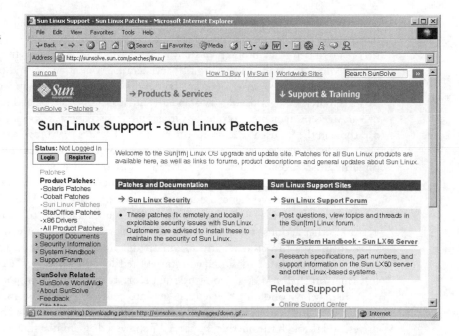

FIGURE 17.6

Apple also has downloadable updates for its easy-to-use operating system.

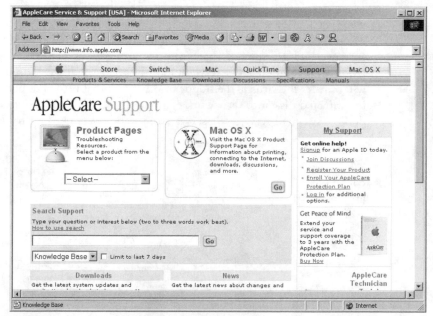

Install a Good, Industry-Standard Antivirus Program

A networked computer without an antivirus scanner is like an automobile without headlights: sure you can operate the machine without them, but it's dangerous, and you're probably going to crash hard if you do it for long. As we mentioned, more than 60,000 documented computer viruses are floating around on the Internet. Everything from Melissa to Code Red is still alive out there; it's just that with new patches to operating systems and programs that prevent their exploits, along with antivirus scanners, they're not much of an inconvenience any longer. Naturally, new viruses frequently crop up (according to Trend Micro, more than 400 a month) and demand your attention and treatment. To protect your computer systems and servers, you can take some basic steps to remain virus-free.

First, purchase a good, industry-standard antivirus program such as Trend Micro's suite of products or McAfee's or Symantec's products. Other antivirus scanners are available, but these products are the top three in the industry. Each suite offers various features that protect your entire enterprise, as well as the individual desktop. They're highly customizable, and some even provide informative reports on virus attack attempts, desktops in the enterprise that have been infected, and so forth. If you only need to protect a single machine, obtain the individual desktop version of the antivirus software.

Generally, you can configure the antivirus software, such as Trend Micro's PC-cillin, to automatically clean viruses from files when it finds one. If PC-cillin is unable to clean the file, you can tell it to perform other actions such as delete the file or quarantine it so that you can deal with the file later. Quarantining a file prevents any automatic deletion of what may be an important file that just happened to get infected. Once you know the file is infected, you can take steps to extract the information that you need from the file before removing it from your system.

You may be wondering how viruses get into your computer system. Code Red debuted the first virus that exploited every known method of spreading infection—through e-mail, through networked drives, and through the Internet. Figure 17.7 shows a diagram that illustrates potential security breaks. Many computers connect to your server internally. The server is communicating with the Internet using TCP/IP and retrieving e-mail, browser pages, and so forth. You need a virus scanner that can protect all these points of entry into your network. You need protection not only from the Internet, but also for each machine on your network. Your colleagues may be transferring files from work to home and vice versa in order to get their work done. An infected home computer will transfer the virus to the floppy or other disk that is used to port the files. Once the user sticks the infected disk into their work computer, your network could become infected. This is why desktops, e-mail servers, file servers, and web servers need up-to-date antivirus protection.

FIGURE 17.7
Viral infection can come from many sources.

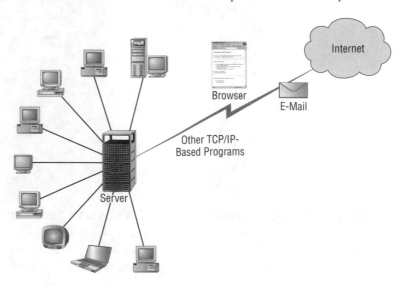

Browser

Internet

E-Mail

Other TCP/IP-
Based Programs

Server

Make Sure You Have a Good, Properly Configured Firewall in Place

Firewalls are so named because they help keep something from spreading, much like an architectural firewall keeps fire from spreading to other parts of an inflamed building. They consist of either software or hardware devices that sit between your system and the Internet, much as Figure 17.8 shows. Firewalls mask your system from the Internet and allow you to halt communication across certain TCP/IP ports and your network. Hackers, crackers, and viruses can take advantage of various ports and exploit their weaknesses in certain operating systems and in web and mail servers.

FIGURE 17.8

A typical firewall placement

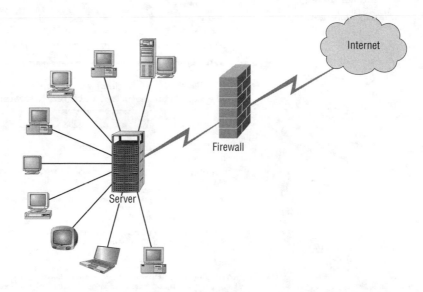

Ports, in reference to the Internet, are basically communication points (think of phone lines) that allow various types of programs to work across the Internet. For example, port 80 is the common HTTP (Hypertext Transfer Protocol) port that allows you to see a page when you load your browser. Port 21 is commonly used for FTP (File Transfer Protocol), and port 25 is used for e-mail. And, of course, many other ports are in use.

There are as many configurations of firewalls and network systems as there are companies that employ them. Some use two or more firewalls, depending on their server configuration and which groups need access to the varied TCP/IP ports available. For example, company policy may be that no one should be able to play RealPlayer files, and the system administrator blocks those ports through the firewall. However, marketing may need access to those types of streaming media files in order to keep an eye on the competitor. A different firewall configuration would allow one group access to ports restricted from the company as a whole.

Following along these lines, to really lock down your network, turn off all unneeded ports. That is, you might want to close off every port and just open those that you know you'll use, such as ports 80, 25, 110, and so forth. You'll need a good understanding of how ports and firewalls work before you start configuring them. This job, needless to say, is typically left to your network or system administrator.

For those of you who are interested in finding out whether your system is open and vulnerable, check out Gibson Research Center's Shields Up page, found at http://grc.com. The GRC has made a name for itself pointing out and offering workarounds for security and privacy flaws in Internet software. Figure 17.9 shows the beginning of a sample result screen of the Shields Up test. Your computer's IP address will normally appear in the center of the page where we've masked our IP. You'll get feedback on what ports might be open and what it might mean to your security if they are.

FIGURE 17.9

Gibson Research Center offers a quick-check security tool that will give you an idea of how secure your computer is.

Shields UP!!

NanoProbe Technology Internet Security Testing for Windows Users
by Steve Gibson, Gibson Research Corporation.

Shields UP! is checking **YOUR** computer's Internet connection security . . . currently located at IP:

Please Stand By. . .

Attempting connection to your computer. . .
Shields UP! is now attempting to contact the **Hidden Internet Server** within your PC. It is likely that no one has told you that your own personal computer may now be functioning as an **Internet Server** with neither your knowledge nor your permission. And that it may be serving up all or many of your personal files for reading, writing, modification and even deletion by anyone, anywhere, on the Internet!

Your Internet port 139 does not appear to exist!
One or more ports on this system are operating in FULL STEALTH MODE! Standard Internet behavior requires port connection attempts to be answered with a success or refusal response. Therefore, only an attempt to connect to a nonexistent computer results in no response of either kind. **But YOUR computer has DELIBERATELY CHOSEN NOT TO RESPOND** (that's very cool!) which represents advanced computer and port stealthing capabilities. A machine configured in this fashion is well hardened to Internet NetBIOS attack and intrusion.

Protect Your Database

Now that you've locked down your system and have a method for keeping prying eyes away from files and servers that they shouldn't see, let's take a look at how to protect the database itself. You'll want to follow the same procedures we outlined earlier when it comes to giving people rights to the database directory. Remember, the least-privilege rule applies to all aspects of security. Unless someone specifically needs access to the database, remove access rights to it. Your web server user account should be given access rights to the database, of course; otherwise it won't be able to modify the database through your website. That is, your site wouldn't be able to accept things such as user registrations.

The website should be open to the world to view (if indeed it is a public website), so your web server account must have rights to display the folder's files through TCP/IP. Your web server software typically sets this permission scheme for you, so you probably won't have to worry about manipulating the security settings for your web folder. Many folks new to web development tend to put their database in the website files folder, like that shown in Figure 17.10. Don't do this!

When you place your database inside your web server, you make it available for downloading and other attacks. Your database should live in its own folder or directory, preferably on its own server, as shown in Figure 17.11.

FIGURE 17.10
Many people new to web development make the mistake of putting their database in the same folder as their web files.

FIGURE 17.11
Your database should at least be in its own secure directory or folder, if not its own server.

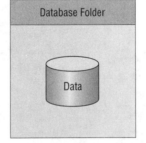

Using Dreamweaver MX to Apply Security to Your Pages

At this point, we've covered how to secure your computer system and the database. That portion of security doesn't involve Dreamweaver MX, obviously, but is important. Now let's explore adding security to your individual web pages—that is, restricting access to your site and your site's pages by allowing only users who have the proper permissions to access your pages.

Create the User Authentication Page

Before you can properly secure or restrict access to your website, you need to know who is trying to log in. Dreamweaver MX provides a quick method for creating a login page and verifying that the user is who they claim to be. Using the User Authentication Server Behavior, you simply point to your database, choose a couple of field names, and then save your new login page. Let's take a look at how to do it.

First, you need a database that contains the proper user information along with username and password fields. For our purposes, we're going to use the tblBorrowers table from the Books database. This table includes two database fields with the names of *Username* and *Password*. If you're not using the sample database on the CD, make sure your database has fields corresponding to the username and password information. (For this example, we're assuming you've already established a database connection through the Databases tab of the Application panel. For more on how to do this, see Chapter 2.)

Next, let's create a simple form with two text fields in which the user will type a username and password. Figure 17.12 shows our version containing a table with the two text fields appropriately named. You'll also want to create two more pages, one to which the successful login will take the user and the page that the unsuccessful login presents. We're calling ours `Welcome.asp` and `LoginFailed.asp`, respectively.

FIGURE 17.12

Although this form isn't pretty, it contains the required elements for a login page.

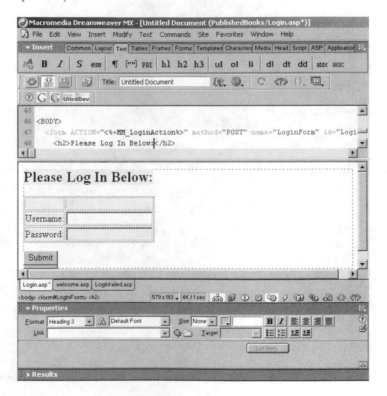

Next, we're going to add the User Authentication Server Behavior to this page. Just as with the other behaviors in Dreamweaver MX, adding this behavior pops up a window into which you specify the proper field names and so forth. To add the behavior, click the plus sign (+) on the Server Behaviors tab of the Application panel, as we did in Figure 17.13, and choose User Authentication ➤ Log In User to open the Log In User dialog box shown in Figure 17.14. We've filled ours out, as you can see.

TIP *Dreamweaver MX doesn't inherently include the User Authentication Server Behavior for PHP (Hypertext Preprocessor) or ASP.NET. However, from the Macromedia Exchange for Dreamweaver you can download a PHP user authentication behavior created by Felice Di Stefano. Log in to the Macromedia Exchange and search for PHP User Authentication. For more information about adding extensions to Dreamweaver MX, see Chapter 24.*

FIGURE 17.13

Dreamweaver MX lets you quickly build a login form.

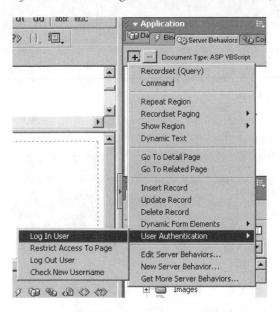

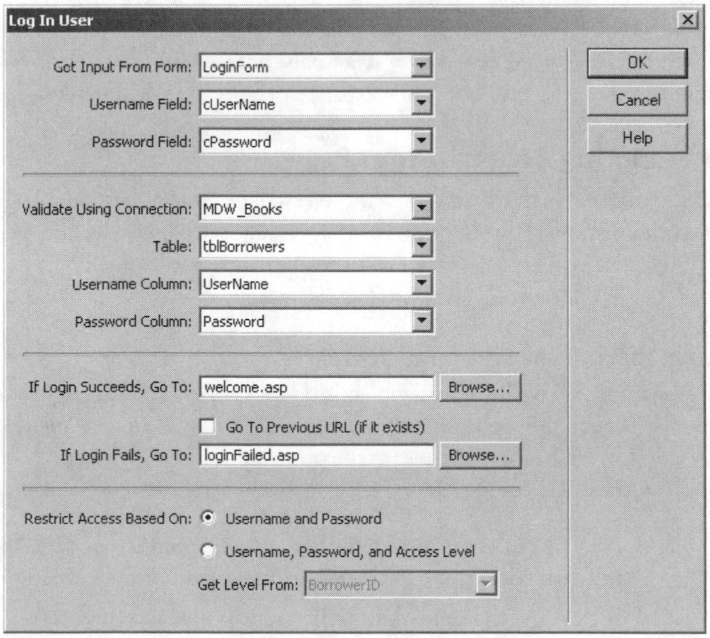

FIGURE 17.14

Choose the proper login options in the Log In User dialog box, and Dreamweaver MX will do the rest.

WARNING   *If you don't see User Authentication, you may first need to save your page with an extension so that Dreamweaver MX knows which language to use. Once you do, click the plus sign (+) on the Server Behaviors tab, and you should then see User Authentication. Dreamweaver MX doesn't show you some of the behaviors until it knows which type of page you're creating—ASP, ColdFusion, and so forth.*

Enter or choose the settings for the following fields:

Get Input From Form   Choose the form's name from this drop-down menu.

Username   Specify the text field on your form that corresponds to the username entry.

Password   Specify the text field on your form that corresponds to the password entry.

Validate Using Connnection   From this drop-down menu, you'll need to select the database connection that contains the table with username and password fields. When you do, Dreamweaver MX will look up the fields and add the fields to the next three drop-down menus.

Table   Choose the proper table from this drop-down list.

Username Column   Choose the table column that contains the usernames.

Password Column   Choose the table column that contains the passwords.

If Login Succeeds, Go To   Enter the name of the page the user should see if they log in successfully.

If Login Fails, Go To   Enter the name of the page the user should see if their login fails.

After you complete the fields, click OK and save your page. That's all there is to creating a login page. Test your page by attempting a login with a proper username and password and then with an improper set. You should see that indeed your pages redirect just as you'd hoped. That was easy!

Suppose that you need to restrict page access based on security levels. Dreamweaver MX allows you to quickly build that kind of behavior as well. We'll explore that next.

Restricting Access to Your Page

Once a user logs in, you might want to restrict them to particular pages. Perhaps this person shouldn't see administration pages, or maybe they should see pages that only pertain to them. Dreamweaver MX will let you quickly build pages that restrict access in two ways. You can simply test whether the user has logged in, or you can restrict access based on varying levels you set.

JUST TESTING FOR LOGGED-IN STATUS

In Chapter 20, we'll be creating an Update Category Data page. We're going to apply access rights to that page in our next couple of examples. First, we'll add the method for just testing logged-in status. We do this in the same manner as the prior method we mentioned—through the Server Behaviors tab. Follow these steps:

1. Click the plus sign (+) on the Server Behaviors tab on the Application panel and choose User Authentication to open the Restrict Access To Page dialog box, shown in Figure 17.15.

2. For this first example, choose the first option, and then enter into the If Access Denied text box the name of the page to which the user should be taken if they don't have rights to view the page.

FIGURE 17.15

You can test for whether the user is logged in or whether the user meets specified level criteria.

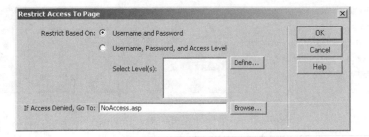

3. Click OK.

4. Save the page, and then test it.

If you've previously logged in, the server may remember that and let you in. So we'll build a log-out page next. (We'll get to restricting access by levels in a moment.) If you weren't allowed in the Book Category page, you should be taken to your NoAccess.asp page, as we were, as you can see in Figure 17.16.

FIGURE 17.16

Our login failed, so we see our No Access page.

CREATING A LOG OUT PAGE

The Dreamweaver MX login and access right behaviors work by using session variables. Session variables are special web server variables that keep track of a user's time on your site. Session variables only exist while the user is logged in and active. If the user leaves the site or doesn't perform any action for a period of time dictated by the web server (and the system administrator), the server erases the session variables and effectively logs the user out.

To create a log out page and clear the user's session variables, follow these steps:

1. Create a new page called Logout.asp or something appropriate.

2. To add the Log Out User Server Behavior, click the plus sign (+) button in the Server Behaviors tab of the Application panel and choose User Authentication ➢ Log Out User to open a dialog box similar to that in Figure 17.17.

FIGURE 17.17
Dreamweaver MX
will automatically
create a log out script
for you.

You can have the log out procedure execute when the page loads by clicking Page Loads or, as we did, by having Dreamweaver MX add a Log Out link to the page for us.

1. Enter a page that the user should be taken to when they log out, typically back to the login screen, and click OK.

2. Save your page and load `logout.asp`. You should see something similar to that in Figure 17.18.

FIGURE 17.18
Our log out screen
will remove our
session variables and
take us back to the
login screen.

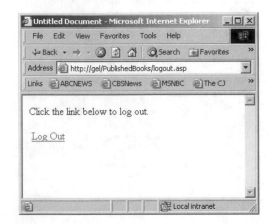

Once you log out, try to load the BookCategory page again. The system shouldn't let you in because you've just logged out. Now, suppose you want to allow people with administrator rights to access the BookCategory page, since they might want to make changes to the database, but you want to keep everyone else out. Dreamweaver MX will let you do that easily too.

RESTRICTING ACCESS BY LEVELS

Let's modify our BookCategory page and restrict user access rights by levels. To do that, we need to go back to the actual login page, because the access rights are pulled from the same table that contains the username and password. Follow these steps:

1. Go back to your login screen and double-click the Log In User Server Behavior that you added earlier to open the behavior so that you can modify what you've already entered.

   This time, we're going to select username, password, and access level, as you can see in Figure 17.19.

2. From the Get Level From drop-down list box, select the field that contains your user security levels. We added a field called SecurityLevel that contains Admin, Power, and User as the varying values among our users, so we select the SecurityLevel field.

3. Click OK and save the page.

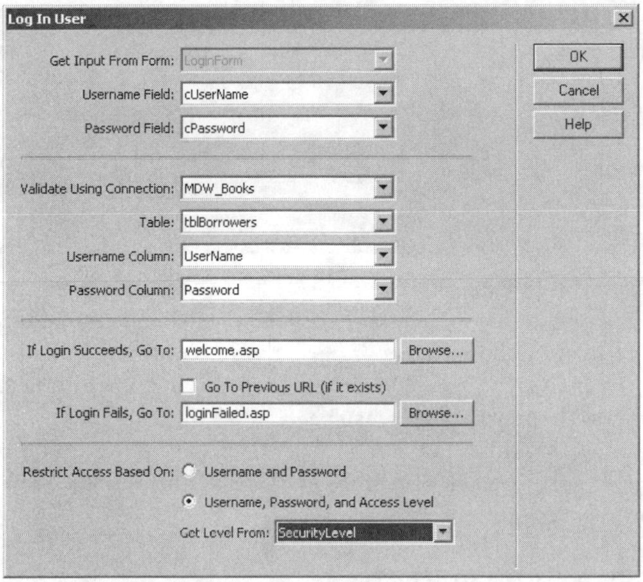

FIGURE 17.19

This time, we're going to use security levels in our login process.

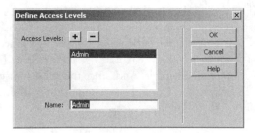

4. Go back to your BookCategory page and double-click the Restrict Access To Page Server Behavior so that you can modify it.

5. Select the Username, Password, and Access Level links.

6. Click the Define button to open the Define Access Levels dialog box, as shown in Figure 17.20.

FIGURE 17.20

You specify the levels to which you want to give access to this page.

7. Add the levels that you want to give access to by typing them in the Name text box and clicking the plus sign (+).

The names that you enter here must already exist in the table you specified back in your login screen. For example, since we specified Admin, Power, and User as our varying levels of access, we have to enter any of those three levels here. If we enter a name that doesn't exist in the table, SuperUser, for example, the page won't let us have access. We're going to add Admin as the only level that should have access to this page.

1. Enter **admin**, and click OK. Now our Restrict Access To Page dialog box looks like that shown in Figure 17.21.

2. Save your page and log back in through your browser.

FIGURE 17.21
We've just given
Admin-level users
access to this page.

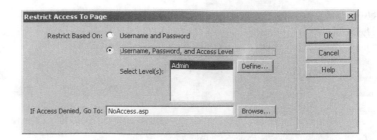

We're going to log in as Susan, since our database has Susan listed with a level of Power. When we try to load the BookCategory page, the system won't let us in, as it shouldn't. Now, log out and log in as Darren. Since Darren has the level of Admin in the database, we succeed when we try to access the BookCategory.asp page.

As you can see, Dreamweaver MX provides some powerful functionality with only a few mouse clicks and a small amount of typing. The User Authentication Server Behaviors provide an excellent way to apply security to your web pages.

ALLOWING A VISITOR TO REGISTER

Suppose you want users who don't have a login username and password to be able to register on the site as well. You'll need to make sure that usernames are unique among your users, and since you certainly don't want to manually check every name visitors could enter, you need to ensure that usernames are unique programmatically. Dreamweaver MX can help you with that as well, through the Check New Username Server Behavior.

Let's modify our system a bit to provide a smooth flow between our login, registration, and new username pages. We'll be adding the registration form to this mix, so let's start with it.

The registration page is basically just a form from which we'll insert data. The exception is that we'll add the Check New Username Server Behavior to this page as well. So let's start with an insert form, similar to that in Figure 17.22. We're adding fields to this form that correspond to the important user information from our table. And, since this table houses a security level as well, we're adding a default hidden field called Level that we're setting to the value of User.

After you create your form, follow these steps:

1. To add the Insert Record Server Behavior click the plus sign (+) on the Server Behaviors tab of the Application panel.

2. Choose Insert Record to open the Insert Record dialog box, as shown in Figure 17.23, and enter the appropriate information, making sure that the fields in Form Elements map correctly.

3. Click the plus sign (+), and choose User Authentication ➤ Check Username to open that the Check New Username dialog box, as shown in Figure 17.24.

4. From the Username Field drop-down list box, select the field that contains your username, and then enter a page that the user should see if the entered username is already on file.

The page we're using for the notice is called UsernameExists.asp and is rather simple, with just a notice and `<a href="javascript:history.go(-1)">go back</a>` as the link. The use of javascript should save the users' entries and let them simply reenter a username and password without having to retype all the other information. You can see our page in Figure 17.25.

FIGURE 17.22

Registration starts with an insert form.

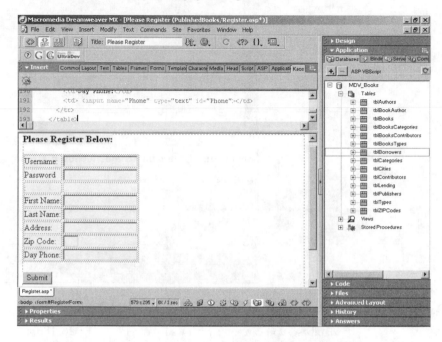

FIGURE 17.23

We use an Insert Record Server Behavior as the first step in our registration page.

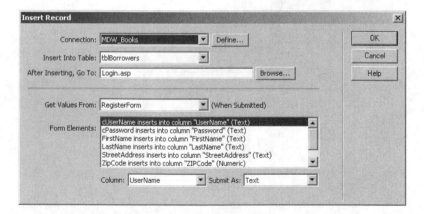

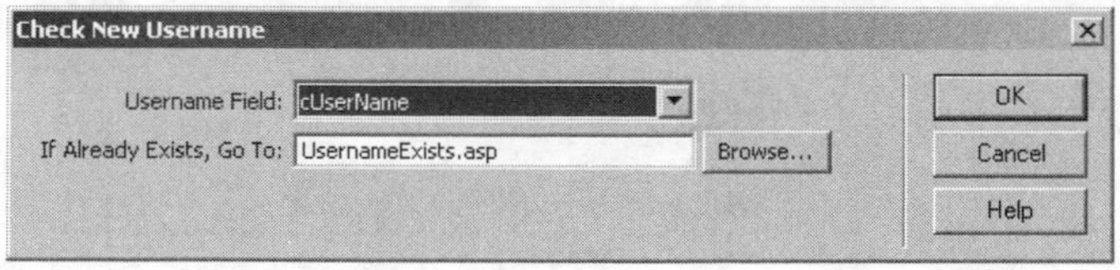

FIGURE 17.24

Specify your username field and the page the user should see if the username exists.

FIGURE 17.25

Our Username Exists notice page is rather simple, but includes a `javascript :history` link.

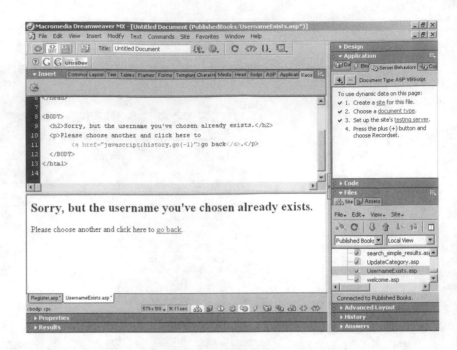

1. Test your page by entering information into the Registration form. If you're using our sample database, you can enter what we have in Figure 17.26. If not, enter some new user information then save it.

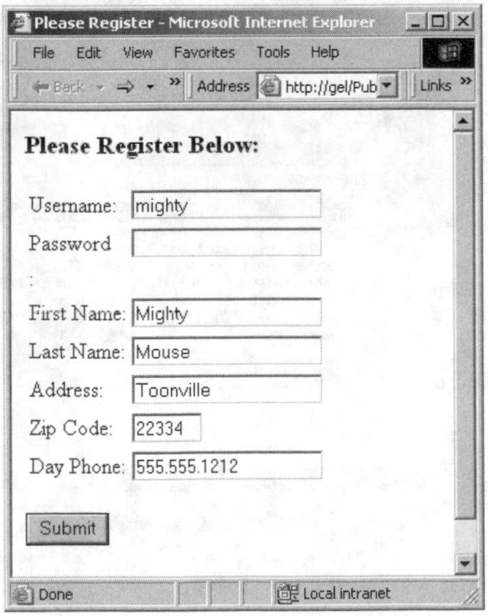

FIGURE 17.26

We're entering a "new" user's information.

2. Go back and reenter the same username to force a duplicate error. Click Submit, and you should see the notice shown in Figure 17.27.

FIGURE 17.27

Dreamweaver MX found our username to be duplicated, so it's sending us to our notification page.

FOR MORE INFORMATION

Network, database, and Internet security are the subjects of far too many books, magazines, online discussions, and so on to list here. A good comprehensive source from the publisher of this book is *Mastering Network Security* (2nd edition), by Chris Brenton and Cameron Hunt (Sybex, 2002). If you're implementing security in a Linux environment, check out *Linux Security (Craig Hunt Linux Library)*, by Ramón J. Hontañón (Sybex, 2001).

Summary

Security in terms of the Internet encompasses many aspects of computing. To create secure systems, you not only need to make sure only those with proper permissions get access to your website, but you must also look behind the scenes to the networking infrastructure. You must try to make the web server, database server, and indeed the entire enterprise as attack-proof as possible. We've given you a good start on securing your systems. But there's much, much more to security than we've covered. Make sure you have a security-minded network administrator, system administrator, and development team that stays abreast of the latest security threats, patches, and theories.

Part IV

Using and Manipulating the Data

In the following section, you'll learn how to:

◆ Work with Structured Query Language
◆ Get Data
◆ Build Update Forms
◆ Build Master Detail Forms
◆ Search
◆ Use Templates
◆ Add Dreamweaver MX Database Extensions

Chapter 18

Structured Query Language

As a web developer, you might not have any input in the design, maintenance, and administration of the database that supplies data to your website. However, not only will you need to access that database, you'll need to automate the process so visitors to your site can retrieve and perhaps even modify data. That's your job—to coordinate access to the data without really having any real influence over the design of the database. Sometimes your job is challenging.

The key to success is to talk to the database in a language it understands. That's where SQL comes into the picture. Structured Query Language (SQL) is the defacto language of relational databases. It doesn't matter one bit what relational database management system (RDBMS) was used to create the database because they all respond to you if you speak in a language they understand.

This chapter introduces SQL. You'll learn the basic statements and syntax that you'll need to communicate with most any relational database.

This chapter covers the following topics:

- ◆ What is SQL?
- ◆ Standardization
- ◆ Syntax and structure
- ◆ Using Data Manipulation Language to retrieve and modify data
- ◆ Using Data Definition Language to manage database objects
- ◆ SQL operators
- ◆ Delimiting and concatenating
- ◆ SQL Aggregate functions

What Is SQL?

SQL is a support language for relational databases, but it's much more. SQL is also the industry standard, which means dozens of vendors produce products—from desktop applications to the largest mainframe systems—that use SQL.

TIP *SQL Server, the subject of Chapter 8, is a relational database system that Microsoft distributes. It uses a vendor-specific version of SQL, known as Transact-SQL. SQL Server is not SQL; SQL is a language. If you're unfamiliar with database systems and languages, it can be easy to confuse the two because the names are similar. SQL is a language that almost all relational database systems support. SQL Server is an RDBMS.*

SQL is the language of choice for almost every relational database in use today because it provides a standardized method for storing and retrieving data. At this point, you're probably wondering just how one language can speak to so many systems.

A relational or SQL database is composed of tables that store data in a column/row format. Each system tracks these tables by indexing them in a sort of data dictionary or catalog that contains a list of all the tables in the database. The list also stores pointers to each table's location. The dictionary can store additional information as well, such as table definitions and even data specific to the database itself.

NOTE *Chapter 5 provides more information on relational databases and relational database theory.*

When you send a request to the database using SQL, the database locates the requested table in the dictionary—without any additional instructions from you. All you need to do is specify the name of the table, and the database will do the rest. SQL works independently of the internal structure of the database.

The database then processes the request, sometimes called a query—a term you have already run into many times in this book. In generic terms, a query is simply a question. In SQL terms, a *query* is a structured request to the database. You can think of a query as a type of sentence, with nouns, verbs, clauses, and predicates. For example, let's turn the English request, "Show me all the employees in the Employees table that live in the southwest region," into a query. The subject in this case is the database. The verb is, "show me." The phrase "in the Employees table" is a clause, and "that live in the southwest region" is a predicate. The resulting SQL statement resembles the following:

```
SELECT *
FROM Employees
WHERE Region = 'Southwest'
```

Processing the request usually entails returning data, which, in SQL terms, we call a view. A *view* can best be defined as a virtual table based on the parameters you passed to the database via your SQL statement.

A BIT OF SQL HISTORY

Chapter 5 includes a short discussion about Dr. E. F. Codd, who began the relational database revolution with his paper on relational database theory. At the time, Dr. Cobb worked for IBM as a researcher. On the strength of this paper, IBM created a new research group known as System/R. This group produced a relational database known as System/R, which eventually evolved into SQL/Data System (SQL/DS) and later DB2.

The support language written for and implemented with this new technology was called Structured English Query Language, or SEQUEL. That's why some developers pronounce SQL as *sequel*, instead of S-Q-L. You could say they're showing their age, but the truth is, they're exposing their experience. More than likely, these developers have been using SQL for a long time, or they were trained by someone who did. Eventually, the product was named SQL to avoid a legal conflict with another product whose name was pronounced *sequel*.

Standardization

Earlier, we mentioned that SQL was the industry standard for relational databases. Computer standards are adopted, coordinated, and maintained by the American National Standards Institute (ANSI), a privately run and not-for-profit organization. You can learn more about this organization at www.ansi.org. The International Organization for Standardization (ISO) and the U.S. government have also adopted SQL as the standard support language for relational database systems.

What standardization means is that software producers and developers have a universally agreed upon set of statements and syntax rules that they can quickly learn and apply to their own work. In a nutshell, if you know SQL, you can quickly learn how to communicate with almost any relational database.

ANSI published the first SQL standard in 1986. To date, the standard has been updated twice, in 1992 and again in 1998. Electronic copies of the 1992 and 1998 versions of these standards are available at http://webstore.ansi.org for $18.00 each. When searching for the standards, refer to the document number X3-135. If you prefer, you can purchase hard copies from American National Standards Institute, 1819 L Street, NW, Suite 600, Washington, DC 20036. Hard copies are, as a rule, expensive.

VENDOR DIALECTS

Despite standardization, many dialects of SQL exist. That's because software vendors expound on the standards by adding numerous customized features known as vendor-specific *extensions* to their proprietary versions. Consequently, every RDBMS that supports SQL offers its own brand, or dialect, of SQL. Generally, these extensions are available only through specialized code, which, of course, is specific and unique to the system. Standard SQL may be all you ever need, but make an effort to learn the system's extensions. Often, these extensions include specialized options and features that you might otherwise have to create on your own.

Syntax and Structure

Standard SQL is simple and straightforward. In fact, once you get the hang of it, you'll probably agree with most developers that it is the easiest language to learn and implement. The bulk of the language is composed of keywords, and learning how to arrange those keywords in the proper order is all you really have to master. The following is a list of a few grammar terms you'll see throughout this chapter:

Keyword   An individual word with a predefined meaning or purpose

Clause   A keyword complete with arguments

Statement   A complete request that the RDBMS can interpret

A SQL statement can be as simple as one keyword and an argument, but most have a little more to them than that. A basic statement generally takes the form of the following:

```
action argument FROM datasource WHERE condition
```

In this statement, `action` specifies the type of task or request being sent to the database, `argument` usually identifies the specific columns of data involved, `datasource` is a table or query that contains the data, and `condition` is a criteria expression that limits the data acted upon in the request.

NOTE SQL can do far more than just retrieve and modify data. SQL can create and delete tables, define indexes, define relationships, and so on. Most of these tasks are more administrative and aren't needed in the average data request from a website. In this chapter, we'll provide a more in-depth review of the standard SQL statements and syntax that you'll need to retrieve and modify data.

Using Data Manipulation Language to Retrieve and Modify Data

SQL performs many tasks, which we can categorize in two ways: manipulating data and modifying database objects. This chapter is mainly concerned with Data Manipulation Language (DML), the terminology that manages data by manipulating or acting upon it. You can think of DML as the data entry manager that performs the following tasks:

- Retrieves data
- Modifies and deletes existing data
- Adds new data

The DML statements we'll review in this section are the SELECT, SELECT INTO, UPDATE SET, DELETE, and INSERT INTO statements. All the examples in this chapter ignore security restrictions and assume you have permission to retrieve, change, insert, and even delete data. (Chapter 17 covers security restrictions.)

NOTE We'll use SQL Server's Query Analyzer to send SQL requests to one of the sample databases that come with SQL Server to process all our SQL statements. You can use any interface and database you like. The only stipulation is that you be somewhat familiar with the database's tables and fields and that system's unique requirements, especially in regard to delimiting data. For more information on delimiters, see the section on delimiters and concatenating later in this chapter.

Retrieving Data with a *SELECT* Statement

By far, the most frequently used SQL statement is the SELECT statement. It's easily the workhorse of the entire language because it retrieves data for viewing so that you can browse and even analyze data, depending on the format in which you present the data.

The SELECT statement combines with five clauses to specify and limit the data that's retrieved using the following syntax:

```
SELECT ALL | DISTINCT column1[As alias[, column2...]]| *
FROM datasource
[WHERE condition]
[GROUP BY column1[, column2...]]
[HAVING condition]
[ORDER BY column1[, column2...] [ASC | DESC]]
```

The FROM clause is the only clause that's mandatory. The ALL predicate is the default and assumed if omitted, but not optional. You can include it for documentation purposes if you like. The following examples start with the simplest form of the statement and add clauses to restrict the data that's retrieved or how it's presented.

TIP The asterisk character (*) used as an argument in the SELECT clause retrieves all the columns in the underlying datasource. Avoid using this character unless you truly need all the columns, because the more data you retrieve, the slower the query's performance.

THE SIMPLEST *SELECT*

In its simplest form, the SELECT statement retrieves all the columns from all the records in a table using just the mandatory FROM clause

```
SELECT *
FROM datasource
```

For example, the following statement retrieves all the columns and records from the Employees table in the Northwind sample database that comes with SQL Server 2000:

```
SELECT *
FROM Employees
```

The results are shown in Figure 18.1, although we can't show the complete records, since some of the columns scroll off the screen. (Notice that we chose Northwind in the database drop-down list.) You'll seldom retrieve an entire table's worth of data.

FIGURE 18.1

Use SELECT to retrieve data.

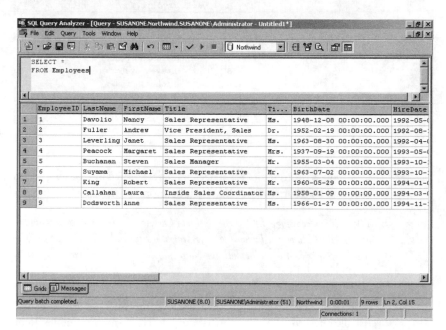

NOTE *Throughout this chapter, we'll use the same general format conventions for SQL statements. First, all keywords will use uppercase. Second, most clauses appear on individual lines, which makes the statements more readable. SQL ignores line breaks. Third, some developers include a semicolon character (;) at the end of each statement. SQL Server doesn't require this, so we've omitted it from our examples. Check with your system's documentation to determine whether the semicolon is required. Some systems will accept multiple statements. When this is the case, you will definitely need the semicolon to separate the statements, but we won't be working with anything that complex in this chapter.*

The AS Clause

You're not stuck using column names from the supporting database. Using an AS clause you can create a temporary name, or alias, for the column. The clause is optional, and when it is omitted, SQL uses the column's name. To modify a column name use the syntax

```
SELECT column1 [AS alias[, column2...]]
```

Figure 18.2 shows the concatenated first and last name entries in a column named EmployeeName:

```
SELECT EmployeeID, FirstName + ' ' LastName AS EmployeeName
```

FIGURE 18.2

Use the AS clause to create an alias for any column.

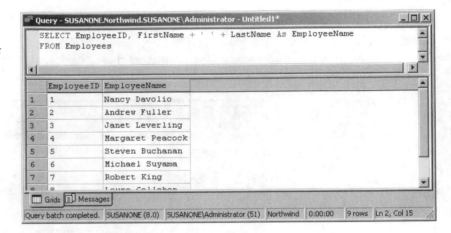

If you want to include a space character in the alias, be sure to enclose the alias in brackets ([ ]) if required by your system. (We include more information on concatenation later in this chapter.)

TIP   *If you're using ADO (ActiveX Data Objects) to carry on a conversation with the supporting database, you might also use the Field object. Furthermore, you might use the Field object's Name property to return that field's name. If you use the AS keyword to set an alias, the Name property will return the alias, not the field's actual name.*

The FROM Clause

The FROM clause specifies the datasource from which the SELECT statement will retrieve data. This clause usually refers to one table or query, but can refer to multiple tables. When it does, use the following syntax:

```
FROM onetable jointype manytable ON onetable.primarykey = manytable.foreignkey
```

(For more information on the types of joins, see Chapter 5.)

LIMIT DATA BY SPECIFYING COLUMNS

The first statement (in "The Simplest SELECT" section) uses the asterisk (*) to retrieve all the data from the Employees table, but you'll seldom want to work with that much data at one time. The first step to limiting data is to limit the columns by identifying only the columns you need in the following form:

```
SELECT column1[, column2...]
FROM datasource
```

When using this form, you must specify at least one column. If you include a list, separate each with a comma character (,). List the columns in the order you want them displayed in the resultset. The following statement returns the EmployeeID, LastName, and FirstName columns from the Employees table:

```
SELECT EmployeeID, LastName, FirstName
FROM Employees
```

The results are shown in Figure 18.3.

FIGURE 18.3

Limit the retrieved data by specifying columns.

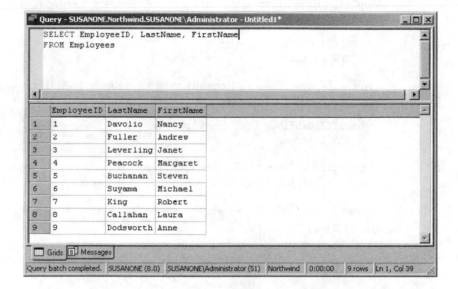

SQL PREDICATES

By default, the SELECT statement returns all records because SQL assumes the ALL predicate (the default). The two following statements return the same records:

```
SELECT ALL * FROM Employees
SELECT * FROM Employees
```

In contrast, the DISTINCT predicate limits the results to only unique values in the field that follows its use:

```
SELECT DISTINCT column1[, column2...]
```

This predicate returns a list of unique values in *column1* based on the entire SELECT statement. Additional columns are considered, but the elimination of duplicate values takes precedence from left to right; so additional columns should have no effect on the values returned from column1. For instance, the following statement

```
SELECT DISTINCT City
FROM Customers
```

returns a unique list of 69 cities from the Customers table in Northwind. The statement

```
SELECT DISTINCT City, Country
FROM Customers
```

returns the same unique list of 69 cities, but also lists the country for each. The DISTINCT predicate eliminates records only if the combined values create a duplicate record.

This predicate presents a chicken or the egg scenario because the first column is already unique; so it's impossible to create a duplicate record. This doesn't seem important if you're really eliminating duplicates from left to right. However, it can produce unexpected results, depending on the order of the columns. For instance, the statement

```
SELECT DISTINCT Country
FROM Customers
```

returns the unique list of 21 countries shown in Figure 18.4. If you include the City column in the recordset but add it to the right of Country instead of to the left

```
SELECT DISTINCT Country, City
FROM Customers
```

the unique list climbs to 69, as shown in Figure 18.5. As you can see, the leftmost column, Country, is not a unique list. This may or may not be what you want.

FIGURE 18.4

The DISTINCT predicate returns a unique list of 21 countries.

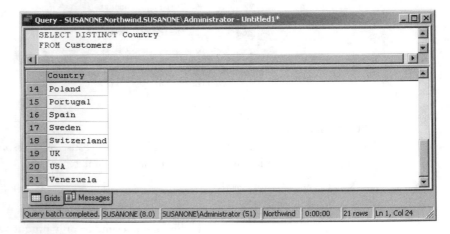

WARNING   *The* DISTINCT *predicate returns a recordset that cannot be updated. That means you can't modify the underlying data via the query results. For more information on updateable queries, see "Updateable Queries" later in this chapter.*

NOTE   *Access provides the* DISTINCTROW *predicate, which eliminates duplicates based on all the columns in the datasource. The* DISTINCT *predicate considers only the columns specified in the* SELECT *statement. You can use the asterisk character (*) with* DISTINCTROW.

FIGURE 18.5

The DISTINCT predicate returns unique records, not just values.

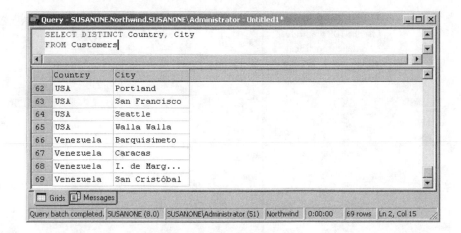

The TOP predicate is optional and returns the top *n* rows or top *n* percent of records, based on the SELECT clause. This predicate is useful when you want to return a subset of records that meet all the other criteria. SQL processes the TOP predicate only after it completes all other criteria—joins, predicates, grouping, and sorts.

The TOP predicate uses the form

```
TOP n [PERCENT]column1[,column2...]
```

and can be combined with other predicates in the form

```
SELECT [ALL | DISTINCT][TOP n [PERCENT]column1[,column2...]]
```

For example, let's use the TOP predicate to return the five most expensive items from the Northwind products list. To do so, run the following statement:

```
SELECT TOP 5 ProductID, ProductName, UnitPrice
FROM Products
ORDER BY UnitPrice DESC
```

The DESC keyword specifies a descending sort. As you can see in Figure 18.6, the query returns only five records—the five records with the largest values in the UnitPrice column.

Similarly, you can use the ASC keyword to return the five least expensive items. To do so, run the following statement

```
SELECT TOP 5 ProductID, ProductName, UnitPrice
FROM Products
ORDER BY UnitPrice ASC
```

as we've done in Figure 18.7. By specifying ascending (ASC) order, we're telling the system to start with the lowest value and work up.

FIGURE 18.6

Use the TOP predicate
to return a portion
of records.

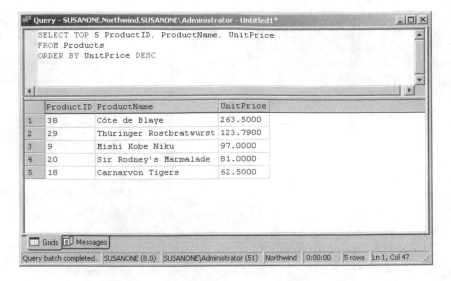

FIGURE 18.7

The ASC keyword
reverses the ORDER
BY order.

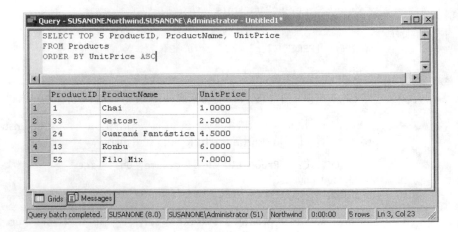

Now let's return five percent—as opposed to just five records—of the most expensive products using the following statement:

```
SELECT TOP 5 PERCENT ProductID, ProductName, UnitPrice
FROM Products
ORDER BY UnitPrice DESC
```

As you can see in Figure 18.8, the results aren't the same. The first few records are the same, but instead of returning five actual records, the PERCENT version returns only four records. There are 77 product records, and 5 percent of 77 is 3.85. The TOP predicate always rounds up to the next highest integer, so we end up with four records.

FIGURE 18.8

The TOP predicate
also returns a
percentage of
records.

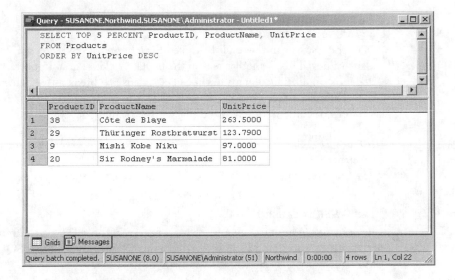

We jumped the gun a bit by including the ORDER BY clause, which we'll review later in this chapter. Most TOP queries simply don't make sense without the ORDER BY clause, although you can run them. Without an ORDER BY clause, SQL returns what may seem like a meaningless set of records. Figure 18.9 shows the result of our previous TOP 5 statement without the ORDER BY clause. In the absence of any sort, SQL returns the first five records in the table, which appear in entry order (as verified by the values in the Identity column, ProductID).

FIGURE 18.9

Without the ORDER
BY clause, the TOP
predicate makes
little sense.

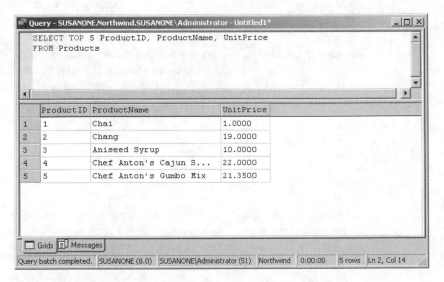

If the TOP predicate finds duplicate records that meet the SELECT statements criteria, it returns both records and includes both in its count. For instance, if another product had a price of $81.00, the query in Figure 18.6 would have bumped Carnarvon Tigers from the results and displayed both $81.00 products.

If the last row in the result has an equivalent record, SQL returns both (or all) rows with equivalent values. This is another reason the ORDER BY clause is so important. Without this clause, SQL depends on all the columns in the SELECT clause to break a tie. Otherwise, SQL depends only on the columns in the ORDER BY clause. (This rule can vary from system to system, so check your system's documentation if you don't get the results you expect.)

NOTE   *The SELECT statement is by far the most versatile of all the DML statements. For that reason, we'll introduce not just the SELECT clause, but the many clauses that work with SELECT that make it so flexible and powerful. However, these clauses aren't restricted to the SELECT statement. You can use them with many of the action clauses.*

THE *WHERE* CLAUSE

Just as you can limit the columns that are retrieved, the WHERE clause limits the records (rows) that are retrieved by specifying a condition that a record must meet before SQL will include that record in its results. Use the clause in the following form:

```
SELECT [ALL | DISTINCT] column1[As alias[, column2...]]| *
FROM datasource
[WHERE condition]
```

The *condition* argument is stated as a conditional expression and can be as simple as a comparison to a literal value or a complex expression. Think of the WHERE clause as a filter that eliminates records from the final resultset.

Use the AND and OR operators to link expressions in the form:

```
WHERE expression1 AND | OR expression2 ...
```

The number of columns or expressions in this clause is limited by each system, so refer to your system's documentation for specifics. (Read more about SQL operators later in this chapter.)

Let's start with a simple example that compares the data to a literal value. The following statement returns only beverage products from the Northwind Products table:

```
SELECT *
FROM Products
WHERE CategoryID = 1
```

The results, shown in Figure 18.10, include only beverage products (the CategoryID value 1 indicates a beverage).

Adding criteria complicates the WHERE clause but gives you more control over the results. For example, let's suppose you want to return only beverages from a specific supplier, Exotic Liquids. The following statement uses an AND operator to include both conditions in one WHERE clause:

```
SELECT *
FROM Products
WHERE CategoryID = 1 AND SupplierID = 1
```

FIGURE 18.10

Use the WHERE clause to filter records.

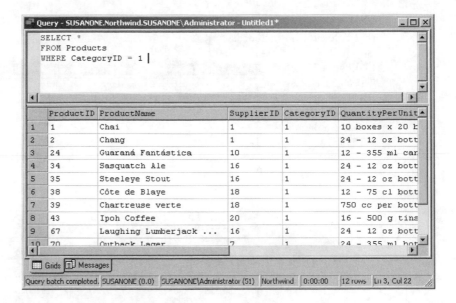

This time, the resulting recordset includes only two records, as shown in Figure 18.11. (The value 1 is Exotic Liquids' SupplierID value.)

FIGURE 18.11

Use an AND or OR operator to include more than one condition in a WHERE clause.

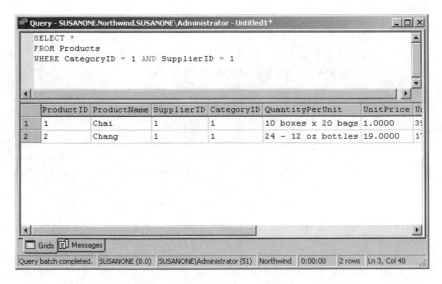

The WHERE clause is flexible. You can refer to columns that aren't in the SELECT clause—as long as the column's in the underlying datasource. For instance, the previous statement includes all the columns, including the CategoryID column. You don't have to include the CategoryID column in the results. For example, the following statement

```
SELECT ProductName, SupplierID, UnitPrice
FROM Products
WHERE CategoryID = 1
```

return the results shown in Figure 18.12—the results correspond to the CategoryID value 1, although that column isn't included.

FIGURE 18.12

The WHERE clause can handle column references that aren't included in the SELECT clause.

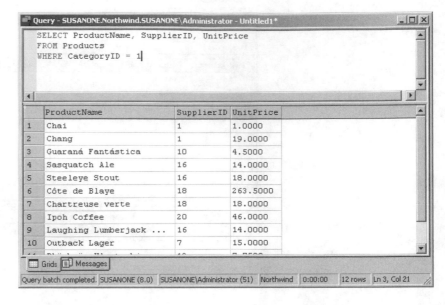

TIP   Nulls present a special problem when filtering records. Specifically, SQL tends to ignore Null values when filtering records. If a column contains a Null value, SQL usually eliminates it from the results. To include Null values, add the expression OR column Is Null *to the* WHERE *clause. Your system may respond differently, so consult your system documentation for more information on Null values.*

THE *ORDER BY* CLAUSE

The ORDER BY clause doesn't limit records; it only sorts them in ascending or descending order, with an ascending sort being the default. You can sort by text, numeric, and date/time columns. Referencing any other type of column returns an error. Similarly to the WHERE clause, the ORDER BY clause can reference a column that isn't in the SELECT clause.

The ORDER BY clause uses the following syntax:

```
ORDER BY column1 [ASC | DESC][,column2 [ASC | DESC][,...]]
```

Although that looks rather complicated, simply put, you specify the column or columns you want to sort by, in the order of preference from left to right. If you want an ascending sort, the ASC keyword isn't required, as it's the default. We'll start with a simple example that sorts customers by name:

```
SELECT *
FROM Customers
ORDER BY CompanyName
```

SQL performs an alphabetic, ascending sort, as shown in Figure 8.13, because CompanyName is a text column.

FIGURE 18.13

The ORDER BY clause sorts a text column alphabetically.

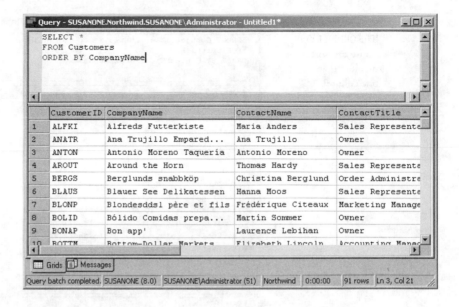

Now let's try something more complicated. The following statement sorts by the ContactTitle first and then performs a second sort, within the first group (ContactTitle), on the ContactName column:

```
SELECT ContactTitle, ContactName, CompanyName
FROM Customers
ORDER BY ContactTitle, ContactName
```

Figure 18.14 shows the results. We've scrolled down just a bit so you can see both sort groups, Accounting Manager and Assistant Sales Agent, at work. Notice that the ContactName entries are alphabetically sorted within the Accounting Manager group until Marketing Assistant resets the sort for the ContactName entries.

NOTE *Some systems allow you to reference columns by position instead of name. For instance, the clause* ORDER BY 3 *performs an ascending sort on the third column in the datasource. We don't recommend it unless the column's position, within the context of the task, is more important than the column's name. Names are simply more explicit and less prone to errors; a number isn't as accurate or as self-documenting as a name.*

THE *GROUP BY* CLAUSE

An Aggregate function evaluates an entire column, and an aggregate query works in a similar fashion. The GROUP BY clause defines groups that you might want to evaluate in some calculation as a whole. When this is the case, the result is a summary of the underlying data. The GROUP BY clause doesn't actually summarize data; it just groups the data. Any calculations for summarizing that data must be provided in the form of Aggregate functions.

You can group data without summarizing it; however, you can't summarize data without grouping it first. When summarizing, the group might not be apparent since you generally see only the results of the Aggregate function and not the data that the function evaluated.

FIGURE 18.14

The ORDER BY
clause can sort
by more than
one column.

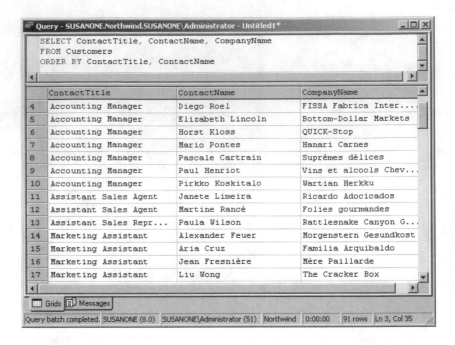

The syntax for the GROUP BY clause is simple:

```
GROUP BY column1[, column2...]
```

The column arguments can reference actual columns by name, calculated fields (as long as the expression doesn't reference an Aggregate function), or constants.

All fields in the SELECT clause must also be present in one of the following positions:

◆ An argument to an Aggregate function

◆ In the GROUP BY clause

As a result of this restriction, every column in the resultset either defines a group or evaluates a group. On the other hand, a column needn't be part of the SELECT clause to be included in the GROUP BY clause, as long as that column is in the underlying datasource. Keep in mind that SQL displays only those columns specified in the SELECT clause.

The GROUP BY clause defines groups based on the columns, in the order you specify them in the clause (from left to right). The results are presented in ascending order.

Figure 18.15 shows the results of a simple grouping statement:

```
SELECT OrderID, OrderDate, ShippedDate
FROM Orders
GROUP BY OrderDate, ShippedDate, OrderID
```

It appears to simply sort the results by the OrderDate, then the ShippedDate, and then the OrderID value. As is, the resultset probably isn't useful and closely resembles the data entry order. (Check the Orders table to compare.)

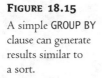

FIGURE 18.15

A simple GROUP BY clause can generate results similar to a sort.

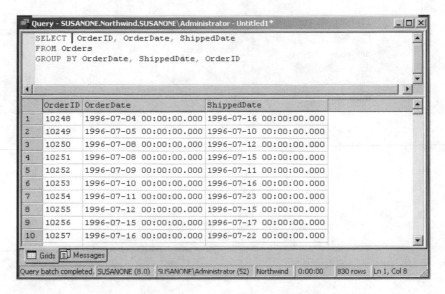

When using the GROUP BY clause, you'll usually want to summarize at least one column. Otherwise, as you just saw, an ORDER BY clause might be a better solution because of GROUP BY's restrictions. It makes more sense to use GROUP BY when you want to evaluate a column in some way. For instance, the following statement groups the records by the OrderDate column and displays a total for the number of orders placed on that day.

```
SELECT OrderDate, Count(OrderID) AS Total
FROM Orders
GROUP BY OrderDate
```

Each unique date value is now a group, and instead of displaying each value, SQL displays just one along with the result of the Count() function, as shown in Figure 18.16. Also notice that the OrderID column isn't in the GROUP BY clause. As long as it's part of an Aggregate function in the SELECT clause, it isn't necessary to include it in the GROUP BY clause.

NOTE   Systems vary in the way they respond to GROUP BY. First, your system may or may not include Null values in the results. Second, your system probably won't group on a memo or image type column—there's nothing on which to base a group. Third, the number of GROUP BY fields you can include in one clause may be restricted by your specific system.

LIMITING THE GROUP'S RESULTS

You can limit the results of a grouped query in two ways:

◆ By adding a WHERE clause to eliminate records you don't want grouped

◆ By adding a HAVING clause to act as a filter on the group, eliminating records from the group

These two choices aren't interchangeable, although sometimes they return the same results. One eliminates records before the GROUP BY clause ever considers them, and one eliminates records after SQL applies the GROUP BY clause. (We'll discuss HAVING in the next section.)

FIGURE 18.16

Use GROUP BY to define a group you want to evaluate using an Aggregate function.

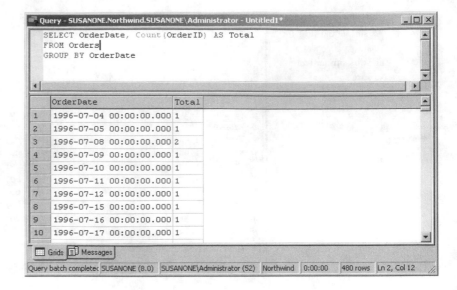

Technically, when you add a WHERE clause to a GROUP BY statement, you're not eliminating records from each group. You're limiting the results of the SELECT clause and thereby limiting the records that get grouped by the GROUP BY clause. For instance, the previous query shown in Figure 18.16 doesn't really limit data; it just groups data. Each date in the OrderDate column appears in the results; it just appears once.

Let's limit the records that make it to the GROUP BY process using a WHERE clause to eliminate all orders that were placed before January 1, 1998. To do so, use the following statement:

```
SELECT OrderDate, Count(OrderID) AS Total
FROM Orders
WHERE OrderDate >'12-31-1997'
GROUP BY OrderDate
```

WARNING *Don't forget to add the appropriate date delimiter if you're not using SQL Server. For instance, Access users would use the statement* WHERE OrderDate >#12-31-1997#.

Figure 18.17 shows the results, which are still grouped. However, the results no longer display dates prior to 1998.

THE *HAVING* CLAUSE

Using SQL's HAVING clause is another way to limit the results of a group. Just remember that the HAVING clause is applied after the data is grouped. This is especially useful when you want to filter records based on a summarized evaluation for each group. This clause uses the syntax

```
SELECT ALL | DISTINCT column1[As alias[, column2...]]| *
FROM datasource
[GROUP BY column1[, column2...]]
[HAVING condition]
```

in which *condition* can be one or more expressions combined by the AND or OR operators in the form:

```
HAVING expression1 AND | OR expression2 ...
```

FIGURE 18.17

The WHERE clause eliminates records before they're grouped by the GROUP BY clause.

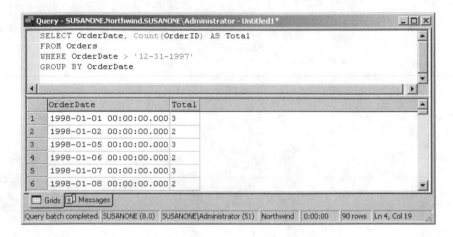

We can illustrate the HAVING clause by returning to an earlier example that returned order dates and the number of each placed on each date. Now, let's suppose you want to eliminate all the date groups that have two or fewer orders. To do so, add a HAVING clause as follows:

```
SELECT OrderDate, Count(OrderID) AS Total
FROM Orders
GROUP BY OrderDate
HAVING Count(OrderID) > 2
```

The results shown in Figure 18.18 are grouped just as before but include only those dates on which three or more orders were placed.

The previous two sections show different ways to limit the results of a grouped recordset at different times during processing. The WHERE clause eliminates records before they're grouped, and the HAVING clause eliminates records after grouping. It's possible to include both limiting clauses in the same statement.

Our last example used the HAVING clause to eliminate dates with fewer than three orders for the day, but the results still had those pre-1998 dates. We can have both. Figure 18.19 shows the results of the following statement, which includes only dates with three or more orders for orders occurring on or after January 1, 1998:

```
SELECT OrderDate, Count(OrderID) AS Total
FROM Orders
WHERE OrderDate > '12-31-1997'
GROUP BY OrderDate
HAVING Count(OrderID) > 2
```

FIGURE 18.18

The HAVING clause eliminates dates that had two or fewer orders to show for the day.

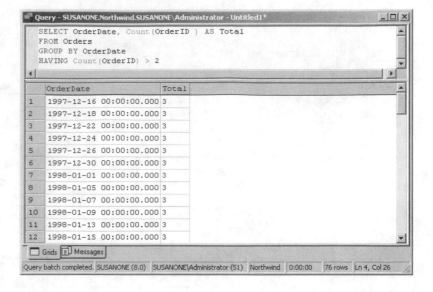

FIGURE 18.19

You can combine the WHERE and HAVING clauses.

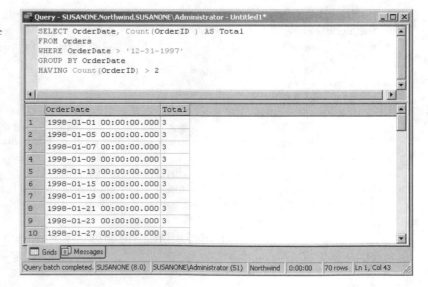

Modify Data with *UPDATE*

Websites are no longer confined to just displaying data. Users can actually modify data via your website. For instance, a human resources manager might update employee files via an intranet that all managers can access. Thanks to SQL, the human resources manager doesn't need to know a thing about the underlying database—they simply call up the appropriate employee record using a web page designed by the web developer. After making the appropriate changes, they submit those changes by simply clicking a button designed for that purpose, and SQL updates the underlying database behind the scenes.

You can use SQL's UPDATE statement to modify existing data, whether you're updating one record or thousands. SQL UPDATE uses the following syntax:

```
UPDATE datasource
SET column1 = expression1[, column2 = expression2][,...]
[WHERE condition]
```

The *datasource* can be a table or an *updateable query*—a query that refers to a resultset that passes along changes to the underlying datasource. (There's a section on updateable queries later in this chapter.) The SET *expression* arguments can be constants or expressions.

WARNING *We recommend you work with a copy of any table you attempt to modify using the examples in the sections on updating and deleting. Use the* **SELECT INTO** *statement discussed in a later section of this chapter to create a copy. (Be sure to give the copy a unique name.)*

For instance, let's change each occurrence of the title Sales Representative in the Employees table to Account Executive using the following UPDATE statement:

```
UPDATE Employees
SET Title = 'Account Executive'
WHERE Title = 'Sales Representative'
```

The UPDATE statement doesn't return a resultset, but your system may return a message identifying how many records were updated, as shown in Figure 18.20. If you like, run the statement

```
SELECT *
FROM Employees
```

to confirm the update, which we've done in Figure 18.21.

FIGURE 18.20

Use UPDATE to change existing entries.

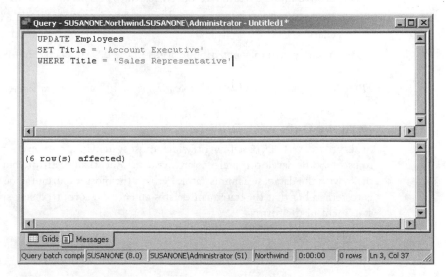

FIGURE 18.21

We changed the Title entries from Sales Representative to Account Executive.

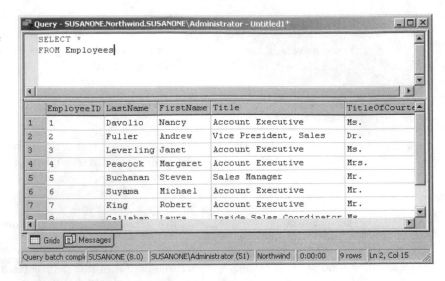

NOTE *Modifying, inserting, and deleting data can violate referential integrity rules, and requests can return errors, unless you plan for the possibility in your design.*

The UPDATE statement isn't quite as versatile as the SELECT statement, but it doesn't need to be. Much of what UPDATE can't do makes sense:

◆ Your system probably can't handle an UPDATE statement that includes a GROUP BY clause. It doesn't really make sense to update just one record in a group of records, and that would be the result; so most systems simply don't support such a request.

◆ UPDATE doesn't return a resultset, so you won't need ORDER BY.

◆ Your system may not support subqueries in the SET clause. (We'll cover subqueries later in this chapter.)

◆ Your system may not support joins in the UPDATE clause, but most do.

TIP *Before updating critical data, it's a good idea to create a copy of the table you're modifying.*

Remove Data with *DELETE*

SQL provides a DELETE statement, which most systems support, even though you might choose never to use it. Some developers prefer to archive data rather than destroy it, but that's a decision you'll need to make with the database administrator. Perhaps the most important issue to hurdle, in regard to DELETE, is to remember that the statement deletes an entire record; to delete specific entries, use the UPDATE statement in the form:

```
UPDATE table
SET column = Null
```

To delete entire records, use the DELETE statement in the form:

```
DELETE
FROM datasource
[WHERE condition]
```

You can specify a field in the DELETE clause, but doing so is useless since you can't delete data from a specific field. Nor do you need to include the asterisk character (*) to indicate that you're deleting all the columns—in fact, SQL won't accept the asterisk character in the DELETE clause.

The simplest form of this statement deletes all the records from a table:

```
DELETE
FROM datasource
```

We recommend that you back up the table before running such a command.

Let's look at a simple example that deletes all the discontinued items from the Northwind Products table. First, a quick review of the Products table shows that Chef Anton's Gumbo Mix (ProductID of 5) has been discontinued—you can tell by the value 1 in that record's Discontinued column. In this context, the value 1 represents a True value, meaning the product has been discontinued. Next, run the following statement to delete that item and any others that have been discontinued:

```
DELETE
FROM Products
WHERE Discontinued = 1
```

Figure 18.22 lets us know that eight rows were deleted.

FIGURE 18.22

The DELETE statement removes eight records from the Products table.

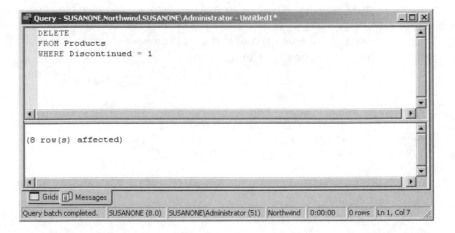

To browse the Products table, run the following SELECT statement:

```
SELECT ProductID, ProductName, Discontinued
FROM Products
WHERE Discontinued = 1
```

However, as you can see in Figure 18.23, there are no records to browse.

FIGURE 18.23

No records in the
Products table have
been discontinued.

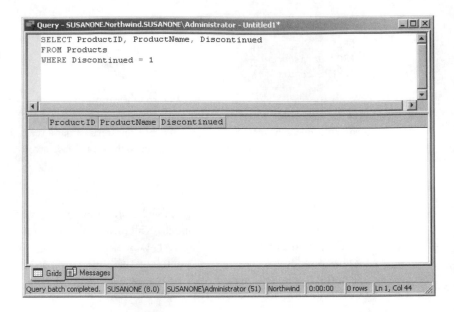

Add a New Table Using *SELECT INTO*

Copying a table is a fairly straightforward process with SQL's SELECT INTO statement. It's similar to a SELECT statement in that you specify columns and a datasource, and the statement supports the WHERE and the ORDER BY clauses. However, you also specify the name of a new table.

In a nutshell, you have a source table, which contains data you want to copy. You specify the columns you want to copy and include clauses to limit the actual data copied and the order in which it's copied using the syntax:

```
SELECT [column1, column2, ... | *] INTO newtable
FROM sourcetable
[WHERE condition]
[GROUP BY column1[, column2,...]]
[HAVING condition]
[ORDER BY column1[, column2, ...]]
```

In its simplest form, you can copy an entire table using the form:

```
SELECT * INTO newtable
FROM sourcetable
```

For instance, let's create a copy of the Northwind Products table using the statement:

```
SELECT * INTO ProductsCopy
FROM Products
```

You can browse the new table using the statement

```
SELECT *
FROM ProductsCopy
```

as shown in Figure 18.24.

FIGURE 18.24

After creating a new products table, run a **SELECT** statement to view the records.

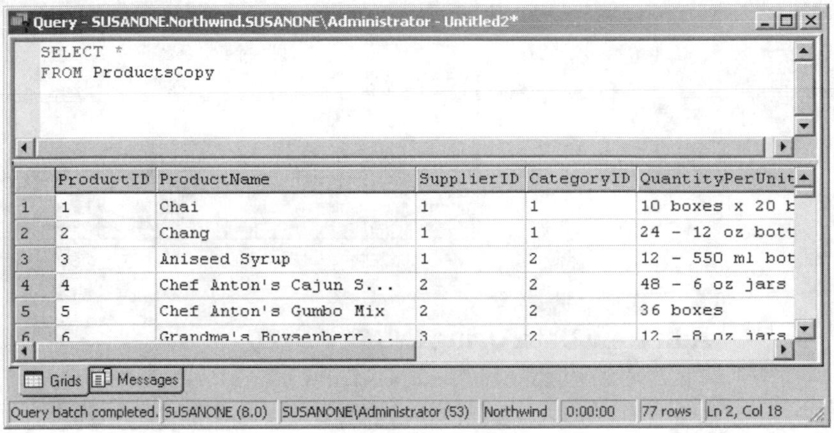

Or, to limit the product records copied to the new table, you might use a statement similar to the following:

```
SELECT * INTO ProductsCopy
FROM Products
WHERE ProductID = 1
```

This time, we copied only one record to the newly created table ProductsCopy—the one record in Products with a ProductID value of 1. Use the simple **SELECT** statement from Figure 18.24 to see the results of the latest **SELECT * INTO**. The resulting recordset, shown in Figure 18.25, contains only one record. Similarly, you can use the **GROUP BY**, **SORT BY**, and **HAVING** clauses to further define the copied recordset.

To copy a table's structure, but not its data, use the form:

```
SELECT * INTO newtable
FROM sourcetable
WHERE False
```

SQL copies the table, but because no record can equal False, no data is copied to the new table.

NOTE   *Your system probably won't make an exact duplicate of the source table. In particular,* **SELECT INTO** *may not set a primary key for the new table, even if the source table has one. In addition, check the new table's indexes and properties—your system may not set anything other than the defaults.*

WARNING   *The* **SELECT INTO** *clause sometimes replaces an existing table if one exists when you execute the* **SELECT INTO** *request. Fortunately, most systems will warn you first. But that may not be enough if your system deletes the table even if you cancel the request (Access does). We recommend that you always back up any table with the same name when creating a new table using* **SELECT INTO**.

FIGURE 18.25

We copied just
one product to
the new table.

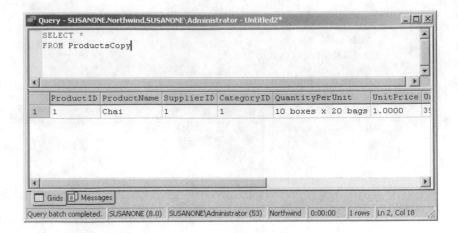

Add New Data Using *INSERT INTO*

The INSERT INTO statement does double duty. It copies data from one table to another, and it inserts new data. As such, you probably won't use this statement for routine data entry. However, it can be efficient when copying data from one source to another, whether you're copying just one record or many.

To copy records into a target table, use the statement's simplest form:

```
INSERT INTO target
SELECT source
[WHERE condition]
[ORDER BY column1[, column2, ...]]
```

In this statement, *target* is the table you're inserting data into, and *source* is the existing data, most likely another table. This statement copies all the records from the source table into the target table.

WARNING   *Your system may not support the asterisk character (*) in the* INSERT INTO *clause.*

This statement can be problematic if you're not aware of some of its requirements:

- The target table must exist. This statement won't create a new table. (Use SELECT INTO if you need to also create the table with the same statement.)
- You can't insert columns (data) that don't already exist in the target table. The table structures don't have to match; they just have to share the columns you're inserting.

Now, let's suppose you want to combine the employee and customer records and you run the following statement in that attempt:

```
INSERT INTO Customers
SELECT Employees.*
FROM Employees
```

SQL returns the error message shown in Figure 18.26—the structures must match. The error message gives us the necessary clue that the column names don't match. The error message won't tell you what columns are missing; you'll have to run a SELECT query using the asterisk character (*) to view the column names.

FIGURE 18.26

SQL returns an error message if the table structures don't match.

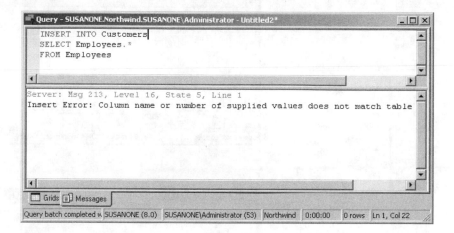

Now, let's copy all the records from the Shippers table into the Shippers table. Yes, you read that correctly. Ordinarily, you wouldn't want to duplicate records in a table this way. However, we need an example that actually works; that is, we need a target table with the same structure as the source, and the Northwind tables are all unique. So copying into the same table is one way to accomplish that. (For the most part, you probably won't find any database with two or more tables that share the same structure; it just isn't efficient. You can learn more about table design in Chapter 5.)

First, run the statement

```
INSERT INTO Shippers
SELECT Shippers.CompanyName, Shippers.Phone
FROM Shippers
```

as shown in Figure 18.27.

Notice that we didn't use the asterisk character (*) in this statement. Doing so would return an error message because the primary key column contains duplicate values, which isn't allowed. Therefore, we explicitly specified all the columns except the primary key column.

Afterward, run the following statement to review those records, shown in Figure 18.28.

```
SELECT *
FROM Shippers
```

The second form of this statement inserts a single row into a table:

```
INSERT INTO target [column1[, column2, ...]]
VALUES (value1[, value2, ...])
```

FIGURE 18.27

Insert all the shipper records into the Shippers table.

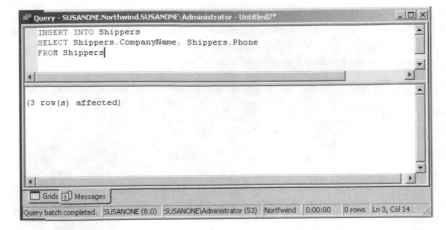

FIGURE 18.28

We inserted three new records in the Shippers table.

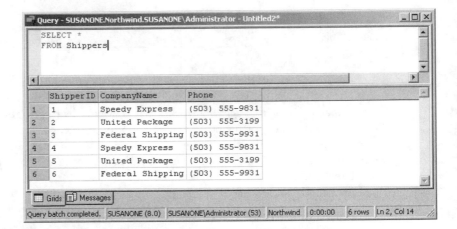

You must remember a few rules when using this form:

◆ The column references in the INSERT INTO clause are optional. When omitted, you must include a value for each column in the target table. This particular instance is impossible to fulfill if the target table has an autonumber type column because you can't insert a value into such a column. (Such columns are system generated.)

◆ The arguments in the VALUES clause must match the order of their corresponding target columns in the target table.

◆ If you include column references, you must include values for the referenced columns, and those values must be in the same order as the referenced columns in the INSERT INTO clause.

◆ The order of the columns does not have to match the order in which they occur in the target table. This last behavior is convenient when you want the column order to be different from that of the source table.

Now let's add a new shipper to the Shippers table using the following statement:

```
INSERT INTO Shippers (Companyname, Phone)
VALUES ('United Shipping', '(555) 555-1234')
```

SQL lets us know that one row was added, as shown in Figure 18.29. Now, run the following statement to see the new shipper record shown in Figure 18.30:

```
SELECT *
FROM Shippers
```

FIGURE 18.29

Use INSERT INTO to add a new record to a table.

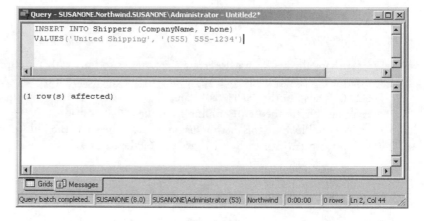

FIGURE 18.30

We added a new shipper record to the Shippers table.

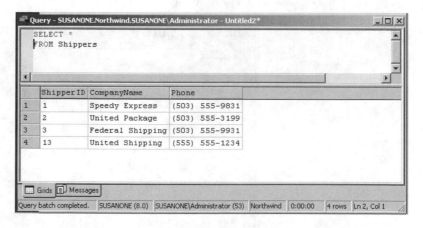

Keep in mind that any data you insert is still subject to the table's underlying properties, such as validation rules, constraints, properties, datatypes, and so on. If you attempt to insert data that doesn't comply with all the table's rules, SQL will return an error message and reject the data.

Use *TRANSFORM* to Create a Crosstab Query

Crosstab queries summarize data by categories, using an Aggregate function of some type. Their usefulness lies in the amount of data they can display because of their specialized format—there's always a least one column heading, and one summary column. Use SQL's TRANSFORM statement in the following form to generate a crosstab query:

```
TRANSFORM aggregate
SELECT statement
PIVOT column
```

The SELECT clause argument is any valid SELECT statement with a GROUP BY clause and specifies the row heading. The PIVOT clause identifies the column headings. In addition, the TRANSFORM statement doesn't support the HAVING clause.

NOTE *Not all systems support the* TRANSFORM *statement. SQL Server doesn't, so we'll use Access to execute our crosstab examples.*

Perhaps the easiest way to create a crosstab is to start with a grouped SELECT statement. Then, insert a TRANSFORM clause before the SELECT statement and move the Aggregate function from the SELECT clause to the TRANSFORM clause. Then, add a PIVOT clause that uses one of the GROUP BY columns. Delete the PIVOT column from the GROUP BY clause.

We can illustrate this method using Access to generate the following GROUP BY query to return the number of items per each order grouped by the date:

```
SELECT OrderDate, CustomerID, Count(OrderID) AS ItemsPerOrder
FROM Orders
GROUP BY OrderDate, CustomerID
```

The grouped results are shown in Figure 18.31.

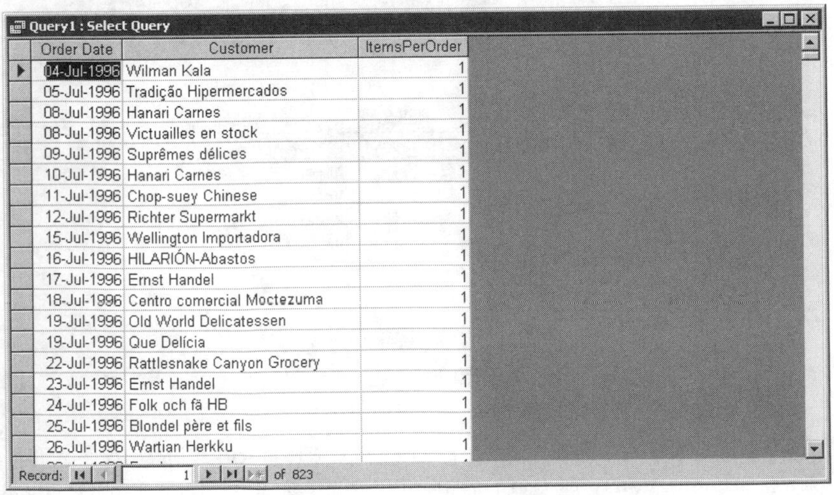

Order Date	Customer	ItemsPerOrder
04-Jul-1996	Wilman Kala	1
05-Jul-1996	Tradição Hipermercados	1
08-Jul-1996	Hanari Carnes	1
08-Jul-1996	Victuailles en stock	1
09-Jul-1996	Suprêmes délices	1
10-Jul-1996	Hanari Carnes	1
11-Jul-1996	Chop-suey Chinese	1
12-Jul-1996	Richter Supermarkt	1
15-Jul-1996	Wellington Importadora	1
16-Jul-1996	HILARIÓN-Abastos	1
17-Jul-1996	Ernst Handel	1
18-Jul-1996	Centro comercial Moctezuma	1
19-Jul-1996	Old World Delicatessen	1
19-Jul-1996	Que Delícia	1
22-Jul-1996	Rattlesnake Canyon Grocery	1
23-Jul-1996	Ernst Handel	1
24-Jul-1996	Folk och fä HB	1
25-Jul-1996	Blondel père et fils	1
26-Jul-1996	Wartian Herkku	1

FIGURE 18.31
We'll convert this Access grouped query to a crosstab.

NOTE *The CustomerID field's Caption property is "Customers." Therefore, throughout these examples, you will see Customers used instead of CustomerID, the actual field's name.*

Once you have a valid grouped query, a crosstab is within easy reach. First, slip in a TRANSFORM clause before the SELECT clause, and then move the Aggregate function from the SELECT clause to the new TRANSFORM clause:

```
TRANSFORM Count(OrderID) AS ItemsPerOrder
SELECT OrderDate, CustomerID
FROM Orders
GROUP BY OrderDate,CustomerID
```

Next, add a PIVOT clause to the end of the statement, and move at least one of the GROUP BY columns to this new clause. Knowing just which column to move may be difficult until you get the hang of this technique. Move the column that most accurately represents the crosstab's column headings. In our example, CustomerID will be the column heading, so move that column to the PIVOT clause:

```
TRANSFORM Count(OrderID) AS ItemsPerOrder
SELECT OrderDate, CustomerID
FROM Orders
GROUP BY OrderDate
PIVOT CustomerID
```

The resulting crosstab report shown in Figure 18.32 displays the number of items ordered by each customer on a particular date. In this case, SQL ignores the AS clause we tacked on to the counting field. That's because SQL displays the CustomerID value as each column's heading. You could easily omit the AS clause.

FIGURE 18.32

Use TRANSFORM and PIVOT to convert a GROUP BY query to a crosstab.

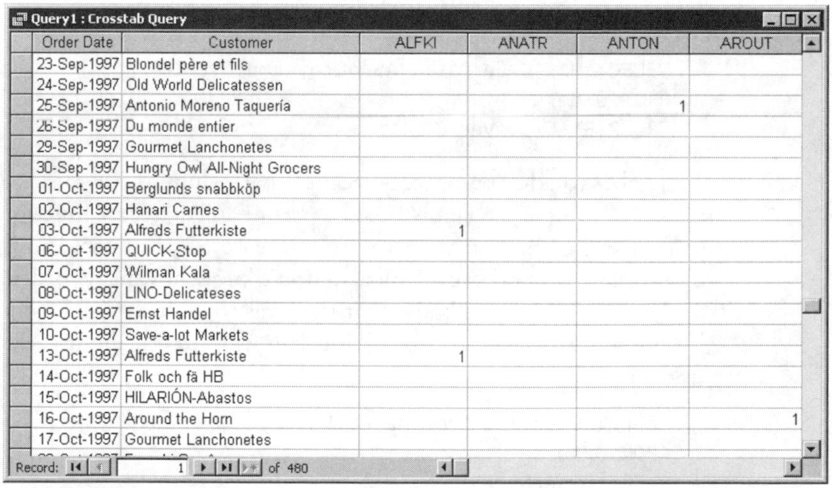
Query1 : Crosstab Query

Order Date	Customer	ALFKI	ANATR	ANTON	AROUT
23-Sep-1997	Blondel père et fils				
24-Sep-1997	Old World Delicatessen				
25-Sep-1997	Antonio Moreno Taquería			1	
26-Sep-1997	Du monde entier				
29-Sep-1997	Gourmet Lanchonetes				
30-Sep-1997	Hungry Owl All-Night Grocers				
01-Oct-1997	Berglunds snabbköp				
02-Oct-1997	Hanari Carnes				
03-Oct-1997	Alfreds Futterkiste	1			
06-Oct-1997	QUICK-Stop				
07-Oct-1997	Wilman Kala				
08-Oct-1997	LINO-Delicateses				
09-Oct-1997	Ernst Handel				
10-Oct-1997	Save-a-lot Markets				
13-Oct-1997	Alfreds Futterkiste	1			
14-Oct-1997	Folk och fä HB				
15-Oct-1997	HILARIÓN-Abastos				
16-Oct-1997	Around the Horn				1
17-Oct-1997	Gourmet Lanchonetes				

Record: 1 of 480

Customer is the Caption property for the CustomerID field, and it takes precedence over the field name. It's also a lookup field, so it displays the corresponding Customer Name instead of the customer's primary key value. This is an Access feature and is built into the Northwind example database.

Subqueries

The more complex the question, the more complex the query, and sometimes just one query won't get the job done. That's when you need what's known as a subquery or subselect.

A *subquery* combines two queries by embedding one SELECT statement within another. The embedded query becomes part of the main query's conditional search, behaving similar to a filter. The embedded query is known as an inner select, and the main query is called an outer select. To create a subquery, use one of the following WHERE forms to define the inner select:

```
WHERE value or expression [NOT] IN (SELECT statement)
WHERE column ANY | SOME | ALL (SELECT statement)
WHERE [NOT] EXISTS (SELECT statement)
WHERE column comparison operator (SELECT statement)
```

Subqueries are often the solution of choice when displaying extraneous data in a GROUP BY query. That's because you can't include such data in a grouped query. Every column must be part of an aggregate or one of the GROUP BY clause's arguments. In either case, the addition of the column will change the group dynamics. An alternate solution is a nested query.

NOTE   *A nested query is simply one query based upon another. We don't recommend you convert nested queries into subqueries unless you have a specific reason for doing so. As a general rule, a subquery won't perform any better than its nested counterparts.*

For example, let's suppose you want to display the number of items per order, but you also want to identify the employee responsible for each order. The following GROUP BY query will return the date for the latest order:

```
SELECT Max(OrderDate) AS Date, EmployeeID
FROM Orders
GROUP BY EmployeeID
```

We're able to add EmployeeID because that column's part of the GROUP BY clause. Remember, in this type of query, a column must be part of an Aggregate function or in the GROUP BY clause. This query displays the results shown in Figure 18.33. The problem is, there's no way to identify the order or any order details. You also don't know how many orders were placed by each employee on that day—you only know that that was the last day each employee placed an order.

One way to view the information you want to see about each order is to run the following subquery:

```
SELECT OrderID, OrderDate, EmployeeID
FROM Orders
WHERE OrderDate IN
(SELECT Max(OrderDate) AS Date
FROM Orders
GROUP BY EmployeeID)
ORDER BY EmployeeID
```

The inner select, which is the same as the previous query, except for the omission of the EmployeeID reference in the SELECT clause, returns the same list of dates shown in Figure 18.33.

However, this query also displays the OrderID value with each record, as shown in Figure 18.34. The outer query returns data from the specified fields in the SELECT clause where the OrderDate value occurs in the result of the inner select. As you can see, the results are different from the previous query—there's a record for each order.

FIGURE 18.33

This simple query returns the latest order date for each employee.

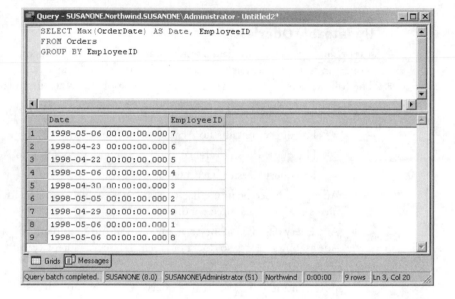

FIGURE 18.34

The subquery can handle the OrderID column.

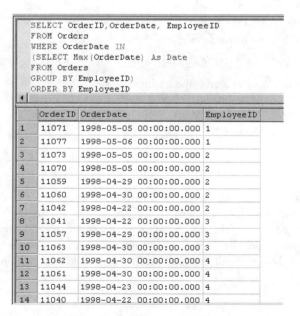

NOTE   *Notice that column references include a table reference. That's because we're using a join, and the only way to avoid ambiguous reference errors is to explicitly declare the source. Throughout this chapter, we reference only the column to keep the examples as simple as possible. However, most developers include the source's entire reference in the form* `owner.table.column` *for all references, even if there's no join. Chapter 3 discusses good coding practices, like this one.*

Updateable Queries

Just because you can return data doesn't mean you can modify it, because not every query is updateable. A query must be updateable in order to update the underlying data as you make changes via the query. The following is a list of general rules you can apply to create an updateable query:

- Any query based on a single table is updateable if:
  - The query contains no Aggregate functions.
  - The query doesn't refer to another query that contains an Aggregate function.
  - The query doesn't have a `GROUP BY` clause.
- Any query based on more than one table with a one-to-one relationship is updateable (if it also meets the previous three conditions).
- Any query based on a one-to-many relationship should allow you to update data on the many side as long as doing so does not violate referential integrity (and the three previous conditions are met).

Keep in mind that an updateable query doesn't ensure success. Some other factors are involved:

- You must have permission to modify the underlying datasource.
- The table can't be read-only.
- The record you're trying to update must not be locked by another user.

In addition, a few queries aren't updateable:

- Crosstab
- SQL pass-through
- `UNION`
- Queries based on three or more tables based on a many-to-one-to-many relationship.

SQL pass-through queries bypass Jet, thereby allowing you to work directly with foreign data without interpretation by (or interference from, as the case may be) Jet. The `UNION` operator joins records from two similar tables. A crosstab query summarizes data by categories, using an Aggregate function of some type. We'll review the `UNION` operator later in this chapter. The other two query types are beyond the scope of this chapter. Check your documentation to see if your system supports these query types.

NOTE   As we've said throughout this chapter, all systems are unique. Please check your system's documentation in regard to updateable queries.

SQL Operators

Earlier in this chapter, we introduced the AND and OR logical operators. *Operators* are symbols that represent mathematical, comparison, logical, and concatenation actions in an expression. Tables 18.1 through 18.3 list the SQL operators. Almost all systems support most SQL operators, but not all, so be sure to check your system documentation for more specific information.

TABLE 18.1: SQL MATHEMATICAL OPERATORS

SYMBOL	REPRESENTATIVE OF OR DESCRIPTION	NOTES
+	Addition	
-	Subtraction	
-	Changes the sign of an operand	
*	Multiplication	
/	Division	
\	Integer division	Not in MySQL
^	Exponentiation	Not in MySQL
%	Returns the remainder of division by an integer	Not in MySQL; use MOD in Access

TABLE 18.2: SQL COMPARISON OPERATORS

SYMBOL	REPRESENTATIVE OF OR DESCRIPTION	NOTES
=	Equals	
>	Is greater than	
<	Is less than	
>=	Is greater than or equal to	
<=	Is less than or equal to	
<>	Is not equal to	MySQL also recognizes the exclamation character (!).
IS	Compares two object reference variables	
LIKE	Compares string values by character	

TABLE 18.3: SQL LOGICAL OPERATORS

SYMBOL	REPRESENTATIVE OF OR DESCRIPTION	NOTES
IN	Compares a value to a list of values	
OR	Meets any one condition	MySQL also recognizes the double pipe (││).
AND	Meets all conditions	MySQL also recognizes the double ampersand (&&).
BETWEEN	Falls between two values and includes both comparison values	
NOT	Negates the result of an expression	MySQL also recognizes the exclamation character (!).

NOTE   An operand *is a literal value, variable, reference, or function that's evaluated by an operator.*

The UNION statement isn't a statement in the same sense as the others we've discussed, although you'll use it in the same manner. The UNION statement is really an operator that combines records from two tables. Use the form:

```
SELECT * | column1[, column2, ...]
UNION [ALL]
SELECT * | column1[, column2, ...]
```

Both SELECT statements must represent compatible tables or queries. That means the column order must be identical in both datasources. SQL doesn't care if the names are the same, but the datatypes must match, column per column. When corresponding datatypes aren't compatible, SQL selects the datatype that's most compatible with the data in both columns. We recommend you avoid allowing SQL to choose unless you have specific reasons to do so because SQL's decision isn't predictable.

By default, the UNION operator omits duplicate records. In this form, SQL sorts the form by the first column. This is the result of an internal sort necessary for SQL to omit duplicate records. You can include all records by adding the ALL predicate to the UNION clause.

A good use for a UNION query is combining similar tables. For instance, another branch might send you a new table full of data that you need to combine with your own. If the structure is the same, a UNION might be the most efficient solution.

There really isn't a good example for this in the Northwind sample database, but let's suppose an employee sends you a table with new customer data. You could re-enter the data, but because the table structure is the same, you can run the following query to combine both tables:

```
SELECT *
FROM CustomersNew
UNION
SELECT *
FROM Customers
```

Include the ALL predicate in the UNION clause in the form

    UNION ALL

when you want to return all records, including duplicates. In addition, you can improve performance by using this predicate if you know there are no duplicates but a lot of data. The predicate omits the comparison step and, as a result, responds faster.

WARNING   *The results of a UNION query are read-only.*

Delimiting and Concatenating

The examples in this chapter are simplified in that they don't contain variables or literal values that require delimiter characters. Concatenating literal values and variables is common practice, and unless you know the rules, a statement can produce errors. Systems aren't uniform in this regard, and we recommend you refer to your system's documentation to learn the specific characters and rules for concatenating. SQL Server uses the plus sign (+) as its concatenation character, and our examples reflect this requirement. Table 18.4 lists the concatenation characters for the systems we use throughout this book.

TABLE 18.4: CONCATENATION CHARACTERS

CHARACTER	RDBMS	NOTES
+	SQL Server	
&	Access	
||	Oracle	
||	MySQL	Only if MySQL is launched with the `--ansi` option. Use the native CONCAT( ) function instead.

A simple example of concatenation is displaying the first and last names from the Employees table, in the same column. To do so, use the simple statement:

    SELECT FirstName + ' ' + LastName AS Employee

SQL displays both names in the same column as shown in Figure 18.35.

General concatenation rules stipulate that you should delimit literal values; each system is unique in its requirements, so check your documentation. In this context, value can be a string, number, or date. Table 18.5 lists the delimiters and their purpose for the systems used throughout this book. For the most part, you won't delimit values.

TIP   *Access accepts single or double quotation marks as a string delimiter. However, we recommend you get in the habit of using the single quotation mark since that's the character SQL Server uses. Should upsizing be in your future, replacing string delimiters is one headache you can avoid.*

FIGURE 18.35

Use your system's concatenation character to combine data.

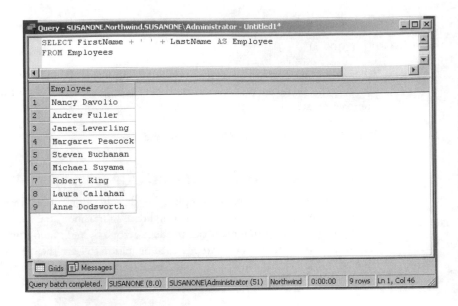

TABLE 18.5: DELIMITERS

CHARACTER	NAME	SYSTEM	PURPOSE	EXAMPLE
'	Single quotation mark	SQL Server and Access	Delimits literal strings and dates	`'string'`
"	Double quotation mark	Access	Delimits literal strings	`"string"`
#	Pound sign	Access	Delimits dates	`#datestring#`

SQL statements are treated as strings in a script, and you must delimit them accordingly. For instance, you might send a request to retrieve all the employee records using the ADO Execute method in the form:

```
Set rst = Conn.Execute("SELECT * FROM Employees")
```

The request returns an error message if you omit the double quotation delimiters.

When passing a literal string as criteria, delimit the string using the single quotation mark character in the form

```
strSQL = "SELECT * FROM Employees WHERE LastName = 'Harkins'")
Set rst = Conn.Execute(strSQL)
```

If you omit the single quotation marks, SQL assumes Harkins is a variable and returns an error message (unless, of course, there really is a variable named *Harkins*, which creates an entirely different problem).

Don't forget that some systems also delimit date values. For instance, SQL Server uses the single quotation mark with dates and literal strings; Access uses the pound character to delimit dates. Both of the following statements are correctly delimited, depending on the system:

```
strSQL = "SELECT * FROM Orders WHERE ShippedDate < '8-1-1977'"
strSQL = "SELECT * FROM Orders WHERE ShippedDate < #8-1-1977#"
```

The first statement works in SQL Server, but returns an error message in Access. The second statement works in Access but returns an error message in SQL Server. Knowing what your system expects is vital to the success of your script.

Passing a variable requires a bit of concatenation, and delimiters can also be required, depending on the requirements of your system. For instance, the following statements request all the records in which the UnitPrice equals the value stored in a variable named intUnitPrice:

```
strSQL = "SELECT * FROM Products WHERE UnitPrice = " + intUnitPrice
strSQL = "SELECT * FROM Products WHERE UnitPrice = " & intUnitPrice
```

If the variable stores a string or (in some systems) a date, you need to delimit that string using the syntax:

```
strSQL = "SELECT * FROM Employees WHERE LastName = '"& strLastName & "'"
```

Remember to use the appropriate delimiter for the value's datatype and to meet system requirements.

SQL Aggregate Functions

The earlier section, "The HAVING Clause," introduces that clause as a means of grouping data by a column or columns. Occasionally, you also want to summarize or otherwise evaluate the data in that column. You can do so using SQL Aggregate functions. Some systems have native functions that are similar and may or may not offer extended capabilities. You'll use the following SQL Aggregate functions to return statistical information on your grouped data. SQL Aggregate functions all accept one argument, which must be the reference to a column (field).

Avg(ALL | DISTINCT column)   SQL's Avg() function returns the average or mean value of a group of values. For instance, the following statement returns the value 26.2185—the average unit price:

```
SELECT Avg(UnitPrice) AS AvgPrice
FROM [Order Details]
```

The ALL predicate is the default; adding the DISTINCT keyword as follows returns the average value of 28.9207:

```
SELECT Avg(DISTINCT UnitPrice) AS AvgPrice
FROM [Order Details]
```

Count(ALL | DISTINCT column | *)   The Count() function returns the number of non-Null values in a group of values. The following statement returns the number of OrderID values in the Order Details table, which is 2155—the number of individual items, not orders:

```
SELECT Count(OrderID)
FROM [Order Details]
```

Adding the DISTINCT predicate returns the number of orders, which is 830:

```
SELECT Count(DISTINCT OrderID)
FROM [Order Details]
```

Using the asterisk character (*) instead of referencing an actual column returns the total number of rows in the underlying datasource. For instance, the following statement returns the number of employee records in the Employees table, which is 9:

```
SELECT Count(*)
FROM Employees
```

In contrast, the following statement references a column that contains Null values and the Region value and returns the value 5:

```
SELECT Count(Region)
FROM Employees
```

Sum(ALL | DISTINCT column)   The Sum() function adds all the values in a group of values. For instance, the sum of all the UnitPrice entries in the Products table is $2,222.71:

```
SELECT Sum(UnitPrice) AS TotalPrice
FROM Products
```

Adding the DISTINCT predicate changes the sum to $1,948.81:

```
SELECT Sum(DISTINCT UnitPrice) AS TotalPrice
FROM Products
```

Min(column)   The Min() function returns the smallest value in a group of values. For instance, the following statement returns the minimum UnitPrice entry of $2.50:

```
SELECT Min(UnitPrice) AS TotalPrice
FROM Products
```

This function doesn't support the DISTINCT predicate because it considers only one value in its results.

Max(column)   The Max() function is similar to the Min() function except it returns the largest value in a group of values. The following statement returns the value $263.50:

```
SELECT Max(UnitPrice) AS TotalPrice
FROM Products
```

Similarly to the Min() function, the Max() function doesn't support the DISTINCT predicate.

StDev(column)   The StDev() function estimates the standard deviation for a group of values. The following statement returns the standard deviation for freight, 44.41, in the RJ region:

```
SELECT StDev(Freight)
FROM Orders
WHERE ShipRegion = 'RJ'
```

StDevP(column) The StDevP() function evaluates the population for a group of values. For instance, the following statement returns the population for freight, 43.75, in the RJ region:

```
SELECT StDevP(Freight)
FROM Orders
WHERE ShipRegion = 'RJ'
```

Var(column) The Var() function estimates variance. For instance, the following statement estimates the variance for freight, 1971.85, on orders shipped to the RJ region:

```
SELECT  Var(Freight)
FROM Orders
WHERE ShipRegion = 'RJ'
```

VarP(column) The VarP() function evaluates the variance by population. The following statement evaluates the variance across the population for the freight, 1913.86, shipped to the RJ region:

```
SELECT VarP(Freight)
FROM Orders
WHERE ShipRegion = 'RJ'
```

FOR MORE INFORMATION

Nowadays developers wear many hats, and the luxury of specializing in one language is long gone. SQL is probably the one skill that all web developers share because you must use SQL to interact with the database. You must do more than learn the basics; you must become proficient at SQL. This chapter has served as an introduction only. We encourage you to explore further sources of information on your own. One of the best sources of information about all aspects of SQL is Martin Gruber's *Mastering SQL* (Sybex, 2000). Another good choice for anyone working with Microsoft Access and SQL Server is *SQL: Access to SQL Server*, by Susan Sales Harkins and Martin W. P. Reid (Apress, 2002).

Summary

Structured Query Language (SQL) is the defacto language of relational databases. This chapter has introduced the most important features of SQL that you need to understand in order to do database development on the web. You've learned the basic operators and functions, and you've learned how to use SELECT and other commands to construct queries into your database.

In the next chapter, you'll start grabbing real live data.

Chapter 19

Getting the Data

As you know by now, the specific language and database you choose to develop your site will have a subtle effect on how you deal with dynamic data. However, for the most part, Dreamweaver MX deals with data, programming languages, and databases in a consistent way. For example, regardless of the language or database, Dreamweaver MX pulls data from your database through a data connection and places the data in a recordset. As you recall from previous chapters, a recordset is simply a collection of data from your database. From that recordset, you can manipulate and display data in your web pages using Server Behaviors such as master/detail page sets, dynamic text, dynamic table, repeating regions, and so on.

Dreamweaver MX also uses these Server Behaviors to treat ASP, ASP.NET, ColdFusion, JSP, and PHP a bit differently. Not every Server Behavior is available to each language. For example, master/detail page sets are only available to ASP, ColdFusion, and JSP. But we'll get to that in Chapter 21. Before we can really begin our "Getting the Data" discussion, we need to take care of some website house-keeping tasks such as properly configuring your site's testing server so that you can view and preview your dynamic web pages. Then we'll discuss creating recordsets from data we pull through data connections. Finally, you'll learn the many ways to output dynamic data to your script page.

This chapter covers the following topics:

- ◆ Previewing your pages
- ◆ Setting the testing server options
- ◆ Creating dynamic pages
- ◆ Recordset server behavior
- ◆ Displaying data

Previewing Your Pages

You can preview your dynamic web pages in three ways. First, you can view your dynamic pages through Design mode. When you view your pages in Design mode, Dreamweaver MX substitutes dynamic data with placeholder text enclosed in curly braces ({ }), as shown in Figure 19.1.

Substituting dynamic data with placeholder text is standard for Dreamweaver MX. There's nothing you must configure or turn on. Design mode is the best view in which to design and format the static layout elements of your page.

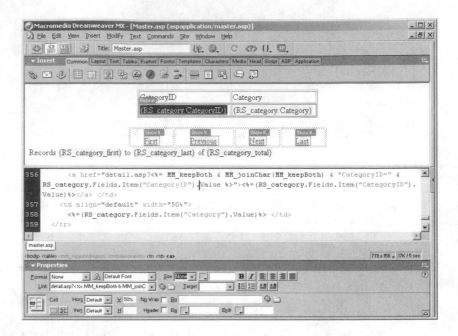

Second, you can preview your dynamic web pages by placing them on a web server and previewing the results in a web browser, as shown in Figure 19.2. Dreamweaver MX lets you instantly preview a page you're editing in a web browser. When you preview a page, Dreamweaver MX dynamically builds a web address to view a temporary copy of the current page through a web browser. To build the web address, Dreamweaver MX appends the name of the temporary script page to the address defined in your testing server. Using a web server is the truest test for determining the final look of your page.

Third, you can view your pages in Live Data view, which requires you to define a testing server in your Dreamweaver MX site. However, instead of launching a web browser to display the HTML (Hypertext Markup Language) results of your script page, Live Data view previews your page within Dreamweaver MX. As you can guess, Live Data view uses the testing server to render the HTML results of your script page and then displays the results within your Dreamweaver MX page, as shown in Figure 19.3. Live Data view is the best view in which to design and format the dynamic layout elements of your pages.

FIGURE 19.2

Viewing dynamic pages in a web browser

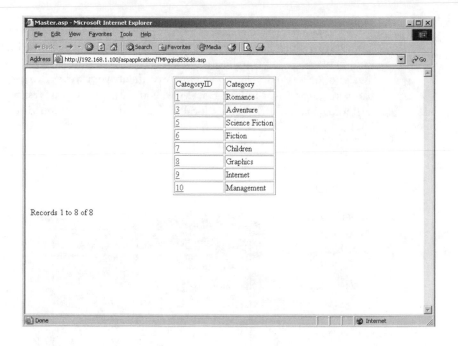

FIGURE 19.3

Viewing dynamic pages in Live Data view

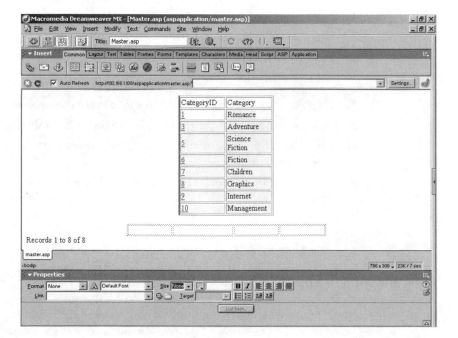

Setting the Testing Server Options

Your testing server can be your local computer, a web server on the Internet, or a web server on your local network. The pivotal criterion is that the server must have the ability to process the type of dynamic pages you develop. To properly configure your website to use a testing server to preview web pages in a browser or in Live Data view, you must define your testing server to use a specific server technology, you must specify a local path to your website home directory, and you must specify a URL to your website.

To define your testing server, follow these steps:

1. Choose Sites ➤ Edit Sites to open the Edit Sites dialog box, which is shown in Figure 19.4.

FIGURE 19.4

The Edit Sites dialog box

2. Select your website, and then click the Edit button to open the Site Definition dialog box.

3. Click the Advanced tab, and select Testing Server from the Category list.

4. In the Testing Server section, be certain your website script language is properly defined in the Server Model drop-down list box.

5. In the Access drop-down list box, choose a method for accessing your testing server. If your server is hosted by an ISP, you'll want to configure FTP (File Transfer Protocol) as your testing server access method. If you have local network access to your testing server, choose Local/Network.

6. In the URL Prefix text box, enter the URL of your testing server. The URL is the web address Dreamweaver MX will use to preview the HTML results of your script file. For example, Figure 19.5 shows the testing server configuration for our ASP (Active Server Pages) application website. Notice we have specified ASP VBScript as our server model, set the access to our testing server through our local network, entered the local file path to the site directory, and inserted the URL to get to our ASP application website through a web browser.

FIGURE 19.5

The ASP website testing server configuration

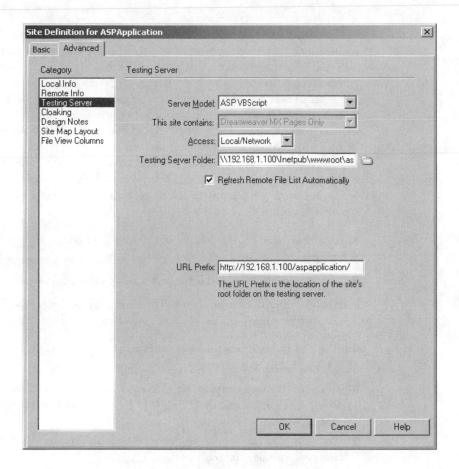

Previewing Pages in a Browser

Standard practice for all web developers throughout the development cycle is to preview their pages on the web server in a browser. Dreamweaver MX speeds up this process by allowing you to instantly preview any page you create with the Preview In Browser command. To do so, choose File ➤ Preview in Browser or press the F12 key. Dreamweaver MX creates a temporary version of your web page on your testing server, opens your choice of web browsers (typically Internet Explorer or Netscape Navigator), and displays the temporary file.

Dreamweaver MX creates only a temporary version of the current file on the web server. Dreamweaver MX does not create temporary files for related or included files that the current file may reference. Therefore, you might need to upload a related or an included file. To do so, choose Site ➤ Site Files to open the Site panel, select the appropriate files, and click the blue arrow.

Previewing Pages in Live Data View

As we mentioned, Live Data view displays the HTML results of the current script file within Dreamweaver MX. This may sound inconsequential, but it has a dramatic effect on the way most coders and designers develop. In the past, web developers scripted a bit of code, saved the file, jumped out to a web browser to preview the result, and then jumped back to the code. Live Data view allows you to visually design and modify your script page with real dynamic data all from within Dreamweaver MX. To switch from Design to Live Data view and back again, choose View ➢ Live Data.

What's more, Macromedia realizes that most dynamic pages require that some parameter be passed to render the proper result. Therefore, Macromedia accounts for these requirements in Live Data view. You can actually set Dreamweaver MX to create and pass any type of variable or value to your page. To demonstrate, let's create a URL variable to pass to the Live Data view of an ASP page. Follow these steps:

1. Create or open an ASP website in Dreamweaver MX.
2. Set the testing server as we've described earlier in this chapter.
3. Open a new VBScript ASP file and name it `LiveDataView.asp`.

In the body of the document, you need to insert labels and output statements to print a query string (or URL) variable named *varQueryString* and a form variable named *varForm* to the browser window.

4. Type **varQueryString:** in your script page.
5. Choose Insert ➢ ASP Objects ➢ Output.
6. Choose Trimmed QueryString Element from the ASP Objects menu. Dreamweaver MX inserts the output and the Trimmed QueryString Element request code line in your ASP script page.
7. Position your cursor between the quotes of the Trimmed QueryString Element request code and type **varQueryString**.

Now duplicate the process to insert an output statement that prints a form variable named *varForm* to the browser window.

8. Insert a <BR> statement after the *varQueryString* output statement to separate the variables with a line break.
9. Enter **varForm:**, then choose Insert ➢ ASP Objects ➢ Output.
10. Choose Trimmed Form Element from the ASP Objects menu. Dreamweaver MX inserts the output and the Trimmed Form Element request code line in your ASP script page.
11. Position your cursor between the quotes of the Trimmed Form Element request code and type **varForm**.

Figure 19.6 shows the completed output line to display the Trimmed QueryString Element named *varQueryString* and the Trimmed Form Element named *varForm* in the browser window.

FIGURE 19.6

The *varQuery-String* and *varForm* output line

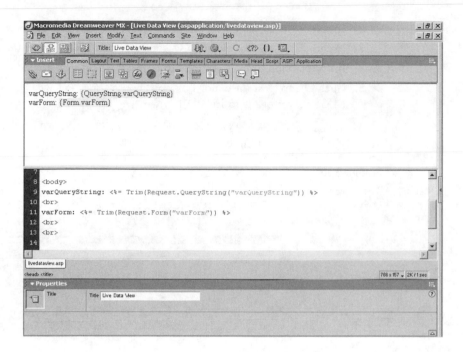

Now let's set Dreamweaver MX to pass the *varQueryString* variable and value to display the value in Live Data view. Follow these steps:

1. Choose View ➤ Live Data Settings or click the Settings button on the toolbar of your Dreamweaver MX script file to open the Live Data Settings dialog box, which is shown in Figure 19.7.

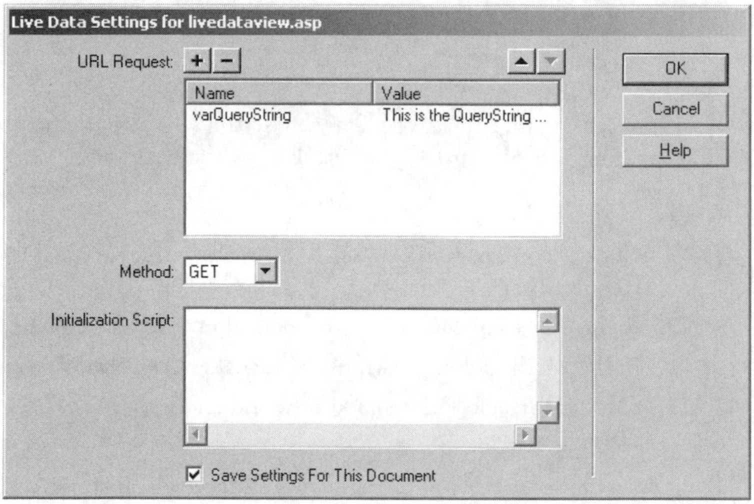

FIGURE 19.7

The Data View Settings dialog box

2. In the Name column of the URL Request list, enter **varQueryString**.

3. In the Value column of the URL Request list, enter **This is the varQueryString value**.

4. In the Method drop-down list box, select GET.

5. Click OK to close the dialog box, and choose View ➢ Live Data to switch your Dreamweaver MX ASP script file to Live Data view.

As you can see in Figure 19.8, our script page displays the value of the QueryString variable *varQueryString* that Dreamweaver passed.

FIGURE 19.8

The Live Data view of *varQueryString*

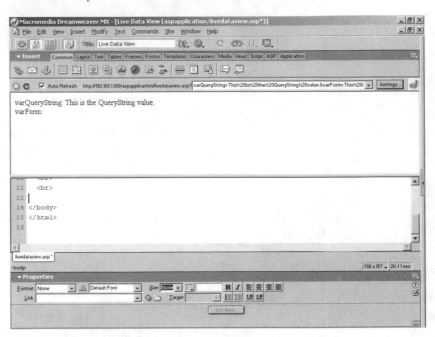

Now, let's change the Live Data view settings to pass the form variable *varForm* instead of the QueryString variable *varQueryString*. Follow these steps:

1. Open the Live Data Settings dialog box, which is shown in Figure 19.9.

2. Click the minus sign (–) button to remove the *varQueryString* variable from the URL Request list.

3. In the Name column, enter varForm, and in the Value column, enter **This is the varForm value**.

4. In the Method drop-down list box, change the method from GET to POST.

5. Click OK to close the dialog box, and choose View ➢ Refresh Design to refresh the Live Data view.

As you can see in Figure 19.10, the Live Data view now shows the value of the passed form variable *varForm*.

FIGURE 19.9

The *varForm*
Live Data Settings
dialog box

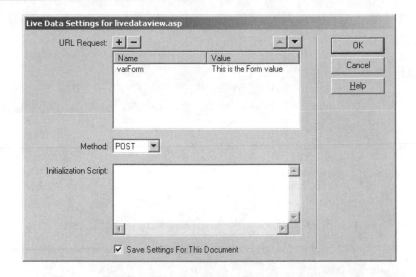

FIGURE 19.10

The Live Data
view of *varForm*

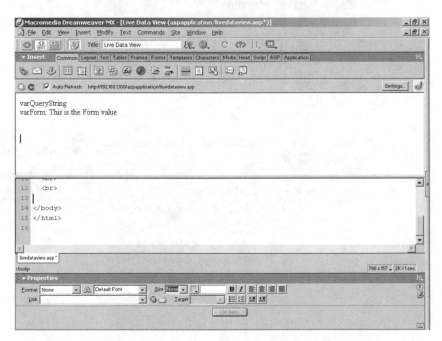

In addition to QueryString and Form variables, you can also use Live Data view to initialize application, session, and cookie variables before Dreamweaver MX previews your script file. As we've mentioned in previous chapters, an application variable is available to all pages running in your web application. A session variable is tied to the user and is available to every page the user accesses. A cookie is a text file written to the user's computer and is available to every page on your website. To set Live Data view to initialize an application, a session, and a cookie variable before it previews your ASP page, follow these steps:

1. Open the Live Data Settings dialog box.
2. Place your cursor in the Initialization Script text area.
3. Enter the following lines to create a *varApplication* application variable, a *varSession* session variable, and a *varCookie* cookie:

```
<%
application("varApplication") = "This is the varApplication value"
session("varSession") = "This is the varSession value"
response.cookies("varCookies") = "This the varCookie value"
%>
```

4. Click OK to close the Live Data Settings dialog box.

Now alter the `LiveDataView.asp` script file to display the application, session, and cookie variables.

5. Add the following lines to your ASP script file.

```
varApplication: <%= application("varApplication") %><br>
varSession: <%= session("varSession") %><br>
varCookies: <%= request.cookies("varCookies") %><br>
```

6. Choose View ➤ Refresh Design to refresh Live Data view.

As you can see in Figure 19.11, Dreamweaver MX runs the initialization code to create the application, session, and cookie variables and values and previews them in Live Data view.

FIGURE 19.11

Live Data View of application, session, and cookie variables

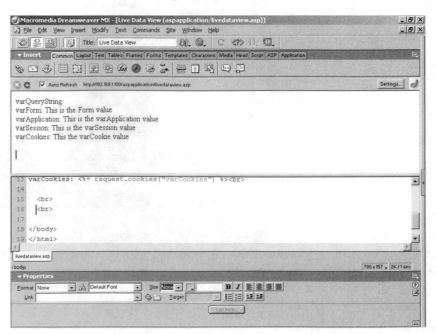

Live Data view is a great tool, but it does behave in a unique way that is different from previewing a script page in a browser. You should know about the following behaviors:

◆ Although we've already covered this, for the sake of thoroughness, let's restate. Live Data view uses the testing server to generate the HTML results of your script page and then displays the results in your Dreamweaver window. Therefore, your Dreamweaver MX website testing server must be configured correctly and accessible through a URL.

◆ While displaying a Live Data view, you can alter the layout using the page-design tools. You can add, modify, or delete dynamic content; add, modify, or delete Server Behaviors; and edit the code in your script page.

◆ Depending on the way you've configured Dreamweaver MX, Live Data view might not automatically refresh its view once you make changes to your script page. To refresh the Live Data view, choose View ➢ Refresh Design or click the Refresh icon (a circle-arrow) on the toolbar of your script page. Likewise, to set Live Data view to automatically refresh, select the Auto Refresh check box in the toolbar of your script page.

◆ Saving your file turns off Live Data view.

◆ Links do not function in Live Data view.

◆ To properly render the active script page, related or included files must be available to the testing web server. To upload a related or an included file, choose Site ➢ Site Files to open the Site panel, select the appropriate files, and click the blue arrow.

NOTE *Throughout the chapter, we mention that the Recordset Server Behavior is universal to all Dreamweaver MX–supported languages. That is true with one exception—ASP.NET uses a DataSet in place of a recordset. Although dramatic differences separate the definition and functionality of a recordset and a DataSet, the Dreamweaver MX interfaces to create a recordset or a DataSet are virtually the same. Therefore, for this chapter only, we'll refer to both as a recordset.*

Creating Dynamic Pages

As we've mentioned, regardless of the scripting language you choose, Dreamweaver MX lets you quickly create dynamic pages from a database using a three-step process:

1. Establish the database connection.
2. Create a recordset (or DataSet in ASP.NET) with a SQL statement or stored procedure.
3. Output the results of that recordset.

Chapter 10 covered establishing a database connection. Now let's create a recordset (or DataDet in ASP.NET) with that database connection.

To create a recordset, we can use the Dreamweaver Recordset (or DataSet in ASP.NET) Server Behavior with a SQL statement or the Stored Procedure Server Behavior. As you know by now, a SQL statement is simply a set of instructions passed to the database to retrieve data. A stored procedure is an SQL statement stored in the database that can be called to retrieve data. Let's begin with the Recordset Server Behavior using an SQL statement and then move on to the Stored Procedure Server Behavior.

Recordset Server Behavior

When you insert a Recordset Server Behavior in your script page, Dreamweaver MX first displays the Recordset dialog box, shown in Figure 19.12, which you can use to set the parameters of the Server Behavior.

FIGURE 19.12

The Recordset dialog box

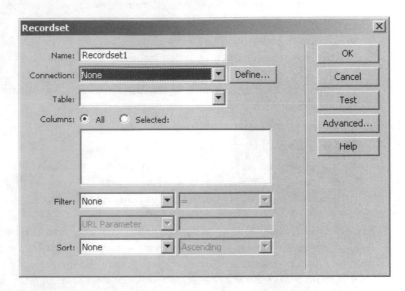

Every Recordset Server Behavior requires three items to function properly:

◆ A name for the recordset. The recordset name should be one word and free of characters such as ',", and /. Traditionally, developers use an RS_ prefix in a recordset name, such as RS_CATEGORY.

◆ A functioning data connection. We created a functioning data connection for each Dreamweaver MX–supported language in Chapter 10. Dreamweaver MX lists each available data connection in the Connection drop-down list box in the Recordset dialog box.

◆ An SQL statement that pulls data from your database.

SQL Statements

You can let Dreamweaver MX craft the SQL statement for you, or you can write your own SQL statement. To write your own SQL statement in the Recordset dialog box, click the Advanced button to switch to Advanced mode, which is shown in Figure 19.13.

FIGURE 19.13

The Recordset
dialog box in
Advanced mode

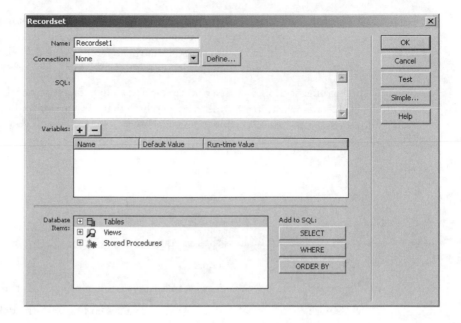

FIGURE 19.13

The Recordset
dialog box in
Advanced mode

Now, we're ready to create a recordset. In our example, the recordset will contain data from the Category table of our Books database. Follow these steps:

1. Open Dreamweaver MX and then open a new page in your defined site.

2. Save the file.

3. To insert a Recordset Server Behavior (or DataSet in ASP.NET) in your script page, choose Insert ➤ Application Objects ➤ Recordset to open the Recordset dialog box.

4. In the Name text box, enter **RS_Category**.

5. In the Connection drop-down list box, select your Books database connection. Notice that Dreamweaver MX populates the Table list box with the tables available in the Books database.

At this point, we'll create the SQL statement that actually pulls data from the database and inserts it into the recordset. As we mentioned, you can let Dreamweaver MX craft an SQL statement based on the table and columns you choose in the Recordset dialog box, or you can switch the Recordset dialog box to Advanced mode and write your own SQL statement. Let's examine both methods.

A SIMPLE RECORDSET

To let Dreamweaver MX generate a SQL statement based on your database table and column choice, follow these steps:

1. From the Table drop-down list box, select tblCategories. Notice that Dreamweaver MX populates the Columns section with the available columns in the tblCategories table.

2. You can set the generated SQL statement to return all table columns, or you can select specific columns. To return every column in the table, click the All radio button in the Columns section. To specify which columns the SQL statement returns, click the Selected radio button and choose the specific columns from the Columns list. (Hold down the Ctrl key to select multiple columns.)

In the Filter section, you set a comparison and a value for a specific table column. Doing so intructs the SQL statement to return only data matching that comparison and that value. Dreamweaver MX allows you to choose the following comparisons:

=	Equal
>	Greater than
<	Less than
>=	Greater than or equal to
<=	Less than or equal to
<>	Not equal to
begins with	Wildcard search for values beginning with the defined value
ends with	Wildcard search for values ending with the defined value
contains	Wildcard search for values containing the defined value

After you specify the comparisons, you must set a value. Dreamweaver MX provides the following six value types:

URL parameter	A variable and a value passed to the page through the URL
Form parameter	A variable and a value passed to the page through a submitted form
Cookie	A variable and a value stored in a cookie on the user's computer
Session variable	A variable set in the web server's memory and available to all pages the user visits
Application variable	A variable available to every page in your web application
Entered value	A value you enter in the recordset SQL statement

In the Sort section, you can sort the data returned to the recordset based on a specific column in the table and a direction you specify in the Direction list box. Dreamweaver MX automatically populates the Sort Column list box with the column names from the selected table in the Table drop-down list box.

Back to our example:

3. To set the SQL statement to return records that have a value of 1 in the CategoryID column, select CategoryID from the Filter drop-down list box, select = from the Comparison list box, select Entered Value from the Value list box, and enter **1** in the Value text box in the Filter section.

4. To sort the returned data alphabetically, select Category from the Column list, and select Ascending from the Direction list box in the Sort section.

The final configuration should appear similar to Figure 19.14. Now let's create the same SQL statement in the Advanced mode of the Recordset dialog box.

FIGURE 19.14

The final simple Recordset configuration

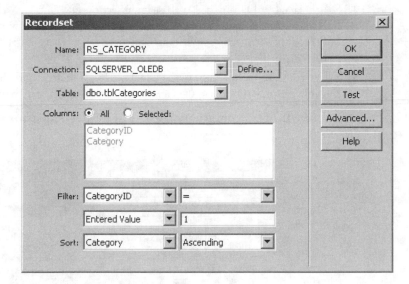

AN ADVANCED RECORDSET

Any time you need to populate a recordset with data from more than one table, you will need to craft your own SQL statement. In Advanced mode, the Recordset dialog box allows you to use a custom SQL statement in Dreamweaver MX to populate a recordset. Let's briefly review the properties of the Advanced dialog box, which is shown earlier in this chapter in Figure 19.13.

◆ A recordset name and data connection are required.

◆ An SQL text area allows you to write a custom SQL statement. Although you can write the SQL statement from scratch, Dreamweaver MX provides a point-and-click interface to help you build SQL using the Variables and Database Items sections.

◆ The Variables section allows you to name a variable and define its default value and runtime value. The default value is used in the absence of the runtime value. The runtime value can be a static value or a dynamic variable defined in your script page.

◆ The Database Items section allows you to create your SQL statement from the tables and columns available through the chosen data connection. You can add a table or column with the SELECT, WHERE, or ORDER BY clause by clicking the appropriate button.

To create the SQL statement in our example, follow these steps:

1. In the Database Items section, select tblCategories.

2. Click the SELECT button. Dreamweaver MX adds a simple SQL SELECT statement targeting the tblCategories table.

3. If you want the SQL statement to return specific columns from a table, choose a column from the table in the Database Items section and click the SELECT button.

4. Select CategoryID from the Database Items section, and click the WHERE button. Dreamweaver MX adds a WHERE clause to the SQL statement. Remember we want the SQL statement to pull only records with a CategoryID that matches 1. Therefore, enter =1 to the right of CategoryID in the WHERE clause.

5. Select the Category column in the Database Items section and click the ORDER BY button. Dreamweaver MX adds an ORDER BY clause to the SQL statement.

You can see the final configuration of the Recordset dialog box in Advanced Mode in Figure 19.15.

FIGURE 19.15

Create an SQL statement in the Recordset dialog box in Advanced mode

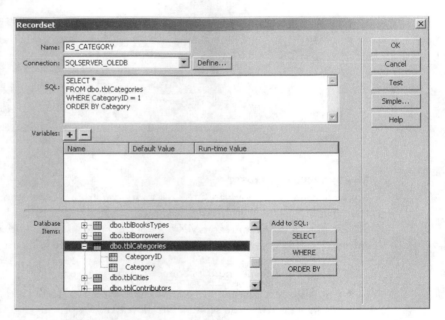

TESTING YOUR RECORDSET

Regardless of the method you use to construct your SQL statement, you can test its validity from within the Recordset dialog box. To do so, click the Test button to open the Test SQL Statement dialog box, which is shown in Figure 19.16. If the SQL statement test is successful, you should see all the data your SQL statement returns.

Once you're confident the recordset is valid, click OK in the Test SQL Statement dialog box, and then click OK in the Recordset dialog box to create the recordset. Dreamweaver MX places the required connection code and recordset code into the script file—ready to go.

FIGURE 19.16

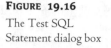

The Test SQL
Statement dialog box

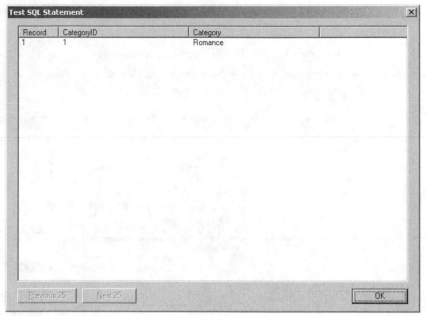

Stored Procedures

Stored procedures are SQL statements that are saved in a database and can be triggered to retrieve data. Since stored procedures are already in the database and can make use of more powerful database-specific functions, stored procedures are ultimately faster and more powerful than SQL statements passed to the database through a web server. The Server Behavior to create a recordset with a stored procedure varies with the scripting language of your website. Nonetheless, the interface to call a stored procedure is similar to the Recordset dialog box. It requires a name, a data connection, a name for the resulting recordset, and the SQL to activate the stored procedure. The following list shows the Server Behavior you use to call a stored procedure per scripting language. (MySQL and Microsoft Access databases do not support stored procedures.)

Microsoft ASP	Command
Microsoft ASP.NET	Stored Procedure
JSP	Callable (Stored Procedure)
Cold Fusion	Stored Procedure

To demonstrate how to use a Server Behavior to activate a stored procedure and return a recordset, we need access to a stored procedure. Obviously, detailing how to create a stored procedure for every type of database that Dreamweaver MX supports is out of the scope of this chapter. Therefore, let's limit our discussion to a common database such as Microsoft SQL Server. Let's create a simple stored procedure that targets the tblCategories table and filters data based on a value passed to the procedure. To do so, follow these steps:

1. Open Microsoft SQL Server Enterprise Manager, and select the Books database.
2. Choose Action ➤ New ➤ Stored Procedure to open the Stored Procedure Properties dialog box, which is shown in Figure 19.17.

FIGURE 19.17

The Stored Procedure Properties dialog box

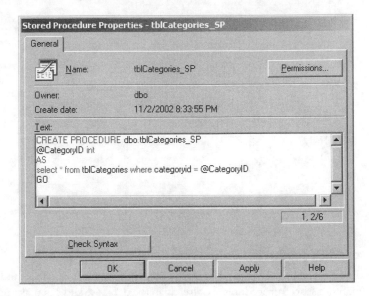

3. Enter the code in Listing 19.1.
4. Click OK to save the stored procedure.

You'll find all the listings in this chapter on the accompanying CD.

LISTING 19.1: TBLCATEGORIES_SP

```
CREATE PROCEDURE dbo.tblCategories_SP
@CategoryID int

AS
select * from tblCategories where categoryid = @CategoryID

GO
```

Now we'll add a Dreamweaver MX Server Behavior to a script file to activate the stored procedure and return a recordset. Since each language has its own way of activating a stored procedure, let's take it one language at a time.

Microsoft ASP

ASP uses the Command Server Behavior to activate a stored procedure. To activate a stored procedure in ASP, follow these steps:

1. Open a new script file in your ASP website, and name it `storedprocedure.asp`.
2. Choose Window ➢ Server Behaviors to open the Server Behaviors panel.
3. Click the plus sign (+) on the panel and choose Command to open the Command dialog box, which is shown in Figure 19.18.

FIGURE 19.18

The Command dialog box

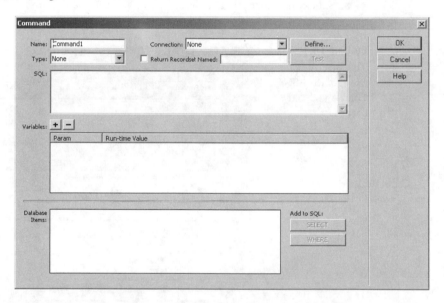

The interface for the Command Server Behavior is similar to the Advanced mode of the Recordset Server Behavior interface. The Command Server Behavior requires a name for the command, a data connection, a name for the returned recordset, and the SQL statement to activate the stored procedure. In addition, there is a Variables section and a Database Items section to help you create the SQL statement. As before, the Variables section allows you to set a test, or default value, and a runtime value. The Database Items section provides you with a point-and-click interface to choose your stored procedure.

4. To set the Command Server Behavior to activate the `tblCategories_SP` stored procedure, enter **Cmd_Category** in the Name text box.
5. Select a data connection from the Connection drop-down list box.
6. Click the the Return Recordset Named check box and enter **RS_Category** in the text box.

As you choose the data connection, Dreamweaver MX populated the Database Items section with the tables, views, and stored procedures available in the Books database.

7. To target our stored procedure, simply expand the Stored Procedure node of the Database Items section and select `tblCategories_SP` from our list. Doing so inserts the name of the

stored procedure into the SQL text area and populates the Variables section with the variables needed for the stored procedure to function.

The `@Category` parameter of our stored procedure requires a size, a test or default value, and a runtime value for the variable. A runtime variable is simply a variable passed to or set in the script page. If the runtime variable does not exist, Dreamweaver MX substitutes the test or default value. Fortunately, Dreamweaver MX inserts a default runtime value, `Request("CategoryID")`, that is based on the parameter name.

8. Click the `@CategoryID` row and enter **4** in the Size column and **1** in the Value column of the `@CategoryID` row, as shown in Figure 19.19.

FIGURE 19.19

The final configuration of the ASP Command Server Behavior

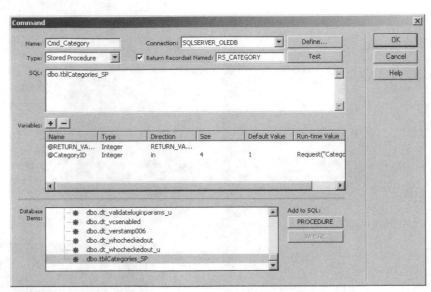

9. Click the Test button to preview the data that the stored procedure returns.

10. Once you are satisfied that the Command Server Behavior works correctly, click OK to save your settings and insert the code in your script page.

The final code should look similar to Listing 19.2.

LISTING 19.2: THE ASP COMMAND SERVER BEHAVIOR

```
<%@LANGUAGE="VBSCRIPT" CODEPAGE="1252"%>
<!--#include file="Connections/SQLSERVER_OLEDB.asp" -->
<%

Dim Cmd_category__CategoryID
Cmd_category__CategoryID = "1"
```

```
if(Request("CategoryID") <> "") then _
Cmd_category__CategoryID = Request("CategoryID")

%>
<%

set Cmd_category = Server.CreateObject("ADODB.Command")
Cmd_category.ActiveConnection = MM_SQLSERVER_OLEDB_STRING
Cmd_category.CommandText = "dbo.tblCategories_SP"
Cmd_category.Parameters.Append Cmd_category.CreateParameter("@RETURN_VALUE", 3, 4)
Cmd_category.Parameters.Append _
Cmd_category.CreateParameter("@CategoryID", 3, 1,1,Cmd_category__CategoryID)
Cmd_category.CommandType = 4
Cmd_category.CommandTimeout = 0
Cmd_category.Prepared = true
set rs_category = Cmd_category.Execute
rs_category_numRows = 0

%>
<html>
<head>
<title>Stored Procedure</title>
<meta http-equiv="Content-Type" content="text/html; charset=iso-8859-1">
</head>

<body>
</body>
</html>
```

Microsoft ASP.NET

ASP.NET uses the Stored Procedure Server Behavior to activate a stored procedure and return a DataSet. To use the Stored Procedure Server Behavior to return a recordset, follow these steps:

1. Open a new script file in your ASP.NET website and name it `storedprocedure.aspx`.
2. Choose Window ➤ Server Behaviors to open the Server Behaviors panel.
3. Click the plus sign (+) on the panel, and choose Stored Procedure to open the Stored Procedure dialog box shown in Figure 19.20.

The interface for the Stored Procedure Server Behavior is similar to the Advanced mode of the Recordset Server Behavior interface and the Command Server Behavior interface. The Stored Procedure Server Behavior requires a name, a data connection, a name for the returned DataSet, and the stored procedure to activate. In addition, there are a Parameters section in which to define variables to pass to the stored procedure and an On Success, Go To and On Failure, Go To sections that allow you to further specify what the web server should do in case of success or failure.

4. To set the Server Behavior to activate our `tblCategories_SP` stored procedure, enter **SP_Category** in the Name text box.

FIGURE 19.20

The ASP.NET
Stored Procedure
Server Behavior

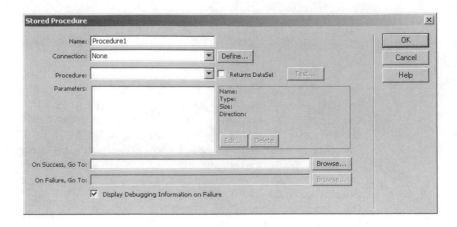

5. In the Connection drop-down list box, select a data connection.

6. Click the Return DataSet check box, and choose **tblCategories_SP** from the list of available stored procedures provided by the selected data connection. As you choose the stored procedure, Dreamweaver MX populates the Parameters section with variables required for the stored procedure to function.

7. To set the value for the **@Category** parameter, you must choose a datatype for the variable, a size, a test or default value, and a runtime value. To do so, select **@CategoryID**, and click the Edit button to open the Edit Parameter dialog box, which is shown in Figure 19.21.

FIGURE 19.21

The ASP.NET Edit
Parameter dialog box

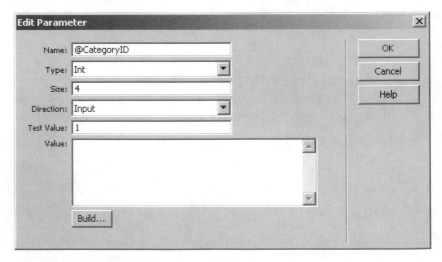

8. From the Type drop-down list box, choose Int.

9. In the Size text box, enter **4**.

10. In the Direction drop-down list box, select Input.

11. In the Text Value text box, enter **1**.

At this point, you can enter a value for `@CategoryID` or let Dreamweaver MX help you create a runtime variable for the value. The source of the runtime variable can be set from a URL or QueryString or from a form, application, session, or cookie value.

12. To let Dreamweaver MX help you create a runtime variable as the value of the `@CategoryID` stored procedure parameter, click the Build button to open the Build Value dialog box, which is shown in Figure 19.22.

FIGURE 19.22

The ASP.NET
Build Value
dialog box

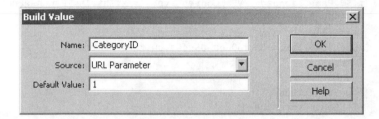

13. Enter a name for your runtime variable, choose a source, and enter a value as the default value for the runtime variable.

For our stored procedure, we set CategoryID as the variable name, URL Parameter as the source, and 1 as the default value.

14. Click OK to close the Build Value dialog box and return to the Edit Parameter dialog box.

As you can see in the Value text area of the Edit Parameter dialog box shown in Figure 19.23, Dreamweaver MX has built the ASP.NET code to check for the existence and value of a URL parameter named CategoryID. If the URL parameter exists and has a value, the code passes the value to the stored procedure. If the URL parameter does not exist or does not have a value, the code passes the default value of 1 to the stored procedure.

FIGURE 19.23

The ASP.NET Edit
Parameter dialog box
with generated code

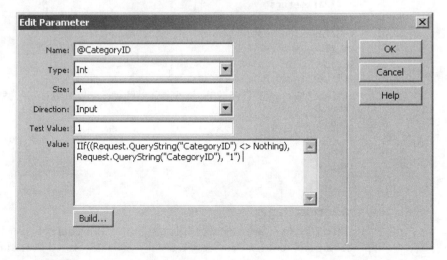

15. Click OK to close the Edit Parameter dialog box.

16. In the Stored Procedure dialog box, click the Test button to check the validity of your settings. If all went well, Dreamweaver MX displays the returned data.

17. Once you are satisfied that the configuration of the Stored Procedure Server Behavior is correct, click OK to add the ASP.NET code to your script page, as shown in Listing 19.3.

LISTING 19.3: THE ASP.NET STORED PROCEDURE SERVER BEHAVIOR

```
<%@ Page Language="VB" ContentType="text/html" ResponseEncoding="iso-8859-1" %>
<%@ Register TagPrefix="MM" Namespace="DreamweaverCtrls" _
Assembly="DreamweaverCtrls,version=1.0.0.0,_
publicKeyToken=836f606ede05d46a,culture=neutral" %>
<MM:DataSet
runat="Server"
id="SP_Category"
IsStoredProcedure="true"
CreateDataSet="true"
ConnectionString='<%# System.Configuration.ConfigurationSettings._
AppSettings("MM_CONNECTION_STRING_BookTrackingSQL") %>'
DatabaseType='<%# System.Configuration.ConfigurationSettings._
AppSettings("MM_CONNECTION_DATABASETYPE_BookTrackingSQL") %>'
CommandText="dbo.tblCategories_SP"
Debug="true"
>
  <Parameters>
    <Parameter  Name="@RETURN_VALUE"  Type="Int"  Direction="ReturnValue" />
    <Parameter  Name="@CategoryID"  _
Value='<%# IIf((Request.QueryString("CategoryID") <> Nothing), _
Request.QueryString("CategoryID"), "1") %>'  _
Type="Int"  Size="4"  Direction="Input" />
  </Parameters>
</MM:DataSet>
<MM:PageBind runat="server" PostBackBind="true" />
<html>
<head>
<title>Stored Procedure</title>
<meta http-equiv="Content-Type" content="text/html; charset=iso-8859-1">
</head>
<body>

</body>
</html>
```

JavaServer Pages

JavaServer Pages (JSP) uses the Callable (Stored Procedure) Server Behavior to activate a stored procedure and return a DataSet. To use the Callable (Stored Procedure) Server Behavior to return a recordset, follow these steps:

1. Open a new script file in your JSP website and name it `storedprocedure.jsp`.
2. Choose Window ➤ Server Behaviors to open the Server Behaviors panel.
3. Click the plus sign (+) on the panel and choose Callable (Stored Procedure) to open the Callable (Stored Procedure) dialog box, which is shown in Figure 19.24.

FIGURE 19.24

The JSP Callable (Stored Procedure) Server Behavior

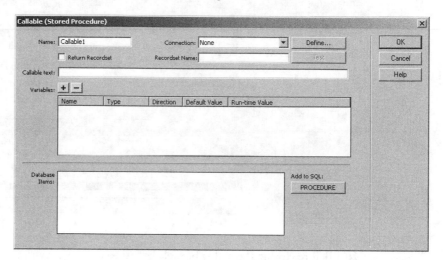

As expected, the interface for the Callable (Stored Procedure) Server Behavior is similar to the previous stored procedure Server Behavior interfaces. The JSP Callable (Stored Procedure) Server Behavior requires a name, a data connection, a name for the returned DataSet, and the stored procedure to activate. In addition, there are a Variables section in which to define variables to pass to the stored procedure and a Database Items section providing a point-and-click interface for you to choose the stored procedure.

4. To set the Callable (Stored Procedure) Server Behavior to activate our `tblCategories_SP` stored procedure, enter **SP_Category** in the Name text box.
5. In the Connection drop-down list box, select a data connection.
6. Click the Return Recordset check box, and enter **RS_Category** in the Recordset Name text box.

As you choose the data connection, Dreamweaver MX populates the Database Items section with the tables, views, and stored procedures available in the Books database.

7. To target the stored procedure, simply expand the Stored Procedure node of the Database Items section, and select `tblCategories_SP` from the list. Doing so inserts the name of the stored procedure in the Callable Text text area and populates the Variables section with the variables needed for the stored procedure to function.
8. To set the value for the `@Category` parameter, you must set a test or default value and a runtime value. To do so, select the `@CategoryID` row and enter **1** in the Default Value column.

9. In the Run-time Value column, Dreamweaver MX places the code to pull a value from a variable passed to our script page. However, it leaves the variable naming up to you. Therefore, click the Run-time Value column cell and insert **CategoryID** between the quotes of the JSP code, as shown in Figure 19.25.

FIGURE 19.25

Setting a runtime value in the Callable (Stored Procedure) Server Behavior

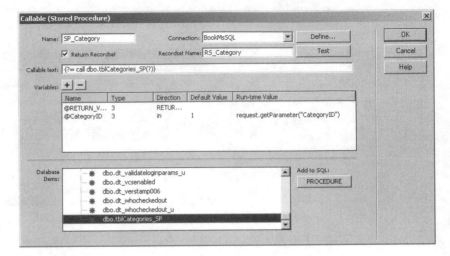

10. Before closing the dialog box, click Test to check the validity of your Callable (Stored Procedure) Server Behavior configuration. If successful, Dreamweaver MX displays the data that will be placed in the recordset.

11. Once you are satisfied the configuration of the Callable (Stored Procedure) Server Behavior is correct, click OK to add the JSP code to your script page, as shown in Listing 19.4.

LISTING 19.4: THE JSP CALLABLE (STORED PROCEDURE) SERVER BEHAVIOR

```
<%@ page contentType="text/html; charset=iso-8859-1" _
language="java" import="java.sql.*" errorPage="" %>
<%@ include file="Connections/BookTrackingMsSQL2.jsp" %>
<%

String SP_Category__CategoryID = "1";
if(request.getParameter("CategoryID") != null)_
{ SP_Category__CategoryID = (String)request.getParameter("CategoryID");}

%>
<%

Driver DriverSP_Category = _
(Driver)Class.forName(MM_BookTrackingMsSQL2_DRIVER).newInstance();
```

```
Connection ConnSP_Category = _
DriverManager.getConnection(MM_BookTrackingMsSQL2_STRING,_
MM_BookTrackingMsSQL2_USERNAME,MM_BookTrackingMsSQL2_PASSWORD);
CallableStatement SP_Category = ConnSP_Category._
prepareCall("{?= call dbo.tblCategories_SP(?)}");
SP_Category.registerOutParameter(1,Types.LONGVARCHAR);
SP_Category.setString(2,SP_Category__CategoryID);
Object SP_Category_data;
SP_Category.execute();
ResultSet RS_Category = SP_Category.getResultSet();
boolean RS_Category_isEmpty = !RS_Category.next();
boolean RS_Category_hasData = !RS_Category_isEmpty;
Object RS_Category_data;
int RS_Category_numRows = 0;

%>
<html>
<head>
<title>Stored Procedure</title>
<meta http-equiv="Content-Type" content="text/html; charset=iso-8859-1">
</head>

<body>
</body>
</html>
<%
ConnSP_Category.close();
%>
```

ColdFusion

ColdFusion uses the Stored Procedure Server Behavior to activate a stored procedure. To use the Stored Procedure Server Behavior to return a recordset, follow these steps:

1. Open a new script file in your ColdFusion website, and name it storedprocedure.cfm.
2. Choose Window ➢ Server Behaviors to open the Server Behaviors panel.
3. Click the plus sign (+) and choose Stored Procedure to open the Stored Procedure dialog box, which is shown in Figure 19.26.

The interface for the Stored Procedure Server Behavior is slightly different from the previous Server Behavior interfaces we've looked at. The ColdFusion Stored Procedure Server Behavior requires a data source, a name for the returned recordset, and the name of the stored procedure to activate. In addition, there are a Parameters section and a Page Parameters section that allow you to set a test or default value and a runtime value to pass to the stored procedure and set a script page variable with a default value.

FIGURE 19.26

The ColdFusion
Stored Procedure
dialog box

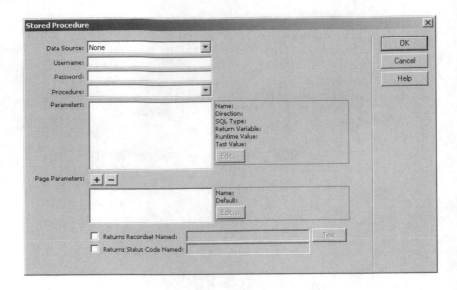

To set the Stored Procedure Server Behavior to activate our **tblCategories_SP** stored procedure, follow these steps:

1. Select a data connection in the Data Source drop-down list box and enter the username and password if applicable.
2. Select the **tblCategories_SP** from the list of available stored procedures in our SQL Server database.
3. Click the Returns Recordset Named check box and enter **RS_Category** in the text box.
4. To set a script page variable named CategoryID with a default value of 1, click the plus sign (+) in the Page Parameters section to open the Add Parameter dialog box, which is shown in Figure 19.27.

FIGURE 19.27

The ColdFusion
Add Parameter
dialog box

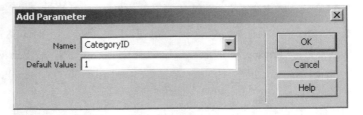

5. Enter **CategoryID** in the Name text box, and enter **1** into the Default Value text box.
6. Click OK to return to the Stored Procedure dialog box.

As you selected the stored procedure, Dreamweaver MX populated the Procedure section with the variables required for the stored procedure to function. To set the value for the **@Category** parameter of our stored procedure, you must set an SQL datatype, a runtime value for the variable, and a test or default value.

7. Select @CategoryID in the Parameters section, and click the Edit button to open the Edit Stored Procedure Variable dialog box, which is shown in Figure 19.28.

FIGURE 19.28

The ColdFusion Edit Stored Procedure Variable dialog box

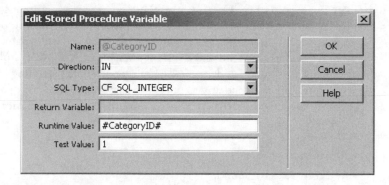

8. Dreamweaver MX guesses the direction, SQL type, and runtime value for the @CategoryID parameter. All that you must do is confirm that the Dreamweaver MX guesses are correct. If they are correct, enter **1** in the Test Value text box.

9. Click OK to return to the Stored Procedure dialog box.

10. Now you're ready to test your stored procedure configuration. To do so, click Test. If successful, Dreamweaver MX displays the data that will be placed in the recordset.

11. Once you are satisfied that the configuration of the Stored Procedure Server Behavior is correct, click OK to add the ColdFusion code to your script page, as shown in Listing 19.5.

LISTING 19.5: THE COLDFUSION STORED PROCEDURE SERVER BEHAVIOR

```
<cfparam name="CategoryID" default="1">
<CFSTOREDPROC procedure="dbo.tblCategories_SP" datasource="MsSQLServer_Book">
  <CFPROCPARAM type="IN"
   dbvarname="@CategoryID"
   value="#CategoryID#" cfsqltype="CF_SQL_INTEGER">
  <cfprocresult name="RS_CATEGORY">
</CFSTOREDPROC>
<html>
<head>
<title>Stored Procedure</title>
<meta http-equiv="Content-Type" content="text/html; charset=iso-8859-1">
</head>

<body>
</body>
</html>
```

Displaying Data

At this point, we're all up to speed establishing the database connection and retrieving data from a database as a recordset (or DataSet in ASP.NET). The missing step is to output the results of that recordset. Numerous Dreamweaver MX Server Behaviors can help you output data to your dynamic pages. More, your chosen scripting language might even have dynamic data output unique to its technology, such as DataGrid and DataList available in ASP.NET. Following is a list of the Server Behaviors available to output dynamic data categorized under scripting languages. Keep in mind that there is often more than one way to output dynamic data to a script page.

For ASP, Dreamweaver MX provides the following Server Behaviors to output dynamic data:

- Dynamic Text
- Dynamic Table
- Recordset Navigation Bar
- Recordset Navigation Status
- Repeat Region
- Master/Detail Page Set

For ASP.NET, Dreamweaver MX provides the following Server Behaviors to output dynamic data:

- Dynamic Text
- DataGrid
- DataList
- DataSet Navigation Bar
- DataSet Navigation Status
- Repeat Region

For JavaServer Pages, Dreamweaver MX provides the following Server Behaviors to output dynamic data:

- Dynamic Text
- Dynamic Table
- Recordset Navigation Bar
- Recordset Navigation Status
- Repeat Region

For Macromedia ColdFusion, Dreamweaver MX provides the following Server Behaviors to output dynamic data:

- Dynamic Text
- Dynamic Table

- Recordset Navigation Bar
- Recordset Navigation Status
- Repeated Region
- Master/Detail Page Set

For PHP, Dreamweaver MX provides the following Server Behaviors to output dynamic data:

- Dynamic Text
- Dynamic Table
- Recordset Navigation Bar
- Recordset Navigation Status
- Repeated Region

The Dynamic Text Server Behavior

The Dynamic Text Server Behavior allows you to place data pulled from a database anywhere in your script page. You can place dynamic text as text in the HTML body, as attributes of HTML tags, or as attributes of embedded objects such as Macromedia Flash. For example, in the following ColdFusion script, we use the Dynamic Text Server Behavior to set the title of the script page and the source of an image tag and to add text to the script page.

```
<cfquery name="RS_Category" datasource="MsSQLServer_Book">
SELECT * FROM dbo.tblCategories
</cfquery>
<html>
<head>
<title><cfoutput>#RS_Category.Category#</cfoutput></title>
<meta http-equiv="Content-Type" content="text/html; charset=iso-8859-1">
</head>
<body>
 <img src="images/<cfoutput>#RS_Category.CategoryID#</cfoutput>.gif">
 <h2>#RS_Category.Category#</h2>
</body>
</html>
```

Let's walk through the process we used to create this script. First let's place dynamic text in the body of our script page and apply the H2 style. To place dynamic text into a script page, you of course need an active recordset or DataSet. Follow these steps:

1. Place your cursor at the page position where you want the dynamic text to appear.
2. Choose Insert ➤ Application Objects ➤ Dynamic Text to open the Dynamic Text dialog box shown in Figure 19.29.

FIGURE 19.29

The Dynamic Text
dialog box

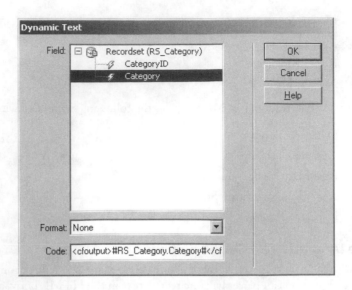

Dreamweaver MX displays the available data columns of the active recordset in the Field section and displays a Format drop-down list box, and a Code text box. The Field section is a point-and-click interface you can use to select the data column you want to use to populate your dynamic text. The Format list box allows you to format the data value of the dynamic text. You can choose to format text, numbers, or dates. For example, you can choose to display 01/01/2003 as January 01, 2003. Dreamweaver MX populates the Code text box based on your choices in the Field section and the Format list box. However, you can alter the resulting code.

3. Select your options, and then click OK to add the dynamic text to your script page.

4. Simply apply the H2 heading style to the dynamic text.

Next let's set the source of an image to dynamic text. For example, you've created an icon image for each category in the Books database. One way to comply with web filename restrictions and tie each icon image to a category in the database is to name the icon image according to the primary key of the category. This allows you to reference the appropriate category icon image by referencing the CategoryID of the tblCategories table.

1. Choose Insert ➢ Image to open the Select Image Source dialog box, which is shown in Figure 19.30.

2. Click the Data Source radio button to view the data columns in the active recordset on your script page.

3. To set the source of the image tag to a data column, simply select a data column.

4. Click OK to close the dialog box and insert the image tag in your script page.

FIGURE 19.30

The Data Source view
of the Select Image
Source dialog box

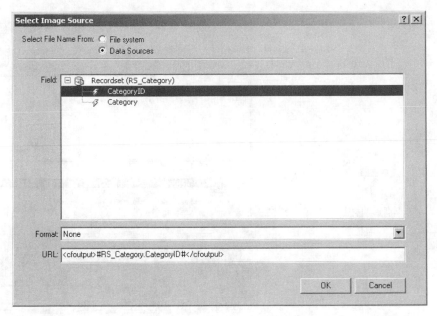

If you decide to edit the SRC attribute or add dynamic data to a new attribute, simply select the image and activate the Bindings panel. To do so, follow these steps:

1. Choose Window ➤ Bindings to open the Bindings panel.
2. To change the attribute attached to the dynamic data, click the drop-down list box next to the CategoryID data column.

The drop-down list box contains every attribute of the selected image tag. You can also choose a format for the dynamic data through the Format drop-down list box.

3. To attach new dynamic data to another attribute of the selected image tag, select another data column and choose an attribute from the Bind To drop-down list box located at the bottom of the Bindings panel, as shown in Figure 19.31.

Yet another way to add dynamic data to your script page is drag-and-drop. To demonstrate, let's add the Category data column to the <TITLE> tag of our script page. To do so, follow these steps:

1. Switch to Code view.
2. In the Bindings panel, click and drag the Category data column to your script page and drop it between the opening and closing <TITLE> tags. Dreamweaver MX places the dynamic text with the appropriate output code into the proper position of your script page.

As you can see, you can add dynamic data to your script pages in many ways. Although the three methods we've shown you are fast and incredibly easy, they are limited to one piece of a recordset at a time. Dreamweaver MX has even other methods for adding an entire recordset of dynamic data to your script pages—Server Behaviors.

FIGURE 19.31

Attach dynamic data to HTML attributes through the Bindings panel

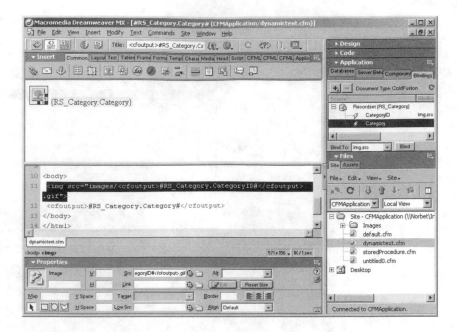

The Repeat Region Server Behavior

The Repeat Region Server Behavior loops through all records of the recordset. Whatever logic or HTML display code is inside the Repeat Region is run or output for each record in the recordset. To demonstrate the Repeat Region Server Behavior, let's create an HTML table to hold each record of the tblCategories data table. To do so, we want to repeat a single row of the table and not the table itself. Follow these steps:

1. Create a table that has one row and two columns.

TIP   *The simplest way to add a table is to choose Insert ➤ Table to open the Table dialog box. Enter 1 in the Row text box, and enter 2 in the Column text box. Click OK to close the dialog box and insert your table in your Dreamweaver page.*

2. Following the procedure we outlined earlier, add dynamic text for the CategoryID and Category columns of tblCategories to each table column. Your table should now look similar to Figure 19.32.

Now let's add the Repeat Region Server Behavior.

3. Select only the row of the table. You can do so in many ways, but the simplest is to place your cursor in the table and select <TR> from the footer of your script file document window.

FIGURE 19.32

Creating a table for
the Repeat Region
Server Behavior

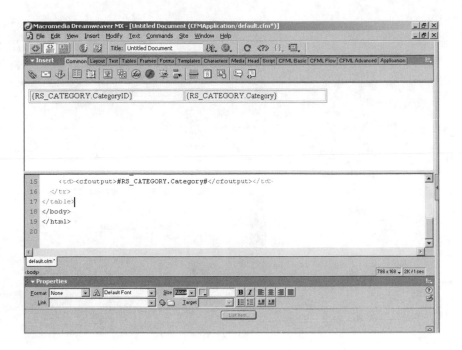

FIGURE 19.32

Creating a table for
the Repeat Region
Server Behavior

4. Choose Insert ➤ Application Objects ➤ Repeat Region to open the Repeat Region dialog
box, which is shown in Figure 19.33.

FIGURE 19.33

The Repeat Region
Server behavior
dialog box

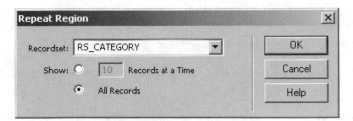

FIGURE 19.33

The Repeat Region
Server behavior
dialog box

5. From the Recordset drop-down list box, select a recordset, and then set the number of records
to display.

6. Click OK.

Dreamweaver MX wraps the table row with the Repeat Region Server Behavior code. You can
see the result in Live Data view in Figure 19.34. It couldn't get any simpler, could it? But wait,
it can!

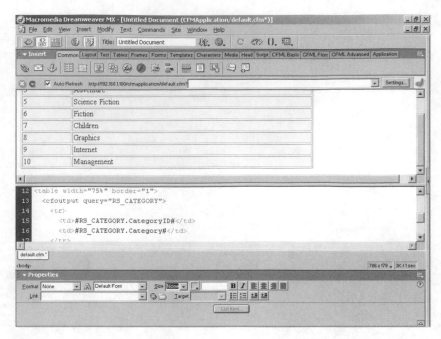

FIGURE 19.34

The live data results of the Repeat Region Server Behavior

The Dynamic Table Server Behavior

The Dynamic Table Server Behavior fully automates the creation and population of an HTML table with dynamic data using the Repeat Region Server Behavior. Don't tell your boss, but the only thing you have to do is create a recordset and attach it to the Dynamic Table Server Behavior. To add a Dynamic Table Server Behavior to your script page, follow these steps:

1. Choose Insert ➤ Application Objects ➤ Dynamic Table to open the Dynamic Table dialog box shown in Figure 19.35.

FIGURE 19.35

The Dynamic Table dialog box

2. Select the recordset with which to populate the table and choose the number of records to display per page plus the cell padding and cell spacing of the HTML table.

3. Click OK to create a table to output all the values of our recordset as shown in Live Data view in Figure 19.36.

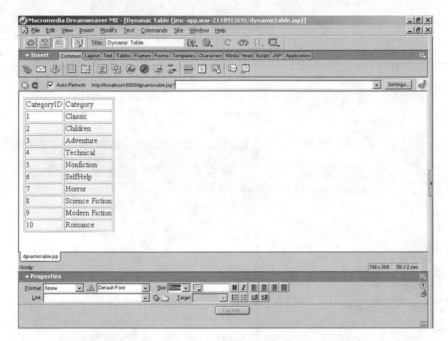

The Recordset Navigation Bar Server Behavior

Up to this point, each Server Behavior we've demonstrated outputs all available records in a recordset. At times, this behavior is not appropriate. For example, a recordset that contains hundreds of records would slow down the creation and display of a web page to an unacceptable level. When these situations arise, you can use Repeat Region and Recordset Navigation Bar to limit the amount of data sent to a web browser—thereby maintaining a fast download and response speed. In addition, the Recordset Navigation Bar Server Behavior also empowers the user to navigate through the data at their leisure.

The first step is to set the Repeat Region or the Dynamic Table Server Behavior to display a limited number of records. You then add the Recordset Navigation Bar Server Behavior to your script page. The Recordset Navigation Bar is a collection of Server Behaviors that create links that display the beginning, end, previous, or next record in the recordset. Further, the Server Behavior takes care of all the logic associated with navigating through a recordset, such as "Is there another record to display or is the current record displayed the last record in the recordset?"

To add a Recordset Navigation Bar to your script page, follow these steps:

1. Choose Insert ➤ Application Objects ➤ Recordset Navigation Bar to open the Recordset Navigation Bar dialog box shown in Figure 19.37.

FIGURE 19.37

The Recordset
Navigation Bar
Server Behavior
dialog box

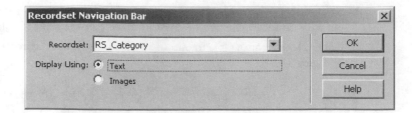

2. Choose the recordset, and select the navigation links to appear as text or images.

3. Click OK to create the text recordset navigation bar or the image recordset navigation bar. You can see examples of both in Figure 19.38.

FIGURE 19.38

The Recordset
Navigation Bar
Server Behavior

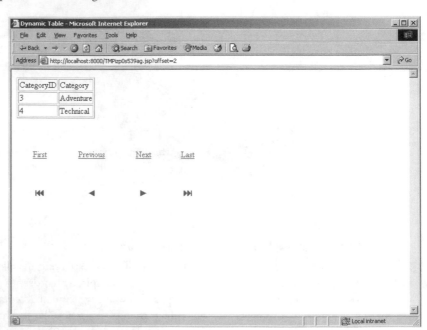

Although the Recordset Navigation Server Behavior is listed as one Server Behavior, it actually consists of several Server Behaviors. The following Server Behaviors make up the Recordset Navigation Bar:

◆ Show If Recordset Is Empty

◆ Show If Not First Record

◆ Move To First Record

◆ Move to Previous Record

◆ Move To Next Record

◆ Show If Not Last Record

◆ Move To Last Record

The Recordset Navigation Status Server Behavior

The Recordset Navigation Status Server Behavior goes hand in hand with the Recordset Navigation Bar Server Behavior. The Recordset Navigation Status Server Behavior displays the current record out of the total number of records in the recordset; the Navigation Bar becomes a less powerful tool without it. To add the Recordset Navigation Status Server Behavior to your script page, follow these steps:

1. Choose Insert ➤ Application Objects ➤ Recordset Navigation Status to open the Recordset Navigation Status dialog box shown in Figure 19.39.

FIGURE 19.39

The Recordset Navigation Status Server Behavior

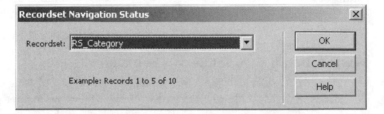

2. In the Recordset drop-down list box, select the appropriate recordset and click OK.

Figure 19.40 shows the browser result of the Recordset Navigation Status Server Behavior.

FIGURE 19.40

The browser result of the Recordset Navigation Status Server Behavior

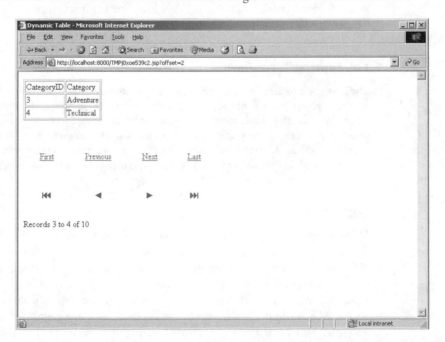

ASP.NET-Specific Server Behaviors—Repeater, DataList, DataGrid

ASP.NET provides three unique Server Behaviors to output data from a data source—Repeater, DataList, and DataGrid. Repeater is similar to the Repeat Region server control that all the scripting languages provide, but it has a unique twist. Instead of simply repeating whatever might be inside the repeating region, the ASP.NET Repeater Server Behavior allows you to define various templates of code. You can set these templates to execute only during specific events. For example, you can create templates to alternate display rows in a table or display a certain visual style only for the column headings of a recordset. Similarly, DataList and DataGrid are unique Server Behaviors that also display data based on defined templates. DataList is similar to the Repeater Server Behavior, but gives the user the ability to interact and modify the data presented in the browser window. Even more powerful than DataList is the DataGrid Server Behavior. DataGrid generates a multicolumn table from a DataSet. Each generated column is of a specific type—data, button, hyperlink, template, or custom. In Chapter 15, we delved deeply into these and more ASP.NET server controls.

Master/Detail Page Set Server Behavior

Using the Master/Detail Page Set Server Behavior is a quick and effiicient way to present information to a user. A master/detail page set consists of two pages—the master page and the detail page. The master page lists limited amounts of information about the records in a recordset. Each record is displayed with a link to a detail page, which displays more information about the record the user clicked in the master page. Dreamweaver MX doesn't provide the Master/Detail Page Set Server Behavior for every supported language. However, using other Server Behaviors you can build your own master/detail page set. We'll leave further discussion of the whats, wheres, and hows of master/detail page sets for Chapter 21.

FOR FURTHER INFORMATION

The best place to find and research Server Behaviors and other Dreamweaver MX extensions is the Macromedia Exchange site at `http://dynamic.macromedia.com/bin/MM/exchange/main.jsp?product=ultradev`. Another resource for the latest and greatest Server Behaviors is `www.dmxzone.com` and `www.dwteam.com`. If you're more interested in creating your own Server Behaviors, check out the Macromedia technotes articles at `www.macromedia.com/support/ultradev/content/creating_sbs/` and `www.macromedia.com/support/ultradev/behaviors/create_extensions/create_extensions04.html`.

Summary

In this chapter, we've introduced you to the Server Behaviors that let you create recordsets (DataSets in ASP.NET) from SQL statements and stored procedures. Further we introduced you to the Server Behaviors that allow you to output and navigate through the dynamic data of a recordset. You've seen that you can output dynamic data in your script pages in many ways. You also learned that some Dreamweaver MX Server Behaviors are actually collections of other Server Behaviors. Although Dreamweaver MX is shipped with many Server Behaviors to make your development life easier, Macromedia and other third parties are constantly creating new and more specialized Server Behaviors. As such, before you spend time hand-coding a script page, look around. Some one has probably made a Server Behavior to do just what you want.

Chapter 20

Building Update Forms

FORMS—THEY'RE EVERYWHERE. You fill out forms when buying a car, when renting an apartment, even when joining a community bowling league. We just can't seem to function without forms. Well, the World Wide Web is no different. To obtain data from visitors to your website, you must use HTML forms. Chapter 4 introduced these forms. As you saw there, Dreamweaver MX provides the tools you need to build and manipulate HTML forms. Since HTML forms almost always update data, we're going to refer to them in this chapter as "update" forms. Using Dreamweaver MX, you can quickly and rather painlessly create useful, meaningful update forms to gather information within your sites.

This chapter covers the following topics:

- ◆ Creating an HTML form
- ◆ A few form rules
- ◆ Inserting a form in Dreamweaver MX
- ◆ Adding web controls to a form
- ◆ Creating an insert page
- ◆ Updating a record
- ◆ Deleting a record

Creating an HTML Form

HTML (Hypertext Markup Language) forms are the basis for communicating with website users on the Internet. They are the "telephone" that creates two-way communication between the user and the web server. For example, the form in Figure 20.1 allows the user to enter information that will be sent through an e-mail message. Forms gather data from the user, send it to the server, and many times present data back to the user based on what the user entered in the form. Shopping carts wouldn't be functional without HTML forms. You wouldn't be able to order your favorite books through Amazon.com without HTML forms, for example. HTML forms are basically a programming structure, and like all programming structures, HTML forms must follow a few rules.

NOTE *Although we discussed these rules in Chapter 4, we're reprising them here as a reminder.*

FIGURE 20.1

This form elicits feedback for an e-mail message.

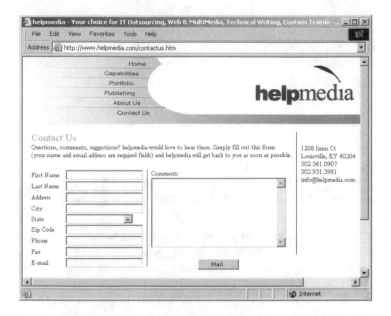

A Few Form Rules

It should come as no surprise that there are, naturally, rules applied to HTML forms. We are discussing programming for the web, right? HTML forms are easy to create and easy to use as long as you make sure they adhere to a few basic rules and guidelines.

Rule #1: Every Form Needs a Data Connection to Be Functional

In order for a form to be functional, it must have a connection to a database through a web server. That is, a form sends its data to a page on the web server that then saves that data to a database or perhaps performs some type of manipulation of the data. Since a form gathers data from the user, it only makes sense that you store that data on the server once you've massaged it to meet the website's needs. You define the page that the form will use in the form's ACTION attribute. We'll cover that later.

Now it is possible, of course, to create an HTML form that doesn't have an ACTION attribute. Forms are often used in conjunction with JavaScript to use an event (onClick) to call a script when the submit button is clicked. In this chapter, though, we'll concentrate on forms and databases.

Rule #2: Forms Cannot Be Nested

Forms can be thought of as containers, since they contain web controls such as text boxes and check boxes. This container is a self-contained item, as well. As such, a form or any HTML element, for that matter, cannot be split across pages, nor can it be nested within another <form> tag. The <form> </form> tag pair must not contain another <form> tag, although you can put multiple <form> </form> tag pairs on a page.

If you're going to put multiple <form> tags on a page, make sure that you end the current form before starting another form. The following is an invalid form structure:

```
<form>
    <form>
```

```
    </form>
</form>
```

but the following structure is perfectly legal on a single page according to HTML rules:

```
<form>
</form>
<form>
</form>
```

Rule #3: Forms Should Be Named

As you do with most tags in HTML, you should name a form. This practice let's you refer to the form in JavaScript and other code. Give the form a descriptive name that explains a bit about what the form contains. For example, the following code

```
<form action="" method="get" name="GetAddress"></form>
```

creates a form that has been named `"GetAddress"` because it's going to contain text fields that ask a user for address information.

Inserting a Form in Dreamweaver MX

As we've pointed out before, Dreamweaver MX provides many ways to accomplish a specific task. Adding a form to your HTML page is no different. As we mentioned in Chapter 4, you can add a form in several ways. You can choose Insert ➤ Form, you can click the Forms tab's Form control as shown in Figure 20.2, or you can simply type the tags in the Code window.

FIGURE 20.2

You can also add a form by clicking the Form control on the Forms tab.

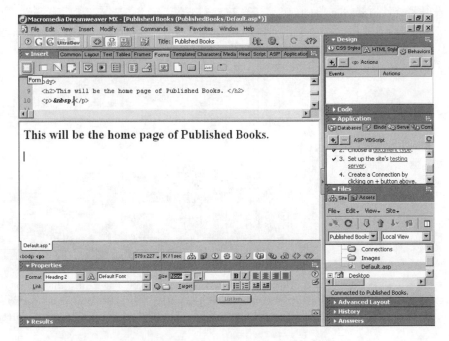

If the cursor is in the Code window when you insert a form, Dreamweaver MX displays the Tag Editor dialog box, as shown in Figure 20.3. If your cursor is in the Design window, you won't see the Tag Editor dialog box. In either case, once you insert the form and put the cursor in the Design window, Dreamweaver MX displays a dashed red line indicating that the form is present, as you can see in Figure 20.4. You can also see that we have the Property inspector open so that we can see the form properties that we can change.

FIGURE 20.3

In the Tag Editor dialog box, you can specify the properties for your `<form>` tag.

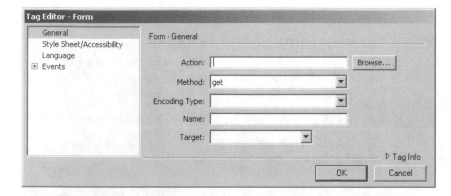

FIGURE 20.4

Dreamweaver MX adds a dashed red line to indicate the form boundaries.

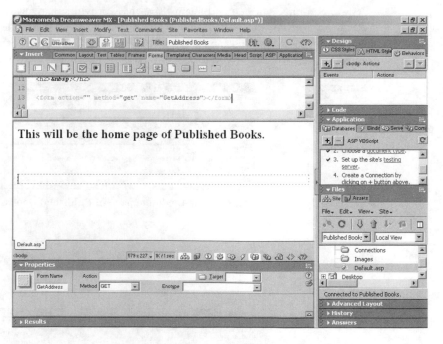

You can modify form properties in either the Tag Editor dialog box or the Property inspector. You can verify this by comparing Figures 20.3 and 20.4. But you can also see that you have a few more options in the Tag Editor dialog box than the Property inspector offers. Let's take a look at those.

INVISIBLE FORM ELEMENTS

If you added a form but don't see the red line we mentioned, you may not have the switch turned on that allows viewing of "invisible" elements. Dreamweaver calls these elements invisible, because even though the element is there, the user will not necessarily see it. To turn on the display of invisible elements, choose View ➢ Visual Aids ➢ Invisible Elements from the Dreamweaver MX main menu. When the item is active, you'll see a check mark next to it, as you can see here.

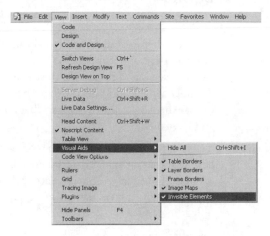

If you still can't see the dashed, red-line boundary after turning on the display of invisible elements, you may need to flip the Form Delimiter switch. Choose Edit ➢ Preferences, and click the Invisible Elements category:

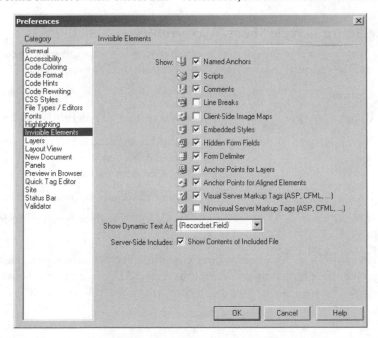

Tag Editor—General

A form tag has five basic, yet optional, attributes that you can specify. That is, the `<form>` tag won't generate an error if you leave any or all of them out of the code, but it doesn't necessarily perform any kind of functionality if you do so. Under the General option of the Tag Editor for Form, you'll see the following five basic options.

Option	Description
Action	Specifies the page that should receive the `<form>` data.
Method	Can be either Post or Get. Get is limited in the amount of data it can pass to a page, and it appends this data to the end of the URL where the user can see it and modify it. Post is used more than Get because it doesn't have the limits or restrictions of Get. It also doesn't immediately expose the data to the user. (See Chapter 4 to learn more about the Get and Post methods.)
Encoding Type	Tells the form what type of data to expect. Typically, this value is set to `application/x-www-form-urlencoded`, which specifies that the data is standard URL data. You can enter other values here as well, such as `text/plain` for e-mail data or `multipart/form-data` when you're uploading a file.
Name	Specifies the name of the form.
Target	Redirects the form results to a specific window or frame.

Tag Editor—Style Sheet/Accessibility

The options in this category let you specify the information needed to apply style sheets and accessibility options to your form. These options are shown in Figure 20.5.

Option	Description
Class	Lets you specify the custom class defined in Cascading Style Sheets (CSS).
ID	You can use this field as an identifier to refer to a specific form object with CSS, JavaScript, and other scripting languages. Check the Dreamweaver MX help file for more information on this.
Style	Lets you specify an embedded (or "inline") style.
Title	Gives the form a title for accessibility purposes. Screen readers will read this title, for example.

If you'd like to learn more about Cascading Style Sheets, check out the World Wide Web Consortium's information at `www.w3.org/Style/CSS/`, or simply visit your favorite web search engine. You'll find many resources on the Internet to aid you in learning CSS.

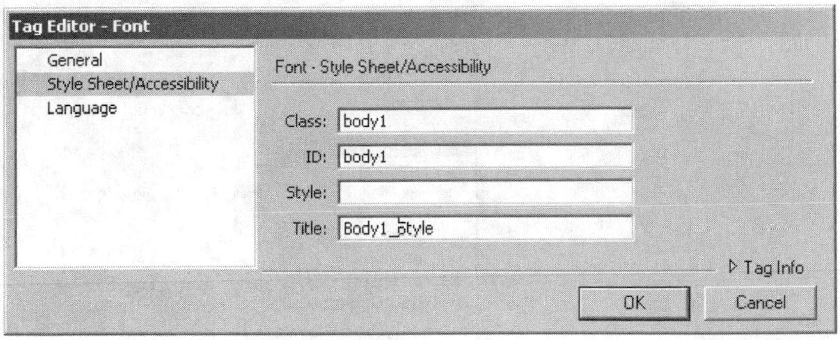

FIGURE 20.5

You set these options to control how your form will look and behave.

Tag Editor—Language

You can specify the language in which you're creating your form and specify how the text should be handled using the Language category options that you can see in Figure 20.6. This doesn't create the form in the particular language, but it tells the server that the form contains data in a specific language, which lets the server display and handle the information appropriately.

Option	Description
Direction	Specifies that the language is read right to left or left to right
Language	Specifies the ISO (International Organization for Standardization) setting for language choices

FIGURE 20.6

You set these options to control the language settings of the form.

Tag Editor—Events

The Events category lets you specify code to be executed for any of the many events associated with a form. These are events such as `onClick`, `onMouseOver`, and so forth. As you can see in Figure 20.7, once you expand the Events tree, you have access to the various events and can enter code in the Code window on the right.

FIGURE 20.7

Even forms have events associated with them.

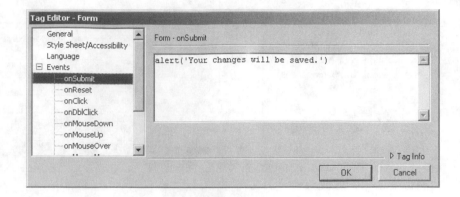

Adding Web Controls to a Form

A form isn't much use by itself—it's just a container. It's the objects, or controls, you put in that container that make functional pages possible. HTML provides several types of controls, and you'll find the basic controls all listed in Chapter 4. We're not going into detail about those controls here, but we will show you how Dreamweaver MX allows you to quickly add them to the form. And we'll cover a couple that Dreamweaver MX packages and provides as well.

You can add controls by typing the code in the Code window, by choosing Insert ➤ Form Objects, as shown in Figure 20.8, or by choosing the appropriate control from the Forms tab of the Insert bar, as shown in Figure 20.9. Figure 20.9 also points out the types of the controls corresponding to the individual icons.

FIGURE 20.8

The Insert menu lets you add various form controls.

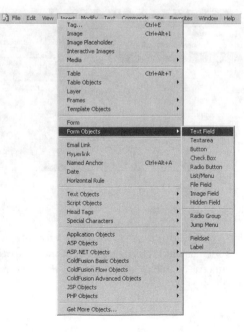

FIGURE 20.9

The Forms tab of the Insert bar lets you quickly add controls by clicking the proper icon.

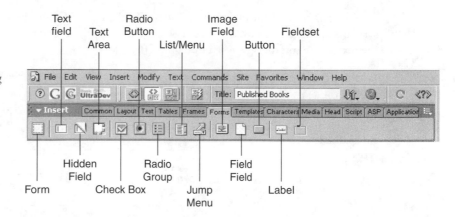

Just as when you're adding a form, adding a form control to the form opens the Tag Editor dialog box, in which you can specify properties appropriate to that control. Dreamweaver MX provides a couple of nonstandard controls that help in the creation of forms: the Radio Group control and the Jump Menu control.

WARNING   If you try to add a form control to the page, Dreamweaver MX automatically adds a <form> tag around the control unless you're already inside a <form> tag when you add the control. Make sure your cursor is within the form to which you want to add a control before you insert it in the page.

The Radio Group Control

Traditionally, when you want to create a radio button group—a group of radio buttons that act as one unit so that only one in the group can be selected—either you add a series of radio buttons to the form and then rename them all the same, or you copy and paste a single radio button. Dreamweaver MX lets you quickly add a series of buttons and actually format them just by clicking a single button. Click the Radio Group button to open the Radio Group dialog box, as shown in Figure 20.10. (You'll open this dialog box regardless of whether your cursor is in the Code window.)

FIGURE 20.10

The Radio Group dialog box lets you quickly add a formatted group of radio buttons to your form.

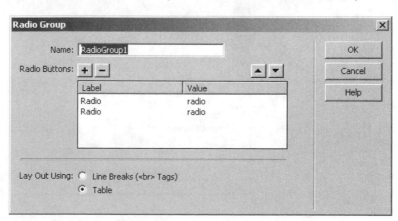

You can control the quantity of buttons in the Radio Group by clicking the plus and minus symbols to add and remove buttons. You can change the label and the value of each button by clicking the text in the middle, as shown in Figure 20.11.

FIGURE 20.11

We've changed the label and value for each button to suit our application's needs.

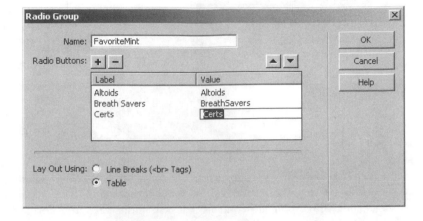

The Lay Out Using option is a handy item that makes us wish Macromedia had included a Checkbox Group as well. This option lets you control how the radio button group will be displayed in your HTML page, either by separating the items with line breaks or by putting the items in a table. Figure 20.12 shows an example of this behavior; you can see that indeed the group is enclosed within a table. You can see the table code in the Code window, as well.

FIGURE 20.12

Dreamweaver MX will automatically put the button group in a table for you.

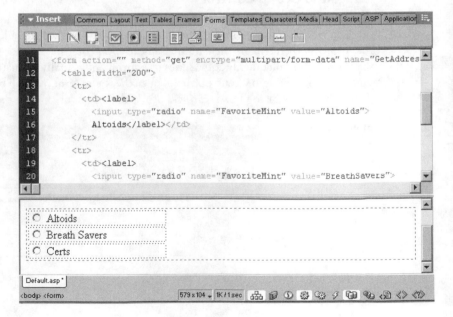

The Jump Menu Control

You can use the Jump Menu control to quickly and easily add a drop-down navigation menu to your pages. You specify the name and the URL for each item in the Jump Menu control, and Dreamweaver MX does the rest. It's that easy! You don't have to worry about creating all the JavaScript behind the scenes, because Dreamweaver MX does it for you. So let's add a Jump menu that let's the user jump to bookseller websites.

Click the Jump Menu icon to open the Insert Jump Menu dialog box, which is shown in Figure 20.13. We've added Amazon.com, Barnes & Noble, and Hawley-Cooke to our list. Notice that the URLs include `http://`. Without `http://`, the Jump Menu control assumes you're specifying a relative link—a link to a page that's on the same server as the menu's page. Once you test your menu, you'll see a functional drop-down list similar to that in Figure 20.14.

FIGURE 20.13

The Jump Menu control lets you quickly add a drop-down menu to your pages.

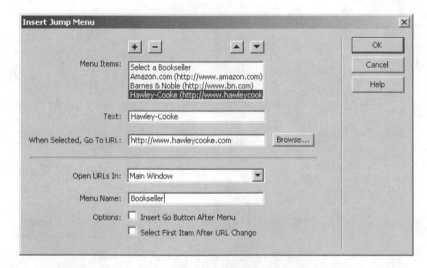

FIGURE 20.14

Our menu includes links to booksellers.

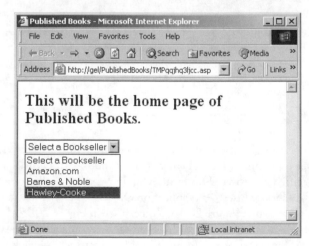

Now that we've covered the basics for adding an HTML form, let's look at how to make them useful. Next, we'll work with actual data.

Creating an Insert Page

Naturally, when you gather data from website visitors, you'll invariably need to store some of it in your data tables. You can quickly insert data into tables using Dreamweaver MX. As you might have guessed, Dreamweaver MX provides a method for inserting the data just by clicking a few buttons.

For this example, we're going to use the Books database included on the CD. We're going to add new categories to the Books database, so let's build a form for displaying the information we currently have and then let the user add a new record.

Showing the Current Data

We want to show the user the current data in the category table before letting them add a new item, so first let's build a recordset. Figure 20.15 shows our ShowCategories recordset. We've already established our DSN (see Chapter 10 for more information on setting up a DSN) called MDW_Books, and we're choosing to work the tblCategories table. (To add your recordset, click the plus sign [+] on the Bindings tab of the Application panel.) We're also going to sort by the Category field as a default.

FIGURE 20.15

We've defined a recordset for our insert page.

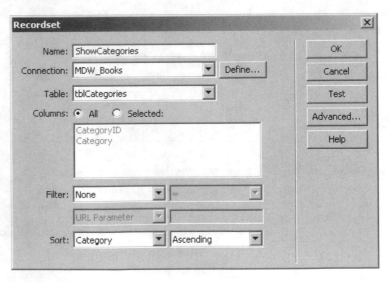

Now, we're going to use that recordset in conjunction with a Dynamic Table object, another Dreamweaver MX time-saver. A Dynamic Table automatically fills an HTML table with the data from the specified recordset. This means you don't have to hard-code the repeating behavior for this common task. Choose Insert ➤ Application Objects ➤ Dynamic Table from the Dreamweaver MX main menu, as shown in Figure 20.16. You can see in Figure 20.17 that we selected the recordset we just created. We're going to opt to show only five records at a time, so we enter 5 in the Show x Records At A Time text box. We add a bit of formatting and click OK to add our repeating table to our form, as you can see in Figure 20.18.

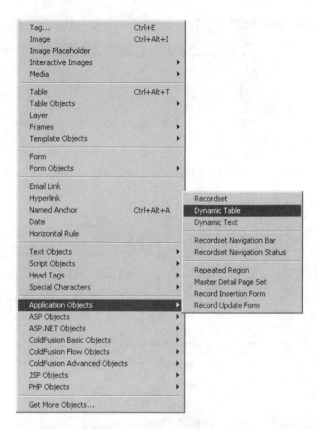

FIGURE 20.16

The Dynamic Table object will save you time when displaying records from a table.

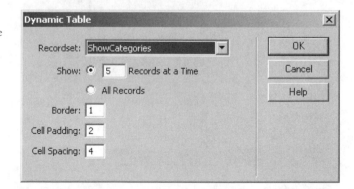

FIGURE 20.17

The Dynamic Table dialog box lets you specify settings for the Dynamic Table you're about to add to your form.

You can see in Figure 20.18 that Dreamweaver MX adds a Repeat outline to the table. This signifies the repeating region. If you don't see something similar to that shown in Figure 20.18, you might need to turn on Show Invisible Elements, as we described earlier. Preview the page in your browser (press F12) to see a display similar to Figure 20.19. Indeed, the table data is repeated for us, all quite painlessly.

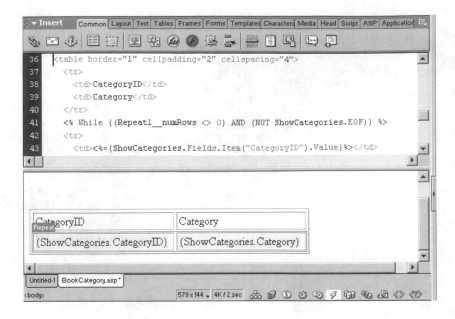

Now that we have the data in the table showing in a list, let's give the user a way to navigate between the records. We'll do that next with the Recordset Navigation Bar object.

Including Navigation Buttons

Our form contains the data from our Categories table, broken out in groups of five. We know that because we can see the first five records. Now, how do we view the rest of the records? Well, we can hand-code the proper ASP (or whatever language you're using) to move the records, but wouldn't it be nice if Dreamweaver MX would just let us plop in a button set to move through the records? Well, of course, Dreamweaver MX can do that—through the Recordset Navigation Bar object. We'll add one of those to our form in a second. First, let's make a place for it within our current table.

Right-click inside the last row of the table that contains the Repeated Region, and choose Table ➢ Insert Rows And Columns to open the Insert Rows Or Columns dialog box, which is shown in Figure 20.20. Add three rows below the current selection, and click OK. Dreamweaver MX adds three rows to the bottom of the table.

FIGURE 20.20

We're adding new rows to the table to accommodate the Navigation bar.

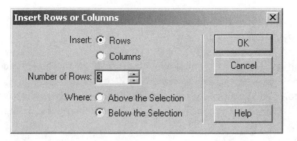

These three rows are currently within the repeating region, however, and will be repeated for every row in the table. This isn't the behavior we want, so we're going to simply move them down a bit, outside the repeating region. Follow these steps:

1. Place the cursor inside the first blank column in the newly added rows. Dreamweaver MX jumps to that column in the Code window, as you can see in Figure 20.21.

FIGURE 20.21

Dreamweaver MX jumps to the selected object in the Code window.

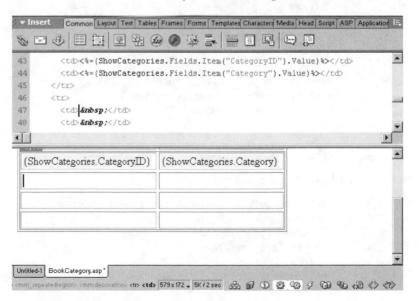

2. Select the newly inserted rows in the Code window by clicking the <TR> tag just above the cursor point and scrolling down to the closing </TR> tag that finishes the third row.

3. Hold down Shift and click the end of that tag to select the three rows.

4. Drag the three rows down to just beyond the closing ASP bracket (or tag or statement, depending on the language you're using) that is below the Wend statement. You want to make sure that the newly inserted rows are outside the repeating loop.

The table code goes from looking like the following:

```
<table border="1" cellpadding="2" cellspacing="4">
  <tr>
    <td>CategoryID</td>
    <td>Category</td>
  </tr>
  <% While ((Repeat1__numRows <> 0) AND (NOT ShowCategories.EOF)) %>
  <tr>
    <td><%=(ShowCategories.Fields.Item("CategoryID").Value)%></td>
    <td><%=(ShowCategories.Fields.Item("Category").Value)%></td>
  </tr>
  <tr>
    <td> </td>
    <td> </td>
  </tr>
  <tr>
    <td> </td>
    <td> </td>
  </tr>
  <tr>
    <td> </td>
    <td> </td>
  </tr>
  <%
Repeat1__index=Repeat1__index+1
Repeat1__numRows=Repeat1__numRows-1
ShowCategories.MoveNext()
Wend
%>
  </table>
```

to looking like the following code:

```
<table border="1" cellpadding="2" cellspacing="4">
  <tr>
    <td>CategoryID</td>
    <td>Category</td>
  </tr>
  <% While ((Repeat1__numRows <> 0) AND (NOT ShowCategories.EOF)) %>
  <tr>
    <td><%=(ShowCategories.Fields.Item("CategoryID").Value)%></td>
    <td><%=(ShowCategories.Fields.Item("Category").Value)%></td>
```

```
        </tr>
        <%
    Repeat1__index=Repeat1__index+1
    Repeat1__numRows=Repeat1__numRows-1
    ShowCategories.MoveNext()
  Wend
  %>
        <tr>
          <td> </td>
          <td> </td>
        </tr>
        <tr>
          <td> </td>
          <td> </td>
        </tr>
        <tr>
          <td> </td>
          <td> </td>
        </tr>
      </table>
```

Now if you preview the form in a browser, you should see the first five records followed by three blank lines, as Figure 20.22 shows. We're going to merge the columns in the bottom row so that the Navigation bar will be centered within our table. Select the bottom row, and merge the columns by clicking the Merge icon in the Property inspector. Click inside the newly merged bottom row, and choose Insert ➢ Application Objects ➢ Recordset Navigation Bar to open the Recordset Navigation Bar dialog box, as we did in Figure 20.23.

FIGURE 20.22

We're making room for the Navigation bar.

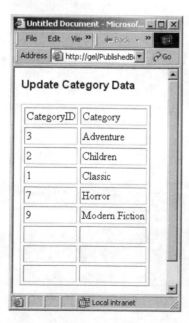

FIGURE 20.23

Insert the
Navigation bar
into the table.

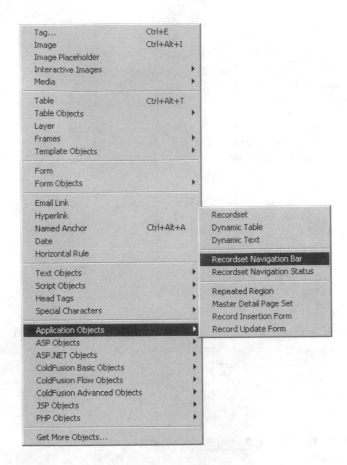

Figure 20.24 shows the Recordset Navigation Bar dialog box, in which you choose the recordset you want to navigate and specify whether you want the navigation links to be text or images. If you select the Images option, the Navigation bar uses VCR-style buttons. You must define the recordset before applying the Recordset Navigation Bar object—this option does not allow you to build one on the fly. Once you click OK, your table should look similar to our snapshot in Figure 20.25. Preview your page, and you'll see the actual buttons displayed in the table. Click a button to move the record pointer through the table and change the records accordingly.

FIGURE 20.24

You use the options
in the Recordset
Navigation Bar
dialog box to control
the appearance of
your Navigation bar.

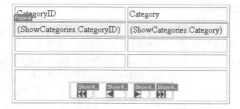

FIGURE 20.25

Dreamweaver MX inserts a placeholder guide in the page.

Inserting the Record Navigation Status

We can now move through the table with ease, thanks to the tools Dreamweaver MX provides. But where exactly in the table are we? Which record of how many total are we viewing? Dreamweaver MX lets you quickly add a status bar to the page as well.

Let's go back to our table and merge the cells in the row above our Navigation bar. Follow these steps:

1. From the main menu, choose Insert ➤ Application Objects ➤ Recordset Navigation Status to open the Recordset Navigation Status dialog box, as shown in Figure 20.26.

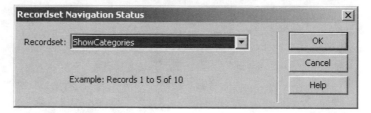

FIGURE 20.26

Dreamweaver MX includes a status bar that you can quickly drop into your pages to show where the record pointer is within the table.

2. Choose the proper recordset for which you want to navigate and click OK.

Add a bit more formatting and preview your page, and you should end up with something similar to Figure 20.27. Now, what about that thing we started with…inserting new data? Well, it's just as easy as adding navigation.

FIGURE 20.27

Your final table should look similar to ours, with the Navigation bar and status bar at the bottom.

Inserting a New Record

Now that the user can see the categories that are already there, let's add a spot for adding a new category to the table. (And, uh, keep in mind that a graphic artist hasn't had a go at this formatting, okay?) We're going to add three more rows to the bottom of the table and merge the cells as we did before. That makes room for our next Dreamweaver MX handy tool, the Record Insertion Form.

To set properties for the form Dreamweaver MX is going to automatically create for you, choose Insert ➤ Application Objects ➤ Record Insertion Form to open the Record Insertion Form dialog box (see Figure 20.28). This form allows you to enter new values for the fields you specify and inserts them into the table.

FIGURE 20.28

Save time and effort by letting Dreamweaver MX create an insertion form for you.

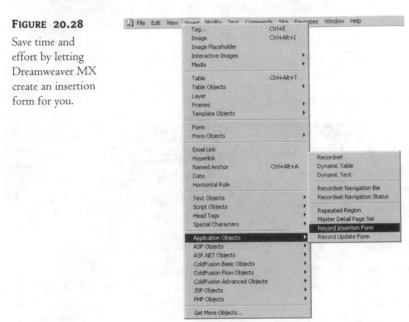

As you can see in Figure 20.29, we've chosen the proper recordset, the table into which we want to insert the data, and the page we want to go to after a new record is inserted. This location can be a fully qualified URL or a relative link, as we've specified in our example.

The Form Fields panel allows you to add fields from the table to the form or remove fields you've already specified. By default, Dreamweaver MX grabs all the fields in the recordset. You'll notice that CategoryID is in our Form Fields panel, but we're going to remove it. CategoryID is an Access AutoNumber field. You can't insert data into an autonumber field, so in order to prevent an error upon insertion of the data, we're going to remove the CategoryID field from our list. Click the CategoryID field, and then click the minus sign (−) to remove it.

The Label field lets you specify a new label for the selected Form field. This will appear to the left of the Form field so that you know what data you're entering. You use the Display As and Submit As drop-down lists to control how the data appears in the form as well as how it should be submitted to the table. We'll look at this in more detail shortly. For now, just click OK to place an insert form in your table, similar to that shown in Figure 20.30.

FIGURE 20.29

In the Record Insertion Form dialog box, you specify all the properties necessary to set up a form for inserting data.

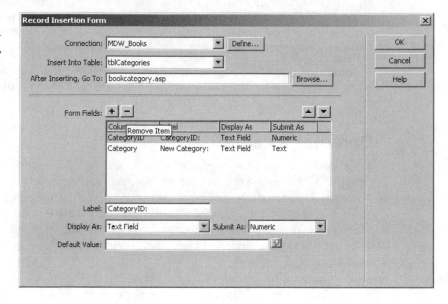

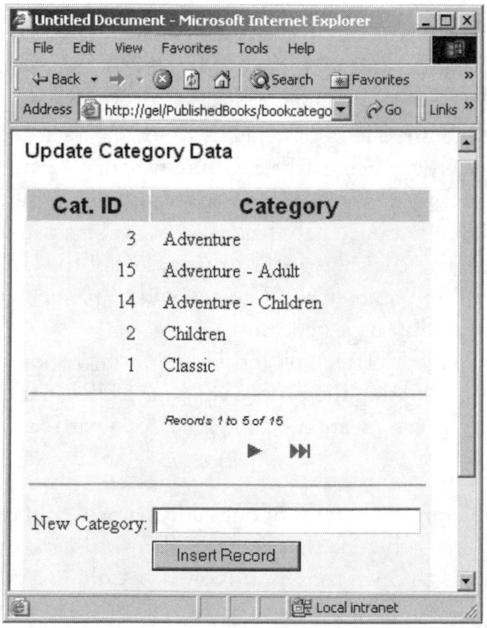

FIGURE 20.30

Our update form now has a means of allowing a user to add a new record to the table.

SERVER BEHAVIORS DO THE WORK

All these fantastic Dreamweaver MX tools that save you time and effort may seem like magic, but they're really just Server Behaviors that Dreamweaver MX applies to your pages behind the scenes. For proof of this, check the Server Behaviors tab on the Application panel after adding any of the objects we've covered. You'll see items such as Dynamic Text, Move To First Record, Show If Not Last Record, and so forth.

You could manually add all these Server Behaviors yourself by clicking an object and choosing the appropriate behavior from the Server Behaviors panel. But why do so when you don't have to?

Updating a Record

We've created a means for a user to see the data and add a new record to the data. Now, let's add the capability for the user to update a record. Naturally, Dreamweaver MX provides a method for doing that, as well. Although this time, we're going to need to involve another page.

Dreamweaver MX provides the Record Update Form menu option, which lets you quickly create a form that will update the current record. Since we've opted to show the user several records at a time, it doesn't make much sense to add an update form to our current page. How would we specify which record is to be updated?

By putting the update form on a second page and using the Go To Detail Page Server Behavior, we can easily accomplish our goals. Before we do so, however, let's examine the Go To Detail Page Server Behavior a bit more.

The Go To Detail Page Server Behavior

Dreamweaver MX employs a series of mechanisms called the Master-Detail Forms concept, by which you can organize sets of pages into a hierarchical structure allowing the site visitor to drill down through your data to the desired level of detail by following a series of links. You'll learn more about creating a master/detail structure in Chapter 21. But we can use part of that concept for our purposes. The Go To Detail Page Server Behavior let's you create a link around an image, text, or whatever is linkable that passes a URL parameter to the linked page. This parameter consists of a singular value from a recordset. Generally, this value is the primary key of the table. You can also choose to pass existing URL and/or Form parameters. (These would be parameters passed into the calling page—not parameters that the calling page generates.)

If you put this Go To Detail Page link inside a repeating region, Dreamweaver MX repeats it for each value in the region, assigning the proper key to the URL parameter that corresponds to the current record. Hence, you can create dynamic links for a particular record with ease. Let's add this to our current form.

1. To add a new column to the right of our table that will contain the word *Update*, right-click the rightmost table cell—the one that contains the word *Category*—and choose Table ➤ Insert Rows Or Columns to open the Insert Rows Or Columns dialog box.

2. Add one column to the right of the selection by clicking Column and then clicking After Current Column. Dreamweaver MX adds a thin column, but leaves the cursor in that newly inserted column.

3. Enter **Options** in the header cell. You'll need to add the same formatting to this text as the other cells in order to make it all pretty. We're adding the plural form because we're also going to add a link to let the user delete a record from this column in a later section.

4. Click below the Options header in the empty cell, and enter **[Update]**. (Include the brackets.)

Your table should now look similar to Figure 20.31.

FIGURE 20.31
We've added an
Update column
to our table.

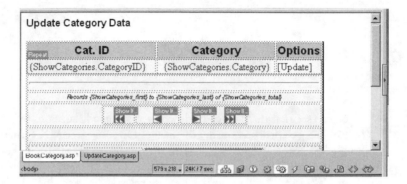

Now that we have the text we want to use as the link, let's apply the Server Behavior that will send the proper information to our page. Follow these steps:

1. Select the text you want for the link—in this case, the [Update] text you just entered.

2. In the Server Behaviors tab on the Applications panel, click the plus symbol, and then choose Go To Detail Page, as you can see in Figure 20.32, to open the Go To Detail Page dialog box, as shown in Figure 20.33.

FIGURE 20.32
Go To Detail
Page lets us create
a dynamic link to
another page.

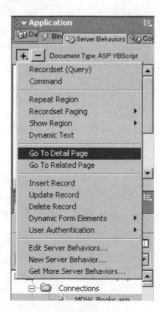

FIGURE 20.33

You can choose which field to send as a URL parameter in the Go To Detail Page dialog box.

You can see that the Link drop-down list box already contains our desired link text as a selection. You can change this by choosing the images Dreamweaver MX gathers from the page and adds as possible links as well. Since we want to use our link text, we'll not choose another image.

In the Detail Page text box, enter the name of the page to which you want to link. Even though we haven't created ours yet, we'll enter **UpdateCategory.asp** since that's what we're going to call our update page.

The Pass URL Parameter text box is tied directly to the Column drop-down list box. If you change the Column drop-down list by selecting different values, the selected value will pop into this field. You can also type over the text in the box. If you enter a parameter name that is different from those listed in the Column drop-down list, Dreamweaver MX will not overwrite your text.

In the Recordset drop-down list box, you choose a recordset from those that you've defined for this page. The Column category will change to reflect columns within the chosen recordset. In our case, we're going to select from the only recordset we've currently defined, ShowCategories. We want to use the CategoryID primary key as the parameter to pass, so we select that as well. Now, click OK and preview your page. It should look similar to Figure 20.34. If you look in the status bar of your browser window as you move your mouse over the Update links, you'll see that the CategoryID parameter is indeed updating properly for each record.

Adding Our Update Page

To create our update page, we're going to employ a couple of other Server Behaviors that Dreamweaver MX provides to make our development lives a little easier. Plus, we're going to use the Filter option available when defining a recordset, which we'll do first. Follow these steps:

1. Create a new page.
2. Add a title across it such as Update Book Category.
3. In the Bindings tab on the Application panel, click the plus sign and choose Recordset to open the Recordset dialog box.
4. In the Name box, enter **GetCat**.

5. Choose MDW_Books (or whatever your DSN is) as the connection.

6. Select the tblCategories table, and make sure that the All option is selected for Columns.

We've added an update link using the Go To Detail Page Server Behavior.

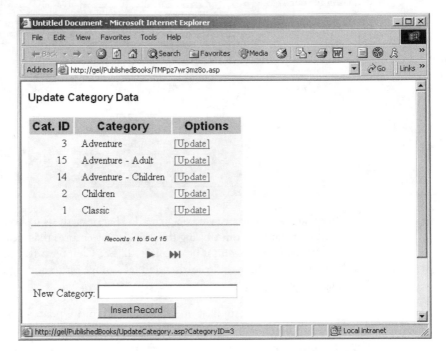

Now, we're going to create a filter for our recordset, which tells Dreamweaver MX to obtain only the records matching the specific criteria we're about to choose.

7. In the Filter drop-down list box, choose CategoryID.

8. Dreamweaver MX default to equals (=) in the next drop-down list box, which is good in this case, but you could choose from any of the logical operators in the list.

9. You use the Filter drop-down list box to tell the filter what type of data to look for. You can choose from among six types, including Session Variable, Cookie, and URL Parameter, which is what we want in this instance.

10. The next drop-down list box is tied to the first drop-down list and should currently contain CategoryID. If you write the filter out, it should look like this: CategoryID = URL Parameter CategoryID.

Your Recordset dialog box should now look similar to that in Figure 20.35.

11. To verify that everything works as it should, click the Test button and enter one of the CategoryIDs from the table, 3 for instance, in the field. Dreamweaver MX should return the record corresponding to that CategoryID.

FIGURE 20.35

This is the recordset definition for our update page.

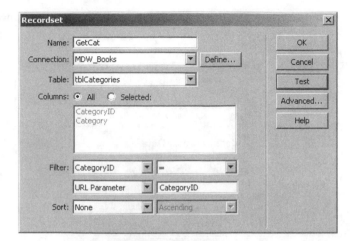

Notice that we're only receiving one record. That's exactly as it should be since we're only going to update one record at a time. Using the primary key ensures that we're going to get only one record back since a primary key cannot be duplicated. (See Chapter 5 for more information on databases and their behavior.) Save the recordset and let's move on to adding the Update Record. Follow these steps:

1. Choose Insert ➤ Application Objects ➤ Record Update Form to open the Record Update Form dialog box.

2. Choose the proper Connection (MDW_Books) and Table To Update (tblCategories) settings again.

3. Select the recordset you just created—in our case, GetCat—if it's not already chosen for you.

4. Select the primary key column CategoryID for the Unique Key Column field, if its not already chosen for you.

5. Since we want the user to go back to the UpdateCategory page when they finish updating, add UpdateCategory.asp to the After Updating, Go To field.

You should, by now, see the tblCategories field in the Form Fields panel. Remember that we can't update an autonumber field, which is the data type of our CategoryID field. So we could remove it from the panel by selecting it and clicking the minus button, or we could change the way Dreamweaver MX will handle it.

We want the user to be able to see the category ID so that they're sure they're editing the proper record.

6. Click the CategoryID field.

7. From the Display As drop-down list box, select Text.

The Display As field controls how the data will be displayed on the form. Submit As controls how Dreamweaver MX should format the data when sending it to the server. Since we chose to display the data as text, Dreamweaver MX deactivates the Submit As field, hence removing any chance for an erroneous update to this field.

8. Click OK and save your page as `UpdateCategory.asp`.

Your page should now look similar to that in Figure 20.36.

FIGURE 20.36

Our update page is ready.

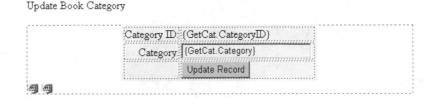

Let's Test It

OK, now we're ready to test our work. Go back to the `BookCategory.asp` page and either preview it or open it in a browser. Paging through the data, we see that "Selfhelp" is misspelled, as Figure 20.37 shows. This should be "Self Help," so click the Update link next to it, change the text in the Update Record window (see Figure 20.38) and click Update Record. It works, as you can see in Figure 20.39.

FIGURE 20.37

"Selfhelp" is misspelled.

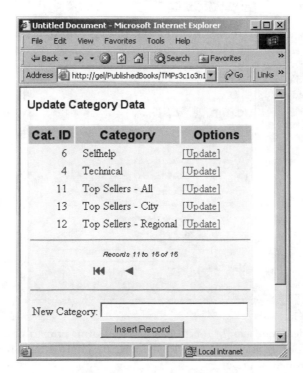

FIGURE 20.38
Click Update to open the Update Record window, and correct the text.

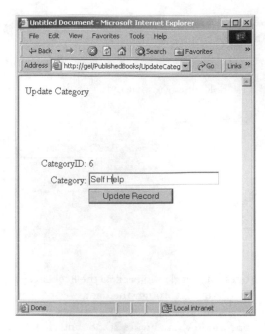

FIGURE 20.39
Open the `BookCategory.asp` page in a browser, and see that indeed the spelling of the category changed.

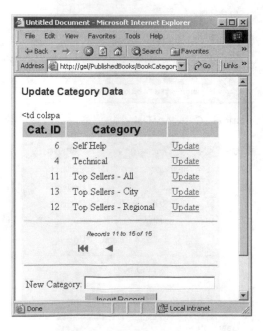

We've added quite a lot of functionality to our forms primarily just by clicking options. Such is the power of Dreamweaver MX! Now lets add an option to delete a record, in case the user wants to remove an erroneous category.

Deleting a Record

We're going to follow a slightly different method for deleting a record than we did for updating a record. This time, we're going to use the Delete Record Server Behavior. Follow these steps:

1. Add [Delete] next to the Update link in the Table column.
2. Highlight the [Delete] link, and add the Go To Detail Page Server Behavior to the link, just as we did before, only this time specifying `DeleteCategory.asp` as the Detail Page.
3. Create a new blank page, and add a header such as Delete a Category.
4. Add a recordset similar to the one we added earlier, except name this one something like DelCat.
5. Make sure you filter the recordset on the URL parameter CategoryID, as we've done in Figure 20.40.

FIGURE 20.40

Our recordset for our delete page is similar to the update page recordset.

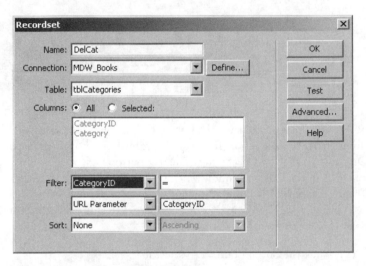

Next, we're going to manually create a data display and form on our delete page.

6. Insert a table that has two columns and two rows.
7. In the top row, add the table headers Category ID and Category.

Next, we're going to manually add the fields from the recordset to our page. It's easy to do, since we just have to click and drag the fields.

8. Expand the recordset DelCat on the Bindings tab of the Application panel.
9. Drag each of the fields CategoryID and Category to the appropriate second-row spot in the table, as we did in Figure 20.41.
10. To add a Submit button to the page, click the Button icon on the Forms Insert bar. Make sure you choose Submit as the button type.

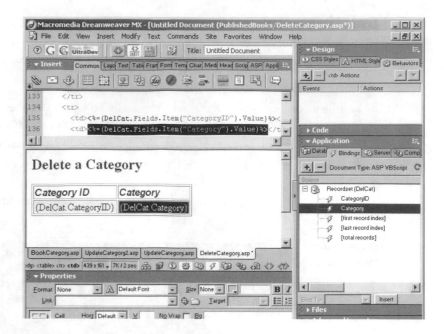

FIGURE 20.41
We're manually creating a display for the delete page.

You might want to name the button Delete Record or some other more meaningful name since this is an irreversible action. If you don't already have a form on the page (which we don't at this time), Dreamweaver MX adds a form around the button for you. (Dreamweaver MX adds the form if your cursor is in the Design window when you add the button. If your cursor is in the Code window, Dreamweaver MX will not automatically add the form.)

Normally, we'd name our form, but since we're only using the button here, we're going to leave the default name of form1.

11. Click the Submit button to select it.

12. Add the Delete Record Server Behavior following the technique described earlier.

13. Again, as you can see in Figure 20.42, we're using the same definitions to define the data connection. Since our recordset name has changed to DelCat, we select it in the Select Record From drop-down list box.

FIGURE 20.42
Your Delete Record definition should resemble this one.

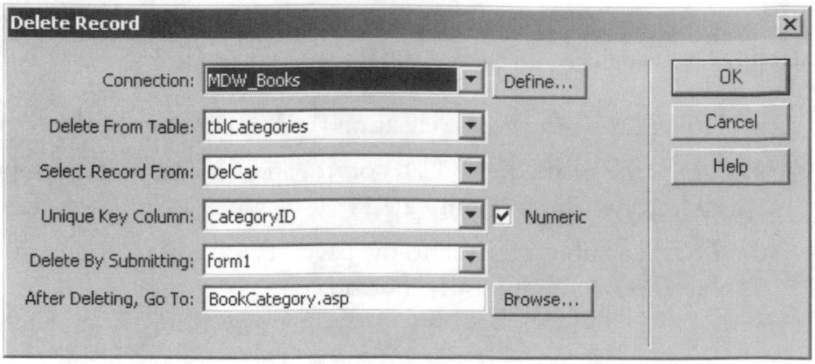

14. Click OK to add this behavior to the button. Delete Record will delete the current record once the user submits the form.

As all good delete actions should behave, ours should ask the user if they really want to pursue this process. We'll accomplish that by adding an OnClick event to the Behaviors tab in the Design panel. Since Submit is a unique button to HTML with a specific purpose, we'll find access to its events by right-clicking the button itself and choosing Edit Tag to open the Tag Editor dialog box. Expand the Events category, click OnClick, and add the following

```
javascript: return confirm('Are you sure you wish to delete this record?')
```

into the Input window as we did in Figure 20.43.

FIGURE 20.43

The Submit button's events are hidden in the Tag Editor dialog box.

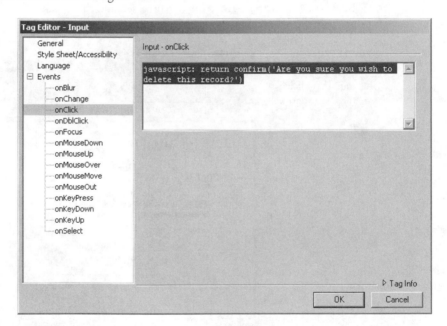

This code is, of course, a piece of JavaScript that will pop up a confirm message box with the "are you sure" message when the user submits the form. If the user clicks OK in the confirm message box, the submit will continue, and the code will delete the record. If the user clicks Cancel, the submit is canceled, and the record is preserved. Make sure you include the keyword `return` in the JavaScript; otherwise, the buttons will not function as you intend.

We should also give the user a way to cancel, or back out of, this delete process from the main page. We'll do that by adding another button with an OnClick method that simply jumps back to the `BookCategory.asp` page. Follow these steps:

1. Add another button, name it Cancel, and then select the button.

2. In the Behaviors tab, choose the Go To URL behavior to open the Go To URL dialog box, as shown in Figure 20.44.

3. Add the `BookCategory.asp` page in the URL box, and click OK. You'll now see the onClick Go To URL behavior listed in the Behaviors tab when the button is selected.

FIGURE 20.44

Dreamweaver MX provides a behavior that lets us jump to a URL.

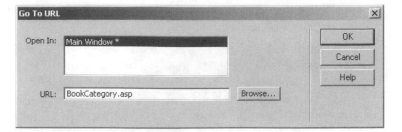

4. Save your page as DeleteCategory.asp.

5. Load BookCategory.asp in your browser, and then click the Delete button. You should see a confirm window like that in Figure 20.45.

FIGURE 20.45

The confirmation message after clicking the Delete button

6. Click OK to delete the record. If you click Cancel, the record is preserved, and the BookCategory page is displayed again.

Summary

Dreamweaver MX provides many mechanisms that make web development quicker and easier than writing code by hand. Using items such as the Application Objects, Server Behaviors, and so forth, you can create an entire Add, Edit, Delete module with very little coding involved. Using the techniques you've learned here, you should be able to quickly display forms, get data from the user, and let the user update and also delete that data. Naturally, larger systems are going to involve more pages, which will incorporate even larger sets of data. But the techniques of using Dreamweaver MX to massage that data are basically the same, regardless of the size of your DataSet.

Chapter 21

Building Master/Detail Page Sets

THE WAY YOU CHOOSE to organize information in your web application will ensure its success or failure. The tried-and-true method is to organize information into a hierarchy that allows the site visitor to "drill down" from general categories in a top-level or master list of information to the specific item they want.

As a web developer, you'll find yourself coding script pages that use the drill-down model again and again and again. Luckily, Dreamweaver MX provides tools to help you quickly build web applications based on the drill-down model. You can build a master/detail page set in Dreamweaver MX in two ways. If you are writing Active Server Pages (ASP) or JavaServer Pages (JSP) script or working with ColdFusion MX, you can use the Master Detail Page Set Server Behavior. If you are working in ASP.NET or PHP (Hypertext Preprocessor), you can use Dreamweaver MX Server Behaviors such as Repeat Region and Go To Detail Page to build your master/detail page set component by component. This chapter describes how to build master/detail pages using both methods, and both are easy to use.

This chapter covers the following topics:

- ◆ The drill-down model
- ◆ Building master/detail page sets
- ◆ Using the Master Detail Page Set Server Behavior
- ◆ Building master/detail page sets in ASP and JSP
- ◆ Building master/detail page sets in ColdFusion
- ◆ Building master/detail page sets using components
- ◆ Building master/detail page sets in ASP.NET and PHP

The Drill-Down Model

The drill-down, or master/detail, model of site organization is widely used and is familiar to most web surfers. The site first presents a master list of options. For example, a movie ticket site might first display a master list of current movie titles. Users browse this list and click a title to drill down for more information. At this point, the web application returns detailed information based on their choice, namely, a detail page displaying the specifics of the movie. The drill-down model is always constructed with a master list and a detail page. Of course, the drill-down model doesn't have to stop at two levels of information. In fact, our movie detail page most likely shows a master list of theaters showing the chosen movie. Click a movie theater to drill down again to show the detailed show times.

Likewise, the drill-down model isn't limited to one direction. In fact, to complete the interface model, many sites let users drill through information in every direction—eventually forming a circuit of information. For example, the page that displays movie show time information for a specific theater also contains lists of other movies currently playing at the theater. The user drills through that movie list to the original detail page that displays the specifics of the selected movie. From there the user drills through to the specific show times for the selected movie and also sees additional links to movies playing at the target theater. See the circular pattern? Using the drill-down model, you ensure that the user always feels your site is responsive and quick because the information they want is always a click away.

In addition to publicly displayed information, the drill-down model is also well suited for any database administration pages you provide for site maintenance. For example, the administration page for the movie ticket site might first display a master list of current movies. The site administrator can click a movie title to display a detail form in which movie specifics can be modified.

Building Master/Detail Pages

As we mentioned, Dreamweaver MX helps you quickly create master and detail pages that allow a user to drill down to find the most relevant information. Let's begin with a brief look at the master/detail structure you'll need to implement, whether using built-in Server Behaviors or scripting your own components, and then move on to build examples using the various Dreamweaver-compatible tools.

A master page lists records held in a recordset. Each of these records is displayed with a link to a record detail page that displays more information about the record the user clicked in the master page. To create a master page, you need several elements: a connection to your database, a recordset of data, and a link between each displayed record on the master page to that more comprehensive record on the detail page. As well, the detail page requires a connection to your database and a recordset of data filtered to show only the record passed from the master page. Figure 21.1 shows this process visually.

FIGURE 21.1

The Master/Detail model

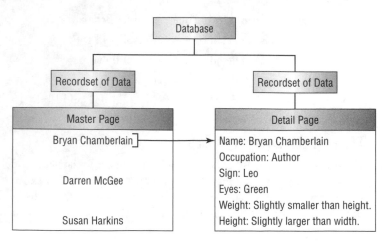

The glue that binds the master and detail pages is the link the user clicks on the master page to view the detail page. This link tells the detail page which record the user has clicked so that the detail page can display more information about that record. To allow the detail page to know which record detail to display, the master page must pass some record identification value in a variable to the detail page. The best way to identify which record was clicked on the master page and which record should be displayed on the detail page is to pass a variable containing the primary key of the record. For example, if the master page displays three records from our tblCategories table, each record passes its primary key to the detail page. The detail page catches the primary key and looks up the record information for only that record. This may sound complex, but creating a master/detail page set is simple using Dreamweaver MX.

Using the Master Detail Page Set Server Behavior

The fastest and easiest way to create a master/detail page set in Dreamweaver MX is to use the Master Detail Page Set Server Behavior. Choosing a Dreamweaver Server Behavior from the Server Behavior panel inserts pre-existing code into your dynamic page. With a small amount of configuration accomplished through dialog boxes, this inserted code is ready to run. Further, once you configure and insert this code, Dreamweaver MX continues to see the inserted code as an object, allowing you to easily modify the behavior through the same configuration dialog boxes. That is, by choosing Insert ➢ Application Objects (or by clicking the plus sign on the Server Behaviors tab of the Application panel), you can automatically create both the master page and the detail page at one time from the same data connection and recordset. This eliminates the typographic errors that often accompany such repetitive tasks as scripting a page and connecting to the data connection and the recordset. Let's create a master/detail page set using ASP and then JSP.

Creating a Master/Detail Page Set Using ASP

To demonstrate how to create a a master/detail page set using ASP, let's again use our Books database from previous chapters as an example. We'll create a master page that initially displays each book category listed in the tblCategories table. Later, we'll drill down to see the contents of each category.

1. In Dreamweaver MX, open a new page in your defined ASP site and save the file as Master.asp.

2. Using the BookTrackingOLEDB or BookTrackingAccess database connection we created in Chapter 10, create and add a recordset of the items in the tblCategories table. To do so, choose Insert ➢ Application Objects ➢ Recordset (or click the plus sign in the Server Behaviors tab of the Application panel and select the Recordset option) to open the Recordset dialog box, as shown in Figure 21.2.

3. Name the recordset RS_Category and choose your data connection from the Connection drop-down list box. Notice that Dreamweaver MX populates the Table drop-down list box with the tables available in the Books database.

4. Select the tblCategories table, and then select Category in the Sort list box.

5. Click OK to create the recordset.

FIGURE 21.2

The Recordset
dialog box

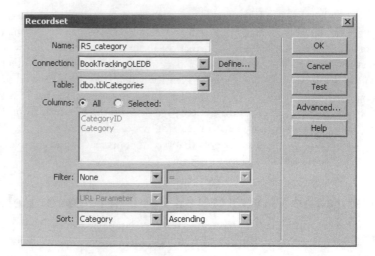

As you can see in Listing 21.1, Dreamweaver MX inserts the ASP `include` statement to reference the BookTrackingOLEDB data connection and the code to create the RS_Category recordset into the `Master.asp` script file.

LISTING 21.1: THE RECORDSET

```
<%@LANGUAGE="VBSCRIPT" CODEPAGE="1252"%>
<!--#include file="Connections/SQLSERVER_OLEDB.asp" -->
<%
Dim RS_Category
Dim RS_Category_numRows

Set RS_Category = Server.CreateObject("ADODB.Recordset")
RS_Category.ActiveConnection = MM_SQLSERVER_OLEDB_STRING
RS_Category.Source = "SELECT * FROM dbo.tblCategories ORDER BY Category ASC"
RS_Category.CursorType = 0
RS_Category.CursorLocation = 2
RS_Category.LockType = 1
RS_Category.Open()

RS_Category_numRows = 0
%>
<html>
<head>
<title>Master</title>
<meta http-equiv="Content-Type" content="text/html; charset=iso-8859-1">
</head>
<body>
```

```
</body>
</html>
<%
RS_Category.Close()
Set RS_Category = Nothing
%>
```

At this point, you're ready to insert the master/detail page set. To do so, follow these steps:

1. Choose Insert ➤ Application Objects ➤ Master Detail Page Set or click the Master Detail Page Set icon in the Application tab of the Insert bar to open the Insert Master-Detail Page Set dialog box, as shown in Figure 21.3.

FIGURE 21.3

The Insert Master-Detail Page Set dialog box

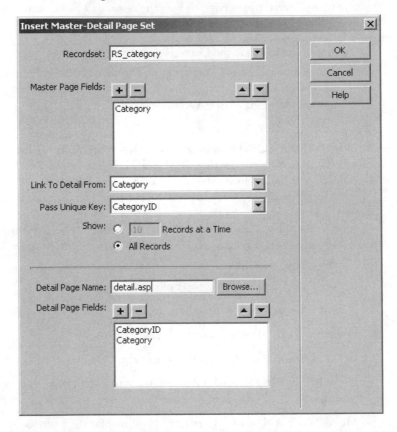

2. In the Recordset drop-down list box, select RS_category.

3. Select the table column fields that you want to on the master page. For our example, we want Category to appear in a list.

4. Choose the table column field that will link the master page to the detail page. Since we are displaying only one table column field in our example, our choice is simple—Category.

5. Choose the record identifier that the master page will pass to the detail page through the link. In our example, we want to use CategoryID, which is the primary key of the tblCategories table, so choose CategoryID from the Pass Unique Key drop-down list box.

Finally, the Show option allows you to divide all returned records into sets or pages of records. The default is to display 10 records at a time. Choosing this option inserts page record navigation links to allow the user to move forward and backward through the recordset 10 records at a time.

1. To keep our example relatively simple, in the Show section, click the All Records option.

At this point we've finished configuring the master page of our master/detail page set. Now let's configure our detail page. (Even though the result will be as many pages as there are categories, we only configure a single detail page.)

1. Enter **Detail.asp** in the Detail Page Name text field.

2. Much as we did for the master page, choose the table column fields you want the detail page to display for the record. Select both CategoryID and Category. Figure 21.3 shows our completed Insert Master-Detail Page Set dialog box.

3. Click OK.

When you click OK, Dreamweaver MX creates the `Master.asp` and `Detail.asp` script pages and inserts the code shown in Listings 21.2 and 21.3. As you can see, the amount of code produced by Dreamweaver MX is considerable, and it is code you do not have to write. To understand a bit more of what Dreamweaver MX is inserting in your pages, take a look at the Server Behavior panel for `Master.asp`.

Notice that there is not a Master Detail Page Set Server Behavior listed. That's because the Master Detail Page Set Server Behavior is actually a collection of the following Dreamweaver MX Server Behaviors.

Recordset   Creates the recordset of data

Repeat Region   Loops through the recordset of data

Dynamic Text   Outputs the data in the recordset

Go To Detail Page   Creates the link to the Detail page

Show If Not First Record   A Boolean test to output page set navigation if the first record of the recordset is not displayed in the page set of records in the current page

Move To First Record   Creates a link to display the page set of records containing the first record in the recordset

Move To Previous Records   Creates a link to move to the previous page set of records

Show If Not Last Record   A Boolean test to output page set navigation if the last record of the recordset is not displayed in the page set of records in the current page

Move To Next Records   Creates a link to move to the next page set of records

Move To Last Record   Creates a link to display the page set of records containing the last record in the recordset

 You'll find all the listing files in this chapter on the CD accompanying this book. Throughout this chapter, code has been formatted to fit the book page. The character _ appearing at a line ending marks a break introduced by the publisher to fit the page width; it is not part of the actual source code.

LISTING 21.2: *MASTER.ASP*

```asp
<%@LANGUAGE="VBSCRIPT" CODEPAGE="1252"%>
<!--#include file="Connections/BookTrackingOLEDB.asp" -->
<%
Dim RS_category
Dim RS_category_numRows

Set RS_category = Server.CreateObject("ADODB.Recordset")
RS_category.ActiveConnection = MM_BookTrackingOLEDB_STRING
RS_category.Source = "SELECT * FROM dbo.tblCategories"
RS_category.CursorType = 0
RS_category.CursorLocation = 2
RS_category.LockType = 1
RS_category.Open()

RS_category_numRows = 0
%>
<%
Dim Repeat1__numRows
Dim Repeat1__index

Repeat1__numRows = 10
Repeat1__index = 0
RS_category_numRows = RS_category_numRows + Repeat1__numRows
%>
<%
'  *** Recordset Stats, Move To Record, and Go To Record: declare stats variables

Dim RS_category_total
Dim RS_category_first
Dim RS_category_last

' set the record count
RS_category_total = RS_category.RecordCount

' set the number of rows displayed on this page
If (RS_category_numRows < 0) Then
  RS_category_numRows = RS_category_total
```

```
      Elseif (RS_category_numRows = 0) Then
        RS_category_numRows = 1
      End If

      ' set the first and last displayed record
      RS_category_first = 1
      RS_category_last  = RS_category_first + RS_category_numRows - 1

      ' if we have the correct record count, check the other stats
      If (RS_category_total <> -1) Then
        If (RS_category_first > RS_category_total) Then
          RS_category_first = RS_category_total
        End If
        If (RS_category_last > RS_category_total) Then
          RS_category_last = RS_category_total
        End If
        If (RS_category_numRows > RS_category_total) Then
          RS_category_numRows = RS_category_total
        End If
      End If
%>
<%
      ' *** Recordset Stats: if we don't know the record count, manually count them

      If (RS_category_total = -1) Then

        ' count the total records by iterating through the recordset
        RS_category_total=0
        While (Not RS_category.EOF)
          RS_category_total = RS_category_total + 1
          RS_category.MoveNext
        Wend

        ' reset the cursor to the beginning
        If (RS_category.CursorType > 0) Then
          RS_category.MoveFirst
        Else
          RS_category.Requery
        End If

        ' set the number of rows displayed on this page
        If (RS_category_numRows < 0 Or RS_category_numRows > RS_category_total) Then
          RS_category_numRows = RS_category_total
        End If

        ' set the first and last displayed record
        RS_category_first = 1
        RS_category_last = RS_category_first + RS_category_numRows - 1
```

```
    If (RS_category_first > RS_category_total) Then
      RS_category_first = RS_category_total
    End If
    If (RS_category_last > RS_category_total) Then
      RS_category_last = RS_category_total
    End If

End If
%>
<%
Dim MM_paramName
%>
<%
' *** Move To Record and Go To Record: declare variables

Dim MM_rs
Dim MM_rsCount
Dim MM_size
Dim MM_uniqueCol
Dim MM_offset
Dim MM_atTotal
Dim MM_paramIsDefined

Dim MM_param
Dim MM_index

Set MM_rs      = RS_category
MM_rsCount     = RS_category_total
MM_size        = RS_category_numRows
MM_uniqueCol = ""
MM_paramName = ""
MM_offset = 0
MM_atTotal = false
MM_paramIsDefined = false
If (MM_paramName <> "") Then
  MM_paramIsDefined = (Request.QueryString(MM_paramName) <> "")
End If
%>
<%
' *** Move To Record: handle 'index' or 'offset' parameter

if (Not MM_paramIsDefined And MM_rsCount <> 0) then

  ' use index parameter if defined, otherwise use offset parameter
  MM_param = Request.QueryString("index")
  If (MM_param = "") Then
    MM_param = Request.QueryString("offset")
```

```
        End If
        If (MM_param <> "") Then
          MM_offset = Int(MM_param)
        End If

        ' if we have a record count, check if we are past the end of the recordset
        If (MM_rsCount <> -1) Then
          If (MM_offset >= MM_rsCount Or MM_offset = -1) Then ' past end or move last
            If ((MM_rsCount Mod MM_size) > 0) Then ' last page not a full repeat region
              MM_offset = MM_rsCount - (MM_rsCount Mod MM_size)
            Else
              MM_offset = MM_rsCount - MM_size
            End If
          End If
        End If

        ' move the cursor to the selected record
        MM_index = 0
        While ((Not MM_rs.EOF) And (MM_index < MM_offset Or MM_offset = -1))
          MM_rs.MoveNext
          MM_index = MM_index + 1
        Wend
        If (MM_rs.EOF) Then
          MM_offset = MM_index   ' set MM_offset to the last possible record
        End If

      End If
%>
<%
' *** Move To Record: if we don't know the record count, check the display range

If (MM_rsCount = -1) Then

  ' walk to the end of the display range for this page
  MM_index = MM_offset
  While (Not MM_rs.EOF And (MM_size < 0 Or MM_index < MM_offset + MM_size))
    MM_rs.MoveNext
    MM_index = MM_index + 1
  Wend

  ' if we walked off the end of the recordset, set MM_rsCount and MM_size
  If (MM_rs.EOF) Then
    MM_rsCount = MM_index
    If (MM_size < 0 Or MM_size > MM_rsCount) Then
      MM_size = MM_rsCount
    End If
  End If
```

```
' if we walked off the end, set the offset based on page size
If (MM_rs.EOF And Not MM_paramIsDefined) Then
  If (MM_offset > MM_rsCount - MM_size Or MM_offset = -1) Then
    If ((MM_rsCount Mod MM_size) > 0) Then
      MM_offset = MM_rsCount - (MM_rsCount Mod MM_size)
    Else
      MM_offset = MM_rsCount - MM_size
    End If
  End If
End If


' reset the cursor to the beginning
If (MM_rs.CursorType > 0) Then
  MM_rs.MoveFirst
Else
  MM_rs.Requery
End If


' move the cursor to the selected record
MM_index = 0
While (Not MM_rs.EOF And MM_index < MM_offset)
  MM_rs.MoveNext
  MM_index = MM_index + 1
Wend
End If
%>
<%
' *** Move To Record: update recordset stats

' set the first and last displayed record
RS_category_first = MM_offset + 1
RS_category_last  = MM_offset + MM_size

If (MM_rsCount <> -1) Then
  If (RS_category_first > MM_rsCount) Then
    RS_category_first = MM_rsCount
  End If
  If (RS_category_last > MM_rsCount) Then
    RS_category_last = MM_rsCount
  End If
End If

' set the boolean used by hide region to check if we are on the last record
MM_atTotal = (MM_rsCount <> -1 And MM_offset + MM_size >= MM_rsCount)
%>
<%
```

```vb
' *** Go To Record and Move To Record: create strings for
' *** maintaining URL and Form parameters

Dim MM_keepNone
Dim MM_keepURL
Dim MM_keepForm
Dim MM_keepBoth

Dim MM_removeList
Dim MM_item
Dim MM_nextItem

' create the list of parameters which should not be maintained
MM_removeList = "&index="
If (MM_paramName <> "") Then
  MM_removeList = MM_removeList & "&" & MM_paramName & "="
End If

MM_keepURL=""
MM_keepForm=""
MM_keepBoth=""
MM_keepNone=""

' add the URL parameters to the MM_keepURL string
For Each MM_item In Request.QueryString
  MM_nextItem = "&" & MM_item & "="
  If (InStr(1,MM_removeList,MM_nextItem,1) = 0) Then
    MM_keepURL = MM_keepURL & MM_nextItem &_
  Server.URLencode(Request.QueryString(MM_item))
  End If
Next

' add the Form variables to the MM_keepForm string
For Each MM_item In Request.Form
  MM_nextItem = "&" & MM_item & "="
  If (InStr(1,MM_removeList,MM_nextItem,1) = 0) Then
    MM_keepForm = MM_keepForm & MM_nextItem &_
  Server.URLencode(Request.Form(MM_item))
  End If
Next

' create the Form + URL string and remove the intial '&' from each of the strings
MM_keepBoth = MM_keepURL & MM_keepForm
If (MM_keepBoth <> "") Then
  MM_keepBoth = Right(MM_keepBoth, Len(MM_keepBoth) - 1)
End If
If (MM_keepURL <> "")  Then
  MM_keepURL  = Right(MM_keepURL, Len(MM_keepURL) - 1)
```

```
End If
If (MM_keepForm <> "") Then
  MM_keepForm = Right(MM_keepForm, Len(MM_keepForm) - 1)
End If

' a utility function used for adding additional parameters to these strings
Function MM_joinChar(firstItem)
  If (firstItem <> "") Then
    MM_joinChar = "&"
  Else
    MM_joinChar = ""
  End If
End Function
%>
<%
' *** Move To Record: set the strings for the first, last, next, and previous links

Dim MM_keepMove
Dim MM_moveParam
Dim MM_moveFirst
Dim MM_moveLast
Dim MM_moveNext
Dim MM_movePrev

Dim MM_urlStr
Dim MM_paramList
Dim MM_paramIndex
Dim MM_nextParam

MM_keepMove = MM_keepBoth
MM_moveParam = "index"

' if the page has a repeated region, remove 'offset' from the maintained parameters
If (MM_size > 1) Then
  MM_moveParam = "offset"
  If (MM_keepMove <> "") Then
    MM_paramList = Split(MM_keepMove, "&")
    MM_keepMove = ""
    For MM_paramIndex = 0 To UBound(MM_paramList)
      MM_nextParam = Left(MM_paramList(MM_paramIndex),
        InStr(MM_paramList(MM_paramIndex),"=") - 1)
      If (StrComp(MM_nextParam,MM_moveParam,1) <> 0) Then
        MM_keepMove = MM_keepMove & "&" & MM_paramList(MM_paramIndex)
      End If
    Next
    If (MM_keepMove <> "") Then
      MM_keepMove = Right(MM_keepMove, Len(MM_keepMove) - 1)
    End If
```

```asp
      End If
    End If


    ' set the strings for the move to links
    If (MM_keepMove <> "") Then
      MM_keepMove = MM_keepMove & "&"
    End If


    MM_urlStr = Request.ServerVariables("URL") & "?" &_
    MM_keepMove & MM_moveParam & "="

    MM_moveFirst = MM_urlStr & "0"
    MM_moveLast  = MM_urlStr & "-1"
    MM_moveNext  = MM_urlStr & CStr(MM_offset + MM_size)
    If (MM_offset - MM_size < 0) Then
      MM_movePrev = MM_urlStr & "0"
    Else
      MM_movePrev = MM_urlStr & CStr(MM_offset - MM_size)
    End If
%>
<html>
<head>
<title>Master.asp</title>
<meta http-equiv="Content-Type" content="text/html; charset=iso-8859-1">
</head>

<body>
<table align="center" border="1">
  <tr>
    <td align="default" width="50%"> CategoryID </td>
    <td align="default" width="50%"> Category </td>
  </tr>
  <%
While ((Repeat1__numRows <> 0) AND (NOT RS_category.EOF))
%>
  <tr>
    <td align="default" width="50%">
      <a href="detail.asp?<%= MM_keepBoth & _
MM_joinChar(MM_keepBoth) & "CategoryID=" & _
RS_category.Fields.Item("CategoryID").Value %>">_
<%=(RS_category.Fields.Item("CategoryID").Value)%></a> </td>
    <td align="default" width="50%">
      <%=(RS_category.Fields.Item("Category").Value)%> </td>
  </tr>
  <%
  Repeat1__index=Repeat1__index+1
  Repeat1__numRows=Repeat1__numRows-1
  RS_category.MoveNext()
```

```
Wend
%>
</table>
<br>
<table border="0" width="50%" align="center">

  <tr>
    <td width="23%" align="center"> <% If MM_offset <> 0 Then %>
      <a href="<%=MM_moveFirst%>">First</a>
      <% End If ' end MM_offset <> 0 %> </td>
    <td width="31%" align="center"> <% If MM_offset <> 0 Then %>
      <a href="<%=MM_movePrev%>">Previous</a>
      <% End If ' end MM_offset <> 0 %> </td>
    <td width="23%" align="center"> <% If Not MM_atTotal Then %>
      <a href="<%=MM_moveNext%>">Next</a>
      <% End If ' end Not MM_atTotal %> </td>
    <td width="23%" align="center"> <% If Not MM_atTotal Then %>
      <a href="<%=MM_moveLast%>">Last</a>
      <% End If ' end Not MM_atTotal %> </td>
  </tr>
</table>
Records <%=(RS_category_first)%> to <%=(RS_category_last)%> of
      <%=(RS_category_total)%>
</body>
</html>
<%
RS_category.Close()
Set RS_category = Nothing
%>
```

```
<%@LANGUAGE="VBSCRIPT" CODEPAGE="1252"%>
<!--#include file="Connections/BookTrackingOLEDB.asp" -->

<%
Dim RS_category__MMColParam
RS_category__MMColParam = "1"
If (Request.QueryString("CategoryID") <> "") Then
  RS_category__MMColParam = Request.QueryString("CategoryID")
End If
%>


<%
Dim RS_category
Dim RS_category_numRows
```

```
Set RS_category = Server.CreateObject("ADODB.Recordset")
RS_category.ActiveConnection = MM_BookTrackingOLEDB_STRING
RS_category.Source = "SELECT * FROM dbo.tblCategories WHERE CategoryID = " +
    Replace(RS_category__MMColParam, "'", "''") + ""
RS_category.CursorType = 0
RS_category.CursorLocation = 2
RS_category.LockType = 3
RS_category.Open()

RS_category_numRows = 0
%>

<html>
<head>
<title>Detail.asp</title>
<meta http-equiv="Content-Type" content="text/html; charset=iso-8859-1">
</head>

<body>
  <table align="center" border="1">
  <tr>
   <td align="default" width="50%">CategoryID</td>
   <td align="default" width="50%"><%=(RS_category.Fields.Item("CategoryID")
      .Value)%></td>
  </tr>
  <tr>
   <td align="default" width="50%">Category</td>
   <td align="default"
      width="50%"><%=(RS_category.Fields.Item("Category").Value)%></td>
  </tr>
  </table>

</body>
</html>
<%
RS_category.Close()
Set RS_category = Nothing
%>
```

Figures 21.4 and 21.5 show the results of Master.asp and Detail.asp in a web browser. As you can see, Master.asp displays the list of categories. Each category has an HTML hyperlink to pass its primary key identifier to the Detail.asp page through a url variable. As the Detail.asp receives the primary key, it displays all information for the Category record with the passed primary key. Pretty slick. However, our example doesn't exactly do our drill-down principle justice. At this point, our detail page simply shows the user the item they click in the master page. A useful detail page shows much more relevant information, such as the books belonging to the clicked category.

FIGURE 21.4

Viewing the results of `Master.asp`

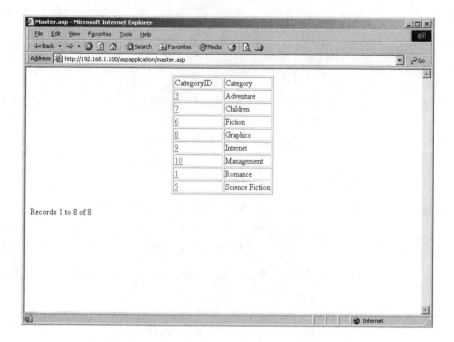

FIGURE 21.5

Viewing the results of `Detail.asp`

A More Realistic Master/Detail Page Set

Now that we have the basics down, let's create a more traditional drill-down example. To demonstrate, let's alter our `Detail.asp` script page to display all the books that belong to the passed category. Follow these steps:

1. Open the `Detail.asp` script page and choose Window ➢ Server Behaviors to open the Server Behaviors panel.

`Detail.asp` is using the following server behaviors:

Recordset   Creates a recordset of data based on the tblCategories primary key passed from the `Master.asp` script page

Dynamic Text   Displays the data in the recordset

To alter the `Detail.asp` script page, we'll alter the data pulled by the recordset, add a Repeat Region to loop through the returned recordset, and alter the Dynamic Text to output the data.

2. To alter the Recordset, double-click the Recordset Server Behavior shown in the Server Behaviors panel.

To change the recordset to select all of the book titles currently belonging to the passed category, we'll need to modify the SQL statement to use joins. If you recall from Chapter 18, a join allows you to link two tables together based on one common field. We'll join the tblCategories table to the tblBooksCategories table and then to the tblBooks table.

3. To modify the SQL, we'll use the Advanced view of the Recordset Server Behavior. In the resulting Recordset dialog box, click the Advanced button to display the SQL statement that defines the data collected into the recordset.

4. Replace the existing SQL statement with the following:

```
SELECT      tblCategories.CategoryID,
            tblCategories.Category,
            tblBooks.BookID,
            tblBooks.Title,
            tblBooks.PageCount,
            tblBooks.Lending
FROM        (tblBooks
INNER JOIN  tblBooksCategories
ON          tblBooks.BookID = tblBooksCategories.Book)
INNER JOIN  tblCategories
ON          tblBooksCategories.Category = tblCategories.CategoryID
WHERE       tblCategories.CategoryID = MMColParam
```

5. The Recordset dialog box should now look similar to Figure 21.6. Click OK to close the dialog box and save the changes to the recordset.

FIGURE 21.6

The Recordset
dialog box

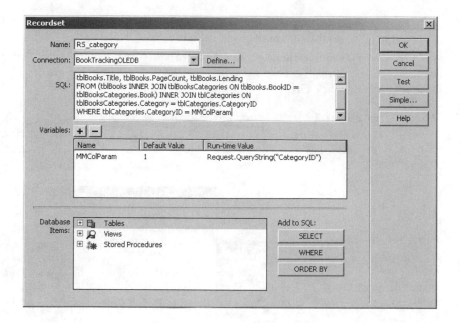

The next step is to loop through the results of the new recordset and output the book ID and titles. First change the Dynamic Text of `Detail.asp` to output the book title instead of the category ID and category name. To do so, follow these steps:

1. Double-click Dynamic Text(RS_category.CategoryID) in the Server Behaviors panel to open the Dynamic Text dialog box, which is shown in Figure 21.7. Dreamweaver displays the available table columns from our modified recordset.

FIGURE 21.7

The BookID
Dynamic Text
dialog box

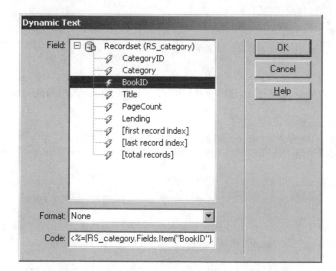

2. To change the Dynamic Text to display the BookID instead of the CategoryID, choose BookID from the Field list box. Click OK.

3. Double-click Dynamic Text(RS_category.Category) in the Server Behaviors panel to open the Dynamic Text dialog box and choose Title from the Field list box as shown in Figure 21.8. Click OK.

FIGURE 21.8

The Title Dynamic Text dialog box

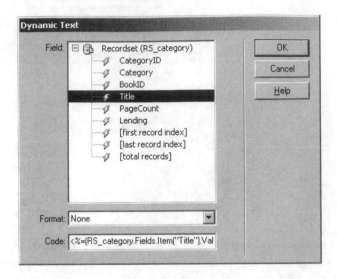

Once you complete the Dynamic Text modifications, update "CategoryID" and "Category" in the HTML of Detail.asp to "BookID" and "Book Title" to reflect the new BookID and Title Dynamic Text. Your code should appear similar to the code in Listing 21.4.

LISTING 21.4: DISPLAY CODE OF *DETAIL.ASP*

```
<table align="center" border="1">
<tr>
 <td align="default" width="50%">BookID</td>
 <td align="default" width="50%"><%=(RS_category.Fields.Item("BookID").Value)%></td>
</tr>
<tr>
  <td align="default" width="50%">Book Title</td>
  <td align="default" width="50%"><%=(RS_category.Fields.Item("Title").Value)%></td>
</tr>
</table>
```

Now you're ready to add a Repeat Region to the Detail.asp page to loop through the recordset results. To do so, follow these steps:

1. Select the table rows and cells of the table in the display code.

2. Choose Insert ➢ Application Objects ➢ Repeated Region to open the Repeat Region dialog box, which is shown in Figure 21.9.

FIGURE 21.9

The Repeat Region dialog box

3. In the Recordset drop-down list box, select RS_category and choose to show all records in the recordset.

4. Click OK to save the Repeat Region to Detail.asp.

Now our Detail.asp script page will display the books under the category chosen from the Master.asp script page. Listing 21.5 shows the updated code of the Detail.asp script page. Figure 21.10 shows the web browser result of Detail.asp.

LISTING 21.5: *DETAIL2.ASP*

```
<%@LANGUAGE="VBSCRIPT" CODEPAGE="1252"%>
<!--#include file="Connections/BookTrackingOLEDB.asp" -->
<%
Dim RS_category__MMColParam
RS_category__MMColParam = "1"
If (Request.QueryString("CategoryID") <> "") Then
  RS_category__MMColParam = Request.QueryString("CategoryID")
End If
%>
<%
Dim RS_category
Dim RS_category_numRows

Set RS_category = Server.CreateObject("ADODB.Recordset")
RS_category.ActiveConnection = MM_BookTrackingOLEDB_STRING
RS_category.Source = "SELECT tblCategories.CategoryID, tblCategories.Category,
    tblBooks.BookID, tblBooks.Title, tblBooks.PageCount, tblBooks.Lending FROM
    (tblBooks INNER JOIN tblBooksCategories ON tblBooks.BookID = tblBooksCategories
    .Book) INNER JOIN tblCategories ON tblBooksCategories.Category = tblCategories
    .CategoryID  WHERE tblCategories.CategoryID = " + Replace(RS_category__
    MMColParam, "'", "''") + ""
RS_category.CursorType = 0
RS_category.CursorLocation = 2
RS_category.LockType = 3
RS_category.Open()
```

```
RS_category_numRows = 0
%>
<%
Dim Repeat1__numRows
Dim Repeat1__index

Repeat1__numRows = -1
Repeat1__index = 0
RS_category_numRows = RS_category_numRows + Repeat1__numRows
%>
<html>
<head>
<title>Detail.asp</title>
<meta http-equiv="Content-Type" content="text/html; charset=iso-8859-1">
</head>

<body>

  <table align="center" border="1">
  <%
While ((Repeat1__numRows <> 0) AND (NOT RS_category.EOF))
%>
  <tr>
    <td align="default" width="50%">BookID</td>
    <td align="default" width="50%"><%=(RS_category.Fields.Item("CategoryID")
      .Value)%></td>
  </tr>
  <tr>
    <td align="default" width="50%">Book
      Title</td>
    <td align="default" width="50%"><%=(RS_category.Fields.Item("Title").Value)%></td>
  </tr>
  <%
  Repeat1__index=Repeat1__index+1
  Repeat1__numRows=Repeat1__numRows-1
  RS_category.MoveNext()
Wend
%>
</table>

</body>
</html>
<%
RS_category.Close()
Set RS_category = Nothing
%>
```

FIGURE 21.10

Viewing the result of
the Detail2.asp

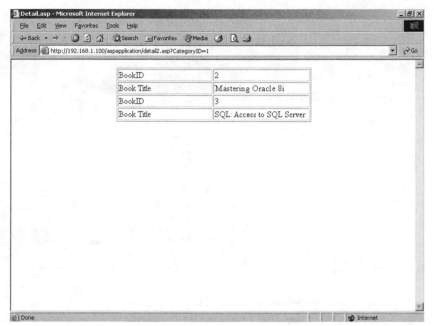

Creating a Master/Detail Page Set Using JSP

Now that you've seen how the Master Detail Page Set Server Behavior functions using Microsoft
ASP, you can easily implement the same behavior using JSP. To demonstrate, let's replicate our ASP
example of the master category list page drilling down to the books belonging to each category. To
review the process, you add a recordset to a JSP page and then insert a Master Detail Page Set Server
Behavior. To do so, follow these steps:

1. Activate the JSP website we've been using throughout the book.

2. Open a new page and name it Master.jsp.

As before, use the data connection we created in Chapter 10 to create the RS_Category recordset.

1. Choose Insert ➤ Application Objects ➤ Recordset (or click the plus sign in the Server Behaviors
   tab of the Application panel and select the Recordset option) to open the Recordset dialog
   box, which is shown in Figure 21.11.

2. Enter **RS_Category** in the Name text field.

3. Choose your data connection from the Connection drop-down list box.

4. In the Table drop-down list box, select the tblCategories table, and choose Category in the
   Sort drop-down list box.

5. Click OK to create the recordset.

FIGURE 21.11

The JSP Recordset dialog box

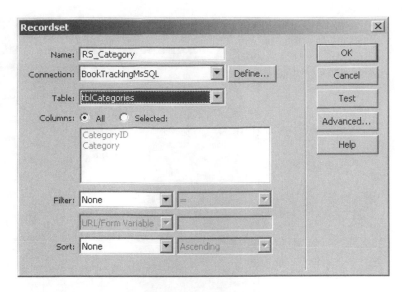

As you can see in Listing 21.6, Dreamweaver MX inserts the JSP `include` statement to reference our data connection and the code to create the RS_Category recordset into the Master.jsp script file.

LISTING 21.6: JSP RECORDSET CODE

```
<%@ page contentType="text/html; charset=iso-8859-1" language="java"
    import="java.sql.*" errorPage="" %>
<%@ include file="Connections/BookTrackingMsSQL.jsp" %>
<%
Driver DriverRS_Category =
    (Driver)Class.forName(MM_BookTrackingMsSQL_DRIVER).newInstance();
Connection ConnRS_Category=DriverManager.getConnection_
(MM_BookTrackingMsSQL_STRING,_
MM_BookTrackingMsSQL_USERNAME,_
MM_BookTrackingMsSQL_PASSWORD);
PreparedStatement StatementRS_Category = ConnRS_Category.prepareStatement("SELECT
    tblCategories.CategoryID, tblCategories.Category, tblBooks.BookID,
    tblBooks.Title, tblBooks.PageCount, tblBooks.Lending FROM (tblBooks INNER JOIN
    tblBooksCategories ON tblBooks.BookID = tblBooksCategories.Book) INNER JOIN
    tblCategories ON tblBooksCategories.Category = tblCategories.CategoryID  ORDER BY
    tblCategories.Category  ");
ResultSet RS_Category = StatementRS_Category.executeQuery();
boolean RS_Category_isEmpty = !RS_Category.next();
boolean RS_Category_hasData = !RS_Category_isEmpty;
Object RS_Category_data;
int RS_Category_numRows = 0;
%>
<html>
<head>
```

```
<title>master.asp</title>
<meta http-equiv="Content-Type" content="text/html; charset=iso-8859-1">
</head>

<body>
</body>
</html>
<%
RS_Category.close();
StatementRS_Category.close();
ConnRS_Category.close();
%>
```

Now we're all set to insert the Master Detail Page Set Server Behavior. To do so, follow these steps:

1. Choose Insert ➤ Application Objects ➤ Master Detail Page Set to open the Insert Master-Detail Page Set dialog box, which is shown in Figure 21.12.

FIGURE 21.12

The JSP Insert Master-Detail Page Set dialog box

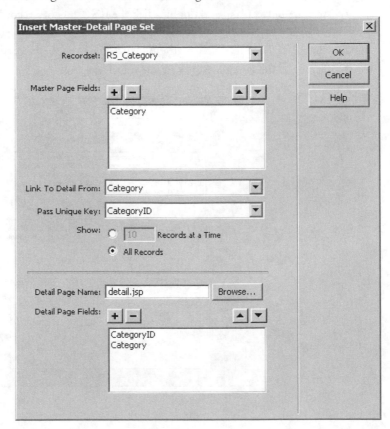

2. In the Recordset drop-down list box, choose RS_Category. As before, Dreamweaver MX lists the available recordset columns in the Master Page and Detail Page Fields box.

3. Choose the Category table column field as the link between the master page and the detail page.

4. Choose CategoryID from the Pass Unique Key drop-down list box to set it as the record identifier that the master page passes to the detail page through the link.

5. In the Show section, click the All Records option.

6. To configure the detail page, enter **Detail.jsp** in the Detail Page Name text field.

7. Select both Category and CategoryID from the Detail Page Fields list box.

Remember, we are going to pass the CategoryID value of each record in the master page to a detail page. That detail page will display the book titles belonging to that passed category. Obviously, the Category column field is incorrect, but we'll fix that in a moment.

8. Click OK to close the Insert Master-Detail Page Set dialog box.

Once Dreamweaver MX has added code to `Master.jsp` and `Detail.jsp`, we can modify `Detail.jsp` to display the book titles of the passed category. To do so, follow these steps:

1. Activate `Detail.jsp` and double-click the RS_Category recordset in the Server Behaviors panel to open the Recordset dialog box.

2. Click Advanced to switch to the Advanced view of the Recordset dialog box.

3. Insert our joined table SQL statement into the SQL text box as shown in Figure 21.13.

FIGURE 21.13

The JSP Recordset dialog box

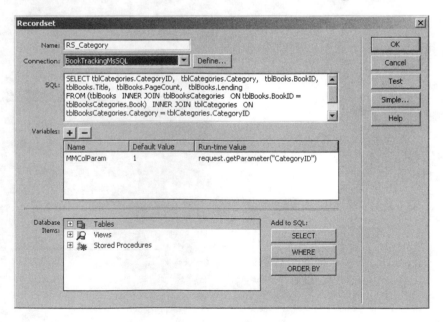

Notice that we added an ORDER BY statement to sort book titles alphabetically.

```
SELECT          tblCategories.CategoryID,
                tblCategories.Category,
                tblBooks.BookID,
                tblBooks.Title,
                tblBooks.PageCount,
                tblBooks.Lending
FROM            (tblBooks
INNER JOIN      tblBooksCategories
ON              tblBooks.BookID = tblBooksCategories.Book)
INNER JOIN      tblCategories
ON              tblBooksCategories.Category = tblCategories.CategoryID
WHERE           tblCategories.CategoryID= MMColParam
ORDER BY        tblBooks.Title
```

Now we change the dynamic text to display book titles instead of categories. To do so, follow these steps:

1. Double-click the Dynamic Text elements in the Server Behaviors panel to open the Dynamic Text dialog box.
2. Change the column fields to BookID and Title.
3. To loop through the recordset, add a Repeat Region around the rows and cells of the table in the HTML display code. To do so, select the rows and cells and choose Insert ➤ Application Objects ➤ Repeated Region to open the Repeat Region dialog box.
4. Select the RS_Category recordset and click OK.

That's it. We've completed the master/detail page set that displays a list of categories with links to view the books that belong to each category. Listings 21.7 and 21.8 show the final code for the Master.jsp master page and the Detail.jsp detail page. Figures 21.14 and 21.15 show the web browser results of Master.jsp and Detail.jsp.

LISTING 21.7: MASTER.JSP

```
<%@ page contentType="text/html; charset=iso-8859-1" language="java"
    import="java.sql.*" errorPage="" %>
<%@ include file="Connections/booktrackingAccess.jsp" %>
<%
Driver DriverRS_Category = (Driver)Class.forName(MM_booktrackingAccess_DRIVER)_
.newInstance();
Connection ConnRS_Category = DriverManager.getConnection_
(MM_booktrackingAccess_STRING,MM_booktrackingAccess_USERNAME,_
MM_booktrackingAccess_PASSWORD);
PreparedStatement StatementRS_Category = ConnRS_Category.prepareStatement_
("SELECT tblCategories.CategoryID, tblCategories.Category    FROM  tblCategories_
ORDER BY tblCategories.Category");
ResultSet RS_Category = StatementRS_Category.executeQuery();
```

```
boolean RS_Category_isEmpty = !RS_Category.next();
boolean RS_Category_hasData = !RS_Category_isEmpty;
Object RS_Category_data;
int RS_Category_numRows = 0;
%>
<%
int Repeat1__numRows = 10;
int Repeat1__index = 0;
RS_Category_numRows += Repeat1__numRows;
%>
<%
// *** Recordset Stats, Move To Record, and Go To Record: declare stats
     variables

int RS_Category_first = 1;
int RS_Category_last  = 1;
int RS_Category_total = -1;

if (RS_Category_isEmpty) {
  RS_Category_total = RS_Category_first = RS_Category_last = 0;
}

//set the number of rows displayed on this page
if (RS_Category_numRows == 0) {
  RS_Category_numRows = 1;
}
%>
<%
// *** Recordset Stats: if we don't know the record count, manually count them

if (RS_Category_total == -1) {

  // count the total records by iterating through the recordset
    for (RS_Category_total = 1; RS_Category.next(); RS_Category_total++);

  // reset the cursor to the beginning
  RS_Category.close();
  RS_Category = StatementRS_Category.executeQuery();
  RS_Category_hasData = RS_Category.next();

  // set the number of rows displayed on this page
  if (RS_Category_numRows < 0 || RS_Category_numRows > RS_Category_total) {
    RS_Category_numRows = RS_Category_total;
  }

  // set the first and last displayed record
  RS_Category_first = Math.min(RS_Category_first, RS_Category_total);
```

```
      RS_Category_last  = Math.min(RS_Category_first + RS_Category_numRows - 1,
         RS_Category_total);
}
%>
<% String MM_paramName = ""; %>
<%
// *** Move To Record and Go To Record: declare variables

ResultSet MM_rs = RS_Category;
int       MM_rsCount = RS_Category_total;
int       MM_size = RS_Category_numRows;
String    MM_uniqueCol = "";
          MM_paramName = "";
int       MM_offset = 0;
boolean   MM_atTotal = false;
boolean   MM_paramIsDefined = (MM_paramName.length() != 0 &&
     request.getParameter(MM_paramName) != null);
%>
<%
// *** Move To Record: handle 'index' or 'offset' parameter

if (!MM_paramIsDefined && MM_rsCount != 0) {

  //use index parameter if defined, otherwise use offset parameter
  String r = request.getParameter("index");
  if (r==null) r = request.getParameter("offset");
  if (r!=null) MM_offset = Integer.parseInt(r);

  // if we have a record count, check if we are past the end of the recordset
  if (MM_rsCount != -1) {
    if (MM_offset >= MM_rsCount || MM_offset == -1) {  // past end or move last
      if (MM_rsCount % MM_size != 0)    // last page not a full repeat region
        MM_offset = MM_rsCount - MM_rsCount % MM_size;
      else
        MM_offset = MM_rsCount - MM_size;
    }
  }

  //move the cursor to the selected record
  int i;
  for (i=0; RS_Category_hasData && (i < MM_offset || MM_offset == -1); i++) {
    RS_Category_hasData = MM_rs.next();
  }
  if (!RS_Category_hasData) MM_offset = i;  // set MM_offset to the last
      possible record
}
%>
```

```
<%
// *** Move To Record: if we dont know the record count, check the display range

if (MM_rsCount == -1) {

  // walk to the end of the display range for this page
  int i;
  for (i=MM_offset; RS_Category_hasData && (MM_size < 0 || i < MM_offset +
    MM_size); i++) {
    RS_Category_hasData = MM_rs.next();
  }

  // if we walked off the end of the recordset, set MM_rsCount and MM_size
  if (!RS_Category_hasData) {
    MM_rsCount = i;
    if (MM_size < 0 || MM_size > MM_rsCount) MM_size = MM_rsCount;
  }

  // if we walked off the end, set the offset based on page size
  if (!RS_Category_hasData && !MM_paramIsDefined) {
    if (MM_offset > MM_rsCount - MM_size || MM_offset == -1) { //check if past
      end or last
      if (MM_rsCount % MM_size != 0)  //last page has less records than MM_size
        MM_offset = MM_rsCount - MM_rsCount % MM_size;
      else
        MM_offset = MM_rsCount - MM_size;
    }
  }

  // reset the cursor to the beginning
  RS_Category.close();
  RS_Category = StatementRS_Category.executeQuery();
  RS_Category_hasData = RS_Category.next();
  MM_rs = RS_Category;

  // move the cursor to the selected record
  for (i=0; RS_Category_hasData && i < MM_offset; i++) {
    RS_Category_hasData = MM_rs.next();
  }
}
%>
<%
// *** Move To Record: update recordset stats

// set the first and last displayed record
RS_Category_first = MM_offset + 1;
RS_Category_last  = MM_offset + MM_size;
```

```
    if (MM_rsCount != -1) {
      RS_Category_first = Math.min(RS_Category_first, MM_rsCount);
      RS_Category_last  = Math.min(RS_Category_last, MM_rsCount);
    }

    // set the boolean used by hide region to check if we are on the last record
    MM_atTotal  = (MM_rsCount != -1 && MM_offset + MM_size >= MM_rsCount);
%>
<%
    // *** Go To Record and Move To Record: create strings for maintaining URL and Form
       parameters

    String MM_keepBoth,MM_keepURL="",MM_keepForm="",MM_keepNone="";
    String[] MM_removeList = { "index", MM_paramName };

    // create the MM_keepURL string
    if (request.getQueryString() != null) {
      MM_keepURL = '&' + request.getQueryString();
      for (int i=0; i < MM_removeList.length && MM_removeList[i].length() != 0; i++) {
      int start = MM_keepURL.indexOf(MM_removeList[i]) - 1;
        if (start >= 0 && MM_keepURL.charAt(start) == '&' &&
            MM_keepURL.charAt(start + MM_removeList[i].length() + 1) == '=') {
          int stop = MM_keepURL.indexOf('&', start + 1);
          if (stop == -1) stop = MM_keepURL.length();
          MM_keepURL = MM_keepURL.substring(0,start) + MM_keepURL.substring(stop);
        }
      }
    }

    // add the Form variables to the MM_keepForm string
    if (request.getParameterNames().hasMoreElements()) {
      java.util.Enumeration items = request.getParameterNames();
      while (items.hasMoreElements()) {
        String nextItem = (String)items.nextElement();
        boolean found = false;
        for (int i=0; !found && i < MM_removeList.length; i++) {
          if (MM_removeList[i].equals(nextItem)) found = true;
        }
        if (!found && MM_keepURL.indexOf('&' + nextItem + '=') == -1) {
          MM_keepForm = MM_keepForm + '&' + nextItem + '=' +
            java.net.URLEncoder.encode(request.getParameter(nextItem));
        }
      }
    }

    // create the Form + URL string and remove the intial '&' from each of the strings
    MM_keepBoth = MM_keepURL + MM_keepForm;
```

```
if (MM_keepBoth.length() > 0) MM_keepBoth = MM_keepBoth.substring(1);
if (MM_keepURL.length() > 0)  MM_keepURL = MM_keepURL.substring(1);
if (MM_keepForm.length() > 0) MM_keepForm = MM_keepForm.substring(1);
%>
<%
// *** Move To Record: set the strings for the first, last,
//     next, and previous links

String MM_moveFirst,MM_moveLast,MM_moveNext,MM_movePrev;
{
  String MM_keepMove = MM_keepBoth;  // keep both Form and URL parameters for
    moves
  String MM_moveParam = "index=";

  // if the page has a repeated region, remove 'offset' from the maintained
        parameters
  if (MM_size > 1) {
    MM_moveParam = "offset=";
    int start = MM_keepMove.indexOf(MM_moveParam);
    if (start != -1 && (start == 0 || MM_keepMove.charAt(start-1) == '&')) {
      int stop = MM_keepMove.indexOf('&', start);
      if (start == 0 && stop != -1) stop++;
      if (stop == -1) stop = MM_keepMove.length();
      if (start > 0) start--;
      MM_keepMove = MM_keepMove.substring(0,start) + MM_keepMove.substring(stop);
    }
  }

  // set the strings for the move to links
  StringBuffer urlStr = new StringBuffer(request.getRequestURI()).append('?')
    .append(MM_keepMove);
  if (MM_keepMove.length() > 0) urlStr.append('&');
  urlStr.append(MM_moveParam);
  MM_moveFirst = urlStr + "0";
  MM_moveLast  = urlStr + "-1";
  MM_moveNext  = urlStr + Integer.toString(MM_offset+MM_size);
  MM_movePrev  = urlStr + Integer.toString(Math.max(MM_offset-MM_size,0));
}
%>
<html>
<head>
<title>master.jsp</title>
<meta http-equiv="Content-Type" content="text/html; charset=iso-8859-1">
</head>

<body>
<table align="center" border="1">
```

```
   <tr>
     <td align="default" width="100%"> Category </td>
   </tr>
   <% while ((RS_Category_hasData)&&(Repeat1__numRows-- != 0)) { %>
   <tr>
     <td align="default" width="100%">
       <a href="detail.jsp?<%= MM_keepBoth + ((MM_keepBoth!="")?"&":"") +
         "CategoryID=" + _
(((RS_Category_data = RS_Category.getObject("CategoryID"))==null ||
   RS_Category.wasNull())_
?"":RS_Category_data) %>"> <%=(((RS_Category_data = RS_Category.getObject_
("Category"))==null || RS_Category.wasNull())?"":RS_Category_data)%></a> </td>
   </tr>
   <%
   Repeat1__index++;
   RS_Category_hasData = RS_Category.next();
}
%>
</table>
<br>
<table border="0" width="50%" align="center">

   <tr>
     <td width="23%" align="center"> <% if (MM_offset !=0) { %>
       <a href="<%=MM_moveFirst%>">First</a>
       <% } /* end MM_offset != 0 */ %> </td>
     <td width="31%" align="center"> <% if (MM_offset !=0) { %>
       <a href="<%=MM_movePrev%>">Previous</a>
       <% } /* end MM_offset != 0 */ %> </td>
     <td width="23%" align="center"> <% if (!MM_atTotal) { %>
       <a href="<%=MM_moveNext%>">Next</a>
       <% } /* end !MM_atTotal */ %> </td>
     <td width="23%" align="center"> <% if (!MM_atTotal) { %>
       <a href="<%=MM_moveLast%>">Last</a>
       <% } /* end !MM_atTotal */ %> </td>
   </tr>
</table>
Records <%=(RS_Category_first)%> to <%=(RS_Category_last)%> of <%=(RS_Category_
   total)%>
</body>
</html>
<%
RS_Category.close();
StatementRS_Category.close();
ConnRS_Category.close();
%>
```

LISTING 21.8: *DETAIL.JSP*

```jsp
<%@ page contentType="text/html; charset=iso-8859-1" language="java"
    import="java.sql.*" errorPage="" %>
<%@ include file="Connections/booktrackingAccess.jsp" %>

<%
String RS_Category__MMColParam = "1";
if (request.getParameter("CategoryID") !=null) {RS_Category__MMColParam =
    (String)request.getParameter("CategoryID");}
%>

<%
Driver DriverRS_Category =
    (Driver)Class.forName(MM_booktrackingAccess_DRIVER).newInstance();
Connection ConnRS_Category = DriverManager.getConnection_
(MM_booktrackingAccess_STRING,MM_booktrackingAccess_USERNAME,_
    MM_booktrackingAccess_PASSWORD);
PreparedStatement StatementRS_Category = ConnRS_Category.prepareStatement_
    ("SELECT tblCategories.CategoryID,_
    tblCategories.Category,   tblBooks.BookID,   tblBooks.Title,   _
tblBooks.PageCount,   tblBooks.Lending  FROM (tblBooks   _
INNER JOIN tblBooksCategories   ON tblBooks.BookID = _
    tblBooksCategories.Book)   INNER JOIN tblCategories   _
ON tblBooksCategories.Category = tblCategories.CategoryID _
WHERE tblCategories.CategoryID= " + RS_Category__MMColParam + "  _
ORDER BY tblBooks.Title");
ResultSet RS_Category = StatementRS_Category.executeQuery();
boolean RS_Category_isEmpty = !RS_Category.next();
boolean RS_Category_hasData = !RS_Category_isEmpty;
Object RS_Category_data;
int RS_Category_numRows = 0;
%>
<%
int Repeat1__numRows = -1;
int Repeat1__index = 0;
RS_Category_numRows += Repeat1__numRows;
%>
<html>
<head>
<title>detail.jsp</title>
<meta http-equiv="Content-Type" content="text/html; charset=iso-8859-1">
</head>

<body>
  <table align="center" border="1">
  <% while ((RS_Category_hasData)&&(Repeat1__numRows-- != 0)) { %>
  <tr>
```

```
        <td align="default" width="50%">BookID</td>
        <td align="default" width="50%">_
<%=(((RS_Category_data = RS_Category.getObject("BookID"))==null ||_
 RS_Category.wasNull())?"":RS_Category_data)%></td>
    </tr>
    <tr>
        <td align="default" width="50%">Book Title</td>
        <td align="default" width="50%">_
<%=(((RS_Category_data = RS_Category.getObject("Title"))==null || _
RS_Category.wasNull())?"":RS_Category_data)%></td>
    </tr>
    <%
    Repeat1__index++;
    RS_Category_hasData = RS_Category.next();
}
%>
</table>

</body>
</html>
<%
RS_Category.close();
StatementRS_Category.close();
ConnRS_Category.close();
%>
```

The browser result
for Master.jsp

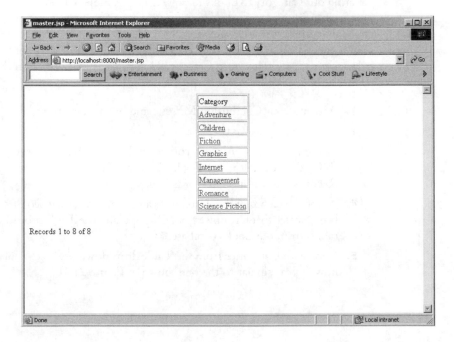

FIGURE 21.15
The browser result
for `Detail.jsp`

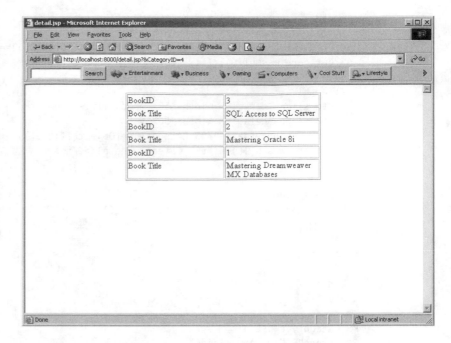

Creating a Master/Detail Page Set Using Macromedia ColdFusion MX

Creating our Category to Books master/detail example in ColdFusion MX is similar to the creation process in ASP. You use a data connection to contact your database and create a recordset. You then attach the recordset to a Dreamweaver MX Master Detail Page Set Server Behavior. Dreamweaver MX creates the master and detail page code. You modify the detail page to return a list of book titles belonging to the URL-passed CategoryID. Simple as that. Let's run through the example at a more deliberate speed. Follow these steps:

1. Activate your ColdFusion MX site and open a new page.
2. Save the page as `Master.cfm`.
3. Using the data connection you created in Chapter 10, create a recordset of the data in the tblCategories table in our Books database. To do so, choose Insert ➢ Application Objects ➢ Recordset to open the Recordset dialog box.
4. Name the recordset RS_Categories and choose your data connection from the Data Source list box. Notice that Dreamweaver MX populates the Table drop-down list box with the available tables from our Books database.
5. Choose tblCategories from the Table drop-down list box. Your Recordset dialog box should now appear similar to the one shown in Figure 21.16.

FIGURE 21.16

The Recordset dialog box

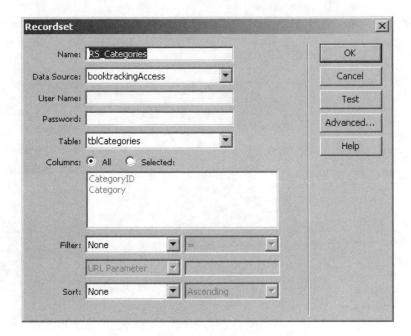

Now we're ready for the Master Detail Page Set Server Behavior. To create the Master Detail Page Set Server Behavior, follow these steps:

1. Choose Insert ➣ Application Objects ➣ Master Detail Page Set (or click the plus sign in the Server Behaviors tab of the Application panel and select the Recordset option) to open the Recordset dialog box.

2. In the Recordset drop-down list box, select RS_Categories. Dreamweaver MX populates the dialog box with the available data columns.

3. Select the table column fields that you want to appear on the master page. For our example, we want only Category to appear in a list, so remove CategoryID from the Master Page Fields list box.

4. To set the Category table column field as the field that links the master page to the detail page, choose Category from the Link To Detail From list box.

5. Choose the record identifier that the master page will pass to the detail page through the link. In our example, we use the primary key of the tblCategories table—CategoryID. Choose CategoryID from the Pass Unique Key drop-down list box.

6. In the Show section, click the All Records option.

7. To configure the settings for the detail page, enter **Detail.cfm** in the Detail Page Name text field.

8. Much as we did for the master page, choose the table column fields to display in the page. Our complete Insert Master-Detail Page Set configuration is in the dialog box shown in Figure 21.17.

FIGURE 21.17

The Master Detail Page Set dialog box

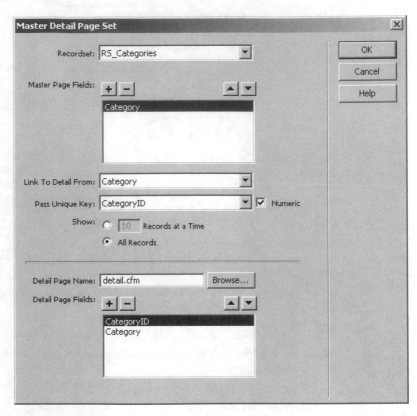

9. Click OK to close the Master Detail Page Set dialog box and create the code for `Master.cfm` and `Detail.cfm`.

You can see the `Master.cfm` code in Listing 21.9. Figure 21.18 shows the browser result of `Master.cfm`.

LISTING 21.9: *MASTER.CFM*

```
<cfquery name="RS_Categories" datasource="booktrackingAccess">
SELECT * FROM tblCategories
</cfquery>
<html>
<head>
<title>master.cfm</title>
```

```
<meta http-equiv="Content-Type" content="text/html; charset=iso-8859-1">
</head>

<body>
<table border="1" align="center">
  <tr>
    <td>Category</td>
  </tr>
  <cfoutput query="RS_Categories">
    <tr>
      <td><a href="detail.cfm?recordID=#RS_Categories.CategoryID#">
      #RS_Categories.Category# </a>
      </td>
    </tr>
  </cfoutput>
</table>
<br>
<cfoutput>#RS_Categories.RecordCount# Records Total</cfoutput>
</body>
</html>
```

FIGURE 21.18

The browser result of Master.cfm

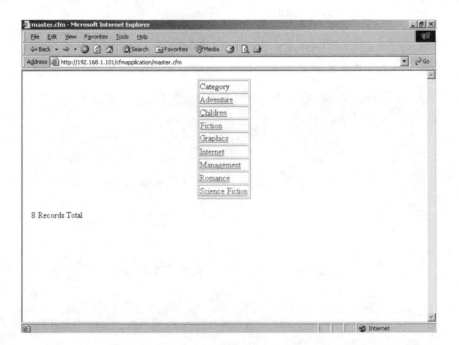

Now let's reconfigure Detail.cfm to display the book titles belonging to the category passed by the master page. To do so, we'll modify the SQL statement in the recordset to join several tables.

Follow these steps:

1. Activate `Detail.cfm`.
2. Choose Windows ➤ Server Behaviors to display the Server Behaviors panel.
3. Double-click the recordset in the Server Behavior panel to open the Recordset dialog box.
4. To alter the SQL statement, click the Advanced button to switch the Recordset dialog box to Advanced view. Notice that Dreamweaver MX is using the URL-passed CategoryID parameter to filter the data selected by the SQL statement.
5. Even though we are altering the SQL statement, we want to keep that filter. To do so, replace the SQL statement with the following code.

```
SELECT      tblCategories.CategoryID,
            tblCategories.Category,
            tblBooks.BookID,
            tblBooks.Title,
            tblBooks.PageCount,
            tblBooks.Lending
FROM        (tblBooks
INNER JOIN  tblBooksCategories
ON          tblBooks.BookID = tblBooksCategories.Book)
INNER JOIN  tblCategories
ON          tblBooksCategories.Category = tblCategories.CategoryID
WHERE       tblCategories.CategoryID=#URL.recordID#
```

The Recordset dialog box should now appear similar to Figure 21.19.

FIGURE 21.19

The `Detail.cfm` Recordset dialog box

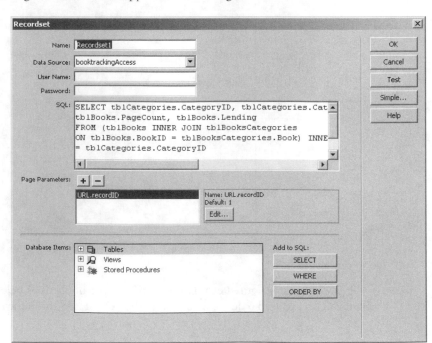

6. Click OK to close the dialog box.

The final step is to change the dynamic text that displays the contents of our recordset. To do so, double-click the Dynamic Text Server Behaviors in the Server Behavior panel and change them to display BookID and Title. You also want to change the static text label that identifies the dynamic text. Then change the CFOUTPUT tag to loop through the recordset. Normally you would insert a Repeat Region Server Behavior. However, ColdFusion MX is so easy to work with that you can simply change the opening <CFOUTPUT> tag to <CFOUTPUT QUERY="Recordset1">. You can see the final Detail.cfm in Listing 21.10 and the browser result in Figure 21.20.

LISTING 21.10: *DETAIL.CFM*

```
<cfparam name="URL.recordID" default="1">
<cfquery name="Recordset1" datasource="booktrackingAccess">
SELECT tblCategories.CategoryID, tblCategories.Category, tblBooks.BookID,
    tblBooks.Title,
tblBooks.PageCount, tblBooks.Lending FROM (tblBooks INNER JOIN
    tblBooksCategories
ON tblBooks.BookID = tblBooksCategories.Book) INNER JOIN tblCategories ON
    tblBooksCategories.Category
= tblCategories.CategoryID WHERE tblCategories.CategoryID= #URL.recordID#
</cfquery>
<html>
<head>
<title>detail.cfm</title>
<meta http-equiv="Content-Type" content="text/html; charset=iso-8859-1">
</head>

<body>
<table border="1" align="center">
  <CFOUTPUT QUERY="Recordset1">
  <tr>
      <td>BookID</td>
      <td>#Recordset1.BookID#</td>
  </tr>
  <tr>
    <td>Title</td>
      <td>#Recordset1.Title#</td>
  </tr>
  </cfoutput>
</table>


</body>
</html>
```

FIGURE 21.20

The browser result of `Detail.cfm`

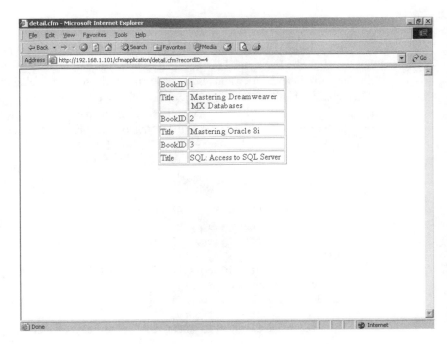

Creating a Master/Detail Page Set from Components

As we've mentioned, Dreamweaver MX uses a collection of Server Behaviors to build master/detail page sets. As you know by now, all but two Dreamweaver MX–supported languages let you build a master/detail page set using one simple interface for the Master Detail Page Set Server Behavior. However, the Dreamweaver MX ASP.NET and PHP interface does not offer the Master Detail Page Set Server Behavior. Still, both language interfaces do support the component Server Behaviors that collectively make up a master/detail page set. Therefore, you can easily build your own version of the master/detail page set using component Server Behaviors of ASP.NET and PHP.

Creating a Master/Detail Page Set Using ASP.NET

As you know, Dreamweaver MX does not offer the Master Detail Page Set Server Behavior for ASP.NET-based websites. Therefore, creating a master/detail page set in ASP.NET requires a slightly different process than simply inserting the straightforward Master Detail Page Set Server Behavior. We must create the master/detail page set component by component. That said, it's still quite simple to create a master/detail page set using standard Dreamweaver MX Server Behaviors. Let's create a master/detail page set of our running book category example. First we need to create a master page and a detail page. Follow these steps:

1. Open a new page in the ASP.NET website we defined earlier in the book.

2. Save the page as `Master.aspx`.

3. Open another new page and save that page as `Detail.aspx`.

To create our master page, we'll pull data from the Books database, so we'll need an active data connection. Luckily, we created a data connection in Chapter 10. Check that the pages can access that data connection. To do so, choose Windows ➢ Databases to activate the Databases panel. You should see the data connection(s) we created in Chapter 10. Using a data connection, create a DataSet of the information we need from the database. Follow these steps:

1. To create a DataSet for the master page, choose Insert ➢ Appplication Objects ➢ DataSet (or click the plus sign in the Server Behaviors tab of the Application panel and select the DataSet option) to open the DataSet dialog box, which is shown in Figure 21.21.

FIGURE 21.21

The DataSet dialog box

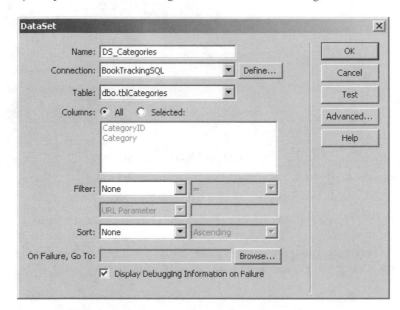

2. In the Name text box, enter **DS_Categories**.

3. In the Connection drop-down list box, select your data connection.

4. Dreamweaver MX populates the Table drop-down list box with the tables available through the chosen data connection. Choose tblCategories from the Tables list box. At this point, the DataSet dialog box should appear similar to Figure 21.21.

5. Click OK to close and save the DataSet to the master page.

Now we need to display the information in the DataSet on the page—making sure to include links to our detail page. To do so, we'll use a DataGrid. As you recall from Chapter 15, a DataGrid is an ASP.NET server control that generates multicolumn tables from data sources such as a DataSet. You can format the columns in a DataSet in a variety of ways—data, button, hyperlink, templated, and so on. If your're not familiar with a DataGrid, take a moment to review Chapter 15.

To insert a DataGrid in the master page, follow these steps:

1. Choose Insert ➢ ASP.NET Objects ➢ DataGrid to open the DataGrid dialog box, which is shown in Figure 21.22.

FIGURE 21.22
The DataGrid
dialog box

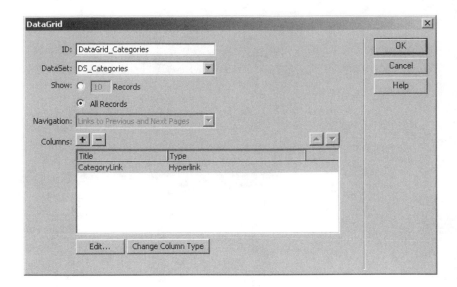

2. In the ID text box, enter **DataGrid_Categories**.

3. In the DataSet drop-down list box, select DS_Categories.

4. In the Show section, click the All Records option.

Now configure the columns of the DataGrid. As you can see in the DataGrid dialog box, Dreamweaver MX has added the CategoryID and Category column by default to our DataGrid. However, we want to show only the records from the Category column—each linked and passing its CategoryID to the detail page. To do so, first remove CategoryID from the DataGrid.

5. Select CategoryID from Columns section. Then click the minus (–) button to remove the column.

6. To configure the Category column as a Hyperlink column, select the Category column from the Columns list box.

7. Click the Change Column Type button to choose Hyperlink from the Change Column Type pop-up menu to open the Hyperlink Column dialog box, which is shown in Figure 21.23.

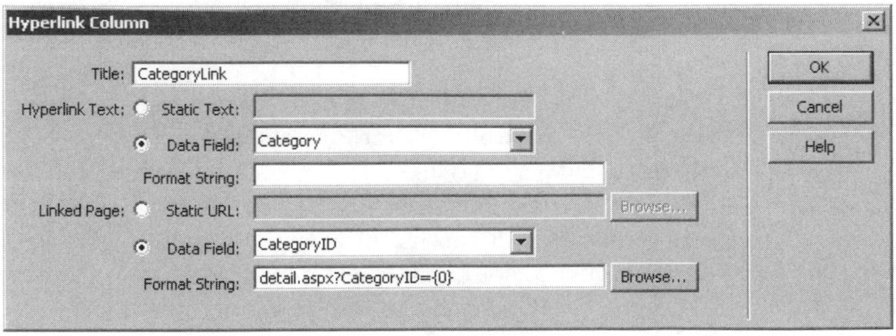

FIGURE 21.23
The Hyperlink
Column dialog box

8. In the Title text box, enter a title for the Hyperlink column such as **CategoryLink**.

Following the Title text box are the Hyperlink Text and Linked Page sections. In the Hyperlink Text section, you set the text that will display to the user. The text can be static text, such as "View Book in…" or dynamic text, such as the data in the Category column. For our example, we want to apply the link directly to the information displayed in the Category column.

9. To apply the link to the information in the Category column, click the Data Field option button, and select Category in the Data Field drop-down list box.

In the Linked Page section, you build the URL of the Hyperlink column. You can set a static URL that will display for each item in the Hyperlink column, such as `detail.aspx?categoryid=1`. Alternatively, you can choose to dynamically create the URL for each item in the Hyperlink column. In our example, we want each item to have a unique URL that passes the CategoryID to the `Detail.aspx` page.

10. Click the Data Field option button and select CategoryID from the Data Field drop-down list box.

Next, build the URL that passes the CategoryID of each record in the Hyperlink column to the `Detail.aspx` page. Not sure how to do that? No problem, Dreamweaver MX can build this URL for you.

11. Click the Browse button, which opens a Browse dialog box, to locate and select our detail page, `Detail.aspx`.

12. Click OK to return to the Hyperlink Column dialog box.

Notice that Dreamweaver MX has crafted the URL from the name of the selected file, the selected data field, and a default value. Figure 21.23 shows our completed Hyperlink Column dialog box.

13. Click OK to return to the DataGrid dialog box.

14. Click OK to insert the DataGrid into the master page.

Listing 21.11 shows the generated code of `Master.aspx`. Figure 21.24 shows the browser results of `Master.aspx`.

LISTING 21.11: *MASTER.ASPX*

```
<%@ Page Language="VB" ContentType="text/html" ResponseEncoding="iso-8859-1" %>
<%@ Register TagPrefix="MM" Namespace="DreamweaverCtrls" _
Assembly="DreamweaverCtrls,version=1.0.0.0,_
publicKeyToken=836f606ede05d46a,culture=neutral" %>
<MM:DataSet
id="DS_Categories"
runat="Server"
IsStoredProcedure="false"
ConnectionString='<%# System.Configuration.ConfigurationSettings.AppSettings(_
"MM_CONNECTION_STRING_BookTrackingSQL") %>'
DatabaseType='<%# System.Configuration.ConfigurationSettings.AppSettings(_
```

```
                "MM_CONNECTION_DATABASETYPE_BookTrackingSQL") %>'
                CommandText='<%# "SELECT * FROM dbo.tblCategories" %>'
                Debug="true"
                > </MM:DataSet>
                <MM:PageBind runat="server" PostBackBind="true" />
                <html>
                <head>
                <title>master.aspx</title>
                <meta http-equiv="Content-Type" content="text/html; charset=iso-8859-1">
                </head>
                <body>
                <form runat="server">

                  <asp:DataGrid id="DataGrid_Categories"
                  runat="server"
                  AllowSorting="False"
                  AutoGenerateColumns="false"
                  CellPadding="3"
                  CellSpacing="0"
                  ShowFooter="false"
                  ShowHeader="true"
                  DataSource="<%# DS_Categories.DefaultView %>"
                  PagerStyle-Mode="NextPrev"
                >
                    <HeaderStyle HorizontalAlign="center" BackColor="#E8EBFD" ForeColor="#3D3DB6" _
                Font-Name="Verdana, Arial, Helvetica, sans-serif" Font-Bold="true" _
                Font-Size="smaller" />
                    <ItemStyle BackColor="#F2F2F2" _
                Font-Name="Verdana, Arial, Helvetica, sans-serif" Font-Size="smaller" />
                    <AlternatingItemStyle BackColor="#E5E5E5" _
                Font-Name="Verdana, Arial, Helvetica, sans-serif" Font-Size="smaller" />
                    <FooterStyle HorizontalAlign="center" _
                BackColor="#E8EBFD" ForeColor="#3D3DB6" _
                Font-Name="Verdana, Arial, Helvetica, sans-serif" _
                Font-Bold="true" Font-Size="smaller" />
                    <PagerStyle BackColor="white" _
                Font-Name="Verdana, Arial, Helvetica, sans-serif" Font-Size="smaller" />
                    <Columns>
                      <asp:HyperLinkColumn
                        HeaderText="CategoryLink"
                        Visible="True"
                        DataTextField="Category"
                        DataNavigateUrlField="CategoryID"
                        DataNavigateUrlFormatString="detail.aspx?CategoryID={0}"/> </Columns>
                </asp:DataGrid>
                </form>
                </body>
                </html>
```

FIGURE 21.24

The browser result
of `Master.aspx`

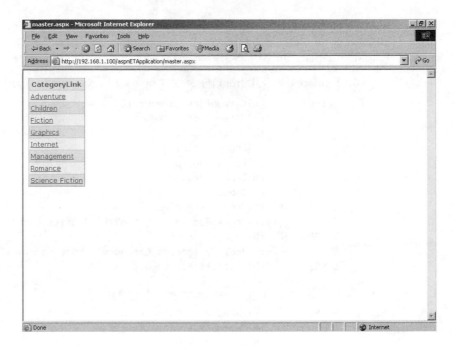

The Detail Page

To create the detail page, we follow a path similar to the one to create the master page. We use the data connection to contact our database and pull information into a DataSet. We then use the DataGrid to display the data. Let's begin.

First create a DataSet. This DataSet will be slightly different because we want to pull only the books that belong to the category of the CategoryID passed in the URL. To do so, we'll use a custom SQL statement that joins several tables together through their primary keys filtered on the URL-passed CategoryID. Follow these steps:

1. Choose Insert ➢ Application Objects ➢ DataSet(Query) to open the DateSet dialog box.

2. In the Name text box, enter **DS_Categories** and choose your data connection from the Connection list box.

At this point, we really should switch to the Advanced view to enter our custom SQL statement. However, we like to let Dreamweaver MX do as much of our work as possible. So before we switch to Advanced view, we want Dreamweaver MX to create the filter for the URL-passed CategoryID.

3. Select tblCategories from the Tables list box.

4. Select CategoryID from the Filter list box, and select URLParameter.

5. Now click the Advanced button to switch to Advanced view.

As you can see in the SQL text area and in the Parameters area, Dreamweaver MX has generated the appropriate code to filter the data based on the CategoryID URL parameter. Sweet! All we have to do is replace the basic SQL statement with our custom SQL statement.

6. Replace the SQL from the SELECT up to the equal sign (=) with the following code.

```
SELECT      tblCategories.CategoryID,
            tblCategories.Category,
            tblBooks.BookID,
            tblBooks.Title,
            tblBooks.PageCount,
            tblBooks.Lending
FROM        (tblBooks
INNER JOIN  tblBooksCategories
ON          tblBooks.BookID = tblBooksCategories.Book)
INNER JOIN  tblCategories
ON          tblBooksCategories.Category = tblCategories.CategoryID
WHERE       tblCategories.CategoryID
```

Your SQL statement should now be as follows:

```
SELECT      tblCategories.CategoryID,
            tblCategories.Category,
            tblBooks.BookID,
            tblBooks.Title,
            tblBooks.PageCount,
            tblBooks.Lending
FROM        (tblBooks
INNER JOIN  tblBooksCategories
ON          tblBooks.BookID = tblBooksCategories.Book)
INNER JOIN  tblCategories
ON          tblBooksCategories.Category = tblCategories.CategoryID
WHERE       tblCategories.CategoryID  = @CategoryID
```

Now create the DataGrid to display the data in the DataSet. To do so, follow these steps:

1. Choose Insert ➤ ASP.NET Objects ➤ DataGrid to open the DataGrid dialog box.

2. In the ID text box, enter **DG_Books**, and choose the DS_Categories DataSet from the DataSet list box.

3. In the Show section, click the All Records option, and remove all columns from the Columns list box but BookID and Title.

4. Click OK to insert the DataGrid into the detail page.

That's it. You've just created a master/detail page set in ASP.NET. Listing 21.12 shows the code generated by Dreamweaver MX. Figure 21.25 shows the browser results of Detail.aspx.

LISTING 21.12: *DETAIL.ASPX*

```
<%@ Page Language="VB" ContentType="text/html" ResponseEncoding="iso-8859-1" %>
<%@ Register TagPrefix="MM" Namespace="DreamweaverCtrls" _
Assembly="DreamweaverCtrls,version=1.0.0.0_
```

```
publicKeyToken=836f606ede05d46a,culture=neutral" %>
<MM:DataSet
id="DataSet1"
runat="Server"
IsStoredProcedure="false"
ConnectionString='<%# System.Configuration.ConfigurationSettings.AppSettings(_
"MM_CONNECTION_STRING_BookTrackingSQL") %>'
DatabaseType='<%# System.Configuration.ConfigurationSettings.AppSettings("_
MM_CONNECTION_DATABASETYPE_BookTrackingSQL") %>'
CommandText='<%# "SELECT tblCategories.CategoryID, _
tblCategories.Category, tblBooks.BookID, tblBooks.Title, _
tblBooks.PageCount, tblBooks.Lending FROM (tblBooks INNER JOIN _
tblBooksCategories ON tblBooks.BookID = tblBooksCategories.Book) _
INNER JOIN tblCategories ON .tblBooksCategories.Category = _
tblCategories.CategoryID _
WHEREtblCategories.CategoryID = @CategoryID" %>'
Debug="true"
>
  <Parameters>
    <Parameter  Name="@CategoryID"  _
Value='<%# IIf((Request.QueryString("CategoryID") <> Nothing), _
Request.QueryString("CategoryID"), "") %>'  Type="Int"   />
  </Parameters>
</MM:DataSet>
<MM:PageBind runat="server" PostBackBind="true" />
<html>
<head>
<title>detail.aspx</title>
<meta http-equiv="Content-Type" content="text/html; charset=iso-8859-1">
</head>
<body>
<form runat="server">

  <asp:DataGrid id="DG_Books"
  runat="server"
  AllowSorting="False"
  AutoGenerateColumns="false"
  CellPadding="3"
  CellSpacing="0"
  ShowFooter="false"
  ShowHeader="true"
  DataSource="<%# DataSet1.DefaultView %>"
  PagerStyle-Mode="NextPrev"
>
    <HeaderStyle HorizontalAlign="center" _
BackColor="#E8EBFD" ForeColor="#3D3DB6" _
Font-Name="Verdana, Arial, Helvetica, sans-serif" _
Font-Bold="true" Font-Size="smaller" />
    <ItemStyle BackColor="#F2F2F2" _
```

```
Font-Name="Verdana, Arial, Helvetica, sans-serif" _
Font-Size="smaller" />
    <AlternatingItemStyle BackColor="#E5E5E5" _
Font-Name="Verdana, Arial, Helvetica, sans-serif" _
Font-Size="smaller" />
    <FooterStyle HorizontalAlign="center" _
BackColor="#E8EBFD" ForeColor="#3D3DB6" _
Font-Name="Verdana, Arial, Helvetica, sans-serif" _
Font-Bold="true" Font-Size="smaller" />
    <PagerStyle BackColor="white" _
Font-Name="Verdana, Arial, Helvetica, sans-serif" _
Font-Size="smaller" />
    <Columns>
      <asp:BoundColumn DataField="BookID"
        HeaderText="BookID"
        ReadOnly="true"
        Visible="True"/>
      <asp:BoundColumn DataField="Title"
        HeaderText="Title"
        ReadOnly="true"
        Visible="True"/> </Columns>
</asp:DataGrid>
</form>
</body>
</html>
```

FIGURE 21.25

The browser result of Detail.aspx

Creating a Master/Detail Page Set Using PHP

As we mentioned, Dreamweaver MX does not provide the Master Detail Page Set Server Behavior when you create a website using PHP. However, Dreamweaver MX does provide the core Server Behaviors that compose a master/detail page set. Therefore, you can create a master/detail page set component by component. To see how to create a master/detail page set using PHP, follow these steps:

To begin, first activate your PHP website and

1. Open two new PHP files.

2. Save one file as Master.php, and save the other as Detail.php.

3. To establish a connection to our MySQL database, create a connection as we detailed in Chapter 10.

4. To create a recordset to hold the contents of the tblCategories table, choose Insert ➤ Application Objects ➤ Recordset to open the Recordset dialog box.

5. In the Name text box, enter **RS_Category**.

6. Select your data connection from the Connection list box, and select tblCategories from the Table list box, as shown in Figure 21.26.

FIGURE 21.26

The PHP recordset

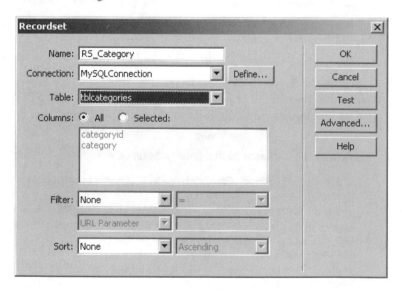

7. Click OK to close the Recordset dialog box and add the code to your page.

The next step is to display the results of the recordset in our page. You can do so in several ways, but one of the easiest is to use the Dynamic Table Server Behavior. The Dynamic Table Server Behavior is a quick way to construct a Repeat Region of dynamic text based on the contents of our recordset. Follow these steps:

1. Position your cursor in the body of the master page.

2. Choose Insert ➤ Application Objects ➤ Dynamic Table to open the Dynamic Table dialog box, as shown in Figure 21.27.

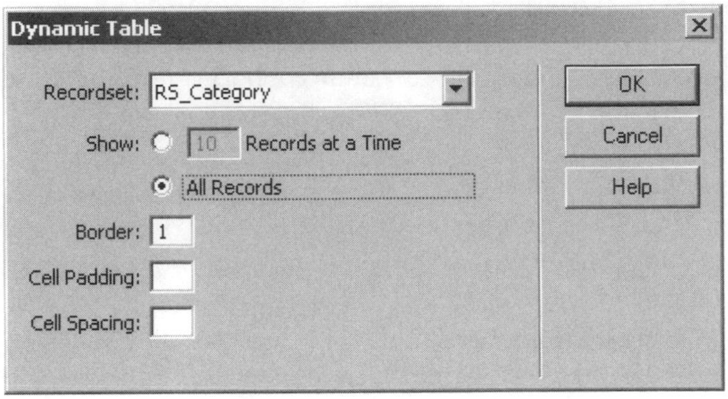

FIGURE 21.27

The Dynamic Table dialog box

3. In the Recordset list box, select RS_Category.

4. In the Show section, click the All Records option.

5. The Border, Cell Padding, and Cell Spacing parameters affect only display properties, so set them as you will.

6. Click OK to close the dialog box and add the appropriate code to our Master.php page.

Listing 21.13 shows the code, and Figure 21.28 shows our browser result at this point. As you can see in the code and in the browser result, the page is displaying the proper records. However, there isn't a link to pass the CategoryID to our detail page. That's our next step.

LISTING 21.13: DYNAMIC TABLE CODE IN *MASTER.PHP*

```php
<?php require_once('Connections/MySQLConnection.php'); ?>
<?php
mysql_select_db($database_MySQLConnection, $MySQLConnection);
$query_RS_Category = "SELECT * FROM tblcategories";
$RS_Category = mysql_query($query_RS_Category, _
$MySQLConnection) or die(mysql_error());
$row_RS_Category = mysql_fetch_assoc($RS_Category);
$totalRows_RS_Category = mysql_num_rows($RS_Category);
?>
<html>
<head>
<title>Untitled Document</title>
<meta http-equiv="Content-Type" content="text/html; charset=iso-8859-1">
</head>

<body>
```

```
<table border="1">
  <tr>
    <td>categoryid</td>
    <td>category</td>
  </tr>
  <?php do { ?>
  <tr>
    <td><?php echo $row_RS_Category['categoryid']; ?></td>
    <td><?php echo $row_RS_Category['category']; ?></td>
  </tr>
  <?php } while ($row_RS_Category = mysql_fetch_assoc($RS_Category)); ?>
</table>

</body>
</html>
<?php
mysql_free_result($RS_Category);
?>
```

FIGURE 21.28

The Dynamic Table browser result

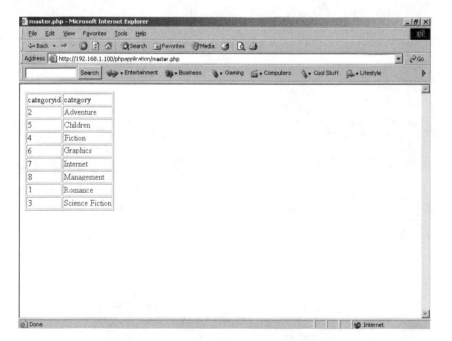

To create a link to pass the CategoryID for each record in the Dynamic Table, follow these steps:

1. To copy the code that outputs the CategoryID value from our recordset, in Code view select and copy `<?php echo $row_RS_Category['categoryid']; ?>` from the left column of the table.

2. Select <?php echo $row_RS_Category['category']; ?> from the right table column.

3. Go to Windows ➤ Properties to activate the Properties panel.

4. In the Link text box, enter **"detail.php?categoryid="**. Paste your copied contents at the end of the line.

Now PHP will add the appropriate URL parameter to each link it creates around a Category record as shown in Figure 21.29. Your code should now be identical to Listing 21.14. You can see the browser results in Figure 21.30.

FIGURE 21.29

The browser results of Master.php

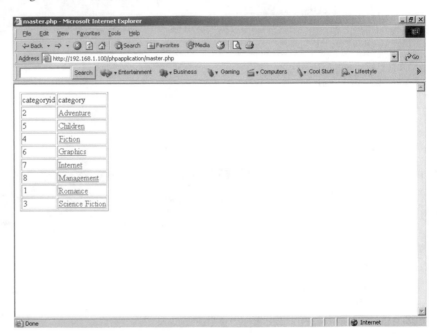

LISTING 21.14: *MASTER.PHP*

```php
<?php require_once('Connections/MySQLconnection.php'); ?>
<?php
mysql_select_db($database_MySQLconnection, $MySQLconnection);
$query_RS_Category = "SELECT * FROM tblcategories";
$RS_Category = mysql_query($query_RS_Category, $MySQLconnection) or
    die(mysql_error());
$row_RS_Category = mysql_fetch_assoc($RS_Category);
$totalRows_RS_Category = mysql_num_rows($RS_Category);
?>
<html>
<head>
```

```
<title>master.php</title>
<meta http-equiv="Content-Type" content="text/html; charset=iso-8859-1">
</head>

<body>

<table border="1">
  <tr>
    <td>categoryid</td>
    <td>category</td>
  </tr>
  <?php do { ?>
  <tr>
    <td><?php echo $row_RS_Category['categoryid']; ?></td>
    <td><a href="detail.php?categoryid=_
<?php echo $row_RS_Category['categoryid']; ?>">_
<?php echo $row_RS_Category['category']; ?></a></td>
  </tr>
  <?php } while ($row_RS_Category = mysql_fetch_assoc($RS_Category)); ?>
</table>

</body>
</html>
<?php
mysql_free_result($RS_Category);
?>
```

FIGURE 21.30

Create a filter for the CategoryID URL parameter.

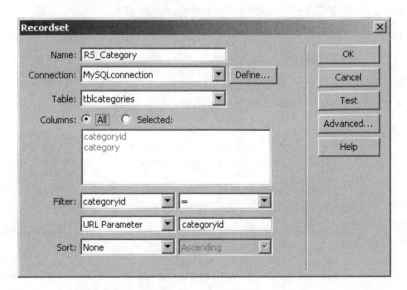

Our final step is to create our detail page to output the books belonging to the passed CategoryID URL parameter. To do so, follow these steps:

1. Open Detail.php.
2. Choose Insert ➢ Application Objects ➢ Recordset to open the Recordset dialog box.

If you recall the previous examples, we will use a custom SQL statement to return the appropriate book titles. In addition, we use a filter to return only the book titles attached to the passed CategoryID.

3. To create the filter, name the recordset RS_Category, and choose our data connection from the Connection list box.
4. Choose tblCategories from the Table list box.
5. In the Filter section, choose CategoryID, =, and URL Parameter, and enter **CategoryID** in the text box, as shown in Figure 21.30.
6. Click the Advanced button to switch the Recordset dialog box to Advanced. Notice that Dreamweaver kindly keeps the filter we created.
7. To add our custom SQL statement, select from the beginning of the existing SQL statement to the equal sign (=).
8. Replace your selection with the following custom SQL statement.

```
SELECT      tblBooks.BookID,
            tblBooks.Title
FROM        (tblBooks
INNER JOIN  tblBooksCategories
ON          tblBooks.BookID = tblBooksCategories.Book)
INNER JOIN  tblCategories
ON          tblBooksCategories.Category = tblCategories.CategoryID
WHERE       tblCategories.CategoryID =
```

Your SQL statement should now be the following:

```
SELECT      tblBooks.BookID,
            tblBooks.Title
FROM        (tblBooks
INNER JOIN  tblBooksCategories
ON          tblBooks.BookID = tblBooksCategories.Book)
INNER JOIN  tblCategories
ON          tblBooksCategories.Category = tblCategories.CategoryID
WHERE       tblCategories.CategoryID = colname
```

9. Click the Test button to be certain the SQL is accurate.
10. Click OK to close the Recordset dialog box and return to Detail.php.

We're almost done. The final task is to output the recordset result to the screen. To do so, we can use the Dynamic Table Server Behavior again. Follow these steps:

1. Choose Insert ➢ Application Objects ➢ Dynamic Table to open the Dynamic Table dialog box, which is shown in Figure 21.31.

FIGURE 21.31

Create a filter for the CategoryID URL parameter

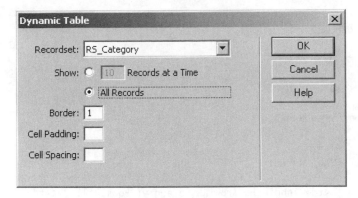

2. Select our recordset.

3. In the Show section, click the All Records option.

4. Click OK to close the Dynamic Table dialog box.

We're done! Now when a user clicks a category link on Master.php, Detail.php displays all book titles listed for that category. Listing 21.15 shows the final code for Detail.php, and Figure 21.32 shows the browser result.

LISTING 21.15: *DETAIL.PHP*

```php
<?php require_once('Connections/MySQLconnection.php'); ?>
<?php
$colname_RS_Category = "1";
if (isset($HTTP_GET_VARS['categoryid'])) {
  $colname_RS_Category = (get_magic_quotes_gpc()) ? _
$HTTP_GET_VARS['categoryid'] : _
addslashes($HTTP_GET_VARS['categoryid']);
}
mysql_select_db($database_MySQLconnection, $MySQLconnection);
$query_RS_Category = sprintf("SELECT  tblBooks.BookID, _
tblBooks.Title FROM (tblBooks INNER JOIN  tblBooksCategories _
ON      tblBooks.BookID = tblBooksCategories.Book) _
INNER JOIN  tblCategories  ON        _
tblBooksCategories.Category = tblCategories.CategoryID _
WHERE tblCategories.CategoryID  = %s", $colname_RS_Category);
$RS_Category = mysql_query($query_RS_Category, $MySQLconnection) _
or die(mysql_error());
$row_RS_Category = mysql_fetch_assoc($RS_Category);
$totalRows_RS_Category = mysql_num_rows($RS_Category);
?>
<html>
<head>
<title>detail.php</title>
```

```
    <meta http-equiv="Content-Type" content="text/html; charset=iso-8859-1">
    </head>

    <body>

    <table border="1">
      <tr>
        <td>BookID</td>
        <td>Title</td>
      </tr>
      <?php do { ?>
      <tr>
        <td><?php echo $row_RS_Category['BookID']; ?></td>
        <td><?php echo $row_RS_Category['Title']; ?></td>
      </tr>
      <?php } while ($row_RS_Category = mysql_fetch_assoc($RS_Category)); ?>
    </table>

    </body>
    </html>
    <?php
    mysql_free_result($RS_Category);
    ?>
```

FIGURE 21.32

The browser result for Detail.php

FOR MORE INFORMATION

To learn more about Master/Detail Page Sets, consult the Macromedia knowledge base at www.macromedia.com and the Dreamweaver help documentation. To get an inside perspective on how your peers are using Master/Detail Page Sets, browse the Macromedia Forums at http://webforums.macromedia.com/dreamweaver.

Summary

In this chapter, we introduced you to master/detail page sets. The master/detail information organization model, more commonly referred to as the drill-down model, is an excellent way to present the staggering amount of information in a website. Each language Dreamweaver MX supports provides several methods to create master/detail page sets. The easiest method to use is the Master Detail Page Set Server Behavior. The Master Detail Page Set Server Behavior is essentially a wizard that allows you to create the many Server Behaviors that actually construct the master/detail page set. The Master Detail Page Set Server Behavior is available in Microsoft ASP, JavaServer Pages, and Macromedia ColdFusion MX. To create master/detail page sets in ASP.NET and PHP, you must manually add the component server behavior.

Chapter 22

Searching with Dreamweaver MX

SEARCHING THROUGH DATA IS obviously one of the tasks that a computer does best. It's also one of the fundamental reasons for storing data in a database. What good is storing your 5000-title comic-book collection in a database if you can't search to verify that you have a particular title?

Dreamweaver MX lets you quickly build search pages for your databases. It provides a simple, single field search or a more advanced, multiple-field search, all created with a few clicks of the mouse (and just a little data entry.)

This chapter covers the following topics:

◆ Searching in general
◆ Performing a simple search
◆ Performing a more advanced search

Searching in General

Searching for data can take many forms. In today's computing environment, you can search through data in many ways. The term *data* is also defined in different ways when you're referring to searching. For example, the data for which you're searching can be found in user records stored in a single table or across an entire database. Perhaps the data consists of all the word-processing documents in a particular folder on your hard drive. Possibly the data is found in a series of websites and their HTML pages. Or maybe it's found in a combination of both files and databases.

Searching myriad data sources can sometimes be complex, which is why various software packages organize and index the data you've specified into *collections* or other types of prebuilt indexed files. Generally, these types of search software packages provide fast search speeds and varying levels of complexity and accuracy in creating and delivering search results.

Examples of search software include Microsoft's Full-Text Search, which is part of Microsoft's SQL Server, and Verity's suite of products that have been licensed to Macromedia for inclusion in ColdFusion. These search engines scan your data, indexing and building information stores that yield faster search results when you perform a search. Windows 2000 and Windows XP include the Indexing Service, which uses Full-Text Search to build an index of your files so that Windows can deliver your results faster when you search for files.

When you're dealing with websites, however, as a developer, you typically need to search through database tables in order to return information such as customer orders, product lists and inventories, and so forth. Dreamweaver MX lets you build both simple and more advanced search pages quickly. We'll look at both types of searches, starting with the simple search page.

Performing a Simple Search

A simple search to Dreamweaver MX is a search that looks for data based on a single criterion. For example, looking for all congressional members who have the last name of Jackson or all car models made in 1973 are searches that use a single qualifier—*Jackson* in the former and *1973* in the latter—to filter the data. Let's build a simple search that lets us look for records with a last name of Mouse.

A Simple Search Form

Start with an HTML form that contains a text field into which the user can type the name for which they're looking. Figure 22.1 shows our simple page, which we're calling `Search_Simple.asp`. You'll need to specify an action for your HTML form. We're entering `Search_Simple_Results.asp` as the action for ours. Add a Submit button to your HTML form and save your page. We'll create the actual page named `Search_Simple_Results.asp` next.

FIGURE 22.1

A simple form starts our search engine.

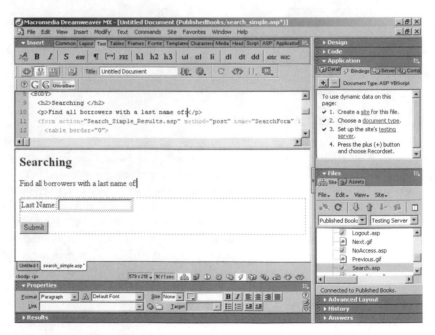

A Simple Search Form Action Page

The action page for our search results is where Dreamweaver MX does the actual work of searching for and displaying our requested data. It accomplishes this through the use of the Recordset Server

Behavior. To start building this page, create a new, blank, dynamic ASP (Active Server Pages) page and save it as `Search_Simple_Results.asp`.

ADDING A RECORDSET

To this search page, we're going to add a recordset, as we've done before. But we're going use the Filter option to grab only the records that match the criteria we enter into our search page's LastName text field. So click the Server Behaviors tab on the Application panel, click the plus sign (+), and choose RecordSet(Query) from the menu to open the Recordset dialog box, similar to that in Figure 22.2. We've already filled out the options in our example, so let's review them.

FIGURE 22.2

The Recordset dialog box effectively acts as our search filter.

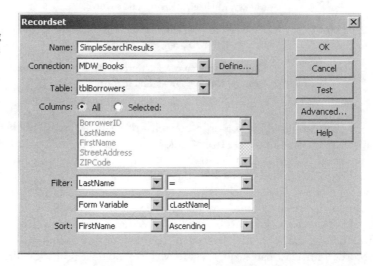

You need to give this recordset a name. We've entered SimpleSearchResults in the Name: field.

The Connection drop-down list box contains the database connection you want to use. We assume you're creating this search engine using an already-defined site that has a database connection assigned to it. If you don't have a database connection, click Define and create a database connection to the database you want to use. For more information on creating your database connection, see Chapter 10.

Once you've specified a database connection, the Table drop-down list box will fill with the tables contained within that database. Select the table upon which you want to perform a search. As you can see, we're choosing the tblBorrowers table.

Next, you choose the table columns you want the search to return. We're interested in seeing all the table columns, so we're going with the default of All. If you only want a few of the columns returned, you can click Selected and then select the columns in the list by pressing Ctrl and clicking the column name you want to see.

SETTING THE FILTER

Filter, in this case, is the magic wielder for our search. By specifying a filter, we tell Dreamweaver MX to return only the records that match our previous page's form search field. Since we're interested in searching by LastName, in the first Filter box, we're going to choose LastName from the list of column names. In the second Filter box, we're going to choose the equal sign (=) since we want only the records that match exactly the name we're entering. We could choose any of the logical operators or three special operators from this list. Table 22.1 lists and explains the special operators.

TABLE 22.1: SPECIAL OPERATORS

OPERATOR	PURPOSE
Begins with	Finds records that begin with the criteria we enter. For example, an entry of Mic would find Mickey, Michael, Michelle, and so forth.
Ends with	Finds records that end with the criteria we enter. For example, an entry of en would find Lauren, Karen, Darren, and so forth.
Contains	Finds records that contain the criteria we enter. For example, an entry of am would find Sammy, Tammy, James, and so forth.

The third Filter box is a drop-down list that lets us choose the type of variable we want to use as the filter. We can choose from Cookie, URL Variable, and so forth, but for our purposes here, we want to use a Form Variable, so choose Form Variable from the list.

The fourth Filter box is where you put the name of the variable you chose in the third box. So here, we enter cLastName, which is the name of our form field from the prior page. Naturally, you'll want to enter the name of your form field if it doesn't match ours.

The Sort drop-down list box lets you specify a column on which to sort the data. You can choose whether the data should be sorted in ascending or descending order. Since we're only looking for records with a last name equivalent to what we enter, we're already filtering our records by last name. Therefore, to sort our records in proper order, we can sort on the FirstName field.

Now that we've got our search complete, we need a place in which to display it. Click OK, and let's add a Dynamic Table to this form.

ADDING A DYNAMIC TABLE

If you recall from Chapter 19, Dreamweaver MX includes an Application object called Dynamic Table that automatically creates a repeating region and table to display the results from a query. We're going to use one of those to display our search results. Follow these steps:

1. Choose Insert ➤ Application Objects ➤ Dynamic Table, as we did in Figure 22.3, to open the Dynamic Table dialog box, as shown in Figure 22.4.

2. Choose the recordset name you created earlier from the Recordset drop-down list box. This may already be chosen for you.

3. Set your table options, such as how many records the table should display at once, the border, and cell spacing and padding, and then click OK. Dreamweaver MX should add to your page a table, complete with repeating regions, similar to that you can partially see in Figure 22.5.

4. Save your page, and open the search page in your browser.

FIGURE 22.3

Add a Dynamic
Table to display the
search results.

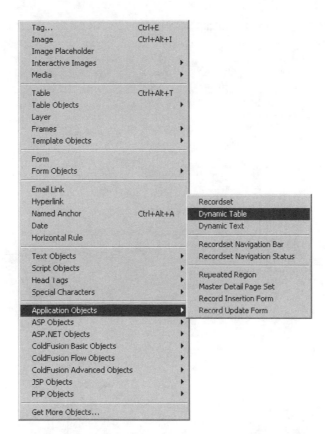

FIGURE 22.4

Set the options for
your Dynamic Table.

PERFORMING THE SEARCH

When you open your search page in a browser, you should see something similar to Figure 22.6, which shows our version. If you're using our sample database and search for "mouse" you should get results similar to that shown in Figure 22.7. Our search yields the records with the last name of Mouse, and, indeed, they're sorted by the first name.

FIGURE 22.5

Dreamweaver MX has added to our page a table to display the record list.

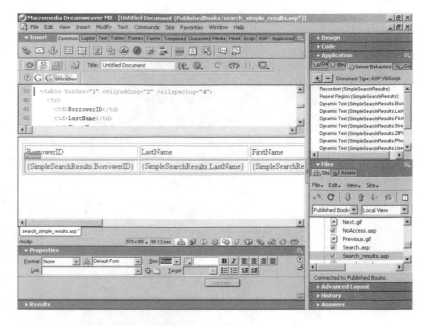

FIGURE 22.6

Our simple search form

FIGURE 22.7

We found all the records matching "Mouse".

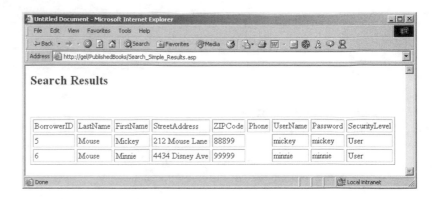

It would be nice to repeat what the user searched for, wouldn't it? We should probably include a statement that reminds the user about the search criteria they used to get these results. And notice the missing table cells under Phone? Let's get rid of those too.

TWEAKING THE RESULTS DISPLAY

Let's go back to our search results page. First, let's add a search criteria form variable to our bindings so that we can display it to the user. Follow these steps:

1. Click the Bindings tab on the Applications panel, click the plus sign (+), and then choose Request Variable to open the Request Variable dialog box.

2. From the Type drop-down list box, select Request.Form, since this is how ASP refers to form variables.

3. In the Name box, enter **cLastName** (or whatever you named your search form text field), as we did in Figure 22.8.

FIGURE 22.8

When creating ASP pages, Dreamweaver MX offers Request .Form variables as a new binding type.

4. Click OK, and Dreamweaver MX adds the Request binding to your Bindings panel, as you can see in Figure 22.9.

FIGURE 22.9

We've added a new variable binding to our page.

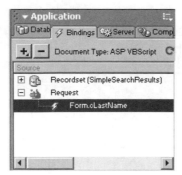

5. Add some text such as "You searched on," and drag the form variable from the Bindings panel onto the appropriate space on your page, as we did in Figure 22.10.

    Now let's prevent empty table cells from breaking the flow of the table.

6. Add a nonbreaking space to each table cell, at the end of the variable. You can either enter ** ** in the Code window at the appropriate place, or you can choose the nonbreaking space character from the Characters tab on the Insert bar.

7. Save your page, and you should see a modified search results screen similar to that in Figure 22.11.

FIGURE 22.10

We're adding a search reminder for the user.

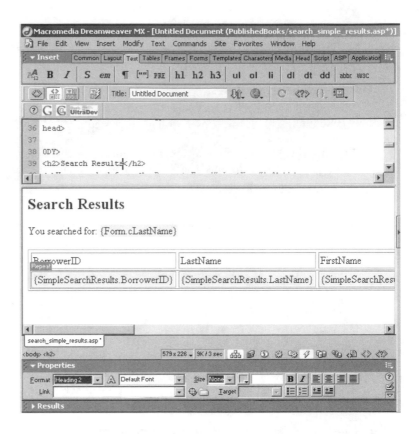

FIGURE 22.11

Our modified search results page

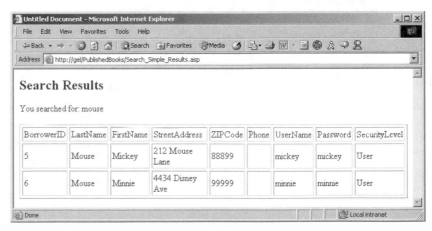

NOTE *Since we're using ASP to create our search, we'll be choosing Request variables here. If we were creating a different type of dynamic page, a ColdFusion page, for instance, we'd see Form Variable. Keep in mind that Dreamweaver MX changes to reflect names that are appropriate for the type of dynamic page you're creating.*

Performing a More Advanced Search

To Dreamweaver MX, a more advanced search is a search in which you filter records by multiple criteria. Perhaps you need to find all customers who live in Colorado that bought snow skis last year. You'd specify those two criteria in the search in order to filter the records in your database. Dreamweaver MX allows us to quickly add such a search using very nearly the same technique we used to build the simple search.

Modifying the Search Form

Let's add a couple more fields to our search field, letting the user specify Last Name and Admin Level, for instance. Figure 22.12 shows our modified search form, which we're saving as `Search_Advanced.asp`. Now we're ready to modify our search results page. We're going to save it under the name `Search_Advanced_Results.asp`, so that both versions can be included on the CD.

FIGURE 22.12

We're adding multiple fields upon which to search.

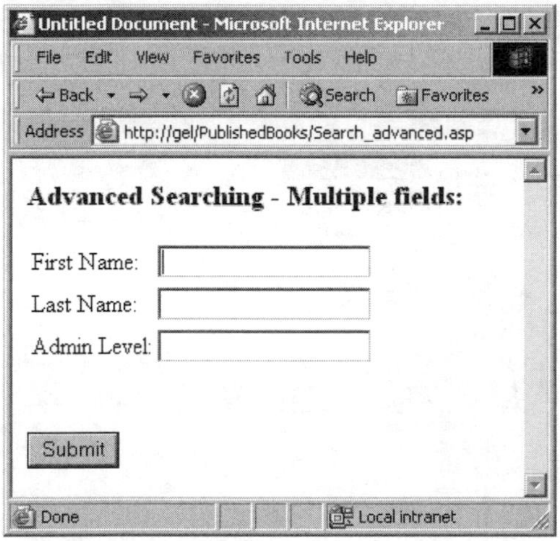

Reviewing the Advanced Recordset Dialog Box

We need to modify the recordset on the search results page, so double-click the recordset on the Bindings tab of the Application panel. Click the Advanced button in the Recordset dialog box, shown in Figure 22.13, to open the advanced version of this dialog box. Your dialog box should now look similar to Figure 22.14.

As you can see, the dialog box contains a few features we should explore a bit. You're familiar with the first two fields—Name and Connection. The SQL, Variables, and Database Items sections let you customize the recordset even further, which helps when you're building a multiple-field search engine.

The SQL section contains the SQL code that Dreamweaver MX generated for our simple search. You can edit the SQL code directly by entering new text in the SQL section. You can also modify the SQL code by selecting and entering options in the remaining two sections as well.

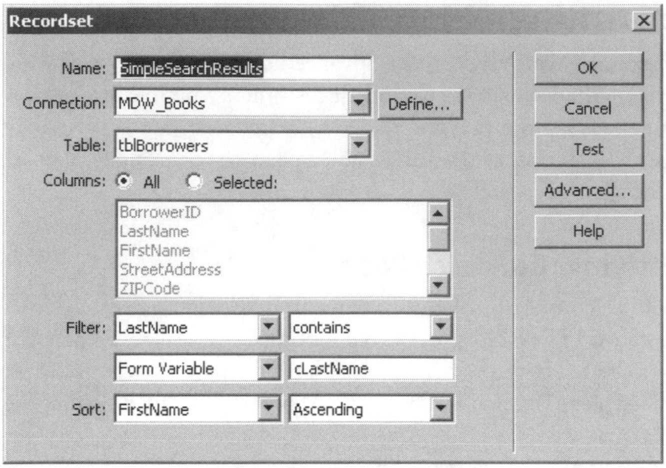

FIGURE 22.13

Click the Advanced button to open the advanced version of the Recordset dialog box.

FIGURE 22.14

The advanced options in the Recordset dialog box.

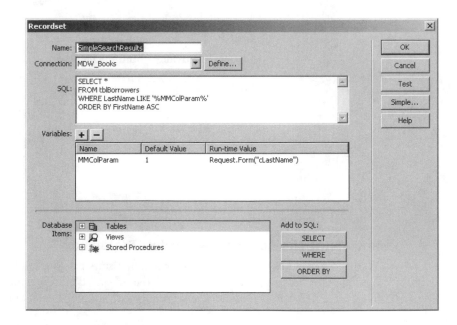

The Variables section lets you specify variables that are to be used in the SQL statement as further filter criteria. You can see that Dreamweaver MX created a variable called *MMColParam* and assigned it the value of our form variable *cLastName*. Notice that since we're using ASP for this example, the form variable is referred to as *Request.Form("cLastName")*. You can also assign a default value to the variable.

Those of you more accustomed to SQL may wonder why you'd want to go through the trouble of assigning a variable in this area instead of just typing in the full SQL statement. If you use the variables feature, Dreamweaver MX takes care of all the weird syntax that sometimes languages such as ASP require. Plus, Dreamweaver MX adds code that takes care of commas and quotes that may exist in the user input. And you can have a default value for the variable. So you see, this feature can be quite handy.

The Database Items section allows you to add the respective items to the SQL statement as well. That is, if you open the Table view, choose a table, and click Select, Dreamweaver MX adds the table name to the FROM portion of the SQL statement. This feature helps you remember your table names, views, and stored procedures and reminds you where they should go in the SQL statement. But that's about all it does. Once you're comfortable with SQL, you probably won't use this much.

Modifying the Search Results Page's Recordset

OK, now we're ready to actually modify this window. Since we need to add the new search criteria to our SQL code, we need to add two more variables in the Variables area. Follow these steps:

1. Click the plus sign (+) next to Variables to add a new, highlighted blank line to the Variables section.

2. Click Name, and enter **FN**.

3. Enter "" in the Default Value column.

4. Click the Run-time Value column, and enter **Request.Form("cFirstName")**.

5. Add another new line by clicking the plus sign (+) and entering **Rights** in the Name column.

6. Enter "" in the Default Value column.

7. Enter **Request.Form("cAdminLevel")** in the Run-time Value column.

Now that we've defined the variables, we can add them to the SQL. We actually have to type the variables into the SQL code, so let's modify the SQL so that it looks like the following:

```
SELECT *
FROM tblBorrowers
WHERE LastName LIKE '%MMColParam%'
    AND FirstName LIKE '%FN%'
    AND SecurityLevel LIKE '%Rights%'
ORDER BY FirstName ASC
```

Your window should now look similar to that in Figure 22.15.

Since we're using LIKE and the percent signs (%) surrounding our variables (the wildcard in Microsoft Access), our search will look for records containing the text we enter. The text doesn't have to exactly match the record in order for the record to be selected.

Save your page and load your new search page. If you're using our sample database from the CD, enter **Mickey**, **Mouse**, and **User** in First Name, Last Name, and Admin Level, respectively. You should now see Mickey Mouse's information on your screen. Try the search again, leaving one of the criteria blank. You should get an empty recordset and no user records returned to your browser when you search.

FIGURE 22.15

After adding the new search criteria to your query, your advanced Recordset dialog box should look similar to this.

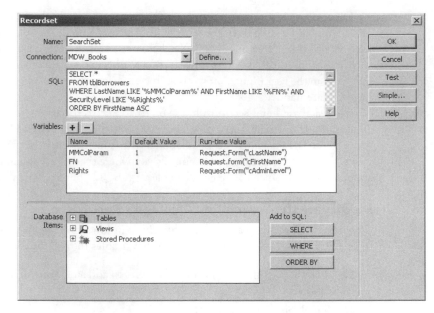

Summary

Building a search page isn't difficult with Dreamweaver MX. Using the tools that Dreamweaver MX provides, you can quickly create the data entry form and the results display form. In this chapter, we've shown you how to create both the simple search form and a more advanced search form using ASP. You can use this method to create a search form in any of the languages Dreamweaver MX supports, since it handles the wildcard searches (begins with, ends with, and contains) for you.

Chapter 23

Using Templates

Whether you consider yourself a web developer or a web designer, page layout is one of the most important aspects of your job. How many times have you abandoned a site you were visiting because it was hard to use or just too confusing or busy? If you're like most of us, you probably don't spend too much of your valuable time trying to unlock a site's biggest mysteries—there should be no mystery. The site's purpose should be clear, and the functionality should be simple to discern and implement, from page to page.

You're not creating great works of art (well, most of you aren't)—you simply want each page to quickly tell its story and grab the visitor's interest before they leave without exploring the really good stuff. That sounds like a lot of work, but it doesn't have to be. One way to reduce wear and tear on yourself and get your site up and running quickly is to make the Dreamweaver MX template your new best friend. Doing so will reduce your work load by quickly reproducing your design from page to page. In this chapter, you'll learn how to put templates to work for you.

This chapter covers the following topics:

◆ The benefits of using templates
◆ Template anatomy
◆ Creating a template
◆ Creating a new page from a template
◆ Applying a template to an existing document
◆ Building a template
◆ Creating a template-based page
◆ Viewing a template-based page

The Benefits of Using Templates

A *template* is a special type of page (document) that shares layout from page to page. Dreamweaver MX templates won't make you a more creative web designer, but they will increase your efficiency and make your job easier. Think of a template as a shell that contains site-level design qualities and behaviors, but little content. For instance, your template might contain a company logo, menu links, and other basic elements. When you're ready to add a new page to your site, you begin with the template instead of a blank page and avoid the repetitive task of re-creating those elements each time you add a new page—all the ingredients are already in the template.

Using templates has several benefits:

◆ Templates help new Dreamweaver developers get up and running faster. Macromedia provides a number of ready-to-go design templates you can use with your own site. You can download them at `www.macromedia.com/software/dreamweaver/download/templates/`.

Even the experienced developer can get a head start on a design using one of these templates. (You must have a valid Dreamweaver MX license to use these templates.)

◆ They reduce construction time by eliminating repetitive design tasks. Place shared design elements in a template, and start each new document from the template instead of from scratch.

◆ They let you update multiple pages at once. When the design changes, there's no need to modify each page. Simply open the template and make the necessary modifications once. Dreamweaver MX will update all the linked documents accordingly (unless you purposely disconnected the document when you created it).

◆ They let the site designer standardize the design, controlling the elements that individual page authors will be able to edit by including noneditable and editable sections in the template. Content in a noneditable section can't be modified anywhere but in the template.

◆ Templates also permit groups of developers to work on a website and not have to worry about page style and layout. All developers can work from a central template pool in a convenient place on the company intranet.

◆ The database programmer is not in many cases a web designer and has limited knowledge of web page design. Using templates, the programmer needs to know little about the actual page design.

Templates significantly aid the construction process and make the finished site easier to maintain. The consistent design qualities and behaviors in the template provide continuity between pages, making your site easier to use. In addition, you can quickly update your entire site by making changes to just the template.

NOTE *Dreamweaver MX refers to design pages as* documents. *We'll refer to such a document as a* page. *The term* template-based page *refers to a new page you base on a template. Web design usually refers to the creator of a page as an author. A template author is the person creating the template; a page author, within the context of templates, is the person creating a template-based page.*

Template Anatomy

Every template-based page has regions the page author can edit and regions that can't be edited. As such, a template can contain text, images, styles, and editable regions. In this section, we'll review the components that make up a template. There are four regions in each template page that can contain text, images, page layout, and styles. These four regions are:

- Editable region
- Repeating region
- Optional region
- Editable tag attribute

The template author determines which regions are editable by including editable regions or editable parameters. An *editable region* is simply an unlocked area that you can modify. When basing a new page on a template, the page author can make changes only to editable regions. All other regions are locked. For this reason, a template should contain at least one editable region.

Repeating regions do just what their name implies—they repeat areas of a web page, typically tables. There are two types of repeating regions:

Repeating tables When you are designing a page, particularly using HTML tables, it is difficult to determine in advance how many table or cell elements page authors might require. Using a repeating region, you can permit a page author to simply repeat as many tables or table cells as needed. The number of rows might be different from page to page, which doesn't matter to the template. A repeating region repeats sections, but it isn't editable unless you add an editable region to the repeating region.

Repeating regions A repeating region is similar to a repeating table. However, in this case, it can be applied to almost any page element, even to a small bit of text. By default, the repeating region isn't editable. You must make the region editable.

Use optional regions for text or images that are part of the template's basic design but that may or may not appear in every page of the site. When creating the new templated-based page, the page author controls whether the page displays the optional content.

Each new template-based page isn't restricted to all the template's design elements. Using an editable tag attribute, you can unlock a template tag, allowing the page author to edit that tag in the new page. For instance, the basic design might call for a graphic that should normally be left-aligned, but you as template author anticipate that on some pages this placement will need to be adjusted. Because the graphic needs to appear on every page, it must be a repeating region, but by making the `align` attribute an editable tag, you allow the page author to align the graphic as needed. You'll learn more in "Using Editable Tag Attributes" later in this chapter.

Creating a Template

You can begin the process of creating a Dreamweaver MX template in three ways:

- Create it from scratch by choosing File ➤ New. This way, you begin with a new, blank page. You then lay out the elements of the site design you've planned and save the page as a template.
- You can also base a template on an existing document. This way, all the elements of your design are in place (if you've planned the master document carefully), and you just need to designate which elements are repeating, which are editable, and so on.

◆ For many sites you will begin without a template. In this case you are often forced to apply new templates to existing content. In general, you create a new template and then base documents on the new template.

With any of these methods, Dreamweaver MX saves the template file with the .dwt extension in a special Templates folder in the active site's local root folder. This folder probably won't exist the first time you add a template to your site, but don't worry—Dreamweaver MX will create the folder for you.

WARNING *Dreamweaver MX documentation warns you not to remove templates from the Templates folder or store nontemplate files in this reserved folder because either action will result in errors. The truth is, as long as your templates are properly linked, it doesn't really matter where you store them. And there's nothing special about other formats that will cause your application to suddenly crash if a nontemplate file is encountered in your Templates folder. It's simply a warning to keep you from unintentionally breaking links or creating links to the wrong type of file.*

Creating a Template from a New Page

To create a template from a new blank page, follow these steps:

1. Choose File ➢ New to open the New Document dialog box, as shown in Figure 23.1.

FIGURE 23.1

Choose a page category and type.

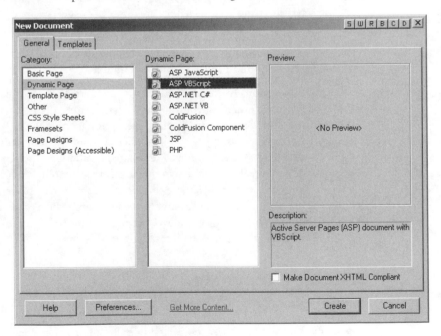

2. Make sure the General tab is selected, and then select Basic Page, Dynamic Page, or Template Page from the Category list. The list to the right updates accordingly to display basic or dynamic page types. Clicking the Templates tab will give you access to any templates stored in a Dreamweaver site. In this case, we've chosen Dynamic Page, because the template we will build later in the chapter will be based on an ASP (Active Server Pages) page.

3. Choose the appropriate page type from the Dynamic Page list, and then click Create. Don't select Template Page at this point—we're using templates to lay out the design and structure of the page.

At this point, your work has just begun. Now you need to build the template, adding the elements of the site design you've planned. You'll work through a complete example of that process in the upcoming section, "Building a Template."

4. Once the elements are in place, Select File ➤ Save As Template and give your template a name.

Creating a Template from an Existing Page

To create a template from an existing page, follow these steps:

1. Choose File ➤ Open to open the Open dialog box, and select the document.

2. You can double-click a document to open it, or select it and click Open. After opening the document, choose File ➤ Save As Template to open the Save As Template dialog box, which is shown in Figure 23.2.

FIGURE 23.2

Identify the site to which you're adding the template.

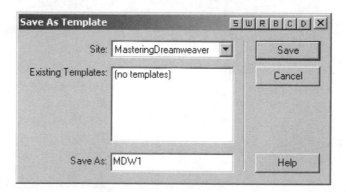

3. Identify the site to which you want to add the template, and name the template. In our example, we've chosen the MasteringDreamweaver site and named the template MDW1. Also notice that currently, we have no other templates.

4. Click Save.

NOTE   *When you save the template at this point, Dreamweaver MX might display a warning that the template doesn't contain any editable regions. That's because you haven't designated any yet. Click OK to continue or click Cancel to abandon the current save task. If you choose Cancel, Dreamweaver MX won't create a template from the current document. You can disable this warning by clicking the Don't Warn Me Again option, but you probably shouldn't.*

5. Click F11 to display the Assets window, shown in Figure 23.3. As you can see, Dreamweaver MX added the new template to this window. Simply double-click a template item in the list to open that template's document.

FIGURE 23.3

You can access a template in the Assets window.

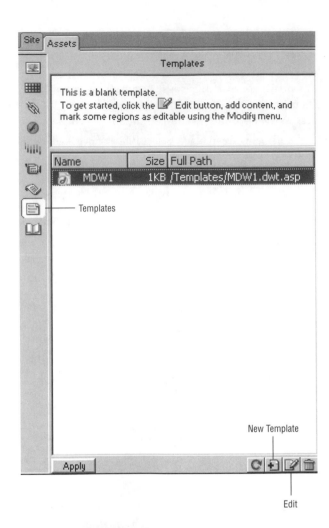

Creating a Template from the Assets Window

You can also create a template from the Assets window. To do so, follow these steps:

1. In the Assets window, click the Templates button to select the Templates category.

2. Click the New Template button, or right-click the list area and choose New Template from the shortcut menu. Figure 23.4 shows the results. Dreamweaver MX adds a new, as yet unnamed template to the list.

3. While the name is highlighted, type a name for the document.

4. To open the new template in the Document window, double-click it in the Assets list or click the Edit button.

FIGURE 23.4

Dreamweaver MX lists templates in the Assets window.

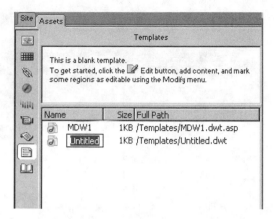

Now you can add the elements of your site design to the template, as you'll do in the "Building a Template" section.

TIP *To open the Assets window, choose Window ➤ Assets or press F11.*

Creating a New Page from a Template

Once you have a template or even a variety of templates to work with, you'll start most new pages with a template to avoid repetitive design tasks. You can base a new page on an existing template in a number of ways. Perhaps the quickest route is to use the Assets window. Just remember, this list contains only templates in the active site. Follow these steps:

1. Open the Assets window and click the Templates tool in the Assets panel.

2. Right-click the template, and choose New From Template from the shortcut menu.

3. Choose File ➤ New to open the New From Template.

   The New From Template dialog box provides a few benefits that the Assets window doesn't:

   ◆ It displays all templates for all your defined sites.

   ◆ You can disconnect the new page from the template.

4. Click the Templates tab. Dreamweaver MX displays all the templates for all your Dreamweaver MX–defined sites, as shown in Figure 23.5.

5. To select a template, choose a site in the Templates For list. The templates in the Site list to the right update accordingly.

6. From the Site list, choose the appropriate template.

7. Click Create to open the new document in the Document window.

WARNING *Deselecting the Update Page When Template Changes option will create an independent HTML file. Be careful when doing so—Dreamweaver MX will not update the page when you modify the template.*

FIGURE 23.5
The Templates tab displays all your templates.

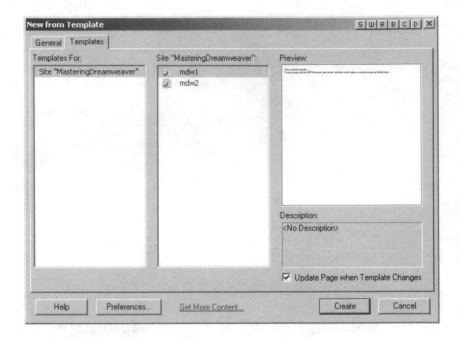

Applying a Template to an Existing Document

You won't always get to start with a template. You may find yourself working with an existing page that you need to update by applying a template. If the page contains editable regions, Dreamweaver MX must reconcile those regions to the template's editable regions. When regions match, Dreamweaver MX retains the content from the page, but applies the template's editable region attributes. When there's no match, Dreamweaver MX returns an error.

To apply a template to an existing page, open the page, and then apply the template in one of the following ways:

◆ With the page active, choose Modify ➢ Templates ➢ Apply Template To Page to open the Select Template dialog box, as shown in Figure 23.6. Select a template, and then click Select. (We haven't created any templates yet, so right now there are no templates to display.)

◆ With the page active, select the template in the Templates list of the Assets window, and then click the Apply button (at the bottom-left corner of the Assets window).

◆ With the page active, drag the template from the Templates category of the Assets window to the Document window's Design view.

NOTE *To detach a page's template, open the page and choose Modify ➢ Templates ➢ Detach From Template. You must detach a template in order to edit a page's locked regions.*

FIGURE 23.6

Choose a site, and then specify a template.

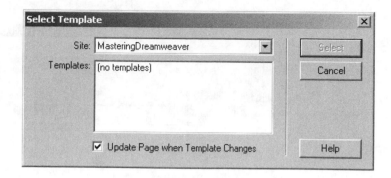

Building a Template

Now, let's create a template that you might use as a base page for a small electronic magazine site.

First, we'll create a new template and add a few graphics and editable regions. Once the template is complete, we'll base a new page on the template. Follow these steps (or use one of the methods reviewed in the earlier section, "Creating a Template"):

1. Choose File ➢ New to open the New Document dialog box.
2. Select Template Page from the Categories list.
3. Select ASP VBScript Template from the Template Page list.
4. Click Create.

Before you start this next section, copy the two graphic files, `backfence2.jpg` and `rtracsban.gif`, from the accompanying CD to the Images folder in your web root folder. You might need to create the folders at this point.

We'll be working with the MasteringDreamweaver folders off the IIS root, wwwroot:

`C:\inetpub\wwwroot\MasteringDreamweaver\images`

`C:\inetpub\wwwroot\MasteringDreamweaver\Chapter23`

`C:\inetpub\wwwroot\MasteringDreamweaver\Templates`

These folders simply constitute our example environment; yours may be different. The Template folder might not exist on your system yet. Dreamweaver MX will create the folder for you when you save your first template file.

Now, let's insert a few graphics that make up the company's logo. Follow these steps:

1. With the Layout View window active, choose Insert ➢ Image ➢ Open the Images folder.
2. Select `backfence2.jpg`.
3. If Dreamweaver MX displays an information message about relative paths in saved documents, click OK to clear it. Figure 23.7 shows the graphic in the Layout View window.
4. Insert a return after the graphic and repeat steps 1 through 3 to insert the second graphic file, `rtracsban.gif`, beneath the first graphic, as shown in Figure 23.8.

FIGURE 23.7
Insert the fence graphic.

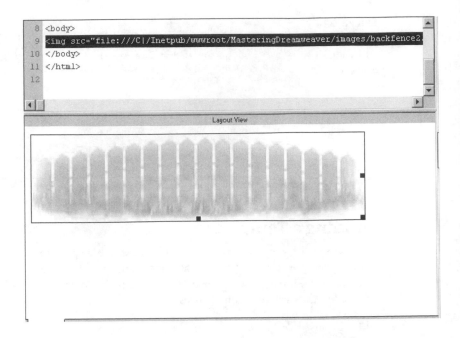

FIGURE 23.8
Insert the banner graphic below the fence graphic.

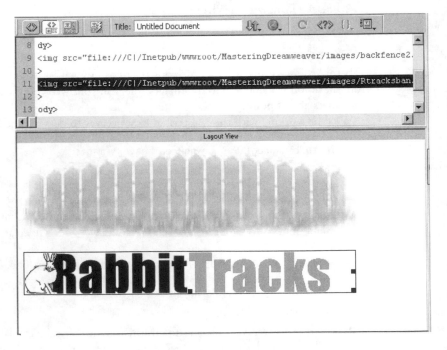

NOTE *Throughout this chapter, the Document window is set up to display both the Code and Design view when possible so you can view each item's relevant code.*

5. Dreamweaver MX aligns both graphics to the left, by default. To center both graphics, select both (hold down the Shift key while you click both graphics), and then choose Text ➤ Align ➤ Center.

6. Before we do anything else, save the template by choosing File ➤ Save As Template.

7. When Dreamweaver MX displays the message that the template contains no editable regions, click OK.

8. Specify the site you want to save the template in (we're working in MasteringDreamweaver), enter a name for the site, as we've done in Figure 23.9, and click Save.

FIGURE 23.9

After adding the graphics, save the template.

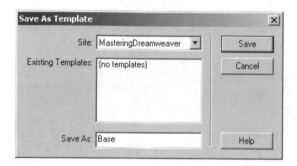

Dreamweaver MX automatically saves the file to the appropriate site's Templates folder. If the Templates folder doesn't exist yet, Dreamweaver MX creates it.

Inserting Locked Content

A template can contain content that's not editable. Simply enter the content right onto the page; don't define it as any kind of region. That content is *locked*, which means the page author can't edit that content.

Our template doesn't contain any content as yet, so position the insertion point below the banner and enter the text **A Harey Tale.** Then right-align the text, as shown in Figure 23.10.

FIGURE 23.10

Enter text directly into the page to lock it, meaning no one can edit it outside the template.

Dreamweaver MX prohibits the page author from modifying that text in any way. Each subsequent page contains the two logo graphics and the small line of text just below. The page author can neither modify nor delete them. The template author must open the template and make any modifications, but doing so will affect all pages based on (and still actively connected to) that template.

Inserting an Editable Region

Let's continue with our example by assuming that the title, byline, and article content changes from issue to issue. You can handle this situation easily by adding a few editable regions to the template. That way, the page author can update the title, byline, and content as required. An *editable region* is an area of content that you might want to modify in subsequent pages. You can enter the content and then select it, or you can insert the editable region and then enter the content into the region.

WARNING   *Make sure you're actually working with a template page before adding an editable region to a page. If you add an editable region to a page and then save it, Dreamweaver MX will automatically save the page as a template, whether you meant to or not.*

To insert an editable region, follow these steps:

1. Move the insertion point to a blank line.
2. Click the Editable Region button on the Insert bar, shown in Figure 23.11, to open the New Editable Region dialog box, which is shown in Figure 23.12. (Click the Templates tab in the Insert bar to display the Template objects.)

FIGURE 23.11

Use the Insert bar to quickly insert regions.

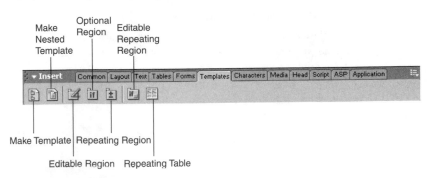

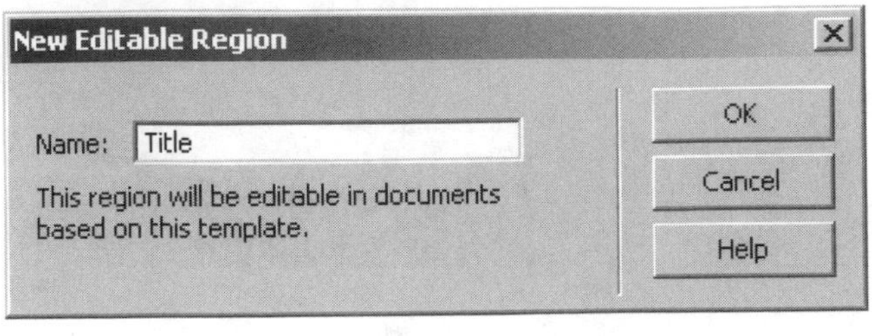

FIGURE 23.12

In the Name box, enter a name for the new editable region.

3. In the Name box, enter a name for the region, and click OK.

4. Center the region.

As you can see in Figure 23.13, the region's tab contains the region's name. Since the editable region is empty (has no content), the content area also displays the region's name. If you create an editable region that includes content, that content will be displayed.

FIGURE 23.13

Dreamweaver MX highlights the new region's border.

5. Repeat steps 1 through 3 to add two more editable regions to the template. Name them Byline and Article, as shown in Figure 23.14. Be sure to include a few blank lines between each region; otherwise, Dreamweaver MX will combine the regions on the same line.

FIGURE 23.14

Add a total of three editable regions to the template.

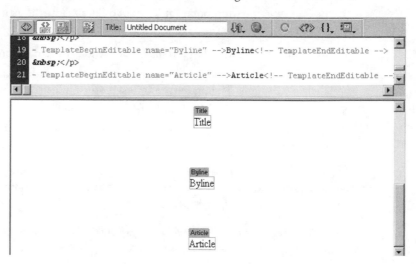

TIP *Things change, and that's what templates are for. At any time, you can lock content by simply changing the template. To remove an editable region, open the template, select the editable region, and then choose Modify ➤ Templates ➤ Remove Template Markup. You won't delete any content, just the editable tags. Remember, you can't lock or unlock content in a subsequent page; you must change the template.*

ALTERNATE METHODS FOR CREATING AN EDITABLE REGION

Dreamweaver MX provides several ways to insert a region. Besides clicking the appropriate button on the Insert bar, you can use one of the following methods:

◆ Choose Insert ➤ Template Objects and then choose one of the following options: Editable Region, Optional Region, Repeating Region, Editable Optional Region, Repeating Table.

◆ Right-click the content, choose Templates and then select one of the following options: New Editable Region, New Optional Region, New Repeating Region.

Inserting a Repeating Region

The next element we want to add to our template is a credits area, in which we acknowledge contributors that aren't part of the staff. That means the page author will edit this data each issue. It's even possible that there will be no acknowledgments. We'll use a repeating region to accommodate this content.

A *repeating region* enables you to replicate a region. Use them the same as you would an editable region, except that these regions aren't editable. Use them to control the layout of repeated data that won't change from page to page, such as a list of contacts, employees, products—any kind of data that you might want to list.

Although a repeating region isn't editable, you can include an editable region in a repeating region to make it editable, and that's what we'll do in this section. Follow these steps:

1. Position the insertion point (at least) two lines below the article region.
2. Click the Repeating Region button on the Insert bar.
3. In the New Repeating Region dialog box, enter the name **Contributors**, and click OK.
4. At this point, the region isn't editable, so double-click the body of the repeating region, and click the Editable Region button to insert an editable region within the repeating region.
5. Name this region **EditableContributors**, and click OK.
6. Left-align the nested regions if necessary, as shown in Figure 23.15. Later, we'll add names to this region.

If you just want to add a series of names, you can use an editable region. When there's more than one contributor, we want to repeat the formatting for each contributor; that's why we're using a repeating region instead of an editable region.

NOTE *Alone, a repeating region isn't editable by a page author. You must open the template and edit any content. This may affect other pages created from the template.*

FIGURE 23.15

Add a repeating region for items you might want to repeat.

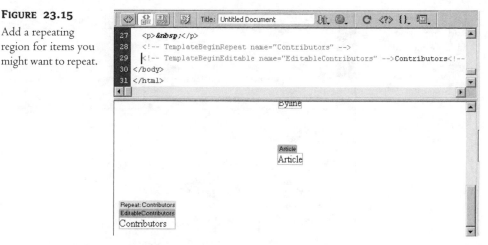

Inserting a Repeating Table

The next section will list staff contributors that will remain permanent for the most part. In this case, you might use a repeating table region. A *repeating table* is similar to a repeating region except it includes repeating rows of table cells that include editable regions. You specify which rows in the table are included in the repeating region.

Inserting a repeating table is similar to inserting any other region. To add a repeating table to our sample template, follow these steps:

1. Position the insertion point a few lines below the contributors region.
2. Click the Repeating Table tool on the Insert toolbar to open the Insert Repeating Table dialog box, which is shown in Figure 23.16.

FIGURE 23.16

Define a two-column repeating table.

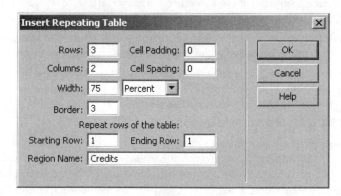

3. Change the default settings as shown in Figure 23.16, and name the region Credits.
4. Enter six cells of content like the two cells shown in Figure 23.17.

FIGURE 23.17
Add a repeating
table for monthly
contributors.

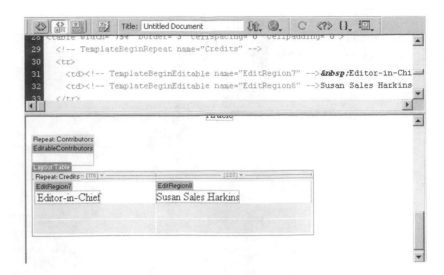

THINGS TO KNOW ABOUT REPEATING TABLE SETTINGS

The Repeating Table settings are fairly self-explanatory, but you might want to keep a few things in mind, particularly if you are more familiar with database development than with web development.

◆ The Cell Padding property determines the number of pixels between a cell's content and the cell's boundaries.

◆ The Cell Spacing property determines the number of pixels between adjacent table cells. If you don't assign a value for either the Cell Padding or the Cell Spacing setting, most browsers default to a padding value of 1 and a spacing value of 2. If you want no padding or spacing, enter the value 0 for both properties. Similarly, if you don't specify a border setting, most browsers default to a setting of 1 pixel. Set the property to 0 if you want no border.

◆ The Width property specifies the width of the table in pixels or as a percentage of the browser window's width. Simply choose Percent or Pixels from that property's drop-down list accordingly.

◆ The Repeat Rows Of The Table options specify the rows displayed in the repeating region.

Inserting an Optional Region

An *optional region* allows you to show or hide content. For instance, you might use a template to display product prices. In this case, you'd put the wholesale prices in an optional region because you wouldn't want retail customers to have access to wholesale prices. You use template parameters and conditional statements to determine whether the page displays the optional content. In addition, depending on the type of optional region object used, the template user may be able to edit the content in addition to determining whether the region is shown or hidden.

To insert an editable optional region that displays, by default, the cost of a single issue, follow these steps:

1. Position the insertion point a few lines below the repeating table.

2. Click the Optional Region tool on the Insert toolbar to open the New Optional Region dialog box, which is shown in Figure 23.18.

FIGURE 23.18

Name and determine whether the optional regional is displayed by default in the template-based page.

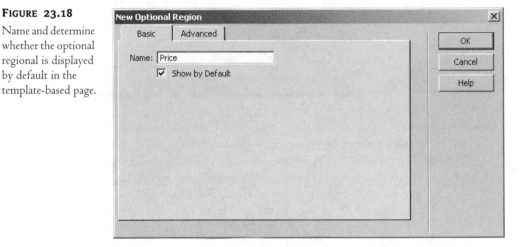

NOTE *The accompanying example inserts an editable optional region. That means the page author can edit the content when basing a new page on the template. If you don't want an editable optional region, enter the content in the template, select it, and then add the optional region using the instructions in this section.*

3. In the Basic tab, name the optional region, which currently has only its default name, OptionalRegion1. The Show By Default option—checked by default—determines whether the region is visible by default. Clearing this option sets the default value property to False.

4. Click the Advanced tab, which is shown in Figure 23.19, to display additional options.

In the Advanced tab, you'll create parameters and define conditional statements that control the visibility of the region's content. You can use simple true or false operations or more complex conditional expressions. To use a parameter, accept the default Use Parameter option. Then, simply choose the parameter from the drop-down list to the right. For now, we're just exploring the options, so close the dialog box by clicking Cancel. Right now we need to add a parameter, and then we'll add an optional region and connect it to that parameter.

FIGURE 23.19

You can define the optional region's visibility to be based on a parameter or an expression you enter.

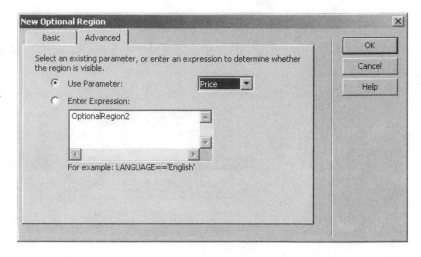

USING A PARAMETER TO CONTROL AN OPTIONAL REGION

Parameters help you control content display in template-based pages. In this section, we'll use a parameter to determine whether the page displays the optional content in the Price region.

Each parameter must have a unique name (which is case sensitive), a datatype, and a default value. Dreamweaver MX encloses a parameter in @@ symbols and evaluates the parameter as a simple expression. The difference is that a parameter requires additional data, which the page author is expected to supply when creating the new template-based page. You define a template parameter in the head section using the following syntax:

```
<!-- TemplateParam name datatype value -->
```

Now, let's use a simple true/false parameter to determine the state of an optional region, with true being the default. To accomplish this behavior, add the following tag (in the Code window) to the template's head section, as shown in Figure 23.20:

```
<!-- TemplateParam name="price" type="boolean" value="true" -->
```

TIP   You don't have to manually add this tag. You can create a parameter in the Optional Regions dialog box, and it automatically inserts the appropriate code in the head section.

FIGURE 23.20

Insert a parameter tag so a page author can determine whether the price content is displayed.

TIP   The TemplateParam tag is case sensitive. If you use uppercase with a datatype or defined value (such as true or false), Dreamweaver MX will return an error.

ADDING THE OPTIONAL REGION

To add the optional region, follow these steps:

1. Return to the bottom of the page in Design view.
2. Click the Optional Region button to open the New Optional Region dialog box.
3. On the Basic tab, name the region Price.
4. Click the Advanced tab, click the Use Parameter option, and choose the optional region from the drop-down list.
5. After Dreamweaver MX adds the optional region, enter the current price of **$3.00**, as shown in Figure 23.21.

FIGURE 23.21

Enter the price per issue in the optional region.

By default, this region is displayed in any new template-based page. However, the page author can modify the parameter's value so as to hide the region. We'll show you how to do so later in this chapter.

Depending upon your circumstances, you can choose to use an expression to determine the fate of the optional region. For instance, the price may be discounted for certain viewers.

When this is the case, click the Enter Expression option in the Advanced tab and enter the appropriate expression. The expression can be as simple as a true or false value or complex enough to contain multiple conditions. We're going to stick with the parameter example. Later, we'll modify the parameter in a template-based page so you can see the full effect of this flexible feature.

Editing a Region

Editing a region's properties is a fairly common task, but not exactly intuitive in Dreamweaver MX. Follow these steps:

1. Choose Window ➤ Properties or press Ctrl+F3 to open the Properties Inspector, as shown in Figure 23.22.

FIGURE 23.22

Use the Properties Inspector to quickly modify a region's properties.

2. Select the Price optional region to display the Properties Inspector with the Edit button, as shown in Figure 23.23.

FIGURE 23.23

Click the Edit button to open the New Optional Region dialog box.

3. Click the Edit button to reopen the New Optional Region dialog box, and make the desired changes in the Basic and/or Advanced tabs.

Using Editable Tag Attributes

Template text, images, and regions are editable within the template, but not always in the template-based page. You can change that by defining an editable tag attribute. For instance, both of the images we dropped into our example template page are centered between the left and right margins. You can allow a bit of flexibility by letting the page author re-align the images in the template-based page. To do so, follow these steps:

1. In the Code window, select the align attribute that precedes the fence image. You might find it easier to first select the image in Design view and then select the div tag to the left of the image tag, as shown in Figure 23.24. You can select the entire statement, as shown in the figure, or just the attribute; the resulting Editable Tag Attributes dialog box is the same in either case.

FIGURE 23.24

Be sure to select the appropriate tag.

2. Choose Modify ➤ Templates ➤ Make Attribute Editable to open the Editable Tag Attributes dialog box, which is shown in Figure 23.25.

FIGURE 23.25

Name the new attribute and modify the default setting if necessary.

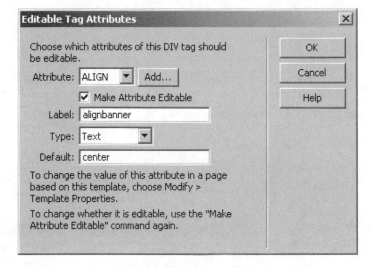

3. Check the Make Attribute Editable option. Dreamweaver MX will fill in the remaining fields for you, even assigning a name for the editable tag.

4. In the Label box, enter a unique label for the attribute. We entered **alignbanner**.

5. Click OK.

In a template-based page, the page author can change the alignment of either image. We'll show you how later in this chapter.

TIP   When naming editable attributes, try to include the type of attribute and identify the item. That way, the page author doesn't have to guess at the parameter's purpose—the name makes it very clear.

Figure 23.26 shows the new editable tag. Notice that the center attribute has been replaced with the string @@(alignbanner)@@. The @@ symbols define align banner as a parameter. You might also be wondering why we didn't repeat the previous steps with the rabbit banner. Since both image tags are contained within the <div> tag with the editable align attribute, any changes to the align attribute will affect both images. Simply enter a new <div> tag between the two images if you want to treat the images differently. Save your template and close it. You're ready to create a new page based on the template you just created.

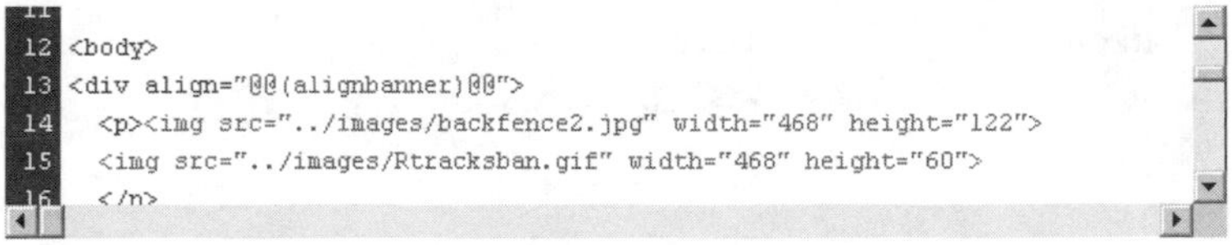

FIGURE 23.26

We replaced the original alignment tag with an editable tag.

```
11
12 <body>
13 <div align="@@(alignbanner)@@">
14    <p><img src="../images/backfence2.jpg" width="468" height="122">
15    <img src="../images/Rtracksban.gif" width="468" height="60">
16    </p>
```

Creating a Template-Based Page

Once you have a template, you can quickly create many new pages with the same design elements in the template. Simply base a new page on the template. To do so, follow these steps:

1. Open the Assets window (click F11).
2. Click the Templates button in the Assets category list on the left side of the Assets panel.
3. Right-click the template (we named ours Base), and choose New From Template from the shortcut menu.
4. To save the new page, choose File ➤ Save As to open the Save As dialog box, which is shown in Figure 23.27, and specify the appropriate web folder. Remember to specify the file type—we're working with an `.asp` file.

NOTE   *We saved our new page to Chapter23 in the MasteringDreamweaver folder and named our new page October to denote an issue.*

FIGURE 23.27

Save the new page.

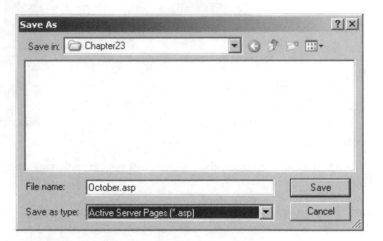

5. Click Save.

To customize the template-based page for the October issue, add text to the three editable regions, as defined in Table 23.1. Your template-based page should resemble the one shown in Figure 23.28.

TABLE 23.1: NEW CONTENT

REGION	TEXT
Title	October's Hare-Raising Trouble
Byline	By Susan Sales Harkins
Article	yada, yada, yada

FIGURE 23.28

Add content to the editable regions of the repeating table.

Now let's acknowledge a few contributors. To do so, follow these steps:

1. Position the insertion point inside the EditableContributors editable region inside the Contributors repeating region.
2. Enter **Special thanks to:**.
3. Click the repeating region's plus sign (+) to display a new editable region.
4. Enter the name **Alexis Stanley**, as shown in Figure 23.29.

FIGURE 23.29

Enter a contributor in the repeating region.

5. Right now the repeating table displays just the Editor-in-Chief. Click the plus sign (+) twice, and Dreamweaver MX will duplicate the repeating row just below the first row. Edit the new lines, as shown in Figure 23.30.

FIGURE 23.30

Add a second row to the repeating table.

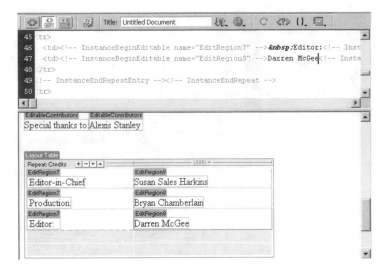

6. The final step is to determine whether you want the optional price region to show. In this case, let's disable it. To do so, choose Modify ➤ Template Properties to open the Template Properties dialog box, which is shown in Figure 23.31.

FIGURE 23.31

Deselecting the Show OptionalPrice option hides the optional region.

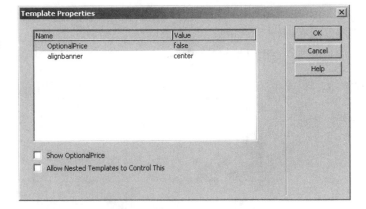

7. Select OptionalPrice in the list, which will enable the Show OptionalPrice option. Deselect that option. Notice that Dreamweaver MX updates the OptionalPrice parameter's value to false.

8. Click OK to close the Template Properties dialog box.

9. Save the new page and close it.

Viewing a Template-Based Page

Viewing the new page is the easiest leg of our adventure. Simply open your browser and enter the appropriate URL for your page. Ours is

```
http://localhost/masteringdreamweaver/chapter23/October.asp
```

The results are shown in Figures 23.32 and 23.33.

FIGURE 23.32

After adding unique content, display your template-based page in a browser.

FIGURE 23.33

Scroll down to see the rest of the page.

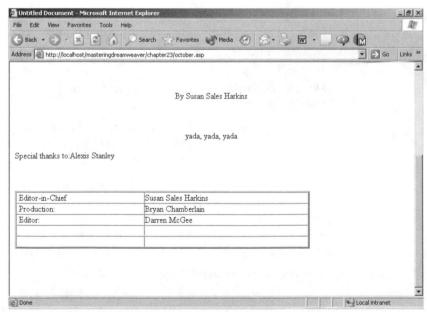

You may not be totally pleased with the results, and that's not a problem. For instance, the contributor content would probably be more easily managed in an editable region. You probably don't need a repeating region. In addition, the repeating table displays two seemingly empty rows because when we set up the repeating table, we only included the first row in the repeating region. Make changes to the template, not to the template-based page.

Adding Dynamic Text

So far, all the examples we've shown you have dealt with static data that the page author will update when creating the new page. A template can also include dynamic text. By dynamic, we mean that the template will display text from the site's database, and the page author doesn't have to do a thing. To illustrate this capability, we'll add dynamic text to the template that displays the last new book added to the sample Books database.

First, you must connect the template to the book site by defining the site. You learned how to do that in Chapters 2 and 10, so we won't repeat those instructions here. We're also working with a system data source name (DSN) named BooksConnection. (You can learn how to create a DSN in Chapter 4.) We're still working in the local system we mentioned earlier in this chapter:

```
C:\inetpub\wwwroot\MasteringDreamweaver\Chapter23
```

It doesn't matter where your copy of the sample books database is, but we'll be working with a copy that's in the Chapter23 folder for this example.

Now, let's update the template by adding a dynamic text control that displays the last book entered into the database. That way, the page will always show the most recently donated (and available) book. Follow these steps:

1. Open the Application window and click the Server Behaviors tab.

2. Click the plus sign (+) and choose Recordset (Query) from the submenu.

3. Name the recordset ShowMostRecentBook, and add the following SQL to the SQL control, as shown in Figure 23.34:

```
SELECT Last(tblBooks.Title) AS LastOfTitle
FROM tblBooks
```

The Connection option should default to your books connection (ours is the DSN Books-Connection). If you like, click Test to see the results of the SQL statement, and then click OK to return to the Recordset dialog box.

4. Click OK, and Dreamweaver MX will warn you about code lying outside the `<html>` section. You'll need to add the `<TemplateInfo>` template tag to the `<head>` section in order for Dreamweaver MX to update pages based on the template. Without this statement, pages won't display the dynamic text. Click OK to clear the message.

5. Display the template's code, if necessary, and locate the `<head>` section and add the following tag:

```
<!--TemplateInfo CodeOutsideHTMLISLOCKED="true"-->
```

as shown in Figure 23.35. Make sure it's in the `<head>` section—we placed ours just before the closing `</head>` tag.

6. Return to Design view and add a new line after the right-aligned text, "A Harey Tale."

7. Click the Application tab in the Insert bar.

FIGURE 23.34

Create a recordset that will retrieve the dynamic text.

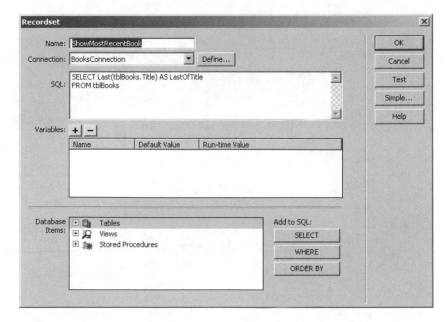

FIGURE 23.35

Add the `<Template Info>` tag to the `<head>` section.

8. Click the Dynamic Text tool to display the Dynamic Text dialog box, which is shown in Figure 23.36.

9. Select LastOfTitle, and click OK.

10. Left-align the text by choosing Text ➤ Align ➤ Left.

11. Save the change by choosing File ➤ Save.

12. When Dreamweaver MX prompts you to update existing template files, select `October.asp`, click Update, and then click Close. You may see another warning about code outside the `<html>` tag. Click OK to clear it, and then close the base template.

13. In your browser, enter the address to `October.asp`. Ours is `http://localhost/masteringdreamweaver/chapter23/october.asp`. If the page is current, click Refresh. You may need to hold down the Shift key while clicking Refresh. The page in Figure 23.37 shows the dynamic text. The displayed book title will change when you add a new book to the database.

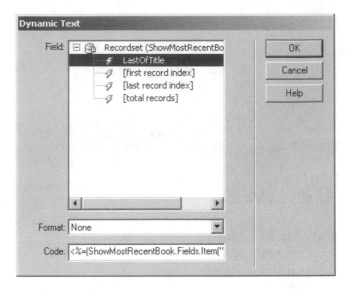

Summary

This chapter introduces you to templates—a feature that reduces production and maintenance tasks. There's a lot to learn, and most of it will be through trial and error. The different regions provide flexible layout opportunities and parameters, and editable tags give you the control you need. The next chapter explores Dreamweaver MX extensions.

Chapter 24

Dreamweaver MX Add-Ins

DREAMWEAVER MX, WHILE CERTAINLY a fantastic tool that saves you time and aids in creating websites, unfortunately doesn't include everything that everyone could want. Naturally, such a piece of software couldn't possibly be built—it would be too large to install, too slow to run, too expensive to buy, too cost-prohibitive to create, too huge a project to manage—just too everything. Dreamweaver MX does an excellent job of providing the necessary tools to quickly and effectively build websites, but Macromedia realized that there would be a benefit to letting third parties add to Dreamweaver MX. Therefore, they built into Dreamweaver MX the ability to let us, the users, expand it via pieces of code called *extensions*.

We'll cover Dreamweaver MX's ability to utilize extensions and some of the many types of extensions that are already available to you. Using Dreamweaver MX extensions, you just might make Dreamweaver MX do everything you could possibly want it to do.

This chapter covers the following topics:

◆ Dreamweaver MX Extensions

◆ The Macromedia Exchange

◆ Some extensions we find particularly useful

Dreamweaver MX Extensions

Dreamweaver MX extensions are actually pieces of code written by either Macromedia or third parties that add new capabilities or extend the capabilities of Dreamweaver MX. By adding new features to Dreamweaver MX, you can customize it to behave in a manner more to your liking or add new functionality that helps you in your daily work. Extensions are typically created by Dreamweaver MX users who have a technical background in JavaScript and XML (Extensible Markup Language) usage and placed on Macromedia's Dreamweaver Macromedia Exchange, which you can find at: `http://dynamic.macromedia.com/bin/MM/exchange/main.jsp?product=dreamweaver`, or just go to `www.macromedia.com/dreamweaver` and click Dreamweaver Macromedia Exchange. We'll cover more about Dreamweaver Macromedia Exchange in a moment. First, let's look at what you'll need before you can use extensions.

TIP *Even though we're going to cover quite a bit about extensions in this chapter, we highly recommend that you check out the Dreamweaver Macromedia Exchange on Macromedia's website. New extensions and new information are added frequently.*

Getting to Know Macromedia's Extension Manager

Before you can install new extensions in Dreamweaver MX, you need Macromedia's Extension Manager version 1.5 (or later) installed on your system. Dreamweaver MX should install this additional program by default, but you can quickly verify that you have it in a couple of ways: choose Start ➢ Programs ➢ Macromedia and check for Macromedia Extension Manager, or simply choose Commands ➢ Manage Extensions from the Dreamweaver MX main menu bar, as shown in Figure 24.1.

FIGURE 24.1

Launch the Macromedia Extension Manager from Dreamweaver MX's Commands menu.

You can check the version number of your copy of the Macromedia Extension Manager by choosing Help ➢ About from the Extension Manager main menu. Figure 24.2 shows the About screen in which we've highlighted the version number.

FIGURE 24.2

You must have version 1.5 or later of Macromedia's Extension Manager in order to use extensions with Dreamweaver MX.

If you don't have the Macromedia Extension Manager, you can download it from Macromedia's website at `http://dynamic.macromedia.com/bin/MM/exchange/em_download.jsp`.

TIP *Before you can download anything from the Macromedia Exchange, you'll need to become a member by registering an e-mail address and a password.*

The Extension Manager, which also lets you manage Fireworks MX and Flash MX extensions, lets you quickly and easily install extensions into Dreamweaver MX. In fact, you won't be able to extend Dreamweaver MX without it. Once you launch the Extension Manager, you'll see a window similar to that in Figure 24.3 that lists the extensions you have installed along with information about each extension.

FIGURE 24.3

The Macromedia Extension Manager lets you install and control the extensions you add to Dreamweaver MX.

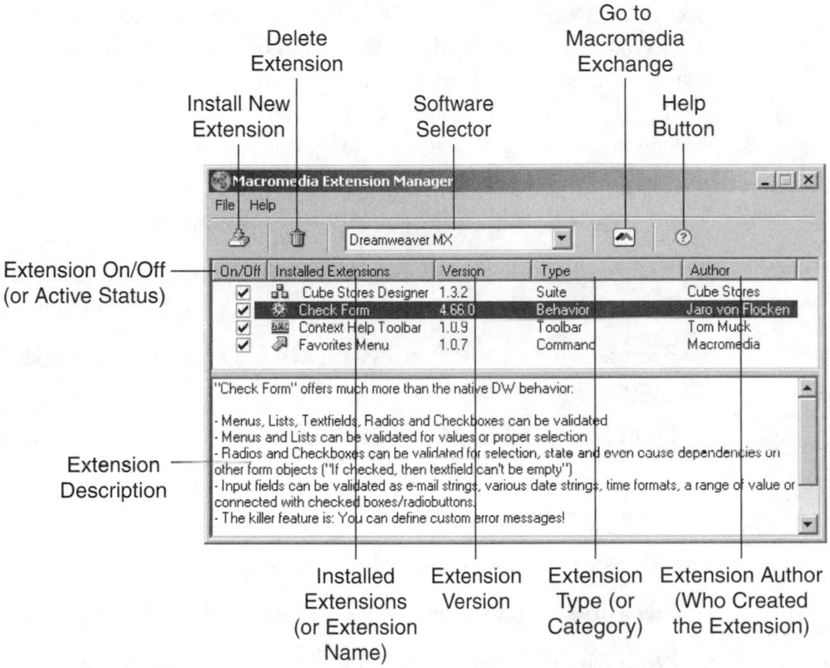

To install new extensions for Dreamweaver MX, click the Install Extension button to open the File Open dialog box through which you point to extensions you've downloaded and are ready to install. You'll probably have to stop Dreamweaver MX (if its running) and restart it before the change takes effect. We'll look at how to install a new extension later in this chapter.

To remove an extension from Dreamweaver MX, select the extension you wish to delete then click Delete Extension. The Extension Manager will ask you for confirmation before it actually deletes an extension. You'll probably have to stop Dreamweaver MX (if it's running) and restart it before the change takes effect.

Using the Software Selector drop-down list box, you can choose to manage extensions for Dreamweaver MX, Fireworks, or Flash. Extension Manager displays the extensions installed for these pieces of software once you select the title in the Software Selector.

Click Go To Macromedia Exchange to open the Macromedia Exchange website in your web browser.

Click Help to open the Macromedia Extension Manager help file. You can find here everything you ever wanted to know and were afraid to ask about Extension Manager.

The On/Off, or Extension Active Status, column lets you control whether the installed extension is on or off—that is, whether it's active in Dreamweaver MX. If an extension is set to inactive, or off, it is removed from Dreamweaver MX, but not deleted from the Extension Manager. Again, you'll probably have to stop and restart Dreamweaver MX for the changes to take effect.

The Installed Extensions column, or Extension Name column, lists the extensions you have installed. You can sort the extensions by name by clicking the column header. Click once to sort the column in ascending order. Click again to sort the column in descending order.

The Version column lists the version number of the particular extension you have installed. This is useful for determining if you have the latest version of an extension. Exchange Manager will detect if you're trying to install the same version of an already-installed extension, but knowing the version number can save you from downloading the same version again.

The Type, or Extension Category, column shows you the category to which the extension belongs. Macromedia has created several categories into which an extension can fall:

Accessibility　Provide features for making your web pages W3C Accessibility compliant. See Chapter 3 for more information on accessibility.

App Servers　Help you connect to, query, format, and view dynamic content from the web application servers that Dreamweaver MX supports, such as ColdFusion, JSP, and ASP.

Browsers　Assist with browser detection and redirection, handle types of browser issues, and so forth.

DHTML/Layers　Add DHTML (Dynamic HTML) objects and behaviors to a web page.

E-Commerce　Aid you in performing e-commerce functions such as building catalogs and transaction processing.

Extension Development　Aid developers in creating and deploying extensions.

Fireworks　Aid you in using Fireworks within Dreamweaver.

Flash Media　Aid you in using Flash Media within Dreamweaver.

Learning　Give you educational or instructional aids that you can either use in Dreamweaver or add to your site.

Navigation　Help you provide various navigation features to your site.

Productivity　Let you improve or add to Dreamweaver MX's tools, ease of use, or behavior.

Rich Media　Provide third-party multimedia tools, effects, or controls to deliver a better experience to your users.

Scripting Tools　Help developers create extensions and scripts for Dreamweaver MX, browsers, and media players.

Security　Let you build security measures into your web pages.

Style and Format　Give you greater flexibility to format and stylize your pages.

Tables　Make creating HTML tables and formatting and manipulating them faster and easier.

Text　Provide better and faster text editing and formatting.

The Author column indicates who created the extension. Creators can be anyone, of course—individuals, third-party companies, or even Macromedia.

The Description pane shows you information about the extension. This information is generally a description of the features of the extension but can contain any text the author chooses to enter.

Now that you've learned the basics of Extension Manager, let's look at how to actually use it. It's simple, effective, and elegant.

Using Extension Manager

In your day-to-day operation, you'll normally be primarily involved in installing extensions, removing extensions, and turning them on and off. Before you can use an extension, of course, you have to install it.

As we've mentioned, you can find extensions on Macromedia's Dreamweaver Macromedia Exchange. The next section will explain more about the Macromedia Exchange. For now, let's assume you have downloaded an extension called Downloads Counter.

INSTALLING AN EXTENSION

To install an extension, you'll take the following steps:

1. Click the Install Extension button, to open the Select Extension To Install dialog box, as shown in Figure 24.4.

FIGURE 24.4

Extensions come in Macromedia Extension Packages, files with a `.mxp` extension.

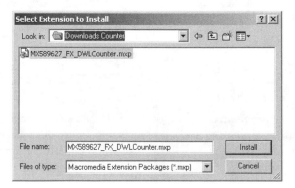

2. Point to the file, called a Macromedia Extension Package, you want to install and click the Install button. Macromedia Extension Manager displays a disclaimer (see Figure 24.5) that you must accept in order to continue.

3. Click Accept to open an "Installing…" window followed by a message that tells you the extension has been installed, as in Figure 24.6.

Notice the message that tells you to stop and restart Dreamweaver MX. Be sure to save your work.

TIP   If you're working with a lot of open files and find restarting inconvenient because you'll have to remember all the files you have open, we'll show you an extension later—the Favorites extension—that will let you quickly add and open files from a Favorites menu, much like your browser's Favorites menu.

FIGURE 24.5

You must accept the disclaimer in order to install a new extension.

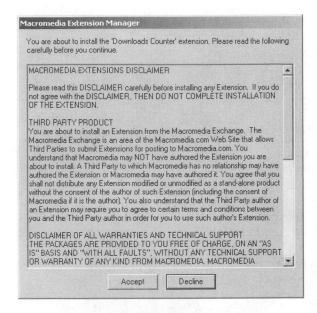

FIGURE 24.6

Our installation is a success.

This particular extension is a Server Behavior that aids us in tracking the number of times a file has been downloaded (or a link clicked). It installs into a developer-named menu called FELIXONE, as you can see in Figure 24.7. (FELIXONE isn't a default Dreamweaver MX Server Behavior name.)

FIGURE 24.7

Extensions can show up anywhere in Dreamweaver MX, depending on their type and function.

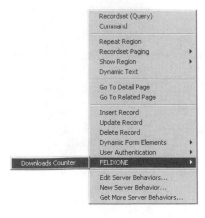

4. Click Downloads Counter to open the configuration dialog box associated with this extension.

DISABLING AN EXTENSION

Let's assume that you want to disable the extension we just installed until you're sure you're going to need it. Perhaps your Dreamweaver MX menus have become too crowded due to all the extensions you've installed, and you want to temporarily remove those you don't use every day. Instead of removing the extension completely, you can simply disable it, which removes it from Dreamweaver MX, but keeps it in Extension Manager for later reinstallation and use.

To disable an extension, or turn it off, open Extension Manager and clear the check mark in the On/Off column next to the name of the extension you want to disable. Figure 24.8 shows that we've disabled the Downloads Counter extension, and, dutifully, Extension Manager is telling us that we'll have to stop and restart Dreamweaver MX in order for this change to take effect.

FIGURE 24.8

Extension Manager lets you temporarily disable an extension.

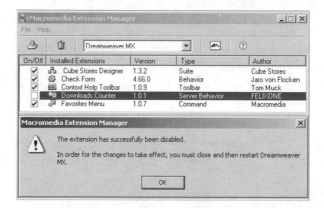

REMOVING AN EXTENSION

Now suppose that a couple of months later, you realize that you're not using that extension any longer and would like to clean up Extension Manager. You can remove the extension from Extension Manager, which also removes it from Dreamweaver MX if it happenes to be enabled. Removing an extension from Extension Manager does not remove the original installation file from your disk; so if you need to reinstall the extension later, you can, provided you have the file.

TIP Keep your extensions organized in a single directory or folder with a name such as Dreamweaver MX Extensions. Then, store each extension in its own folder by the extension name, such as Downloads Counter. That way, if you ever need to reinstall the extension, you have the exact version to which you became accustomed.

To remove the file, you simply click the name of the extension you want to remove and click the Remove Extension button—the trash can button. After a verification pop-up makes sure you want to remove the extension, Extension Manager removes the extension and verifies success. And, as you can see in Figure 24.9, you'll have to stop and restart Dreamweaver MX for the removal to take effect.

"Fine!" you say. "Where do I get these nifty extensions?" On the Macromedia Exchange, of course. Let's look at that next.

FIGURE 24.9

You can also permanently remove an extension in Extension Manager.

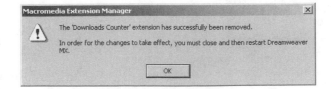

The Macromedia Extension Manager

The 'Downloads Counter' extension has successfully been removed.

In order for the changes to take effect, you must close and then restart Dreamweaver MX.

OK

The Macromedia Exchange

The Macromedia Exchange is the one-stop shop for all your Dreamweaver MX extension needs. Macromedia has set up the Macromedia Exchange to act as the one source for obtaining, learning about, creating, and sharing extensions. Macromedia tests the extensions that are on their site, so you can rest assured that you're getting something that is functional and meets a set of criteria. Now Macromedia doesn't guarantee the quality of that functionality, but they do give their approval to many of the extensions posted. Let's dig in and explore this site a bit.

Getting Started on the Macromedia Exchange

Figure 24.10 shows the home page of the Macromedia Exchange. As you can see, there are extensions, tags, and other goodies for just about every product Macromedia offers, and it's all accessible from this page.

FIGURE 24.10

The Macromedia Exchange is the best source for extensions for all your Macromedia products.

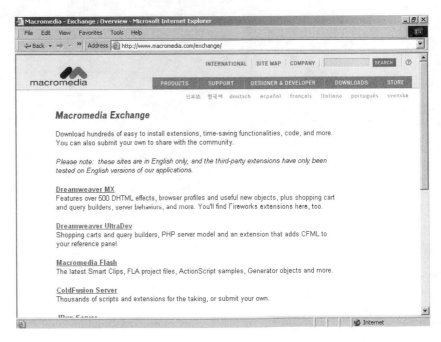

Notice that Dreamweaver also contains Fireworks extensions and that Dreamweaver UltraDev still has its own category. At the time of this writing, Macromedia had only recently added Dreamweaver MX extensions to the Macromedia Exchange, so you can really get to the Dreamweaver MX extensions from either Dreamweaver link. Click the Dreamweaver link to open a screen similar to that in Figures 24.11, 24.12, and 24.13.

FIGURE 24.11

You'll have to log in to use the Macromedia Exchange.

FIGURE 24.12

More of the Macromedia Exchange main page

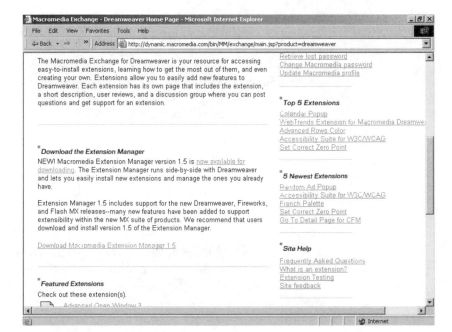

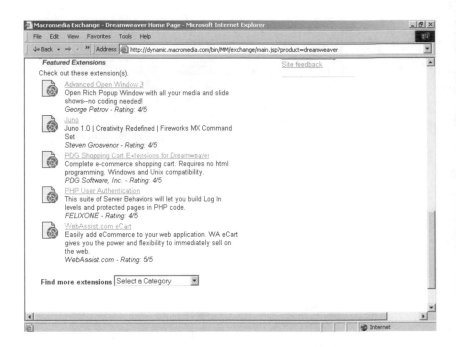

FIGURE 24.13

The rest of the Exchange main page

Before you can download extensions from the Macromedia Exchange, you'll have to log in. Most of the extensions are free, so registering wasn't a problem for us. There are several items of interest on this page as well.

The Macromedia Exchange for Dreamweaver home page lists news about Dreamweaver MX, as well as categories showing the top five downloaded extensions, the five newest extensions added to the Macromedia Exchange, and a link to the newest version of Macromedia Extension Manager.

To find extensions, you can search by extension type by clicking the Browse Extensions drop-down list box at the top of the page. You'll see a list of extensions that fall into the category you chose. For example, we chose "Learning" from the drop-down list, which yielded the results shown in Figure 24.14.

NOTE   Most of the extensions on Macromedia Exchange are free. They're added to the site by nice, community-minded developers who are giving back to the Dreamweaver MX community. You must pay for some extensions listed on the site. Developers who make their living by bringing you excellent, commercial-grade code to make your development life easier provide these extensions. Whatever your needs, you're sure to find an extension or two to add to your copy of Dreamweaver MX.

You can also search for extensions by keyword or phrase by entering text in the Search Extensions text box at the top of the page. Again, you'll be presented with a list of extensions that match your criteria. But the best way to find confirmed Dreamweaver MX extensions is through the Advanced Search, shown in Figure 24.15.

FIGURE 24.14

Quickly find extensions by choosing a category from the Browse Extensions drop-down list box.

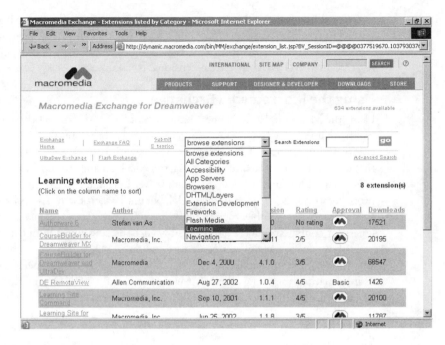

FIGURE 24.15

The Advanced Search page lets you find Dreamweaver MX–specific extensions.

Macromedia Exchange for Dreamweaver   601 extensions available

| Exchange Home | | Exchange FAQ | | Submit Extension | | browse extensions ▼ | | Search Extensions | | | go |

UltraDev Exchange | Flash Exchange   Advanced Search

Advanced Search
Search for extensions by specifying any or all of the following items.

Your Product   [Dreamweaver MX ▼]   Date added   [Any ▼]

Extension   [   ]   Extension   [   ]
Name   Author

Category   [Any ▼]   Extension Type [Any ▼]

Approval   [Any ▼]   Rating   [Any ▼]   Popularity [Any ▼]

Platform   [Any ▼]

Server Environment

☐ ASP JavaScript ☐ ASP VBScript
☐ ASP.Net C#   ☐ ASP.Net VB
☐ ColdFusion   ☐ Java Server Pages
☐ PHP MySQL   ☐ Other

Check All | Uncheck All

[Search]

Select Dreamweaver MX from the Your Product drop-down list box, and then select any other criteria you'd like to use to filter your search. As you can see, you can narrow your search to be as specific as you could possibly get with extensions. Now why, you may ask, would you want to look for Dreamweaver MX–specific extensions? Read on.

Using the Macromedia Exchange

Using the Macromedia Exchange is basically just like using any web-based search engine—you enter the criteria that match what you're looking for and wait for the results. But, at this time, Macromedia hasn't completed its testing of the prior extensions with Dreamweaver MX; therefore, it can't guarantee that every extension you find on the Macromedia Exchange for Dreamweaver works with Dreamweaver MX. Many Dreamweaver 4 and Dreamweaver UltraDev extensions have yet to be tested. They will probably work fine in Dreamweaver MX, but until Macromedia has a chance to test them all (more than 600 at this writing), they recommend that you search for Dreamweaver MX–specific extensions—unless, of course, you don't mind possibly encountering errors with those untested extensions.

So how do you know which are Dreamweaver MX–specific and have been tested? Aside from searching for Dreamweaver MX specifically, you can check the specific extension's page for a variety of information, including whether it works specifically with Dreamweaver MX. Figure 24.16 shows you an example of an extension page.

FIGURE 24.16

The extension information page for the Abbreviation and Acronym extension

This page, which extends for several screens beyond the area illustrated, contains tons of information about the particular extension, which will help you select the correct one for your needs. Let's explore this information:

Category   Identifies the category of the extension and also links back to the Category page or the main Exchange page.

Name   The extension's complete name

Features   A description of what the extension does

Developer URL   The web page of the developer of the extension

Support Info   Any special information needed to use the extension or get it working

Discuss   You can discuss the extension with other Macromedia Exchange users by clicking the Discussion Forum link.

Review   You can read reviews—if any—and post your own about the extension.

Sample URL   Generally, the developer will include a URL link to a web page where the extension is in use or will include a link to more information about the extension.

Download Extension   You can download the extension in either Macintosh or Windows version. Notice the installation instruction information? This is just generic information about how to download and use Macromedia Extension Manager.

Author   The author's name

Date   The date the extension was added to the Macromedia Exchange.

Version   The version of the particular extension

Type   What type of extension this is (the extensions category)

Environment   Lists whether the extension works only for a particular server or development environment, such as PHP.

Downloads   Tells you how many times the extension has been downloaded (which could be a gauge to its popularity).

Rating   Gives you information about its user rating—what score it has out of 5—if the extension has been rated. Macromedia Exchange encourages the user community to rate the extensions it uses.

Approval   Lets you know whether the extension passes basic testing or whether it passes the more rigorous testing to receive the Macromedia Approved rating. Extensions that have Macromedia Approved rating status will have the Macromedia "M" logo in this entry.

Browsers   Lists any browser restrictions for this extension

Platforms   Lists the platforms on which the extension works

Required Products   Lists the minimum requirements for using the extension

Supported Products   Lists the products for which the extension has been tested and confirmed to work

TIP   Read the reviews of the extension before you download it! The reviews will help you decide if an extension is right for your needs. They frequently point out pitfalls or praises, which can save you time in the long run. Also, once you use an extension, give back a little to the Dreamweaver MX community by writing a review about it. It'll help everyone and give you a warm fuzzy about yourself.

Once you've confirmed that this is the extension you want, download it and install it using Macromedia Extension Manager. That's all there is to it. You've mastered extensions. Now, let's take a look at some of the many extensions that we've found to be particularly useful.

Some Extensions We Find Particularly Useful

As we mentioned, there were more than 600 extensions on the Macromedia Exchange at the time of this writing. Needless to say, we've not explored nor can we cover all of them. However, we'd like to point out a few extensions that we hope you'll find useful in your development. These are listed in no particular order, by the way.

Check Form

Check Form, in the Scripting category, was written by Jaro von Flocken. It gives you more flexibility in validating a form in Dreamweaver MX. Figure 24.17 shows some of the many types of validation you can perform. In particular, some of the capabilities this extension adds include the ability to verify e-mail addresses and dates and to require that other fields be checked at the same time. You can even define your own error messages. This is much better than the default Dreamweaver MX Validate Form behavior. We highly recommend this one.

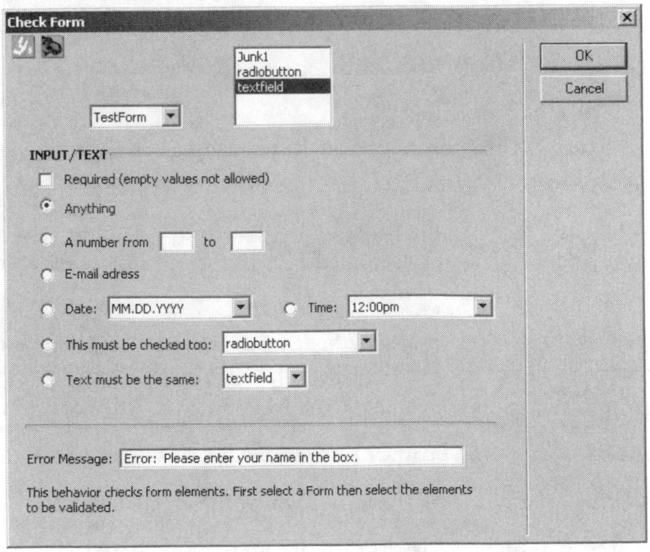

FIGURE 24.17

Check Form gives you more control over validating your forms.

Author   Jaro von Flocken

Category   Scripting

URL   www.yaromat.com

Platform   Windows 98/Me/NT/2000/XP

Features

- ◆ Defining your own error messages
- ◆ Dependent states for radio buttons and check boxes, such that you can create something like "if this radio button is checked, that text field can't be empty"
- ◆ Validating fields with acceptable range values

Cube Stores Designer

Cube Stores Designer, from Cube Stores, is in the E-Commerce category. It provides a suite of tools that let you quickly build online storefronts that interface with Cube Stores online store and e-commerce solutions. Figure 24.18 shows the help system along with tutorials that Cube Stores Designer provides.

FIGURE 24.18
Cube Stores installs new menus and object panels, as well as a help system to get you started quickly.

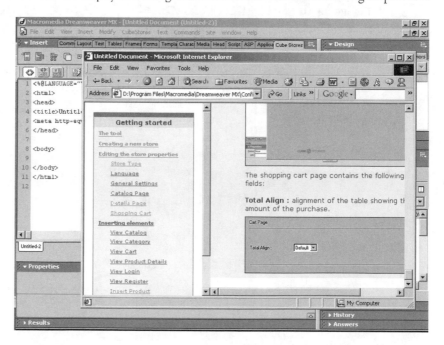

Author   Cube Stores

Category   E-Commerce

URL   www.cubestores.com

Platform Windows 98/Me/NT/2000/XP, Mac OS 9 or later

Features

◆ Visual tools to aid in designing e-commerce sites quickly using the Cube Stores tools and e-commerce capabilities

◆ Integrated help system and tutorials

Context Help Toolbar

This handy extension, written by Tom Muck, is listed in the Toolbar category. That doesn't mean it helps you build a toolbar on a site you're designing; instead, it builds a toolbar that provides contextual help for your own use in development. It lets you quickly find help on language tags, statements, and functions just by clicking the tag in question and clicking a help button. It's "smart" enough to work with each of Dreamweaver MX's supported languages except JSP (JavaServer Pages). You can see an example of its function in Figure 24.19. Notice the added buttons in the development window? The LiveDocs website popped up by clicking the CFIf tag and clicking the question mark button. We highly recommend this one.

FIGURE 24.19
Context Help Toolbar is one of the handiest extensions you'll find. It provides contextual help on just about every tag Dreamweaver MX can handle.

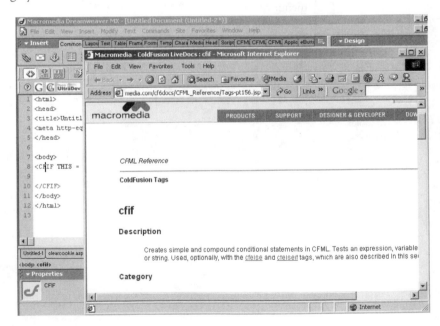

Author Tom Muck

Category Toolbar

URL www.dwteam.com/Tutorials/contexthelp/

Platform Windows 98/Me/NT/2000/XP, Mac OS 9 or later

Features

- Context-sensitive help for ColdFusion, VBScript, JScript, C#, VB, and PHP.
- Provides help directly within Dreamweaver.
- Searches a number of sources to provide useful information.
- You get help for whatever tag or keyword that your cursor is on in Code View, but you can also highlight words as help targets.
- You can add your own help to the extension via XML.

Favorites Menu

Favorites Menu, from Macromedia, is found in the Productivity category. This extension adds an item to your Dreamweaver toolbar that anyone familiar with a web browser would recognize—a Favorites list. This Favorites list, however, lets you immediately open a file just by selecting it from your Favorites menu, even across different sites. Favorites you might want to add to this list include Constants pages such as adovbs.inc, a code snippets page, or other references you use in your development. Figure 24.20 shows the Favorites menu in action. You also have complete capability to edit the menu, change its order, and so forth.

FIGURE 24.20
Favorites Menu gives you quick access to files you use frequently.

Author   Macromedia

Category   Productivity

URL   www.macromedia.com

Platform   Windows 98/Me/NT/2000/XP, Mac OS 9 or later

Features

- Adds a Favorites list to Dreamweaver MX
- Works just like your web browser Favorites feature
- Uses the HTML <Title> tag to name the document if it has anything other than Untitled Document in the tag

Drop Down Menu Builder for IE

This extension, written by Rabi Sunder Raj, is a DHTML/Layers tool that lets you effortlessly build drop-down menus for Internet Explorer. And, unlike most of the extensions we've encountered, you can update this one—you don't have to delete the code and rebuild it if you want to change something. Figure 24.21 shows the Drop Down Menu Builder for IE interface.

FIGURE 24.21

Drop Down Menu Builder for IE lets you quickly build drop-down menus for Internet Explorer.

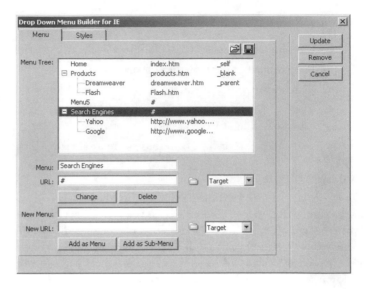

Author   Rabi Sunder Raj

Category   DHTML/Layers

URL   www.dreamweaver-extensions.com/

Platform   Windows 98/Me/NT/2000/XP, Mac OS 9 or later

Features

- ◆ Creates a drop-down menu for Internet Explorer.
- ◆ Has an easy-to-use interface that lets you build the drop-down menu.
- ◆ The menu appears as a text link in Netscape, so you don't lose your navigation.

Average Distribute Extension

This extension, written by Myhyli@blueidea.com, is a handy extension in the Tables category that aids your HTML table layout. It adds a series of commands to the Modify ➤ Table menu, as you can see in Figure 24.22, that lets you evenly distribute among a table's cells the width and height of the table. If you know you want a table a certain height and width, but want the cells distributed evenly within that table, size the table and then select these options. This extension calculates the average width and height of each cell and applies those calculations to your table. Its easy, quick, and cool.

Author   Myhyli@blueidea.com

Category   Tables

URL   www.blueidea.com/user/myhyli

Platform   Windows 98/Me/NT/2000/XP, Mac OS 9 or later

Features

- ◆ Quickly distribute table cells among the width and height of your table.
- ◆ You can use percentages or pixels as the distribution calculation.

FIGURE 24.22

You can quickly size your table cells with this extension.

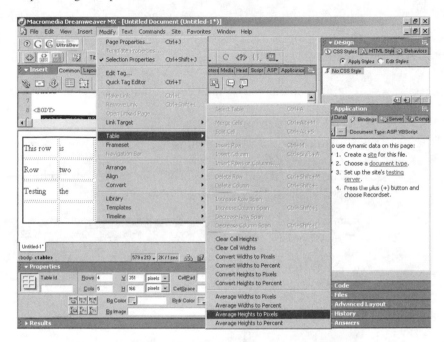

The CFML Form Tab

This extension, written by Neil Clark and found in the Productivity category, adds a new CFML Form tab to your Insert bar that appears when you're creating CFML pages. This new tab, which you can see in Figure 24.23, let's you quickly insert CFML Form objects such as CFForm, CFApplet, CFInput, CFTree, and so forth. If you use CFForm in your ColdFusion pages, you'll definitely want this extension.

FIGURE 24.23

This extension adds a tab to the Insert bar that Dreamweaver MX was missing—the CFML Form tab.

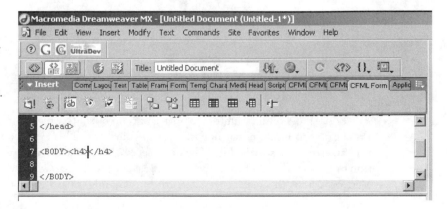

Author   Neil Clark

Category   Productivity

URL   www.fluidik.com

Platform   Windows 98/Me/NT/2000/XP, Mac OS 9 or later

Features

◆ Adds a CFForm object tab to your CFML Insert bar.

◆ You can quickly add CFForm objects from the Insert bar.

Go To Line Number

Two extensions in the Productivity category let you jump to a specific line number while you are working in the Code View window. Go To Line Number and Go To Line Number V2, by Public Domain, LTD and Paul R. Boon - DWTeam, respectively. Both apply a new menu option to the right-click pop-up menu. Right-click in the Code window, and you'll see something like that in Figure 24.24.

FIGURE 24.24

Go To Line Number (both versions) lets you immediately jump to a line number in the Code View window.

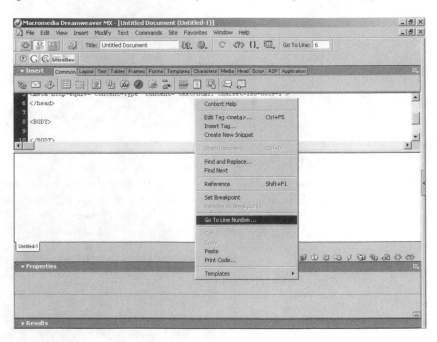

Choose Go To Line Number to open a pop-up box into which you type the line number you want. Press Enter to jump to that line number in your code. This extension is handy when you need to find an error on a specific line. The difference between the original version and version 2 is the addition of the Go To Line box in the Dreamweaver MX toolbar, which you can also see in Figure 24.24. Version 2 adds this quick access feature, but you might need to hide the Panels column to see it.

Author   Original—Public Domain, LTD

Version 2—Paul R. Boon - DWTeam

Category   Productivity

URL   Original—`www.publicdomain.to`

Version 2—No URL available

Platform   Windows 98/Me/NT/2000/XP, Mac OS 9 or later

Features

- Both versions add an option to the right-click pop-up menu that lets you jump to a code line number in the Code View window.
- Aids you when trying to debug code.
- Version 2 also adds an option to the Dreamweaver MX toolbar that lets you enter the line number without having to right-click.

Close All Documents

This extension, written by Katsuyuki Sakai and available in the Productivity category, adds a welcome function to the File menu, a Close All option. Choose this command, shown in Figure 24.25, to close all the windows currently open without closing Dreamweaver MX. This saves time when you're ready to work on a new site or batch of pages. One oddity about this extension, though, is that when you open new pages after using this extension, the pages open in an un-maximized window. But you can restore the familiar maximized window in tab format by simply maximizing one of the newly opened windows.

FIGURE 24.25

This extension closes all open documents.

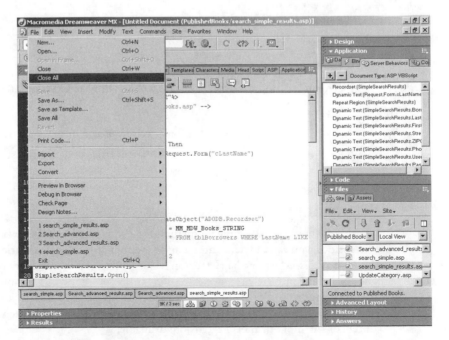

Author   Katsuyuki Sakai

Category   Productivity

URL   No URL available

Platform   Windows 98/Me/NT/2000/XP, Mac OS 9 or later

Features

- ◆ Quickly closes all open documents without closing Dreamweaver MX
- ◆ Clears the workspace so you can start work on a new site

No Right-Click

This extension, written by Paul Davis and found in the Security category, adds a security feature that's becoming popular among web developers. It prevents a right-click on a web page. Many times, developers like to discourage saving of images or viewing of source code that a right-click pop-up menu provides. This extension prevents that menu from popping up, as you can see in Figure 24.26. We right-clicked the web page and received this message. Now, there are ways around the right-click limitation, but the less web-savvy among us probably won't know about them.

Figure 24.26
Quickly prevent right-clicks in your web pages using No Right-Click.

Author   Paul Davis

Category   Security

URL   www.kaosweaver.com

Platform   Windows 98/Me/NT/2000/XP, Mac OS 9 or later

Features

- ◆ Intercepts the right-click on a web page and displays an error message to the user
- ◆ Prevents the right-click pop-up menu from appearing, restricting access to saving images and other items

Summary

We've covered the Macromedia method for enhancing Dreamweaver MX in this chapter. Using extensions, you can add new features and functionality to the already rich set of options Dreamweaver MX provides. Macromedia Extension Manager lets you manage extensions with ease. You can add, disable, and completely remove extensions from your copy of Dreamweaver MX. Macromedia also provides approved extensions (extensions that have passed a series of tests) on the Macromedia Exchange website. We've described how to use the Macromedia Exchange site and also shown you a few of the more than 600 extensions available.

Appendix

Datatypes and Functions Compared

MOST OF US WORK with more than one database system, and often we have to make those systems talk to one another. Knowing the compatible functions and datatypes is essential. Unfortunately, that's easier said than done. The following tables will help you quickly find counterpart functions and datatypes for the four systems we use throughout this book: SQL Server, Access, Oracle, and MySQL.

Not every function and datatype has an equivalent function or datatype in each system, so there are gaps. We've left those gaps so you can fill in your custom solutions for future reference. For instance, you might use the Access FORMAT() function to truncate values. In this case, you would enter FORMAT(*value,code*) as the Access equivalent to the MySQL and Oracle truncating functions, TRUNCATE and TRUNC, respectively. We didn't list this function because it returns a string, not a number. Consequently, it isn't a good match for our purposes, but it might be fine for yours. Also keep in mind that where equivalents are listed, they are rarely exactly alike. You'll still want to refer to the particular system's documentation, but at least you'll know where to start.

Functions in Dreamweaver MX–Compatible Database Management Systems

There's no way any of us can memorize all the functions in one system, let alone several. The following tables compare functions by task for each of the systems we use in our examples in this book.

TABLE A.1: AGGREGATE FUNCTIONS IN DREAMWEAVER MX–COMPATIBLE DATABASE MANAGEMENT SYSTEMS

SQL SERVER	ACCESS	ORACLE	MYSQL
AVG(*domain*)	DAVG(*field,domain, criteria*)	AVG(*domain*)	AVG(*domain*)
COUNT(*domain*)	DCOUNT(*field,domain, criteria*)	COUNT(*domain*)	COUNT(*domain*)

Continued on next page

TABLE A.1: AGGREGATE FUNCTIONS IN DREAMWEAVER MX–COMPATIBLE DATABASE MANAGEMENT SYSTEMS *(continued)*

SQL SERVER	ACCESS	ORACLE	MYSQL
MAX(*domain*)	DMAX(*field,domain, criteria*)	MAX(*domain*)	MAX(*domain*)
MIN(*domain*)	DMIN(*field,domain, criteria*)	MIN(*domain*)	MIN(*domain*)
SUM(*domain*)	DSUM(*field,domain, criteria*)	SUM(*domain*)	SUM(*domain*)
STDEV(*domain*)	DSTDEV(*field,domain, criteria*)	STDEV(*domain*)	STDEV(*domain*)
STDEVP(*domain*)	DSTDEVP(*field, domain,criteria*)	STDEVP(*domain*)	STDEVP(*domain*)
VAR(*domain*)	DVAR(*field,domain, criteria*)	VARIANCE(*domain*)	
VARP(*domain*)	DVARP(*field,domain, criteria*)	VARP(*domain*)	
	DLOOKUP(*field, domain,criteria*)	DECODE(*expr1,expr2*)	

TABLE A.2: NUMERIC FUNCTIONS IN DREAMWEAVER MX–COMPATIBLE DATABASE MANAGEMENT SYSTEMS

SQL SERVER	ACCESS	ORACLE	MYSQL
ABS(*value*)	ABS(*value*)	ABS(*value*)	ABS(*value*)
		GREATEST(*value1, value2*)	GREATEST(*value1, value2*)
		LEAST(*value1,value2*)	LEAST(*value1,value2*)
ROUND(*value,length, function*)		ROUND(*number,decimal places*)	ROUND(*value, precision*)
		TRUNC(*number,decimal places*)	TRUNCATE(*value, precision*)
CEILING(*value*)			CEILING(*value*)
FLOOR(*value*)			FLOOR(*expr*)
RAND(*value*)	RND(*value*)		RAND(*seed*)

TABLE A.3: STRING FUNCTIONS IN DREAMWEAVER MX–COMPATIBLE DATABASE MANAGEMENT SYSTEMS

SQL SERVER	ACCESS	ORACLE	MYSQL
	FORMAT(*string,code*)		
LEN(*string*)	LEN(*string*)	LENGTH(*string*)	LENGTH(*string*)
LOWER(*string*)	LCASE(*string*)	LOWER(*string*)	LCASE(*string*) / LOWER(*string*)
SUBSTRING (*searchstring,begin, length*)	INSTR(*start,string1, string2,compare*)	SUBSTR(*string, length*)	INSTR(*string, searchstring*)
UPPER(*string*)	UCASE(*string*)	UPPER(*string*)	UCASE(*string*) / UPPER(*string*)
SOUNDEX(*string*)			SOUNDEX(*string*)
DIFFERENCE (*string,...*)			
STUFF(*string,start, length,substring*)			
ASCII(*character*)	ASC(*character*)	ASCII(*character*)	
CHAR(*value*)	CHR(*value*)		
LEFT(*string,number*)	LEFT(*string,number*)		LEFT(*string,number*)
LTRIM(*string*)	LTRIM(*string*)		LTRIM(*string*) / TRIM(*string*)
SPLIT operator	SPLIT(*string, delimiter*)		
RIGHT(*string, number*)	RIGHT(*string, number*)		RIGHT(*string,number*)
RTRIM(*string*)	RTRIM(*string*)		RTRIM(*string*) / TRIM(*string*)
SPACE(*value*)	SPACE(*value*)		SPACE(*value*)
STR(*value*)	STR(*value*)		
	STRCOMP(*string1, string2*)		
	STRREVERSE(*string*)		
	VAL(*string*)		

Continued on next page

TABLE A.3: STRING FUNCTIONS IN DREAMWEAVER MX–COMPATIBLE DATABASE
MANAGEMENT SYSTEMS *(continued)*

SQL SERVER	ACCESS	ORACLE	MYSQL
CONCATENATION operator			CONCAT(*string1, string2,...*)
	MID(*string,begin, number*)		

TABLE A.4: DATE FUNCTIONS IN DREAMWEAVER MX–COMPATIBLE DATABASE
MANAGEMENT SYSTEMS

SQL SERVER	ACCESS	ORACLE	MYSQL
DATEADD(*code, interval,date*)	DATEADD(*code, interval,date*)	ADD_MONTHS(*date, numberofmonths*)	DATE_ADD(*date, interval,type*)/ ADDDATE(*date, interval,type*)
		LAST_DAY(*date*)	
DATEDIFF(*code,date, datestring*)	DATEDIFF(*code, interval,date*)	MONTHS_BETWEEN (*date1,date2*)	PERIOD_DIFF (*date1,date2*)
		NEXT_DAY(*date, dayname*)	
		ROUND(*date/ time,format*)	
GETDATE()	NOW(),DATE()	SYSDATE()	NOW(),SYSDATE()
		TRUNC(*date/time*)	
DATEPART(*code,date*)	DATEPART(*code,date*)		
DAY(*date*)	DAY(*date*)		DAYOFWEEK(*date*), WEEKDAY(*date*), DAYNAME(*date*)
MONTH(*date*)	MONTH(*date*)		MONTH(*date*)
YEAR(*date*)	YEAR(*date*)		YEAR(*date*)
	DATESERIAL(*year, month,day*)		
	DATEVALUE(*datestring*)		

Continued on next page

TABLE A.4: DATE FUNCTIONS IN DREAMWEAVER MX–COMPATIBLE DATABASE MANAGEMENT SYSTEMS *(continued)*

SQL SERVER	ACCESS	ORACLE	MYSQL
DATEPART('hh',time)	HOUR(time)		HOUR(time)
DATEPART('mi',time)	MINUTE(time)		MINUTE(time)
DATEPART('ss',time)	SECOND(time)		SECOND(time)
DATEPART('dw',date)	WEEKDAY(date)		DAYOFWEEK(date), WEEKDAY(date)
	TIMESERIAL(hour, minute,seconds)		
			DAYOFYEAR(date)
			DAYNAME(date)
			MONTHNAME(date)

TABLE A.5: CONVERSION FUNCTIONS IN DREAMWEAVER MX–COMPATIBLE DATABASE MANAGEMENT SYSTEMS

SQL SERVER	ACCESS	ORACLE	MYSQL
CAST(expression AS datatype), CONVERT(datatype, expression)	CDATE(value)	TO_DATE (expression,format)	CAST(expression as date)
CAST(expression as datatype), CONVERT(datatype, expression)		TO_CHAR (date,format)	
CAST(expression as datatype), CONVERT(datatype, expression)		TO_NUMBER (string,format)	
CAST(expression as datatype), CONVERT(datatype, expression)	CBOOL(value)		

Continued on next page

TABLE A.5: CONVERSION FUNCTIONS IN DREAMWEAVER MX–COMPATIBLE DATABASE MANAGEMENT SYSTEMS *(continued)*

SQL SERVER	ACCESS	ORACLE	MySQL
CAST(*expression as datatype*), CONVERT(*datatype, expression*)	CBYTE(*value*)		
CAST(*expression as datatype*), CONVERT(*datatype, expression*)	CDBL(*value*)		
CAST(*expression as datatype*), CONVERT(*datatype, expression*)	NZ(*variant, valueifnull*)	NVL(*expression1, expression2*)	
CAST(*expression as datatype*), CONVERT(*datatype, expression*)	CINT(*value*)		CAST(*expression as signed|unsigned*)
CAST(*expression as datatype*), CONVERT(*datatype, expression*)	CLNG(*value*)		
CAST(*expression as datatype*), CONVERT(*datatype, expression*)	CSNG(*value*)		
CAST(*expression as datatype*), CONVERT(*datatype, expression*)	CSTR(*value*)		

Datatypes in Dreamweaver MX–Compatible Database Management Systems

Datatypes are easier to remember than functions, but knowing the equivalents across several systems can be difficult, if not impossible, for most of us. Unfortunately, if you guess the wrong datatype, you can actually destroy data; so it's important that you have the most precise match possible.

TABLE A.6: DATATYPES IN DREAMWEAVER MX—COMPATIBLE DATABASE MANAGEMENT SYSTEMS

CATEGORY	SQL SERVER	ACCESS	ORACLE	MYSQL
Binary	BINARY		RAW	BINARY
	VARBINARY			
Text/Character	CHAR		CHAR	CHAR
	VARCHAR	TEXT	VARCHAR	VARCHAR
	NCHAR		NCHAR	
	NTEXT		NCLOB	
	NVARCHAR		NVARCHAR	
	TEXT	MEMO	CLOB	
				TINYTEXT, TINYBLOB
				TEXT, BLOB
				MEDIUMTEXT, MEDIUMBLOB
				BIGTEXT, BIGBLOB
Numeric	BIT	YES/NO		BIT, TINYINT
	BITNULL			
	NUMERIC		NUMBER	
	NUMERIC NULL			
	DECIMAL	DECIMAL		DECIMAL
	DECIMAL NULL			
	REAL	FieldSize = Single		DOUBLE
	FLOAT	FieldSize = Double		FLOAT
	REAL NULL			
	FLOAT NULL			
	TINYINT	FieldSize = Byte		TINYINT

Continued on next page

TABLE A.6: DATATYPES IN DREAMWEAVER MX–COMPATIBLE DATABASE MANAGEMENT SYSTEMS *(continued)*

CATEGORY	SQL SERVER	ACCESS	ORACLE	MYSQL
Numeric *(cont.)*	SMALLINT	FieldSize = Integer		SMALLINT
	INT	FieldSize = Long		INT
	TINYINT NULL			
	SMALLINT NULL			
	INT NULL			
				MEDIUMINT
				BIGINT
Date/Time	DATETIME	DATE/TIME	DATE	DATETIME
	SMALLDATETIME			DATE
	DATETIME NULL			
				TIME
			TIMESTAMP	TIMESTAMP
			INTERVAL	YEAR
Currency/Money	SMALLMONEY	CURRENCY		
	MONEY			
	SMALLMONEY NULL			
	MONEY NULL			
Image	IMAGE	OLE OBJECT		
			BFILE	

Index

Note to the reader: Throughout this index **boldfaced** page numbers indicate primary discussions of a topic. *Italicized* page numbers indicate illustrations.

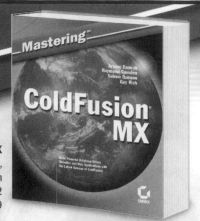